This is a time of critical transformation for infrastructure industries with profound implications for relevant networks and underlying market design. This book provides a rare and systematic overview about the recent evolution of the different network industries and includes case studies, insights about perspectives – a treasure for all those concerned by the future of our infrastructure networks.

Christoph Frei, Secretary General, World Energy Council, UK

Network industries constitute the physical presence of past development. They provide the contemporary infrastructure for future value creation. Modern technology and global economics lump together former vastly different industrial sectors in the emergence of new service systems and innovative enterprises. This book provides a unique and comprehensive overview. It pairs functional development to underlying principles, crossovers and dynamics. It asks what is to be done about it in terms of policy, management and regulation. This book constitutes a standard and indispensable reference for understanding the complexities of modern strategic infrastructure development.

Theo Toonen, Dean, Faculty of Behavioral, Management and Social Science and Professor, University of Twente, the Netherlands

All over the world, network industries have undergone profound transformations as a result of their liberalization since the late 1980s. This unique publication documents this transformation in the nine main infrastructure sectors. In the process, it analyzes the details of the changes at the industry, policy and firm level in quite a pedagogical way. It is probably the most systematic, self-contained and up-to-date overview of network industry transformation currently available.

Antonio Estache, Professor, Université Libre de Bruxelles, Belgium

The Routledge Companion to Network Industries

In recent decades, network industries around the world have gone through periods of de- and re-regulation. With vast amounts of sometimes conflicting research carried out into specific network industries, the time has come for a critical over-arching assessment of this entire industry in order to provide a platform of understanding to aid future research and practice.

This comprehensive resource provides an orientation for academics, policy makers and managers as to the main economic, regulatory and commercial challenges in the network industries. The book is split into sections covering market, policy, regulation and management perspectives, whilst all of the key network industries are covered, including energy, transport, water and telecommunications.

Overseen by world-class editors and experts in the field, this inter-disciplinary resource is essential reading for students and researchers in international business, industrial economics and the network industries.

Matthias Finger holds the Swiss Post Chair in Management of Network Industries at EPFL, Switzerland. He is also the Director of the Florence School of Regulation's Transport Area in Florence, Italy.

Christian Jaag is Managing Partner at Swiss Economics and Lecturer in Economics at the Universities of St Gallen and Zürich as well as at EPFL, Switzerland.

Routledge Companions in Business, Management and Accounting

Routledge Companions in Business, Management and Accounting are prestige reference works providing an overview of a whole subject area or sub-discipline. These books survey the state of the discipline including emerging and cutting edge areas. Providing a comprehensive, up to date, definitive work of reference, Routledge Companions can be cited as an authoritative source on the subject.

A key aspect of these Routledge Companions is their international scope and relevance. Edited by an array of highly regarded scholars, these volumes also benefit from teams of contributors which reflect an international range of perspectives.

Individually, Routledge Companions in Business, Management and Accounting provide an impactful one-stop-shop resource for each theme covered. Collectively, they represent a comprehensive learning and research resource for researchers, postgraduate students and practitioners.

Published titles in this series include:

The Routledge Companion to Fair Value and Financial Reporting
Edited by Peter Walton

The Routledge Companion to Nonprofit Marketing
Edited by Adrian Sargeant and Walter Wymer Jr

The Routledge Companion to Accounting History
Edited by John Richard Edwards and Stephen P. Walker

The Routledge Companion to Creativity
Edited by Tudor Rickards, Mark A. Runco and Susan Moger

The Routledge Companion to Strategic Human Resource Management
Edited by John Storey, Patrick M. Wright and David Ulrich

The Routledge Companion to International Business Coaching
Edited by Michel Moral and Geoffrey Abbott

The Routledge Companion to Organizational Change
Edited by David M. Boje, Bernard Burnes and John Hassard

The Routledge Companion to Cost Management
Edited by Falconer Mitchell, Hanne Nørreklit and Morten Jakobsen

The Routledge Companion to Digital Consumption
Edited by Russell W. Belk and Rosa Llamas

The Routledge Companion to Identity and Consumption
Edited by Ayalla A. Ruvio and Russell W. Belk

The Routledge Companion to Public-Private Partnerships
Edited by Piet de Vries and Etienne B. Yehoue

The Routledge Companion to Accounting, Reporting and Regulation
Edited by Carien van Mourik and Peter Walton

The Routledge Companion to International Management Education
Edited by Denise Tsang, Hamid H. Kazeroony and Guy Ellis

The Routledge Companion to Accounting Communication
Edited by Lisa Jack, Jane Davison and Russell Craig

The Routledge Companion to Visual Organization
Edited by Emma Bell, Jonathan Schroeder and Samantha Warren

The Routledge Companion to Arts Marketing
Edited by Daragh O'Reilly, Ruth Rentschler and Theresa Kirchner

The Routledge Companion to Alternative Organization
Edited by Martin Parker, George Cheney, Valerie Fournier and Chris Land

The Routledge Companion to the Future of Marketing
Edited by Luiz Moutinho, Enrique Bigne and Ajay K. Manrai

The Routledge Companion to Accounting Education
Edited by Richard M. S. Wilson

The Routledge Companion to Business in Africa
Edited by Sonny Nwankwo and Kevin Ibeh

The Routledge Companion to Human Resource Development
Edited by Rob F. Poell, Tonette S. Rocco and Gene L. Roth

The Routledge Companion to Auditing
Edited by David Hay, W. Robert Knechel and Marleen Willekens

The Routledge Companion to Entrepreneurship
Edited by Ted Baker and Friederike Welter

The Routledge Companion to International Human Resource Management
Edited by David G. Collings, Geoffrey T. Wood and Paula Caligiuri

The Routledge Companion to Financial Services Marketing
Edited by Tina Harrison and Hooman Estelami

The Routledge Companion to International Entrepreneurship
Edited by Stephanie A. Fernhaber and Shameen Prashantham

The Routledge Companion to Non-Market Strategy
Edited by Thomas C. Lawton and Tazeeb S. Rajwani

The Routledge Companion to Cross-Cultural Management
Edited by Nigel Holden, Snejina Michailova and Susanne Tietze

The Routledge Companion to Financial Accounting Theory
Edited by Stewart Jones

The Routledge Companion to Ethics, Politics and Organizations
Edited by Alison Pullen and Carl Rhodes

The Routledge Companion to Management and Organizational History
Edited by Patricia Genoe McLaren, Albert J. Mills and Terrance G. Weatherbee

The Routledge Companion to Mergers and Acquisitions
Edited by Annette Risberg, David R. King and Olimpia Meglio

The Routledge Companion to Ethnic Marketing
Edited by Ahmad Jamal, Lisa Peñaloza and Michel Laroche

The Routledge Companion to Critical Management Studies
Edited by Anshuman Prasad, Pushkala Prasad, Albert J. Mills and Jean Helms Mills

The Routledge Handbook of Responsible Investment
Edited by Tessa Hebb, James P. Hawley, Andreas G. F. Hoepner, Agnes Neher and David Wood

The Routledge Handbook to Critical Public Relations
Edited by Jacquie L'Etang, David McKie, Nancy Snow and Jordi Xifra

The Routledge Companion to Consumer Behaviour Analysis
Edited by Gordon R. Foxall

The Routledge Companion to Philosophy in Organization Studies
Edited by Raza Mir, Hugh Willmott and Michelle Greenwood

The Routledge Companion to Network Industries
Edited by Matthias Finger and Christian Jaag

The Routledge Companion to Network Industries

Edited by Matthias Finger and Christian Jaag

Routledge
Taylor & Francis Group
LONDON AND NEW YORK

First published 2016
by Routledge
2 Park Square, Milton Park, Abingdon, Oxon OX14 4RN

and by Routledge
711 Third Avenue, New York, NY 10017

Routledge is an imprint of the Taylor & Francis Group, an informa business

British Library Cataloguing in Publication Data
A catalogue record for this book is available from the British Library

Library of Congress Cataloging in Publication Data
The Routledge companion to network industries / edited by Matthias Finger and Christian Jaag. -- 1 Edition.
pages cm. -- (Routledge companions in business, management and accounting)
Includes bibliographical references and index.
1. Computer industry. 2. Computer networks. I. Finger, Matthias, editor. II. Jaag, Christian, editor. III. Title: Companion to network industries.
HD9696.2.A2R68 2016
338--dc23
2015021501

ISBN: 978-1-138-78282-2 (hbk)
ISBN: 978-1-315-76898-4 (ebk)

Typeset in Bembo
by Saxon Graphics Ltd, Derby

MIX
Paper from responsible sources
FSC
www.fsc.org
FSC® C013056

Printed and bound in Great Britain by
TJ International Ltd, Padstow, Cornwall

Contents

Figures

Tables

Contributors

Laticia Argenti, Captain, US Coast Guard, retired, OK, United States of America.

Raimonds Aronietis, Transport Analyst, International Transport Forum at the OECD, Paris, France.

Sergio Ascari, Gas Adviser, Florence School of Regulation, European University Institute, Florence, Italy.

Janice A. Beecher, Professor and Director, Institute of Public Utilities, Michigan State University, East Lansing, United States of America.

Reto Bleisch, Director of Regulatory and International Affairs, Swiss Federal Railways, Berne, Switzerland.

Gert Brunekreeft, Professor for Energy Economics, Bremen Energy Research, Jacobs University Bremen, Germany.

Marius Buchmann, Research Associate, Bremen Energy Research, Jacobs University Bremen, Germany; Research Associate, Fraunhofer IFAM, Bremen, Germany.

Kenneth Button, University Professor, School of Policy, Government and International Affairs, George Mason University, Arlington, United States of America.

Aad Correljé, Associate Professor, Economics of Infrastructures Faculty of Technology, Policy and Management, Delft University of Technology, Delft, Netherlands, Associate Fellow Clingendael International Energy Programme.

Damian Dominguez, Scientific Collaborator, Water Division, Federal Office for the Environment, Bern, Switzerland.

Hervé Dumez, Director of research, i3-CRG, École polytechnique, CNRS, Université Paris-Saclay, Paris, France.

Matthias Finger, Swiss Post Chair Management of Network Industries, Ecole Polytechnique Fédérale Lausanne (EPFL), Switzerland; Director, Transport Area, Florence School of Regulation, European University Institute, Florence, Italy.

Peter Forsyth, Adjunct Professor of Economics, Monash University, Victoria, Australia and Adjunct Professor, Southern Cross University, Australia.

Paula Gori, Research Associate, Communications and Media Area, Florence School of Regulation, European University Institute, Florence, Italy.

Michelle Hallack, Adjunct Professor, Universidade Federal Fluminense, Rio de Janeira, Brazil.

Christian Jaag, Managing Partner, Swiss Economics, Zürich, Switzerland; Lecturer, Universities of St Gallen and Zürich as well as Ecole Polytechnique Fédérale Lausanne (EPFL), Switzerland.

Tooraj Jamasb, Professor of Energy Economics, Durham University Business School and Durham Energy Institute, Durham, UK.

Alain Jeunemaître, Professor, Director of research, i3-CRG, École polytechnique, CNRS, Université Paris-Saclay, Paris, France.

Bruce Lambert, Executive Director, Institute for Trade and Transportation Studies, New Orleans, United States of America.

Benjamin Lehiany, Assistant Professor, SKEMA Business School, Paris, France; Research Associate, i3-CRG, École polytechnique, CNRS, Université Paris-Saclay, Paris, France.

Wolter Lemstra, Senior Research Fellow Economics of Infrastructures, Department Technology, Policy and Management, Delft University of Technology, the Netherlands; Visiting Senior Research Fellow, Center for Communications, Media and Internet Technologies, Aalborg University Copenhagen, Denmark.

Eva Lieberherr, Group Leader of Natural Resource Policy, Institute for Environmental Decisions, Swiss Federal Institute of Technology Zurich, Switzerland.

Antonio Massarutto, Professor, University of Udine, Udine, Italy.

Bernhard Meier, Delegate Public Affairs, Swiss Federal Railways, Berne, Switzerland.

William H. Melody, Emeritus Director of LIRNE.NET; Emeritus Professor Economics of Infrastructures, Department Technology, Policy and Management, Delft University of Technology, the Netherlands; Guest Professor, Center for Communications, Media and Internet Technologies, Aalborg University Copenhagen, Denmark.

Roland Meyer, Research Associate, Bremen Energy Research, Jacobs University Bremen, Germany.

Fumitoshi Mizutani, Professor of Public Utility and Transport Economics, Graduate School of Business Administration, Kobe University, Kobe, Japan.

Beat Mueller, Director International Markets, Swiss Postbus, Berne; PhD student, Institute of Technology and Public Policy, Ecole Polytechnique Fédérale Lausanne (EPFL), Switzerland.

Jürgen Müller, Professor, Berlin School of Economics and Law (HWR), Berlin, Germany.

Eri Nakamura, Associate Professor of Business Economics, Graduate School of Business Administration, Kobe University, Kobe, Japan.

Chris Nash, Research Professor, Institute for Transport Studies, University of Leeds, Leeds, UK.

Elena Navajas Cawood, Scientific Officer, European Commission, Joint Research Centre (JRC), Institute for Prospective Technological Studies, Sevilla, Spain.

Hans-Martin Niemeier, Professor of Logistics, Director, Institute for Transport and Development, Bremen University of Applied Sciences, Germany.

Pier Luigi Parcu, Professor, Director, Communications and Media Area, Florence School of Regulation, European University Institute, Florence, Italy.

Michael G. Pollitt, Professor of Business Economics, Judge Business School, University of Cambridge, Cambridge, UK; Assistant Director, Energy Policy Research Group, University of Cambridge, Cambridge, UK.

Rahmatallah Poudineh, Lead Research Fellow, Oxford Institute for Energy Studies, Oxford, UK.

Gregory Smith, Analyst Regulatory and International Affairs, Swiss Federal Railways, Berne, Switzerland.

Maria Luisa Stasi, Research Associate, Communications and Media Area, Florence School of Regulation, European University Institute, Florence, Italy.

Christa Sys, BNP Paribas Fortis Chair Transport, Logistics and Ports, Department of Transport and Regional Economics, University of Antwerp, Belgium.

Wenche Tobiasson, Durham University Business School, Durham, UK.

Bernhard Truffer, Professor of Geography of Transitions, Utrecht University, Utrecht, the Netherlands; Head of Department, Environmental Social Sciences, Swiss Federal Institute of Aquatic Science and Technology, Dübendorf, Switzerland.

Shuji Uranishi, Associate Professor of Industrial Economics, Graduate School of Economics, Osaka City University, Osaka, Japan.

Didier M. van de Velde, Researcher, Faculty of Technology, Policy and Management, Delft University of Technology, Delft, the Netherlands; Director, inno-V consultancy, Amsterdam, the Netherlands.

Thierry Vanelslander, Research Professor of Transport, Logistics and Ports, Department of Transport and Regional Economics, University of Antwerp, Belgium.

Lorenzo Vannacci, Scientific Support Officer, European Commission, Joint Research Centre (JRC), Institute for Prospective Technological Studies, Sevilla, Spain.

Miguel Vazquez, Professor, Universidade Federal Fluminense, Rio de Janeira, Brazil.

Thomas Wakeman, Research Professor and Deputy Director, Davidson Laboratory, Stevens Institute of Technology, Hoboken, New Jersey, United States of America.

1
Introduction

Matthias Finger and Christian Jaag

Network industries have witnessed around 20 years of de- and re-regulation, as well as deep changes in their underlying technologies. It is time for a critical assessment and a look into the future. This book's ambition is to provide an orientation for academics, policymakers, and managers as to the main economic, regulatory, and commercial challenges – and potential solutions – in nine network industries: telecommunications, postal services, electricity, gas, maritime transport, railways, air transport, urban public transport, and water.

Network industries can be categorized into four domains (see Figure 1.1): communications, transport, energy, and water. While most industries clearly belong to one of these domains, the postal sector is somewhat hybrid in that it provides a means of communication (letter mail), but also transportation (parcel services).

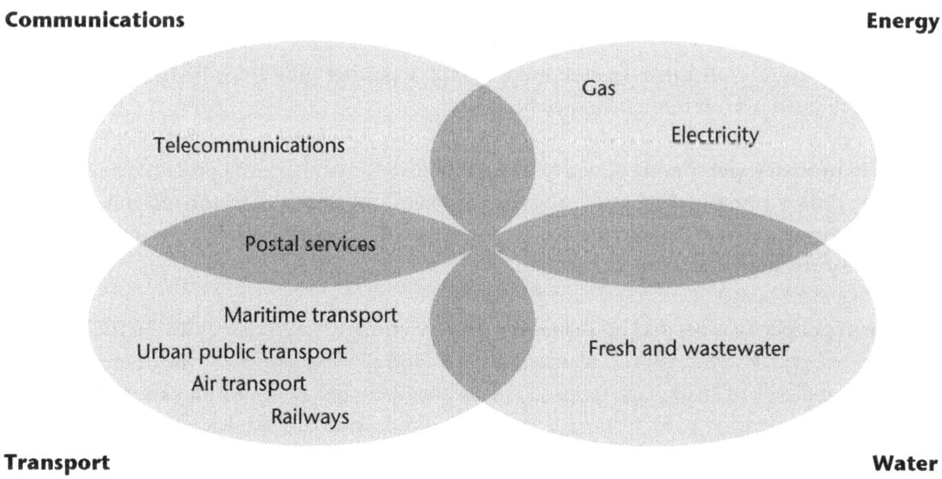

Figure 1.1 Network industries

Source: Authors' own elaboration

Network industries are interesting from an engineering, economics, and policy perspective for three main reasons:

- First, they share a common layered structure that determines their heterogeneous economic characteristics (see Table 1.1). The passive network-infrastructure layer comprises the physical infrastructure with a high fraction of irreversible fixed cost and strong economies of scale and/or bundling. This results in naturally monopolistic bottlenecks. The second layer (active infrastructure) is part of the infrastructure as well, but investment cycles are shorter and the cost may be reversible. The services layer uses the other layers to provide services to customers. The cost structure is more flexible and competition is easier to implement than in the infrastructure layers. This layered structure necessitates a differentiated (disaggregated) and well-targeted regulatory approach (see Knieps, 2000). A major organizational issue is the unbundling of the three different layers, since an integrated firm may have incentives to bar others from being active in the (potentially competitive) services layer. Hence, access to the infrastructure is an important issue, both commercially and from a regulatory perspective.
- Second, they exhibit network effects, also called network externalities (see Katz and Shapiro, 1985; Farrell and Saloner, 1985). This is the effect that a user of a service has on the value other people derive from that service. As a result, the value of a product or service is dependent on the number of others using it. The telephone is a classic example: the more people who own telephones, the more valuable the telephone is to each owner. The network effect may be present on all three layers of network industries. It creates commercial and regulatory challenges as well.
- Network industries also consist of, and provide platforms with, two- or multi-sided markets. This means that they serve two or several distinct user groups that provide each other with network benefits (Rochet and Tirole, 2006). Multi-sided platforms produce value for all users or parties that are interconnected through it by playing an intermediary role, and therefore those parties may all be considered customers (unlike in the traditional seller–buyer dichotomy). This creates a potential for pricing issues and a strong tendency towards concentration, and therefore motivates regulatory oversight.

In order to capture all these aspects and provide a unified view, the book approaches the network industries from three main perspectives:

- The **industry perspective,** with a focus on current market developments and dynamics.
- The **policy perspective,** discussing the rationales and aspects of sector-specific regulation.
- The **management perspective,** focusing on the strategic challenges resulting from regulatory and technological change.

The three perspectives depend on each other and are strongly interrelated (see Figure 1.1). The industry perspective observes the market outcome and its development over time. It captures the entry and exit of market participants, as well as their behavior and market position. The behavior of the market participants is expressed by their business models, their product range offered, and their pricing strategy. These strongly depend on the legal and regulatory framework that prohibits, enables or incentivizes certain business models and may determine the market structure and the organizational structure of the market participants.

Table 1.1 Layered structure of network industries

	Layer 1: Passive infrastructure	*Layer 2: Active infrastructure*	*Layer 3: Services*
Economic characteristics	Mainly irreversible fixed cost Long-term investment cycle	Mixed cost structure Medium-term investment cycle	Mainly reversible cost Short-term investment cycle
Market structure	Naturally monopolistic bottlenecks	Actual and potential competition	Actual and potential competition
Telecommunications	Ducts, cables	Routers, switches	Voice and data services
Postal services	Streets, buildings	Post offices, sorting centers	Letter and parcels conveyance services
Electricity	Transmission and distribution networks	Power plants (nuclear, hydro, coal, oil, gas), pump storage, batteries	Energy services, metering services, balancing services
Gas	Pipelines, liquefied natural gas converting facilities	Refinement	Energy services
Maritime transport	Channels	Harbors, ships	Transportation services, harbor-related services
Railways	Tracks, on-track signaling systems	Train stations, on-train signaling systems, rolling stock	Transportation services
Air transport	Air traffic control infrastructures	Airports	Air transport, airport-related services
Urban public transport	Streets, tracks, tunnels	Rolling stock	Transportation services
Water and wastewater	Water distribution and wastewater pipes	Water and wastewater treatment plants	Water services

Recent developments in the legal framework of the network industries can be structured in terms of regulation, liberalization, and privatization:

- Regulation refers to the entirety of legal constraints on economic activity in the sector. Network industries are characterized by a dense regulatory framework (see Figure 1.1). Economic regulations may be concerned with fair competition, and be symmetrically targeted to all operators in the sector (market regulation). Additionally, regulations may focus on correcting market failures by providing a socially desired level of service quality or redistribution, or fostering environmental protection. This second kind of intervention (provision regulation, such as universal service obligations [USOs]) is often asymmetric and costly, which has long been the main motivation for establishing state monopolies. Such monopolies have necessitated further regulations to deal with market dominance.

  In addition to economic regulation, in network industries there are safety regulations (in energy, railways, and air transport), data protection (in telecommunications and postal services) and security of supply and national independence (in energy).

- Liberalization is the abolishment of reserved areas and the opening of markets for new operators. In recent years, most network industries have become liberalized in many countries. In addition, technological change - which is mostly driven by information and communication technologies - is substantial in some of the network industries and often goes in parallel with market dynamics. As a result, sectors have converged, stimulating indirect competition between different industries (for example, postal services and telecommunications).
- Privatization is the process of transferring ownership of a network operator from the public sector (government-owned) to the private sector. The precursor to privatization is corporatization, which transforms government agencies into corporations. Privatization often takes place in parallel with liberalization (or prior to it) in order to ensure a level playing field for all firms in the sector.

In parallel with liberalization and increased competition, sector-specific regulation in the different network industries has become a widely discussed topic among academics, policy makers, industry economists and regulators themselves. The focus of these debates has usually been on whether such regulation is necessary, and, if so, what its optimal design should be. Some argue for deregulation (that is, the abolishment of price regulation or USOs), whereas others propose re-regulation, which involves the replacement of pre-existing (monopoly-related) regulations with new regulations that aim to safeguard service levels and competition. The resulting compromise is often somewhere in between de- and re-regulation. The current and future challenges in network industries mainly pertain to the dynamics in the industries' regulatory frameworks. Therefore, regulation is one of the main focal areas of this book.

From an economics perspective, the principal rationale for regulation is to remedy market failure; that is, the deviation of the market outcome from an efficient allocation. Markets can fail (in theory and in practice) for four major reasons (see, e.g., Viscusi *et al.*, 2005; Armstrong *et al.*, 1994; Laffont and Tirole, 1993):

1. Market power: If one firm or several firms (oligopoly or a cartel) can profitably raise their price above the competitive level, then the market is not efficient as the price exceeds the marginal opportunity-cost of production. A monopoly may naturally develop due to high fixed and irreversible cost to build infrastructure. Remedies for the abuse of market power are primarily price and access regulation, sometimes combined with quality of service standards.
2. Externalities: Economic activities may impose losses or benefits on third parties that the market participants do not take into account. Since their choices do not consider the social cost and benefit, their actions are distorted. This implies that the externality-creating activities are under- or over-provided relative to the efficient level. Pollution and congestion are examples in which the social cost is higher than the private cost. Typical remedies for externalities are taxation, production quota, or, more recently, cap-and-trade mechanisms.
3. Public goods: The consumption of a public good is neither rivalrous nor excludable. A competitive market fails to provide an efficient level of a public good due to freeriding and the inability of the suppliers to appropriate an adequate return. Security of energy supply and load balancing is an example of a public good. Spectrum for mobile telecommunication services has been made a private good by first defining and allocating corresponding property rights.
4. Asymmetric information: Imperfect information gives rise to two problems – adverse selection and moral hazard. These issues arise often in situations in which risk is involved.

In addition to economic regulation as a remedy of market failure, a further rationale is distributive concerns. Redistribution is often implemented in the form of price control, cross-subsidies or USOs.

In practice, not only markets but also regulation may fail due to its being costly and creating its own distortions (see, e.g., Coase, 1960). This has resulted in the development of a framework of government failure (Wolf, 1988; Demsetz, 1969) and later the New Institutional Economics approach (Williamson, 1985).

The market outcome in network industries is primarily determined by regulatory policies in two domains: first (on the left-hand side of Figure 1.2) market regulation aims to ensure fair competition. It governs market access (for example, through a reserved area or a licensing regime) and network access to monopolistic bottlenecks (especially to the passive infrastructure). It also regulates interconnection (provisions related to numbers and addresses, for example in telecommunications, see Laffont and Tirole [1996], or in postal services). Flanking measures may pertain to the regulation of labor conditions in labor-intensive industries such as postal services. Second (on the right-hand side of Figure 1.2), provision regulation intends to remedy the under- or over-provision of certain goods or their quality. In telecommunications or postal services, this is ensured through USOs concerning the provision of quality services to the entire population in all regions of a country. Conversely, regulations may be concerned with environmental pollution or energy efficiency. After the identification of an under- or over-provision, the first aspect to be governed is the concrete definition of obligations. In a second step, one or several operators have to be designated if the market does not spontaneously provide the desired level of service quality. If the (asymmetric) regulatory intervention constitutes a binding economic constraint and a relevant burden on the designated operator(s), a financing mechanism is needed for compensation.

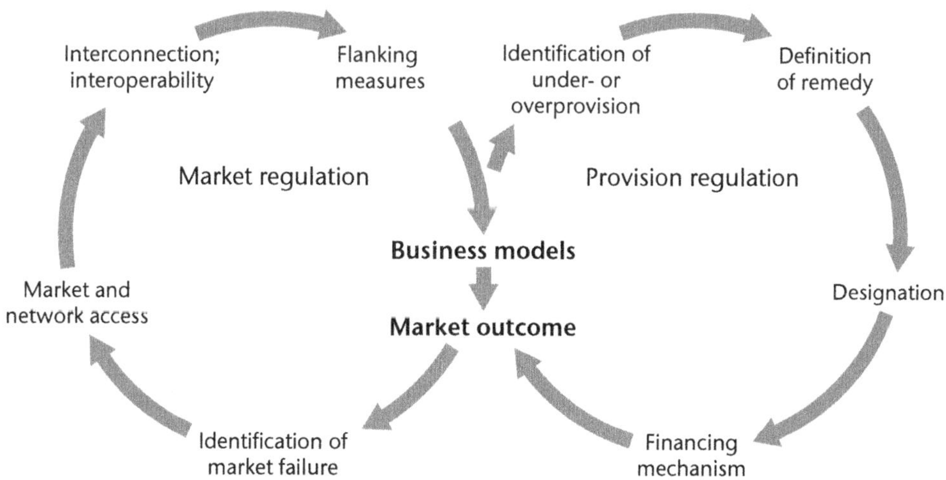

Figure 1.2 Illustration of interactions

Source: Based on Jaag and Trinkner (2011)

This book covers the main institutional levels of policy and regulation; namely, the global level (airlines, maritime transport, and telecommunications), the regional level, especially Europe (railways, air traffic control, electricity and gas), the national level (postal services, and road transport), as well as the local level (water and wastewater, urban public transport and airports). The remaining chapters discuss the concrete interactions between regulation, technology and market forces in each industry sector in detail. For each of the nine network industries, a separate chapter gives a view from a sector/market perspective, the policy/regulation perspective, and a management/strategy perspective.

References

Armstrong, M., Cowan, S. and Vickers, J. (1994) *Regulatory Reform: Economic Analysis and British Experience*. Cambridge, MA: MIT Press.

Coase, R. (1960) The problem of social costs, *Journal of Law and Economics* 3, 1–44.

Demsetz, H. (1969) Information and efficiency: Another viewpoint, *Journal of Law and Economics*, 12, 1–22.

Farrell, J. and Saloner, G. (1985) Standardization, compatibility, and innovation, *Rand Journal of Economics* 16, 70–83.

Jaag, C. and Trinkner, U. (2011) A general framework for regulation and liberalization in network industries, in M. Finger and R. Künneke (eds) *International Handbook for the Liberalization of Infrastructures*. Cheltenham: Edward Elgar Publishing, pp. 26–53.

Katz, M.L. and Shapiro, C. (1985) Network externalities, competition and compatibility, *American Economic Review*, 75(3), 424–440.

Knieps, G. (2000) Access to networks and interconnection: A disaggregated approach, in C.D. Ehlermann and L. Gosling (eds), *European Competition Law Annual 1998: Regulating Communications Markets*. Oxford and Portland, OR: Hart Publishing, pp. 151–170.

Laffont, J.J. and Tirole, J. (1993) *A Theory of Incentives in Procurement and Regulation*. Cambridge, MA: MIT Press.

Laffont, J.J. and Tirole, J. (1996) Creating competition through interconnection: theory and practice, *Journal of Regulatory Economics*, 10(3), 227–256.

Rochet, J.C. and Tirole, J. (2006) Two-sided markets: A progress Report, *The RAND Journal of Economics*, 35(3), 645–667.

Viscusi, W.K., Harrington, J.E. and Vernon, J.M. (2005) *Economics of Regulation and Antitrust* (4th Edition). Cambridge, MA: MIT Press.

Williamson, O.E. (1985) *The Economic Institutions of Capitalism*. New York: Free Press.

Wolf, C. (1988) *Markets or Governments: Choosing Between Imperfect Alternatives*. Cambridge, MA: MIT Press.

Part I

The market and industry perspective

2

Telecommunication networks

Technology and market development

Wolter Lemstra and William H. Melody

Introduction

Telecommunication is widely considered an important contributing factor to economic productivity and growth, as reflected in a strong correlation between gross domestic product (GDP) per capita and teledensity. With the emergence of the Internet, the role of the telecoms industry has become even more important, as economic and social activity is increasingly electronically mediated and transacted online.

In the OECD, business and private spending on telecommunications moved from a plateau of just above 2 percent of GDP in the period 1985–1995, to a peak of 3.5 percent in 2001; this slowly declined to a level just below three percent from 2011 onward. This is linked to an underlying increase in the proportion of household expenditure on telecommunication; from an index of 100 in 1990, it increased to approximately 130 in 2003 and remained relatively flat in later years (OECD, 2003; 2005; 2007; 2011; 2013).

As the industry has evolved from connecting homes to connecting people, and more recently to connecting devices, it has become increasingly global. This applies in particular to the supply industries that provide infrastructure equipment. With the emergence of the Internet, the content conveyed is becoming increasingly important and, hence, so is the relationship with the computer and media industries. This has both global and very local policy dimensions.

This chapter is structured as follows: first the historical developments of the telecommunications industry are captured. The development trajectories in both fixed and mobile communications are summarized, as well as the convergence between these. The way in which the Internet is subsuming the role of traditional telecoms receives special attention. Subsequently, the development of broadband markets, from the year 2000 onward, is discussed. This is followed by a discussion of the challenges in the transition to ultra-fast next-generation access networks and concluding remarks close the chapter.

This chapter should be read in conjunction with Chapter 11 on Electronic communications policy and regulation in Europe, and Chapter 20 on Innovative and disruptive effects of the Internet on strategy in the communications and media markets.[1]

Overview of major developments – technologies and markets

Telecommunications development has been linked to the application of new network technologies for the provision of specific services; for example, telegraph, telephone, video, mobile voice and data. Improvements in technologies led to the expanded capability of these networks to provide additional services, thereby creating a degree of overlap and competition for the provision of some services. It has now reached the point where infrastructure networks are increasingly capable of providing most, if not all, telecommunication services. The range and variety of services are also expanding rapidly as they are applied innovatively in all sectors of the economy, including the other network industries. One of the main challenges today is to ensure that next-generation networks (NGN) will have the capacity and quality to support the anticipated rapid growth in new applications of telecommunications services.

Telephone network

The telecommunications industry originated in the invention of the electrical telegraph in 1832, and the telephone in 1876. Telephone services started through private entrepreneurship; however, following the expiry of the Bell patent in 1893, many competing networks were built in US cities and towns. AT&T maintained its market dominance primarily by refusing to interconnect with new competitors. Under the threat of being charged with violation of US competition laws, AT&T lobbied the federal government to establish a regulation that would sanction its monopoly. In return AT&T agreed to enable universal service, meaning it would interconnect with other operators serving neighboring areas (Falk, 1984; ITU, 1965; Mueller, 1997).

In Europe in the early 1900s, most private and municipal telephone networks transitioned to central government ownership, whereby public administrations (PTTs) became responsible for the national telephone infrastructure and service provision. These developments resulted in a private monopoly under regulatory supervision operating in the US, Canada, the Philippines, and a few other countries, and national public monopolies operating in Europe and most other countries. The infrastructure equipment supply was also largely a national affair. Hence, a vertically integrated industry structure resulted, according to the model of 'one country – one operator – one (main) supplier' (Lemstra, 2006).

The AT&T monopoly was successfully challenged in the late 1960s by an independent terminal provider (Carterfone) and an alternative provider of long-distance communication using microwave transmission (MCI). This stimulated support for market liberalization throughout the 1970s from the electronics, satellite manufacturing, and computer industries. The latter wished to use telephone lines to connect computers and data terminals. The break-up of AT&T in 1984 for its violations of US competition laws, and a gradual erosion of the monopoly, changed the industry environment dramatically, culminating in full liberalization under the Telecommunications Act of 1996 (Falk, 1984; Melody, 1997).

In Europe, pressure for market liberalization caused the publication of a Green Paper by the European Commission on creating a harmonized market for telecommunications, and liberalization of the telecommunication services industry in 1987 (EC, 1987). January 1, 1998, was set as the target date for full liberalization of the telecom markets. In Japan, liberalization started in 1985 with the privatization of NTT, and regulations were eased gradually. South Korea began to open its telecom markets in the early 1990s (Mizutani, 2012; Oh and Larson, 2011).

A dedicated telephone network was developed, and optimized for transmission of the human voice. A two-way connection was set up for the duration of each call, known as circuit switching. Later, data was encoded for transmission within the voice band (300–3400 Hz); this enabled the development of facsimile and data communication at data rates up to 56 kbit/s. Higher data rates could be provided using leased lines. The local loop – the connection between the home and the central office – remained analogue until the Integrated Services Digital Network (ISDN) was introduced in the mid-1980s in the US, and in the early 1990s in Europe. ISDN offered two user connections at 64 kbit/s. Interconnection of networks was facilitated through standardization of the equipment interfaces at national, regional, and global level.

Mobile networks

Wireless communication using radio-based transmission was introduced around 1950 and used by telephone operators for intercity transmission of phone calls and relaying television signals. The introduction of cellular systems, using small cells with lower power and allowing the reuse of radio frequencies, occurred around 1980. NTT in Japan was the first to use such technology. These were the first-generation (1G) analogue systems for mobile phone service (using Frequency Division Multiple Access [FDMA]). Fully digital systems were introduced in the early 1990s. The European GSM system, using Time Division Multiple Access (TDMA) became the world's leading second-generation (2G) system (King and West, 2002; Manninen, 2002; Meurling and Jeans, 1994).

In the late 1980s, Qualcomm, in close cooperation with PacTel, demonstrated a Code Division Multiple Access (CDMA) prototype, which provided a tenfold capacity increase compared to TDMA systems. In the mid-1990s, the CDMA standard was ratified by the US Telecommunications Industry Association and adopted by PCS PrimeCo, Airtouch and Sprint. Other early adopters were Hutchison in Hong Kong and Korea Mobile Telecom (Mock, 2005).

In the late 1990s, Wireless Application Protocol (WAP) served as an early attempt to provide access to the Internet. The introduction of General Packet Radio Service (GPRS) provided for a packet-switched overlay with a data rate of up to 170 kbit/s. The capacity was extended through Enhanced Data for Global Evolution (EDGE) to rates of 200–700 kbit/s (GSM Association, 2009).

Initially, licenses allowing the use of the radio frequency spectrum for mobile telephony were granted by the national governments to the incumbent PTTs. During the early 1980s in the US, two licenses were granted in each market, one for the wire line carrier and one for a non-wire-line carrier. Through the acquisition of local cellular operations, McCaw built the nation's largest cellular company, which was sold to AT&T in 1993 (Corr, 2000).

During the 1990s in Europe, second licenses were typically issued through a 'beauty contest'. This marked the start of competition, which was not controversial as the mobile market was booming. Vodafone was one of the first mobile operators to build a multinational presence, extending its operations from the UK to Europe, Japan and the US. In the late 1990s, additional licenses were auctioned. Over time, consolidation usually reduced the number of competitors to three to five. Competition has been enhanced through Mobile Virtual Network Operators (MVNOs), which lease infrastructure capacity from Mobile Network Operators (MNOs) to provide their services, typically targeting special user groups or leveraging a consumer brand.

In rural areas, mobile communication has become a substitute for a lack of fixed communication. This applies to many countries in Africa, South East Asia and Latin America, but also to countries in central and eastern Europe, where fixed penetration has peaked at a density of approximately 60 percent of households (Skouby and Williams, 2014).

The introduction of prepaid service in the early 1990s unlocked telecommunications for many users with irregular earning patterns at the 'bottom of the pyramid'. This also applied to the Grameen Village Phone program in Bangladesh, which brought phones to 45 percent of all villages using microfinance to turn mobile phones into payphones. The microtelcos in Latin America and the Caribbean also enabled mobile services to be used by the poor (Lirneasia, 2014; Mahan, 2005, Samarajiva and Zainudeen, 2008).

The Internet

The Internet had a different starting point and a totally different development trajectory compared to the telecom networks. In the mid-1960s in the US, the Advanced Research Projects Agency (ARPA) sponsored a study to be executed by universities and research centers on the cooperative network of time-sharing computers. The invention of packet switching in the mid 1960s in the US and the UK led to the ARPANET project, with the first research centers being connected through packet switching in 1970; this was the precursor of the Internet (Abbate, 2000).

In packet switching, a data message is split into a number of relatively short packets, to which an address is added to enable routing of the packet through the network. This method is much better suited for computer communication, which is very wide-ranging in terms of the volume of data to be transmitted; it is asymmetric, with most data being transmitted in one direction; and sometimes involves a short transmission time compared to the set-up time of a circuit switched connection.

In the 1980s, the Internet was so named and the 1000 host computers switched en masse to the use of the newly agreed protocols set for data transmission – transmission control protocol and Internet protocol (TCP/IP). International connections to universities and research institutes were established from the late 1980s onward. A spin-off of one of the regional research centers started to provide TCP/IP network services to business customers. In the early 1990s, a number of US-based Internet service providers (ISPs) created the non-profit organization Commercial Internet Exchange (CIX), to connect their networks through gateways. The operation was financed through a membership fee, and traffic from any other member network was handled free of charge (peering). A similar function was soon established in Europe (through RIPE) and other regions of the world (Abbate, 2000).

In hindsight, four major events can be identified as instrumental in the Internet's development towards its current-day popularity: (1) the creation of the TCP/IP protocol in 1972, under the leadership of Vint Cerf, to be used universally across the Internet for information exchange; (2) the creation of the World Wide Web using the principle of hypertext developed in 1989 by Tim Berners-Lee – the application (html) that would unlock information stored in computers on a worldwide basis; (3) the introduction of the first popular browser, Mosaic, by Marc Andreesen in 1993; and (4) the transition of the Internet in 1995 from a research domain to an open-network resource. Fundamental to the development of the Internet has also been the popularization of computing through the introduction of the PC, notably the Apple in 1977, followed by the IBM PC in 1981 and more recently the laptop and the tablet (Lemstra, 2006).

Cable TV networks

Another infrastructure development trajectory that is important in the context of broadband access to the Internet is the cable TV (CATV) network. CATV networks emerged for the distribution of radio and television (RTV) signals to apartment buildings, using a common antenna system. Through interconnection and consolidation, these systems typically evolved into municipal and regional systems using coax cables for signal distribution and fiber cables in the backbone network. To provide data communication services, these CATV networks had to be upgraded from one-way analogue RTV signal distribution to two-way digital communication.

These CATV networks were typically developed by private entrepreneurs in North America. In Europe, they were more often owned by housing corporations or municipalities, and at the time of liberalization transferred into private ownership or to a utility firm, such as the electricity provider. In most countries, a consolidation wave led to a number of large players operating in non-overlapping service areas, such as each being a monopoly provider in the area they served.

Convergence of networks

Leading up to the broadband era, which started around the year 2000 in most countries, three network development trajectories came together: those related to the two fixed networks, and to the mobile network. To this we must add the trajectory of the Internet. Figure 2.1 shows a stylized representation of the innovation avenues.

The coming together of the worlds of circuit switching and packet switching produced a clash between two engineering cultures and two different technology paradigms, represented on the one side by the 'Bell Heads' from the telecoms industry and on other by the 'Net Heads' from the computer industry (Dosi, 1982; Lemstra, 2006).

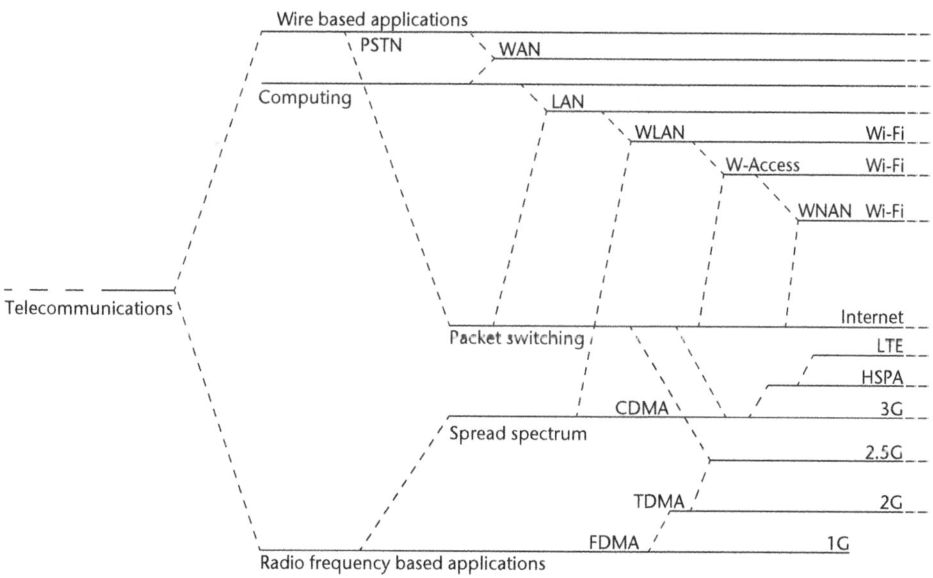

Figure 2.1 Wi-Fi and Internet innovation avenues re-combine

Legend: PSTN: 1–3G: first- through third-generation mobile; CDMA: Code Division Multiple Access; FDMA: Frequency Division Multiple Access; HSPA: High-Speed Packet Access; LAN: Local Area Network; LTE: Long-Term Evolution, 4G; PSTN: Public Switched Telephone Network; TDMA: Time Division Multiple Access; WAN: Wide Area Network; WLAN: Wireless LAN; WNAN: Wireless Neighborhood Area Network.

Source: Lemstra et al. (2010). Reprinted with permission from Cambridge University Press.

The early packet networks were inadequate for real-time applications, such as voice and video. Today, with higher data rates, the Internet is increasingly used for all types of services. Moreover, a difference in quality is often accepted, as the services are typically included 'free'; that is, as part of the subscription fee.

Broadband market dynamics

The final decennium of the twentieth century was a defining period for the telecommunications industry. It featured active implementation of market liberalization policies in many countries around the world. Varying degrees of competition were introduced, and in many countries the incumbent operator was privatized. The market dynamics were fueled by a strong interest from the financial industry, leading to a period of market euphoria. The period marks the beginning of the end of the era of traditional telephone systems based on circuit switching, and the start of the era of packet switching and the Internet. The ubiquitous use of TCP/IP enables an effective decoupling of the underlying transmission infrastructure from the services and applications provided over those networks. It marks the end of the era of dedicated networks and the beginning of over-the-top (OTT) services provisioning.

In the late 1990s, the exponential growth of Internet traffic led to a wave of investments in the construction of fiber backbone links. In the US, incumbents such as AT&T, MCI WorldCom, Sprint, and Qwest, and new entrants, such as Global Crossing, Williams Communications, Level 3, and Enron, deployed close to 900,000 route miles. In Europe, operators such as Telia, Interoute, KPNQwest, COLT, and Global Crossing built competing pan-European fiber networks. Competition in the backbone networks drove down prices for long-distance connections, directly impacting prices for leased lines and long-distance calling. Liberalization also provided more freedom and opportunities for the equipment suppliers who now had many new potential customers (Lemstra, 2006).

Following the collapse of the stock price bubble in 2000, the telecom services sector became subject to consolidation. Incumbent operators refocused on their core services and core markets (Lemstra, 2006). Many of the more recent market entrants had insufficient cash flows to survive. The OECD reported 142 filings for bankruptcy with a total default of US$183 billion, for the period 1999–2003. Infrastructure investments dropped to 30–50 percent of previous levels, which led to the bankruptcy of Nortel Networks, the merger between Alcatel and Lucent Technologies, and Siemens and Nokia merging their telecom networking activities (Lennin and Paltridge, 2003).

Despite this setback, Internet traffic continued to grow although at a slightly lower rate. As the leading supplier of Internet routers and switches, Cisco was least affected. Huawei and ZTE from China started to make important inroads as telecom equipment suppliers.

In the following sections we capture the developments, with a focus on broadband.

Infrastructure-based competition

With the inherently higher bandwidth of the coax cable, the CATV companies became drivers of the competition on speed. A series of upgrades of the DOCSIS modems (data over cable service interface specification – from version 1.0 through 3.0) allowed data rates of up to 120 Mbit/s to be provided. As in the cable network, a group of end users share the capacity of the final part of the access network, at higher data rates the degree of sharing needs to be reduced and fiber is deployed in the feeder network towards the street cabinet.

For access to the Internet using the public switched telephone network (PSTN), asymmetrical digital subscriber line (ADSL) equipment was introduced in the access part of the network, starting with a data rate of up to 2 Mbit/s downstream and 512 kbit/s upstream. ADSL uses a high-frequency band on the local loop and hence could be provided in addition to telephony and ISDN. Subsequent technological upgrades (ADSL2, ADSL2$^+$) allowed for data rates of up to 24 Mbit/s downstream and 1 Mbit/s upstream. As higher data rates required shorter copper loops, fiber was deployed in the access network up to the street cabinet, with very high data-rate DSL (VDSL) equipment used on the remaining part of the copper loop. Data rates per user were further increased to around 80 Mbit/s through bonding (using a double wire pair) and vectoring (active canceling of cross-talk in copper cables).

It should be noted that infrastructure-based competition is a result of the extent to which the legacy networks have been deployed. The PSTN has reached the highest penetration levels, with close to 100 percent of households in the most developed nations, approximately 60 percent in Central European countries, and much lower levels in, for instance, Central African countries. Cable TV networks have been built in urban areas only, and are completely absent in some countries. In Europe, the penetration is highly varied, with close to 100 percent in the Netherlands and Belgium, to being fully absent in Italy and Greece. In the US, the cable networks have a very high penetration level (Lemstra and Melody, 2015).

Competition also emerged based on the opening of the internal communication networks of utility firms; in particular, electricity companies have deployed fiber along the electricity grid. A typical example is KEPCO in South Korea (Oh and Larson, 2011).

Access-based competition

Infrastructure-based competition has been viewed by many analysts as more effective than access-based competition, whereby new entrants provide services competition, facilitated by access to the incumbent operator's infrastructure network. However, in the absence of a cable network, opening the PSTN was the only means to create fixed network competition. This required regulation in order to create a level playing field for entrants. Recent econometric analysis of developments in Europe shows that the combination of access-based and infrastructure-based competition provides the best possible outcome (Lemstra, Van Gorp and Voogt, 2015).

Access regulation became linked to the so-called ladder of investment concept. At the lowest rung of the ladder, the market entry barrier is also the lowest, and very little investment is required from the alternative operator to enter the market. Having established a customer base using a product such as resale or bitstream, the alternative operator would be enticed to decrease its dependency on the incumbent and the fees to be paid by investing more in its own infrastructure (Cave, 2006). As the alternative operators change from resale and bitstream to partial and full local loop unbundling (LLU), their investments per end user connected increases, as does their ability to innovate in the service provision. The progression on the ladder is illustrated in Figure 2.2, using France as an example.

Free/Iliad, an alternative operator in France, is a salient example of an operator having reached the highest rung of the ladder by deploying fiber in the major cities in France. This started with Paris, where the deployment was facilitated by the use of the sewer system and later by access to the duct systems of incumbent France Telecom/Orange (Lemstra and Van Gorp, 2013).

With the CATV network as the most important competitor to the PSTN, regulators refrained from applying access regulation. More recent attempts to open the CATV network show that this is difficult due to the different technologies and network architectures applied. In the US, with a broad deployment of CATV networks, access regulation was abolished in the mid-2000s, with the aim of improving the incentives for investment in fiber to the home.

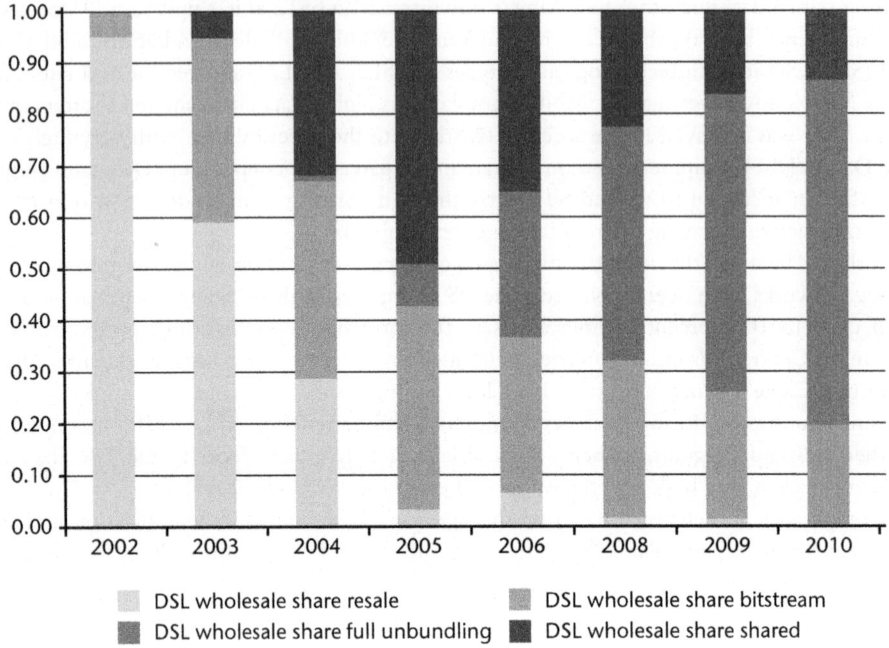

Figure 2.2 DSL share by wholesale type in France, 2002–2010

Source: Lemstra and Van Gorp (2013)

Competition from mobile

The unexpected success of text messaging, or Short Message Service (SMS), as part of 2G, indicated the potential of mobile cellular technology for providing data communication. The introduction of i-mode services by NTT DoCoMo in Japan in the late 1990s illustrates the point: within six months, one million subscribers had been achieved; after 18 months the 10 million mark was reached; and soon thereafter, one third of the user base (Natsuno, 2000).

The development of a standard for broadband communication with data-rate capacity in the range of Mbit/s started in the mid-1980s, gaining traction in the mid-1990s through the 3rd Generation Partnership Project (3GPP), which involved standards and industry organizations from Europe, the US, Japan, and Korea. In 1999, the dispute over intellectual property rights that had emerged in 1995 between Ericsson and Qualcomm was settled and a 3G standard could be concluded, with three modes to assure compatibility with each major 2G standard.

The success of 2G mobile voice technology, combined with the success of the Internet, raised high expectations for mobile broadband networks. This was reflected in the initial willingness by operators to pay very high prices at auction for 3G licenses. The first auction was held in the UK in 2000, with five licenses on offer. The gross proceeds amounted to US$33.3 billion, or US$650 per inhabitant. This auction coincided with the peak of the financial market euphoria (Lemstra, 2006; Melody, 2001).

Later in the year, SK Telecom in Korea introduced the first commercial 3G offering, based on the CDMA 1X standard. NTT DoCoMo of Japan followed a year later. In 2002, Verizon launched 3G services in the US. In the fall of 2007, 132 operators had deployed 3G with high-speed packet access (HSPA), with data rates between 1.8 and 7.2 Mbit/s on the downlink, and

56 operators were providing high data-rate uplinks of 1.4–5.7 Mbit/s. The setback after the period of financial euphoria and delays in providing a range of 3G terminals caused the introduction of 3G to take much longer than that of 2G.

In those countries where people have no or limited fixed services, mobile broadband is the preferred infrastructure for accessing the Internet. With increasing data rates, the number of mobile-only households in other countries is also increasing, reflecting a substitution of mobile for fixed services.

Market dynamics

Competition for access to the Internet has resulted in the quick convergence of prices and strong price competition. In recent years, the competition has become focused on offering higher data rates at relatively constant prices, with ADSL and DOCSIS providing 'always on' connections to the Internet for a flat subscription fee. For mobile access to the Internet, maximum limits were set for the amount of data that could be transferred without additional charges.

Competition in mobile telecommunication has become complex, with many different types of smartphone, applications platform providers and related stores (Apple and the Appstore; Google and Google Play), and service providers. While the BlackBerry was one of the first and most popular smartphones by the Canadian supplier Research in Motion, Taiwanese (such as HTC) and Korean (such as Samsung) suppliers have become market leaders, next to US-based Apple. In terms of the underlying technology, the competition is between the platform operating systems of Apple (iOS), Google (Android), and, to a lesser degree, Microsoft (Windows Mobile). Android is considered to be a more open platform, being built on open source software, while Apple and Microsoft use proprietary software.

Competition in fixed broadband is increasingly driven by bundles of services being offered. From the early combination of Internet plus telephony to triple-play and quadruple-play, the latter includes Internet, telephony, TV, and mobile.

At home, in businesses, in hotels, and at public places (hotspots) high data-rate wireless access to the Internet is provided using WLAN, known as Wi-Fi. Wi-Fi is considered to compete with mobile broadband, but is also a complement for offloading data traffic. Wi-Fi operates in the license-exempt 2-GHz and 5-GHz frequency bands, and has become popular as it is typically provided free of charge. Municipalities have taken up the deployment of Wi-Fi-based networks to improve their services to the public. The low barrier to the technology has allowed the creation of community Wi-Fi networks in underserved areas, such as the Nepal Himanchal network, the Dharamsala network in India, the Mérida network in Venezuela, and the Knysna and Mpumalanga networks in South Africa (Lemstra, Hayes and Groenewegen, 2010).

Over-the-top services and applications

Although not designed for data services, short message service (SMS) has become a very popular and profitable technology in this area. It was also the first service to be absorbed by the Internet in the form of instant messaging (IM), first among BlackBerry users, and later among iPhone users, and has become widely used through WhatsApp. As a result, SMS traffic has fallen by 30–50 percent in recent years.

Voice over the Internet protocol (VoIP) has become popular through Skype, which is a closed community network but is connected to the PSTN through an off-net calling feature.

Most PSTN operators, including incumbents, now provide IP-based telephony services as part of their All-IP strategy.

This also applies to IP-based TV. The PSTN operators have been able to gain a significant share of the RTV distribution from the CATV operators – up to 15–25 percent in some countries. Internet TV is watched mostly in delay mode, using video streaming, replacing the traditional recording of TV programs at home, or by using video-on-demand services, such as those provided by Netflix. In addition, music on demand, which uses platforms such as Apple's iTunes store, or radio-streaming services (including most of the traditional radio stations) provided by a multitude of companies can be received via the Internet.

The market structure

Infrastructure networks (both fixed and mobile broadband), and access to them are necessarily local and national in supply. Hence, competition is still largely influenced by national policies. Alliances have been created between operators, such as 'Concert' between AT&T and BT; Unisource between KPN, Swiss Telecom and Telia; and a joint purchasing agreement between France Telecom and Deutsche Telekom. However, they did not survive. The cross-border supply to multinational corporations, such as by AT&T and BT, consists largely of a combination of own and locally procured services.

More characteristic for the fixed market in 2015 is a combination of the incumbent operator(s), one or two major alternative operators, and a few (specialized) smaller players. In the mobile sector the structure is different, with many more cross-border activities and regional/global branding, such as by Vodafone, T-Mobile, Telefónica and Hutchison. Typically, three to five mobile operators compete in each territory, often with a large number of virtual network operators representing 5–15 percent of the market.

After liberalization, incumbents wishing to expand their business had to go abroad or expand vertically. Hence, the ownership of incumbent operators has become much more diversified and international. See Figure 2.3 for an illustration of the expansion of Telefónica in the 1990s; the figure reflects both geo-political and language preferences, in addition to the opportunity to invest.

Where ownership rules have been liberal, we can also observe private equity funds taking control of the PSTN incumbent, such as in Ireland and Denmark, and of many CATV operators. US-based Liberty Global has become a major player in cable in Europe (Melody, 2007; Lemstra and Groenewegen, 2009).

Through the application of the TCP/IP protocol, telecom services have become decoupled from the underlying infrastructure and can be supplied 'over the top' (OTT). Service provision is no longer bound by geographical borders, but only by language limitations or legal borders. This has emphasized the two-sided market characteristic of the telecoms network infrastructure. Network operators contend that as these OTT service providers (in particular providers of film and video that require very large bandwidth capacity) pay only access charges but not transport and delivery fees, the incentive to invest in access networks is reduced. A recent contract between Netflix and the US-based cable company Comcast suggests a further willingness to pay, as well as a possible move away from flat-fee subscriptions by Comcast. The willingness to invest by content providers is also shown in the deployment of content distribution networks (CDNs), which assure high-quality access close to ISPs.

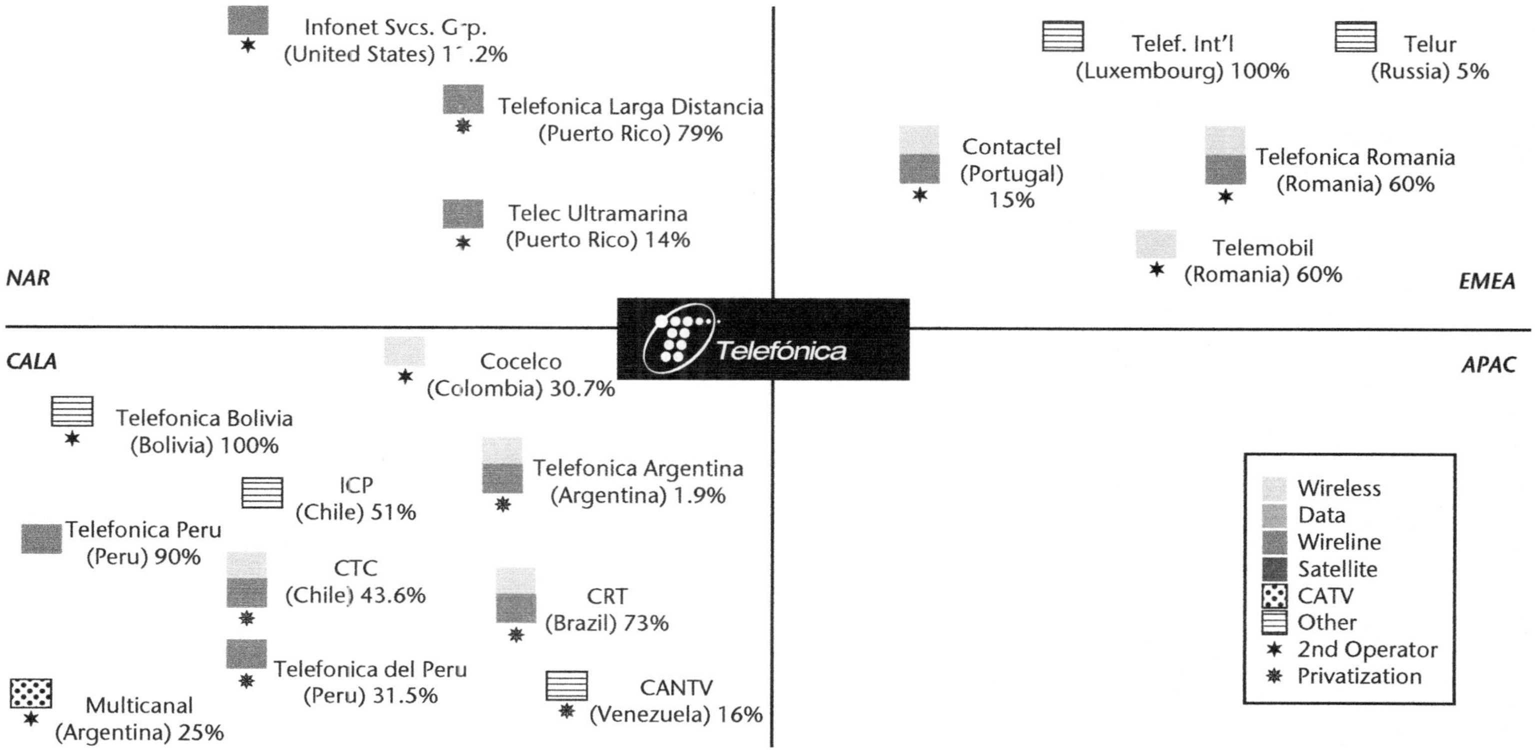

Figure 2.3 Expansion of Telefónica

Legend: APAC: Asia and Pacific; CALA: Caribbean and Latin America; EMEA: Europe, Middle East and Africa; NAR: North America Region.

Source: Courtesy Lucent Technologies.

Realizing next-generation access networks

The use of the Internet intensifies with more subscribers, more data-intense applications and more devices, in particular smartphones, tablets, and an increasing variety of communication-capable terminal devices and machines. This growth in demand drives the transition towards next-generation fixed and mobile networks. These transitions represent major investment challenges for the network operators, as data demand is growing while revenues remain flat.

Next-generation fixed – Fiber to the Home (FttH)

As the full replacement of copper by fiber requires major investment in trenching between the street cabinet and the customer's premises, Fiber to the Home (FttH) deployment has become a gradual process. Demand aggregation is important to reach a viable business case; an initial 20–30 percent take-up rate is typically required. Cost reductions in terms of using existing ducts and rights-of-way are also important, and collaboration in civil works among utility providers is being considered. The low-end offer on fiber is typically 100 Mbit/s symmetrical (that is, in the up- and downlink) and the offers extend into the gigabit range.

Different countries show different trajectories in the transition towards next generation fiber access. A few examples are provided below.

In Korea, a number of factors combine to explain the early take-up of fiber. From 1980 onwards, the Korean Electric Power Corporation built fiber-optic connections to most of the country's high-rise apartment buildings, which became accessible to ISPs through regulation. Around 2000, in the wake of the Asian crisis, the Korean government offered ISPs attractive loans to invest in broadband, which, for instance, Hanaro Telecom used to build optical cables to 4,700 high-rise apartment complexes. Moreover, the use of fiber was subject to exemption from unbundling after 2004, and in 2008 regulations allowed IP-TV providers to offer real-time broadcasting, thereby boosting demand (Kushida and Oh, 2006).

In the Netherlands in the early 2000s, because of the lack of fiber investment by established operators, municipalities declared a 'market failure'. In collaboration with housing corporations, providing demand aggregation and funding, many municipal FttH projects were initiated. This triggered a construction company to build passive open-access fiber networks in competition with the established operators (Lemstra and Melody, 2015).

In Sweden, a large country with low population density outside the major cities, 60 percent of the 290 municipalities are involved in fiber deployments. To ensure these networks are deployed on the basis of market principles, they are all open-access networks with service-level competition. The ownership and operation of the passive infrastructure is typically separated from the active network layer, whereby the operators are selected through a tendering process (Forzati and Mattson, 2015). See Figure 2.4 for the network layering and variety of business roles.

In the US, to facilitate the transition to fiber the regulator exempted it from unbundling in 2003. In 2005, the transition was further stimulated by the abolishment of local loop unbundling. However, investment by both incumbents has been significantly lower than originally anticipated.

In Japan, fierce competition in DSL stimulated the transition to fiber-based competition, which is facilitated by aerial deployments. The incumbents NTT-East and NTT-West, in which the government still has a large interest through a 50 percent share in the NTT Holding Company, lead fiber deployments. Fiber-based competition was stimulated by providing access to fiber, rolled out by the utility companies. By the first quarter of 2008, the number of FttH lines already exceeded the number of DSL lines (Mizutani, 2012).

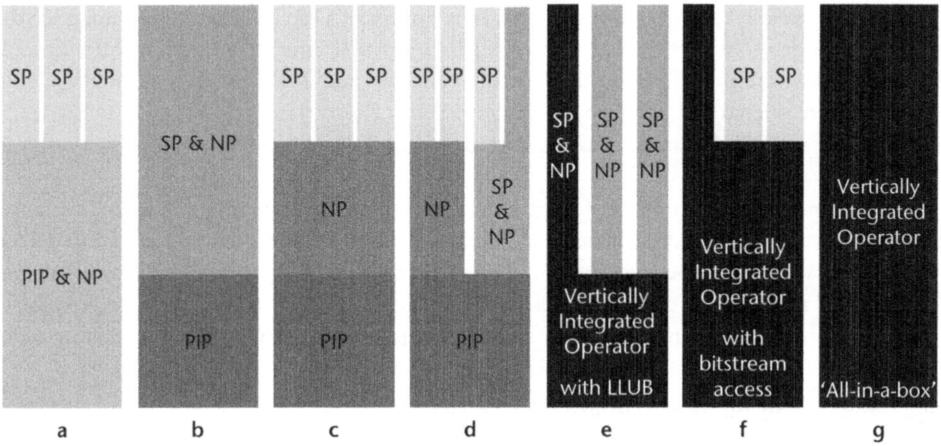

Figure 2.4 Access network business models

Legend: LLUB: Local Loop Unbundling; NP: Network Provider; PIP: Passive Infrastructure Provider; SP: Service Provider.

Source: Lemstra and Melody (2015). Reprinted with permission from Cambridge University Press.

In Australia, in 2008 the federal government opted for a National Broadband Network (NBN), which included the establishment of a new company to build and operate a national fiber network to reach 90 percent of homes, schools, and workplaces with 100 Mbit/s. As the NBN is being realized, the copper network was to be decommissioned. The 2013 NBN review process found that the plans were forecast to miss the intended completion date by three years, and to cost AU$73 billion rather than AU$48 billion. The government's response was a multi-technology approach that would reduce costs to AU$41 billion and facilitate completion by 2019 (Beltrán, 2013).

Next generation mobile – 4G and beyond

Smart mobile devices, such as tablets, and the use of video content and cloud-based applications, are driving data demand. The cumulative annual growth rate of 50 percent or more is expected to continue in the coming years. Hence, operators are being forced to upgrade the existing 3G systems through HSPA, HSPA$^+$ and HSPA Advanced, which accelerate the transition to the next generation of mobile technology (4G), also known as Long-Term Evolution (LTE).

LTE has become a misnomer as 4G follows on the heels of 3G in order to provide an All-IP solution to meet increasing data demand. To improve the system capacity and capacity per user, LTE uses a combination of techniques including Orthogonal Frequency Division Multiple Access, multiple send and multiple receive antennas, wider frequency channels of up to 20 MHz, the ability to combine frequency channels across different frequency bands, smart antennas with beam forming, and interference mitigation techniques to allow the combined operation of macro, pico, and femto cells, as well as Wi-Fi for offload. LTE provides typical user download rates of between 6 Mbit/s and 26 Mbit/s (Rysavy, 2013).

A typical LTE cell has an average of 42 Mbit/s of download traffic, and to reach its spectrum efficiency it needs to be able to ramp up to 100 Mbit/s instantaneously, which is why LTE typically requires fiber-optic links for connecting cell sites to the core network.

LTE was first used at the end of 2009 by Telia Sonera in Oslo and Stockholm using USB-based data modems. With the availability of LTE-compatible smartphones from Samsung and HTC, services were introduced in the US between 2010 and 2011. By the end of 2013, 256 networks were operational in 97 countries, with South Korea, Japan, and the US in the lead. The upgrade to LTE Advanced was first introduced in 2013, providing a cell capacity of 1.2 Gbit/s.

The performance objectives set for the next generation of mobile (5G) are radically higher data rates (two to three orders of magnitude relative to 2012), much lower round-trip delays (<1 ms), and very high dependability for critical applications, combined with a far lower energy footprint and reduction of exposure to electromagnetic radiation. Implementation will include software-defined networking and network function virtualization, based on 'cloud' computing.

Next generation Internet – Internet of Things

The next step in the evolution of the Internet is the interconnection of uniquely identifiable embedded computing-like devices using the Internet, denoted as the Internet of Things (IoT). IoT requires transition to IPv6, which has a much larger address space of up to 3.4×10^{38}, as well as low data rates with very low energy consumption.

IoT includes the earlier form of machine-to-machine (M2M) communication, which originated in the field of industrial instrumentation. The ubiquitous use of the Internet facilitates M2M communication and expands its range of applications, particularly in tracking and tracing. Previously, this was also denoted as telematics. Many mobile operators have departments dedicated to M2M services. A number of energy utility companies have recently outsourced the collection of smart-meter data to communication providers.

IoT is to include: environmental monitoring; energy management; remote health monitoring and notification; building and home automation, such as the smart city of Songdo in South Korea; smart vehicles; and more. The IoT is expected to encode 50 to 100 trillion objects and will be able to follow these objects (where human beings in urban environments are each surrounded by 1,000–5,000 traceable objects). This raises new issues around privacy and security, as well as of autonomy and control (Höller *et al.*, 2014).

Conclusion

Over the first 100 years of telecoms development, the end-user perception of the telephone service largely remained the same. This has fundamentally changed in the past 25 years through the introduction of mobile and the Internet.

A succession of fixed and wireless technologies has changed the user's experience in accessing the Internet for a host of applications. While increasing data rates on fixed networks have led those on wireless networks by a factor of 10, it is mobility and convenience that makes wireless services combined with smart devices so attractive.

In providing increasing data rates, wireless and wire line technologies are converging, as wireless traffic must be offloaded to the fixed network as quickly as possible. Fiber is the next step in increasing the Internet access capacity at home, and in increasing the backhaul capacity of wireless cells. Wi-Fi in the home is converging with femto cells, leading to the extension of the wireless network into apartment buildings and homes.

Although the liberalization of the industry introduced approximately 25 years ago removed the protected monopoly status of incumbent operators, the deep investment required to sustain the deployment of successive generations of infrastructure technologies has resulted in an oligopoly of private firms. While three to five nationally operating mobile infrastructure providers are still economically feasible, the transition towards next-generation fixed access, such as fiber to the home, suggests a return of the monopoly in fixed access networks. Based on the current trends in technological and market development, outside the main urban areas there will be no viable business case for infrastructure-based competition using fiber access. Hence, access regulation will be necessary in many regions to ensure that natural monopoly fiber networks remain open to competition at the services level.

Note

1 The authors would like to acknowledge the valuable feedback received on an earlier version of this chapter from Peter Anker, Aad Correljé, Nicolai van Gorp, Roshanthi Lucas Gunaratne and Rohan Samarajiva.

References

Abbate, J. (2000) *Inventing the Internet*. Cambridge, MA: MIT Press.

Beltrán, F. (2013) Effectiveness and efficiency in the build-up of high-speed broadband platforms in Australia and New Zealand, *Communications & Strategies, Digiworld Economic Journal*, 91(3), 35–55.

Cave, M. (2006) Encouraging infrastructure competition via the ladder of investment, *Telecommunications Policy*, 30(3–4), 223–237.

Casey Corr, O. (2000) *Money from thin air – The story of Craig McCaw, the visionary who invented the cell phone industry and his next billion-dollar idea*. New York: Crown Business.

Dosi, G. (1982) Technological paradigms and technological trajectories: A suggested interpretation of the determinants and directions of technical change, *Research Policy*, 11, 147–162.

European Commission (EC) (1987) COM (87)2 290: Green paper on the development of the common market for telecommunications services and equipment, European Commission, Brussels.

Falk, J.W. (1984) The environment, in R.F. Rey (ed.) *Engineering and operations in the Bell System*. Murray Hill, NJ: AT&T Bell Laboratories, Inc.

Forzati, M. and Mattsson, C. (2015) Sweden, in Lemstra, W. and Melody, W.H. (eds) *The Dynamics of Broadband Markets in Europe – Realizing the 2020 Digital Agenda*. Cambridge. Cambridge University Press.

GSM Association (2009) History and statistics of GSM, Available at: www.gsmworld.com/about/history/.

Höller, J., Tsiatsis, V., Mulligan, C., Avesand, S., Karnouskos, S. and Boyle, D. (2014) *From Machine-to-Machine to the Internet of Things: Introduction to a New Age of Intelligence*. Amsterdam: Academic Press.

ITU (1965) *From Semaphore to Satellite*. Geneva: International Telecommunication Union.

King, J.L. and West, J. (2002) Ma Bell's orphan: US cellular telephony, 1947–1996, *Telecommunications Policy*, 26(3–4), 189–203.

Kushida, K. and Oh, S-Y. (2006) Understanding South Korea and Japan's spectacular broadband development: Strategic liberalization of the telecommunications sectors, BRIE Working Paper 175. Berkeley, CA: University of California at Berkeley.

Lemstra, W. (2006) The Internet bubble and the impact on the development path of the telecommunication sector. PhD dissertation, Department Technology, Policy and Management, Delft, TUDelft, The Netherlands.

Lemstra, W. and Groenewegen, J.P.M. (2009) Markets and public values – The potential effects of Private Equity Leveraged Buyouts on the safeguarding of public values in the telecommunications sector. Delft, TUDelft, The Netherlands.

Lemstra, W. and Melody, W.H. (eds) (2015) *The Dynamics of Broadband Markets in Europe – Realizing the 2020 Digital Agenda*. Cambridge: Cambridge University Press.

Lemstra, W. and Van Gorp, N. (2013) Unbundling: Regulation is a necessary, but not sufficient conditions to reach the final rung of the investment ladder, Second Annual Conference on the Regulation of Infrastructure Industries in an Age of Convergence, Florence School of Regulation, Florence, Italy.

Lemstra, W., Hayes, V. and Groenewegen, J.P.M. (eds) (2010) *The Innovation Journey of Wi-Fi – The road to global success*. Cambridge: Cambridge University Press.

Lemstra, W., Van Gorp, N. and Voogt, B. (2015) Research building the Broadband Performance Index and Broadband Market Model, *Telecommunications Policy* 39(2015), 253–268. Available at: http://dx.doi.org/10.1016/j.telpol.2015.01.006.

Lennin, P. and Paltridge S. (2003) After the telecommunications bubble, *Economics Department Working Papers*. Paris: OECD.

Lirneasia (2014) National broadband networks: What works and what doesn't. Available at: http://lirneasia.net/wp-content/uploads/2014/06/National-Broadband-Networks-What-works-and-what-doesnt.pdf (accessed 26 May 2015).

Mahan, A.K. (2005) Prepaid mobile and network extension, in A.K. Mahan and W.H. Melody (eds) *Stimulating investment in network development: Roles for regulators*. Copenhagen: LIRNE.NET.

Manninen, A.T. (2002) *Elaboration of NMT and GSM standards: From idea to market*. Jyväskylä, Finland: University of Jyväskylä.

Melody, W.H. (ed.) (1997) *Telecom Reform – Principles, policies and regulatory practices*. Den Private ingeniorsfond, Lyngby, Denmark: Technical University of Denmark.

Melody, W.H. (2001) Spectrum auctions and efficient resource allocation: Learning from the 3G experience in Europe, *Info,* 3(1).

Melody, W.H. (2007) The private equity takeover of telecom infrastructure in Denmark: Implications for network development and public policy. *Nordic and Baltic Journal of Information and Communication Technologies*, 1(1).

Meurling, J. and Jeans, R. (1994) *The Mobile Phone Book – The invention of the mobile telephone industry*. London: Communications Week International.

Mizutani, F. (2012) *Regulatory reform of public utilities – The Japanese experience*. Cheltenham: Edward Elgar Publishing.

Mock, D. (2005) *The Qualcomm Equation*. New York: AMACOM.

Mueller, M.L. (1997) *Universal Service: Competition, interconnection, and monopoly in the making of the American Telephone System*. Cambridge, MA/Washington, DC: MIT Press/AEI Press.

Natsuno T. (2000) *i-Mode Strategy*. Chichester, UK: John Wiley & Sons.

OECD (2003, 2005, 2007, 2011, 2013) Communications Outlook. Paris: OECD Publishing.

Oh, M. and Larson, J.F. (2011) *Digital development in Korea: Building an information society*. Abingdon, UK: Routledge.

Rysavy Research for 4G Americas (2013) Mobile broadband explosion – the 3GPP wireless evolution. www.4gamericas.org/en.

Samarajiva, R. and Zainudeen, A. (2008) *ICT infrastructure in emerging Asia – Policy and regulatory roadblocks*. New Delhi: Sage.

Skouby, K-E. and Williams, I. (eds) (2014) *The African mobile story*. Aalborg: River Publishers.

3

Postal sector development between digitization and regulation

Christian Jaag

Introduction

In recent times, the postal industry has undergone large changes that are shaped by two major forces; technological progress and altered regulatory frameworks. This paper will show how technological progress is influencing postal services in different, or rather opposing ways, as well as outline changes in the regulatory framework, and the aftermath of the past liberalization process that led to new market structures, whereas the universal service obligation (USO) have aimed to ensure the provision of a socially desired level of service quality or redistribution. The various forces and influences described are strongly interrelated, and may even interfere with other, non-sector-specific regulations, such as competition law. It is suggested that the developments in the postal industry should be viewed as a co-evolution process between technological progress and regulation.

The chapter is structured as follows. The second section discusses the twofold effect of technological progress on postal services. It will be shown that where the letter post is threatened by the new developments in electronic communications, parcel services are obtaining new opportunities for growth due to the booming electronic commerce industry. The third section introduces the two regulatory domains of the postal industry and analyzes the ways in which they interact. Postal regulation has the task of governing the functioning of the market for postal services, and more often to ensure a level playing field for all postal operators. Further, it has to deal with new relevant markets for postal operators due to the emergence of e-commerce. The USO should guarantee a minimum range and quality of service for the benefit of all users, but may constitute a financial burden to the universal service provider (USP). The fourth section provides an outlook on competition and regulation in the postal sector and offers suggestions for the future design of the regulatory framework. The fifth section concludes, and summarizes the main findings and contributions of this chapter.

Technological progress

Progress in electronic alternatives of communication is creating opposing trends in the postal services industries. Addressed mail volumes are generally shrinking in all industrialized countries as a result of increased competition from electronic means of communication (e-substitution) (Jaag, 2014). According to Dieke *et al.* (2013), between 2007 and 2011, the European letter post sector declined in terms of revenues and volume: between 2007 and 2010, the volume declined on average by 4.3 percent per year, while the revenue dropped by 5.2 percent per year. Between 2010 and 2011, the decline slowed to 3.3 percent in volume, and 1.4 percent in revenue. Dieke *et al.* (2013) estimated that mail volumes will continue to decline. Parcel volumes are growing due to e-commerce, which is the most important growth area for postal operators and consolidators: according to A.T. Kearney (2012), between 2009 and 2011 the European market for courier, express and parcel services grew 4 percent in revenue and 6 percent in volume.

Mail services and e-substitution

In most developed countries, addressed mail volumes grew robustly during the twentieth century and in parallel with gross domestic product (GDP), but began to fall in the first years of the new millennium (Trinkner and Grossmann, 2006). There seems to be no foreseeable end to this trend, and the decrease will strongly affect the development of postal markets in the future. The volume of letters sent via the United States Postal Service (USPS) has declined from a peak of 213 billion in 2006 to around 158 billion in 2012 (Jaag, 2014). Comparing the development of the GDP per capita and the letter volumes per capita for industrialized and developing countries, it can be observed that the two parameters have diverged in recent years for both country categories. Whereas the trends for letter volumes and GDP per capita were quite similar until the beginning of the 1980s, they started to decouple in the later 1980s for the developing countries, and after the turn of the millennium for industrialized countries. Today, there is a wide spread between the evolution of mail volumes and GDP, especially in developing countries (Universal Postal Union UPU, 2014).[1]

Increased indirect competition from electronic substitutes may indicate that the definition of relevant markets applied by regulation and competition law may change. Dietl (2012) argued that the increasing substitutability of letters with electronic means implies that they should both be considered to belong to the same market. This issue is important in the context of several competition cases (mainly in the direct-mail and unaddressed-items segments), which refer to predatory pricing and rebate issues. For example, in 2009 the Danish Competition Council concluded that there was still a separate market for direct mail products that did not include other (electronic) forms of advertisement (The Danish Competition Appeals Tribunal, 2010). In addition, Brennan and Crew (2014) argued that the observed decline in volume was not, on its own, a basis for deregulation. They showed that a product that reduces demand for the firm's services does not necessarily mean that, despite the displacement of demand, the firm no longer has significant market power. In terms of market definition, the original product and the displacing product need not be in the same market. It remains to be seen whether the current market definition will be upheld in the course of the ongoing substitution process.

Being forced to fight competition on two fronts – direct competition due to liberalization of the postal market and indirect competition caused by e-substitution – the concern of cost efficiency arises both for the USP and the regulatory authority. The costs of some elements of the universal postal service are presumably high; therefore, USPs seek ways to mitigate these costs (Maegli *et al.*, 2011). As a result, an increasing number of postal operators have started to invest in digital solutions to combine them with traditional physical postal services (Maegli *et al.*, 2007). Current pilot projects include virtual mailboxes (for example, Belgian Post, Post Denmark, and Canada Post), electronic billing, and e-government efforts like e-health and e-voting. A project that seems to have been quite successful is the Danish electronic communication system e-Boks, which started its service in 2001 and was used by 3.8 million receivers and 20,000 senders in 2012 (Dieke *et al.*, 2013). The company offers public institutions and companies a way to communicate electronically with customers and citizens through a secure platform. With the adaption of the Danish Public Digital Post Act, all individuals above the age of 15 and with a Danish civil registration number had to register for digital post from public authorities by November 1, 2014. As of November 1, 2014, 65.9 percent of the Danish population had already registered for digital post, whereas 24 percent were registered automatically and 10.1 percent remained exempted[2] (Danish Agency for Digitisation, 2014).

Parcel services and e-commerce

While shopping in a retail store, the customer is immediately handed the purchased good after payment. The situation is quite different with customers buying goods through e-commerce; since customer and retailer are not located in the same place at the time of purchase, there is a need for a delivery operator who transports the product from the retailer to its customers. This obviously constitutes a great opportunity for postal operators, since the amount of purchases made via the Internet are increasing significantly (Jaag *et al.*, 2014b). Stengg (2013) estimated the average European growth of e-commerce to be 17 percent in 2013, and even up to 23 percent (Germany) or 30 percent (Russia) in some countries. Ecommerce Europe (2014) estimated the share of the European Internet economy in the European GDP at 2.2 percent and argued that the percentage is set to double by 2016 and to triple by 2020. In 2013, e-commerce in the US made €315.4 billion in turnover, followed by China with €247.3 billion in turnover (Ecommerce Europe, 2014). Regarding the relation between e-commerce and parcel delivery, it is not surprising that, in contrast to the letter market, the European parcel sector, for example, is growing in terms of volumes, as well as revenue, and therefore attracts various kinds of competitors. Okholm *et al.* (2013) distinguished between three main key players in the delivery markets:

- National postal operators: incumbent postal firms, which are typically subject to a USO;
- Global integrators: multi-national operators, such as DHL, FedEx, TNT Express or UPS;
- Couriers and other express and parcel specialists, which differ from the already mentioned categories with respect to services, coverage and business models.

Even though incumbent postal operators still have a strong position in the domestic parcels market and a share of above 20 percent in most European countries, international integrators play an important role and can be seen as serious competitors to the USPs. The domestic parcel market is mainly dominated by the three largest operators offering parcel services in the specific country, since in most European countries the three largest operators achieve a combined market share of above 60 percent (Meschi *et al.*, 2011).

Keeping the high growth rates of e-commerce turnovers in mind, it might be surprising that the majority of purchases are made within national borders, and that only 11 percent of consumers shopped online across borders in 2013 (Stengg, 2013). This circumstance could be attributed to higher prices, poorer quality of service, or lacking information comparing domestic and cross-border parcel delivery (Meschi *et al.*, 2011). Okholm *et al.* (2013) found that prices for cross-border deliveries are three to five times higher than those for domestic deliveries of similar items. A possible explanation for this observation is that competition for cross-border parcel services may differ from that of the domestic market, and that market power is higher in cross-border markets. This point seems to provide an adequate explanation for observed price differences, since cross-border parcel distribution markets are highly concentrated (Jaag *et al.*, 2014b). There are four main competitors; DHL, TNT, UPS, and FedEx, and it is interesting to see that USPs do not hold a dominant market position (Dieke *et al.*, 2013). In addition, Meschi *et al.* (2011) observed that higher cross-border competition has had a strong impact on cross-border price differentials. They found that in the six largest European countries in terms of mail volume (France, Germany, Italy, Netherlands, Spain, and the UK), where competition is highest, cross-border price differentials are significantly lower.

Although postal operators can benefit from e-commerce to boost their business, the quality of delivery services has to be improved to promote (in particular) cross-border e-commerce and thus parcel flows. Even though services such as track-and-trace are standard for most postal operators, customers and retailers have great concerns considering cross-border delivery (Okholm *et al.*, 2013). Therefore, the development and advancement of delivery services and models are important to gain competitive advantages. Such advancements include different insurance options, various speeds of delivery, delivery confirmations, returns services, parcel pick up boxes, etc. However, optimizing and diversifying delivery services should not be the only step postal operators should take to profit from the boom in e-commerce. For example, Finger (2014) suggested that postal operators should widen their service and also take on the roles of information and financial intermediaries (for example, e-retailing platforms and credit card companies) in the e-commerce value chain, since, unlike the physical intermediaries (for instance, delivery operators), those players would capture the most value. There are already several national postal operators that have expanded their service outside the delivery business and started to offer payment solutions (such as Post NL), support for e-retailers (such as La Post, Royal Mail and bpost) or even e-commerce platforms (including DHL Paket).

Regulatory framework and competition

Market regulation and competition

Bypass and access are the two generic forms of competitive entry in the postal sector (Jaag, 2014). With bypass, each postal organization operates its own delivery network. Typically, this entails partial area coverage serving only the most densely populated areas. Hence, the entire value chain is under competition end-to-end. Sweden is a prominent example of postal end-to-end competition in selected market segments. CityMail, the only notable competitor to Sweden's USP Posten AB, entered the Swedish mail market after it was fully liberalized in 1993 (Jaag, 2014). CityMail chose to only deliver pre-sorted bulk mail to the most densely populated areas in Sweden, with a lower delivery frequency of twice a week (and later every third business day). With the adaption of this business model, CityMail could keep costs low since it did not have to invest in expensive sorting technologies and had low delivery costs from not delivering every day, and could offer its services at lower prices than Posten AB. Today, as a subsidiary of the Norwegian incumbent Posten Norge, it is operating under the new brand Bring Citymail and is mainly active in the bulk mail segment. Bring Citymail covers about 54 percent of the delivery points and has an approximate market share of 12 percent in volume and 6 percent in turnover. This shows that end-to-end competition in the mail market is possible even in the presence of strong economies of scale (ERGP, 2014b).

Access gives competing operators the choice to deliver on their own, or to (partly) use the incumbent's delivery network. In the latter case, only upstream processes are competitive, while delivery remains monopolistic. In the US, with its work-sharing system, only USPS's express mail and package delivery services are subject to end-to-end competition, which comes primarily from FedEx and UPS. USPS's monopoly prevents other companies from delivering first-class and standard mail, with an exception for urgent mail. Furthermore, private companies are not allowed to place their deliveries in mail boxes (Jaag, 2014). Panzar (2002) argued that giving downstream access to the network, coupled with economic incentives, increases the contestability of the market for upstream postal services. This results from strong economies of scale and scope in delivery, potentially prohibiting entry for end-to-end services. With access to the incumbent's delivery, market entry is facilitated since only upstream processes (which exhibited weaker economies of scale and scope) have to be operated by the entrants. Experience in the US confirms this: in 2000, approximately 70 percent of all mail was work shared to some degree (Haldi and Olson, 2004).

In Europe, large volumes are work shared (mostly presorted), even though competing postal operators and consolidators are allowed to deliver their items themselves. An example of an access regime in Europe is the UK, where the first access agreement was established in 2004, between the incumbent USP Royal Mail and its competitor UK Mail. Since then, competitors have been able to perform upstream activities, such as collecting, sorting, or transportation for the USP. In return, they received rebates of up to 33 percent of the end-to-end price of Royal Mail. However, since mandatory downstream access resulted in a major loss of business for Royal Mail, significant changes in the treatment of access were introduced with the adaption of the new Postal Services Act in 2011. Since then, the new postal regulator Ofcom may not impose a condition requiring access to the USP's network unless it appears to it that a condition is appropriate for each of the following purposes: (1) promoting efficiency; (2) promoting effective competition; and (3) conferring significant benefits on the users of postal services (ERGP, 2012). Another example of access competition can be found in Germany, where 11.4 percent of the letter items the incumbent Deutsche Post Group distributed were injected into the incumbent's network by competitors. This can be considered a relatively high percentage, since the only country with access competition above 5 percent is Slovenia (7.6 percent). The ERGP examined several hypotheses to explain the different developments of access competition, such as maturity and timing of liberalization, regulation, demographics, mail characteristics, and the existence of rival operators. The ERGP concluded that the emergent patterns are largely heterogeneous, and stated that the developments seem to be based on country-specific factors (ERGP, 2014b). Since access competition is more directly reliant on supporting regulation, country-specific access regimes seem to be an important factor for the emergence of competition, which, for example, is the case (as already discussed) in the UK.

Although market liberalization has not yet led to radical changes in the competitive position of the letter markets, there are few examples where competition has emerged. Out of the 29 countries that participated in an ERGP survey, end-to-end market shares of new entrants have exceeded 5 percent in 10 countries (Bulgaria, Estonia, Germany, Latvia, Lithuania, Netherlands, Poland, Romania, Slovakia, Sweden) (ERGP, 2014b). In the countries that opened up their markets before 2012, competition appears to have largely stabilized at a low rate (ERGP, 2014b). An example of the nearly absent end-to-end competition can be found in the UK, where the postal services regulator Ofcom, acknowledged in 2013 that the incumbent operator Royal Mail had delivered over 99 percent of all mail items in 2011 (Eccles, 2014). Potential reasons for the high incumbent market shares for letters include their good reputation, substantial economies of scale, small margins, high overall quality, and the rather risky sector outlook in terms of declining mail volumes and competitive pressure from electronic means of communication.

The focus of postal regulation has shifted from regulatory aspects, which evolved in the context of the liberalization process, concerning a level playing field for competition and access to the incumbent's network to e-commerce services including both domestic services and cross-border delivery. This has also been acknowledged by the European Commission (EC) (Jaag *et al.*, 2014b). In 2012, the EC published a Green Paper with the objective of boosting e-commerce through establishing an integrated parcel-delivery market in the European Union (EU), and to discuss the problems and challenges faced by consumers and e-retailers (EC, 2012). The key elements of the Green Paper can be summarized according to the following three priorities:

- Improving convenience of delivery services for consumers and e-retailers;
- Ensuring more cost-effective delivery solutions and better prices;
- Promoting improved interoperability of delivery services between operators, and between operators and e-retailers.

The Green Paper was followed by a 'Roadmap for completing the Single Market for parcel delivery' (EC, 2013). Therein, the EC set three main objectives: (1) increased transparency and information for customers and e-retailers; (2) improved delivery solutions; and (3) enhanced complaint handling and redress mechanisms for consumers. The roadmap outlines a portfolio of actions that must be taken in the 18 months following publication by retailers, delivery operators, member states, and the EC itself. E-commerce constitutes a difficult field for regulation, since it is an extremely dynamic market and needs different services in order to function. However, focusing regulation on individual components could create inefficiencies and distortions due to asymmetries. Therefore, the role of regulation should be to enable, rather than to patronize, suggesting that regulation be handled with prudence to avoid unintended consequences.

Universal service regulation and competition

Authors such as Cremer *et al.* (2008) have shown that profit-maximizing postal operators would choose a suboptimal quality of delivery in a fully liberalized postal market. The USO defined a minimum set of services to be provided as a possible solution to this problem. In the following, the illustration of the USO will strongly refer to the concept that is applied in the EU. In Europe, the Postal Directive prescribes a minimum set of postal services of specified quality, which must be available and affordable for all users in all member states (Knieps *et al.*, 2009). Besides affordability, the Third Postal Directive obliges member states (Jaag, 2014) to ensure:

- One collection is completed from appropriate access points every working day;
- One delivery is completed to all addresses every working day;
- The above must include postal items and packages weighing up to 20 kg;
- Uniformity (independent from distance) of prices for single pieces of mail;
- A service is offered for registered or insured items.

The concrete specification and implementation is country specific. As documented in Dieke *et al.* (2013), there are several differences between European countries in the scope of services considered to be universal: 11 countries (Bulgaria, Czech Republic, Germany, Estonia, Finland, Lithuania, Netherlands, Poland, Slovenia, Sweden, and the UK) have defined a minimal range of services including single-piece letters and parcels only. Eight countries (Austria, Belgium, Denmark, Ireland, Luxembourg, Malta, Romania, and Slovakia) with a share of about nine percent of the European letter post market include all non-express postal services, such as bulk letters and parcels, in the USO.

To ensure the provision of universal services, the Postal Directive allows member states to employ one or a combination of three options, respecting the principles of transparency, non-discrimination, and proportionality (Knieps *et al.*, 2009):

- Reliance on market forces;
- Designation of one or more USPs;
- Public procurement.

In practice, almost all EU member states have designated the incumbent operator as the single USP for the entire national territory, without considering alternatives. To name an exception, in Germany the NRA has concluded that Deutsche Post and other operators provide satisfactory universal services to the entire national territory in response to market forces (Dieke *et al.*, 2013). The idea of public procurement to strengthen competition and increase efficiency will be applied in Belgium, where postal operators (including specialized press-distribution firms) will get the opportunity to bid for a concession for the distribution of newspapers and periodicals from 2016 onwards (EC, 2014).

The USO may represent a financial burden, and therefore a competitive disadvantage; in this case, the USPs should be compensated appropriately. In Europe, the USO cost and financing is laid out in the Third Postal Directive. Article 7 of the Directive states that only the net cost of the USO that constitutes an unfair financial burden should be subject to compensation. The net cost of the USO according to profitability cost is the difference in the USP's profit with and without this obligation. Further, what should be regarded as 'unfair' is not defined; however, the Directive imposes criteria on compensation, such as objectivity, transparency, non-discrimination, proportionality, least distortion, or neutrality (Jaag *et al.*, 2014a).

With full liberalization and the abolishment of reserved areas, the need for alternative funding sources for the USO has risen. Often, USPs receive compensation for fulfilling the USO, which can happen through direct state funding, or compensation funds to which operators contribute. These contributions might be waived if an operator provides universal services ('pay or play'). An alternative means of financing that the USO includes is adjusting prices, in the USO case, such that the USP's profit remains unchanged compared to the situation without the USO. This financing mechanism only makes sense if there is price regulation, as is the case in Europe, and if it can be assumed that the USP enjoys a certain degree of market power, so that price changes are supported by demand (Jaag, 2013). According to Dieke *et al.* (2013), 22 EU member states have authorized the establishment of a compensation fund, but only four of these (Cyprus, Estonia, Italy and Slovakia) have actually established one. Three member states (Italy, Poland and Spain) make use of state funding. Compensation of USPs for the unfair burden of the USO remains a controversial topic, since, as noted above, the term 'unfair', as well as the calculation methods for the net cost of USO, are not clearly defined in the Postal Directive. Moreover, intangible benefits of the USO (for instance, exemption from value-added tax [VAT]) may reduce the need for financial compensation.

Interactions between market and universal service regulation

Although regulation of the USO and of the market relevant for postal services has been discussed separately, it is important to understand that the two domains are strongly interrelated. Authors such as Jaag and Trinkner (2011a) argued that various elements of market regulations and universal service regulations should not be viewed independently of each other. Thus, for example, many measures related to the USO and its costing and financing have an impact on the levelness of the market playing field. The USO is often shaped asymmetrically by binding only one operator in the marketplace. The financing of the USO either removes the burden from the USP by granting compensation, or shares the burden with other operators via a USO fund (Jaag, 2014). Jaag and Trinkner (2011c) showed that the net cost of USO – defined as the difference in the USP's profit with and without the USO – very much depends on the design of the compensation mechanism. Their simulations showed that if all operators (including the USP) contribute to a compensation fund the USP would be under-compensated, whereas a compensation fund from which the USP is excluded would lead to an over-compensation of the USP. Only if the USP is compensated from the general government budget is the market equilibrium not (or only insignificantly) affected and the operators' decisions not distorted. Jaag and Trinkner concluded that it does not suffice to just calculate the deficit of unprofitable products: as the financing affects profitable products, these should not be ignored in the cost of the USO.

The process of defining the financing scheme for the net cost of universal services does not only have to include considerations about impacts on the competition conditions and the market equilibrium; it also has to take into account legal aspects, or rather restrictions, due to competition law. To illustrate this potential conflict in the financing mechanism for postal universal services, Switzerland serves as a good example (Jaag and Maegli, 2014). In contrast to the EU, there is no additional examination of whether the burden is to be considered as unfair. In addition, in contrast with the Postal Directive, there is no financing mechanism in Switzerland that envisages state funds or a contribution by competitors towards financing the USO. However, Swiss Post permitted a reserved area for letters up to 50 grams. The medium-term sustainability of the USO financed by the residual monopoly is jeopardized by the increasingly intensive competition from electronic means of communication. At the same time, there is strong price regulation for Swiss Post services. For mail in the reserved area, Article 18 of the Postal Act authorizes the Federal Council to define and approve the adaptation of regulated prices for individual services. Outside of the reserved service another (non-sector-specific) authority, the Price Supervisor, is responsible for price control, provided that the prices are not the result of effective competition. This price regulation is cost-based, which prevents services arising that generate a significant surplus to Swiss Post. However, it also prevents these services from covering losses from unprofitable services due to the USO. Article 51 of the Ordinance on the new Postal Act resolves this conflict by means of a specific financing instrument, known as net cost rebalancing. Swiss Post is allowed to reallocate the net cost of the USO through transfer payments between its units and subsidiaries. It can charge these costs to the services, for which it is able to generate high prices in order to relieve unprofitable services (Jaag, 2011). By shifting costs to the more profitable services, it increases costs and can enforce higher prices under price regulation, which is cost-based. This interplay between financing of the USO and price regulation makes it possible for Swiss Post to provide universal services without external financing.

A further approach to improving the competitive position of USPs is to exclude universal postal services from VAT. This may reduce the need for financial compensation, but could be seen as a violation of the level playing field for all postal operators (see Dietl *et al.*, 2011a). For example, TNT legally challenged the UK's USP, Royal Mail, for this reason in 2009, and argued that VAT should be charged on all services in liberalized markets in order to avoid market distortion (Dietl *et al.*, 2011a). Conversely, Sweden did not provide VAT exemptions to postal services at all. In both cases, the European Court of Justice clarified that VAT exemptions for universal services have to be applied by all USPs, regardless of whether universal services are provided by a public or a private operator (Gramlich, 2014).

Outlook on competition and regulation in the postal sector

The digitalization trend of recent decades has resulted in a number of new technologies that have allowed letters to be increasingly replaced and substituted. Jaag and Trinkner (2012) argued that the postal market and the telecommunications market are converging, and that e-substitution is a reflection of letter mail's loss in market share in the communications market. Figure 3.1 illustrates the structural change of the postal industry due to the convergence of transaction-based markets.

Finger *et al.* (2005) postulated a conceptual framework which suggests that infrastructure systems have to be regarded as the result of a co-evolution process involving technologies on the one hand, and institutions on the other. According to Finger *et al.*, a satisfactory functioning of infrastructures requires coherence between technologies and institutions. Therefore, interrelations between these two domains may not be neglected, or rather have to be coordinated. The increasing convergence between postal products and telecom applications is a new phenomenon, which needs a corresponding co-evolution of regulation in order to exploit synergies and find proper universal service definitions in line with changing customer needs. Thus, rethinking the communications USO in general, and the postal USO in particular, is necessary.

Various countries have adjusted the definition of their USO to counter financial difficulties and decreasing letter volumes. The modifications already made to the national USO have mainly focused on the removal of bulk mail and direct mail, the redefinition of coverage of the USO scope, and adjustment to the weight categories that are included in the USO. For example, Lithuania, Poland, and the UK removed bulk mail; Austria, the Czech Republic, Latvia, Portugal, and Slovenia reduced parcel weight to 10 kg; and Italy and the Netherlands reduced delivery from six to five days per week (ERGP, 2014a). The observed pattern shows that in most cases, changes can be summarized as a limitation of the scope of the USO, such as a restriction of the products and services offered within it. This might be a solution for the short run and should be viewed as a transitional step; however, in the longer run, convergence between the postal and telecommunications sector has to be taken into account to reform not only the scope, but, even more importantly, the concept of the USO. This would suggest that it

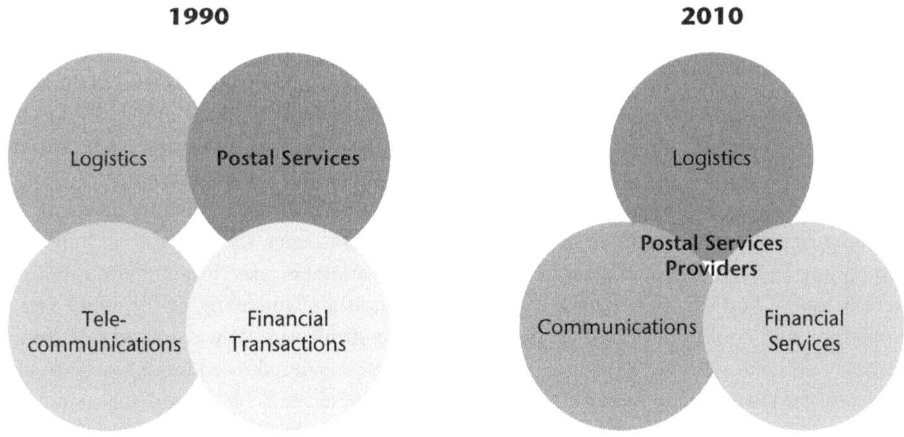

Figure 3.1 Convergence of (transaction) markets

Source: Dietl et al., 2011b.

should not only be focused on the question of *what* services are provided (within the scope of the USO), but also *how* services are provided. One possible answer to the latter question could be that the provision of universal postal services should not depend on a certain technology (Maegli *et al.*, 2011).

Borsenberger (2014) argued that accessibility and proximity in connection with the USO should also contain a 'virtual' dimension regarding progresses in information and communication technologies. She saw online services, which complement and extend physical postal services, as a solution to reduce economic and social costs of the USO. Jaag and Trinkner (2011b) took a similar path by presenting an outline for a future-oriented postal USO, which includes electronic complements and substitutes to traditional postal services. Their newest USO concept combines old and new means to provide universal service and is based on the following five principles: output orientation, technological neutrality, product neutrality, necessity, and viability. In contrast to the current definition of USO, this concept would allow USPs to adjust the universal service individually to the needs of their customers, to the portfolio of available products, and to the technological progress. Due to the convergence of the postal and telecommunications markets, Jaag and Trinkner (2011b) proposed to establish an intermodal USO for postal and telecommunications services. Such an intermodal USO would consist of two basic services. The first is a physical delivery service for items of all kinds meeting certain speed, reliability, affordability, and uniformity requirements. The second is a fast broadband service provided at an affordable, fixed rate. While the first service would require good accessibility and availability measured from the point of residence, the second service would need to be available everywhere.

Most European countries have already merged the postal and telecom regulators organizationally in order to realize economies of scale and concentrate their expertise, as well as experience. But, even if several countries cover regulation of the two markets in the same bill, the responsibilities are still separated institutionally because the responsibilities for the two markets are typically completely segregated in the different departments of the regulatory authority. However, the transformation of regulatory institutions argued for here suggests the need for a more unified and coordinated approach across postal and telecommunications, not only from an organizational, but also from a regulatory point of view (see Maegli *et al.*, 2011).

Conclusion

This chapter discussed the two major forces that shape the postal industry. First, technological progress has a two-fold effect on postal services. E-substitution threatens the postal mail business, and also initiates the advancement of traditional letter post services. E-commerce creates new business opportunities for postal operators and outside the parcel delivery business.

Second, market and universal service regulation are the two regulatory domains that determine market equilibrium in the postal sector. The chapter showed the way in which competition has evolved, and how recent regulatory attempts may foster e-commerce and parcel delivery. Further, the chapter examined how cost and financing of the USO impacts competition and could interfere with the aims of competition law. It was argued that the two regulatory domains strongly interact, and should not be considered or addressed individually.

Finally, the current rigid definition of the USO was questioned. New approaches, including new technologies for the provision of universal services, should be taken into account. The chapter presented the idea of technological neutral postal services, and recommended establishing an intermodal USO for postal and telecommunications services in order for the sector to reach its potential.

Notes

1 Comparing the parameter values from 2011 to their level in 1980; the industrialized countries showed a level of letter volumes p.c. of 118 percent and of GDP p.c. of 174 percent; the developing countries showed a level of letter volumes per capita (p.c.) of 41 percent and of GDP p.c. of 227 percent.

2 There are several reasons for exemption, for example: disability that prevents from receiving post digitally; no computer access; being homeless; language difficulties.

References

Borsenberger, C. (2014) Accessibility/proximity in the digital age: what does it mean for postal networks and postal services?, in M.A. Crew and T.J. Brennan (eds) *The Role of the Postal and Delivery Sector in a Digital Age (Advances in Regulatory Economics Series)*. Cheltenham: Edward Elgar Publishing, pp. 267–279.

Brennan, T.J. and Crew, M.A. (2014) Gross substitutes vs. marginal substitutes: Implications for market definition in the postal sector, in M.A. Crew and T.J. Brennan (eds) *The Role of the Postal and Delivery Sector in a Digital Age (Advances in Regulatory Economics Series)*. Cheltenham: Edward Elgar Publishing, pp. 1–15.

Cremer, H., Donder, P., Boldron, F., Joram, D. and Roy, B. (2008) Social costs and benefits from the universal service obligation in the postal market, in M.A. Crew and P.R. Kleindorfer (eds) *Competition and Regulation in the Postal and Delivery Sector (Advances in Regulatory Economics Series)*. Cheltenham: Edward Elgar Publishing, pp. 23–35.

Danish Agency for Digitisation (2014) Digital post from public authorities, Available at: http://www.digst.dk/Servicemenu/English/Policy-and-Strategy/Digital-Post-from-public-authorities (accessed 30 December 2014).

Dieke, A., Bender, C., Campbell Jr., J.I., Cohen, R.H., Müller, C., Niederprüm, A. *et al.* (2013) *Main Developments in the Postal Sector (2010–2013)*, Study for the European Commission, DG Internal Market and Services.

Dietl, H. (2012) Wie die Grundversorgung den Wettbewerb verzerrt und regulatorische Eingriffe erfordert, in U. Meister (ed.) *Mehr Markt für den Service Public*. Zürich: NZZ.

Dietl, H., Jaag, C., Lang, M., Lutzenberger, M. and Trinkner, U. (2011a) Impact of VAT exemptions in the postal sector on competition and welfare, in M.A. Crew and P.R. Kleindorfer (eds) *Reinventing the Postal Sector in an Electronic Age (Advances in Regulatory Economics Series)*. Cheltenham: Edward Elgar Publishing, pp. 267–280.

Dietl, H., Jaag, C. and Trinkner, U. (2011b) Reform des Postsektors in der Schweiz: Eine Standortbestimmung/La réforme du secteur postal en Suisse: état de lieux, *Die Volkswirtschaft*, 4, 43–46.

Eccles, R. (2014) The regulatory treatment of end-to-end competition in the UK postal sector, in M.A. Crew and T.J. Brennan (eds) *The Role of the Postal and Delivery Sector in a Digital Age (Advances in Regulatory Economics Series)*. Cheltenham: Edward Elgar Publishing, pp. 93–105.

Ecommerce Europe (2014) European B2C E-commerce Report 2014. Facts, Figures, Infographics & Trends of 2013 and the Forecast of the European B2C E-commerce Market of Goods and Services. Available at: http://www.adigital.org/sites/default/files/studies/european-b2c-ecommerce-report-2014.pdf (accessed 12 December 2014).

European Commission (EC) (2012) An integrated parcel delivery market for the growth of e-commerce in EU. Green Paper.

European Commission (EC) (2013) A roadmap for completing the single market for parcel delivery – building consumer trust in delivery services and encouraging online sales. Initiative.

European Commission (EC) (2014) High quality and competitive postal services for citizens and business – state aid control in the postal sector. *Competition Policy Brief*, 6.

European Regulators Group for Postal Services (ERGP) (2012) Report on 'Access' to the Postal Network and Elements of Postal Infrastructure.

European Regulators Group for Postal Services (ERGP) (2014a) Discussion paper on the Implementation of Universal Service in the Postal Sector and the Effects of Recent Changes in Some Countries on the Scope of the USO. Brussels: ERGP.

European Regulators Group for Postal Services (ERGP) (2014b) Report on End-to-End Competition and Access in European Postal Markets. Brussels: ERGP.

Finger, M. (2014) Postal operators as information intermediaries? *The Postal Industry*, 2(2).

Finger, M., Groenwegen, J. and Künneke, R.W. (2005) The quest for coherence between institutions and technologies in infrastructures, *Journal of Network Industries*, 6(4), 227–260.

Gramlich, L. (2014) Das Postrecht in den Jahren 2013/2014, *Netzwirtschaft & Recht*, 6, 277–286.

Haldi, J. and Olson, W. (2004) An evaluation of USPS worksharing: postal revenues and costs from workshared activities, in M.A. Crew and P.R. Kleindorfer (eds) *Competitive Transformation of the Postal and Delivery Sector (Topics in Regulatory Economics and Policy Series)*, 46. Boston, MA: Springer, pp. 185–198.

Jaag, C. (2011) What is an unfair burden? Compensating the net cost of universal service provision, *Review of Network Economics*, 10(3).

Jaag, C. (2013) Price regulation and the financing of universal services in network industries, *Review of Law & Economics*, 9(1), 125–150.

Jaag, C. (2014) Postal-sector policy: From monopoly to regulated competition and beyond. *Utilities Policy*, 31, 266–277.

Jaag, C. and Maegli, M. (2014) Market regulations and USO in the revised Swiss Postal Act: Provisions and authorities, *Swiss Economics Working Paper 48.*

Jaag, C. and Trinkner, U. (2011a) A general framework for regulation and liberalization in network industries, in M. Finger and R.W. Künneke (eds) *International Handbook of Network Industries: The Liberalization of Infrastructure.* Cheltenham: Edward Elgar Publishing, pp. 26–53.

Jaag, C. and Trinkner, U. (2011b) The future of the USO – Economic rationale for universal services and implications for a future-oriented USO, *Swiss Economics Working Paper 26.*

Jaag, C. and Trinkner, U. (2011c) The interaction of universal service costing and financing in the postal sector. A calibrated approach, *Journal of Regulatory Economics*, 39(1), 89–110.

Jaag, C. and Trinkner, U. (2012) Defining and financing an intermodal USO, *Swiss Economics Working Paper 35.*

Jaag, C., Trinkner, U. and Uotila, T. (2014a) Regulation and the burden of the net cost resulting from the universal service obligation, in M.A. Crew, and T.J. Brennan (eds) *The Role of the Postal and Delivery Sector in a Digital Age (Advances in Regulatory Economics Series).* Cheltenham: Edward Elgar Publishing, pp. 204–213.

Jaag, C., Trinkner, U. and Yusof, J. (2014b) *Assessment of EU Post Sector Policy during the Second Barroso Administration (2010–2014),* Robert Schuman Centre for Advanced Studies Research Paper (2014/117).

Kearney, A.T. (2012) *Europe's CEP Market: Growth on New Terms.* Berlin: A.T. Kearney.

Knieps, G., Zenhäuser, P. and Jaag, C. (2009) Wettbewerb und Universaldienst in europäischen Postmärkten, in G. Knieps (ed.) *Fallstudien zur Netzökonomie. 1. Aufl.* Wiesbaden: Gabler (Lehrbuch), pp. 87–109.

Maegli, M., Jaag, C., Koller, M. and Trinkner, U. (2011) Postal markets and electronic substitution: implications for regulatory practices and institutions in Europe, in M.A. Crew and P.R. Kleindorfer (eds) *Reinventing the Postal Sector in an Electronic Age (Advances in Regulatory Economics series).* Cheltenham: Edward Elgar Publishing, pp. 109–122.

Maegli, M., Jaag, C. and Schaad, C. (2007) Triebkräfte der Innovation im Postmarkt, *Innovation Management*, 2, 70–73.

Meschi, M., Irving, T. and Gillespie, M. (2011) Intra-community cross-border parcel delivery: A study for the European Commission.

Okholm, H.B., Thelle, M.H., Möller, A., Basalisco, B. and Rolmer, S. (2013) E-commerce and delivery. A study of the state of play of EU parcel markets with particular emphasis on e-commerce. Study for the European Commission, DG Internal Market and Services.

Panzar, J. (2002) Reconciling competition, downstream access, and universal service in postal markets, in M.A. Crew and P.R. Kleindorfer (eds) *Postal and Delivery Services. Delivering on Competition (Topics in Regulatory Economics and Policy Series)*, 44, Boston, MA: Springer, pp. 93–118.

Stengg, W. (2013) Parcel delivery services and cross-border e-commerce, *Königswinter, 11/26/2013.*

The Danish Competition Appeals Tribunal (2010) *Kendelse afsagt af Konkurrenceankenævnet den 10. maj 2010 i sag nr. 2009-0019768.* Available at: https://www.kfst.dk/Indhold-KFST/Nyheder/Presse meddelelser/2010/~/media/FB8665FBA40C4980953E4A713C485621.pdf.

Trinkner, U. and Grossmann, M. (2006) Forecasting Swiss mail demand, in M.A. Crew and P.R. Kleindorfer (eds), *Progress Toward Liberalization of the Postal and Delivery Sector (Topics in Regulatory Economics and Policy Series)* 49. New York, NY: Springer, pp. 267–280.

Universal Postal Union (UPU) (2014) *Development Strategies for the Postal Sector: An Economic Perspective.* Bern: UPU.

4

New developments in electricity markets following large-scale integration of renewable energy

Gert Brunekreeft, Marius Buchmann and Roland Meyer

Introduction

Renewable energy supply (RES) is no longer a niche market; projections indicate that RES will likely cover a very substantial part of electricity supply from 2030 onwards. Today, 14 percent of European energy demand is met by RES. In some countries, such as Sweden, Austria, and Latvia, more than 30 percent of gross final energy consumption is met by renewable energies (Eurostat, 2014). In Germany, one quarter of gross electricity production is provided by RES (BMWi, 2014). Germany has plans to increase this share to 50 percent by 2030, and 80 percent in 2050 (BMWi, 2010). Relying on current policies, it is safe to conclude that RES is no longer a negligible part of the market; RES has already grown to be a serious player. What does this all mean for electricity markets? It seems that it changes the entire playing field.

This chapter focuses on a selection of important developments; however, it does not claim to be comprehensive. In particular, we discuss the following fields of developments in electricity markets and market design:

- The borderline between subsidy schemes and the electricity market: The experience is that a system with fixed feed-in charges is very successful for a niche market, but if RES is actually a large part of total supply the system reaches its limits. More market-oriented approaches are necessary.
- Third parties: Perhaps the most important development in the electricity sectors is far-reaching fragmentation of the sector. Following liberalization and environmental policy, the sector witnessed a constant growth of new third-party participants. As a result, the sector needs institutions to efficiently coordinate these decentralized actions among parties with widely diverging interests.
- Disruptive challenges for conventional players: Large-scale integration of RES has placed conventional generation under severe financial stress, to the extent that industry observers talk about 'disruptive challenges' (e.g., EEI, 2013). Clearly, the golden age of coal- and gas-fuelled centralized supply with high and stable load factors and profit margins has come to a halt. Energy companies will have to rethink their business model.

- Capacity markets: Worries are increasing that the (energy-only) markets do not provide adequate investment incentives for reserve capacity. Hence, there is a wide and controversial discussion about the necessity and details of capacity markets.

This chapter intends to provide general insights applicable to any country with large-scale integration of RES. However, we draw on examples, numbers and lessons, especially from Germany, because Germany is currently experiencing a challenging large-scale integration of RES. The entire German electricity supply sector is changing as we speak. In this chapter, the first section provides a brief overview of the electricity sector from an economics perspective. The subsequent sections discuss the developments mentioned above: the second section explores the borderline between subsidy schemes and the electricity market; the third section discusses the emergence of third parties; the fourth section describes the disruptive challenges as faced by conventional players; and the fifth section steps into capacity markets.

Electricity markets

Figure 4.1 depicts the electricity value chain. Usually, an economist would distinguish the following stages: (1) generation, which is the production of electricity; (2) the high-voltage transmission network; (3) the low- and medium-voltage distribution networks; (4) retail, which is the sale of electricity to end users; and (5) wholesale trade of electricity between producers and retailers. The networks do not play a role in this chapter and we will thus neglect them. Generation and retail are potentially competitive stages; promoting competition at these stages has been the primary focus of the European Commission (EC).

Until recently, in a typical market, at the generation stage we would find four to eight companies, largely with centralized conventional power plants, nuclear, lignite, coal, gas, and, where applicable, large-scale hydro. The large-scale conventional power plants are typically connected to the high-voltage transmission network. In most markets, competition has long been a matter of concern, but it seems safe to say that generation in most markets is fairly competitive. In Europe, most retail markets have been liberalized and are in fact competitive; end users can choose their supplier and, provided they are motivated to do so, will find it easy to switch suppliers. In other parts of the world, most notably the US, retail market competition has not been a policy focus. At the stage of wholesale trade, we find marketplaces. These can be centralized spot markets, but also virtual platforms for bilateral contracting. Anything goes and any type of contract, be it physical trade or pure financial risk-hedging, seems to exist. Most markets do well and are fairly liquid.

RES enters at both the generation and retail stages. Much of RES is what is called distributed generation; that is, RES tends to be decentralized, small-scale, and connected to low-voltage distribution networks. In fact, RES can be supplied by residential users (also called end users or 'prosumers'), especially through the use of photovoltaics (PV). It is here that we find the strongest current developments. Managing the large-scale feed-in of decentralized RES is technically challenging and requires the grids to become smart; smart grids are based on high-tech information and communication technology (ICT). The actions of decentralized third parties, all of which are participating in one interactive system, need to be coordinated institutionally. 'Smart markets' need rules, responsibilities, and regulations, which are currently being developed.

Worldwide, RES is growing very rapidly. Figure 4.2 shows the global development of RES in electricity output (TWh) and as a share in total electricity production; already in 2016 RES output will exceed output of nuclear or gas. It shows that, apart from hydro,[1] onshore wind is

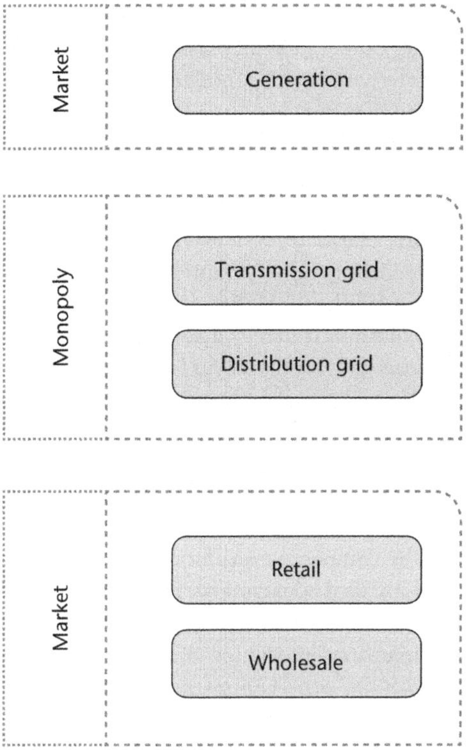

Figure 4.1 Overview of the electricity value chain

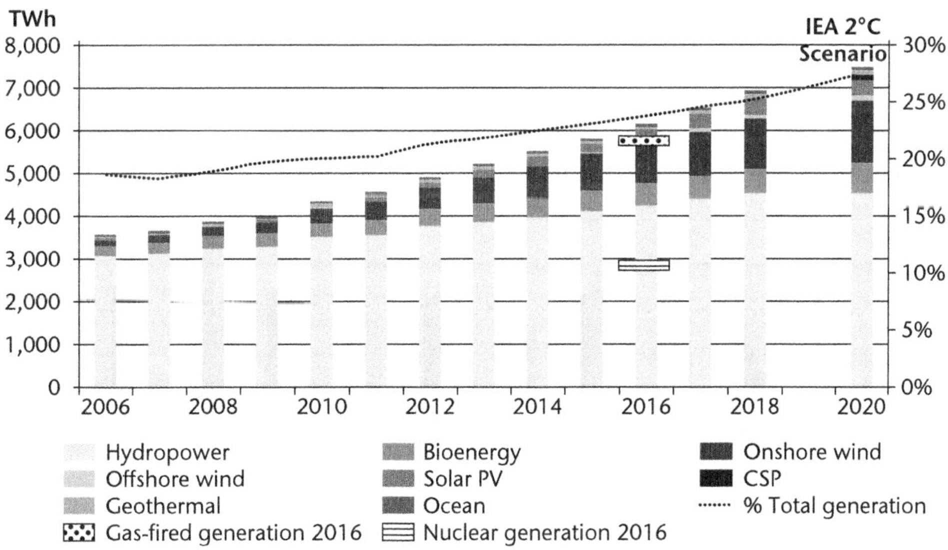

Figure 4.2 Projected RES global installed capacity and expansion until 2020

Source: IEA, 2013, Renewable Energy – Medium-Term Market Report 2013.

growing especially rapidly. Solar is growing as well, but its increase is less considerable when expressed in terms of electricity output (TWh); expressed in capacity, the growth is much more marked. Note also that offshore wind is still considered small.

Figure 4.3 depicts projected installed capacity (in GW) for Europe following projections by the European Network of Transmission System Operators. The letters A, B, and V depict different scenarios. Note that current load in Europe is approximately 525 GW and is expected to grow only moderately (ENTSOE, 2014: 11). Starting in 2014, RES growth in Europe will be substantial, or even explosive. Around 2030, even in moderate scenarios, total installed RES capacity will already be in the vicinity of maximum load.

Figure 4.4 depicts the projected share of RES in total electricity consumption in Germany.[2] The 'medium' scenario B-2024 projects that by 2024 no less than 50 percent of total electricity consumption will be from renewable sources. This will be composed largely of onshore wind, offshore wind, and solar; hydro will not play a major role in Germany.

Large-scale integration of RES: The borderline between subsidy schemes and the electricity market

RES is still too expensive to be competitive against conventional generation without subsidies (especially if these are already installed conventional power plants and capital costs are sunk). As long as RES is a niche market, non-market-based subsidy schemes will work well and do no harm to the market. With large-scale integration of RES, non-market-based subsidy schemes start to come into conflict with the non-RES market, and we have to think carefully about a market-oriented subsidy scheme. The German experience illustrates a market-driven evolution from the non-market-based, command-and-control scheme with fixed feed-in charges to a

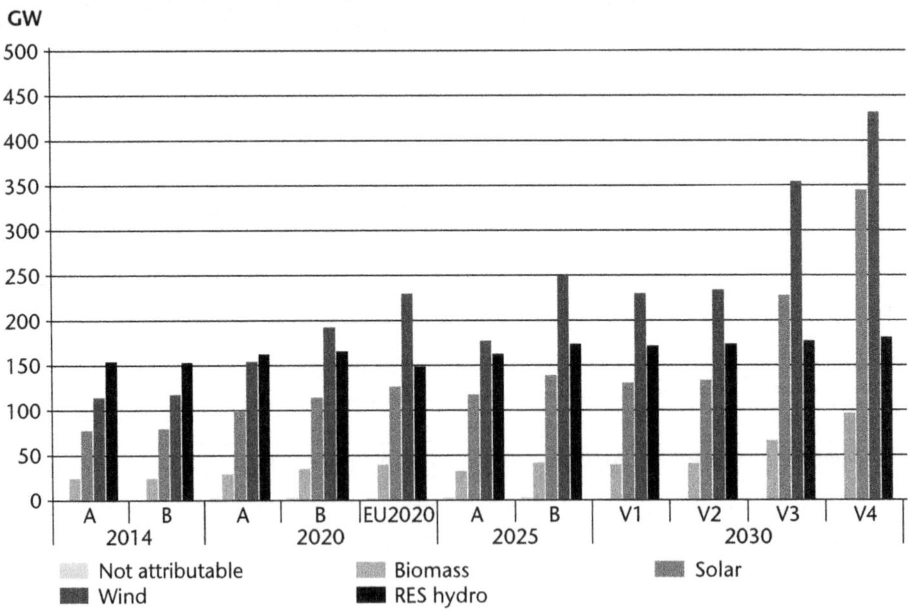

Figure 4.3 Projected RES installed capacity and expansion in Europe

Source: ENTSOE (2014: 51).

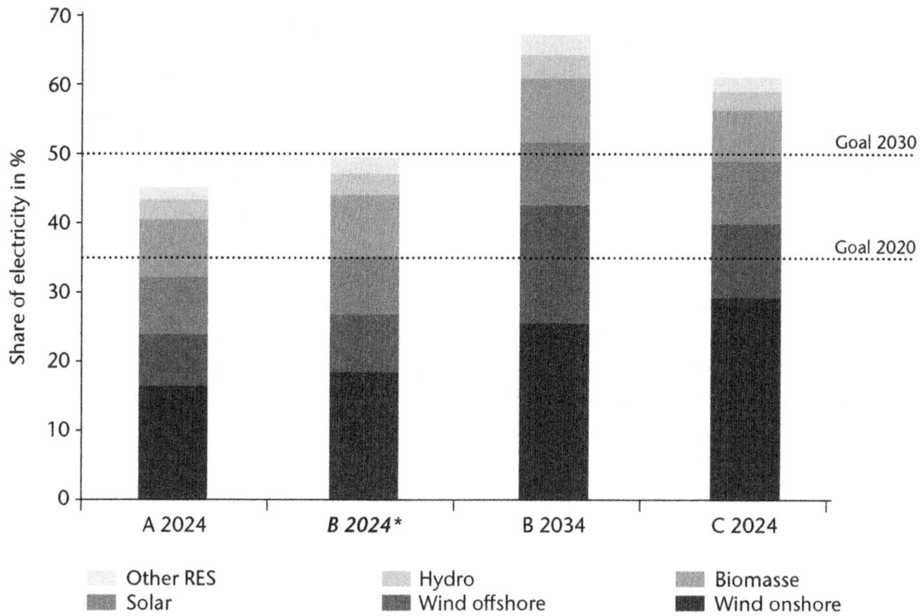

Figure 4.4 Projected RES installed capacity and expansion in Germany

Source: (2014: 51) Based on NEP.
** indicates a difference between scenario B and B* in NEP (2014)*

more market-based system. In this section, we will illustrate what can go wrong with the electricity market if large-scale integration of RES is supported with a non-market-based subsidy scheme.

Until recently, the RES support system in Germany was a typical example of a feed-in system with fixed-feed charges. The main arguments for this system are that it lowers investors' risks and is thus more cost-effective (Klessmann *et al.*, 2008; Bauknecht *et al.*, 2014). It is considered to have been very successful and to be responsible for the rapid expansion of RES in Germany. It was established with the Renewables Energies Act (*Erneuerbare-Energien-Gesetz* [EEG]) in 2000. In 2014, the EEG was substantially reformed, indicating that the system with fixed feed-in charges had reached the limits of incompatibility with the market as a whole. Until the 2014 reform, the EEG had the following key elements (which remain valid for RES installed before the reforms):

- Fixed feed-in charges for every kWh fed into the system: the charges were/are determined by law and updated at regular intervals.
- A take-off obligation: the Transmission System Operators (TSO) have to take off RES and bring this to the market. A take-off obligation is clearly necessary if feed-in charges are higher than market prices.
- RES priority: in case of network constraints, RES had priority.
- No RES curtailment: again, in case of network constraints or, more generally, excess supply, the TSOs were not allowed to curtail RES, unless necessary for system reliability.

The system was the victim of its own success. The growth of RES was vastly greater than anticipated, which caused many problems. First, the subsidy system was far more expensive than anticipated, creating pressure on politicians to interfere (Hiroux and Saguan, 2010). Second, RES at this scale began pushing conventional generation out of the market, creating massive financial pressure for conventional generators. Third, network congestion at all voltage levels requires significant network expansion to integrate RES. Fourth, the non-market-based subsidy scheme started to become a burden for the market; the system had simply reached its limits.

Since 2009, wholesale markets have shown negative prices. Albeit unintuitive at first glance, negative prices can basically be efficient for non-storable goods such as electricity. However, analysis quickly reveals that the overall situation was economically inefficient (see Brandstätt *et al.* 2011b); if wholesale prices reach negative levels, economically speaking, RES (wind and solar) with zero marginal costs should stop producing or be curtailed. This did not happen for two reasons: first, as explained above, the possibilities for curtailment of RES production were strongly restricted by law. If RES generators are curtailed while conventional plants are still running for economic, rather than reliability, reasons, the foregone production of RES would impede climate policy goals. Second, the fixed feed-in charges insulate the RES producers from market signals. The signal of the negative wholesale price does not reach the RES producers, who consequently do not respond to this signal.

Meanwhile, the subsidy-system for RES has changed; the reform of 2014 contains two significant changes. First, the government has tried to control the exploding cost of the subsidy scheme. Second, the subsidy scheme has been reformed to allow more market elements.

The EEG subsidy scheme has become very expensive. Depending on technology, the feed-in charges are considerably higher than wholesale prices; they are funded in the form of an explicit surcharge on the end-user electricity price. In 2014, the surcharge was 5.28 eurocents/kWh on a total end-user price of roughly 30.11 eurocents/kWh. The total annual subsidy amount was approximately €19 billion (BNetzA, 2014). Figure 4.5 shows the development of the RES surcharge in the electricity price.

The absolute sums are high. Moreover, the surcharge system to fund the subsidies is not a progressive tax. The income redistribution effects are similar to a value-added tax: everyone pays the same. However, since low-income households tend to spend a larger share of their income on electricity, the surcharge system is effectively digressive. As long as RES is small, this is all academic; but with large-scale RES, these issues get political. With the 2014 EEG reform,

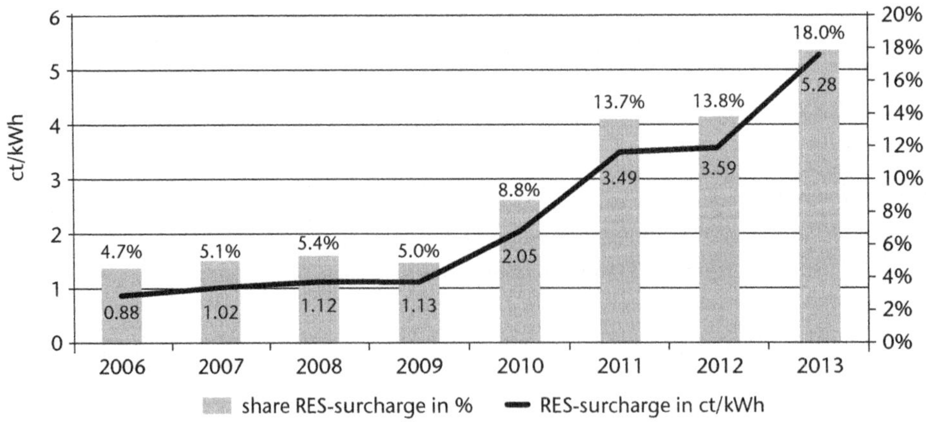

Figure 4.5 Development of the RES surcharge in the electricity price

Source: BNetzA 2014.

the government decided to control the growth of the costs of the RES subsidy scheme. For new RES investment, the feed-in charges have been lowered (depending on technology). Additionally, the annual quantity of new RES is capped. When the cap is reached, the subsidy charges for new RES will be lowered automatically.

The second pillar of the 2014 reform was to introduce more market-based elements. Under the former EEG, direct sale of RES on the market was already possible as an exception. In that case, the RES producers did not receive the feed-in charge, but rather the wholesale prices. Basically, direct sale has now become the rule rather than the exception; since August 2014, direct sale is mandatory for all larger, newly built RES generators (above 500 kW). Only small RES remains under a feed-in charge. As wholesale prices do not suffice to recover full costs of RES, the subsidy is a surcharge premium in addition to the wholesale price. The sum of the wholesale price and the premium should be high enough to recover full costs. In total, this is similar to the system in Spain, which is currently suspended due to the economic crisis (Binda Zane *et al.*, 2012). This change is important as it creates a corridor for market signals. The premium ensures that the overall remuneration suffices to recover full costs. The wholesale prices ensure that RES responds to market prices. However, this response is effectively one-sided, as RES has zero marginal costs. So, whenever prices are positive, RES is simply offered into the market as base load. On the other hand, whenever the wholesale starts to become negative, RES will not be offered on the market; instead, RES operators will seek to be curtailed. In other words, the market will give priority to inflexible plants.

Decentralization: The emergence of 'third parties'

The main effect of the EEG and the resulting increase in RES is the decentralization of the energy system. This decentralization has resulted in a substantial increase of market entries of new players in the electricity sector. Irrespective of whether these new market entrants are energy-related businesses, we call all non-incumbent players 'third parties'. Furthermore, third parties may or (increasingly) may not be energy-related parties. ICT is the obvious example, as smart grids require a certain amount of ICT.

Coordination of these new third parties with incumbents then becomes a key challenge for the institutional design of the future energy system. This is especially true for the distribution system operators (DSOs), as most RES are being connected to the distribution grids; for example, in Spain, roughly 50 percent; Portugal, 75 percent of all wind (Lopez and Ackermann 2007); and in Germany, 90 percent. Markets will play a key role in facilitating the integration of third parties.

The increasing diversity on the investment side for RES in Germany might serve as a good example for the relevance of third parties in the future energy system. The DSOs need to coordinate with many more investors compared to prior to the energy transition. Specifically, residential users become active as private investors in RES. In 2012, 6 percent of all households in Germany had their own RES installed (TNS EMNID, 2013). These renewable-energy installations have, in most cases, a small capacity (<100 kW). Therefore, the number of applications for grid connection of small renewable power plants has increased. These applications need to be processed by the DSO within a limited time frame. Similar effects have resulted from the increasing importance of energy cooperatives. Today, more than 2000 energy cooperatives invest in RES in Europe (Vansintjan 2014), 650 of which are in Germany (Holstenkamp and Mueller, 2013).

In sum, private non-institutional investors (households, energy cooperatives) account for approximately 30 percent of all investments in RES in Germany. Therefore, private households

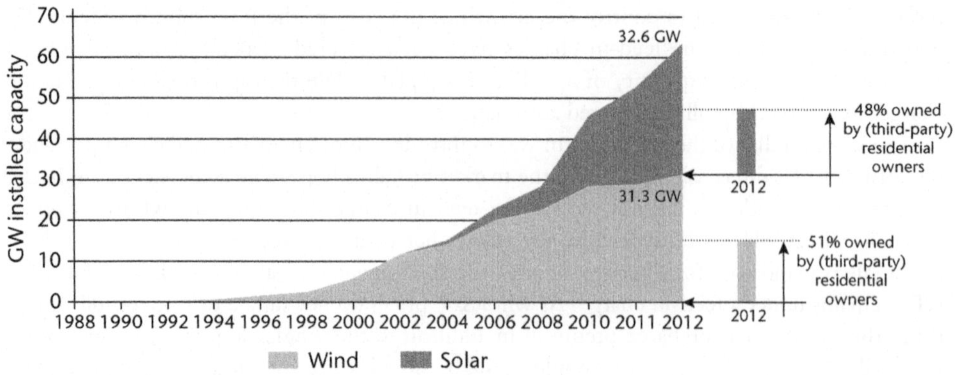

Figure 4.6 Installed RES capacity (PV and wind) in Germany from 1988 to 2012 and private investment in RES in 2012

Source: Based on data from BNetzA 2014 and trend:research Leuphana Universität Lüneburg, 2013.

own roughly 45 percent of total RES capacity (51 percent of PV, 48 percent of onshore wind capacity), while incumbents from the energy sector only own a share of 12 percent of the RES (trend:research and Leuphana Universität Lüneburg, 2013).

The examples above illustrate an important change in the market. The main development is that electricity supply changes quickly from a top-down, closed-shop, single-firm game, into an open, bottom-up, multiple-player system. In such a system, the decentralized activities of multiple agents with diverse incentives need to be coordinated. What used to be intra-firm coordination (hierarchy) should now be coordinated by market mechanisms (Adam Smith's invisible hand). Two market-based approaches serve here as examples of how coordination with third parties could be facilitated.

Smart contracts and flexible pricing demand flexibility, either in the form of demand-side management (DSM) or demand response, requires price signals that reflect the current status of the electricity system. Prices could be flexible either with respect to time or location. Specifically, locational pricing in the distribution system might defer network investment. Smart contracts might serve as a promising coordination mechanism in the future energy system. Smart contracts describe a set of locationally differentiated prices and contracts used by market parties to reduce the need for network investment. These smart contracts will have energy and network components. The point is to incentivize market parties to seek lowest-cost solutions and allow these to be implemented with adequate flexibility (Brandstätt *et al.*, 2011a).

Optimally managing smart distribution grids with many small players, RES feed-in, and DSM requires 'massive data' and opens up a debate on the organization of data management. The collection, aggregation, and distribution of data from smart metering are becoming key tasks to secure efficient market integration of RES. Importantly, this process of data management needs to secure that all eligible market parties can access the data. Therefore, the institutional design of the data management, meaning the governance of information management, needs to ensure that the party responsible for data management is neutral and does not have an incentive to discriminate against any market parties. Here, the analysis of Brandstätt *et al.* (2014) proposed a common information platform, which stressed that a stakeholder-based governance approach that integrates all relevant market parties into the decision process on data management can better facilitate coordination whilst securing competitive neutrality than other concepts currently discussed in the European Union (EU).

Disruptive developments

The rapid growth of RES has started to put wholesale markets under enormous pressure. It seems that the traditional market design is reaching its limit when it comes to large-scale integration of RES.

The merit order is the key element of the wholesale market, as it determines both the order in which generators are dispatched, and the resulting market prices. The merit order corresponds to a supply curve showing the marginal production cost of generators in ascending order. Market price and quantity are both determined at the point of intersection between demand and supply. The so-called 'marginal generator' at this intersection sets the market price, which subsequently determines the revenues for all generators being dispatched. Figure 4.7 illustrates the effect of growing RES capacity on the electricity market; increasing RES capacity shifts the merit order to the right. This merit-order shift actually has two implications representing two sides of the same coin: a 'utilization effect' and a 'price effect'.

The 'utilization effect' results from the fact that electricity production from renewables is characterized by low (or even zero) marginal costs, especially in the case of wind and solar power. The rightward shift of conventional generators, as illustrated in Figure 4.7 means that they will be dispatched less frequently, since RES covers a larger share of electricity demand and is utilized with higher priority. This effect can be measured in terms of the 'load factors', which are defined as the share of hours per year a generator is actually producing. Due to their low marginal cost, RES generators directly compete with traditional base-load generation such as coal, lignite, and nuclear. Those generation units used to run more or less full-time to cover the basic level of electricity demand. This is changing now with higher market shares of RES. As a result of the changing supply structure on electricity markets, load factors of conventional power plants have started to decrease.

The 'price effect' is the second part of the merit-order effect caused by the RES-driven market developments. The price is determined by the highest marginal cost of all producing units. Hence, for any given demand level, the rightward shift of the merit order (as shown in Figure 4.7) leads to lower market prices in the case of RES-dominated energy markets. As a result, the revenues of all generators are undermined by the increasing market share of RES. Figure 4.8 compares the energy input and output prices for coal, gas, and electricity to illustrate the situation in the German electricity market for the two main sources of conventional power.

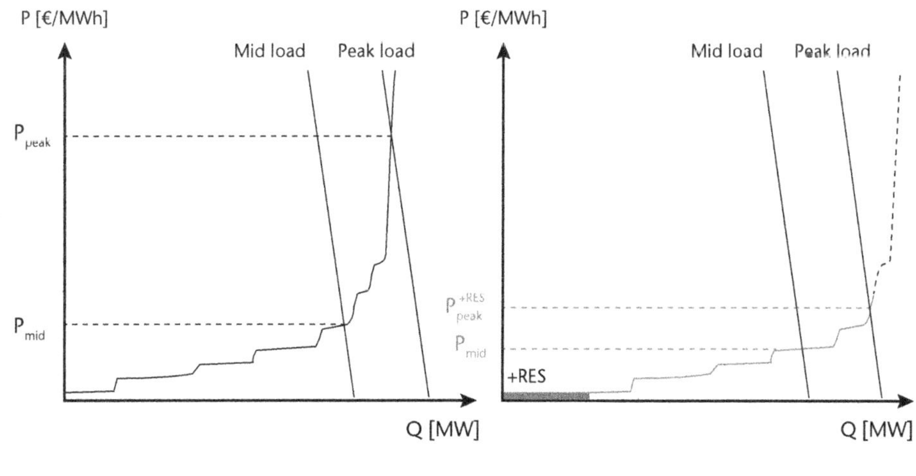

Figure 4.7 Merit-order effect of increasing RES

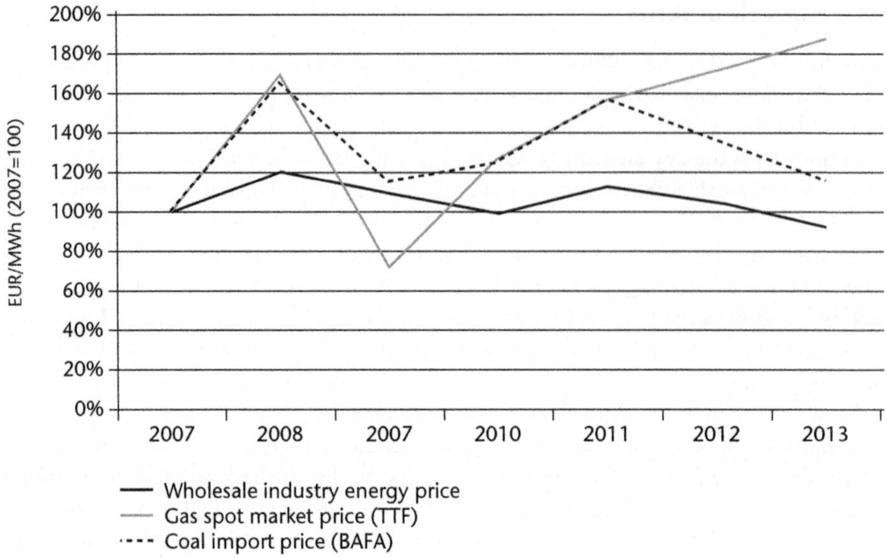

Figure 4.8 Development of energy prices in Germany

The combination of reduced-load factors and lower prices exacerbates the situation for conventional power plants. Gas-fired plants have recently suffered both from a strong decline of load factors since 2010, and negative price developments. The profit margin of gas-fired plants has been too low, given that electricity wholesale prices remained low, while gas input prices increased. Similar effects have occurred in other countries. Ten of Europe's biggest power companies announced the mothballing of a total of 21.3 GW of existing gas power plants in 2013 (Caldecott and McDaniels, 2014). In the case of Germany, the two largest incumbent generating companies, RWE and EON, have recently faced a dramatic collapse of profits due to severe reductions in market prices.

However, the question is: what will happen long term? Apart from regular power production, gas plants serve as reserve capacity for balancing differences between supply and demand. These imbalances are likely to increase with more RES due to intermittency of supply. Therefore, the load factor of gas is likely to be restored later, while the prospects for coal are rather negative. Figure 4.9 shows the projected development of full-load hours per lignite, coal, and gas power plants for different scenarios according to the four TSOs' ten-year network development plan (NEP, 2014). While gas is projected to remain relatively stable, the effect on lignite and coal varies significantly between RES scenarios. In case of a moderate development of RES (scenario A), the full-load hours for coal remain at around 6,300 hours per year, while a strong increase of RES (scenario C) reduces full-load hours of coal plants to 4,000 hours per year, which corresponds to a utilization of less than 50 percent.

Capacity markets and generation adequacy

The market developments described above raise the question of whether the traditional market will be able to cope with large-scale integration of RES, or whether negative effects on generation adequacy, and thereby supply security, have to be expected: that is, the discussion of the so-called 'missing-money' problem and the need for capacity mechanisms (Cramton and

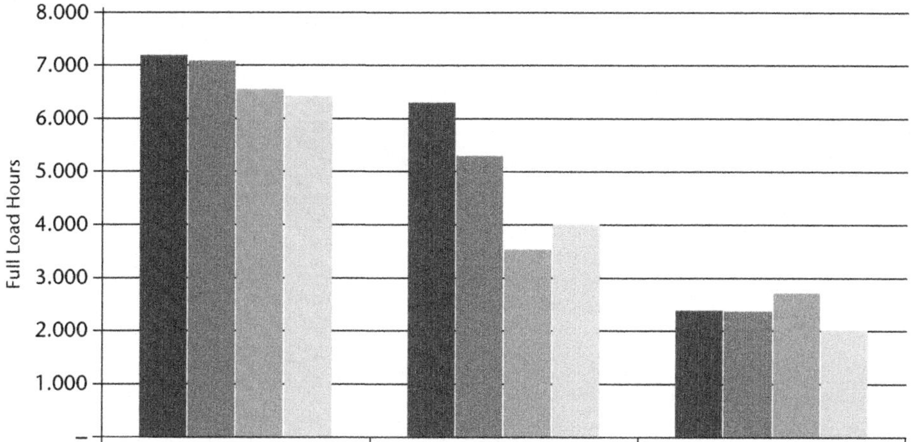

	Lignite	Hard Coal	Gas
A 2024	7.240	6.339	2.406
B 2024	7.109	5.326	2.391
B 2034	6.587	3.533	2.780
C 2024	6.479	4.023	2.070

Figure 4.9 Projection of full-load hours for lignite, coal, and gas plants in Germany

Source: Based on NEP (2014: 49).

Stoft, 2006). The underlying argument is that the revenues of traditional energy markets may not be high enough to cover the fixed cost of conventional generators. As mentioned above, the inframarginal rents generated by prices above marginal cost are the source of revenue to finance the fixed capital cost of power plants. This is due to the traditional market design of 'energy-only markets'; generators only receive money for real power production, not for available capacity. The issue arises as to whether the value of reserve capacity – needed to address extraordinary peak demand or unexpected outages of generators – may not be adequately remunerated to ensure sufficient investment in reserve capacity. The number of times these reserve units actually run and produce power and the corresponding peak prices might be too low to recover capital costs (thus, the 'missing-money' problem).

The theoretical missing-money argument itself is not directly based on the discussion of renewables. Rather, it is a general dispute about whether energy-only markets succeed in attracting adequate generation investment. However, the RES-driven market developments add an important dimension to the problem: the intermittency of RES, notably of wind and solar power plants, significantly increases the volatility of generation, which formerly was only an attribute of demand. As a consequence, even though the utilization of reserve capacity may decline as the market is dominated by RES, conventional reserve capacity will (at least in the near future) remain and play an important role in the electricity market. Flexible reserve capacity such as gas plants are needed to compensate for eventual shortfalls of RES generation, notably in cases of low wind- and solar-power production. Even though the missing-money problem is difficult to prove empirically, several European countries have started to redesign their electricity markets to include capacity mechanisms, or have moved to more elaborate capacity markets. Figure 4.10 provides an overview of capacity mechanisms in Europe.

Capacity mechanisms provide remuneration for generation capacity irrespective of the actual amount of electricity produced by adding a capacity fee onto the energy price. By transforming

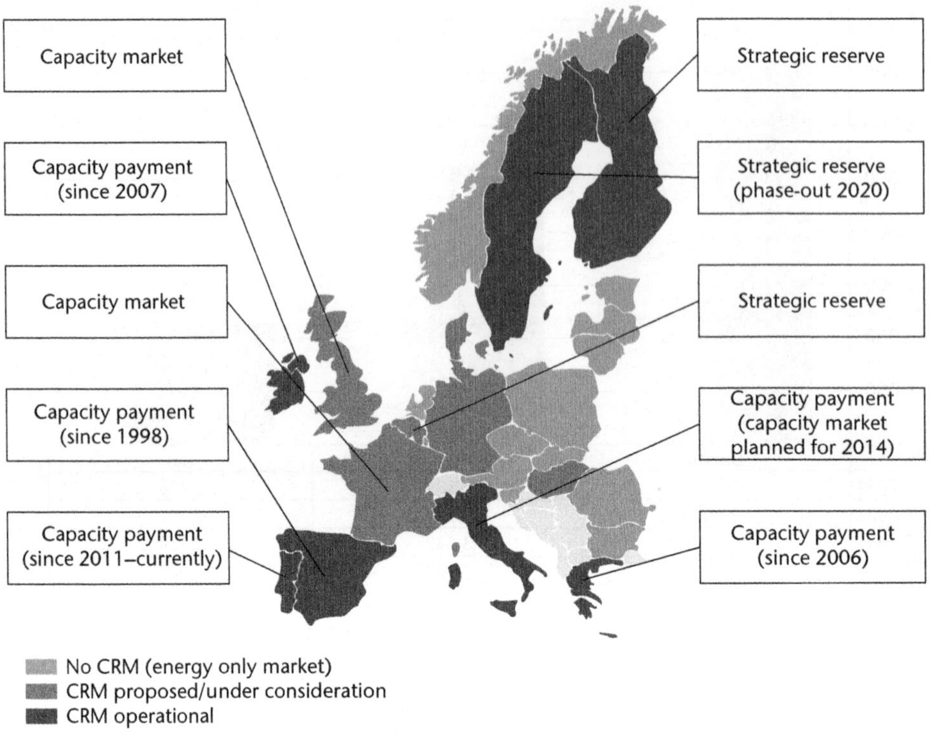

Figure 4.10 Capacity remunerative mechanisms (CRM) in Europe

Source: Adapted from ACER, 2013.

generators' revenues into two-part tariffs, their income is no longer strictly 'energy-only', but is supplemented by payments for available capacity. This reduces the utilization risk, especially for peak generation, and provides more stable revenues to cover fixed capital cost.

As Figure 4.10 reveals, capacity mechanisms exist in multiple forms in Europe and around the world. Each of these mechanisms has its specific pros and cons (e.g., Brunekreeft *et al.*, 2011). In its most simple design, capacity mechanisms consist of capacity payments paid to all or technology-specific forms of capacity. Such a mechanism is 'price-based', since the capacity prices are fixed administratively, while the amount of market capacity ultimately results from investment decisions, which are typically based on the sum of capacity and energy payments. Hence, price-setting for capacity is a difficult task for policymakers if the aim is to avoid both under- and over-investments. Therefore, market distortions are likely to occur. Other versions of capacity mechanisms are 'quantity-based', meaning the overall capacity target is fixed, while capacity prices result from a market mechanism. A common approach for price determination is to use a capacity auction that is either separate from the spot-market auction, or is an integral part of the market – in which case one would use the term 'capacity market'. In a multitude of possible options, below we briefly discuss two: strategic reserves and capacity markets.

A strategic reserve is an example of a relatively cost-efficient version of a quantity-based capacity mechanism. The procedure is similar to the balancing market, though the purpose of a strategic reserve is different. A predetermined amount of generation capacity is tendered and then withheld from the market as a reserve for situations of extreme scarcity. The functioning of the normal energy-only market remains unchanged; the strategic reserves are used only in predefined times of scarcity. This form of capacity mechanism is implemented in Sweden and Finland, and is the focus of discussion in Germany. The market distortions of a strategic reserve are moderate as long as the reserves are used only rarely, and do not suppress normal energy-only market prices (see Brunekreeft *et al.*, 2011). However, the auction design may be a critical issue; a challenge is to evaluate capacity and energy bids in the auction such that both the choice of technology and the dispatch of reserve generators are not distorted (see Brunekreeft *et al.*, 2013).

More elaborate forms of capacity markets are known in the US. PJM is an example of a full-capacity market in which all generation capacity participates in a capacity auction.[3] Retailers are required to have a long-term contract with generation capacity according to their estimated capacity requirements; the latter is determined by the end users that retailers have under contract. This system is also called 'capacity requirements'. The capacity contracts can be (and are) traded on capacity markets. Forward markets up to three years in advance have been established to enhance investment incentives for new capacity. Although such capacity markets may be theoretically efficient, the market design has turned out to be a complex and critical task, as the numerous market design adjustments in PJM have indicated (see Brunekreeft *et al.*, 2011).

Although several European countries have already moved to different forms of capacity mechanisms, the overall discussion in Europe is currently far from conclusive. The optimal market design depends on several aspects. One of the common characteristics in Europe is the movement towards RES-dominated markets, though with different speed and different technology mixes throughout the continent. The underlying philosophy of a strategic reserve is that the energy-only market basically functions well enough to provide investment incentives by shortening capacity and thereby raising the price level on the normal market, while the reserve capacity serves as additional insurance to prevent outages in situations of extraordinary scarcity.

In addition, the choice of capacity mechanism may have implications on neighboring markets. Given the aim of European market integration, national market design decisions may cause cross-border inefficiencies, countervailing the benefits of an internal European energy market. Meyer and Gore (2014) provided a simulation for different capacity mechanisms, showing that coordination of market design changes may be required to prevent negative externalities on neighboring markets. Results also show that full-capacity markets may be theoretically efficient, but there is also a higher risk of inadequate market design, leading to market failures in practice. The negative effects of a strategic reserve may be small as long as it is rarely dispatched, but this may change with the growing shares of RES in the near future.

Conclusion

RES is no longer a niche market; projections indicate that RES is likely to cover a very substantial part of electricity supply; up to 50 percent is no longer a dream, and will therefore be a reality that must be maintained. In a country such as Germany, it is already almost reality; RES output is larger than maximum demand (load) on sunny, windy days. Worldwide, RES is growing very rapidly.

Large-scale integration of RES has a huge impact on the markets and on market design. This chapter focused on a selection of important developments. We discussed four fields of developments in electricity markets and market design:

- The borderline between subsidy schemes and the electricity market;
- Third parties;
- Disruptive challenges for conventional players;
- Capacity markets.

If RES is large and no longer a fringe supply, a non-market-based subsidy scheme will start to conflict with the other electricity markets; therefore, day-ahead and balancing markets and cross-border trade will be adversely affected. The typical RES support scheme with fixed feed-in charges seems to work well in promoting RES, but conflicts with the market if RES grows large. In Germany, where the feed-in system is considered very successful, in 2014, the RES subsidy scheme was reformed; it is now more market compatible.

With an increasing share of RES, the total number of actors in the energy system has increased. Third parties, meaning non-incumbents – not necessarily from the energy sector, but from other segments such as ICT – have entered the energy market and provide new services. Driven by the increasing number of third parties in these four areas, the coordination requirements within the energy supply chain increases. Here, market mechanisms are needed to facilitate this coordination. This requires innovative pricing and contracting schemes, and governance mechanisms.

The rapid increase of RES has put wholesale markets under enormous pressure. Revenues of conventional generation that are needed to back up intermittent RES supply have strongly declined as both prices and load factors have decreased. Companies such as EON and RWE are in severe financial distress and need to drastically rethink their business model.

Several countries have implemented capacity mechanisms to address the so-called 'missing-money' problem. Capacity mechanisms provide remuneration for generation capacity by implementing a capacity fee on top of the energy price. From a European perspective, the main concerns are that one-sided national market design changes may counteract European market integration. The question is whether the EC should take the lead and coordinate changes in market design.

Notes

1 These figures include hydro. It is always debatable whether to include hydro; it is of course zero-CO_2, but hydro has other environmental impacts and is not an option for many countries. Nevertheless, hydro is clearly the largest RES from a global perspective.
2 The letters A, B, and C depict different scenarios for 2024 and 2034. Note that they depict RES production. To achieve this production (TWh), installed capacity (GW) must be far higher.
3 PJM is the largest regional transmission organization in the US and is named after the three states Pennsylvania, New Jersey and Maryland originally involved in its foundation.

References

Agency for the Cooperation of Energy Regulators (ACER) (2013) Capacity Remuneration Mechanisms and the Internal Market for Electricity, Ljubljana, Agency for the Cooperation of Energy Regulators, 30 July 2013.

Bauknecht, D., Brunekreeft, G. and Meyer, R. (2014) From niche to mainstream: the evolution of renewable energy in German electricity market, in P. Sioshansi (ed.) *Evolution of Global Energy Markets*. Elsevier Academic Press.

Binda Zane, E., Piria, R., Frank, R. and Bauknecht, D. (2012) *Integration of Electricity from Renewables to the Electricity Grid and to the Electricity Market – RES-INTEGRATION*, Final Report for DG Energy, Eclareon and Öko-Institute V, Berlin, 13 March 2012.

Bundesministerium für Wirtschaft und Energie (BMWi) (2010) Energy *Concept for an Environmentally Sound, Reliable and Affordable Energy Supply*, Federal Government of Germany, Berlin.

Bundesministerium für Wirtschaft und Energie (BMWi) (2014) *Erneuerbare Energien im Jahr 2013*, Federal Government of Germany, Berlin.

BNetzA (2014) *2009–2014*, Monitoringbericht, Bonn.

Brandstätt, C., Brunekreeft, G. and Friedrichsen, N. (2011a) Locational signals to reduce network investments in smart distribution grids: what works and what not? *Utilities Policy* 19, 244–254.

Brandstätt, C., Brunekreeft, G. and Jahnke, K. (2011b) How to deal with negative power price spikes – Flexible voluntary curtailment agreements for large-scale integration of wind, *Energy Policy*, 39(6), 3732–3740.

Brandstätt, C., Brunekreeft, G., Buchmann, M. and Friedrichsen, N. (2014) Information governance in smart grids – a common information platform (CIP), *Bremen Energy Working Papers No. 18*, Jacobs University, Bremen, accepted for publication in Economics of Energy & Environmental Policy.

Brunekreeft, G., Damsgaard, N., De Vries, L., Fritz, P. and Meyer, R. (2011) *A Raw Model for a North European Capacity Market – A Discussion Paper.* Final Report, Elforsk.

Brunekreeft, G., Meyer, R. and Rammerstorfer, M. (2013) Auction design for a strategic reserve market for generation adequacy: on the incentives under different auction scoring rules, *Bremen Energy Working Papers No. 14*, Jacobs University, Bremen.

Caldecott, B. and McDaniels, J. (2014) Stranded generation assets: Implications for European capacity mechanisms, energy markets and climate policy. *Stranded Assets Programme Working Paper,* Smith School of Enterprise and the Environment, University of Oxford (Oxford, UK).

Cramton, P. and Stoft, S. (2006) *The Convergence of Market Designs for Adequate Generating Capacity.*

Edison Electric Institute (EEI) (2013) *Disruptive Challenges, Financial Implications and Strategic Responses to a Changing Retail Electric Business*, Edison Electric Institute, Washington, DC.

European Network of Transmission System Operators (ENTSOE) (2014) *Scenario Outlook and Adequacy Forecast 2014–2030*, European Network of Transmission System Operators, Brussels.

Eurostat (2014) *Share of Renewable Energy up to 14.1 percent of Energy Consumption in the EU28 in 2012*, Eurostat Press Release, 11 March, STAT/14/37, Luxembourg.

Hiroux, C. and Saguan, M. (2010) Large-scale wind power in European electricity markets: time for revisiting support schemes and market designs? *Energy Policy,* 38(7), 3135–3145.

Holstenkamp, L. and Mueller, J. (2013) *On the State of Energy Cooperatives in Germany – A Statistical Overview as of 31 December 2012*, Working Paper Series in Business and Law, Leuphania University.

International Energy Agency (IEA) (2013) *Renewable Energy – Medium-Term Market Report 2013,* International Energy Agency, Paris.

Klessmann, C., Nabe, C. and Burges, K. (2008) Pros and cons of exposing renewables to electricity market risks – A comparison of the market integration approaches in Germany, Spain, and the UK, *Energy Policy,* 36(10), 3646–3661.

Lopez, E.C. and Ackermann, T. (2007) *Grid Issues for Electricity Production Based on Renewable Energy Sources in Spain, Portugal, Germany and United Kingdom*, Stockholm: Statens Offentliga Utredningar.

Meyer, R. and Gore, O. (2014) *Cross-Border Effects of Capacity Mechanisms: Do Uncoordinated Market Design Changes Harm the Internal European Market for Electricity?* Bremen Energy Working Papers No. 17, Jacobs University, Bremen, published in Energy Economics, 51, 9–20.

Netzentwicklungsplan (NEP) (2014) *Netzentwicklungsplan Strom 2014. Zweiter Entwurf der Übertragungsnetzbetreiber (Network development plan of the four German TSOs),* 50Hertz Transmission GmbH (Berlin), Amprion GmbH (Dortmund), TenneT TSO GmbH (Bayreuth), TransnetBW GmbH (Stuttgart).

TNS-EMNID (2013) Befragung im Auftrag des Verbraucherzentrale Bundesverband (VZBV), TNS-EMNID, Bielefeld.

trend:research, Leuphana Universität Lüneburg (2013) *Definition und Marktanalyse von Bürgerenergie in Deutschland*, Technical Report, Initiative Die Wende – Energie in Bürgerhand, and Agentur für Erneuerbare Energien, trend:research GmbH, Leuphana Universität Lüneburg, Bremen/Lüneburg 2013.

Vansintjan, D. (2014) *REScoop.eu Comments on the DG Competition Draft Guidelines on Environmental and Energy Aid for 2014–2020*, REScoop, Brussels.

5

Natural gas

A tale of three markets

Aad Correljé

Introduction

Today, the world comprises three isolated, but increasingly connected, continental gas markets, in North America, in the European region and in Far East Asia, with Qatar and Trinidad and Tobago as important sources of supply. The three continental markets have their own means of sourcing their gas supply, and, with the exception of Asia, pipelines are the main arteries of transport. Only recently, they were being connected by flows of liquefied natural gas (LNG). This chapter provides a perspective on how these markets are evolving and interacting, taking into account their structural characteristics, institutional features, national policies, and firms' strategies.

Each market is characterized by its particular structure; the physical, geographical, and economic characteristics of the supply and demand side, including the role of gas in energy use, and the competitive position of natural gas vis-à-vis other sources of energy. Crucial in their evolution is the institutional set-up, involving public policy, market regulation, and the public–private coordination of the industry.

The notion of the value chain is used as a device to sketch the functioning of the gas industry, as it allows us to link technical and spatial developments in the gas market with the governance of the system and with economic aspects. First, with regard to the technical system, exploration turns underground gas deposits into reserves that are produced at particular sites. Subsequently, gas is moved via pipelines or LNG vessels, storage facilities, and distribution grids to end users. Second, based on this technical system, the value chain encompasses an institutional framework that determines which activities are undertaken by what actor, how investments are made, how the gas flows are allocated to distribution areas and end users, how these actors are remunerated and billed, and how the added value is distributed among the actors involved, including the state(s).

These value chain dimensions are interacting. Developments in technology allow for new methods of production, transport, storage, and use of natural gas, from both the geographical, as well as the functional, perspective. Such technologies become part of, and require, specific national institutional frameworks for their proper operation. These rules determine how the system is used, how the production and transport takes place, how the gas is traded, and under what conditions. The technologies and rules together determine the costs, revenues, and profits being generated, and their distribution over the actors involved. In turn, these outcomes, or expectations thereof, will drive the actors to develop and apply new technologies, deploy new commercial practices, and take initiatives to change the prevailing sets of rules.

This chapter focuses on the technical/spatial, institutional, and economic developments in the world's main gas markets, and their interconnection. The next section provides a brief overview of the evolving technical and spatial system of the gas industry and its end-use markets. This is followed by an explanation of the issue of economic, commercial, and political coordination, and the tradition of public–private governance of the gas market. The subsequent section will examine how a variety of approaches characterize the liberalization, and restructuring of the markets in the US, Europe, and Asia Pacific. Finally, some remarks are made regarding the further integration of the regional gas markets, and its impact on market governance and regulation in the world energy market.

The evolving technical system

The technical system of the natural gas industry can be described as the segments of a supply chain involving five main functions, as illustrated in Figure 5.1. First, there is the upstream segment comprising the on- and offshore exploration and production activities, the collection of gas from the wellheads, and the treatment of gas to remove the liquid components and impurities. These activities are located in the neighborhood of the gas reserves under exploitation. Second, the gas is transmitted from the production sites to consumer markets. This involves either long-distance high-pressure pipelines, or LNG systems. LNG implies that gas is liquefied by cooling it down to -162°C, for transport by ocean-going tankers to regasification

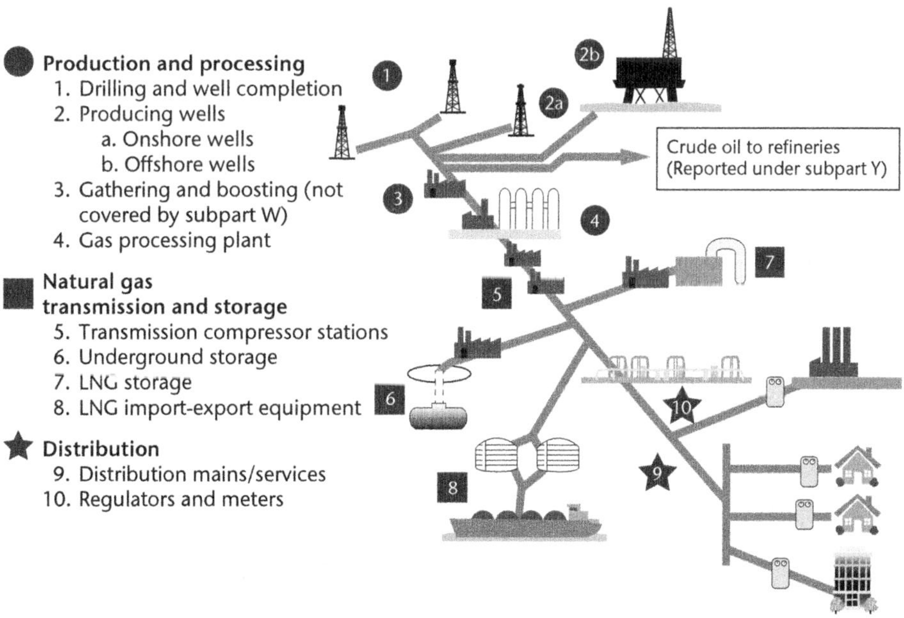

Figure 5.1 The natural gas supply chain

Source: American Gas Association and EPA Natural Gas STAR Program. http://www.epa.gov/ghgreporting/reporters/subpart/w-basicinfo.html.

terminals. From these terminals, the gas flows on via transmission pipelines. The third segment involves the natural gas distribution, delivering the gas to end users. This involves the operation of local or municipal low-pressure pipeline transportation, metering, and billing. Often, large industrial consumers and power plants are supplied directly from the transmission system. The fourth segment involves the storage of gas in any of the three other segments. There are three main types of underground storage: depleted gas reservoirs, aquifers, and salt caverns. Moreover, natural gas can be stored as LNG.

The fifth segment comprises the end use of gas. In its final use, gas has to compete with a variety of other fuels in the energy market, depending on the end-use sector. In the domestic sector, in small businesses, and in schools, hospitals, and other public buildings, gas is used mainly for the purposes of supplying hot water and space heating, where the latter is subject to seasonal load variance. Alternative sources of energy are electric power and heating oil. In large industries, gas is used as a feedstock, for process heating, and for steam supply, possibly involving combined heat and power production. Substitutes are fuel oil, coal, and electric power. The electricity sector is a dynamic market, which, as a system, can relatively easily switch from one source of energy to another; many firms have a portfolio of generating plants. Here, the main alternative fuels are coal, nuclear energy, hydropower, fuel oil, and diesel, and increasingly wind and solar power. Hence, each of these end-use sectors is associated with a particular pattern of daily and seasonal swings and demand elasticity vis-à-vis potential substitute fuels (Naturalgas, 2015; Mokhatab and Poe, 2012).

A crucial consequence of the technical characteristics of the gas system is its spatial-geographic structure. Natural gas deposits are located and fixed underground and determine the location of production sites. Technological advances in constructing increasingly large and long pipelines have driven the geographical expansion of gas systems. Initially, the value chain evolved from a purely local scale, such as city gasworks in the early days, to national systems in which natural gas is transported over longer distances from the production sites to consumers. Later on, where gas reserves and production activities were located in one country, the gas could be transported via transit countries to far-away consumer markets in other countries.

Until the mid-1990s, the main viable form of large-scale gas transport was by pipeline, initially only onshore and later through shallow waters. Hence, the first gas infrastructures developed as national systems. A continental system evolved in North America from the early 1900s onwards. After 1960, a European system started to develop; this was initially supplied from the Netherlands and later from Norway, the USSR and Algeria. In the formerly Eastern Bloc countries an integrated gas supply system was developed, supplied from the USSR. From the 1970s, individual countries in the Asia-Pacific region, including Japan, South Korea, and Taiwan, started to import LNG from overseas suppliers (Leeston *et al.*, 1963; Peebles, 1980; Davis, 1984; Estrada *et al.*, 1988, 1995; Correljé *et al.*, 2003).

However, in many countries the value chain remains national in scope; that is, the gas is being produced and consumed in the same country. In the Middle East, large amounts of gas are produced (often in association with crude oil) and used nationally; only Iran and Qatar export significant volumes. In South America, most of the gas is produced and used nationally; only Trinidad and Tobago (LNG) and Bolivia are significant exporters (BP, 2014).

Over the past two decades, the enhanced economic viability of LNG transport has radically altered the traditional spatial restrictions of the supply chains, allowing for overseas, intercontinental transport (see Figure 5.2). This has two important consequences. First, it has brought about a substantial expansion of the gas resource base. Long-time acknowledged and geologically confirmed gas deposits in areas without a sufficiently large nearby demand potential could be developed as economically feasible resources to supply overseas markets. A second

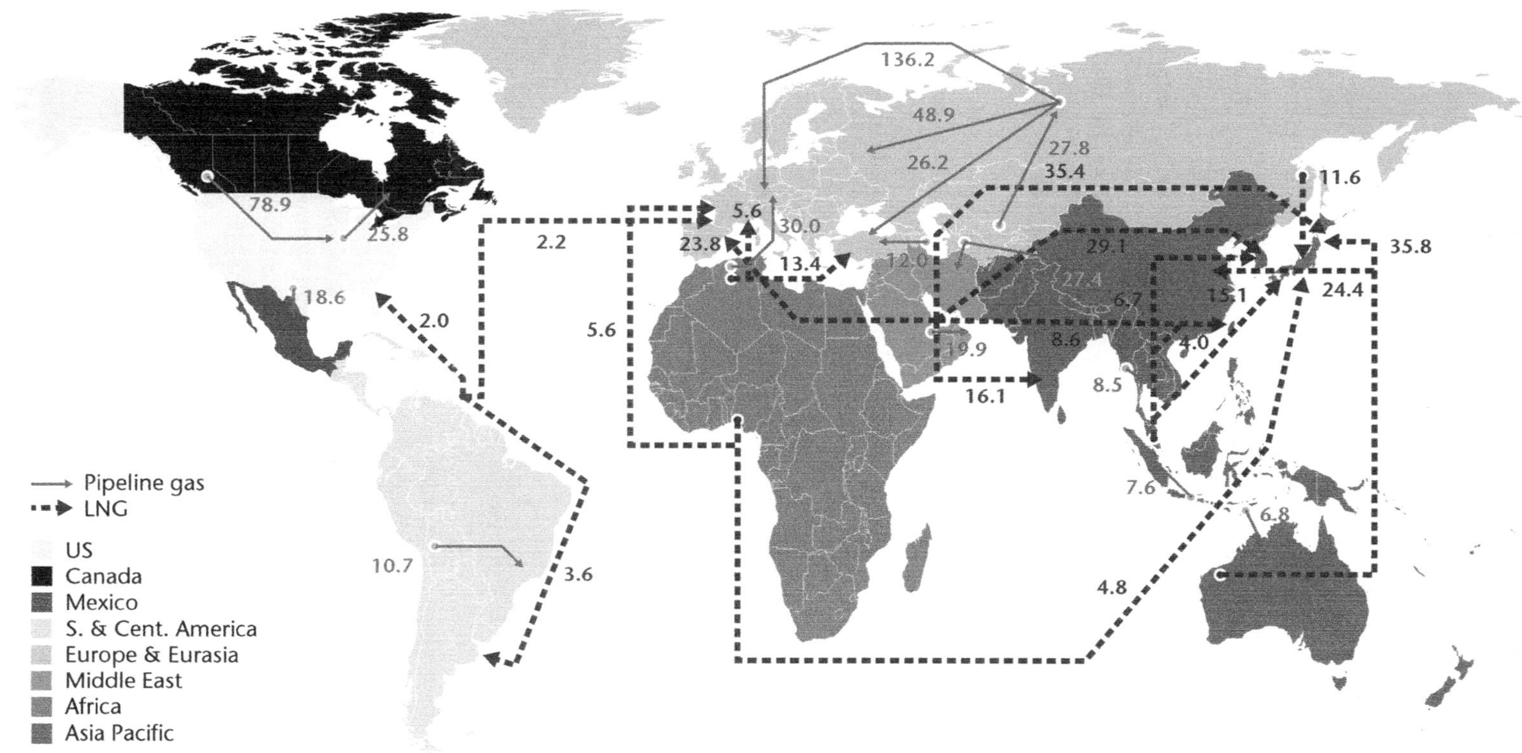

Figure 5.2 Major gas trade movements 2013

Source: Includes data from Cedigaz, CISStat, FGE MENAgas Service, IHS CERA, PIRA Energy Group.

important consequence is that volumes of LNG can be exchanged between the hitherto separate national and continental gas markets. Hence, market dynamics in the different areas have begun to interact. Although the capacities to liquefy and regasify are still modest compared to those available for pipeline-based supply, the traditional pattern of separate regional and national markets is gradually eroding (see Jensen, 2004; GIIGNL, 2014, 2015).

Moreover, ongoing advances in exploration and production technology are making volumes of hitherto un-producible gas available for exploitation; initially onshore, and later offshore. The current development of unconventional (shale) gas production is a next step in this respect (Rao, 2012). By combining deviated directional drilling with hydraulic fracturing, operators can produce gas from source rock with very low permeability, which was not considered possible in the past. Thereby, large 'new' gas reserves have become available for exploitation in more countries. Thus far, the 'shale gas revolution' has materialized only in the US. Yet this has already caused important structural changes in the world gas market. It has liberated large volumes of conventional gas, initially destined for export in the form of LNG to the US, to be available to the rest of the world. In many other countries, including China, Argentina, and Australia, the potential for shale gas development is enthusiastically explored (IEA, 2012).

Finally, there are a number of other emerging technologies on the horizon that deserve attention as potential substitutes for natural gas, such as power-to-gas and bio gas (Gahleitner, 2013). Moreover, in end use, new technologies are expanding the potential use of gas towards new markets, in which gas may substitute other sources of energy in a variety of new applications and appliances, even in the transport sector via small-scale LNG (IEA, 2014). However, these technologies are in the early stages of development and implementation.

Economic, commercial, and political coordination of gas markets

The long-term technical and spatial evolution of the gas supply systems summarized above has coincided with the development of a variety of (national or regional) institutional arrangements by which the technical, economic, and commercial functions are undertaken, and coordinated (Aalto, 2014).

Public policy objectives

As a common starting point, natural gas reserves are considered of national interest, similar to oil reserves. As a result, there is always a degree of state intervention in the exploitation of gas resources. Main elements involve a permit, depletion, and taxation regime, plus environmental and safety requirements. Many countries have established concessionary schemes, regulating the exploration and production activities, investments, and royalties of private industry, such as in the US, the UK, and Australia. In other countries, the state is engaged via (partial) state-ownership, whereby international oil companies (IOCs) form joint ventures with national oil companies (NOCs) and share the profits of the gas exploitation; examples are Algeria, Canada, Indonesia, Netherlands, Norway, Nigeria, Qatar, and Russia. In other cases, IOCs are only allowed to carry out specific tasks as subcontractors. In some countries, the international oil companies are obliged to sell (part of) the gas produced to a state entity, which takes care of the sale and export of the gas (see Baker Institute, 2007; Correljé and van Geuns, 2011; Mommer, 2002; Taverne, 2013; Mitchell and Mitchell, 2014).

Next to energy production, energy supply is often subject to state intervention involving the establishment of taxes and levies on specific products and end-use activities, or their subsidization. These economic instruments may serve a variety of purposes, such as the redistribution of rents among consumer groups and the public budget, or the stimulation, or discouragement, of specific activities (Energy Charter, 2008; EY, 2014). Regarding the latter, sustainability is an important issue, as natural gas is perceived as either a CO_2-emitting fuel, which should be reduced, or as a transition fuel towards a 'carbon-free' energy system. Other parties see a continued role of gas as the cleanest fossil fuel, alongside wind, solar, and other intermittent sources of energy. Depending on the particular perception, policy instruments are applied to achieve the goals chosen, influencing the (future) role of gas in energy supply (CIEP, 2014).

Coordination of the value chain

In addition to these forms of public-policy-driven intervention, the grid-based nature of gas systems and the need for coordination imply that the gas industry was generally perceived to be a natural monopoly, requiring some form of public oversight or control (Correljé *et al.*, 2014; Energy Charter, 2007; Joskow, 2007).

First, there is the need for technical coordination to maintain a constant gas pressure and gas quality, in line with the requirements of the transport system and the connection to it. This requires an adequate and timely balancing of supply and demand, and possibly the use of storage facilities. Moreover, conversion and blending may be necessary to allow different qualities of gas to flow into the system.

Second, there is the need for economic coordination. Huge investments are required both upstream, in the exploration and production facilities, as well as in transport. Investment projects generally involve lead times of around a decade. As demand cannot be predicted with complete accuracy in advance, there is a volume risk involved. This may cause excess capacity in the system, the costs of which cannot be recovered in due time, or a lack of capacity, which causes problems with the certainty of supply.

Third, the production, transmission, and sale of natural gas involve risk as a consequence of physical aspects, such as contingencies affecting production units or pipelines, or seasonal temperature changes affecting demand. Moreover, there are economic aspects, such as changes in the prices of substitute fuels, and long-term economic growth rates. Excess supply of gas in a closed market, in which the actors cannot adjust their supply and demand swiftly, causes the price to drop, whereas shortages cause price spikes. Thus, there is a risk concerning the price.

Historically, such characteristics had brought about a variety of governance relationships between gas producers, transporters, and consumers and their governments, in the US, Europe, the USSR and its satellite states, and Asia. As stated above, exploration and production activities were controlled by the state, including the collection of state revenues. Moreover, the volume and price risk to producers and consumers had been reduced by central planning, regulation, or administered prices and tariffs, and by establishing specific terms of trade for longer periods of time. The risks had often been shared, with producers carrying the volume risk and consumers and/or taxpayers carrying the price risk. In the US, upstream wellhead price regulation had been combined with downstream pipeline and public utility regulation. In Europe, netback pricing, long-term contracting, shared public–private ownership and management of (parts of) these systems had been applied as the solution (Correljé *et al.*, 2003, 2014). In many other countries, such as the USSR, fully state-operated systems had emerged, sometimes involving local public utilities, as in Japan and Korea (Energy Charter, 2007).

International coordination

The gradual internationalization of the gas systems, linking the US and the Canadian systems, linking the systems within Europe (which were later extended towards the USSR and Algeria), and more recently, linking Asia with extensions towards the Middle East, had a number of important consequences. A crucial aspect is that the production, transmission, and distribution activities in the value chain were now located in different countries. These countries often had radically different political and institutional traditions, governed by different national institutional frameworks with a variety of roles, assigned to public and private stakeholders. Moreover, the international gas system(s) had to deal with fundamental differences in the interests of producing countries, transit countries, and consuming countries. Hence, from a strategic energy and economic-policy perspective, the internationalization of the value chain moved natural gas from the realm of national utility and economic policy into the arena of 'high politics' of international affairs among nation states.

Paradoxically, in the past, this situation did not cause too much tension in the industry and between the countries involved. Generally, the commercial contracts between suppliers, transmission companies, and distribution and retail companies were preceded and accompanied by agreements of understanding between the participating nation states. Moreover, these states were often directly involved in the industry, either as public owners, or in joint ventures with private enterprises. Hence, these parties were involved in the coordination of investments upstream, in transit pipelines or LNG ventures. States, but also regional and local public authorities, were also involved in the development of downstream markets and the associated distribution systems. Generally, the distribution of rents along the value chain was negotiated beforehand, while adjustment clauses in the contracts and conflict-resolution procedures took care of managing the impact of unexpected changes in markets. An important device, in this respect, was the application of market-based netback pricing, linking the consumer price for gas to those of oil products in the relevant market in Europe, and initially in Canada, or to the price of imported crude oil in Asia. Primarily, it was ensured that gas was sold at the equivalent value of substitute, though less efficient and technically less convenient, fuels. Moreover, such arrangements made any dispute over market manipulation and unjust pricing irrelevant. The use of the oil price linkage neutralized such antagonisms, as no actor involved in the gas chain could effectively influence the leading oil price (Stewart and Madsen, 2005; Davis, 1984; Estrada *et al.*, 1988, 1995; Correljé *et al.*, 2003; Energy Charter, 2007; Högselius, 2013; Stern, 2008).

In general, the need to balance the interests of private firms in the industry with the public interests in the countries involved, both up- and downstream, was sufficiently recognized to depoliticize conflicts of interest. Generally, the long-term contracts contained protocols for conflict resolution and renegotiation. Moreover, most governments kept gas trade carefully out of international political controversies; on all sides, the stakes were sufficiently high to avoid conflicts. Where structural disputes existed between countries, or between regions, international gas trade simply did not evolve, and potential projects did not mature (see, e.g., Victor *et al.*, 2006).

Towards markets for gas

In the 1980s, important changes began to affect the rationale behind the established value chains, initially in the US, the UK, and Australia, and later in the European Union (EU), some countries in Latin America, and, to a lesser extent in East Asia. The traditional underpinnings of the organization of the gas industry were gradually replaced by neoliberal insights, advocating a 'well-functioning market' in the gas industry. Recognizing the inherent difficulties of bringing about competition in a natural monopoly infrastructure, the new paradigm was based on the unbundling of those segments of the gas value chain that could be conducted under competitive conditions from those that require (strict) regulation (see Jaag and Trinkner, 2011).

Unbundling gas trade and transport

Generally, the exploration and production activities, wholesale gas trading, gas storage, LNG terminals, and the retail business are considered as the segments in the value chain in which competitive markets could be created. State controlled or regulated monopoly operators should give way to competing upstream producers, traders, operators of storage and other facilities and retail sellers. These suppliers and the consumers should decide upon buying and selling on the basis of the individual benefits or utility they expected from their transaction, as signaled by prevailing or expected prices. Such decisions should cover both short-term operating decisions in buying, selling and storing gas, as well as investments involving longer-term horizons. To create dynamic competition, the incumbent monopolistic producers, wholesalers, and retailers would have to be split up into separate firms, while also new parties were expected to enter the newly created markets.

To facilitate access to such a competitive market, the transmission and distribution pipeline systems, with their natural monopoly characteristics, were to be unbundled from the commercial gas trading activities. Creating access to these transport systems became a main regulatory objective in order to facilitate the activities of sellers and traders. A variety of capacity-booking and auctioning arrangements were devised to allocate the pipelines' capacity to these 'shippers'. Tariff regulation forced the monopolistic pipeline operators to control their costs and tariffs (Helm *et al.*, 1989; Armstrong *et al.*, 1995; Newbery, 2001).

Models for restructuring

For smaller gas markets, it was recognized that a lack of economies of scale would preclude the efficiency improvements pursued by full unbundling. Hence, a simple model was promoted in which only gas exploration and production activities would be separated from the downstream industry. By opening the upstream regime for competition, gas producers would then sell their gas to a single-buyer utility, at a price established via competitive bidding. The utility takes care of the transmission and distribution of the gas to the consumers, subject to regulatory oversight to control its monopolistic position (Juris, 1998).

In larger markets, a more comprehensive approach to unbundling would be justified; that is, the separation of the ownership of, and control over, pipeline transport facilities from that of the gas flows through the system. In the traditional approaches, one single integrated company combined the activities of acquiring and selling the gas up- and downstream with the operation of the gas transport system. This had provided such companies with an effective monopoly position, often awarded by the state. To create competition by enabling more parties to engage in the trading of gas, the integrated pipeline companies were forced to provide third-party access (TPA) on their systems to shippers. In this way, a wholesale market could emerge.

Depending on local circumstances, such as the size and the up- and downstream market structure, the unbundling could take various shapes. A relatively soft form of unbundling only required the integrated incumbent gas company to provide access to new traders, which would then purchase gas from producers to be sold in competition with the same incumbent to large industrial users. The producers would benefit from a larger number of potential buyers, whereas end users would benefit from a greater choice of gas suppliers, and from competitive conditions.

The incumbent(s), often retaining the monopoly of supply to small consumers, would also purchase gas at lower prices. Regulatory oversight would only have to assure that the advantages would be passed on to the captive, non-industrial clients.

A more radical solution would involve the full unbundling of ownership of, and control over, the transport functions from supply and wholesale trade, and even storage activities. This would eliminate the incumbent firms' advantages from controlling access of new entrants to the transport systems. In addition, it would create a level playing field for competing producers and traders in the wholesale market to sell gas to large end users and local distribution companies, using the systems of regulated transmission system operators (TSOs). Flexible, short-term contracts and spot markets would emerge to constantly balance supply and demand, yielding prices that reflected the market value of natural gas at a specific location and a specific time. End-use price regulation and regulatory oversight of the distribution companies as local monopolies remained a necessity.

This fully unbundled model has produced two variants that strongly differ in nature. In the US, unbundled pipeline operators provide their transport capacity to traders, or shippers, on a long-term contract basis that underscores the initial investment in pipeline capacity. These long-term capacity rights for transport, storage, and conversion can be retraded in parts and time slices among the shippers in the secondary market, at prices that reflect the market value of the specific capacity and time slot. Thus, the demand for transport services and the value thereof reflects the need for transporting volumes of gas through the country, as a consequence of the commodity transactions in the market. In contrast, in the EU, gas transport capacity is made available to shippers by strictly regulated TSOs that offer their transport capacity at cost, plus tariffs that reflect the cost of using and maintaining the system. Shippers have to 'book' capacity on the systems and pay uniform tariffs (Makholm, 2012; Correljé *et al.*, 2014).

An even more intrusive form of unbundling would provide TPA on the local utilities' low-pressure distribution networks to retail sellers, in competition with the former utilities. The regulated distribution system operators (DSOs) would take care of the gas transport in their service areas, sometimes alongside the provision of electricity distribution and other grid-based services. In this configuration, given effective wholesale and retail competition, the main regulatory functions are maintaining market oversight and checking for anti-competitive behavior, and regulating the transmission and distribution networks, their transport tariffs, and their access conditions.

Regional markets

Since the 1980s, a large variety of approaches emerged regarding the ways in which (groups of) countries restructured their markets. In some countries, there was only a slight change, while others introduced relatively soft forms of restructuring. However, some countries embarked on a process of thorough restructuring, which generally involved a sequence of steps. In the following paragraphs, the approaches applied in the US, Europe, and Asia-Pacific are discussed.

The North American area

After a long history of regulation, in 1978 the US Congress adopted the Natural Gas Policy Act to liberalize the interstate natural gas markets. During the 1980s and 1990s, the Federal Energy Regulatory Commission (FERC) established a framework for a restructured gas market in a series of regulatory orders, which were supported by court decisions. By the turn of the century, a well-functioning interstate gas market with transparent gas-trading practices had emerged, facilitated by an accessible and flexible gas transport system that included short-term capacity resale, shippers' choice in delivery locations on interstate pipeline systems, and the standardization of contracts and pipeline system operation. Capacity and interruptible transportation contracts were traded among pipeline companies and shippers. Nevertheless, at the retail level the regulated utility approach has been maintained, so consumers cannot choose their supplier (see Macavoy, 2000; Leitzinger and Collette, 2002; Correljé *et al.*, 2014; Makholm, 2012; Talus, 2014).

The functioning of a US gas market and transmission system has supported important shifts in the pattern of gas supply and demand. Facing a declining endogenous gas resource base without pipeline connections to overseas suppliers, from 2000 onwards the US industry engaged in developing plans for the construction of a large number of terminals to import LNG. Yet only a decade later, it appeared that US gas demand could be fully satisfied from the production of rapidly developed indigenous shale-gas resources. As a consequence, the short-term price for gas on the US spot market (Henry Hub) fell dramatically and has not yet recovered. Most of the LNG import terminals were mothballed (Wang and Krupnick 2015).

The consequences of these shifts on the global gas and energy market were substantial. First, the US power sector began, rather swiftly, to substitute low-cost gas, and this made large amounts of coal available for export to the world market. Second, the gas production and liquefaction capacity that had been developed elsewhere in the world (GIIGNL, 2014), in anticipation of rising US imports, became available for deliveries wherever existing gasification terminals and contractual circumstances were ready to receive such volumes. Third, in the slipstream of rising shale-gas exploitation and lowering gas prices, the US exploration and production industry moved towards the production of shale oil, or 'wet' unconventional gasses. This reduced the need to import crude oil and placed serious pressure on the world oil price. Finally, the over-supply of low-priced shale gas in the US reopened a long debate in the country about the ban on exports of either crude oil or natural gas to non-affiliated countries. Many investors in (planned) import LNG terminals switched directions and began to convert them into gas export terminals. However, these require acquiescence of the US federal administration and Congress, which is not easy because of the resistance of those states that were consuming gas (Baron *et al.*, 2015).

The European area

The post-1982 restructuring of the British gas industry inspired the EU Commission. In the UK, the introduction of competition and privatization was an unambiguous ideological and political objective, driving the formal dismantlement of monopolistic structures and the creation of market-based trading arrangements (see Helm *et al.*, 1989; Stern, 1990; Armstrong *et al.*, 1995; Newbery, 2001).

In the EU, this process was less straightforward. In a series of Gas Directives (98/30/EC, 2003/55/EC, 2009/73/EC) from 1998 onwards, the EU established increasingly stringent requirements regarding unbundling and operation of the gas industry. At present, the main components involve: (1) regulated TPA for the gas shippers to functionally unbundled national transmission networks, operating as so-called entry/exit areas in which the gas, once entered into the national/regional transport system, can be traded and moved around freely; (2) the introduction of free choice of traders and suppliers to retail customers by abandoning long-term wholesale and retail contracts; and (3) the creation of national regulatory authorities to control and approve transport tariffs (Stern, 1998, 2001; Glachant *et al.*, 2013).

However, this internal gas market is far from being completed. Upstream, the traditional four large pipeline suppliers are still dominant: Russia, Algeria, Norway, and the Netherlands.

Only a few coastal countries have LNG import terminals: Spain (6), the UK (4), France (3), Italy (3), Belgium (1), Greece (1), Lithuania (1), the Netherlands (1) and Portugal (1) (GIIGNL, 2015). At the wholesale level, in many national markets the incumbent companies have remained dominant by controlling the long-term import contracts for pipeline gas and (where applicable) LNG and indigenous production. They rarely enter other national markets as competitors. With the exception of the Northwest European market (the UK, the Netherlands, Belgium, Denmark, and part of Germany), spot-market trading represents only a minor part of gas supply, and new entrants have to procure gas on weakly developed wholesale markets (Glachant *et al.*, 2013; OIES, 2014; Westphal, 2014).

Moreover, in many EU countries traders often lack effective access to the transport networks. Whereas some formerly national TSOs, notably Dutch Gasunie and Belgian Fluxys, have engaged in the operation of gas systems in other member states, many of them are still to be unbundled. Furthermore, the free capacity available on cross-border import pipelines, LNG terminals and storage facilities is limited, as their capacity is booked by incumbent suppliers for the long term (Correljé *et al.*, 2009; Glachant *et al.*, 2013).

As there is no single or common EU energy regulator that is similar to the FERC in the US, a regulatory vacuum exists for cross-border situations. Although an Agency for the Cooperation of National Energy Regulators (ACER) has been established, such cooperation is still voluntary. As a next phase in the institutional evolution, ACER is advocating the Gas Target Model. This should provide cross-border linkages between the national or regional entry/exit areas, which are expected to evolve as well-functioning gas markets. The delivery of long-term contracted volumes of gas, plus the delivery of occasional spot volumes, should then take place at the borders of these entry/exit areas (Vazquez *et al.*, 2012; Yafimava, 2013; ACER, 2015).

Regarding the European sources of supply, a number of critical issues have emerged over the past decade. First, main indigenous sources, such as in the Netherlands and the UK, are in decline. As a European shale gas revolution is not very likely (see Chyong and Reiner, 2015), this implies that the EU will become increasingly dependent on external suppliers. Second, concerns about the security of the gas supply have entered the policy agenda, as the disintegration of the USSR created new transit countries with their own interests. Particularly, the disputes between Russia and Ukraine, and the disruptions of the gas transit flows through the Ukraine caused supply problems in Central and Southeastern Europe (Stern *et al.*, 2009).

The EU Commission's solution to both issues was to intensify its efforts to create a pan-European gas market and to bring about diversification in gas supply. Internally, supported by (new) traders and large consumers, it promotes gas-to-gas competition on spot markets as the preferable trading device, while trying to outlaw the traditional oil-linked long-term contracts between the suppliers and incumbent midstream traders. So far, this has succeeded only partly, creating a hybrid market structure with oil-linked, long-term contracts alongside spot trade (Konoplyanick, 2012; Stern and Rogers, 2011). Moreover, by solving the internal infrastructure constraints it sought to facilitate cross-border flows with the EU, to connect the several areas. This approach requires EU funding for the extra connections between pipelines, reverse-flow facilities, and gas storage, which are not economically feasible in terms of gas business economics. The development of a new supply infrastructure, such as LNG terminals and the Nabucco pipeline from the Caspian Sea area via Turkey to Austria, were expected to invite new gas supplies to the EU market, thereby reducing the dependence on Russia.

However, differences in perception between the EU member states concerning energy vulnerability were strong. The expensive internal infrastructure and the supply diversification pursued by the Commission and some Central European countries are not supported wholeheartedly. With a long-term experience of stable gas cooperation with Russia, Western member states preferred the joint construction of pipelines with Russia, such as the Nord and South Stream, to circumvent transit countries.

Externally, in order to create supply diversification, the Commission seeks to extend its competition policy towards non-EU suppliers, forcing them to unbundle trade and transport while threatening the legality of their long-term supply contracts with European midstream companies and fostering spot market development (Stern and Rogers, 2011). This approach, principally, implies an intervention in established trade arrangements and with the interests of the upstream countries. The escalation of the tension between Russia and the EU about the Ukraine, combined with uncertainties about both the future development of the EU regulatory framework and EU gas market development, are rapidly cooling down relations with Russia.

Within the hybrid EU market structure, the impacts of the post-2008 economic crisis and the abundant supply of coal following the US shale-gas revolution were huge. First, demand for gas declined considerably in the industry. Second, the EU power sector began to substitute low-cost coal, also stimulated by the low value of tradable CO_2 emission rights under the failing EU Emission Trading System (ETS). Moreover, the growth in wind and solar power in several countries began to exert a downward pressure on both gas use and power prices. Third, the gradual growth in gas volumes traded on the spot markets began to reflect this situation, yielding substantially lower spot prices. As a consequence, the incumbent midstream traders could no longer compete with their high-priced oil-linked gas (see Westphal, 2014). Statoil from Norway and GasTerra from the Netherlands reacted by supplying increasing volumes of gas on the spot markets, while the midstreamers managed to renegotiate the price level in their contracts with Gazprom (see Konoplyanik, 2012; OIES, 2014). Only Sonatrach from Algeria has maintained the status quo so far.

Given the uncertain future perspective for EU gas consumption, as well as the evolution of the market and pricing structures, both the EU-sponsored Nabucco pipeline, and the Russian South Stream initiative, were cancelled. So far, alternative gas supplies from the Caspian region or Iran seem to be a remote opportunity (OIES, 2014; ESI, 2014). Currently, supplies of Russian, Caspian and even Middle Eastern gas via Turkey are evaluated as an alternative. Yet, most likely, Europe is either bound to remain largely dependent on its traditional suppliers, or it has to accept the higher prices for LNG, which are paid in Asia. Security of supply and diversification will come at a price. However, the height of that price is a function of the complex interaction of European, US, and Asian markets, influenced by the markets for gas, oil, and coal.

The Asia-Pacific area

The Asia-Pacific gas market is essentially a market for LNG. Pipelines are not viable, as a result of the deep seas between countries and geopolitical tensions between supplier, transit, and consumer countries. Moreover, most (emerging) markets are smaller, and gas has to compete with relatively low-priced substitute fuels. Nevertheless, in Southeast Asia a number of pipelines connect the production areas in Indonesia with Malaysia, and Myanmar with Singapore and Thailand. Consequently, the region consists of a number of national submarkets with their own dynamics, economics, and institutional frameworks (Wybrew-Bond and Stern, 2002; Stern, 2008).

The national markets in Japan, India, China, Taiwan, and Korea are all heavily regulated. Most of the gas is used in power generation and the remainder in industries, directly and domestically. In some countries, natural gas is subsidized, whereas in others it is priced at its full cost. Japan and the other primary LNG users, Korea and Taiwan, import most of their LNG under long-term contracts; the gas price is determined on the basis of the Japanese Crude Cocktail (JCC) plus a premium. The JCC formula reflects the costs of the crude oil imported by Japan, which resulted in relatively high prices until recently. China is negotiating gas pipeline imports with Russia, at prices that match those of the main alternative fuel, indigenous coal. The Fukushima incident and the subsequent closure of the Japanese nuclear power plants caused a huge draw on LNG volumes, which partly offset the reduction in (expected) US demand (OIES, 2014). Future oil prices will strongly determine LNG prices in Asia.

The idea of creating a well-functioning spot market for gas in Asia is considered highly problematic. There are only a few mature markets, while in many countries gas is either a new fuel, or accounts for a relatively small proportion of energy demand. In principle, there is a huge potential for growth in gas consumption in most countries, as well as in gas supply from a few of them. Yet the current JCC-based pricing methodology will hamper further development, as it imposes an additional burden on the subsidizing by states, while it scares away (potential) consumers of natural gas (Vivoda, 2014; Rogers and Stern, 2014).

Conclusion

The international gas market essentially consists of three main market areas and a few supply centers, which are gradually being connected and facilitated by the LNG infrastructure. This is giving rise to a global market, in which regional supply/demand/price dynamics influence conditions elsewhere. Clear evidence is provided that the US shale revolution is having a multidimensional impact on the flows and prices of gas, coal, and petroleum to the rest of the world. Local incidents, such as the Fukushima disaster, the Ukraine crisis, and the failing EU ETS, have specific consequences for each of the regional gas markets, which influence the other markets in the shorter and longer term. This is a fairly new development. Until a few years ago, the isolated regional markets were only indirectly connected by the price of oil.

The interaction between the regional markets is often attributed to an increase in the spot trade of cargos of LNG and even piped gas. And, indeed, spot and short-term contracts (less than 4 years) reached 29 percent in terms of traded volumes in 2014 (GIIGNL, 2015). However, despite the reduction of their duration and the greater flexibility in price and volume conditions while renegotiation has become more regular, long-term contracts have not lost their importance in securing the terms of trade between many suppliers and consumers (Neumann and von Hirschhausen, 2015; Neumann *et al.*, 2015).

In the context of increasing globalization of the gas market, we can observe the emergence of market forces playing an increasingly important role, alongside all kinds of public-policy-based interventions and environmental and other market regulations. Such politically and ideologically inspired interventions may have been relatively harmless in the past, as long as the effects were primarily national. However, in the current global market constellation, they directly affect the interests and objectives of other nation states and, as a consequence, become part of the sensitive realm of international politics. Yet such policies are adopted nationally under the pretense of local economic competition, and environmental, social, or safety policies, often without taking into account the international implications. This is causing serious tensions between (groups of) countries, both within, as well as between, the worlds' regional gas markets (see also Westphal, 2014).

The responses from governments will vary. Some will accept the loss of their role as an effective market coordinator and adopt a more liberal stance. However, others will resist liberalization and actually strengthen their position as a direct actor, owner, or regulator in the industry. Nevertheless, within the context of an international value chain, companies from one jurisdiction must negotiate their terms of trade with governments that may have radically diverging perceptions. This politicizes commercial conflicts, and even the nature of market competition as such.

Finally, regarding regulation of the gas sector, a number of issues are important. First, the determinants of market power and infrastructure regulation in the value chain will always extend beyond the national – or even regional – regulators' span of control. Second, gas markets around the world differ substantially in their stage of development. Some markets have already matured, such as in the US, Japan, and South Korea, while other markets are still in an expansionary phase, such as India and China. Europe covers the full spectrum from emerging to mature markets. Some countries are characterized by (declining) domestic supplies, some by a variety of long-term supply relationships from external resources, and others by their dependency on a single supplier. Third, and even more important, gas systems encompass different countries and world regions, stemming from radically different traditions in terms of their policies and institutional characteristics. Therefore, market regulation will always be politically sensitive. As a consequence, 'one-size-fits-all' recipes for structural reform and liberalization in the gas industry will cause serious conflicts of interest, and create difficulties in establishing mutually acceptable ways of governing transactions in the international gas value chain.

Acknowledgments

This research was financed by a grant from the Energy Delta Gas Research (EDGaR) program. EDGaR is co-financed by the Northern Netherlands Provinces, the European Fund for Regional Development, the Ministry of Economic Affairs, and the Province of Groningen. Wolter Lemstra is gratefully acknowledged for his valuable comments and suggestions.

References

Aalto, P. (2014) Institutions in European and Asian energy markets: A methodological overview, *Energy Policy*, 74, 4–15.

Agency for the Cooperation of National Energy Regulators (ACER) (2015). Available at: http://www.acer.europa.eu/Gas/Gas-Target-Model/Pages/Main.aspx (accessed on 4 May 2015).

Armstrong, M., Cowan, S. and Vickers, J. (1995) *Regulatory Reform: Economic Analysis and British Experience*. Cambridge, MA: The MIT Press.

Baker Institute (2007) *The Changing Role of National Oil Companies in International Energy Markets*. Houston, Texas: Baker Institute Policy Report no. 35, The James Baker III Institute for Public Policy of Rice University.

Baron, R., Bernstein, P., Montgomery, W.D. and Tuladhar, S. (2015) Macroeconomic Impacts of LNG Exports from the United States. *Economics of Energy & Environmental Policy*, 4(1), 37–58.

British Petroleum (BP) (2014) *BP Statistical Review of World Energy: A Consistent and Objective Series of Historical Energy Data*. London: British Petroleum.

Chyong, C.K. and Reiner, D.M. (2015) Economics and Politics of Shale Gas in Europe. *Economics of Energy & Environmental Policy*, 4(1), 69–83.

Clingendael International Energy Programme (CIEP) (2014) *Transition? What Transition? Changing energy systems in an increasingly carbon constrained world*. The Hague: Clingendael International Energy Programme.

Correljé, A. and van Geuns, L. (2011) The oil industry: a dynamic helix, in M. Finger and R. Künneke (eds), *International Handbook of Network Industries: The Liberalization of Infrastructure*. Cheltenham: Edgar Elgar Publishing, pp. 197–214.

Correljé, A., Groenleer, M. and Veldman, J. (2014) Understanding institutional change: The development of institutions for the regulation of natural gas supply systems in the US and the EU, *Competition and Regulation in Networked Industries*, 15(1), 2–13.

Correljé, A., Jong, D. and Jong, J. (2009) *Crossing Borders in European Gas Networks: The Missing Links.* Policy paper, The Hague: Clingendael International Energy Programme.

Correljé, A., Van der Linde, C. and Westerwoudt, T. (2003) *Natural Gas in the Netherlands: From Cooperation to Competition?* The Hague: Oranje Nassau Groep/Clingendael International Energy Programme (CIEP).

Davis, J.D. (1984) *Blue Gold: The Political Economy of Natural Gas,* World Industries Studies 3. London: George Allen & Unwin.

Energy Charter (2007) *Putting a Price on Energy: International Pricing Mechanisms for Oil and Gas.* Brussels: Energy Charter Secretariat.

Energy Charter (2008) *Taxation Along the Oil and Gas Supply Chain: International Pricing Mechanisms for Oil and Gas.* Brussels: Energy Charter Secretariat.

Energy Security Initiative (ESI) (2014) *Business as Usual: European Gas Market Functioning in Times of Turmoil and Increasing Import Dependence,* Energy Security Initiative by Brookings, October, Policy brief 14–05.

Ernst & Young (EY) (2014) *Global Oil and Gas Tax Guide 2014.* Available at: http://www.ey.com/Publication/vwLUAssets/EY-Global-oil-and-gas-tax-guide-2014/$FILE/EY-Global-oil-and-gas-tax-guide-2014.pdf (accessed on 4 May 2015).

Estrada, J., Bergesen, H.O., Moe, A. and Sydnes, A.K. (1988) *Natural Gas in Europe. Markets, Organisation and Politics.* London: Pinter.

Estrada, J., Moe, A. and Dahl Martinsen, K.D. (1995) *The Development of European Gas Markets: Environmental, Economic and Political Perspectives.* Chichester: John Wiley & Sons.

Gahleitner, G. (2013) Hydrogen from renewable electricity: An international review of power-to-gas pilot plants for stationary applications, *International Journal of Hydrogen Energy,* 38(5), 2039–2061.

GIIGNL (2014) The LNG Industry in 2013. Groupe International des Importateurs de Gaz Naturel Liquéfié: Neuilly-sur-Seine.

GIIGNL (2015) The LNG Industry in 2014. Groupe International des Importateurs de Gaz Naturel Liquéfié: Neuilly-sur-Seine.

Glachant, J.M., Hallack, M., Vazquez, M., Ruester, S. and Ascari, S. (eds) (2013) *Building Competitive Gas Markets in the EU: Regulation, Supply and Demand.* Cheltenham: Edward Elgar Publishing.

Helm, D., Kay, J., Thompson, D. (eds) (1989) *The Market for Energy.* Oxford: Clarendon Press.

Högselius, P. (2013) *Red Gas: Russia and the Origins of European Energy Dependence.* (Transnational History Series). New York: Palgrave Macmillan.

International Energy Agency (IEA) (2012) *Golden Rules for a Golden Age of Gas: World Energy Outlook Special Report on Unconventional Gas.* Paris: International Energy Agency.

International Energy Agency (IEA) (2014) *Energy Technology Perspectives: Harnessing Electricity's Potential.* Paris: International Energy Agency.

International Group of Liquefied Natural Gas Importers (GIIGNL) (2014) *The LNG Industry in 2013.* Available at: http://www.giignl.org/fr/home-page/publications/ (accessed on 4 May 2015).

Jaag, C. and Trinkner, U. (2011) A general framework for regulation and liberalization in network industries, in M. Finger and R. Künneke (eds), *International Handbook of Network Industries: The Liberalization of Infrastructure.* Cheltenham: Edgar Elgar Publishing, pp. 26–53.

Jensen, J.T. (2004) *The Development of a Global LNG Market. Is it Likely? If so, When?* Oxford: Oxford Institute for Energy Studies.

Joskow, P.H. (2007) Regulation of natural monopolies, in A.M. Polinsky and S. Shavell (eds) *Handbook of Law and Economics,* Vol. 2. Dordrecht: Elsevier.

Juris, A. (1998) *The Emergence of Markets in the Natural Gas Industry,* Policy Research Working Paper No. 1895. Washington, DC: The World Bank, Private Sector Development Department, Private Participation in Infrastructure Group.

Konoplyanick, A.A. (2012) Russian gas at European energy market: Why adaptation is inevitable, *Energy Strategy Reviews,* (1), 42–56.

Leeston, A.M., Crichton, J.A. and Jacobs, J.C. (1963) *The Dynamic Natural Gas Industry: The Description of an American Industry from the Historical, Technical, Legal, Financial, and Economic Standpoints.* Norman, Oklahoma: University of Oklahoma Press.

Leitzinger, J. and Collette, M. (2002) A retrospective look at wholesale gas: industry restructuring, *Journal of Regulatory Economics,* 21(1), 79–101.

Macavoy, P.W. (2000) *The Natural Gas Market: Sixty Years of Regulation and Deregulation.* London: Yale University Press.

Makholm, J.D. (2012) *The Political Economy of Pipelines: A Century of Comparative Institutional Development*. Chicago and London: The University of Chicago Press.

Mitchell, J.V. and Mitchell, B. (2014) Structural crisis in the oil and gas industry, *Energy Policy*, 64, 36–42.

Mokhatab, S. and Poe, W.A. (2012) *Handbook of Natural Gas Transmission and Processing*. Oxford: Gulf Professional Publishing.

Mommer, B. (2002) *Global Oil and the Nation State*. Oxford: Oxford University Press.

Naturalgas (2015) *Natural Gas – From Wellhead to Burner Tip*. Available at: http://naturalgas.org/naturalgas. (Accessed 4 May 2015).

Neumann, A., Ruester, S., and von Hirschhausen, C. (2015) *Long-term contracts in the natural gas industry – Literature survey and data of 426 contracts (1965–2014)*. Data Documentation 77, Berlin: Deutsches Institut für Wirtschaftsforschung (DIW).

Neumann, A. and von Hirschhausen, C. (2015) Natural gas: An overview of a lower-carbon transformation fuel, *Review of Environmental Economics and Policy*, 9(1): 64–84.

Newbery, D.M. (2001) *Privatization, Restructuring and Regulation of Network Utilities*. Cambridge, MA: The MIT Press.

Oxford Institute for Energy Studies (OIES) (2014) *Reducing European Dependence on Russian Gas: Distinguishing Natural Gas Security from Geopolitics*, OIES Paper NG 92. Oxford: Oxford Institute for Energy Studies.

Peebles, M.W.H. (1980) *Evolution of the Gas Industry*. London: The Macmillan Press.

Rao, V. (2012) *Shale Gas: The Promise and the Peril*. New York: Research Triangle Institute (RTI).

Rogers, H.V. and Stern, J. (2014) *Challenges to JCC Pricing in Asian LNG Markets*, OIES Paper: NG 81. Oxford: The Oxford Institute for Energy Studies.

Stern, J. (ed.) (2008) *Natural Gas in Asia: The Challenges of Growth in China, India, Japan and Korea*. Oxford: OIES/Oxford University Press.

Stern, J.P. (1990) *European Gas Markets: Challenges and Opportunities in the 1990s*. London: Royal Institute of International Affairs, Energy and Environmental Programme.

Stern, J.P. (1998) *Competition and Liberalization in European Gas Markets: A Diversity of Models*. London: RIIA Energy and Environmental Programme.

Stern, J. (2001) *Traditionalists versus the New Economy: Competing agendas for European gas markets to 2020*, Briefing Paper No. 26, November. London: Royal Institute of International Affairs, Energy and Environmental Programme.

Stern, J. and Rogers, H. (2011) *The Transition to Hub-Based Gas Pricing in Continental Europe*, OIES Paper: NG 59. Oxford: The Oxford Institute for Energy Studies.

Stern, J., Pirani, S. and Yafimava, K. (2009) *The Russo-Ukrainian Gas Dispute of January 2009: A Comprehensive Assessment*, OIES Paper: NG 29. Oxford: The Oxford Institute for Energy Studies.

Stewart, D.D. and Madsen, E. (2005) *The Texan and Dutch Gas: Kicking off the European Energy Revolution*. Oxford: Trafford Publishing.

Talus, K. (2014) United States natural gas markets, contracts and risks: What lessons for the European Union and Asia-Pacific natural gas markets? *Energy Policy*, 74 (November), 28–34.

Taverne, B.G. (2013) *Petroleum, Industry, and Governments: A Study of the Involvement of Industry and Governments in Exploring for and Producing Petroleum*. Dordrecht: Wolters Kluwer Law and Business.

Vazquez, M., Hallack, M. and Glachant, J-M. (2012) Designing the European gas market: More liquid & less natural? *Economics of Energy & Environmental Policy*, 1(3) 25–38.

Victor, D.G., Jaffe, A.M. and Hayes, M.H. (2006) *Natural Gas and Geopolitics: From 1970 to 2040*. Cambridge and New York: Cambridge University Press.

Vivoda, V. (2014) Natural gas in Asia: Trade, markets and regional institutions. *Energy Policy*, 74 (November), 80–90.

Wang, Z. and Krupnick, A. (2015) A Retrospective Review of Shale Gas development in the United States: What Led to the Boom?, *Economics of Energy & Environmental Policy*, 4(1), 5–19.

Westphal, K. (2014) Institutional change in European natural gas markets and implications for energy security: Lessons from the German case, *Energy Policy*, 74(November), 35–43.

Wybrew-Bond, I. and Stern, J. (2002) *Natural Gas in Asia – The Challenges of Growth in China, India, Japan, and Korea*. Oxford: Oxford University Press.

Yafimava, K. (2013) *The EU Third Package for Gas and the Gas Target Model: Major Contentious Issues Inside and Outside the EU*, OIES Paper: NG 75. Oxford: Oxford Institute for Energy Studies.

6

Current trends in the global maritime transport sector

Bruce Lambert

Introduction

For most people, international trade shapes their daily lives. As one example, in studying the 'travels' of a T-shirt in the global economy, Planet Money tracked harvested cotton on its course from Mississippi to Indonesia to become fabric, and then followed the fabric, which was shipped to either Bangladesh or Colombia to be printed, before finally returning to the US in the form of a finished T-shirt (National Public Radio, 2013). On any day, transportation patterns depend upon many similar supply chains, as markets demand more complicated parts and consumers more choice. Maritime transport is not necessarily one industry, but a variety of different ships, markets, owners, and cargos. First, there is bulk shipping, which normally carries a single commodity, such as grain, ores, or coal (dry bulk), or petroleum, crude, or other chemicals (liquid bulk). Another category is break-bulk shipping, which, as its name implies, is cargo placed directly in the hold of a ship. This was the traditional means of shipping general or loose cargo before the advent of containerized shipping. The final category is containerized shipping, which has transformed the maritime industry in ways that were unimaginable when Malcolm P. McLean put containers on the top deck of the *Ideal X* in 1956 (Levinson, 2008). Containerized shipping is just that: ships that are designed to carry eight feet and six inches high, eight-foot-wide, 40-foot-long containers, often referred to in 20-foot equivalent units (TEUs) when describing vessel capacity as opposed to deadweight tonnage in the bulk markets.

The maritime industry represents one of the oldest, and most integrated, networked industries, having successfully spread culture, goods, and commerce for thousands of years, and still remains relevant in today's highly connected world (United Nations Conference on Trade and Development, 2013). This chapter outlines the main agents in the maritime industry in the context of networks, followed by a discussion on worldwide maritime networks. After outlining the future of ship operations and the challenges facing the industry, the paper discusses the maritime industry's nature as a networked industry and how this influences the relationship between different agents in maritime shipping. The paper concludes with a section outlining both the similarities and differences of maritime activities to other networked industries, and how the maritime industry responds to changing regulatory oversight.

Principal agents in maritime transport related to network activities

The world's economy has always depended upon maritime transportation, which often served as the primary way to transport people, news, and materials. Over the past 50 years, tied to advanced telecommunications and the adoption of computers, more firms have engaged in international markets and conduct business in real time. Political pressure has resulted in improved trade relationships to cement geopolitical positions and partnerships, as expressed by the mantra that 'free trade is the best path to world peace'.

As with any industry, there are many agents involved, either directly or indirectly, in international shipping. There are four basic agents involved in international maritime shipping: ocean carriers, cargo owners, terminal/port operators, and finally, regulators (policymakers). Labor remains an important component in transportation operations, costs and regulation, but due to their relatively fixed geographical positions, and as a contractual arrangement with ports, vessel owners, longshoreman, crewmen, etc., are not necessarily considered networked agents for this discussion. However, labor concerns may not necessarily serve as a network agent, but their actions, especially in the short term, can significantly influence trade activities.

Between the four main agents, ocean carriers, cargo owners, terminal/port operators and regulators, there are always changing dynamics concerning services, costs, and availability. Over time, regulations, technologies, commodities, and markets have all changed, but the essence of shipping still depends upon carrying cargo safely between different maritime facilities. As with any network, the main agents can be seen as simultaneously complementary and conflicting in their relationships.

This chapter will focus on commercial navigation, and not passenger navigation, such as through ferry services or cruise shipping, fishing or the offshore service industry. Each of these ships must also satisfy the same standards concerning vessel operations and safety conditions, but are not included in this discussion, which primarily focuses on freight-related transportation shipments.

Ocean carriers

Ocean carriers are responsible for managing vessels while they are engaged in international commerce, and as such, they are responsible for the vessel's operation while at port and sea. The ocean carrier, also known as the vessel operator, secure the tonnage (there are many firms that own their own vessels or engage in chartering vessels), crew the vessels, secure the cargo, and are responsible for the vessel's safe passage. Ocean carriers also determine the vessel's maintenance and decisions regarding vessel operations, based on what trades they wish to service.

Operational goal: Normally, vessel operators make their money when the vessel and cargo is moving, and any delays, such as extended port calls, or positioning empty equipment, are considered detrimental to the bottom line.

Terminal/port operators

This report uses terminal and port operators in a common framework as the agent responsible for providing facilities for the loading/unloading of cargo. Labor, which may include stevedores and longshoremen, are considered contractual elements within this category. The port or terminal often directly builds the maritime facility, but may or may not have control over access to that facility (landlord port), or will operate the facility (operating port). The port is often geographically fixed as well as temporally fixed, as it takes time to build new facilities that satisfy not only maritime customers, but also other regulatory/land-use decisions in their respective communities.

For example, in the US, a port may develop its docks but must work with both the US Army Corps of Engineers for any dredging associated with authorized federal channels, and the coast guard for safe operations and aids to navigation. In addition, a port's access to other regions may not be directly controlled by the port, but by other entities, such as highways, railroads, or barge operators. These entities, whether private or publicly owned and operated, may have goals and performance expectations that conflict with those of the port or terminal. Thus, while the port provides a service, it often remains dependent upon other agents to be successful.

Operational goal: Public ports tend to seek to cover all or a portion of their costs, but often they are seen as economic development agencies, so they may focus on long-term leases and regional job creation. As a publicly-owned entity, they may also be subjected to other goals in addition to simply moving cargo through the port complex. The Maritime Administration, American Association of Port Authorities' survey on port expenditures provides a good overview of how ports spend their money on various projects (US Maritime Administration, 2009). Private terminals, that are operated by a privately-owned company, are either seen as an in-house function to manage costs, or, in some cases, may service other cargos to offset operating costs, but do not necessarily have the same public sector demands.

Cargo owners

Cargo owners are responsible for preparing cargo for shipment. They may be responsible for any costs associated with draying equipment to their warehouse or property, in addition to ensuring all appropriate paperwork has been filed – this is often done by a customs house broker for imports or a freight forwarder for exports. There are also stringent requirements concerning when the transfer of ownership of the cargo occurs during international trade. The International Chamber of Commerce develops and maintains International Commercial Terms to provide a common framework for identifying when cargo ownership should be transferred, who determines and pays for transportation and other services, and when payment can be requested between parties. The cargo owner may be concerned with vessel turnaround times, so any delays are seen as an unplanned-for cost. There are current pushes for increased trade facilitation or infrastructure to remove this variable from their operations.

Operational goal: The cargo owners' goal is to handle freight in a timely, safe, and cost-effective manner. Given the diversity of global supply chains, direct management of logistics functions is often contracted out to other trade intermediates such as brokers, forwarders, or third-party logistics firms.

Regulatory oversight

Many groups responsible for the regulatory oversight of the maritime industry exist. These include bodies concerned with environmental issues, such as water or air pollution, those serving as a barrier to prevent dangerous or illegal cargos from moving in international trade, or those to promote trade and maritime activities through either investing in physical infrastructure, such as navigable waterways and channels, or encouraging firms to engage in international trade. There are also several groups that work at an intergovernmental or associational level to ensure that international navigation operates within common standards. Finally, businesses operate in domestic environments, and occasionally changing domestic policies in one country may limit or expand cargo shipments, which often has some unintended consequence that changes the relative cost/efficiency of a particular good or service, and can change trade activity.

Operational goal: Regulators aim to balance the need to enable ships/cargo to be handled in an expedited manner while enforcing any regulations related to tariffs, duties, emissions, mitigating risks, or other statuary authorizations.

What is the global maritime network?

Shipping represents a comprehensive network, with vessels crossing the oceans, sailing in coastal waterways, and even stretching into internal lakes and rivers. The shipping network's largest flows occur among the industrialized markets of Asia, Europe, and North America, but there exists growing trade activities between the northern and southern hemispheres, as well as within the developing countries themselves (UNCTAD, 2013).

When discussing the network, we can do so with reference to two main actions. We can describe the network, and its corresponding activities by function and geography, or as actions undertaken by various agents. Each is important, especially as agents' responsibilities tend to change as the vessel/cargo moves along the network. In many ways, function drives the longer-term physical network that shippers and regulators respond to when determining their business goals, but the feedback loop through the actions of the various agents reinforces or changes the respective network as well. However, global shipping is not necessarily one network, but a series of interconnected networks that only operate upon the same physical structure – waterways and ports – and, in many cases, these associated networks may have little in common beyond the fact that they are vessels for carrying mariners and cargo.

Network function and geography

A network is usually thought of as a relationship of links and nodes; in the case of maritime shipping, the links may represent maritime routes (most ships try to rely on great circle distances to minimize transportation costs) or specific channels or waterways. Nodes can be represented by either ports or specific navigational regions or areas, such as the Port of Long Beach, the Panama Canal, or the Straits of Gibraltar. However, the network only exists to move three things: the vessel, the cargo, and the equipment. Unlike most networks, the equipment must move bi directionally, otherwise all the capacity will leak out of the system. As such, one can view maritime shipping as a series of networks, each of which are defined by the following:

- Aggregate shipping worldwide, which is normally discussed concerning trends in ship building and global operations;
- Aggregate shipping between countries/ports, which is normally discussed in the context of trade policy and market trends;
- Sub-regional networks between ports and their related infrastructure, which is often discussed in relation to access to both international (oceans) and inland (hinterland) markets, or questions of route capacity and shipping rates;
- Specific port networks that occur within a port area, normally associated with performance metrics, regulatory oversight, and other operational matters.

However, even the above broad descriptions are not adequate, since there are definite relationships between the vessel's design and its intended cargo. Each vessel type tends to move specific cargo within regional dependent networks. Bulk shipping tends to move on a consignment basis, sailing to and from ports to pick up/drop off cargo. Container shipping usually operates on a scheduled, or liner, service model, where ships sail between certain ports on a predetermined route. Regarding containerized shipping, there exists a special situation concerning hub cargos and transshipment centers. The basic premise of transshipment is that vessels carry containers from the first port to a second port. At this second port, the container is placed aboard another ship that carries the cargo to its final port destination. This allows carriers to put bigger vessels in service between the various ports, thus improving overall network efficiency (similar to the hub-and-spoke networks used by large airlines). However, as with most networks, an agent's location along a network can determine its relative power to mitigate trade growth, especially when connecting ports to inland markets (Wilmsmeier *et al.*, 2011).

Measuring efficiencies along the network

As such, geography and function sharply influence vessel operations. For a vessel at sea, fuel represents one of the largest daily costs, followed by crew wages. Thus, minimizing fuel use becomes an important element for commercial vessels. As such, operational settings directly influence a vessel's operating costs, and transportation routing decisions or movement along the broad geographic network reflect this concern (Rodrique *et al.*, 2009).

In the drive to improve traffic, many groups are interested in performance metrics that both highlight where 'bottlenecks' exist in the system, and also how markets may be compared to each other regarding freight access or costs. One could use broad comparisons, such as 'total transit time', for routing cargo through different modes or routing options. However, while such comparisons may be useful to a traffic manager, simply measuring the overall system does not provide a mechanism by which to examine the components of the move for all parts involved. In many cases, it is not only the long haul but also the transfer points where productivity challenges exist. Other metrics, such as the World Bank Logistic Index and the UNCTAD (United Nations Conference on Trade and Development); World Bank (UNCTAD) 'Liner Connectivity Index', measure a comparison of either transportation processes or access to markets. The focus on performance measures and improving trade access become proxies not only of maritime productivity, but also of the entire relationship between various parties in the trade and transportation area. However, even identifying that these inefficiencies exist may be complicated by the ability of various groups to respond quickly, such as building or retrofitting vessels or ports, or even changing crewing, paperwork forms, or other administrative tasks.

The operations/regulatory framework of ocean shipping

There always remain questions concerning the interrelated structures that shape the modern world, and correspondingly, a dynamic world economy that shapes demand for maritime transportation. Trade policies, technologies, political pressures, and security concerns have led to different discussions concerning what the world 30 years hence, including the corresponding maritime system, will need to satisfy demand (International Maritime Organization, 2011). Such a list may be fairly broad, so the focus will only highlight those items that are directly tied to accessing the network, operations along the network, and changing networks.

Accessing the network

There remains no barrier to getting into shipping beyond the price of renting, leasing, or purchasing a ship. Anyone who can meet and acquire the necessary permits should be able to operate a vessel between ports. While the regulatory burdens are fairly high – namely with respect to ensuring the vessel's seaworthiness and crew safety – anyone can hire a ship and engage in maritime services. Obviously, there are exceptions to this rule, as firms may be restricted from operating on certain domestic routes due to cabotage laws, even if these routes are fairly long, such as trade between the Netherlands and Sint Maarten. In the US, this is governed by the Jones Act, which limits trade between US states and territories to US-built vessels operating under the US flag with US crews. In many cases, there may exist concerns that shipping companies can charge 'unfair rates' or act in a monopolistic manner, so many countries monitor or approve mergers or other market-share and access-related decisions.

For ports, the developmental costs are fairly high, including not only the placement of wharves and cranes, but also aids to navigation, navigation channels, and other ancillary services, such as customs, labor, and actually working to secure adequate cargo that will pass through the port. Often, there is a question of permission, especially around waterways, and other land-use decisions, which may influence how a terminal is ultimately configured, especially if a port requires permits or other approvals.

For the cargo owner, there are few barriers to engaging in trade, especially as the push for globalization has resulted in more companies routinely engaging in international access. As with all industries, there may be special restrictions, such as preventing the transportation of hazardous materials or contraband materials due to political concerns that firms have to plan and manage for in their ongoing operations. Often, these are addressed through working with a freight specialist, such as a customs house broker or a freight forwarder, to assist in moving the cargo internationally.

Therefore, the question of access from a port/local perspective has become extremely complicated due to increasing competition for access and management by other users. For example, navigation often occurs in fishery areas, and as the demand for fish grows, so too does the conflict between navigation and fishing interests regarding the right to access waterways and oceans. The maritime sector also has to deal with increased demand for access to water and shorelines from both an economic-development and a recreational/access perspective. For the maritime industry, the problem of the commons is a real issue, especially as countries work to expand economic development of their coastlines.

Operating along the network

This is where shipping gets fairly complicated, as the need for improving efficiencies has driven modern supply chains to work on improving operations while balancing other concerns of maritime security and environmental oversight. There are questions concerning managing not only operations of the vessel, but also its environmental effects. For example, ballast water is used to trim a vessel to maintain seaworthiness. As such, a vessel may have tanks that were filled in one ocean area but discharged in another, which can result in the spread of invasive species. A focus on reducing air emissions has led to efforts to reduce ships' emissions, which inevitably leads to changing vessel fuel stocks and operations in coastal waters and in ports.

One of the reasons containerization was readily adopted was to reduce both the manpower used to work ships and the time it took to load/unload a vessel, but it led indirectly to reducing pilferage at maritime terminals and in general port areas. Cargo theft has remained an ongoing problem, but so too have concerns over terrorism, cybercrime, immigration, and piracy, as containers can just as easily be used to ship illegal materials as goods. As such, cargo security standards are normally considered to be the responsibility of the port when the vessel is docked. The US has sought to X-ray or inspect containers entering the US in an effort to reduce the threat of potentially harmful materials entering the US through maritime containers. However, there remain concerns that the cargo itself may be used as a weapon, such as the shipment of a 'dirty bomb', and many countries have worked on prescreening containers before they are loaded onto a vessel or released from customs to reduce the transportation of hazardous materials, illegal immigrants, and other illegal cargos. The question of maritime security continues to be an area of concern (Ritter *et al.*, 2007).

Changing networks

Trade has grown over the past 30 years, and forecasts predict that it will continue to do so, largely due to the continued integration of developing economies into the global market place, as these countries demand more materials to support their economies and expanding middle classes. As most countries continue to encourage trade growth, supporting global trade should lead to greater economic returns. At the same time, there are concerns over the ability of ports to handle increasing cargo volumes and the associated movements to/from inland markets. Stopford (2010) extrapolated that if current rates continued, by 2060 shipping will have increased from 8 billion tons of cargo to over 23 billion, which will place a significant burden on the overall existing network. Part of this cargo growth may occur through new routings, such as transiting through the Arctic Circle, or from expanded facilities, such as through the Panama and Suez Canals.

Answers to this growth depend on how carriers respond. Many have continued to purchase larger vessels, although other options exist. For example, carriers have generally been allowed some degree of collusion when discussing services and rates. Twenty years ago, some container vessel operators explored more direct integrated cooperation; namely, the development of vessel-sharing agreements or consortiums. Consortiums potentially provide for a greater reduction of costs through more efficient equipment utilization and better allocation of capital assets. Thus, regulatory bodies must approve these consortiums, and anti-trust protection to see if carriers are not exploiting shippers by commanding a large market share regarding services or available capacity. Recent consortium approval processes suggest that more consortiums and partnerships will emerge, although it is not clear how regulatory bodies will respond.

Applying network theory to the maritime industry

A network can be defined as 'both a set of links that build the interaction amongst agents, and as a set of agents that adopt a similar behavior for different economic purposes' (Umbhauer, 1998). As with any industry, firms and agents respond differently to various market signals, but in general, everyone seems to encourage economic cooperation and increased trade. As with any networked industry, there are a number of complex relationships, but in shipping every physical shipment also generates informational flows that trigger notifications, including cargo releases, contractual obligations, and charges. As such, the maritime industry meets the four conditions outlined by Shy (2001): that there exists some degree of complementarity, compatibility, and standards; consumption externalities; switching costs and lock-in; and significant economies of scale in production. Each of the four elements is discussed below.

Complementarity, compatibility, and standards

Shipping, like all transportation activities, satisfies a derived demand. No one simply pays for transportation unless there is a need to move cargo or reposition equipment, and even providing storage itself entails some cost. By its nature, transportation complements the needs of other agents who want a product to be stored or shipped, and it must do so in such a manner that the cargo owner can expect to see the product arrive in the same condition in which it was shipped. Standards for operational details, such as container size, vessel operations, and safe navigation, are developed through international treaties, associations or government policies, which work to ensure that the system works fairly well. As more firms engage in international shipping, the standards become more known and accepted, resulting in the chance for additional trade opportunities. Often, the maritime industry will seek to establish standards through international conventions, which avoids the question of balancing one country's laws against those of the broader maritime community.

Consumption externalities

Consumption externalities comprise the fact that as more users begin to use the same product or process, there is a net benefit to all. The growth in world trade, both in terms of total world trade and sea trade, has been a culmination of many regulatory reforms (for example, in the US, the Stagger's Act and the Shipping Act of 1984 were key reform bills that encouraged intermodal interoperability) and firms seeking to benefit from increasing access to offshore production in the developing world. This has been particularly apparent in the growth of containerization. Containerized transportation was adopted worldwide partially as the industry gradually agreed to common standards and other related operational elements, so that the benefits could be shared by many different users throughout the global supply chain. As these technologies were adopted, the net result was a drop in reduced costs on a per ton basis, although services improved.

Over time as service options and costs were better managed, more firms entered the global marketplace. In the US alone, there exist over 400,000 directly engaged cargo owners/intermediaries working in international trade (which includes maritime trade), and these are not necessarily located only in coastal areas (US Department of Commerce, 2014). Ocean shippers benefit from standardized equipment, which has allowed them greater market penetration, especially in the containerized shipping area, to more markets worldwide; while equipment interchangeability has increased operational velocity.

Switching costs and lock-in

Every network industry benefits from more dedicated commitment to a particular system, which allows firms to benefit from stabilized operations and other benefits, such as more sailing or vessel options. For example, intermodalism developed not because of shipper needs, but because carriers reexamined transportation services. During the 1980s, shippers in the US distrusted intermodal services because of the failure of initial attempts (due to service delays, equipment problems, scheduling problems, etc.). As many of the earlier problems associated with intermodalism were removed, shippers began finding intermodal service worth the added cost, and it has been one of the fastest-growing segments of the North American railroad industry (Monios and Lambert, 2013).

There is also a second locked-in effect; namely, the geography of ports and infrastructure. While ships are mobile, ports and maritime terminals are not, and are fairly expensive to build. To accommodate larger ships, terminal operators are developing larger terminals or reconfiguring current land use to provide additional space. As the size of container ships increases, there is a greater demand not only at quayside, but also on the entire terminal to handle and store containers as they move to and from ships (Abt and Lambert, 2006). Ports unable to expand or improve facilities or provide adequate inland transportation reduce their attractiveness to shippers. Conversely, as shippers and supply chains have become concentrated in key corridors, the ability to quickly respond to natural or manmade events can be compromised. As such, in the near term, ports and carriers, etc., may exhibit monopolistic tendencies; however, such gains can often be offset by other corridors, or even changing trade routes and markets.

Economies of scale

Some network industries tend to have fairly large setup costs, but each unit of consumption requires less cost to secure or handle. Such is the case with transportation, which normally has a stepwise function when new capacity is added, despite normal incremental increases that occur from day-to-day operations. It is an expensive industry, not only for vessels, but also for ports, trucking lines, and any other agent involved. It is an industry driven by economies of scale.

For example, when a vessel's size is increased, it must be expanded in length, width and breadth, to remain seaworthy, so there is a geometric cubic progression in volume (carrying capacity) when vessels are made bigger. Despite the high cost of new buildings, carriers continue to order bigger ships. There are several reasons for wanting to place these massive ships into service:

- Various ship lines anticipate that sufficient cargo volumes exist for new vessels.
- Larger ships allow carriers to control costs. Although the ships are more expensive, operating costs do not increase proportionately to the ships' size. As the vessels carry more cargo, costs become spread over a greater amount of revenue-generating containers. This added volume lowers the operating costs for each container slot, thus reducing costs for the carrier.
- Modern ships possess more efficient engines, thus, there is the possibility of reducing transit times or fuel use, which may give carriers a competitive advantage in certain markets.

There exist other benefits and costs. For example, the push to serve larger ships can be seen in the expansion of the Panama Canal. This canal, which opened in 1914, is currently being expanded through not only the addition of a third set of locks, but also a deeper main channel. This will allow larger vessels to transit the channel, potentially allowing access to larger vessels, and lower rates through economies of scale that will make certain routings between Asia and the eastern US more competitive when compared to other regions. This means that cargo owners will benefit from these services, but only if the ports that service those trades are ready to handle these vessels. However, larger vessels also impose costs on the system, as ports and terminals must continue to invest in new facilities and dredge channels to accommodate larger vessels, while regulators must be able to process more containers and their associated paperwork. As with most industries, system-wide increases can be disruptive while potentially changing existing usage patterns.

Comparison of maritime transport to other network industries

In an article entitled 'The 20-Ton Packet', Taggert (1999) explained containerized shipping in terms of a computer network, and compared the container to an information packet that moves through a series of modal exchanges (truck, rail, water, etc.) onto a ship, which itself may be relayed several times on a network before arriving at a port and moving inland. This comparison, which focused on the movement of the cargo and not necessarily the whole network at the same time (that is, the vessel), makes for an interesting comparison to other industries. However, there are other ways to compare other industries based not only on information flows, but ownership of assets, and the relationship between agents in the network (Zacher and Sutten, 1996).

Similarities between the maritime sector and other networked industries

Every network industry has many similarities, especially as the agents work to ensure that the network generally works ultimately to satisfy most customers' demands in a timely and cost-efficient manner. Furthermore, network industries exist to solve problems related to geography or time, such as physically moving goods and materials, or moving information, as in the case of telecommunications or social networks. In all networks, the group generally works to solve issues in ways that encourage network efficiencies – not necessarily for the good of the network, but to encourage or capture some competitive advantage over competitors or to control costs or risks.

Encouraging investment

Every network-based industry suffers from the perception of maintenance, i.e., who is responsible for what asset within the network. Once a network has been developed and is operating sufficiently to satisfy demand, most people are confident that the system will continue to work as promised. The same can be said of the maritime industry, as vessel operators tend to use the 'fix as fails' mentality, since any time away from actual steaming/operations often represents an unrecoverable cost.

From a maritime perspective, vessels are largely in the private domain, while the port infrastructure is normally in the public sector. There do exist many private terminals that handle cargo, but most of these facilities still rely on public-sector infrastructure, either regarding channels, roadways, or other services to work the vessel or move cargo. The high initial costs and timeframes associated with deploying ships or building terminals make planning for the maritime sector somewhat reactive, although speculative investment does occur.

Rates

User rates are based on one direction of shipment, although operational costs emerge on both sides. Forehaul/backhaul transportation also entails a tremendous amount of assets that do not generate any value unless they are physically carrying something. Often, transportation industry officials joke that one of their largest businesses is simply moving air in empty holds, hatches, and containers. Thus while the cargo may move in only one direction, the equipment itself has to move in both directions, so that balancing cargo throughout the voyage is important to manage costs. There are a tremendous number of inefficiencies in the system due to a variance in weight, size, time of day, or seasonal concerns. However, like most industries, rates vary based on volume, frequency, and special needs, and it could be argued that even the rate of globalization has changed rate structures and transportation costs; and identified these costs as arriving from variances in technologies, the quality of a country's infrastructure, and relative market power for the shipping lines (Hummels, 2009).

Dissimilarities between the maritime sector and other networked industries

As shipping represents a diverse network, it has some unique characteristics that distinguish it from other industries. These tend to be items related to ownership and engagement with non-maritime users, as well as the diverse relationship between when regulation begins and ends based on the ship's location along the network.

Flag of registry

Every ship needs to identify its country of registry for both tax and inspection purposes. Often, a vessel owner will register a vessel in their home country, but some countries, including Liberia and Panama, serve as 'flags of convenience', which allow owners to register ships in countries other than their own to manage costs or operating regulations. After World War II, the alignment of merchant marine fleets established worldwide fleet services controlled by increasingly larger (but fewer) shipping companies (UNCTAD, 2013). Despite the reduction in national fleets, certain incentives remain for vessel operators to offer domestic flagged services. First, these may be the only vessels allowed to work in cabotage trades between domestic ports, as in the case of the Jones Act in the US. Second, there are certain cargos that must be carried by domestically flagged vessels, such as military shipments, because of other existing regulatory or political requirements. These different registries and ownership issues can complicate enforcement of (primarily) crewing and tax law.

Network infrastructure needs

From a shipping perspective, vessels are normally owned by the private sector; however, the infrastructure can be owned by either a public or private entity. There are always concerns over land-use development and the local community. At the same time, most construction, either from a vessel or port perspective, may be speculative or tied to a fairly long lease or property agreement. Shipping companies purchase ships based on managing costs, but ships, especially container ships, are often purchased in batches, as they tend to be deployed jointly in a service string. Ports develop terminals in the hope that the anticipated traffic will occur and will actually use the constructed facility once completed. There are plenty of examples of vessel owners missing changing market conditions (such as US Lines ordering slower, but more fuel-efficient ships, which ultimately led to its bankruptcy) or port projects that never reached their intended full development potential until much later than the initial forecast had suggested.

Security and control

As with most industries, there exist concerns over the question of who has access to the vessel, terminal, and cargo. While security is often seen as preventing damage to the network or unlawful use of the system, the maritime industry is fairly open concerning access to international waters, which is one of the main challenges regarding keeping vessels safe from pirate attacks. However, in all points, security remains the responsibility of the vessel, terminal, or cargo owner, depending on whether the ship is in open water or port (that is, in a public space). However, it is the relatively open nature of the seas that makes security such an important consideration to mariners, especially across the vast seas.

User benefits and costs are unequal

Often, public infrastructure is critical in supporting trade through either the deepening or the maintenance of the channel, port, or roadway that connects the terminal to inland users. However, in most places, while supporting regional and national economic goals, improvements are often the responsibility of the local port operator or transportation agency. Furthermore, transportation networks are often criticized for bearing user costs disproportionately along the system, even if the benefits are fairly widespread. For example, port congestion, especially concerning drayage operations and gate movements, remains a major complaint levied against port authorities by local trucking and shipper groups. The same can also be said for rail activity or other transportation services within a port area that may lead to service disruptions. Operationally, the concentration of transportation activity paints a target on the port area to improve transportation around the port, but once the cargo leaves the port area it becomes domestic cargo, and as such is subject wholly to that country's laws. The second-order economic effects thus become fairly difficult to quantify, but nevertheless remain an important consideration (US Department of Transportation, Federal Highway Administration, 2004). In the US, continued calls for a national port strategy have been stymied, as the question of equity and project selection across the range of port needs and sizes makes this a somewhat impossible task (US Department of Transportation, Maritime Administration, 2011).

How does the industry respond to regulatory oversight?

Often, the question of when to respond to a regulatory decision is determined by when that condition can be satisfied. First, vessels are built according to the safety standards in operation at that time, and the costs of retrofitting may be prohibitively expensive, so that vessels are often grandfathered in to satisfy new requirements. Because of the uneven time nature of the approval of national maritime laws, the adoption of these laws through vessel design and construction takes a fairly long time to fully adopt on a global basis.

Historically, access to international oceans represented an open, but contentious, issue, as vessel owners wanted safe passage but governments were concerned with questions of national security and safety. When a vessel is operating in international waters, few inspections currently occur, as it is difficult to practically impose any restrictions in international waters. Additionally, as with most industries, the only time shipping gets any significant press coverage is in the aftermath of a maritime disaster, which often leads to an uncomfortable focus on the industry's operational and regulatory structure. In many cases, this post-event management makes reform fairly hard to institute because of the many difficult jurisdictional issues (George, 2013).

Therefore, the industry tends to focus on international organizations to set up standards regarding vessels and operations, and the respective flags under which ships sail. Nations are able to impose some degree of influence on international shipping through their own legal structures, including preventing ships from entering a country due to various political goals or because the ship's equipment may be considered environmentally below a nation's current standards.

Despite these challenges, the industry remains committed to handling freight shipments in a manner that does not incur additional delays or costs, especially as governments have promoted international trade to spur economic growth. Therefore, speed and efficiencies are important, especially given the growth in just-in-time deliveries and advanced logistical management systems. However, there may always be a tradeoff within any network; that is, how do you encourage, or 'speed up', the process, while still making sure the network itself is secure and meets other social and political goals?

Conclusion

The advancement of containerized shipping was not able to transform global economies without many regulatory activities taking place. First, the ships themselves had to have standardized cargo units, so that the interchange between ships and inland transportation access would not become an additional bottleneck (for example, different rail gauges and operational standards, developed independently of each other, have prevented the development of a fully integrated pan-European freight railroad system). Second, as the cost of ships and equipment increased, largely driven by the deployment of larger vessels to gain economies of scale, encouraging customs and inspection processes to more quickly process freight shipments, including preprocessing cargo before it arrives at its destination country, has been adopted to improve trade facilitation.

As with any network industry, one does not think about the investment and background operations that largely go unheralded unless something significant occurs. In most places, a domestic substitute may be available for imported goods, or export products may be consumed at home, although in many cases there may be questions concerning whether these will generate the same net benefits if trade did not exist. One could argue that trade will remain a critical component of the world's economic future for a number of reasons:

- Increased trade agreements generally experience fairly high growth rates after they are signed.
- Energy (coal, natural gas, and petroleum) and bulk shipments of chemicals and agriculture will remain in heavy demand, especially in developing countries.
- The growing middle class in other markets makes international trade more attractive to firms, especially in relation to container shipping.
- Trade allows for broader consumer and business choices, especially as telecommunications and business transactional barriers decline.

The challenge that exists is: how does the system handle this additional traffic in an efficient, environmentally friendly, and safe manner? Many of those questions will be determined by the network operators themselves, such as the vessel owners, ports, and cargo interests. However, many of their responses will be determined by actions defined by oversight and regulation, either within a country or through some international forum or association.

Maritime transportation represents a somewhat unusual network industry, simply because of the large startup/operating costs, various ownership issues in different parts of the system, and how jurisdictional boundaries influence regulatory control when operating across the network. This complexity ensures that maritime transportation will remain fertile ground for additional studies concerning how various agents continue to balance regulatory oversight among operational efficiencies and social and economic goals.

References

Abt, K. and Lambert, B. (2006) *The Development of Larger Container Vessels at Port Facilities of the Eastern US Container Ports – Changing Port Operations and Infrastructure Investment*. Lisbon, Portugal: PIANC Congress.

George, R. (2013) *Ninety Percent Of Everything: Inside Shipping, the Invisible Industry that Puts Clothes on Your Back, Gas in Your Car, and Food on Your Plate*. US: Metropolitan Books.

Hummels, D. (2009) *Globalization and Freight Transport Costs in Maritime Shipping and Aviation,* International Transport Forum 2009, The Organisation for Economic Co-operation and Development, Paris, France.

International Maritime Organization, (2011) *International Shipping Facts and Figures – Information Resources on Trade, Safety, Security, Environment.* London.

Levinson, M. (2008) *The Box: How the shipping container made the world smaller and the world economy bigger.* Princeton, NJ: Princeton University Press.

Monios, J. and Lambert, B. (2013) Intermodal freight corridor development in the United States, in R. Berqvist (ed.) *Dry Ports – A Global Perspective: Challenges and Developments in Serving Hinterlands.* Surrey: Ashgate Publishing Limited, pp. 197–218.

National Public Radio (2013, December 2) *Planet Money Makes a T-Shirt* (A. Blumberg, ed.), available at: http://apps.npr.org/tshirt (accessed March 12, 2015).

Ritter, L., Barrett, J. and Wilson, R. (2007) *Securing Global Transportation Networks.* McGraw-Hill.

Rodrique, Jean-Paul, Comtois, C. and Slack, B. (2009) *The Geography of Transport Systems* (2nd ed.). Abingdon, Oxon: Routledge.

Shy, Oz. (2001) *The Economics of Network Industries.* New York: Cambridge University Press.

Stopford, D.M. (2010) *How Shipping Changed the World.* Available at: http://ec.europa.eu/competition/consultations/2012_maritime_transport/euda_8_en.pdf (accessed November 4, 2014).

Taggert, S. (1999) The 20-ton packet, *Wired,* 7(10), 246–255.

The International Bank for Reconstruction and Development/The World Bank (2014) *Connecting to Compete 2014 The Logistics Performance Index and Its Indicators.* Washington, DC: The International Bank for Reconstruction and Development/The World Bank.

Umbhauer, G. (1998) Introduction, in P.P. Cohendet (ed.), *The Economics of Networks: Interaction and Behaviours.* Berlin-Heidelberg: Springer, pp. 1–13.

United Nations Conference on Trade and Development (UNCTAD) (2013) *Review of Maritime Transportation (UNCTAD/RMT/2013).* Geneva, Switzerland: United Nations Publication.

United Nations Conference on Trade and Development (UNCTAD) (n.d.) *Liner Shipping Connectivity Index.* Available at: http://unctadstat.unctad.org/wds/TableViewer/tableView.aspx?ReportId=92 (accessed March 12, 2015).

US Department of Commerce, International Trade Administration (2014) U.S. Trading Companies: 2013 Highlights. Available at www.trade.gov/mas/ian/build/groups/public/@tg_ian/documents/webcontent/tg_ian_005410.pdf (accessed August 31, 2015).

US Department of Transportation, Federal Highway Administration (2004) *Freight Transportation Improvements and the Economy,* Washington, DC.

US Department of Transportation, Maritime Administration (2009) *U.S. Public Port Development Expenditure Report,* 2009, Washington, DC.

US Department of Transportation, Maritime Administration (2011) *National Port Summit,* 2011, Chicago, IL.

Wilmsmeier, G., Monios, J. and Lambert, B. (2011) The direction development of intermodal freight corridors in relation to inland terminals, *Journal of Transport Geography,* 19(6), 1379–1386.

Zacher, M.W. and Sutten, B.A. (1996) *Governing Global Networks: International regimes for transportation and communication.* Cambridge: Cambridge University Press.

7

The evolving global railway industry

Chris Nash

Introduction

In the last 50 years, the rail industry has faced growing competition from road and air transport, and has lost its former role of providing comprehensive freight and passenger transport for the transport market as a whole. Nevertheless, in most parts of the world it has found important and growing markets in specific market segments – bulk and long-distance freight (including containers), medium-distance intercity passenger travel, and commuter services into large cities. The first part of this chapter discusses the economic and commercial position of rail, including the major technological advances that have influenced this position (such as double-stack containers, high-speed rail, cab signaling, etc.).

We then turn to the regulatory environment that governs the rail industry. Outside North America, the norm in terms of rail organization in the immediate post-World War II period was to have a single state-owned, vertically integrated rail company responsible for both the infrastructure and passenger and freight services. Discontent with this structure in terms of efficiency and market responsiveness has led to the emergence of a number of other structures. We first consider the way in which the trend towards separation between the network provider and the final supplier, that has been common in network industries in recent decades, has influenced rail organization. We then describe the three basic models of rail organization to be found worldwide – that is, continued government-owned monopolies (Russia, India, and China), deregulated private vertically integrated companies (America, Japan), and separation of infrastructure from operations (Europe, Australia). Each of the models is examined, and their strengths and weaknesses in dealing with particular situations are outlined. From our overview of the three basic models, we then outline our conclusions.

The economic position of rail

Most of the world's railways were originally built as privately owned, profit-seeking companies, and provided extensive passenger and freight services aimed at the entire transport market. With the growth of road competition, rail's position changed dramatically. Much short-distance passenger traffic and small consignments of freight were irrevocably lost to road, whilst rising car ownership and the use of road haulage facilitated changes in land use that generated new transport markets for which rail could never compete (Drew, 2011). However, in many countries rail has found an important role as a specialized transport mode. These changes are discussed for the freight and passenger sectors, respectively, in the next two sections, following which the infrastructure developments that have supported this traffic are explained.

Freight

As shown in Table 7.1, in 2012 the railways of three countries carried more than 2,000 billion ton-km of freight traffic. These were China, the US, and Russia. In comparison, India carried 626 and the European Union (EU) 449. All of these countries had seen rail traffic grow in the preceding 10 years, with growth of around 70 percent in India and China, and 50 percent in Russia. Growth in the US and Europe was much slower, at 10–15 percent.

Traditionally, rail freight has been dominated by bulk commodities, especially coal, and to a large extent this remains the case. These commodities tend to move in large volumes between a small number of locations – such as ports, mines, and power plants. Such locations typically have private sidings so that trains may be loaded directly. The volumes moved are large enough that complete trains may be loaded at one end and unloaded at the other without intermediate marshaling. Technical progress on rail has seen trains of bulk commodities become steadily heavier.

However, in many countries bulk traffic is static or declining, and the growth area of the freight market is in high-value commodities. The growth of high-value commodities has gone hand in hand with the growth of road freight, which is able to offer a flexible, high-quality, door-to-door service for what are typically smaller consignments of high-value articles. High-value goods are also associated with the trend of "just-in-time" deliveries, because firms do not want to keep large stocks of such articles. The way in which rail has traditionally handled smaller consignments is through the operation of wagonload services, where individual wagons or groups of wagons are taken to a marshaling yard and combined with wagons from other locations into full trains for the trunk part of the haul. At the destination end they are remarshaled into groups of wagons for the same or nearby destinations. However, this method of operation tends to involve a great deal of time, as well as increased costs in "trip" workings to and from marshaling yards and in remarshaling. Rail is therefore only competitive with road haulage if there is a long length of haul on which fast speeds and low costs can offset the high costs of trip workings. There is still much wagonload traffic in North America and in Europe, but for domestic traffic in smaller countries it is fast disappearing.

Table 7.1 Rail freight (billion ton-km)

Country	*2012*	*2002*	*2012/2002*
India	626	353	1.77
China	2518	1508	1.67
Russia	2222	1510	1.48
US	2525	2202	1.15
EU	449	426	1.05

Source: World Bank world databank (http://databank.worldbank.org/data/reports.aspx?source=world-development-indicators#).

A more efficient way of handling smaller consignments is by containerization, which makes transfer between modes faster and cheaper. A container depot may cover a wide area so that it can bring together enough traffic to make up complete trains for major destinations, with road transport essentially being used for the consolidation function. Whilst maritime containers are designed to be stacked onboard ships, a variety of less robust non-stackable swap bodies have been designed for purely land transport involving road and rail. Rail is particularly competitive for the transport of containers to and from ports, as much traffic is already containerized, and the port may have a rail container depot on its premises, avoiding the need for collection and delivery. Hence, one major growth area for rail traffic has been containers, and particularly the inland distribution of maritime containers. In the US, this has been facilitated by the development of double-stack container trains, which offer a major increase in capacity for a given length of train. All these developments have required large increases in axle loads, which have had consequences for the construction and maintenance requirements of the infrastructure.

A key issue for rail freight is the terms of competition with road freight. First, this competition depends on the approved technical characteristics of road vehicles permitted. Rail struggles to compete in countries such as the US and Australia, both of which allow road trains of up to 120 tons (sometimes more), compared with Europe, where in many countries the limit for a heavy goods vehicle is 44 tons. However, there has been a major debate over whether to allow so-called megatrucks more widely in Europe. Second, the competitiveness of road competition depends on the charging regime for the use of roads (Nash *et al.*, 2008). Traditionally, many countries have charged for the use of roads by means of a fuel tax plus an annual license duty. The relationship of the fuel tax to the physical and environmental damage done by the vehicle is poor; heavier vehicles tend to burn more fuel, but the relationship is not proportionate to the damage done, and road damage is in any case more related to axle weight than gross vehicle weight. To the extent that the shortfall is made up of a fixed annual charge, this results in overcharging vehicles on short-distance work and undercharging those on long hauls, which are arguably the most susceptible to rail competition. In the EU, policy corrects for this by permitting a kilometer-based charge for heavy goods vehicles, which varies with the characteristics of the vehicle (such as gross weight and axle load and also environmental standards), but very few countries (Austria, the Czech Republic and Germany as well as non-EU member Switzerland) have implemented such a charge, and only in Switzerland does it apply on all roads and not just motorways.

Passenger transport

In terms of passenger traffic, the leading countries in 2012 were India, with 979 billion passenger-km and China, with 796 billion. The EU's 27 states carried 407 billion passenger-km and Japan 245 billion. Again, all these countries had seen growth, except for Japan where traffic had been stagnating. Traffic had grown by 90 percent in India and 75 percent in China in the past ten years.

In passenger transport, technical developments have been more pronounced than in freight. The construction of new high-speed lines, capable of carrying trains at 300 km/h or more, has contributed to the growth of rail in both Europe and Asia. These new lines have enabled rail to recapture traffic on distances of up to 800 km that had been lost to air. Where rail has a station-to-station journey time of less than three hours it typically dominates over air, because of its greater convenience in terms of traveling directly between city centers, allowing passengers to avoid losing time accessing and waiting at terminals. For most people, and particularly business or leisure travelers where one end of their journey is in a large city, accessing and egressing

Table 7.2 Rail passenger traffic (billion passenger-km)

Country	*2012*	*2002*	*2012/2002*
India	979	515	1.90
China	796	456	1.75
EU	418	367	1.14
Japan	245	241	1.02

Source: World Bank database (EU data: EU transport in figures, 2014).

airports is less convenient than rail stations. Upgrading existing lines to achieve speeds of up to 225 km/h, has had a similar impact on shorter-distance routes of up to 300 km. High-speed rail may also capture some car travel over shorter distances (over short distances, the principle competitor to rail in most countries today is the car). However, in competing with the car, rail has a major disadvantage in terms of accessibility and frequency of service, compared with the door-to-door access and on-demand availability of the car. These disadvantages will be less pronounced where traffic, and hence services, are dense, where congestion is severe, where there is good public transport access to intercity rail stations, and where parking is difficult and expensive. Thus, rail tends to be more successful in shorter-distance, interurban transport between large cities and conurbations.

The other major growth area for rail is commutes into very large cities, a function that has expanded with increased urbanization and the growth of service-sector employment. Again, congestion and limited or expensive parking will aid rail against the car, and in some cities parking policies (as in Zurich) or road pricing schemes (as in Singapore, London, and Stockholm) are deliberately used to favor public transport over the car, thereby relieving congestion.

Countries such as Sweden and Switzerland have also seen major growth in shorter-distance regional and interurban traffic as part of a well-integrated network with buses and trams. For suburban and regional traffic, the almost complete displacement of locomotive hauled trains by electric or diesel multiple unit trains has contributed to economy and flexibility.

The above figures on traffic growth undermine the popular conception that rail is a dying mode. In the countries in which rail is most important, it is growing – often very fast. Moreover, rail traffic is not generally subsidized in India, China, and Japan, and nor is freight in the US. However, the same is not true of Europe, where on average around half the costs are borne by government. This is principally the result of the subsidization of substantial passenger networks. In India and China, passenger transport is cross-subsidized by freight.

Infrastructure developments

Growth in traffic has put pressure on the capacity of existing main lines. As noted above, new high-speed or freight lines may help resolve this issue; new high-speed passenger lines release capacity for freight and other passenger trains on existing routes. Many other solutions have also been adopted, such as running longer trains (which may require investment in lengthening station platforms and in reconfiguring track to make this possible), and installing new flyovers to remove conflicting movements at junctions. Problems at city terminals have often been overcome by placing suburban trains in tunnels under the city center so that they run through between suburban stations on opposite sides of the city without having to turn around in the center; this both relieves capacity problems at the city terminal and improves accessibility of services.

In Europe, signaling systems have also seen major advances, culminating in the development of the European Rail Traffic Management System. A key ingredient of this is a cab signaling system, which will remove the need for trackside signals and permit increased capacity utilization on given infrastructure. This was developed as a standard European system, which would avoid the need to equip trains to deal with different signaling systems as they pass from country to country, but it is seeing substantial application elsewhere in the world as well.

Developments in rail network organization

The major trend in network industry organization in recent decades has come from the realization that a natural monopoly lies in the provision of the network infrastructure, and that it is perfectly possible for competing suppliers to use that network. Thus, there has been a trend, particularly in Europe but also elsewhere in the world, to open up the market to new suppliers and to regulate access to the network infrastructure to ensure nondiscrimination. Sometimes, this has been achieved by requiring existing companies to grant access to new entrants to compete with their own downstream activities, but increasingly it has involved complete vertical separation of the network from its users so that multiple electricity, gas, or telecommunications companies make use of the same separately owned network. For instance, in Britain, retailers have a choice of a number of possible companies from which to buy their gas and electricity, but all make use of a common national grid to transport the product to them from the point of generation or supply.

This trend has also extended to railways, with new entrants sharing tracks with existing operators and with separation of provision and operation of the infrastructure from running trains. However, there are reasons why for rail this sharing of network infrastructure may be more difficult than for other industries. In most network industries, final suppliers simply need to buy a certain amount of capacity at a certain time. For rail, the relationship between final supplier and network managers is much more complex. The train operator needs a path on a particular route, which calls at specific points on the way. It demands a particular quality of service in terms of speed and reliability. It needs space at platforms or yards, access to depots, and possibly connection with other services. Moreover, the capacity of a particular route depends heavily on the mix of trains that run over it and the order in which they do so. For example, if a slow train follows a fast train, there will be a long gap before another fast train can follow without being delayed. In terms of real-time control, signalers and controllers have to decide how to recover from delays, which trains to further delay, and which to give priority. Track access agreements that stipulate what, exactly, the train operator is buying in terms of facilities and quality of service, and what flexibility the network manager has regarding rescheduling, are needed.

There are also other important features of the relationship between train and track. Delays may be the fault of either the infrastructure manager or the train operator; in the latter case, the train operator may also delay trains of other operators. The design and state of repair of the rolling stock used will influence the amount of wear and tear on the track, as well as capacity required (better acceleration and braking will reduce the capacity needed). Safety is of course an overriding concern that needs to be ensured.

To a degree, correct incentives for all these issues may be provided by appropriate track access charges and a system of compensation for delays. However, to achieve this fully will require systems of great complexity. Track access charges will need to reflect the amount of capacity required and the damage done by the vehicles in use. The performance regime will need to reflect the importance of delays according to which trains are delayed, their loadings, and importance of the staff and rolling stock being on time for their next duty.

Perhaps the system closest to achieving this at present is that in Britain. Track access charges differentiate between types of vehicles in fine detail, and a capacity charge is levied according to the forecast delay costs an additional train will create by removing some of the slack for recovery in the system. However, the latter charge is only relatively crudely differentiated in time and space, particularly for freight trains. There is also a performance regime with penalties and bonuses based on evidence of the cost of delays. Yet even in Britain there has been concern that vertical separation has brought with it cost penalties. Often, these are identified as transactions costs, which are the additional costs of drawing up and monitoring contracts to cover these issues, rather than simply using "command and control" mechanisms. However, the one attempt to quantify the transaction costs of vertical separation found them to be at most 2–3 percent of total system costs (Merkert *et al.*, 2012). Despite the sophistication of its track access charges and performance regimes, a greater problem in Britain is considered to be misalignments of incentives – the fact that each party in the industry has an incentive to optimize its own system, rather than the system as a whole. The McNulty report (McNulty, 2011) found much evidence of such problems. For instance, infrastructure renewals and enhancements are not fully paid for by operators, who therefore have an incentive to argue for higher standards than they would if they were paying for renewal and enhancement themselves.

As a result of these complexities, there remains ongoing debate about the wisdom of vertical separation in railways. Vertical separation is to be found in Europe, Australia, and some other countries in Asia, but even in Europe, where the European Commission (EC) has pursued it as an objective since 1991, it is not uniform. In some countries the degree of separation is limited, with infrastructure and the main operations in separate subsidiaries of the same holding company, or with the main train operator still undertaking infrastructure activities, such as provision of stations and depots, track maintenance, and signaling. Such arrangements may improve incentives to optimize system costs, but at the expense of making it harder for the regulator to ensure lack of discrimination.

Model I: Government-owned monopolies

Russia, India, and China, along with many smaller countries, have so far stuck largely to the model of a single vertically integrated state-owned operator. Traditionally, these have been run directly by a government ministry, although in both Russia and China the railway has now been separated out into an organization responsible to a new ministry of transport. Only Indian Railways is still run directly by a Ministry of Railways. Most observers (e.g., Oum and Yu, 1994) conclude that railways operate more efficiently when their management is given a reasonable degree of autonomy rather than being under the direct control of a ministry, as in the latter case it is not clear what is a political decision and what is a commercial decision of railway management – a scenario in which accountability suffers.

Both India and China face problems of massive growth in traffic, including unprofitable passenger traffic, but their reactions to this problem have differed. China is rapidly building an extensive network of high-speed lines, which should release capacity on the existing network for freight. India is concentrating on a new freight-dedicated network, whilst still considering limited construction of high-speed rail. As noted above, neither country has explicit subsidies for unprofitable passenger services, so these have to be provided with the profits made on freight traffic. Nor does either country have an independent regulator; charges are regulated directly by government departments.

Whilst discussion of the introduction of competition into the rail networks is intense in all three countries, so far this has only happened at the margins. In Russia, new companies are allowed to own rolling stock and to market their own services, but so far they have to hire not just track capacity but also locomotives and drivers from the state-owned monopoly (Winner and Evdokimov, 2011). In container transport in India, a similar approach has been taken. The argument is that in densely operated networks, it is more efficient for a single company to be responsible for running all trains. Given the importance of planning and operating services to maximize use of limited track capacity, there is extreme nervousness in these countries regarding any consideration of separating infrastructure from operations. Reforms that are under discussion concern giving railway management greater commercial freedom, with more independent regulation to ensure that freedom is not abused. However, the natural accompaniment to this would be the introduction of subsidies for non-commercial activities, though this is not something that is welcomed by governments. Particularly in India, where a number of cities have important commuter rail systems, it would be sensible for a conurbation authority to take responsibility for planning such systems in conjunction with other modes of transport and land use; however, such conurbation authorities do not exist, and local government is very reluctant to take on responsibility for subsidizing rail services.

Providing for massive growth that is entirely funded by the public sector is a problem, and all three countries have shown interest in public–private partnerships (PPPs) as a way of funding investment. However, PPPs in the rail sector are far from easy; rail infrastructure is a very costly, long-lived asset and is viewed by the private sector as a risky investment. Often, it is used by both commercial and social services and heavily influenced by government decisions. As a result, progress in PPPs for rail infrastructure has been limited, although privately funded rolling stock is becoming more common, as noted above.

Model II: Private vertically integrated railways

The North American model (following the Staggers Act in the US and similar measures elsewhere) relies on competition between different privately owned vertically integrated freight rail companies and with other modes in a largely deregulated environment to achieve an efficient rail system. The small amount of passenger traffic is handled by a separate government-owned company (Amtrak in the US) running over the track of freight railroads (except in the busy Northeast corridor, where Amtrak owns its own infrastructure). Earlier controls on prices and on the withdrawal of services have largely been removed. The same general approach has been combined with franchising in South America and parts of Africa. This approach is generally thought to have been extremely successful in North America, with major improvements in productivity, reductions in tariffs, and increases in traffic (Thompson, 2011). However, there is an argument that the lack of competition is limiting rail market share – particularly in manufactured goods, because firms are unwilling to invest in rail facilities when faced with the risk of "capture" by a monopoly railroad (Boyer, 2014) – and that statutory rights of access for competitor operators would therefore be desirable. The South American experience of franchising has been more mixed: whilst there have been big improvements in traffic and productivity, several problems have arisen, particularly concerning investment. The franchise competition itself introduces an added element of competition, but it seems that even long franchises do not provide sufficient incentive to invest in infrastructure (Thompson and Kohon, 2013).

It is difficult to see how such a structure could be brought about in Europe. Much European rail freight is international, and therefore would have to be passed from one company to another unless the vertically integrated companies were themselves international. There is no sign that European governments are willing to privatize rail infrastructure at all (the one attempt, in Britain, was a failure and the resulting company went bankrupt), let alone see it taken over by a foreign company, as they see decisions about rail infrastructure as very much decisions for government. Moreover, passenger services play a major role in Europe, and government intervention is much more predominant in this sector, with many services being subsidized. Governments are resistant to the idea of paying subsidies to private monopolies, preferring franchising as a way of privatizing passenger services, whilst running heavy passenger traffic over the tracks of vertically integrated freight railroads would be problematic in terms of incentives to provide adequate quality of service.

The only country to follow a similar model to the North American one for passenger railways is Japan, where population density and the cost of motoring make rail passenger services largely profitable. Japan has long had private, vertically integrated suburban railways in many parts of the country, but in 1987 it also split up the state-owned operator into six regional, vertically integrated passenger operators, with freight carried over their tracks by a separate freight operator. Three of these companies have now also been privatized via sale of shares (Ishida, 2011).

Model III: Within rail sector competition

In Europe, the EC has tried to encourage competition in train operations over common infrastructure by a degree of separation of infrastructure from operations and allowing entry to new operators (on the main interstate lines Australia has followed suit). So far the success of this measure in Europe has been limited, and the EC has been forced into increasing regulation of the market to try to remove barriers to entry and to ensure nondiscrimination. Directives – which have to be implemented by all member states – require non-discriminatory rules for setting track access charges and allocating capacity, as well as for providing access to stations, freight terminals, depots, and marshaling yards. It is also required that there should be an independent regulator, to whom complaints about discrimination may be addressed.

Table 7.3 shows the level of penetration of operators other than the principal operator in the European rail freight market, ranging from zero in Finland, Ireland, and Latvia to 54 percent in the UK and Romania (the UK is a special case as when it privatized its rail freight business, it deliberately split it into two companies. At the time, one specialized in bulk traffic and the other in containers, but now both compete in both markets). In the freight sector, new entry has largely taken one of two forms: first, small new companies have been set up to address particular niche markets; second, major operators from adjacent countries have entered the market for both domestic and international traffic. In some cases, they have in fact bought the existing operator and thus become the principal operator themselves. Foremost amongst these are Deutsche Bahn, which has bought the major freight operators in Britain, the Netherlands, and Denmark, and has major operations in many other countries; SNCF, which is particularly active in Belgium; Trenitalia, through its international subsidiary TX Logistics; and Austrian Railways, which bought the principal operator in Hungary.

Until recently in the passenger market, most new entry was through winning competition for franchises to operate particular services. In Britain, virtually all passenger services were franchised out to private companies over the period 1994–1997; in Sweden, virtually all subsidized services are franchised; and in Germany an increasing proportion of regional services are franchised out by the individual states rather than the federal government. Some non-core services are also franchised in other countries, including the Netherlands, Portugal, and Denmark. Table 7.4 shows the proportion of regional and suburban services operated by new entrants in countries where such entry exists.

Table 7.3 Percentage of rail freight market held by operators other than the main one

Country	%
Austria	18
Belgium	13
Bulgaria	37
Czech Republic	14
Denmark	27
Finland	0
France	32*
Germany	29
Greece	n.a.
Hungary	32
Ireland	0
Italy	24
Latvia	23
Lithuania	0
Luxembourg	0
Netherlands	36
Norway	38
Poland	33
Portugal	17
Romania	54
Slovakia	12
Slovenia	10
Spain	17
Sweden	n.a.
UK	54

n.a. indicates not available *includes VFLI, a subsidiary of the principal operator (SNCF).
Source: EC, 2014.
Note: the sources for this and subsequent tables refer to the UK whereas the discussion refers to Britain (Northern Ireland Railways remain a state owned vertically integrated monopoly). However, Northern Ireland Railways are so small that this scarcely affects the results.

Table 7.4 Percentage of regional and suburban services provided by new entrants in EU countries where they exist

Country	%
UK	100
Italy	27
Germany	18
Denmark	15
Portugal	12
Netherlands	8

Source: EC, 2014.

The advantage of franchising for passenger services is that governments can continue to determine service levels and fares, in conjunction with plans for other modes of transport and for land use and economic development, whilst introducing competition for the provision of services in order to control costs. In most countries, franchising has been associated with significant reductions in costs. That is not the case, however, in Britain – the country to have made most use of franchising – where train operating costs per train-km have actually increased by 13 percent since the completion of franchising (ATOC, 2013). Such an increase may be partly the result of improved quality of service, but the high increase in staff costs also suggests that having expanding companies competing for skilled labor tends to push wages up. This effect has not been so pronounced where only some services are franchised.

There is also increasing open-access competition in the passenger market. It is permitted in Germany, Italy, Austria, the Czech Republic, and Sweden. In Britain, bids to run open access passenger services are considered by the regulator, which will only permit them if they are expected to bring significant new traffic to the railway rather than simply taking traffic from existing (franchised) operators. However, in no country does it account for more than 7 percent of the intercity passenger market, this being the figure in Austria. In Italy it is 4 percent (Table 7.5).

Which model works best?

A limited number of studies have tried to investigate which of the alternative structures for the rail industry discussed in this chapter work best in which circumstances. Of these, the most recent and comprehensive is that of van de Velde *et al.* (2012), who used data from 26 OECD countries from 1994 to 2010 and looked for relationships between costs and mode share and structure of the rail industry, controlling for other major factors. They found that vertical separation worked best in terms of costs on relatively lightly loaded lines with a preponderance of passenger traffic; high density and a high proportion of freight tended to favor vertical integration. Horizontal separation of freight from passenger services tended to reduce costs, suggesting that where vertical separation exists, it should be with the operator of the predominant type of traffic. Neither structure nor the level of competition appeared to have a significant impact on mode share.

According to these prescriptions, there is good sense behind the variety of railway organizations found around the world. North America, with its dense, predominantly freight operations follows vertical integration for freight operations, with passenger operations being separate. Japan, with dense passenger operations but little freight, has vertically integrated passenger operators and a separate freight operator. Russia, India, and China, with dense operations of both passenger and freight traffic maintain almost complete vertical and horizontal

Table 7.5 Percentage of passenger traffic handled by open access passenger competition in countries where it exists

Country	*%*
Austria	7
Czech Republic	5
Italy	4
UK	<1

Source: EC, 2014.

integration. The less densely used railways of Europe, Australia, and other parts of Asia have experimented most with vertical separation. Yet even here there remains concern that added transaction costs and misalignment of incentives may make vertical separation inefficient. In some countries, this is dealt with by making infrastructure and the main operators separate subsidiaries of the same holding company, with the holding company responsible for coordination of planning and investment (France, having initially opted for a structure in which a separate infrastructure company was responsible for planning and capacity allocation, but contracted signaling and maintenance back to the dominant operator, is now reverting to this model). This will obviously reduce transaction costs and misalignment of incentives, but at the expense of increased risk of discrimination against new entrants. Therefore, it imposes greater burdens on the regulator, and only works where entrants have a relatively small share of the market (otherwise many operations would still be vertically separated). Britain, where passenger services dominate and are mainly franchised, has sought an alternative solution in the form of alliances between infrastructure managers and franchisees. The most extreme case of this approach is that of South West Trains, where the staff of the franchisee and the relevant geographical division of the infrastructure manager have been merged, and where all cost and revenue variations from what was predicted at the time of the agreement are shared equally between the two. This should significantly reduce transaction costs and correct misalignment of incentives, but it leaves other operators using the infrastructure concerned at possible discrimination, and only works where most services belong to a single franchisee. Obviously, to significantly influence infrastructure investment, franchises would need to be very long (it is doubtful whether the current British norm of 10 years is adequate).

Conclusion

Despite being regarded as obsolete in some quarters, the rail industry remains very important and is growing in many parts of the world. However, it has moved from competing in the transport market as a whole to being a specialist carrier of bulk products, containers, and road trailers or swap bodies in the case of freight, and of travelers into and between major cities in the case of passengers. Technological advances, including dieselization and electrification, construction of new high-speed lines, and improved signaling systems, have played their part in this process.

Until 30 years ago, rail companies were almost always vertically integrated, providing infrastructure and passenger and freight services. However, as with other network industries, there has been pressure to separate the natural monopoly infrastructure from the potentially competitive provision of services. However, the rail industry possesses particular characteristics that make it more difficult to introduce intra-industry competition than in other network industries. Whilst it is possible to divide it into a natural monopoly infrastructure sector and a competitive train operating sector, the degree of interaction necessary between the two, and the problems of transaction costs and misaligned incentives, are likely to remain greater for rail. Thus, it is not clear that vertical separation is always worthwhile. Particularly for densely used systems, vertical integration remains the norm. This includes government-owned, vertically integrated monopolies (Russia, China, and India) and privately owned ones (US, Japan). Nevertheless, pressure remains to introduce intra-industry competition, even in the US – which is widely regarded as the most successful freight railway system in the world. It is worth noting that in both the US and Japan, it is the only major form of traffic that is vertically integrated – passenger traffic in the US and freight in Japan are separated.

The main way of introducing competition whilst retaining vertical integration is through franchising, as practiced for freight in South America and passenger transport in Europe, especially Britain. This enables competition with no misalignment of incentives, except for the fact that the time horizon of the vertically integrated company is limited by the length of the franchise. In Britain franchises are not currently vertically integrated, though the growth of alliances between the infrastructure manager and the train operator is a major step in this direction.

A degree of vertical integration through the holding-company model remains possible where there is a dominant operator, as is currently the case in most of Europe. This will permit better alignment of incentives whilst raising the continued fear of discrimination. It will also increase the need for a strong, vigilant regulator wherever there is a desire to allow some competition within the rail sector. However, the evidence to date is that unless franchising is introduced, there will remain a dominant operator. Perhaps the model in which this operator works closely with the infrastructure manager, but smaller competitors keep it on its toes, is not a bad one after all.

References

Association of Train Operating Companies (ATOC) (2013) *Growth and Prosperity. How franchising helped transform the railway into a British success story*. London: ATOC.

Boyer, K. (2014) Why is the rail share of US freight traffic so low? *Journal of Transport Economics and Policy*, 48(2), 333–344.

Drew, J. (2011) Introduction, in J. Drew and J. Ludewig (eds) *Reforming railways: lessons from experience*. Brussels: Community of European Railways, pp. 13–20.

European Commission (EC) (2014) *Commission Staff Working Document*, Brussels: Report from the Commission to the Council and the European Parliament. Fourth report on monitoring development in the rail market. COM (2014) 353 final.

Ishida, Y. (2011) Japan, in J.Drew and J. Ludewig (eds) *Reforming railways: lessons from experience*. Brussels: Community of European Railways, pp. 23–31.

McNulty, Sir R. (2011) *Realising the Potential of GB Rail: Final Independent Report of the Rail Value for Money Study*. London: Department for Transport and Office of Rail Regulation.

Merkert, R., Smith, A.S.J. and Nash, C.A. (2012) The measurement of transaction costs – Evidence from European railways, *Journal of Transport Economics and Policy*, 46(3), 349–365.

Nash, C.A., Menaz, B. and Matthews, B. (2008) Inter-urban road goods pricing in Europe, in H. Richardson and C.H. Bae (eds) *Road congestion and pricing in Europe: implications for the United States*. Cheltenham: Edward Elgar Publishing, pp. 233–251.

Oum, T.H. and Yu, C. (1994) Economic efficiency of railways and implications for public policy: A comparative study of the OECD countries' railways, *Journal of Transport Economics and Policy*, 28(2), 121–138.

Thompson, L. (2011) United States and Canada, in J. Drew and J. Ludewig (eds) *Reforming railways: lessons from experience*. Brussels: Community of European Railways, pp. 47–55.

Thompson, L.S. and Kohon, J.C. (2013) Developments in rail organization in the Americas, 1990 to present and future directions, *Journal of Rail Transport Planning & Management*, 2(3), 51–62.

van de Velde, D., Nash, C.A., Smith, A., Mizutani, F., Uranishi, S., Lijesen, M. and Zschoche, F. (2012) *EVES-Rail. Economic effects of vertical separation in the railway sector*. Brussels: Community of European Railways.

Winner, J. and Evdokimov, A. (2011) Russia, in J. Drew and J. Ludewig (eds), *Lessons from Experience*, Brussels: Community of European Railways, pp. 33–45.

World Bank world databank (http://databank.worldbank.org/data/reports.aspx?source=world-development-indicators#)

8

The evolving global air transport industry

Kenneth Button

This chapter is concerned with the major transformation that air transportation has gone through over the past 40 years, and the directions in which it continues to evolve. While many of these changes have been technical in nature, others have been institutional with significant reforms to the regulation of industrial structures and the provision of international services. While the chapter covers all three legs of the 'air transportation stool' – airlines, airports, and air traffic control – the main focus is on the airlines. We also move beyond traditional boundaries of economic regulation, fares and market access regulation, to offer comments on safety, environmental, and security matters.

Introduction

From an economic perspective, air transport is the archetypal network industry. It provides numerous services between a diversity of nodal airports controlled by a similarly structured networked information system. From a theoretical perspective, air transport is characterized by significant economies of scope[1] that extend through the operations of air traffic control (ATC), airports, and airlines. All three elements in the system handle freight and passenger traffic, but more importantly combine a wide range of freight consignments and person types moving between a diversity of origins and destinations – a classic element of any network industry. In addition, on the demand side there are economies of market presence (or 'positive network externalities') with potential users enjoying significantly larger benefits as the number of possible destinations open to them increases more rapidly than the links added.

The tendency for much of the history of air transport has been for public policymakers to try to regulate the industry with the primary economic objective of spreading services for what were traditionally perceived as reasons related to social welfare maximization – a pattern common to many network industries. This long-established, almost global pattern of aviation regulation began to break down with the deregulation of, first, the US domestic air cargo market in 1977, and then the country's passenger market. This was followed by a gradual liberalization of other national markets and international air transport.

It is this rapid globalization of the air transport sector that concerns us here. However, this cannot be treated in isolation from narrower domestic considerations. The institutional structure, under which international air transport is supplied, emanates from the 1944 Chicago Convention and the establishment of the United Nations International Civil Aviation Organization (ICAO). Crucially, early agreement gave countries complete sovereignty over their air space. This led to divergent approaches in the treatment of domestic markets, over which a country had complete authority, and international markets that entail bilateral agreements between each pair of countries involved. However, there are considerable overlaps between domestic and international aviation: both use the same airports and ATC systems; in many cases, the airlines are engaged in offering services in both markets; and passengers often link to international services using domestic airlines.

This chapter looks at the factors that have led to changes in airline, airport, and ATC systems and assesses the institutional and economic challenges that still exist while moving air transport to a truly global industry. It considers the institutional changes that have taken place over the last 35 years, followed by the impacts of these changes.

The age of regulation

As an embryonic industry there were air transport networks prior to 1939, but these were limited by the technology of the time, with aviation primarily domestic and short haul in nature. However, the Second World War brought significant technical changes in all three legs of the air transport stool – aircraft, airports, and air navigation and control – and institutions to oversee them. The Second World War also left significant hardware that could be quickly and cheaply converted for civilian use. This allowed for the development of relatively reliable medium-range international air services, and longer-distance intercontinental services where a series of flight legs were employed.

Aware of a need to establish an institutional framework in which an international air transport system could successfully function, the Allies convened the Chicago Convention on International Civil Aviation in 1944. Reaching any consensus at the Convention proved problematic; however, it did establish the ICAO for continued debate and rule-making, and provided a structure for the subsequent regulatory environment, and especially the establishment of national sovereignties. Further, a lexigraphy was developed, enabling the resultant bilateral agreements to be structured and modified in similar ways. These latter features helped facilitate the subsequent liberalization of many international air transport markets.

The outcome, as indicated above, was a series of domestic markets that were universally restricted to national air carriers with various controls over their pricing, service provision, and ownership. The general concept that internal transport should be a public service remained in air transport, as it did for most other modes. Internationally, most services were provided under bilateral agreements, with each partner having one 'flag carrier' on a route and each airline offering similar capacities, while fares and revenues were often shared evenly between them. Competition was largely at a secondary level, involving such things as comfort and catering. ATC systems were national, with aircraft being passed from one radar control system to another along their route.

In network terms services were far from seamless, with impediments to efficient functioning over links both in terms of internal airline incentives and moving between various air spaces, and at hubs where efficient airport operations were stymied by the dominance of national carriers and the inability to offer efficient online services. Whether these factors had a serious effect on the development of international aviation in the period after the Second World War, given the technology of the line, is somewhat unclear. The subsequent actions of the ICAO – for example, in areas such as developing common safety standards – did provide a global backdrop against which both the institutional structure of the industry and its associated technology could move forward.

The situation later changed considerably as incomes rose, leisure and business travel demand increased, and new manufactured and perishable agricultural products ('exotics') requiring rapid and reliable transport came on the market. The regulatory structure that emerged from the 1940s, and lingered for over 30 years had become outdated in a global environment where transport had become a commodity and where flexibility and low cost, rather than stability and social cohesion, had become the key requirement of users.

Changing institutional structures of international air transport networks

Deregulation[2] really began with air transport (Button, 2015). While there had been deregulations elsewhere, these, as with trucking in the UK, had relatively small effects and did not attract the widespread attention of the US Airline Deregulation Act of 1978. Although US domestic air cargo airlines had been deregulated a year earlier, the debate surrounding the 1978 legislation, together with the subsequent intensive analysis of its impacts, provided an impetus for both domestic reforms in other countries, and for reviews of the international bilateral air service agreements structure (Morrison and Winston, 1995). Indeed, the US itself initiated an Open Skies policy in 1979, and although arrangements had been signed with 23 minor air service trading partners by 1982, it was not until the 1992 Open Skies Agreement with the Netherlands that the policy had a significant effect. Changes in the other main elements of the international air transport sector, airports and ATC, were even more measured and are still far from embodying a common approach.

The following sections will look in more detail at the changes that have taken place in the three main international aviation industries.

Airlines

Airlines are highly flexible businesses that are subject to a number of inherent economic characteristics; most notably, economies of scope and density on the supply side and market presence on the demand side (Levine, 1987). These features are often seen to lead naturally to hub-and-spoke networks with numerous small flows of traffic being consolidated at a major airport to be combined and relocated to final destinations (Mayer and Sinai, 2003). The constraints on the optimal extent of hubbing are determined by the size of each traffic flow and the congestion arising at the hub as traffic descends in banks upon it. The traditional bilateral model of international aviation led each country to have at least one hub that was dominated by its flag carrier airline. Under bilateral air service agreements, such flag carriers provide 50 percent of international flights at the airport. In addition, airports supplied capacity for purely domestic services provided by the nation's airlines.

The economies associated with hub-and-spoke networks tend to be more pronounced when it comes to long-distance services; there tends to be less traffic between distant origin-destination pairs than between local services. This feature links the institutional structure affecting domestic services with international services. This partly explains why international service deregulation followed the domestic reforms in the US, and why extra-EU reforms followed those within the EU. The stylized picture in Figure 8.1 represents a fairly large domestic air transport market, such as that of the US, EU or India. The deregulation of domestic markets had the type of effect seen within the circle, as quantified in numerous US studies after 1978. Put simply, deregulation creates more domestic traffic because of lower fares and the positive impact it has on the nation's income. However, by reducing fares to international

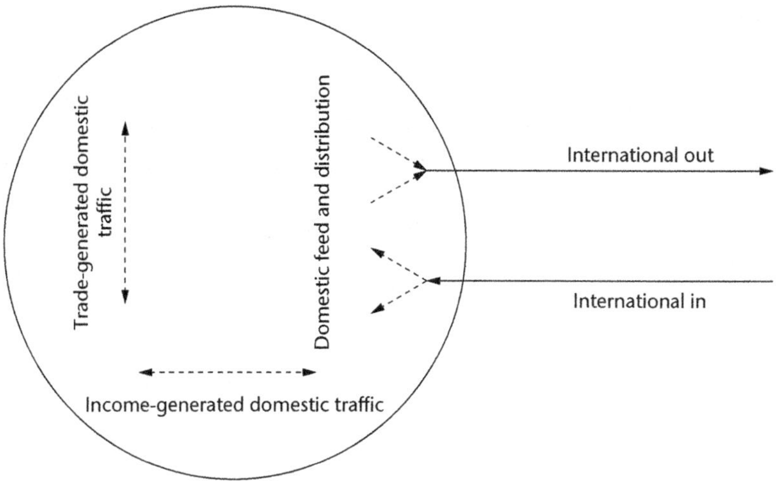

Figure 8.1 The relationship between domestic and international air transport

gateways (and these are classified as domestic flights), this also reduces the overall costs of international travel and pushes up demand for international flights. The existing bilateral air services agreements were simply not capable of handling this demand, or at least not agile enough to adjust quickly. Any general demonstration effects that liberalization had on potential travelers' views on the increased utility of air travel compounded this demand-driven effect.

While liberal bilateral air service agreements have allowed for much of the restructuring of international services, multilateral agreements, often on a regional basis, have also had a role and are increasing in importance (Button, 2015). This may again be seen as a response to interactions across networks, as well as a narrow view that liberalization is desirable.

The largest of these multilateral initiatives has involved the members of the European Union (EU), which, in 1997 after phasing in three 'Packages' of reforms, created a single European Market for air transport. This structure has been expanded as other non-EU European countries have joined, and as the US engaged with this grouping in 2007 within the EU–US Open Skies Agreement, although this latter element falls short of being a free-trade area in that cabotage is not permitted (Button, 2014). Other small, open international markets include the Multilateral Agreement on the Liberalization of International Air Transportation signed in 2001 by the US, Brunei, Chile, New Zealand and Singapore, and the ASEAN Multilateral Agreements on Air Services and Full Liberalization of Air Freight Services that were simultaneously approved in 2009 in Manila by the 10-member Association of Southeast Asian Nations. Progress, however, elsewhere has proved more difficult; for example, while the 1999 Yamoussoukro Decision commits its 44 African signatory countries to deregulate air services, the actual integration of international aviation on the continent has proven problematic (Schlumberger, 2010).

The pressures for this gradual shift from bilateral to multilateral agreements seems to have been quite powerfully influenced by the demonstration and ripple demand effects of the earlier changes in domestic and international regulatory structures. They also reflect a number of other factors, some of which are peculiar to specific cases. The Single European Market for air services was part of a much larger legislative package – the Single European Act of 1996. This act liberalized a multiplicity of markets within the EU. Similarly, the EU–US Open Skies Agreement was partly motivated on the European side by the questionable legality under EU law of the existing US bilateral agreements.

Airports

Until relatively recently, the vast majority of airports have been publicly owned and operated as public utilities. They were seen as part of the essential infrastructure needed to provide both domestic and international air services, but required regulation to contain their natural monopoly power and, in many cases, public ownership to ensure adequate financing. There were difficulties with this, especially with the almost universal interference of governments in the operations and investments in airports. The inability to economically price airports, and the need to conform under the Chicago Convention to accountancy, rather than marginal cost pricing in their charging of international air services, meant that runway capacity was often not allocated efficiently.

In general, this situation changed in the 1990s because of new thinking regarding the efficient provision of infrastructure in general, and specifically because of reinterpretations of the role of airports and how they should function. In some cases a shortage of funding for expansion played a practical role. There now exists a wide range of institutional structures (Carney and Mew, 2003); however, as with airlines, separating out the international air transport elements of the airport system from the domestic is almost impossible. Instead, a general move to greater commercialization of airports in different ways has been a global trend (Button, 2007).

The UK initiated such a change with the privatization of its major airports under the Airports Act of 1986, although other countries have pursued a variety of other, less direct, measures to distance airports from day-to-day interference by government, and to open them up to wider sources of financing. For example, many countries in South America have concessionary arrangements with companies tendering to run and invest in airports under long-term arrangements, with the assets returning to the state after the concession periods (Button, 2008). Other countries have engaged in extensive outsourcing of airport activities, such as terminal operations, while still retaining many operational functions. In many cases the pattern has been to corporatize airports, particularly in Europe. This has generally meant retention in government hands, but with airports free to attract private financing and manage their everyday activities within what amounts to a non-profit business model.

Air traffic control

ATC has been the slowest element of international air transport to experience significant institutional reforms. This is partly explained by the difficulty inherent in modifying a system that is at the core of a functioning air transport network. Such a network provides information and direction both to those using it, and when the actions regarding one nation's system immediately impact the ATC systems of other countries. In addition, ATC has been a monopoly undertaking, traditionally provided as a direct part of a government's activities – a relict of its initial military function. Additionally, there are issues surrounding the nature any reforms may take. For example, limits are often noted regarding the extent to which genuine competition in the market can exist for ATC services, and it is not easy to develop systems of competition for the market.

Reforms have occurred in terms of ownership structures and the ways in which systems are managed. As with airports, the impacts have tended to be slow because of the cost structures involved, and also because air navigation systems and their providers (ANSPs) tend to be much more entwined (Button, 2013). The move away from state ownership and control over ANSPs began in New Zealand in 1987 and in Australia the following year. However, the corporatization of Nav Canada in 1996 was the real catalyst for change and the focus of a marked demonstration effect. It is the world's second largest ATC system handling some 12 million aircraft movements a year. Since then, many countries have adopted the idea of a quasi-independent, non-profit ATC system funded from user charges with a range of nuances (Oster and Strong, 2008).

The situation in the US has proven to be something of an outlier (Gloaszewaki, 2002). Its ANSP is a state monopoly, the Federal Aviation Administration (FAA), with its financing coming largely from taxation. Critics have pointed to excessive government involvement in its operations and finances; for example, there were 23 continuations to 2007 legislation before the 2012 FAA Air Transportation Modernization and Safety Improvement Act was passed. The challenge in financing and introducing the new satellite-based Next Generation (NextGen) ATC system has been another part of the problem (US Federal Aviation Administration, 2013).

European air traffic management is also a substantial undertaking, but the system handles fewer flights, using more centers and airports, and is more labor intensive than the American system to which it is often compared (e.g., EUROCONTROL Performance Review Commission and Federal Aviation Administration, 2013). However, this scale of activity still makes it difficult to modify and update, and the situation is made worse by the regular involvement of national governments in its investment and pricing policies. At another level, there are considerable diversities in the forms of ownership of the monopoly national systems now in place. At one end of the spectrum is the public/private model of NATS, which handles ATC in the UK and has access to private finance markets, and levies user fees (Goodliffe, 2002). At the other end are state-owned systems that are largely financed from taxation.

There are ongoing regional endeavors to consolidate national ATC systems. The diversity of approaches in Europe has proved challenging as economic growth and its geographical concentration in particular parts of the EU, coupled with wider socio-political aspects of integration, has led to serious congestion of several systems. There have been efforts within Europe since 1999, especially since 2004, to integrate these systems into a single entity, which is the Single European Sky initiative (European Commission, 2012). The initiative is composed of several components, including technological programs (SESAR), new Europe-wide safety competencies, and the merger of airspace, currently divided into national region to increase capacity and reduce inefficiencies; for example, the creation of functional airspace blocks. However, progress has been slow and has overlapped with technical and institutional changes in the various national systems.

At a more mesoscale, a number of Central American countries (Guatemala, El Salvador, Honduras, Nicaragua, Costa Rica, and Belize) have come together to form the Central American Corporation for Air Navigation Services. This has allowed common policies on equipment purchases and savings in operational costs, including the ability to retain air traffic controllers for the member countries.

These efforts to integrate ATSs are reliant both on political agreements that have to overcome concerns involving not only relinquishing sovereignty over each nation's skies, but also the way military and civilian airspace interact and the adopting of a common technology. Existing radar-based ATC systems require air control centers and the allocation of responsibility for air space use. These factors are not amenable to large-scale system integration. However, efforts to move to a satellite-based system whereby airlines control their fight paths, as is gradually happening in the US and the EU and is *de facto* used by aircraft flying remote oceanic routes, is proving difficult. Until there is a common software platform and all aircraft are fitted with appropriate hardware, the exiting ATC system will have to coexist with land-based controls.

The impacts of change

There are numerous studies on airline and airport efficiency, though fewer on ATC efficiency. The general conclusion, irrespective of the markets reviewed, the time period covered, or the method of analysis favored, is that liberalization can enhance economic efficiency. Further, much of this efficiency gain has been passed on to passenger and cargo consignors in the form of lower fares and rates, and more extensive networks of services.

Air traffic

The measures to liberalize markets have contributed, along with factors such as enhanced aviation technology and the general increase in global income, to producing more air traffic. For example, the number of globally international passengers rose from 412 million in 1996 to 11,157 million in 2012, and the freight moved from 13.6 million tons to 32.3. However, isolating the pure effects of legal reforms on traffic is difficult. Nevertheless, we can consider the airline industry and how its industrial and operational structure has been transformed. Again, this is not entirely the result of institutional reforms; for example, technological developments of various kinds have been very important and have been key drivers of change.

In the case of short-haul international traffic between relatively small countries, air services had traditionally been between the main airports of each country. There were few intermediate stops to change aircraft. The liberalizations have changed this in a number of ways. First, the carriers providing these services have often changed from the flag carriers to low-cost airlines, such as Ryanair and EasyJet in Europe. In terms of passengers carried, Ryanair is the world's largest international airline. Second, the traditional 'gateway' hubs in many countries are now facing competition from other airports that offer more basic services and conform more to the economic needs of the low-cost airlines. The combination of these factors has led to the growth of 'base' rather than hub airports, where the low-cost carriers provide radial international services, often without any online options. Third, many of the international services are provided by third-party airlines; for instance, the Irish carrier Ryanair serves from Basel to London Stanstead or Frankfurt Hahn Airport to Corfu. This is largely a function of the increase in multilateral air services agreements discussed earlier.

In the case of long-haul services, the traditional pattern of traffic from originating cities to final destinations frequently took a 'dog-bone' or 'dumb-bell' pattern. This initially involved local domestic feeder services taking traffic from the origin cities to a national hub where it was consolidated with other traffic to go to a gateway hub in a destination country. This was usually done by one of the designated flag carriers of either the origin or destination country. Once at the gateway hub, passengers were consolidated onto domestic flights in that country to fly to their final destinations.

The US Open Skies initiatives not only allowed more flexibility in terms of airline services between countries, but also permitted the growth of the strategic alliances of airlines (Star Alliance, Oneworld, and SkyTeam) that now carry about two-thirds of the world's international air traffic. These alliances generally grew with the advent of Open Skies bilateral agreements and subsequent multilateral agreements. They also provide both cost economies to the airlines through their ability to better integrate their services and passenger benefits in terms of offering more online services, as well as more convenient scheduling and integrated loyalty programs.[3]

More recently, technology changes and more liberal air service agreements have led to the greater use of smaller airports over traditional gateway hubs. This has allowed either direct long-haul flights between origins and destinations, or only one stop at a gateway hub. These technology changes have included upgrading the range of some existing medium-sized aircraft, such as the Boeing 737 and 757, and the introduction of new large hardware, most notably the Boeing 787, with its greater fuel efficiency and intermediate passenger capacity. Larger and longer-range aircraft, especially the Airbus A380 and upgraded Boeing 747, also allow lower-cost, direct-trunk services on high-volume routes between a larger number of the world's major hubs.

Added to these are the new network models that have been developed in particular, but not exclusively, by airlines from the Gulf region (Emirates Airlines, Qatar Airways, Etihad Airways) and Turkey, with the aim of linking the rapidly growing Middle East and Asian economies with Europe, and to a lesser extent the US. The airlines involved have made extensive purchases of long-haul jet aircraft, and have developed 'hourglass' networks, each of which is based on a large hub (see Figure 8.2). For example, Emirates' hub at Dubai International Airport is specifically designed to handle online long-haul movements. In this case, the pattern of travel for someone going from 'b' to 'y' (see Figure 8.2) requires just one change, at the hub.

In terms of the type of air carrier engaged in longer-haul international movements, there has been limited development of the low cost model.[4] There are basically fewer cost savings possible in a long-haul operation, making it harder for a low-cost operator to differentiate itself from a conventional airline. In particular, the former typically fly their aircraft for more hours and flights each day than the legacy airlines, which is difficult when long-haul aircraft scheduling is more determined by time zone constraints, and longer flight times mean there is less scope to increase aircraft utilization by adding one or two more very short flights each day.

This does not mean that long-haul international operators have not emerged. For example, Australia's Jetstar Airways has provided low-cost international flights since 2005, when it began services to Christchurch, New Zealand, followed by services from Sydney, Melbourne and Brisbane in 2006 to tourist destinations such as Honolulu, Japan, Vietnam, Thailand and Malaysia. However, the numerous failures that have occurred suggest that airlines have found it difficult to develop a low-cost, long-haul international business model. Unlike domestic air transport markets or routes within integrated economic blocks, lower fares have often resulted from economies associated with strategic alliances of traditional carriers and associated network competition between these alliances, rather than the entry of low-cost airlines.

International airports

The liberalization of international airlines, combined with the growth of the three mega strategic alliances, and of the hourglass model for many long-haul operations (which may involve, as with Turkish Airlines, or not, as with Emirates, an alliance membership), has focused

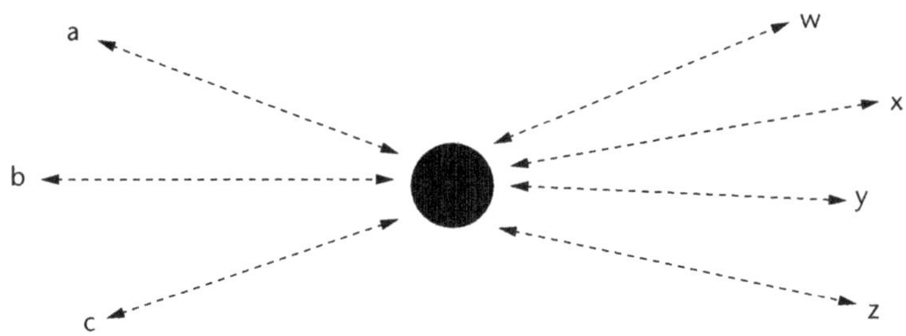

Figure 8.2 The 'hourglass' pattern of international hub-and-spoke operations

traffic on large airports. The general pattern is one of rapid international traffic growth at the largest airports, with particularly pronounced expansion in the Gulf States airports. For example, Dubai is now the world's largest international airport, handling 71 million passengers in 2014. What is also notable, and ties with the development of the long-haul international airline model, is the rapid expansions at Dubai and Atatürk International airports between 2005 and 2013, which are major hubs in large hourglass networks.

While much of the academic and policy debate focuses on passenger traffic, there have also been changes in the use of airports for cargo movements, although the nature of the data makes it difficult to isolate domestic from international traffic. The hourglass model is again relevant, with Dubai increasing its tons handled from 784,997 in 2002 to 2,267,365 in 2014, moving from the world's 21st largest freight airport to its sixth. Equally pronounced is the growth in freight handled by Chinese airports, with Shanghai being the world's third largest cargo airport in 2014, Beijing 14th and Guangzhou 19th (compared to 27th, 26th, and 29th in 2002).

Air traffic control system

The institutional changes that have taken place over recent years would generally seem to have improved the economic and technical efficiency, in terms of delays, of the ATC system. This has helped the system to cope with the considerable growth in aircraft movements (Oster and Strong, 2008), and has also been achieved with no diminution of the system's safety. The problem is that compared to the airline and airport industries, very limited analytical work has been conducted on the various ANSP providers. What has been done has generally been focused on simple analysis of delays relative to the growth in traffic at a very broad level, and for various providers, but without any real consideration of the physical environments under which these providers operate.

However, recent cost analyses of the various European systems that come under EUROCONTROL do provide guidance as to the relative efficiencies of each European national system (Button and Neiva, 2014). There are clear differences between the various systems, and analysis over time also shows that the ranking of the various ANSPs varies temporally; both patterns are also picked up using different techniques in the annual reports of EUROCONTROL's Performance Review Body. From an institutional perspective, further analysis of the data reveals that the move to separate providers from the traditional high level of government oversight has not proven effective in improving efficiency. Although the reasons for this are unclear, it may be due to problems at the interfaces of efficient and inefficient systems, or to the time it takes to adjust the way in which an ANSP operates.

Some additional considerations

There are a number of additional areas of international aviation that have attracted the attention of policymakers often in response to public concerns but also as a reflection of shifting political priorities. These add additional parameters to the ways in which global aviation is evolving. We touch upon a number of these very briefly below.

Security

It would be remiss not to say a little about the security of the international air transport network. This has been a major concern since the use of airliners, albeit on domestic routes, as weapons in the US in 2001. Attacks on international aviation, taking hostages for political reasons, and use of its infrastructure to launch attacks (such as those in the US in 2001) are well documented. The reasons for these attacks are in part because of visibility and the spatial concentrations of people utilizing international air transport, and at the very least provide a focus of media attention. Attacks can also be extremely costly to society when successful (Blunk *et al.*, 2006; Blalock *et al.*, 2007).

For the international air traveler there are obvious costs in meeting security arrangements, many of which are specified under ICAO rules, while others are augmented to meet national or regional concerns. There are direct costs of security measures that are in place at airports, and less transparently at locations such as ATC centers. These immediate costs are covered in a diversity of ways; for instance, by a security fee, by a combination of fees and general taxation (as is the case in the US), or indirectly, whereby airports have to meet security standards and the costs are pushed onto travelers through airport user fees levied on airlines (as in the UK). Adding to these direct costs are those associated with the added time it takes to pass through security, and, in many cases of international travel, the time and financial costs of obtaining documentation. Aircrafts must also meet security specification standards, as must crew and associated workers. These costs funnel through in the form of higher ticket prices.[5]

Much as one may hope for positive changes in the area of security, or at least in terms of its costs, this seems unlikely. Security measures are continually changing, partly to meet new threats, partly to give reassurance to travelers, and partly to reduce the costs of existing measures. It seems unlikely that the threats of attack on the airline network, because of its visibility and the important role that it plays in the modern economy, will diminish, and thus there will remain the inevitable challenge of providing socially acceptable levels of protection for those employed in the sector and those that use its services.

Environment

All modern transport entails environmental costs, and air transport is no exception (Rothengatter, 2010). Local noise around airports has always been an issue with aviation, although the problem has been eased with the adoption of quieter hardware, in part introduced as ICAO initiatives and in part through the use of more noise-sensitive flight paths. The challenge has switched more to that of handling matters related to climate-change gas emissions, particularly CO_2. State-of-the-art technology, such as that embodied in the Boeing 787, has led to a gradual improvement in the fuel efficiency of aircraft, averaging about 1 percent per year over the past 20 years or so. Higher fuel prices have stimulated the purchase of more fuel-efficient hardware and its more fuel-efficient use, and initiatives such as NextGen and the Single European Sky should facilitate even more of the latter.

The larger network effects are likely to be associated with global initiatives of the kind seen in the Kyoto Protocol: that is, measures to seriously reduce carbon emissions across all sectors. Efforts to do this regarding air transport have to date been relatively unsuccessful, with only some regional efforts, such as those of the EU, being developed. The latter, the EU Emissions Trading System, is a cap-and-trade regime designed to statutorily limit overall CO_2 emissions and to allow trade between those most needing to use carbons. In simple terms, airlines would receive tradable allowances covering a certain level of CO_2 emissions from their flights per year and be allowed to buy and sell amongst themselves. The 2008 legislation applied to EU and non-EU airlines, along with flights to and from Iceland, Liechtenstein and Norway, are also covered. In 2013, the EU temporarily suspended the scheme for flights operated from or to non-European countries, while continuing to apply the legislation to flights within and between countries in Europe. It did this to allow the ICAO to reach a global agreement to tackle aviation emissions. Subsequently, it was agreed that a global market-based mechanism would be developed by 2016, to be applied by 2020.

The implications for the environment of the failure to embrace carbon within international air transport were to some extent been mitigated in the short term by the rise in kerosene prices since about 2007. This could be seen as internalizing much of the external environmental costs. However, the issues have not gone away and the ICAO's commitment is still in place; this is a genuinely evolving situation. The impact that a carbon cap-and-trade – or some comparable scheme if universally introduced – would have on air transport is unclear. If fuel prices were to remain high and constrain rising demands for air transport, the impacts of any environmental policy on overall air travel may be muted, although there would inevitably be some effects on the relative costs of different types of air travel, with a larger impact on short-haul, relatively fuel-intensive services (Scheelhaase *et al.*, 2010). Fuel prices have, however, fallen dramatically since 2012.

Safety

Air transport is a remarkably safe mode of transport, particularly when it comes to long-distance international services. In aggregate, globally in 2012 there were 794 fatalities in the 119 commercial aviation accidents involving planes carrying six or more passengers, and this was part of a long-term downward trend. Put another way, there were about 3.2 accidents of one kind or another per million departures in 2012. This data can be compared with the World Health Organization's estimate of 1.24 million deaths in road accidents in 2010. The improvement in safety has also occurred during the period of economic deregulation of the industry (McKenzie and Shughart, 1988)

Aviation safety varies across the global network. Small commercial aircraft are more prone to accidents, in part because they are used on shorter routes involving more takeoffs and landings, the most dangerous parts of flights, and at smaller airports that are often less well equipped. Their pilots also tend to be less experienced. Overlapping these factors, there are large regional variations across the global network, with poorer safety records in Africa and Latin America than in Europe and North America. The transition economies of Central and Eastern Europe have considerably improved their safety record following a poor period in the 1990s.

The impressive safety record of aviation is in part due to continual improvements in technology, better training, and evolving organizational structures. In the last case, there have been a number of regional initiatives, in addition to the role of ICAO, to coordinate safety initiatives; these include the Banjul Accord Group Aviation Safety Oversight Organization, the East African Community Civil Aviation Safety, the Security Oversight Agency in Africa, the Cooperative Development of Operational Safety and Continuing Airworthiness Project for the Commonwealth of Independent States, and the Central European Rotation Group.[6] Added to these have been a number of major acts of bilateral assistance, and funding from international agencies such as the World Bank and the European Investment Bank.

Accidents are now rare events, and even if they do occur there is a very high probability of survival. The safety situation is unlikely to change significantly in the future, although while the probability of being in an accident may decline, as air traffic grows the actual number of incidents could also increase. Nevertheless, in sum, air transport safety has become a global network issue, and with this is evolving a global approach to ensuring uniformly high safety standards, if for no other reason than that a country's nationals could be flying on any airline anywhere in the world.

Conclusion

The global air transport market has undergone a transmogrification over the past 35 years since the initial deregulation of the US domestic market. While the trend is unquestionable, the pattern of liberalization is patchy, and in many cases the process is far from complete. One way of looking at the current era is in terms of viewing it as that of an 'Age of Experimentation'. We see a plethora of different policies in place regarding the many aspects of air transport, and it is still unclear which combination of these actions, if any, will emerge as superior. The market, in one form or another, is playing an increasing role, but the devil is really in the detail. Markets do not exist in a vacuum, but rather within institutional structures that, at the very least, set out property rights. As of now, a number of market forms are being 'experimented' with at various places and in regard to various elements in the global aviation market.

Notes

1 The various economies associated with airline networks are discussed in Button (2002).
2 'Deregulation' is the term largely used in the US. Europeans more accurately tend to talk about 'liberalization' or 'regulatory' reform.
3 See, for example, Oum *et al.* (2000). Similar strategic alliances have developed for airfreight traffic.
4 Their development in many lower income markets has also often been limited both by economic considerations and regulation (Schlumberger and Weisskopf, 2014),
5 There are also social costs associated with individuals switching to less safe modes than aviation, most notably the automobile, as the result of the higher costs and hassle of air travel (Blalock *et al*, 2007).
6 There have also been global initiatives of a wider kind regarding research and rescue activities; for example, the use of national satellite data in the search for the Malaysian airliner MH370 in 2014 was initiated when China activated the 15 signatories of the International Charter on Space and Major Disasters.

References

Blalock, G., Kadiyali, V. and Simon, D.H. (2007) The impact of post-9/11 airport security measures on the demand for air travel, *Journal of Law and Economics*, 50: 731–755.

Blunk, S.S., Clark, D.E. and McGibany, J.M. (2006) Evaluating the long-run impacts of the September 11th terrorist attacks on US domestic airline travel. *Applied Economics*, 38: 363–370.

Button, K.J. (2002) Airline network economics, in D. Jenkins (ed.) *Handbook of Airline Economics*. 2nd ed. New York: Aviation Week, pp. 27–34.

Button, K.J. (2003) Does the theory of the 'core' explain why airlines fail to cover their long-run costs of capital? *Journal of Air Transport Management*, 9: 5–14.

Button, K.J. (2007) The implications of the commercialization of air transport infrastructure, in D. Lee (ed.) *The Economics of Airline Institutions, Operations and Marketing 2*. Oxford: Elsevier, pp. 171–192.

Button, K.J. (2008) Air transportation infrastructure in developing countries: privatization and deregulation, in C. Winston and G. de Rus (eds) *Aviation Infrastructure Performance: A Study in Comparative Political Economy*. Washington, DC: Brookings Institution, pp. 193–221.

Button, K.J. (2012) The efficiency of network nodes: the regulation of airports, *Competition and Regulation in Network Industries*, 13: 19–39.

Button, K.J. (2013) Comparative inefficiency of various air navigation systems, in P. Forsyth, D. Gillen, K. Hüschelrath, H-M. Niemeier, and H. Wolf (eds) *Liberalizing Aviation: Competition, Cooperation and Public Policy*. Burlington: Ashgate, pp. 325–342.

Button, K.J. (2014) Really opening up the American skies, *Regulation*, 7: 2–7.

Button, K.J. (2015) A book, the application and the outcomes; how right was Alfred Kahn in *The Economics of Regulation* about the effects of the deregulation of the US domestic airline market? *History of Political Economy*, 47: 1–39.

Button, K.J. and Neiva, R. (2014) Economic efficiency of European air traffic control systems, *Journal of Transport Economics and Policy*, 47: 65–85.

Carney, M. and Mew, K. (2003) Airport governance reform: a strategic management perspective, *Journal of Air Transport Management*, 9: 221–232.

EUROCONTROL Performance Review Commission and Federal Aviation Administration (2013) *2012 – Comparison of Air Traffic Management-related Operational Performance: US/Europe*. Brussels/Washington, DC: EUROCONTROL/FAA.

European Commission (2012) *Single European Sky*. Available at: http://ec.europa.eu/transport/modes/air/single_european_sky.

Gloaszewaki, R. (2002) Reforming air traffic control: an assessment from the American perspective, *Journal of Air Transport and Management,* 8: 3–11.

Goodliffe, M. (2002) The new UK model for air traffic services – a public private partnership under economic regulation, *Journal of Air Transport and Management*, 8: 13–8.

ICAO (International Civil Aviation Organisation various years) *Annual Report to the Council*, ICAO, Montreal.

Levine, M.E. (1987) Airline competition in deregulated markets: theory, firm strategy, and public policy, *Yale Journal on Regulation* 4: 393–494.

Mayer, C. and Sinai, T. (2003) Network effects, congestion externalities, and air traffic delays: Or why not all delays are evil. *American Economic Review*, 93: 1194–1215.

McKenzie, R.B. and Shughart, W.F. (1988) Deregulation's impact on air safety: separating fact from fiction, *Regulation*, 11: 42–51.

Morrison, S.A. and Winston, C. (1995) *Evolution of the Airline Industry*. Washington, DC: Brookings Institution.

Oster, C. V. Jr. and Strong, J.S. (2008) *Managing the Skies: Public Policy, Organization, and Financing of Air Navigation*, Aldershot, Ashgate

Oum, T., Park, J. and Zhang, A. (2000) *Globalisation and Strategic Alliances: The Case of Airline Industry*. Oxford: Pergamon Press.

Rothengatter, W. (2010) Climate change and the contribution of transport: Basic facts and the role of aviation, *Transportation Research* D, 15: 5–13.

Scheelhaase J., Grimme, W. and Schaefe, M. (2010) The inclusion of aviation into the EU emission trading scheme – Impacts on competition between European and non-European network airlines, *Transportation Research D*, 15: 14–25.

Schlumberger, C.E. (2010) *Open Skies for Africa: Implementing the Yamoussoukro Decision*. Washington, DC: World Bank.

Schlumberger, C.E. and Weisskopf, N. (2014) *Ready for Takeoff? The Potential for Low-cost Carriers in Developing Countries*. Washington DC: World Bank.

US Federal Aviation Administration (2013) *NextGen*. Available at: http://www.faa.gov/nextgen/.

9

Urban public transport

Lorenzo Vannacci[1] and Elena Navajas Cawood[1]

Introduction

The public transport (PT) industry is facing challenging times. The economic crisis and new mobility trends are putting more pressure on the system with higher demand, while operational costs are rising and public support is decreasing due to financial stability requirements. In this historical landscape, boosting revenues and reducing costs should be crucial for all PT operators: it is time to do more with less, as well as serve more customers. In addition, global policy is clearly fixed in the goal of reducing car use in cities and decarbonization of transport. Therefore, increasing PT supply becomes the main objective; however, transport authorities and operators need to solve the financial equation of PT in a period of austerity measures. Looking for alternative resources, mainly from indirect beneficiaries, will be necessary; however, this should not hide the need to improve the performance of the PT network. Economic crisis and austerity measures will be an opportunity to consider the design of the supply differently. A recent study (PTV Group, 2013), aimed to identify what key issues will drive PT in the future. The survey results identified two main drivers, 'climate change and fewer resources' (81 percent) and 'demographic change' (80 percent). Decreasing public subsidies are forcing operators to rethink their business model and seek new revenue streams. Providers are changing, with attempts to go beyond their local borders (merging with major groups), improving travel experiences with real-time and mobile communications and diversifying revenue sources with advertising and consultancy.

Cities are at the heart of the economy, as they make up 80 percent of the world's economic output and more than 50 percent of the world's inhabitants (Pourbaix, 2012). The social advantages of good PT are unquestionable. An efficient mobility system within a city is a necessary condition to create economic opportunities, facilitate trades, and open access to markets and services. The implementation of a good PT service, as the backbone of any efficient urban mobility system, helps cities to be more dynamic, competitive, and create more jobs. As a matter of fact, PT networks play an essential role in the global appeal of cities, which become more appealing to businesses and tourists when movement around the city is easy.

This chapter demonstrates three main pillars that will influence the future outlook of the urban PT industry: budgetary pressure (decreasing budgets, cost control, new business model), mobility pattern changes (increasing in PT demand) and new technologies (social media, smart apps). The first section will introduce the urban PT industry in the historical context and in current situations. The economic crisis, and consequently the decrease of resources, will be discussed together with a necessary new structure of urban transportation firms and growing policy awareness. The second section will analyze the new mobility trends caused by demographic changes and urbanization (in the less developed countries) and urban sprawl (in the more developed countries). The final section will discuss the innovation in demand management and enhancement of users' travel experience.

Industry description

Urban PT is quite an old industry, dating as far back as 1662, when the scientist Blaise Pascal laid down the principles of urban transport services inaugurating a horse omnibus service in the French capital city (European Commission, 2007). Even though this service ran only for a few months, it could be considered the first attempt to introduce a public service to transport passengers along a predetermined itinerary and frequency in exchange for a fare, according to the definition developed by Costa and Fernandes (2012).

In the following years, several efforts to start transportation services were carried out around Europe; however, they did not gain public favor. The beginning of mass transportation as a successful business, and consequently the growing of the industry are related to a horse omnibus services started in Nantes by Mr. Bandry in 1826 (Robert, 1974).

Later, the diffusion of the horse omnibus started in Paris, London, and Prague, and many cities saw local investors involved in the services. The young PT industry saw over the period of a few years many innovations, from the horse omnibus to the horse tram introduced in New York in 1852, and 10 years later in many European cities. The electric tram was a key breakthrough; it was able to provide a cheap form of transportation and caused the first real modal shift to PT (McKay, 1976). In the second half of the nineteenth century, the PT industry evolved into two different levels: surface transport and underground services. Many larger cities in Europe started to experience congestion and began to plan solutions for dedicated PT corridors. The solution of going underground was welcomed in order to save money and avoid destroying buildings. London started the subway trend in 1863, with a steam-powered service that was later converted to an electricity-powered service. Soon after, Glasgow, Budapest, Paris and many other cities around the world established these services.

In parallel, surface services evolved into trolley buses, which were less expensive in terms of maintenance costs. In the beginning of the twentieth century, motorbuses appeared, being capable of flexible services around city roads. This period of around 50 years of great innovation has not been replicated to date by PT industry.

Motorbus services are now widely diffused around the world, as a result of the innovations of engines and the decrease of operational costs. Starting in the middle of the twentieth century, many cities substituted the tram and trolley system. The number of tram systems decreased quickly between 1960 and 1970, but the tram rebirth in Strasbourg at the end of the twentieth century introduced a new transport system called the Light Rail, developing a modern concept of the tram with segregated path and traffic-light priority.

Simultaneously, with the technical innovations and the birth of new systems of passenger transportation, the structure of transport companies and the investors also changed, evolving from an entrepreneurial initial stage to a public involvement phase, including agreements, mergers, and acquisitions. We could argue that the urban PT industry, throughout its history, experienced three different phases (Costa and Fernandes, 2012) but did not necessarily happen at the same time and form for all systems and regions. The phases were as follows:

- **Entrepreneurial transport**: This phase was characterized by great dynamism and market instability needing considerable entrepreneurial ability to survive.
- **Agreements and mergers**: This phase was an attempt to increase profits and achieve market stability, improving operators' prospects of staying in the market. This consolidation was achieved either through fare and service agreements between the operators, or by public authorities via the granting of monopoly licenses.
- **Public involvement**: In this phase, public authorities assumed the responsibility of operating urban PT services.

In some developed regions, the story has returned to the second phase. The process of finding agreements or consolidating operators with mergers and acquisitions has become relevant again in recent years, both due to the financial crisis and the lowering of subsidies. Until the beginning of the twenty-first century, public authorities planned the majority of PT that was run by companies. Often, these two bodies were the same subject. Currently, pressed by the necessary spending review in many countries, outsourcing is opening the market to private involvement. PT operators such as RATP (Regie Autonome des Transports Parisiens), Veolia, Transdev, and Arriva have become global firms that provide services across Europe, Africa America, and Asia. Even in the UK, which had the first deregulated transport market in Europe (Transport Act 1985), there have been several mergers and acquisitions that have recently led to the creation of only a few multinational PT operators.

Clearly, the situation is not developing at the same pace in all world regions. In developing countries, the history has been completely different; we did not see the same evolution of the PT industry in developed countries. In many regions of the developing world, informal and unregulated paratransit operations are the only available services, and are often affected by poorly maintained vehicles and unsafe conditions. Recent efforts have been put in place to regulate these operations as part of an integrated PT. There is no universal solution; however, some good examples of joint land use and transport solutions can be found in Asia, Africa, and Latin America. On the other hand, in fast-growing economies, we are experiencing a modal shift from non-motorized mobility towards a car-centered mobility system.

The actual economic situation

Urban PT is a very peculiar network activity. It is strictly linked to a city's landscape and mobility infrastructure, and social and economic situation, and it develops based on the population's characteristics. For these historical reasons, urban PT presents a less unified policy framework in comparison with other modes of transport such as aviation, and is normally segmented by region. For example, looking at the rates of operational cost coverage by fare revenues, great fluctuation is evident, with some European cities covering more than 50 percent of operational costs, and others far from it (EMTA, 2012). Furthermore, a deep analysis demonstrated that there is no evidence of geographical or social reason for it.

The PT sector is now, more than ever, playing a fundamental role in urban society, and it should be highlighted that this industry is one of the main contributors to cities' economies, in terms of jobs and services supplied. In many European cities (Brussels, Amsterdam, Barcelona, and Paris) PT operators are the largest city employers, with approximately 7.3 million people worldwide and with transport authorities accounting for another 300,000 (UITP, 2011).

The actual economic situation of the sector varies widely, from shortening of subsidies in Western countries, to the need to regulate the market structure in developing countries, and the increase in car use within growing economies. In developed countries, the PT industry is

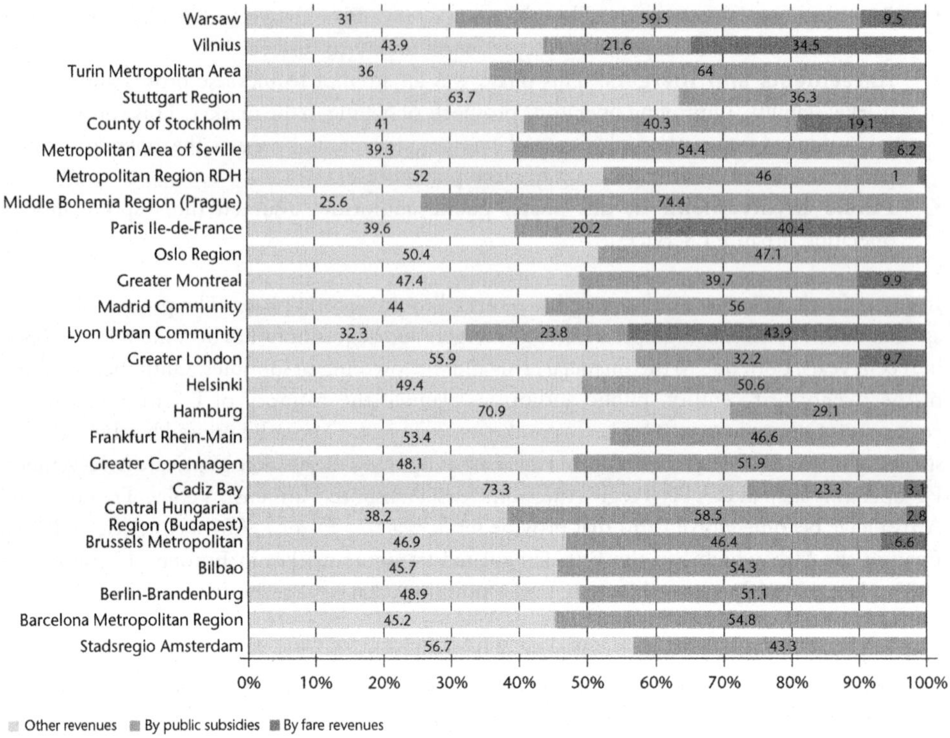

Figure 9.1 Barometer of PT in the European metropolitan areas

Source: (EMTA, 2012).

facing two conflicting events: increasing demand (due to new mobility trends and environmental issues) and a reduction of public funding (due to economic crisis). In addition, many developed countries have recently put in place policies aiming at a decarbonization of transport. This invests the PT industry with a central role in multimodal networks, whereby it gains market shares at the expense of the private car.

This situation is putting operators and politicians in front of a remarkable change in the sector, stimulating the debate about how to straighten the economic solvency of these companies, and at the same time provide better PT with more services as required by new mobility trends, economic development, and new urbanization. This should be enforced with fewer resources and with extraordinary effort to guarantee better services, especially during off-peak periods. In developed economies, some parts of the network are not profitable and are operated as a social service to maintain city accessibility. In many regions, this social aspect is even more present because school transport is the backbone of local PT. The provision of these services is normally heavily subsidized by public agencies, such as central or regional governments. As recent demographic studies show, in the developed world the number of pupils is expected to drop in the next 10 years. Transport firms could lack an important demand driver and also a source of revenue, leading to economic collapse if this situation is ignored.

Developing countries are affected by a strong presence of informal transport services, often bridging the transport needs that are not sufficiently covered by government operators offering accessible and flexible service. However, they are often operated with low safety, using high-environmental-impact vehicles and without any type of regulations, planning or control. Many vehicles are often involved in road accidents and collisions, due to a market structure that encourages 'on-the-road competition' for passengers, in the form of drivers racing to the next bus stop in order to collect fares (Small and Verhoef, 2007). In this context, the government and regulatory authorities should find the resources and skills to professionalize the sector, upgrading their services to integrate the formal PT system in a better way. On the other hand, in many fast-growing cities living standards are changing: the new middle class is experiencing economic growth, and is no longer attracted by PT services. Higher incomes are converted into higher car ownership and higher expectations in terms of better mobility and better quality of service. Given this, it is necessary to implement a PT system with integrated ticketing, multi-modal integration, high-quality service, and safety, which is a prerequisite of quality living standards (GIZ, 2010).

These issues require a complete rebuilding of the system, and new economical, sustainable concepts. In addition, as transit services fit into a broader social framework the system must adapt to policies in other fields (such as the locations of schools or the accessibility to the city for disadvantaged people). This sector is typically a low-margin business, but by developing secondary revenue streams companies can capitalize on their existing assets and knowledge.

The outlook

Pourbaix (2012) reported that in a typical business scenario, energy consumption for urban transport would increase by 30 percent in 2025 in respect to 2005 data, missing the objective of reducing greenhouse emissions without considering the offset of important energy consumption and emissions from avoided private transport activity. This objective is also part of the European Commission's Energy Union strategy (European Commission, 2015), with the intention of pushing for a gradual transformation of the entire transport industry to break from oil dependency and decarbonize transport. The solution should decouple the growth of mobility in urban areas from the related growing environmental costs, and thereby increase market share of PT worldwide. The International Association of Public Transport (UITP) strongly supports the objective of doubling its market share by 2025, in line with this strategy. Therefore, the PT industry should work hard to improve the attractiveness of the system and gain more users, even in an economic context of decreasing resources from the governments. It is time to reinvent PT to encourage the return of the more affluent classes and exploit new ancillary revenue streams. For many years, PT was perceived as an inferior good for low-income citizens (OECD/ITF, 2008): a social service with a medium/low quality. The primary goal of all governments, stressed by recent economic conditions, should be to make the PT sector more efficient, productive and attractive, in order to guarantee at least the same passenger services to the citizens. In many cases, we are facing a new wave of mergers and acquisitions to improve efficiency and productivity, by attaining economies of scale and therefore gains in terms of reduced operational costs; politicians often encourage this. The merger practice, whereby two or more companies merge into one to strengthen their market positions, has been experienced by the bus transport sector in Europe, and elsewhere, since the early 1990s (Odeck, 2008).

Mergers can be classified in two types: vertical and horizontal. The first type considers cases in which two or more operators merge to operate in more locations and increase their market share. The second mainly refers to cases where companies are united through a hierarchy and share a common owner; however, the result may be a different product, which we could define as a total mobility company.

Looking at recent statistics elaborated by the authors using the Orbis database (Bureau van Dijk, 2014), it is evident that in the last eight years, acquisitions were significant (Figure 9.2). Even though the database is not exhaustive, it shows the reduction in the number of PT firms around the world (40 in the UK, 26 in China, and 32 in Japan) (Figure 9.3)

An additional strategy for ensuring the economic viability of the companies is to transform the old style operators – who are simply running the vehicles – into total mobility companies that are able to sell not only passenger transportation, but also advanced services, such as parking, bike rental, or car sharing. Transitioning from production to customer-oriented services is the best way forward in the near future for PT firms in developed cities. Recent research (Little, 2013) has suggested three types of possible structures for long-term urban PT: a company as an aggregator of third-party services; a structure with a vertical integration of services (for example, bus, train, and car sharing); and finally the presence of a single specialist in the market. The growth of car- and bike-sharing systems is evident everywhere. For instance, in Germany the car-sharing market indicates that there are more than 750,000 users and 150 providers. This is an increase of 67 percent since 2013 (UITP, 2014). The bicycle has even turned into a PT vehicle. There are 495 bike-share programs around the world, with 500,000 bikes and a 14 percent annual growth rate (UITP, 2014).

Policies should follow this new phase, encouraging the development of mobility platforms with value-added services, such as booking and payment, thereby removing legal and administrative barriers that maintain the status quo and hinder a larger PT market share. In many developed urban systems, the sector presents overlapping areas of local responsibility, and needs reform to overcome the economic crisis, starting from the examination and construction of new legal and economic arrangements. In many cases, given the limited possibility of network extensions, particularly in urban centers, the transport authorities should be encouraged to develop mobility demand strategies with incentives and penalties to encourage more sustainable transport options.

A different situation is occurring in several developing economies, such as Africa and Asia, where PT is dominated by irregular operators providing services without any registration, and using minibuses, motorcycles, and cars with poor safety records. Such modes represent a significant (if not the only) mode of PT available to many citizens; however, it is necessary to professionalize the sector, regulating the services with personnel that are competent in PT. For example, in Lagos, Nigeria, the Lagos Metropolitan Area Transport Authority was instated in 2002 as a facilitator of a sustainable and effective integrated transport system with the help of the World Bank. A recent report (UN Habitat, 2013) also identified and documented 15 case studies highlighting the solutions implemented to improve informal transport with pro-poor

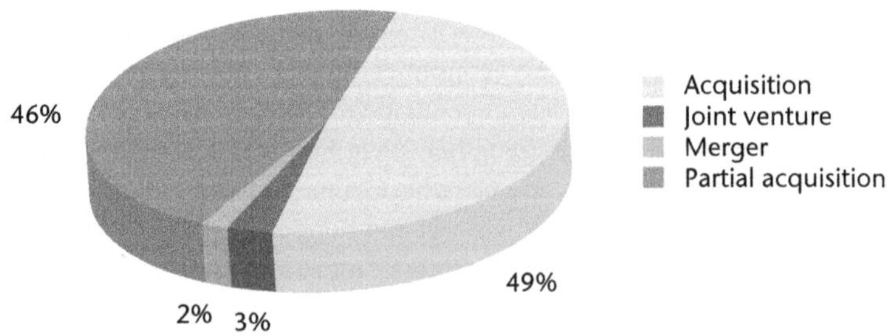

Figure 9.2 Transportation firm deals by type 2005–2013 (Elaboration from Orbis database [Bureau van Dijk, 2014])

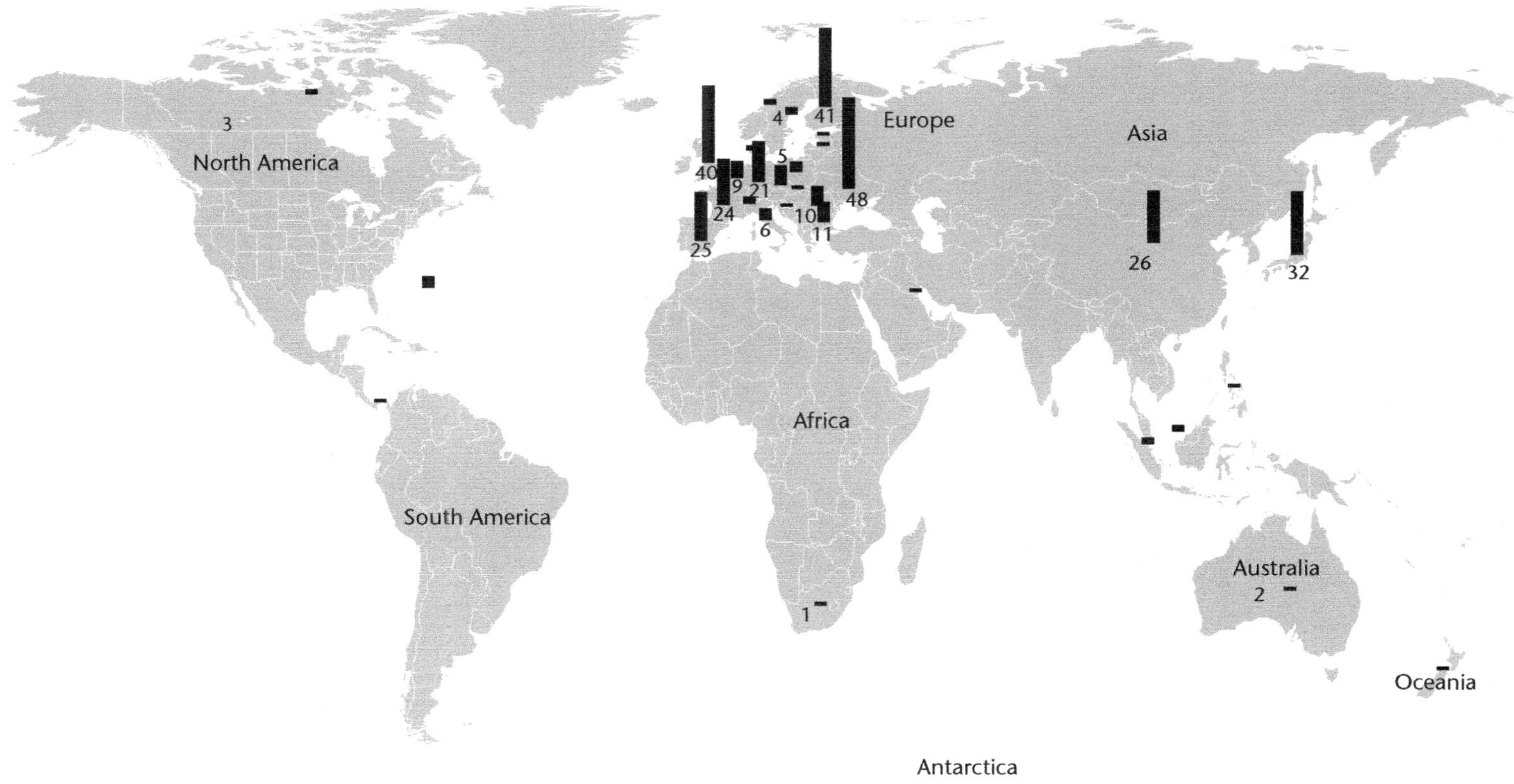

Figure 9.3 Reduction of transport firms in 2005–2013 (Elaboration from Orbis database [Bureau van Dijk, 2014])

mobility projects from the South/South East Asia, Africa, and Latin American Regions. The great number of different schemes identified suggests that there is no universal solution. Each city's mobility system has been developed in that city, tailored to the landscape and the citizens' unique characteristics. In such a context, setting up a policy that promotes strategic joining strategies between transport demand and land use plans is extremely welcome. Prioritizing PT is a must, and could help to avoid the mistakes made in developed cities during the transition phase from personal mobility to PT. This could solve problems in these cities such as congestion, degradation, and safety issues.

The construction and setting up of PT systems has accelerated in recent years, particularly in cities with developing economies where mass transit becomes a clear strategy to improve urban mobility and mitigate congestion, such as in Bangkok (Rodrigue *et al.*, 2013). The Singapore experience (Han, 2010) showed how a range of coordinated policies, including efforts to control the number of cars (ownership and usage) and, at the same time, increased availability and ridership of public transit, contributed to a sustainable transport system. Here, much like other fast-growing economies, such as Hong Kong, Taiwan, and South Korea, the increase of prosperity has pushed the demand for car ownership and motorization, also thereby increasing traffic volumes, traffic jams, urban land expansion, and greenhouse emissions. In Singapore, the attempt to balance motorization with a PT system was made at an early stage of development, and implemented in a short time-span. In contrast to many European cities, such as London, Paris, and Berlin, Singapore had few PT infrastructures and services to start with. It did not take a long time to arrive at its present status from the 67 km of urban rail in 1990 to the actual 182 km, with an average daily ridership of around 640,000 passenger trips (Land Transport Authority Singapore, 2015).

In general, innovative financing mechanisms have evolved because traditional ways of funding PT have been reduced. Governments have become sensitive to the levels of general taxation and expenditures in public services, such as health systems and transportation. Mergers could help companies acquire a scale economy to improve their performance (Odeck, 2008); however, optimizing production costs may not be enough to get sufficient cash flow, and it could be necessary to explore new business models in order to diversify revenues. New methods of financing are necessary to avoid fare increases and service cuts. Traditional PT companies have developed practical knowledge in many areas over the years, and have utilized this knowledge for in-house purposes. This ranges from technical expertise, to planning and project management. Although often overlooked, this knowledge could be an important source of revenue. Some operators are trying to expand into the consultancy sector, selling their expertise in traffic systems or in project management. Others are increasingly considering advertisement solutions in stations or in rolling stock. Ultimately, transport companies are moving from simply local operators towards a more complex, bigger industry that provides additional services and retail investment opportunities (Ubbels and Nijkamp, 2002). Larger operators could also have the opportunity to sell their experience in managing and building transport networks or their products, such as e-ticketing solutions, to other firms or municipalities that, due to their size or situation, would not be able to gain this experience otherwise. Some others could also sell their experience in vehicle maintenance and refurbishment to the transport vehicle industry. At the same time, it is important for operators to contemplate revenues from ancillary activities, such as spaces for advertisement, retail, and property development, telecommunication systems, and their company's brand.

By tapping into the potential of these various assets, PT companies will not only generate incomes, but also be able to improve the journey experience for passengers. For example, converting terminals to commercial areas is a good opportunity for exploiting unused spaces for rentals and public activities, thereby creating profitable commercial revenues for the operators. At the same time, this could provide services to passengers: shops and food and beverage areas help to improve the customer travel experience by developing a warm atmosphere, in and around the stations (Little, 2013). For instance, Japanese stations have increased their non-transport ratio revenues by 32.8 percent through their shopping zones (UITP, 2015). In this context, airports are a good example of the possible growth of commercial offering for urban transport terminals. Furthermore, they have a key characteristic that is not available to airports: they are located in the center of cities, or dense urban areas. The PT terminals of the future should offer retail spaces, business solutions, and food and beverage areas in order to extend their target not only to passengers, but to nearby residents and tourists. An example of this expansion is happening with central railway stations. The capability of operators to rethink their business model, including retail revenues normally outside their core activity, should allow them to capitalize on all of their captive market.

Naming rights are becoming another interesting and popular tool to increase revenues that are catching the attention of the sector. The Massachusetts Bay Transportation Authority has opened bids for the naming rights of nine terminals, expecting around $1 million per station on a five-year contract. Other successful examples include Dubai, Lisbon, and Madrid, which are already obtaining benefits of their cooperation with partners to cover some of the operational expenditure (UITP, 2015). Vodafone will pay Madrid's metro operator €3 million over three years for the re-branding of one of the most popular metro stations in the city, in a deal that will also allow the mobile phone company to publish its logo on Madrid's official Metro map, on platforms, and inside trains. It is the first time in Europe that an entire metro line has changed its name based on a commercial deal, thereby generating new forms of income. In the UK, Transport for London has sold the naming rights for the cable car that runs between Greenwich and the Royal Docks, in a 10-year deal with Emirates airline (Rushton, 2013).

Mobility trends

Mobility is key to economic development and goes hand in hand with it. Policymakers have recently departed from a rigid approach strictly based on infrastructure investment, and have started adopting a holistic view of public urban mobility. In parallel, urban mobility is now recognized as a relevant aspect of transport policy, transcending the local scope that many considered inherent to it. The EU Transport White Paper (European Commission, 2011) explicitly refers to the lack of an integrated urban mobility approach in many EU urban agglomerations as a setback to the development of a more competitive and resource-efficient transport system.

Passenger transport demand has been traditionally shaped mainly by income, household composition, and motorization rates. These factors have accounted for the steady growth in private car travel activity between 1970 and 2000 in most developed countries. Interestingly, this trend has slowed down significantly over the last 10–15 years. Although this change can be partially attributed to policy interventions, particularly at the local level, research is still needed in order to better understand all the reasons behind it. Many of these drivers will also have an impact on urban PT demand, and therefore additional insight into evolving mobility patterns would benefit the whole urban transport sector, from practitioners to local authorities and users. Urban planning and transportation services are increasingly focused on accessibility, rather than indicators strictly based on mobility. However, from a global perspective, many of these developments are limited to the most developed economies, and emerging countries still replicate the move towards higher reliance on private car transport.

Many of the countries showing a stabilization of private car transport also display profound socioeconomic changes that could be behind such a trend. Younger cohorts are fewer in number, and this was traditionally the age group with the largest reliance on cars. Ageing is not the only explanation for such decline, as young adults are also driving less, and present lower car ownership rates (OECD/ITF, 2013), in spite of the fact that the impact of gender in car use is disappearing. Some studies (Davis *et al.*, 2012; Kuhnimhof, 2012) underlined the effect of this demographic group in the overall evolution of road passenger transport, and hint that it stems from a change in transport demand, rather than a shift in preferences between modes. It remains unclear, however, whether this change is the result of new lifestyle choices or limitations, such as high youth unemployment or rising inequality. Alternatively, some authors argue that young people are only delaying their take-up of cars as their main means of transport, as they are also establishing families later in life compared to previous generations.

The high degree of urbanization in these countries shapes the transport demand and puts the focus on land use and urban planning decisions, particularly urban sprawl. Increasing distances for daily commuting patterns, growth of economic activity in the periphery of cities, together with commercial and leisure centers contribute to higher transport demand that is difficult to meet without private cars (Hill *et al.*, 2012). Improved access to services, notably broadband, across developed countries outside the largest urban areas, together with the increasing costs associated with bigger cities, seems to counteract agglomeration forces and foster the growth of small and medium cities (Dijkstra, 2013).

Thanks to recent surveys, the EU has gained insight into Europeans' transport habits (The Gallup Organisation, 2011; TNS Opinion & Social, 2014). In 2014, the Institute for Prospective Technological Studies from the European Commission conducted a survey with Transporti e Territorio and IPSOS, targeting many aspects of daily mobility of citizens, as well as socioeconomic and demographic circumstances. A majority of 56 percent declared that they use the car as their main mode of transport for daily trips. Urban forms of PT, such as bus, coach, tram, and metro, were the preferred choices for these frequent trips for 20 percent of the respondents. Slower modes, such as walking and cycling, added up to 16 percent. The survey also showed a low predominance of mode combination, with 22 percent using two or more means of transport for the most frequent trip. In almost half of the cases, multimodal trips involved car and PT, with a clear prevalence of such a combination in metropolitan areas and large cities. The typology of living area is a determinant of car ownership, travel habits and perception of PT service. While almost 65 percent of people living in metropolitan areas and large cities considered PT service good, the share of residents in rural areas satisfied with PT service dropped to less than 20 percent. Conversely, car ownership rates were the highest in rural areas, with reliance on PT as low as 10 percent for the most frequent trip.

Attitudes towards transport, and particularly urban transport, are also changing. In the EU, awareness of innovative transport options, such as car sharing, is now a fact among a majority of transport users, as this and many other surveys show, albeit with stark differences by living area and country. Subscription to such services remains somewhat low, with only 10 percent already registered clients, 33 percent not interested in car sharing, and 45 percent not showing any discernible inclination to join or not. Notably, half of the respondents who revealed an interest in car sharing did not see this option as an alternative to car ownership. In general, car users mentioned (TNS Opinion and Social, 2014) that among the reasons that would encourage them to use PT more, frequency of services, better coverage, and cheaper or season tickets, were the most relevant. As mentioned earlier, a combination of private and PT is still low, and the main improvements identified (The Gallup Organisation, 2011) as encouraging drivers to combine different modes of transport were ease of transfer from one transport mode to another, as well as better online information on schedules. This stressed the need to reinforce the urban planning dimension of the PT service and the potential benefits of sophisticated urban transport modeling, particularly activity-based modeling, with its huge demands on data.

Environmental concerns might be conditioning citizens to reduce their use of private cars. In a recent public consultation in the European Union ('The urban dimension of the EU transport policy'), the majority of respondents agreed that low-emission zones are an effective measure to improve air quality in cities, although some groups demanded better PT and urban planning as a more efficient way of reducing traffic volumes (COWI, 2013). Congestion also acts as a deterrent to private car use. The same survey illustrated acceptance for congestion charging as an effective measure to improve accessibility, although opposition to such views is far from marginal.

New technologies

Urban PT is consolidated economic activity that, despite some major changes (vehicle and traction system updates), can hardly be considered one of the most innovative industries. Only one transport operator figure ranks in the EU Industrial R&D Investment Scoreboard (European Commision, 2014) that aims to monitor and analyze worldwide trends in industrial R&D. This fact was also confirmed by a report about network industries (European Commision, 2013) that characterized the whole transport industry as one that has experienced limited innovation throughout its history. Many authors, such as Molnar (2008), have questioned whether PT is adequately developed technologically, financially, or commercially, to be a viable alternative to private cars. In many cases in the PT industry, technologies are continuing to operate in isolation. Innovation is welcome as it is acknowledged by the Organisation for Economic Co-operation and Development (OECD) as one of the key sources of competitive advantage in the industry. Due to new financial cuts, many companies should also work to maximize fare revenues that will attract more customers. New technologies are spreading into the sector. While some operators are just starting to establish interactions with customers using mobile technologies, others are only setting up profiles on social networks (mainly Facebook) without any type of interaction with users. In the first case, exploiting the potentiality of smart apps could allow data collection and conducting surveys at lower costs, in order to obtain better insight into demand and provide new services according to specific travel needs of citizens. In addition, using smart technologies, such as e-ticketing, could lead to the opportunity to set dynamic fare schemes (peak and off-peak tickets). The economic recession and relatively high fuel prices are driving lower growth rates of private car use. At the same time, economic crisis has obliged governments to conduct spending reviews, reallocating resources as rationally as possible in order to maintain social and welfare services for citizens. These issues raise the question for PT of better management of resources and a more commercial approach, introducing the question of private involvement (outsourcing), at least in the production phase. According to many researchers, such as (Guittat and Berjoan, 2012), PT industries should try to maximize demand for their services, optimize their mobility capacity, and rethink their business models towards a new direction, also considering that customer expectations on increasing quality of service is becoming an important choice factor.

The growth of information and communication technology (ICT) using social media could encourage the sector to make a step further in the direction of innovation to reward customers. The introduction of web 2.0 technologies could also help to capture more customers, and increase the satisfaction of existing customers with additional or premier services.

In recent years, it has become clear that the operation of PT is not only a matter of moving people, but also reaching and encouraging people to use the whole transport system. Combined and shared mobility works best when it uses the same information technology infrastructure as the city's PT. Software companies are increasingly producing novel integrated mobility solutions for the client side, designing applications that act like personal travel assistants (UITP, 2014). Authorities and operators should become more customer-centric to attract more users from affluent classes to overcome the perception of PT as an inferior good that individuals use less as their incomes rise.

It is therefore mandatory for mobility companies to develop a portfolio of mobile applications able to enhance the travel experience (ticketing, combined mobility, access to travel information). In addition, using social media (web 2.0) could provide transit agencies with an unparalleled opportunity to connect with their customers using real-time mobile and direct communication. In many cases, the use of social media functions has resulted in mostly one-way communication; for example, a transportation provider communicating with passengers, or publishing up-to-date information about a service. A real value-added service will come when the industry truly leverages insight into customer needs and then shapes services accordingly. According to Bregman (2012), in the US and Canada, many public agencies have adopted social media policies to provide guidance for addressing some, or all, of these issues; while 58 percent had a social media policy in development, 27 percent had one in place. If we look at the aviation sector, the first to be truly deregulated, many airlines have already developed applications that allow customers to book flights and reserve their seats (basic services). Several have also introduced advanced services such as hotel booking, shuttle services, reservation, and onboard meal requests. Urban transport operators have a great potential for growth in the tourism sector. Many of them, at the moment, only present very basic applications that display information on timetables and lines; several provide live updates on disruptions and delays; and only a few allow customers to buy tickets with their smartphones.

Table 9.1 How providers are leveraging mobile and direct communication (x=basic, xx=advanced)

Cities	*Maps*	*Real time traffic info*	*Journey planner*	*Intermodality*	*Geopositioning*
Amsterdam		XX	XX	XX	XX
Birmingham	X	XX	X	X	
London	X	XX	XX	XX	X
Madrid	X	XX	XX		XX
Oslo	X	X	XX	XX	X
Paris	X	XX	XX	X	X
São Paulo	X	X			
Seoul	X	XX	X		XX
Singapore	X	XX	XX	XX	XX
Shanghai	X	X	X		X
Toronto	X	XX	XX	XX	
Tokyo	X	X	X	X	X

Source: Guittat and Berjoan, 2012.

In many PT companies, the difficulty of providing these services is strictly linked to the lack of internal process and capabilities to support new technologies, in order to take advantage of the data coming from it. Some operators, especially those with less ICT capabilities or human resources, may also consider increased collaboration through releasing open data so that third-party developers can create apps and other 'extras' for the public. Many operators and authorities around the world have also developed applications within the mobile sphere, or loaded their data into the Google Maps application using the General Transit Feed Specification (GTFS)[2] format (Google, 2014). Analysis of travel applications, based on open data, clearly shows that the added value created for third parties helps to enhance the travel experience (e-ticketing, travel planner, on-time app), and to shape mobility (discounts, personalized fare). For example, Singapore has a smartphone application that goes beyond the goal of providing only transportation information, including attractive features such as an advanced taxi booking system and a contactless tap-and-go fare card, allowing customers to pay fares on all transport modes, including metros, light rail, and buses.

Mobile applications, social media, and ICT services could also permit data collection and analysis of customer behavior without wasting financial resources in studies or surveys on customer satisfaction. Although providers are not yet analyzing data in order to understand the individual movements of passengers (this should be their ultimate goal in mining data to provide new insights), in some places like Singapore and Seoul, advances are being made in that direction (Accenture, 2012). In those cities, travel data is used to optimize capacity. In the future, passengers may be able to choose seats on modes based on their individual preferences and availability, and create personal journey plans.

The next point on the agenda is for authorities and operators to dynamically set prices to reflect preferences and actively shape the mobility demand. Peak and off-peak ticket pricing is already used in some cities, such as London, with more dynamic optimization under development. In recent years, mobile applications for virtual wallet usage (Apple Pay, PayPal, Google Wallet) have increased and their use for mobile ticketing for urban and local transport service grew consequently (LRTA, 2015). At the same time, investing in mobile ticketing and encouraging customers to use it (through promotions and discounts) reduces the need for installation and maintenance of vending machines and kiosks, and produces savings in the cash handling process. With a little investment, this technology could also help in the design of sophisticated fare structures, personalizing the travel experience at its maximum: each customer will have his or her personal fare. Furthermore, electronic payment systems are also valuable for collecting and analyzing data to drive performance in resource allocation, pricing, and customer offerings. They can also support the growing need for multimodality. Rechargeable e-purse public transit cards are increasingly accepted by suburban trains, as well as by parking and taxi providers in some cities, moving toward a unique 'city card' that allows consumers to use PT, pay for parking, rent a bike, enter a museum or cinema, shop, and also take national trains.

For many of the patterns identified, these innovative sources of revenue could form a substantial share of the operating budget, helping local authorities responsible for the provision of PT to seek new ways of financing it. On the other hand, central governments will have more possibilities to make use of existing sources, and less need for new funding techniques.

PT operators already own and manage these wide range of assets, both physical and intangible: they can offer plenty of potential to generate non-fare revenue, but this is often overlooked or underestimated.

Notes

1 The views expressed are purely those of the author and may not in any circumstances be regarded as stating an official position of the European Commission.
2 The GTFS defines a common format for public transportation schedules and associated geographic information. This format was created in 2006 when Google introduced to Google Maps an additional feature, Google Transit. This service helps users to plan public transport trips from origin to destination. The success of GTFS lies in its data format (open and simple), the availability of free validation tools, and the possibility to use a powerful trip planner embedded in Google Maps (Antrim and Barbeau, 2013).

References

Antrim, A., and Barbeau, S.J. (2013). *The many uses of GTFS data–opening the door to transit and multimodal applications*. Location-Aware Information Systems Laboratory at the University of South Florida.

Accenture (2012) Beyond the traditional: Establishing new rules and roles for public transportation. Available at: http://www.accenture.com/SiteCollectionDocuments/PDF/Accenture-Beyond-the-Traditional-Establishing-New-Rules-and-Roles-for-Public-Transportation.pdf (accessed 28 August 2014).

Bregman, S. (2012) *Uses of Social Media in Public Transportation* (Vol. 99). Transportation Research Board.

Buehler, R. and Pucher, J. (2011) Making public transport financially sustainable, *Transport Policy*, 18(1), 126–138.

Bureau van Dijk (2014) Orbis database.

Costa, Á. and Fernandes, R. (2012) Urban public transport in Europe: Technology diffusion and market organization, *Transportation Research Part A: Policy and Practice*, 46(2), 269–284.

COWI (2013) Results of the public consultation: The urban dimension of the EU transport policy. Available at: http://ec.europa.eu/transport/themes/urban/studies/doc/2013-a032862-urban-mobility-public-consultation-report.pdf (accessed 9 February 2015).

Davis, B., Dutzik, T. and Baxandall, P. (2012) Transportation and the new generation: Why young people are driving less and what it means for transportation policy. Boston MA: Frontier Group.

Dijkstra, L.G. (2013) The economic performance of European cities and city regions: Myths and realities, *European Planning Studies,* 21(3), 334–354.

EMTA (2012) Barometer of Public Transport in the European Metropolitan Areas, Association of European Metropolitan Transport Authorities (EMTA). Available at: http://www.emta.com/IMG/pdf/emta_barometer_2012.pdf (accessed 5 August 2014).

European Commission (2007) Outsourcing and industrial relations in city lines of transporting. Available at: http://www.lasaire.net/upload/file/rapporto%20definitivo%20Confservizi%20PDF%5B1%5D.pdf (accessed on 8 September 2014).

European Commission (2011) *WHITE PAPER Roadmap to a Single European Transport Area – Towards a competitive and resource efficient transport system.* (COM/2011/0144 final).

European Commission (2013). *Market Functioning in Network Industries – Electronic Communications, Energy and Transport.* Occasional Papers 129. European Commission.

European Commission (2014) The EU Industrial R&D Investment Scoreboard. Available at: http://iri.jrc.ec.europa.eu/scoreboard.html (accessed on 6 August 2014).

European Commission (2015) Energy Union Package. European Commission.

GIZ (2010) Informal Public Transport. Available at: http://www.sutp.org. (Accessed on 29 August 2014).

Google (2014) General Transit Feed Specification Reference. Available at: https://developers.google.com/transit/gtfs/. (Accessed on 3 December 2014).

Guittat, P. and Berjoan, S. (2012) *Beyond the traditional: Establishing new rules and roles for public transportation.* Accenture. Available at: http://www.accenture.com/SiteCollectionDocuments/PDF/Accenture-Beyond-the-Traditional-Establishing-New-Rules-and-Roles-for-Public-Transportation.pdf (accessed 28 August 2014).

Han, S.S. (2010) Managing motorization in sustainable transport planning: the Singapore experience, *Journal of Transport Geography*, 18 (2), 314–321.

Hill, N.B., Smokers, R., Schroten, A., van Essen, H. and Skinner, I. (2012) *Developing a Better Understanding of the Secondary Impacts and Key Sensitivities for the Decarbonisation of the EU's Transport Sector by 2050.* European Commission.

Kuhnimhof, T.A. (2012) Men shape a downward trend in car use among young adults – evidence from six industrialized countries, *Transport Reviews*, 32(6), 761–779.

Land Transport Authority Singapore (2015) Statistics in Brief 2014. Available at: http://www.lta.gov.sg/content/dam/ltaweb/corp/PublicationsResearch/files/FactsandFigures/Statistics%20in%20Brief%20 2014.pdf (accessed on 20 January 2015).

Little, A.D. (2013) The Future of Urban Mobility 2.0. UITP. Available at: http://www.adlittle.com/future-of-urban-mobility.html (accessed on 19 June 2014).

LRTA (2015) *Tramways & Urban Transit*, 62. Welwyn Garden City (UK): LRTA Publishing.

McKay, J.P. (1976) *Tramways and Trolleys: The rise of urban mass transport in Europe*. Princeton, NJ: Princeton University Press.

Molnar, E. (2008) *Eurotransport* 5, 1–4. Available at http://www.unece.org/fileadmin/DAM/trans/topics/docs/ITSUrbanTransport.pdf (accessed on 29 August 2014).

Odeck, J. (2008) The effect of mergers on efficiency and productivity of public transport services, *Transportation Research Part A: Policy and Practice*, 42(4), 696–708.

OECD/ITF (2008) Privatisation and Regulation of Urban Transit Systems. Paris: OECD Publishing.

OECD/ITF (2013) Long-run trends in car use, *ITF Round Tables*. Paris: OECD Publishing.

Pourbaix, J. (2012) Towards a smart future for cities, *Sharing Urban Transport Solutions*, 36, (7).

PTV Group (2013) Perspective – Public Transport: What moves the sector? Available at: http://vision-traffic.ptvgroup.com/en-uk/lp/ptv-visum/white-paper (accessed on 29 January 2015).

Robert, J. (1974) *Histoire des transports dans les villes de France*. Distributed by the author Robert, J. [s.l.].

Rodrigue, J.P., Comtois, C. and Slack, B. (2013). *The Geography of Transport Systems*. New York: Routledge.

Rushton, K. (2013). Madrid rebrands metro in Vodafone deal. *The Telegraph*. Available at: http://www.telegraph.co.uk/finance/10016166/Madrid-rebrands-metro-in-Vodafone-deal.html (accessed on 4 March 2015).

Small, K.A. and Verhoef, E.T. (2007). *The Economics of Urban Transportation*. New York: Routledge.

The Gallup Organisation (2011) Future of transport, *Flash Eurobarometer*, European Commission. Available at: http://ec.europa.eu/public_opinion/flash/fl_312_en.pdf (accessed on 5 August 2014).

TNS Opinion and Social (2014) Quality of transport. *Special Eurobarometer*, European Commission. Available at: http://ec.europa.eu/public_opinion/archives/ebs/ebs_422a_en.pdf (accessed on 22 December 2014).

Transport Act (1985) UK Parliament Act, Chapter 67.

Ubbels, B. and Nijkamp, P. (2002) Unconventional funding of urban public transport, *Transportation Research Part D: Transport and Environment*, 7 (5), 317–329.

UITP (2011) Observatory of employment in public transport, Report 2. Available at: http://www.uitp.org/sites/default/files/cck-focus-papers-files/Observatory_of_Employment_Report2_2012.pdf (accessed on 4 February 2015).

UITP (2014) Who are the new pioneers of the sharing economy? *The Journal of the UITP World Congress & Exhibition*, 6, 1.

UITP (2015) New ways of financing public transport. Available at: http://www.uitp.org/news/new-ways-financing-event-look-how-public-transport-can-be-more-entrepreneurial (accessed on 4 March 2015).

UN Habitat (2013) *Improving Informal Transport*. Case studies from Asia, Africa and Latin America. Available at: http://mirror.unhabitat.org/downloads/docs/11804_1_594697.pdf (accessed on 29 August 2014).

10

The evolving global water industry

Antonio Massarutto

Fundamentals of economic regulation of water and sanitation

Water and sanitation services (WSS) are a classical prototype of market failure, and economists have traditionally considered them as a prerogative of the state, with very limited options for introducing competition and market-based arrangements. The neoliberal agenda has reached the WSS sector much later than other network utilities, such as electricity, gas, and telecoms (Finger *et al.*, 2006) – and with far less success (Castro and Heller, 2011). This is unsurprising, since most of the theoretical work, even at the apex of the political fortune of the neoliberal approach, has recognized the many sectorial specificities that characterize WSS and make it rather unfit for competitive markets (Kessides, 2004; Noll, 2002; World Bank, 2006).

Factors located both on the demand and on the supply side contribute to making this statement true. On the demand side, WSS cannot be reduced to the supply of water to households; rather, it should be seen as a collective system that ensures organized and disciplined access to the natural resource (Massarutto, 2011). This means that WSS output includes public goods and related positive externalities; for example, concerning public health and environmental protection. While water demand of individuals is stagnant or diminishing, health protection and environmental policy are the key drivers of demand, leading to the imposition of tighter restrictions and quality requirements (Barraqué, 2013).

Bypass of the utility is technically feasible in certain circumstances, especially in rural or suburban areas (such as private wells, rainwater harvesting, and community systems), but not always recommended, precisely because of the negative externalities associated with disorganized and decentralized access to natural resources (Barraqué, 2013; Massarutto, 2011). Moreover, water is an essential good and a basic human right, with formidable implications regarding accessibility and affordability (Gleick, 1999). Assimilating it to a 'commodity', accessible in exchange for a price, is a concept that many people simply reject (Petrella, 2001).

These features have always justified at least some role of the State in the specification of service standards, universal service obligations and cost-allocation patterns, whatever the management model. On the supply side, the dominance of non-replicable essential facilities, asset specificity and the high ratio of fixed over variable costs qualify this industry as a prototype of natural monopoly (National Research Council, 2002; Shirley, 2002). High capital intensity and very long economic life of assets (50 years or more) enhance the economic risk associated with investments. In other network industries, such as energy, telecoms, and railways, the separation of essential facilities from service provision represented a key to liberalization (Newbery, 2000); however, this solution is not particularly useful here, due to the relative unimportance of potentially competitive segments (such as meter reading, billing, and post-meter services) (Kessides, 2004).

Nonetheless, this does not mean that WSS is completely isolated from the market economy. Finger *et al.* (2006) distinguish four different sets of transactions (axes) that characterize WSS:

- Choice of operators and governance of WSS arrangements (axis I);
- Provision of inputs (for example, equipment, specialized services, capital) (axis II);
- Access to water resources (axis III);
- Retail customer service (axis IV).

Each set of transactions eventually implies a choice between market-based and state-governed relations (Table 10.1). For example, WSS systems may compete to access water resources owned by a third party and buy bulk water rights from resource owners; alternatively, resource ownership can accrue to the state, which allocates water-use rights via an authoritative decision. On the opposite side, end users of water may choose not to connect to collective networks, and manage the WSS system on an individual or community basis, or purchase water from water vendors, as is still quite common in developing countries.

Although these cases are possible in principle, and in practice exist somewhere, their practical importance is limited. In turn, axes I and II offer better opportunities for market-based schemes.

With respect to the choice of operator, the affirmation of WSS as a public service ('service of general interest', in European Union jargon) implies that the public has to assume responsibility, but does not inhibit the delegation of operations and investment tasks to a third party, which is eventually selected from the market via a competitive process. Concerning the supply chain, WSS utilities obviously require the purchase of many inputs, which poses the classic make-or-buy alternative. Economies of scale, specific expertise and professional capabilities of the organization in question, along with other factors, may influence the decision. For example, it is straightforward to imagine that most of the infrastructural work is acquired from the construction and equipment industry. Less obvious is whether this is also appropriate for engineering and legal services. Specialized companies – which may eventually be other WSS companies in other areas – can effectively supply many activities that imply economies of scale.

Finance is another field in which external suppliers have become increasingly important (OECD, 2010a; Raftells, 2014). Self-finance at the individual utility level is feasible in some circumstances, but requires adequate scale and a continuous cash flow from depreciation, which is not interrupted for an extended period. Some countries have developed original schemes that allow some self-finance on a collective basis (for example, revolving funds in the US, special-purpose financial facilities operating in other countries), which are eventually funded by earmarked taxation (for example, the French Agences de l'Eau) or activating direct and indirect financial cross-subsidies between different utility sectors (as in the German Stadtwerke) (OECD, 2011).

However, the recourse to market finance (bank loans, corporate bonds, and equity) has become fundamental to bridge the gap between available resources and investment needs, due to the difficulties met by public finance in its various forms. No systematic studies are available, to our knowledge, that have systematically assessed the relative weight of the different financing sources, but it is quite evident that the share of market finance has been growing significantly,

Table 10.1 Examples of market and non-market-based arrangements in the four axes of WSS

Axis	*Counterpart of WSS*	*Regulatory issues*	*Market-based arrangements (examples)*	*Non-market-based arrangements (examples)*
I	Entities responsible for service provision	Incomplete contracts	Full divesture	Direct labor organization
		Transactions costs	Delegation (lease, concession, management contract)	State-owned establishments
		Sunk costs		
		Information asymmetries		
II	Suppliers of inputs along the value chain	Vertical integration	Market-based finance (loans, equity)	Public spending
		Cost of capital for long-run undertakings	Outsourcing	
		Incomplete contracts and transactions costs in procurement	BOT schemes	Public engineering and project services
			Direct purchase of inputs on the market	Centralized procurement facilities
III	Entities holding property rights for water resources	Externalities	Tradable water rights	Public ownership + regulation of access to water resources
		Long-run sustainability	Bulk water sale on a commercial basis	Publicly owned water-transfer schemes
		Transaction cost in the trading of water rights		
IV	End-users	Natural monopoly	Private water-vendors	Public system with universal service obligations
		Output includes public-good components (for example, public health)	Community-based independent systems	Public planning of service extensions
		Accessibility and affordability issues		
		Resilience and flexibility		

Source: Author's own elaboration based on Finger et al., 2006.

regardless of the management form. In other words, whether run publicly or privately, WSS need to access the private financial markets to fund operations and investments (OECD, 2010b).

Many authors have noted that the arrangements in axes II and I are not independent (Kraemer, 1998). Control of the supply chain through vertical integration has revealed a powerful source of competitive advantage for companies competing for the delegation of operation. This explains the long-lasting success on the global market of the French multinationals (Suez and Veolia), whose business model precisely uses delegation of service operation as a 'Trojan horse' for technologies and services that are purchased internally within the vertically integrated group. Vice versa, when the operator is a public company – or at least, if it is not vertically integrated – competition along the supply chain is livelier; this also favors a higher degree of specialization.

Rise and decline of private-sector participation in the global water industry

These rather unfavorable characteristics have not hindered the role of the private sector even before the 'neoliberal era' (Barraqué and Katko, 2011). In fact, until the mid nineteenth century, state and local communities typically organized collective access to water in urban spaces (fountains, lavatories, and washtubs), while individual households provided for the 'last mile' by carrying water to their home, and wastewater was simply thrown away. At the origin of modern water supply systems, the initiative was often that of private enterprises; piped water supply within private premises was initially a prerogative of the rich who could afford to pay for the connection.

However, at the turn of the twentieth century, it became clear that generalized access to controlled water supply, as well as the use of flushing toilets connected to sewers, could dramatically improve public health and effectively reduce the risk of waterborne diseases. Local communities started pressing private developers to extend networks. Nevertheless, this was possible only by accepting repayment of investments over increasing time horizons. Many private utilities underwent serious financial difficulties, and municipal authorities finally took them over in most cases, also assuming new initiatives.

In a few cases, pristine arrangements with the private sector managed to remain in business; for example, Barcelona in Spain or Genoa in Italy. Other countries, and notably France, developed an original governance approach, which allowed the identification of more sustainable means of private undertakings. Yet in most of the developed world, public initiative generally replaced private investors, taking over their assets and assuming the initiative elsewhere. In most of the world the standard scheme – which we refer to as the 'traditional' model – became that of public institutions, which were directly owned and ruled by the state or local authorities, funded by tariffs and local taxes, and relied on public financial facilities for the initial capital. Transfers from general taxation were a diffused source of funding, especially in Mediterranean countries, while in Northern Europe and in the US, the norm was to recover all costs from user charges – although these were frequently more similar to local taxes than to tariffs. Metering itself was not necessarily used everywhere; charges could well depend on wealth indicators, as the size of houses, rather than on actual or presumed consumption (Barraqué, 2013).

During the 1990s, the need to modernize WSS utilities became urgent in the water policy debate in many countries, and especially in the developing world. The main driver of the shift away from the established management forms has been in most cases the need to (re)-start investment cycles and improve service quality, especially on the environmental side, and despite the budget constraints of the public sector (Bel, 2006; Finger *et al.*, 2006). The long economic life of assets, typical of WSS, often encouraged municipal authorities to underprice services, without accounting adequately for depreciation. This created a financial gap and a hidden debt, which at some point would become a major issue (OECD, 2011; Winpenny, 2003).

This does not necessarily imply privatization of WSS companies, but requires at least that the traditional model evolve towards a structure that enables these firms to represent credible counterparts for investors (Raftells, 2014). However, in many cases some involvement of the private sector was deemed necessary, given that many publicly run utilities exhibited poor managerial and administrative records, inefficient billing and revenue collection, unsatisfactory commercial quality, etc. (Finger *et al.*, 2006).

In a handful of countries regulatory reforms have been quite dramatic, introducing a sudden break through a legislative intervention: this is the case of England and Wales (which privatized the former Water Authorities in 1989, separating management from regulation), Portugal, and Italy.

In many other cases, the institutional framework has remained substantially unchanged, but transformation has taken place at the scale of single utilities. Multilateral institutions (such as the World Bank and the OECD) have also played an important role; the former by providing financial support to privatization, and the latter spending its cultural influence on governments in promoting reforms inspired by market principles.

Overall, during the 1990s and the first half of the 2000s, the trend was clearly towards wider involvement of the private sector for the operation and market-based finance for investments. Between 1990 and 2008, over 660 utilities throughout the world underwent privatization processes. More recently, this trend seems to have arrested or even inverted as far as operation is concerned – such as in the heavily advertised case of Paris, which decided to step back from delegation and create a municipally-owned company.

The number of water projects involving private-sector developers more than halved since 2005 with respect to the previous period (Figure 10.1). The financial dimension also drastically reduced from $10–14 billion to the actual $4–5 billion. However, what is most interesting is to look at the typology of contracts.

Utility concessions were more popular and frequent around the end of the 1990s/early 2000s, while the trend in later years was clearly in favor of contracts that implied a more substantial risk share allocated to the public (public–private partnerships [PPPs]), or were confined to specific facilities (BOT and similar contracts). With the notable exception of Brazil, initiatives launched in 2012 are all of this type, and mostly concern sewage treatment plants.

Among awarded contracts, 60 projects (covering 9 percent of the total, but nearly 35 percent of total investment) were terminated or encountered financial troubles; most of the others have remained financially sustainable only after drastic renegotiation (World Bank and PPIAF, 2013). According to Lobina and Hall, 81 WSS contracts with the private sector (47 in developed countries and 34 in developing countries) have been terminated or not renewed after expiration since 1995. The average was one per year at first, but later on stabilized to five cases per year (Lobina and Hall, 2013).

Among these, the case of Paris attracted a great deal of media attention, perhaps because remunicipalization took place in the homeland of the 'French model' of utility privatization, which represented the main source of inspiration for supporters of market-based reforms, and will be discussed in more detail later.

At a global scale, only 10 percent of cities above one million inhabitants are served by (partially or entirely) privatized utilities (Figure 10.2). Although the partition between public and private is not entirely clear – as we will show later, many management forms lie in a grey zone in-between – Figure 10.2 demonstrates that public operation remains the dominant model in both developed and developing countries.

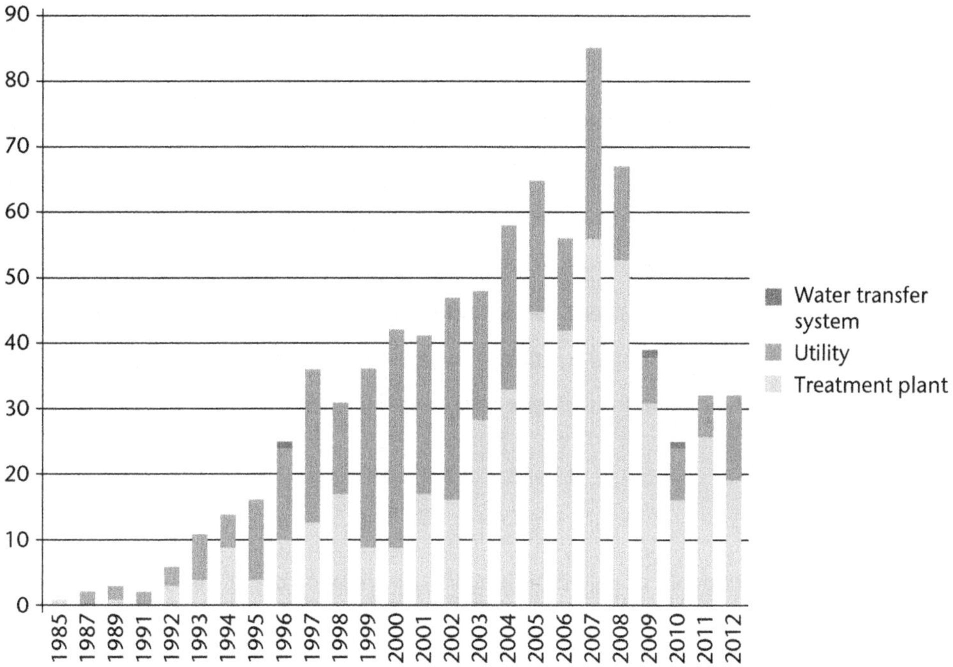

Figure 10.1 WSS projects involving the private sector (n. of projects)

Source: Author's own elaboration based on World Bank and PPIAF, 2013.

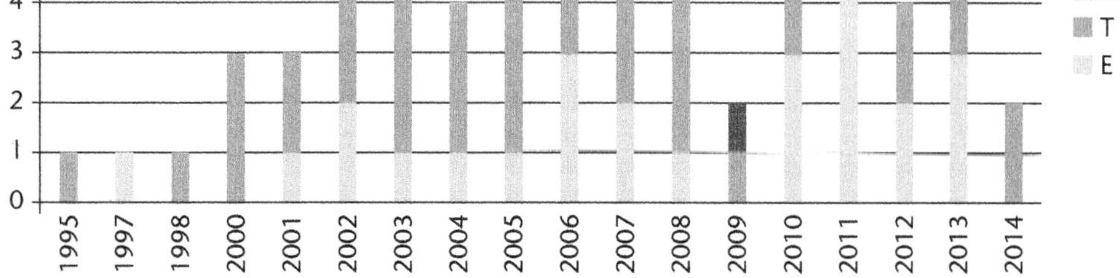

Figure 10.2 Concession contracts terminated (T) or not renewed (E) (n. of contracts)

Source: Author's own elaboration based on Lobina and Hall, 2013.

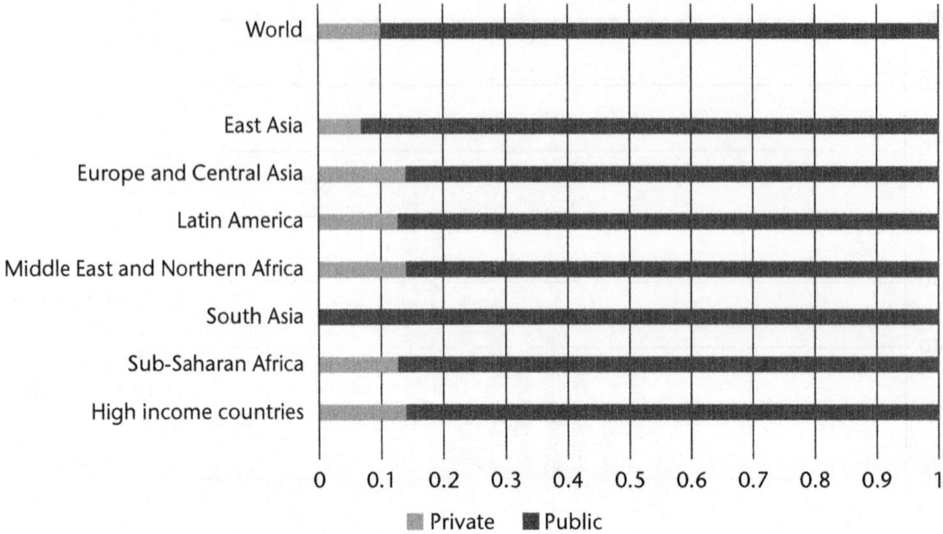

Figure 10.3 Private or public operators in cities with a population over 1 million, October 2006

Source: Author's own elaboration based on Lobina and Hall, 2013.

However, as already mentioned, this data should not hide the important transformation that has occurred within public undertakings as well. In particular, these entail:

- Corporatization: Many publicly owned entities transform into private-law corporate companies and acquire at least some management and financial autonomy, although they may be not completely isolated from the parent authority, which can provide financial guarantees, controls the management board, etc.
- Procurement: Infrastructure may be acquired with turnkey contracts (that is, with an up-front payment covering all investment costs at once), but also with schemes that involve anticipation of the constructor, who will also operate the facility and repay its investment through a certain share of revenues. Many alternative schemes are possible, which combine in different ways the reciprocal rights and duties of concessionaires and public entities.
- Operational outsourcing: The main operator, while remaining responsible for providing the service, delegates certain operational phases and activities to specialized external subjects.
- Financial outsourcing: Funding for operation and investment is provided by market operators (banks, private investors) in various forms.

Another interesting trend is emerging: that of so-called public–public partnerships. In this model, a public WSS company operating in an area collaborates with another by sharing activities or selling specialized services (Kraemer, 2014; Lobina and Hall, 2013). Collaboration between public WSS companies is particularly interesting for finance. For example, in Italy groups of municipal firms have created collective vehicles for issuing corporate bonds, with partial sharing of risk, while others have genuinely merged their own company within a common multi-utility holding firm (as in the case of the Hera Group). In Portugal, the state-owned company AdP raises funds on the open market and acts as a financial facility in the internal market. Once more, the boundary between public and private is not fully clear:

partnerships may originally start within the public sector, but require private legal forms to become operational, and may easily end in the creation of entities that will later play a leading role in the open market.

Conceptual models of WSS organization, theory, and practice

Since WSS remains a natural monopoly, with little chance (if any) to introduce competition in the market, the main way to move from the traditional model is delegation to private companies on a contractual basis (French model) and partial or total divesture of monopoly ownership, accompanied by the creation of independent regulators (British model). However, most of the developed world has maintained public ownership, though very often borrowing governance schemes from the private sector, e.g., by creating publicly owned corporate establishments, with or without the participation of private partners (Ballance and Taylor, 2005; Rouse, 2007). The latter solution is often referred to as the 'German model', although it has been widely adopted in many other countries. In fact, it represents the dominant solution in continental Europe, where legislation even encourages it and sometimes – as in Sweden or the Netherlands – makes it compulsory (Castro and Heller, 2011). Similarly, it dominates the scene in North America, Japan, and even developing countries.

However, this method of classifying management models is probably too narrow, since it actually neglects the many variants that are present. Menard and Peeroo (2011) proposed a more sophisticated classification, where the explanatory factors are the degree of autonomy the operator enjoys with respect to decision-making and property rights over assets and revenues. Rather than clear-cut alternatives, different models appear more as the combination of complementary governance schemes, which may easily overlap.

Within the delegation model, many different contractual approaches are in fact possible (World Bank, 2006). Each one entails a different mix of responsibilities shared between the awarding authority and the operator, and of course different patterns of risk assumption (Table 10.2).

In addition, within the direct public-management scheme, private-sector entities are eventually involved in other ways; for example, through outsourcing or project finance schemes (BOT) that concern individual facilities such as wastewater treatment plants. Public management forms range from municipal departments with little autonomy, and that are hierarchically dependent on the public administration and receive funds from internal budget allocation (US), to publicly owned corporate companies, which operate on a commercial basis and are eventually quoted on the stock exchange (Italy, Germany, and the Netherlands). Other countries have adopted intermediate solutions, such as the French EPIC (enterprises owned by the public, with managerial and financial autonomy, but ruled by public law).

We can also observe that both the delegation model and direct public management can easily trespass into the privatized monopoly scheme. In fact, delegation of investment responsibility usually requires very long contracts and sophisticated clauses that in practice render the incumbent's position virtually unchallengeable even in case of re-tendering. In turn, public entities may gradually become self-referential the more independent they become from the parent administration, as in the case of quoted public corporations.

The three-model scheme is more conceptual than real, since the real world mostly offers a combination of the three, with varying degrees and dosage; it is nonetheless useful for a theoretical discussion. A vast amount of economic literature has discussed, either theoretically or empirically, the relative advantages and disadvantages. Table 10.3 summarizes the key aspects of each model, and the main strengths and weaknesses. Each model entrusts its governance mechanism to a different regulatory principle, and is vulnerable to specific risks.

Table 10.2 Types of contractual arrangements between WSS operator and contracting authority

Type of arrangement	*Operator's duties*	*Selected responsibilities of the operator*	*Stylized typical profit function of the operator*	*Selected risks typically borne by the operator*	*Typical share of total project risks*	*Ownership of operating assets*	*Ownership of infrastructure assets*
Management contract	Supplies management services to the utility in exchange for a fee	Provides management services to the utility (for example, meter reading, billing, pipe maintenance)	Fixed fee +/- bonuses, manages salaries and related expenses	Depend on the nature of the performance bonus	Very small	Contracting authority	Contracting authority
Affermage	Runs the business, retains a fee (generally not equal to customer tariff) based on the volume of water sold, but does not finance investments in infrastructure assets	Employing staff, operating and managing utility	(Affermage fee volume of water sold) – (operating and maintenance costs)	Operating and commercial risk	Significant	Operator	Contracting authority
Lease	Runs the business, retains revenues from customer tariffs, pays a lease fee to the contracting authority, but does not finance investments in infrastructure assets	Employing staff, operating and managing utility	Revenue from customers – (operating and maintenance costs + fee paid to the contracting authority)	Operating and commercial risk	Significant	Operator	Contracting authority
Concession	Runs the business and finances investments, but does not own infrastructure assets	Employing staff, operating and managing utility, financing and managing investment	Revenue from customers (operating and maintenance costs + finance costs + any concession fees)	Operating, commercial and investment-related risks	Major	Operator	Contracting authority
Divesture	Runs the business and finances investments, and owns infrastructure assets	Employing staff, operating and managing utility, financing and managing investment	Revenue from customers – (operating and maintenance costs + finance costs + any license fees)	Operating, commercial and investment-related risks	Major	Operator	Operator

Source: Author's own elaboration based on World Bank, 2006.

Table 10.3 The archetypal models for WSS organization, and their main characteristics

	Delegation	*Private monopoly*	*Direct public management*
Main instrument of governance	Contract	Independent and discretional regulation	Hierarchical control
Main pro-competitive incentives/potential sources of efficiency	Tenders (competition for the market)	Price caps	Procurement
	Threat to go public	Yardstick competition	Outsourcing
		Market for takeovers and corporate control	Threat to privatize
Main pitfalls/potential sources of failure	Incomplete contracts	Asymmetric information	Vulnerability to political influence
	Transactions costs	Regulatory capture	Limited incentives for efficiency
	Competitive advantage of incumbents		
Critical aspects to monitor	Transfer prices (vertical integration)	Cost evaluation and comparison	Overstaffing
	Renegotiation	Investments needs	Loose enforcement
	Responsibility for investment and risk sharing	Cost pass-through of new obligations	Raiding of funds by municipal departments
	Strategic decisions and planning	Hidden profits	Entering a debt spiral due to unwillingness to raise prices
Sources of risks for private investors	Contract enforcement	Expropriation of free cash flows	Political unwillingness to secure cash flows for debt service
	Failure to renegotiate in case costs increase	Setting unrealistic or overly demanding efficiency targets	Political priority to maintain low prices and protect delinquent payers
		Regulators learn how to anticipate progress; companies find it more difficult to outperform benchmarks	
Hybrids (examples)	Lease/management contracts	Quoted multi-utilities	Management contracts, project finance
	Institutional PPPs	Corporate privatization	Community systems, cooperatives

Source: Author's own elaboration.

Table 10.3 highlights a number of trade-offs that impede the simultaneous pursuit of all the desired targets – financial viability, operational efficiency, effectiveness, etc. A key aspect to consider concerns the link between competition, regulation, risk, and the cost of capital (Pedell, 2005). Supporters of neoliberal dogmas often underrated this link, in the belief that private financial markets had become efficient enough to unveil long-term risks associated with infrastructural investment, and price them appropriately. In turn, high capital intensity, heavy initial capital requirements, and extremely long repayment schedules (in the order of many decades), drastically increase investors' risks (OECD, 2010b). Legal instability, political turmoil, monetary turbulence, and other features affecting the macroeconomic context obviously act as multipliers of expected risks.

In order to maintain industry viability, WSS governance rule should adequately guarantee cash-flow generation and control required to sustain debt and asset renewal (Marques, 2010). Hence, regulatory contracts should explicitly target the securitization of operational margins (Baietti and Curiel, 2005); the legal system should be stable and predictable, without experiencing sudden disruptions of any kind (Kessides, 2004). Securing cash flows implies that regulatory conditions need to be flexible enough in order to be adapted to unforeseeable conditions that may occur in the future. This limits the possibility of binding the operator to *ex-ante* commitments. However, if cost pass-through is required too often, the opposite risk arises: private companies may deliberately accept contracts even at very disadvantageous terms, assuming that there will be a possibility to renegotiate them immediately after. Therefore, the very possibility of effectively introducing surrogates of competition (such as competitive tendering, or pricing formulas based on standard costs) and to exploit the consequent incentive effect to reduce costs is limited by the need to leave at least some valves open to future renegotiation. In turn, renegotiation makes it possible to shift at least part of the risk away from the operator; this is a precondition for attracting market investors. This trade-off obviously becomes less advantageous the more investment responsibilities the operator has to assume.

The case for private-sector participation: conflicting perspectives

This dynamism has obviously attracted the interest of applied researchers. During the last 15 years, a considerable number of studies appeared in the literature, with the aim of: (1) comparing the performance of alternative models, and verifying theoretical expectations about each; (2) assessing the outcome of change; and (3) helping to improve regulatory design (Araral and Young, 2013; Massarutto, 2007; Walter *et al.*, 2009).

We can identify two complementary approaches, each of which has strengths and weaknesses. The first, based on case studies, provides the advantage of giving more direct and in-depth information and explicitly addressing qualitative and institutional aspects that are difficult to manage at an aggregate level. However, it is also more likely to suffer from the well-known *confirmation bias*: authors tend to 'cherry-pick' cases that are suited to confirming their point of view, or that focus attention only on the desired aspects. The possibility to generalize results is consequently limited. In this line of research, Lobina and Hall (2003) emphasized the many cases of privatization failures, showing that in a vast number of cases concession contracts have been terminated or led to strong discontent. Quite to the opposite, Marin (2009) presented a number of more successful experiences, where regulatory reforms have delivered positive results.

More recently, the case-study approach was applied by institutional economic researchers, suggesting that management model and ownership are less important explanatory variables than the micro-foundation of regulatory institutions (Glachant, 2009; Massarutto and Ermano, 2012; Menard and Saussier, 2002).

Authors such as Guasch (2004) focused on the difficulties in setting out the regulatory contract due to the continuous necessity to renegotiate its clauses; this literature concludes that contract design is a crucial element, but institutions devoted to discretional regulation along the contract are still more important. In this light, public undertakings may offer a comparative advantage by reducing transactions costs, but also have better opportunities to 'capture' the regulatory agenda so that the interest of (public) shareholders may prevail on that of service customers (Marques, 2010).

The second approach uses an econometrics technique. The technique allows a more neutral comparison, but also forces a more superficial and simplistic characterization of cases. Again, the results of these studies are far from univocal. Generally, they have found that privatization leads to an increase in efficiency, but also in the financial costs and tariffs. Some have concluded in favor of the public, some other in favor of the private operation, but no solution has emerged as the dominant one (Abbott and Cohen, 2009; Caliman and Nardi, 2010; Dore *et al.*, 2004; Elnaboulsi, 2001; Renzetti and Dupont, 2004; Romano and Guerrini, 2011; Wallsten and Kosec, 2005; Walter *et al.*, 2009).

A central reason for this unsettled result rests on the measures used to evaluate WSS performances: an aggregate measure of efficiency is not able to grasp how modifications in the institutional and organization framework affect each individual stakeholder, chiefly because it is not straightforward to identify who the stakeholders are and how big their concern is relative to others. Unsatisfactory outcomes can equally arise because the private sector and competitive markets are unfit, or of poor institutional design and too timid to open to competition (Massarutto *et al.*, 2013).

The same outcome frequently inspires opposite statements, depending on the viewpoint (Barraqué, 2013). Price increase and metering can provoke indignation in those who oppose the 'commodification' of water, and the approval of those who are concerned about financial stability. Often, private companies are entrusted precisely to do the 'dirty job' that politicians are unwilling to undertake: that is, restore managerial control in organizations accustomed to loose command, eliminate rents and privileges, and impose regular bill payments after a long tolerance of abuses.

Critics of privatization may also raise the opposite arguments in case the private contractor fails to achieve the promised investments and service improvements. In the publicized case of Atlanta, conflicts within the company organization and generalized delinquent payment impeded the setup of an efficient customer-service track (Public Citizen, 2005). While this case is often presented as a flagship of privatization failures, it should be noted that failures depend on the fact that the actual distress of the former public organization was much higher than the private company could imagine (Segal, 2003).

In their analysis of Italian reform, Massarutto *et al.* (2013) argued that the initial situation was so bad, in many respects, that one could imagine that the reform would generate Pareto-improvements (gains or no losses for everyone). However, this expectation was soon proven too optimistic: the space for win–win outcomes was rapidly exhausted, and many trade-offs between the different objectives in the agenda became apparent. Political unwillingness to make clear-cut choices about priorities condemned the reform to languish; but as soon as the government announced a breakthrough choice, a wave of discontent arose. The law introducing compulsory competitive tendering and more widespread private involvement triggered the popular referendum of 2011 that affirmed WSS belonged to the public sphere.

In the case of Johannesburg – another well-publicized case of contract termination – the water company reports considered results in terms of billing efficiency, cost recovery, and water saving as remarkable technical and managerial improvements (Suez Environnément, 2010).

From an opposite viewpoint, Bond (2008) considers the same facts as negative outcomes of privatization, blaming the commodification of water, and the subtraction of vital water endowments to the poor.

The benefits of remunicipalization are also controversial, despite the huge interest in experiences such as of Paris and, more recently, Berlin. A recent verbal crossfire between Bernard Barraqué and the deputy mayor of the newly created public company Eau de Paris, published by the journal *Water Policy*, perfectly exemplifies the arguments used in the debate (Barraqué, 2012, 2014; Le Strat, 2014). On the one hand, prices have reduced without apparent quality losses, and efficiency improvements have been achieved on the procurement side. On the other hand, most of the 'savings' in fact owe much to changed depreciation policies and internalization of taxes previously paid to the city, while coordination costs may outweigh the short-term benefits of tenders in the future. Barraqué also pointed out the coordination problems that remunicipalization problems generate at the intermunicipal scale.

Beyond the public–private divide: looking forward

The application of neoliberal policy methods to WSS has generated controversial results, but also marked some points of no return.

History has confirmed what economists knew about water – that is, it is an industry that opposes formidable difficulties to competitive markets. Water is simply too important, even in symbolic terms, to stop ideology and passion from streaming into the public debate. Of course, this does not mean that there is no alternative to public operation and taxpayers' money for funding. The global experience is much less univocal than in the past, and no clear-cut trend is identifiable (Figure 10.4). Instead, rather than preferring one model to the others, it seems that models are increasingly contaminated and mixed.

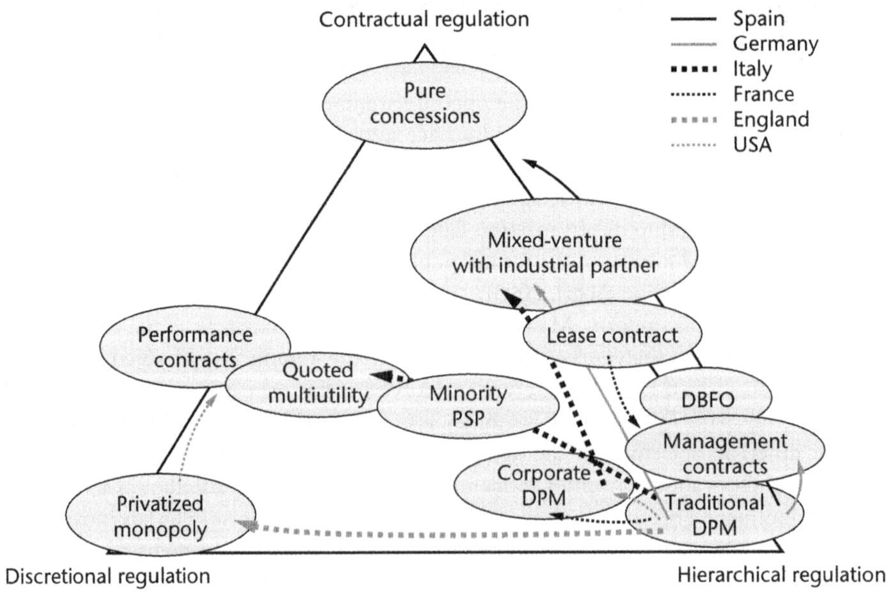

Figure 10.4 Management models for WSS and recent trajectories of change in certain countries

Source: Massarutto, 2011.

The most important lesson arising from the recent experience, in our opinion, concerns the need to refrain from dogmatism. No solution emerges as the winner; instead, the quality of governance and regulation are the key explanatory factors of successes and failures.

A combination of regulatory arrangements – contracts, discretional regulation, command and control – rather than opposite principles should be seen as complementary tools to use at once, and possibly in a coordinated way (Marques, 2010). The search for the optimal mix between *ex-ante* rules and *ex-post* revisions will remain the crucial regulatory issue. The former are needed in order to foster efficiency improvements, while the latter are required in order to reduce risks to a manageable level (Massarutto and Ermano, 2013). Public ownership is not an alternative to regulation, since more formal economic regulation is required even for public organizations (Vinnari, 2006).

Innovative solutions may be experimented with – such as performance-based bonuses and penalties, as recently recommended by the OECD – but no one is likely to turn out to be a neat solution (Marin *et al.*, 2015). Consumers' involvement and public participation is also a key and fundamental value to pursue in the construction of innovative regulatory systems (OECD, 2015).

Subsidies from the state budget can no longer represent the main source of funding, since many other – and possibly more compelling – public expenditure items compete for use of taxpayers' money. State support is nonetheless necessary, but should be parsimonious and targeted towards securitizing financial obligations and shifting some risk away from investors, rather than to the provision of non-repayable block grants. Full-cost recovery is ultimately mandatory, but can also be achieved in ways that are more creative. Earmarked taxes can complement meter-based tariffs; cost and risk sharing arrangements among utilities may facilitate access to credit, and so on.

Competition between models – namely, the reversibility of choices – is a key asset to maintain. The best competitor to a powerful private incumbent is the credible threat to remunicipalize, whereas the best way to force improvements in the public sector is to threaten privatization.

References

Abbott, M. and Cohen, B. (2009) Productivity and efficiency in the water industry, *Utilities Policy* 19, 233–244.

Araral, E. and Wang, Y. (2013) Water Governance 2.0. A review and second generation research agenda, Water Resources Management, 27, 3945–3957.

Baietti, A. and Curiel, P. (2005) Financing water supply and sanitation investments: Estimating revenue requirements and financial sustainability, *Water Supply & Sanitation Research Notes n.* 7. Washington DC: The World Bank.

Ballance, T. and Taylor, A. (2005) *Competition and Economic Regulation in Water: The future of the European water industry*. London: IWA Publishing.

Barraqué, B. (2012) Return of drinking water supply in Paris to public control, *Water Policy*, 14(6), 903–914.

Barraqué, B. (2013) New modes of water supply and sanitation management and emerging business models, *OECD Working Party on Biodiversity, Water and Ecosystems*, ENV/EPOC/WPBWE/RD(2013)7. Paris: OECD.

Barraqué, B. (2014) Author response to right of reply by Anne Le Strat, deputy Mayor of Paris, to the article 'Return of Drinking water supply in Paris to public control', *Water Policy*, 16(2), 422–424.

Barraqué, B. and Katko, T. (2011) Urban water conflicts in recent European history: changing interactions between technology, environment and society, in B. Barraqué (ed.), *Urban Water Conflicts*. London: Routledge, pp. 15–32.

Bel, G. (2006) *Economía y política de la privatización local*, Barcelona: Marcial Pons.

Bond, P. (2008) Water, human rights and social conflict: South African experiences (with Jackie Dugard), *Law, Social Justice and Global Development*, 10, 1, February. Available at: http://www.go.warwick.ac.uk/elj/lgd/2008_1/bond_dugard (accessed on 22 September 2015).

Caliman, T. and Nardi, P. (2010) Technical efficiency drivers for the Italian water industry, *Economia delle fonti di energia e dell'ambiente*, 1, 87–103.

Castro, J.E. and Heller, L. (2011) *Water and Sanitation Services. Public Policy and Management*. London: Earthscan.

Dore, M., Kushner, J. and Zumer, K. (2004) Privatization of water in the UK and France – What can we learn? *Utilities Policy* 12, 41–50.

Elnaboulsi, J.C. (2001 Organization, management and delegation in the French Water industry, in *Annals of Public and Cooperative Economics*, 72(4), 507–547. doi: 10.1111/1467-8292.00180.

Finger, M., Allouche, J. and Luis-Manso, P. (eds) (2006) *Water and Liberalization: European water scenarios*. London: IWA Publishing.

Glachant, J.M. (2009) Regulating networks in the new economy, *EUI Working Papers 2009–5*, Robert Schuman Center for Advanced Studies. Available at: http://cadmus.eui.eu/dspace/bitstream/1814/10622/1/EUI_RSCAS_2009_05.pdf (accessed on 31 January 2015).

Gleick P.H. (1999) The human right to water, *Water Policy*, 1, 5, 487–583.

Guasch, J.L. (2004) *Granting and Renegotiating Concessions: Doing it Right*. Washington, DC: The World Bank.

Guasch, J.L. and Staub, S. (2009) Corruption and concession renegotiations: Evidence from the water and transport sectors in Latin America, *Utilities Policy*, 17(2), 185–190.

Hall, D. (2007) The Watertime project, *Utilities Policy*, 15(2), 61–160.

Hall, D. and Lobina, E. (2010) *The Past, Present and Future of Finance for Investments in Water Systems*. Public Service International Research Unit, University of Greenwich. Available at: www.psiru.org (accessed on 22 September 2015).

Kessides, I.N. (ed.) (2004) *Reforming Infrastructure – Privatization, regulation and competition*. The World Bank.

Kraemer, A. (1998) Privatization in the water industry, *Public Works Management and Policy*, 3(2), 104–123.

Kraemer, A. (2014) Networks of cooperation: Water policy in Germany, *Environmental Politics*, 3(4), 52–79.

Le Strat, A. (2014) The remunicipalisation of Paris water supply service: a successful reform, Reply to B. Barraqué, *Water Policy*, 16(1), 197–204.

Lobina, E. and Hall, D. (2003) *Problems with Private Water Concessions: A review of experience*, Public Service International Research Unit, University of Greenwich. Available at: www.psiru.org.

Lobina, E. and Hall, D. (2013) *Water Privatization and Remunicipalization: International lessons for Jakarta*. Public Service International Research Unit, University of Greenwich. Available at: www.psiru.org.

Marin P., Williams T. and Janssens, J. (2015) *Performance-Based Contracts for Improving Utility Efficiency*. London: IWA Publishing.

Marin, P. (2009) *Public–Private Partnerships for Urban Water Utilities: A review of experiences in developing countries*. Washington, DC: World Bank-PPIAF.

Marques, R.C. (ed.) (2010) *Regulation of Water and Wastewater Services: An international Comparison*. London: IWA Publishing.

Massarutto, A. (2007) Liberalization and private sector involvement in the water industry: a review of the economic literature, IEFE Working Paper 6.

Massarutto, A. (2011) Urban water conflicts: An ecological-economic approach, in Barraqué, B. (ed.), *Urban Water Conflicts*. London: Routledge.

Massarutto, A., Antonioli, B. and Ermano, P. (2013) Assessing the impact of water service regulatory reforms in Italy: A multidimensional approach, *Water Policy*, 15(6), 1046–1063.

Massarutto, A. and Ermano, P. (2013) Drowned in an inch of water. How poor regulation hampered the Italian water reform, *Utilities Policy*.

Menard, C. and Peeroo, A. (2011) Liberalization in the water sector: three leading models, in R. Kuenneke and M. Finger (eds), *Handbook of Liberalization*. London: Edward Elgar Publishing.

Menard, C. and Saussier, S. (2002) Contractual choice and performance: The case of water supply in France, in E. Brousseau and J.M. Glachant (eds) *The Economics of Contracts: Theory and applications*. Cambridge: Cambridge University Press.

National Research Council (2002) Committee on Privatization of Water Services in the United States (2003) *Privatization of Water Services in the United States*. Washington, DC: National Academy Press. Available at: http://books.nap.edu/openbook.php?record_id=10135&page=40 (accessed on 22 September 2015).

Newbery, D.M. (2000) *Privatisation, Restructuring and Regulation of Network Utilities*. Cambridge, MA: The MIT Press.
Noll, R.G. (2002) The economics of urban water systems, in M.M. Shirley (ed.), *Thirsting for Efficiency: The Economics and Politics of Urban Water System Reform*. The World Bank: Elsevier.
OECD (2010a) *Pricing Water Resources and Sanitation Services*. Paris: OECD.
OECD (2010b) *Innovative Financial Mechanisms for Water Supply and Sanitation*. Paris: OECD.
OECD (2011) *Meeting the Challenge of Financing Water and Sanitation: Tools and Approaches*. Paris: OECD.
OECD (2015) *Stakeholder Involvement for Inclusive Water Governance*. Paris: OECD.
Pedell, B. (2005) *Regulatory Risk and the Cost of Capital: Determinants and implications for rate regulation*. London: Springer.
Petrella, R. (2001) *The Water Manifesto: Arguments for a World Water Contract*. London: Zed Books.
Public Citizen (2005) Waves of Regret. What some cities have learned and some others should know about water privatization fiascos in the US. Available at: www.wateractivist.org (accessed on 22 September 2015).
Raftells, G. (2014) *Water and Wastewater Finance and Tariffs: The Changing Landscape*. London: CRC Press.
Renzetti, S. and Dupont, D. (2004) The performance of municipal water utilities: Evidence on the role of ownership, *Journal of Toxicology and Environmental Health*, 67(20–22), 1861–1878.
Romano, G. and Guerrini, A. (2011) Measuring and comparing the efficiency of water utility companies: a data envelopment analysis approach, *Utilities Policy*, 19(3), 202–209.
Rouse, M. (2007) *Institutional Governance and Regulation of Water Services*. London: IWA Publishing.
Segal, G. (2003) *What Can We Learn From Atlanta's Water Privatization?* Reason Foundation. Available at: http://reason.org/news/show/what-can-we-learn-from-atlanta (accessed on 22 September 2015).
Shirley, M. (2002) *Thirsting for Efficiency. The economics and policy of urban water system reform*. Amsterdam: Elsevier.
Suez Environnément (2010) *Water Stories. Johannesburg Management Contract*. Available at: www.suez-environnement.com (accessed on 22 September 2015).
Vinnari, E.M. (2006) The economic regulation of publicly owned water utilities: The case of Finland, *Utilities Policy*, 14(3), 158–165.
Wallsten, S. and Kosec, K. (2005) Public or private drinking water? The effects of ownership and benchmarking competition on US water system regulatory compliance and household water expenditure, *Working Paper 05/05*, AEI, Brookings Center for Regulatory Studies.
Walter, M., Cullmann, A., von Hirschhausen, C., Wand, R. and Zschille, M. (2009) Quo vadis efficiency analysis of water distribution? A comparative literature review, *Utilities Policy*, 17(3–4), 225–232.
Winpenny, J. (2003) Financing water for all. *Report of the World Panel on Financing Water Infrastructure*. World Water Council.
World Bank (2006) *Approaches to Private Participation in the Water Sector: A toolkit*. Washington, DC: The World Bank.
World Bank and Public Private Infrastructure Advisory Facility (PPIAF) (2013) *Infrastructure Policy Unit, PPI data update: Water and sewerage sector 2012*. Available at: http://ppi.worldbank.org/features/December-2013/Water-Note-2013.pdf (accessed on 22 September 2015).

Part II

The policy and regulatory perspective

11

Electronic communications policy and regulation in Europe

Paula Gori and Pier Luigi Parcu

Introduction

The main objectives of the 1990s revolution of the telecommunications sector in Europe were to keep pace with technological changes and to promote consumers' interests. Such a revolution was built around three main drivers: liberalizing the markets, harmonizing the regulatory rules across European Union (EU) member states, and introducing competition (and consequently protecting consumers).[1]

The following chapter first introduces the general regulatory framework of electronic communications in the EU. It then looks at what has been done and achieved so far, as well as what still needs regulatory intervention. This is achieved by analyzing fixed networks, mobile networks, and the Internet. To conclude, we briefly consider possible next steps in the sector and discuss the need for a new, profound change in our regulatory structure.

The European electronic communications regulatory framework

The starting point for liberalization and regulation in the European telecommunications sector is the fixed-line network. This market has been faced with a monopolistic situation with state-owned monopoly operators owning the infrastructure and being the only ones to provide service. The 1987 Green Paper (European Commission, 1987) and the following Open Network Provision (ONP) Framework Directive and the Full Competition Directive (Council of the European Union, 1990; European Commission, 1996) were the first instruments to open the telecommunications market with the explicit aim of introducing competition.

Asymmetric regulation between incumbent operators and new entrants was the first strategic instrument to be introduced, as the former monopolies had to share their infrastructure with new competitors. Indeed, market actors sharing the infrastructure were called to compete on services provided to customers on that same infrastructure.

January 1, 1998 was set as the date for EU member states to enact the proposed liberalization (a number of southern European states received permission for implementation at a later date). All the different provisions introduced before this date are called the '1998 package'. One of the main consequences was the creation in each member state of an independent national regulatory authority (NRA). In the past, the Ministries of Communications and the monopolistic companies had often operated very closely, substantially mixing regulatory and operational capacities. However, once the market was opened such a way to proceed was no longer acceptable, as it would have gravely distorted any competition.

The second driver for European intervention in the telecommunications market was harmonization of national regulatory legislation as a key element necessary to pursue a European single market. Only a harmonized and almost uniform application of European rules in the different member states could guarantee equal treatment for companies competing on the market and for consumers to be able to benefit from their services.

The Open Network Framework Directive (ONP), the Licensing Directive, Radio Equipment and Telecommunications Terminal Equipment Directive (R&TTE) and the Regulation on unbundled access to the local loop (LLU) (Council of the European Union, 1990; European Parliament and Council, 1997, 1999, 2000) are all characterized by the aim of harmonizing regulatory rules at a European level. In particular, the LLU Regulation imposed on incumbent operators, owners of the legacy infrastructure, an unbundling and sharing of access (in a transparent, fair, and non-discriminatory way) of the local copper loops. A local loop is a physical circuit that connects the subscriber's premises to the main distribution frame or equivalent local facility. The aim of this regulatory imposition was to foster immediate (partial) infrastructure competition and stimulate service innovation on the local access market, while recognizing that it was physically and/or economically impossible for new operators to duplicate the local loop in the short to medium term. According to the LLU Regulation, this obligation has to be fulfilled by operators of fixed public telephone networks designated by their NRA as having significant market power (SMP) in the provision of fixed public telephone networks and services under Annex I, Part 1, of Directive 97/33/EC or Directive 98/10/EC (at the time having SMP simply meant owning a market share of 25 percent or more).

The 1998 package was followed in 2002 by the regulatory framework for electronic communications in the EU, also called the Telecoms Package. Today, after the 2009 re-visitation, the latter is composed of a Framework Directive, four specific directives, namely the Authorization Directive, the Access Directive, the Universal Service Directive, and the Privacy and Electronic Communications Directive (European Parliament and Council, 2002a, b, c, d, e), the Roaming Regulation and the Body of European Regulators for Electronic Communications (BEREC) Regulation (European Parliament and Council 2007, 2009a). The rationale behind this reform was the need to take into account digital convergence, as it was clear that, in the light of technological neutrality, a single regulatory framework for all legacy and newly born electronic communications networks was necessary (European Parliament and Council 2002a).

Nonetheless, transmission of content did not fall under the scope of application of the Telecoms Package and is still regulated by the Audiovisual Media Services Directive (European Parliament and Council, 2007). The aim of the Electronic Communications Regulatory Framework, created in 2002, was essentially the same as that already envisaged in the 1987 Green Paper, namely promoting competition, building a European single market in the sector, and promoting consumers' interests (European Parliament and Council, 2002a). The 2002 package was revised in 2009 (BEREC Regulation, Better Regulation Directive and Citizens Right Directive) without changing any of its fundamental tenets (European Parliament and Council, 2009a, b, c).

One of the major points of this new regulatory framework was the key role played by the independent NRAs and their coordination. Following the subsidiarity principle, NRAs, acting impartially, transparently, and in a timely manner, were responsible for any of the regulatory tasks assigned in the regulatory framework. However, in order to ensure harmonization, the very fact of leaving to national regulators the task of applying the framework required strong coordination at the European level. After the spontaneous constitution of the Independent Regulators Group in 1998 and the official institution of the European Regulators Group in 2002, the Regulation (EC) 1211/2009 established BEREC. The final aim of this body is to guarantee a harmonized application of the regulatory framework at a European level, and coordination and collaboration between the different NRAs.

According to the Framework Directive, NRAs shall determine whether undertakings do have SMP, which is now a concept analogous to what in competition law is defined as a dominant position in a relevant market.

The European Commission (EC), in its Recommendations on Relevant Markets, identified those markets requiring analysis for the potential application of *ex-ante* regulatory intervention. This identification process, which is the same as the one that the NRAs have to apply in cases where they want to intervene in other markets that are not listed by the EC, is conducted through the application of the so-called 'three-criteria' test. According to this test, regulation is needed when the following three cumulative criteria are met: (1) presence of high and non-transitory structural, legal, or regulatory barriers to entry; (2) a market structure that does not tend towards effective competition within the relevant time horizon, having regard to the state of infrastructure-based and other competition behind the barriers to entry; and (3) the assessment that competition law alone is insufficient to adequately address the market failure(s) concerned in a timely manner (European Parliament and Council, 2002a).

Where an NRA, taking into account the Recommendation on Relevant Markets, concludes that a relevant market is not competitive, it has to identify the undertaking with SMP and intervene with adequate remedies chosen among those explicitly and exhaustively listed in the relevant directives.

According to Article 7 and 7a of the revised Framework Directive, NRAs shall notify the EC, as well as BEREC and other NRAs, of the possible remedial measures. The bodies then have one month to assess these. Upon receiving the Commission's answer, the NRA must take into '*utmost account*' the Commission's comments as well as those from BEREC and other NRAs when introducing the relevant remedies. Should the Commission have serious doubts about the compatibility of an NRA's proposed remedies with EU law, Phase II is opened and the investigation period prolonged (two months for Article 7 and three for Article 7a). In this case, BEREC must issue an opinion on the serious doubts of the Commission, and, should it confirm them, it should work together with the interested NRA to identify the most appropriate remedies.

The Framework Directive is accompanied by other specific directives, covering four issues where harmonization is needed: authorization, access, universal service, and privacy.

Regarding authorization, the specific directive also applies to the granting of rights to use radio frequencies that involve the provision of an electronic communications network or service, normally for remuneration (Recital 5). The former practice of national states granting individual licenses to telecoms companies has thus been replaced by a general authorization regime. Only in the case of the attribution of scarce resources, frequencies, and numbers is a special license scheme still required. Thanks to the general authorization, undertakings have the right to provide electronic communications networks and services, and to negotiate interconnection with the other undertakings active in the EU. While member states should facilitate the use of frequencies through these general authorizations, there might exist the need to grant individual rights in order to avoid harmful interference, ensure technical quality of service, safeguard efficient use of spectrum, or ensure the fulfillment of other general-interest objectives defined by member states. NRAs have to monitor compliance with the requirements set for the general authorization or the rights of use and specific obligations. In concluding, it is worth mentioning the project contained in the 2013 proposal called Connected Continent Regulation (revising the electronic communications regulatory framework) (European Commission, 2013a), which aims to introduce a European single authorization, meaning that operators that are active in different member states would need to submit a notification only in their home member state.

As far as access is concerned, the specific directive applies to all forms of communications networks carrying publicly available communications services. It establishes both rights and obligations for operators and undertakings that look for access and/or interconnection to their networks. The general principle is to leave the interconnection issue to competitive forces and commercial negotiation. However, should an NRA identify a situation in which there is no effective competition, it has to intervene, imposing obligations on the operator with SMP. Member states have to guarantee that undertakings do not face restrictions on negotiating access and/or interconnection agreements. The fundamental rule introduced by the Access Directive is that all network operators have rights and obligations regarding access and interconnection agreements; the directive thus establishes a general right and obligation, when requested by other undertakings, to give access and to interconnect (European Parliament and Council, 2002c).

The Directive on Universal Service aims to ensure the availability of a minimum set of quality services that are available to all users at an affordable price without distortion of competition, thus imposing some provision obligations to undertakings and granting specific rights to end users. Member states shall ensure that such services are available to citizens in their territory regardless of their geographical location, with a certain quality level, and at affordable prices. (European Parliament and Council, 2002d). Services that fall under the universal service category are: provision of access at a fixed location and telephone services; directory enquiry services and directories; public pay telephones and other access points to publicly available telephone services; and special measures for disabled users. It is up to member states to designate the undertaking(s) on which to impose the universal service obligation. Citizens with low incomes must have access to special affordable tariffs or special assistance to have access to the network. The NRAs set performance targets and monitor compliance with these targets. The net costs sustained by the undertaking(s) are compensated for by member states (be it compensation from public funds and/ or sharing of costs between the providers of networks and services).

Finally, concerning privacy and electronic communications, the relevant directive introduces a general principle of privacy protection of users by the service providers. Service providers have to ensure that personal data is accessed only by authorized persons; protect personal data from being destroyed, lost, or accidentally altered; and ensure the implementation of a security policy in the processing of personal data. The directive also introduces specific principles on confidentiality of communications, data retention, spamming, cookies, and public directories. Member states have to enforce a system of penalties for cases of infringement and must ensure that the relevant national authorities have the necessary powers to monitor and control compliance.

The regulatory debate regarding European networks

With the general framework set, we will now go over the different aspects that characterize the main types of network; namely fixed networks, mobile networks, and the Internet. Although convergence is in progress, these different networks have faced, and still face, different levels of regulatory intervention.

Fixed networks

Concerning fixed networks, it is widely recognized that access and interconnection policy in Europe has been a regulatory success. Indeed, thanks to European regulatory intervention, access has been effectively granted throughout the EU, and many new operators have entered the market.

Once the market was liberalized, regulatory rules were necessary in order to foster competition and to progressively create a level playing field for old and new operators. Indeed, as the infrastructure was unique and owned by the incumbents, *ex-ante* asymmetric regulation was clearly essential for reaching these goals. In order to foster and enhance competition without holding back investments, the ladder of investment (LOI) concept was adopted (Cave and Vogelsang, 2003; Cave, 2006). According to this theory, service-based competition is only the first step in reaching infrastructure-based competition, and in order to do that, access is seen as the key element to trigger competition between different services. While the final aim of regulating access is always to introduce a viable form of competition and finally repeal regulation, leaving market control to *ex-post* antitrust regulation, the access regulation was originally built on competition instruments, such as the definition of relevant markets and the SMP interpreted as a dominant position principle (Parcu and Silvestri, 2014).

Access is a fundamental instrument to open existing networks to competition through regulatory intervention. However, it is still to be demonstrated whether the LOI concept may really lead to infrastructure-based competition. This is of particular interest with regard to investments into the 'final rung' of the LOI. Indeed, in Europe we are witnessing insufficient private investment in next-generation networks (NGN), and it seems that this cannot be explained only by the current financial crisis.

In September 2013, the EC issued a Recommendation on non-discrimination and costing methodologies (European Commission, 2013a), which, according to Recital 3, 'aims to promote efficient investment and innovation in new and enhanced infrastructures whilst recognizing the need to maintain effective competition, which is an important long term investment incentive'. The Recommendation seeks:

> (i) to ensure a level playing field through the application of stricter non-discrimination rules, (ii) to establish predictable and stable regulated wholesale copper access prices, as well as (iii) to increase certainty on the circumstances that should lead to the non-imposition of regulated wholesale access prices for NGA services. Increasing legal and regulatory predictability in this manner should further help to trigger the investment needed in the near to medium-term future.

In order to tackle discrimination between incumbents and new entrants, the Commission considers that the 'equivalence of inputs (EoI)' is the surest principle to protect the latter from discrimination.

The transition between copper-based networks and fiber-based networks is far from being achieved, and broadband speeds vary across countries and geographic areas. This very fact is acknowledged by the European legislator, which, in its 2010 NGA Recommendation, (European Commission, 2010) allows NRAs the possibility of identifying sub-national geographic markets where *ex-ante* regulation is needed when they clearly witness substantially and objectively different conditions of competition. Moreover, in those cases that do not require the definition of sub-national geographic markets, it might be appropriate for NRAs to respond to diverging competitive conditions between different areas of the same geographic market (such as the presence of several alternative infrastructures or infrastructure-based operators) by imposing differentiated remedies and access products (Recital 9).

It is worth mentioning that in recent years we have witnessed a progressive decline in the fixed voice market which is mainly due to its replacement by mobile or voice over Internet protocol technologies (VoIP) (European Commission, 2014). In general, consumers are demanding more and faster bands, be it fixed (and thus NGN) or mobile. In order to foster the transition from traditional networks to NGNs, a possible solution could be to learn from what happened in TV broadcasting with the transition from analog to digital, and to reconsider the possibility of a switch-over policy that is directed/coordinated by member states. Indeed, a mandatory switch-over, which is carefully planned and extremely localized in order to avoid asset depreciation, combined with competition-driven regulation, could represent a serious candidate as a solution to tackle the delay in the transition between copper and fiber in some EU member states.

Another solution, which, as we will see later on, has been suggested to overcome market fragmentation and lack of investment, is favoring an increase in the dimension of the European electronic communications companies. In other words, some favor the idea of a process of consolidation through a wave of intra-EU mergers.

To conclude, the fixed-network markets, while generally competitive thanks to the success of past regulatory policies (especially access and interconnection provisions), are currently characterized by a perceived lack or delay of investment in NGNs in several member states. Applications, videos, games, VoIP, and data quests in general have caused a significant increase in traffic over networks (often referred to as the 'data tsunami'), thereby challenging existing networks' capacities. Moreover, services such as VoIP and instant messaging are directly replacing traditional voice and SMS services offered by telecoms operators, fueling the debate and economic contrast between the 'over the top' (OTT) players and the telecommunications companies. The question of whether European regulatory rigidity represents a disincentive to invest in the new technological scenarios is clearly at the core of many present debates and reflections.

Mobile networks

Contrary to fixed networks, in mobile networks there is essentially symmetrical regulation, as the issue of a single incumbent operator already owning the infrastructure is missing.[2] Regulatory intervention in mobile networks in recent years has almost solved issues such as interconnection rates and roaming, but intervention is still needed when it comes to the efficient use of spectrum.

Network interconnection consists of two networks establishing a link to allow two consumers who have subscriptions with different operators to talk to each other. When user A calls user B, the call starts on the network of the operator of user A and ends on the network of the operator of user B. This means that the network of operator B is essential for the operator of A's network to conclude the call. This puts the operator that terminates the call in a monopolistic situation; the 'natural tendency' was indeed to abuse this position and thus to apply very high termination costs to the calling operator, with evident consequences for consumers' charges.

Europe adopted the so-called calling party network pays (CPNP) system, which means that the originating operator pays the operator that receives the call. This means that users pay for the entire call they make and do not pay for the calls they receive.[3] This, as previously noted, generates a bottleneck, as the terminating operator appears to be de facto in a monopolistic position.

Because of the absence of a former monopoly operator, prima facie one might wonder whether a market failure regarding competition is really at issue. However, it turns out that all operators, quite irrespective of their general market power, were endemically placed in a sort of 'local' monopolistic position, thus creating a generalized competitive bottleneck.

As a consequence of the 2002 regulatory framework, rigid price controls on interconnection charges (mainly on termination) were introduced. However, prices remained very high, especially for fixed-to-mobile charges that were used to cross-subsidize the mobile networks' building and penetration. In 2009, the EC adopted a termination rates Recommendation (European Commission, 2009b), which aimed at removing cross-subsidies between fixed and mobile networks. As stated in Recital 3 of the Recommendation:

> Significant divergences in the regulatory treatment of fixed and mobile termination rates create fundamental competitive distortions. Termination markets represent a situation of two-way access where both interconnecting operators are presumed to benefit from the arrangement but, as these operators are also in competition with each other for subscribers, termination rates can have important strategic and competitive implications. Where termination rates are set above efficient costs, this creates substantial transfers between fixed and mobile markets and consumers.

According to the Recommendation, when imposing price control and cost-accounting obligations on operators with SMP on the fixed and mobile termination markets, NRAs should define termination rates based on the costs incurred by an efficient operator. Moreover, the long-run incremental cost (LRIC) model has been recommended as the relevant cost methodology.

When the Commission issued the above Recommendation, mobile operators claimed that merely lowering termination rates does not imply a price reduction for consumers. They were referring to a possible 'waterbed effect', meaning that as a consequence of lowering termination charges, other charges would have been increased and the reduction of termination rates would not ultimately reach consumers.

A solution to abandon the CPNP system and its necessary regulatory intervention could have lead to the adoption of the 'bill and keep' (BAK) model. This system is based on reciprocity, where no termination charges are paid between the operators. In a competitive market, if it is true that the network of operator B terminates the call of operator A, it is also true that operator B does the same when it receives a call from operator A. This means that termination payments are needed only in case of traffic asymmetries – a phenomenon that is essentially transitory or sporadic among interconnected telecommunications networks regardless of relative dimensions. Not only would this model allow termination regulation to be eliminated, but it would also apply the same method across different technologies. Indeed, it would create a common, technologically neutral charging principle in light of the actual convergence between voice, video, and Internet and of the spread of NGN (the Internet-protocol-based charging system typical of the Internet world that has essentially been a BAK system from the beginning) (Parcu and Silvestri, 2014). However, although it acknowledged that 'technological convergence is considered an important factor driving the need to assess which interconnection regime is appropriate in the long-term', BEREC also considered that in the medium term member states should keep the so-called 'improved' CPNP system (BEREC, 2010). In practice, following the 2009 Recommendations, the NRAs imposed deep reductions in termination rates using the LRIC methodology. Since then mobile termination rates have deeply fallen in Europe, ultimately bringing important price reductions for consumers, showing the waterbed effect to be a theoretical construct of scarce practical relevance.

International roaming was another major challenge for EU regulation, not only from a regulatory harmonization point of view but also in light of the European single market aim. The EC strongly intervened in this sector by imposing a series of deep price reductions, the final goal being the elimination of international roaming between member states and consequently the demolition of artificial and unjustified barriers across the EU for consumers.

International roaming involves the provision of voice, texts, and Internet across different countries. Operators from the different countries negotiated agreements with the operators of hosted consumers and had a clear tendency to overcharge those services. Both consumers' full cost awareness and competition between international users were missing, and prices were both very high and completely unrelated to industrial costs. The first EC intervention dates to 2007, when the Commission imposed price transparency and introduced the Eurotariff for the voice wholesale and retail levels (the price cap was extended to text messaging in 2009). In 2012, the Commission came out with another regulation that foresaw a new price cap, again at wholesale and retail levels, for all services (voice, text, and mobile Internet). According to the regulation, in June 2016 the EC will report to the European Parliament and to the Council. At that stage, if differences between roaming tariffs and national tariffs have not approached zero, the Commission shall make appropriate proposals to the European Parliament and the Council to address this situation. In April 2014, the European Parliament, following a first reading of the proposal for a Connected Continent Regulation, voted for the abolishment of all kinds of roaming charges by December 2015. At present, international roaming in the EU appears to be an issue that is close to reaching a satisfactory solution in the interest of European consumers.

With regard to the constant growth of data traffic, a crucial issue to be solved in European mobile communications markets is radio spectrum availability. The radio spectrum is a limited resource that can be used for various public services and safety, but also for commercial purposes. The rapid development of information and communications technology (ICT) and the explosion of connected devices and data traffic are challenging the spectrum availability, posing the risk of a spectrum crunch. Users are becoming increasingly demanding, in terms of both quantity and quality of their mobile communication. Moreover, spectrum is also a valid alternative for bringing broadband (mobile) into those geographic areas that cannot be easily reached with fixed lines. The solution is, in a sense, already there, as the issue is most likely not absolute scarcity, but the need for a smart and harmonized management of the existing resource. Indeed, the traditional approach has been to assign the right to use a specific band for a specific purpose, with the consequence of being very often stuck in rigid situations of under-exploitation of the resource. Another limit is constituted by the very fact of having local spectrum assignment procedures and different rules in different member states.[4]

The 1998 Green Paper on Spectrum Policy and the subsequent 2002 Radio Spectrum Decision (European Commission, 1998, 2002) were adopted in order to tackle the lack of harmonization and to foster a more efficient use of spectrum. Moreover, two new bodies were established, tasked with assisting the Commission: the Radio Spectrum Policy Group (RSPG), which is a high-level advisory group composed of national government experts to help the Commission develop general radio spectrum policy at the European Community level; and the Radio Spectrum Committee, which assists the Commission in developing technical implementation measures to ensure harmonized conditions across Europe for the availability and efficient use of radio spectrum.

Technological densification of existing mobile networks and the utilization of high-quality bands, formerly reserved for broadcasting, and exploiting the so-called spectrum 'digital dividend', are key elements in satisfying the request for more spectrum, but better regulation can also contribute to solutions. In 2012, the Radio Spectrum Policy Program took an interesting step toward smarter spectrum management, endorsing collective (or shared) use of spectrum. According to a recent opinion of the RSPG, licensed shared access (LSA) might represent the better sharing model, where LSA is defined as a:

> regulatory approach aiming to facilitate the introduction of radio communication systems operated by a limited number of licensees under an individual licensing regime in a frequency band already assigned or expected to be assigned to one or more incumbent users.
>
> (RSPG, 2013)

To conclude, thanks to regulatory intervention, we can affirm that interconnection and roaming are issues that have been essentially solved or are close to reach a satisfactory solution. However, radio spectrum availability remains a crucial aspect in need of an efficient solution, as this represents the only answer to ever-growing data traffic needs.

The Internet

During the 1990s, the electronic communications sector has witnessed the beginning of an incredible revolution: the rise of the Internet.

The Internet completely changed the communications sector by erasing old certainties, destroying original business models, and introducing new services. Thanks to the Internet, which is by definition global, new businesses and economic and innovation opportunities have emerged. However, this is still a work in progress as we continue to look for a new equilibrium in the electronic communications sector. The peculiarity of the Internet is that it started as a new technology and rapidly became a general marketplace, with disruptive consequences for already existing markets. The Internet introduced a parallel virtual reality, though this is only 'virtual' in the sense that it is 'untouchable', and is indeed more than real with regard to the ecosystem it built and the economic effects it is having. During the last decade, many new businesses have started thanks to the Internet, and it was soon realized that Internet markets are often characterized by a 'winner takes all' mentality, where the best performer takes the majority of the business in the market, leaving very little space for competitors. This can easily be seen by looking at search engines, social networks, e-commerce platforms, and so on.

To benefit from the online world an Internet connection is needed; thus, consumers pay Internet service providers for having the connection, which passes through an infrastructure. Once this is done, the door to services and products offered on the World Wide Web is open. This is at the basis of the main discussion between telecommunications companies and OTT companies. The latter are represented by firms having built, or recreated, their business by offering services and products online, such as Skype, Apple, Google, Facebook, and Amazon.

European telecommunications companies (telcos) claim that the Internet access service they provide is an essential element at the very base of OTT businesses, as these OTT firms could not exist without providers offering Internet access to users; however, their businesses are less regulated and have fewer obligations. Moreover, OTTs are offering services such as voice, TV content, and instant messaging, directly competing with those traditionally offered by telcos through their electronic communications networks. This leads to the question of whether the perceived difference in regulatory levels alters the necessary level playing field among competitors.

This is also related to another important aspect of the general European digital debate: all major OTT companies are based outside of Europe (mainly in the US), and the old continent appears unable to keep pace with what is happening beyond its borders. The debate between OTTs and telecommunications operators has a strong impact on network investments, as the latter are facing reductions in revenues and are hardly stimulated in investing in new network capacity as long as investments are perceived as further favoring only OTTs.

Another key issue in the debate between OTTs and European telcos is net neutrality. According to this principle, all traffic shall be treated equally, following a best-effort principle that there shall not be discrimination and/or different price charges among users, content, sites, platforms, applications, equipment, etc. In the spring of 2014, the European Parliament voted for a net neutrality proposal that emphasizes equal treatment. European operators are strongly opposed to this position, as they see the possibility of negotiating agreements with OTTs and content providers for privileged fast-track lanes as a way to recoup their present losses and consequently restart investment in network infrastructures.

The main currency of the Internet ecosystem is data. Apple, Google, Facebook, and Amazon, to name just a few, are collecting an enormous amount of user data, which is a large – possibly even decisive – component of their present economic power. Thanks to these big datasets, these companies can profile users, consequently enhancing their services and, above all, attracting advertisers by offering profiled/behavioral advertising. The current European data protection framework dates back to 1995 and precedes recent technological developments. A new data protection framework, which is strongly based on users' consent, is now under discussion (European Commission, 2012).

Another relevant aspect of the present debate is online copyright. As always, the challenge is to maintain a balance between protecting the rights of the authors and promoting creativity and innovation. Because of the very structure of the Internet, which is characterized by openness and digitization, it is quite easy to copy, at low/zero price, any kind of digital work. Rights enforcement is complicated by the fact that content can be put on the Web from anywhere, subverting traditional national copyright law enforcement (and the difficulties appear from the very beginning, as even copyright itself can be defined differently). This is the rationale behind the intervention of the European legislator in 2001 with the Information Society Copyright Directive (European Parliament and Council, 2001) that focuses on online copyright and aims at establishing a 'harmonized legal framework on copyright and related rights, through increased legal certainty and while providing for a high level of protection of intellectual property' (Recital 4). This directive was followed by the 2008 Green Paper on copyright in the knowledge economy (European Commission, 2008) and the 2009 Communication on Copyright in the Knowledge Economy (European Commission, 2009a). However, online copyright is still an extremely hot and largely unresolved topic that remains very difficult to tackle at both the national and the EU level. We are still witnessing diverging approaches from different member states, and the lack of an effectively unifying EU dimension. As the debate continues, it appears that the issue can be solved only with a global coordinated approach.

To conclude, regulation with regard to the Internet is related to general economic aspects regarding investment resources and the management of the networks, but also to apparently more principled aspects such as data protection, security and freedom of expression. The Internet has definitely revolutionized the electronic communications sector, and the issue now is whether there should be a common level playing field between all the different actors of the Internet scene, and, if so, how to achieve it.

The future of regulation

In the last 25 years in Europe, we have experienced radical changes in the electronic communications sector. This has mainly been due to liberalization of the market – and the consequent competition-oriented regulatory intervention – and to the explosion of the Internet. In a sense, the electronic communications market faced a twist of fate since, once it was almost approaching a new equilibrium, the Internet revolution arrived and reshuffled the dynamics. Furthermore, it is interesting, and also somewhat paradoxical, to note that at the very same moment in which demand for communications services in general is booming, many telecommunications companies are facing a serious crisis.

Looking at what could happen in the near future, there are a series of issues at the core of the current debate that appear to be fundamental for moving forward in the European ICT world, such as the Connected Continent proposal; complementarity/convergence between fixed and mobile broadband; convergence between telecommunications and media; network security; data protection; industry consolidation; and cross-sectorial regulation.

The 2013 proposal for a new Regulation on Connected Continent is an effort by the EC to keep pace with the rapid technological developments, and to tackle US dominance over the Internet. For the moment, it looks more like a revision of the existing framework than a complete revolution; however, the numerous critical reactions to the proposal may have convinced the Commission that a more radical approach is necessary. As an example, in light of the specific goal of moving toward a European single market and, more generally, the acceleration of harmonization, it might be time to enhance the power of BEREC and, perhaps, create a fully-fledged single European regulator.

Another aspect that currently characterizes the sector is the complementarity and convergence between fixed and mobile broadband. Indeed, it seems that mobile is currently giving access to the Internet in those geographic areas where fixed broadband penetration is absent. Looking at this in more general terms, in the future the growth of mobile traffic will certainly require an increase in the support given by fixed broadband. Convergence between fixed and mobile broadband might also represent an advantage for consumers, as they can use services regardless of the type of network (OECD, 2012). Will we retain the distinction between the two in the future? How rapidly will this require a unique fixed/mobile regulatory framework?

Convergence between telecommunications and media is another big issue. While in the past networks delivered single services, the same network is now delivering many different ones (such as broadband transmitted over cable TV networks). However, the media sector has a different regulatory tradition than that of the telecommunications industry. The need for a degree of coordination between regulatory intervention in the two sectors has already been perceived,[5] but is loose coordination sufficient? Are we going in the direction of a regulatory convergence between the two sectors? Some national regulatory authorities have already converged. Should this be a mandatory solution for all media and telecommunications NRAs? At a deeper level, is it time to reunify the existing specific and *ad hoc* media regulations within the general realm of European electronic communication regulation? Are member states – always reluctant to relinquish traditional powers, of which media supervision is one – willing to allow this to happen in the primary interest of the European industries and consumers?

Security is another crucial aspect of the debate. Our habits depend increasingly on what can be done on the Web using a net connection. Thus, the stability of network and information systems is becoming crucial (be it for online shopping or for smart energy management). Indeed, security is a turning point in order to reach many of the EU 2020 goals, and, more generally, it is critical, considering the global tendency to conduct greater amounts of our daily activity online. The 2013 proposal for a directive aiming at introducing a common level of network and information security, in the context of a European cybersecurity strategy, is a first step forward (European Commission, 2013b).

Additionally, data protection is another key element of the debate as many OTTs have built highly successful business models on the foundation of collecting user data and profiling users, with the ultimate goal of attracting advertisers. The data debate is very animated in Europe, especially because OTTs, which are non-European companies, collect massive amounts of data from European residents. A new data protection regulation should be approved soon. This instrument will introduce stricter rules and is pivotal on the issue of (real) consensus by the data subject, with precise rules in case of infringements. It will be interesting to note whether this Regulation will efficiently achieve the aim of protecting the rights of the users while at the same time improving business opportunities in the digital market. The recent EU Court of Justice's Google Spain ruling (Court of Justice of the European Union, 2014) can be seen as a turning point in the debate as it imposes on digital non-European companies the obligation to act differently (granting the right to be forgotten) in respect to European residents.

Industry consolidation in Europe, as has already been mentioned, seems to represent another important element of the picture. The aim of liberalization was to achieve a competition-driven market. Once the market was open, regulatory intervention was set up around the final aim of competition, and thus focused on the control of market power with the introduction of the SMP concept and regulation. Nowadays, a better balance between competition and consolidation could be seen as a possible solution to tackle the crisis in the electronic communications sector and the perceived lack of investment in NGNs. European operators are currently working on a smaller scale compared to US ones, and consolidation would allow them to enlarge and consequently be in a better position to compete and eventually to invest again. But should we accept more consolidation at the price of less competition, and should consolidation be at a national or a European level? Consolidation in light of a European single market might be more forward looking, as the very fact of having fewer operators might make Europe more competitive on the international scene. On the other hand, this would represent a bigger revolution in the traditional competition approach and would probably require a European regulator, or at least a much stronger capability of coordination and harmonization between NRAs' actions than we have observed in the past.

Finally, it is important to mention that the telecommunications sector is closely related to the transport and energy sectors, especially with regard to the push for smart cities – traffic monitoring and smart grids being just two examples. In light of this infrastructure convergence, efficient cross-sectorial regulatory coordination seems to be needed and could become a key topic in the future, possibly suggesting a process of convergence/merging regulatory authorities, as has already begun in countries such as the Netherlands and Spain.

Conclusion

The electronic communications sector is facing a very delicate phase, and this is probably due to the coexistence of different problematic issues (the end of the raison d'être of most of the current regulatory framework, the rise of the Internet and of OTTs, and the prolonged financial crisis). It can be reasonably said that EU regulation has effectively overcome so many important issues that it might even seem that it is no longer needed. Nevertheless, there are still some old, and many new, items to be tackled. In the fixed network segment in Europe, while the problems of access and interconnection have been solved, we are now facing a serious issue regarding low investment in NGNs. Interconnection and roaming appear, at this point, to be stories of success with regard to mobile networks, but adequate spectrum capability is still a fundamental issue that needs a smart and efficient solution. Finally, the Internet revolution is raising important issues on the need for a level playing field among traditional and new players, and has highlighted many new themes related to the trust users have in the networks, such as data protection and security.

For all these reasons, the time is ripe for a new regulatory 'shock' in the electronic communications sector. We see the need for deep-reaching reform that disrupts the existing situation and reshuffles the current regulatory picture. Exactly as was the case with liberalization in the 1990s and with the telecoms package in the 2000s, we perceive the need for major change. The difficulty is that the complexity and the novelty of the issues may call for the contemporaneous adoption of two opposite policy stances; we may have to blend deregulation with new regulation, which is not an easy task. Nevertheless, today the complex, sophisticated, and generally successful regulatory construction of the EU in the electronic communications sector is called to evolve with the same rapid pace at which the world digital industry is dramatically changing.

Notes

1 The sense of the change was originally explained in the 1987 Green Paper on the development of the common market for telecommunications services and equipment COM(87)2 290, and realized and refined by subsequent legislative interventions.
2 An exemption is first-generation mobile licenses that were sometimes granted for free to incumbents. With the introduction (and growth) of second-generation digital networks, competition was introduced early on all over the EU.
3 The European approach diverges from the one applied in the US, which is the receiving party network pays (RPNP), wherein the receiving operator pays a fee to the calling operator and when, by consequence, it is up to the receiving party to pay the cost for the terminating part of the call. In this case, regulatory intervention is less crucial and termination costs remain low, being controlled by the interest of the user that chooses its own operator.
4 Nonetheless, European countries, through their administrations, have a long history of coordination and alignment of radio spectrum use through the International Telecommunications Union (ITU) at global level and the European Conference of Postal and Telecommunications Administration (CEPT) at regional level.
5 As a matter of example, Recital 5 of the electronic communications framework, which does not regulate content, states that 'The separation between the regulation of transmission and the regulation of content does not prejudice the taking into account of the links existing between them, in particular in order to guarantee media pluralism, cultural diversity and consumer protection.'

References

BEREC (2010) Common Statement on Next Generation Networks Future Charging Mechanisms/Long Term Termination Issues, available at: www.berec.europa.eu/eng/document_register/subject_matter/berec/public_consultations/177-berec-common-statement-on-next-generation-networks-future-charging-mechanisms-long-term-termination-issues (accessed on 22 September 2015).

Cave, M. (2006) Encouraging Infrastructure via the Ladder of Investments, *Telecommunications Policy*. Volume 30, Issues 3–4, April–May 2006, 223–237.

Cave, M. and Vogelsang, I. (2003) How Access Pricing and Entry Interact, *Telecommunications Policy*. Volume 27, Issues 10–11, November–December 2003, pp. 717–727.

Council of the European Union (1990), Directive 90/387/EEC on the establishment of the internal market for telecommunications services through the implementation of open network provision, available at: http://eur-lex.europa.eu/legal-content/EN/TXT/?uri=CELEX:31990L0387 (accessed on 18 May 2015).

Court of Justice of the European Union (2014) C-131/12, Google Spain SL and Google Inc. v Agencia Española de Protección de Datos (AEPD) and Mario Costeja González, 13 May 2014, available at http://curia.europa.eu/juris/document/document_print.jsf?doclang=EN&docid=152065 (accessed on 18 May 2015).

European Commission (1987) Green Paper on the development of the common market for telecommunications services and equipment, COM(87)2 290, available at: http://ec.europa.eu/green-papers/pdf/green_paper_telecom_services__common_market_com_87_290.pdf (accessed on 18 May 2015).

European Commission (1996) Directive 96/19/EC amending Directive 90/388/EEC with regard to the implementation of full competition in telecommunications markets, available at: http://eur-lex.europa.eu/legal-content/EN/TXT/?uri=CELEX:31996L0019 (accessed on 18 May 2015).

European Commission (1998) Green Paper COM (1998) 596 on radio spectrum policy, available at http://europa.eu/documents/comm/green_papers/pdf/com98_596.pdf (accessed on 18 May 2015).

European Commission (2002) Decision 676/2002/EC on a regulatory framework for radio spectrum policy in the European community, available at: http://eur-lex.europa.eu/legal-content/EN/TXT/?uri=celex:32002D0676 (accessed on 18 May 2015).

European Commission (2008) Green Paper COM (2008) 466 on copyright in the knowledge economy, available at: http://eur-lex.europa.eu/legal-content/EN/ALL/?uri=CELEX:52008DC0466 (accessed on 18 May 2015).

European Commission (2009a) Communication COM (2009) 532 on copyright in the knowledge economy, available at: http://ec.europa.eu/internal_market/copyright/docs/copyright-infso/20091019_532_en.pdf (accessed on 18 May 2015).

European Commission (2009b) Recommendation 2009/396/EC on the Regulatory Treatment of Fixed and Mobile Termination Rates in the EU, available at: http://eur-lex.europa.eu/legal-content/EN/TXT/?uri=CELEX:32009H0396 (accessed on 18 May 2015).

European Commission (2010) Recommendation 2010/572/EU on regulated access to NGA networks, available at: http://eur-lex.europa.eu/legal-content/EN/TXT/?uri=celex:32010H0572 (accessed on 18 May 2015).

European Commission (2012) Proposal COM (2012) 11 for a Regulation of the European Parliament and of the Council on the protection of individuals with regard to the processing of personal data and on the free movement of such data (General Data Protection Regulation), available at: http://eur-lex.europa.eu/legal-content/en/ALL/?uri=CELEX:52012PC0011 (accessed on 18 May 2015).

European Commission (2013) Recommendation 2013/466/EU on consistent non-discrimination obligations and costing methodologies to promote competition and enhance the broadband investment environment, available at: http://eur-lex.europa.eu/legal-content/EN/TXT/?uri=CELEX:32013H0466 (accessed on 18 May 2015).

European Commission (2013a) Proposal COM (2013) 627 for a Regulation laying down measures concerning the European single market for electronic communications and to achieve a Connected Continent, and amending Directives 2002/20/EC, 2002/21/EC and 2002/22/EC and Regulations (EC) No. 1211/2009 and (EU) No. 531/2012, available at: http://eur-lex.europa.eu/legal-content/EN/TXT/?uri=celex:52013PC0627 (accessed 18 May 2015).

European Commission (2013b) Proposal COM (2013) 48 for a Directive concerning measures to ensure a high common level of network and information security across the Union, available at: http://eur-lex.europa.eu/legal-content/EN/TXT/?uri=celex:52013PC0048 (accessed on 18 May 2015).

European Commission (2014) Staff Working Document on Implementation of the EU regulatory framework for Electronic Communications, available at: http://ec.europa.eu/digital-agenda/en/news/2014-report-implementation-eu-regulatory-framework-electronic-communications (accessed on 18 May 2015).

European Parliament and Council (1997) Directive 97/13/EC on a common framework for general authorizations and individual licences in the field of telecommunications services, available at: http://eur-lex.europa.eu/legal-content/EN/TXT/?uri=CELEX:31997L0013 (accessed on 18 May 2015).

European Parliament and Council (1997) Directive 97/66/EC concerning the processing of personal data and the protection of privacy in the telecommunications sector, available at: http://eur-lex.europa.eu/legal-content/EN/TXT/?uri=CELEX:31997L0066 (accessed on 18 May 2015).

European Parliament and Council (1999) Directive 1999/5/EC on radio equipment and telecommunications terminal equipment and the mutual recognition of their conformity, available at: http://eur-lex.europa.eu/legal-content/EN/TXT/HTML/?uri=CELEX:31999L0005&from=EN (accessed on 18 May 2015).

European Parliament and Council (2000) Regulation (EC) No 2887/2000 on unbundled access to the local loop, available at: http://eur-lex.europa.eu/LexUriServ/LexUriServ.do?uri=CELEX:32000R2887:EN:HTML (accessed on 18 May 2015).

European Parliament and Council (2001) Directive 2001/29/EC on the harmonisation of certain aspects of copyright and related rights in the information society, available at: http://eur-lex.europa.eu/legal-content/EN/TXT/?uri=celex:32001L0029 (accessed on 18 May 2015).

European Parliament and Council (2002a) Directive 2002/21/EC on a common regulatory framework for electronic communications networks and services (Framework Directive), available at: http://eur-lex.europa.eu/legal-content/EN/ALL/?uri=CELEX:32002L0021 (accessed on 18 May 2015).

European Parliament and Council (2002b) Directive 2002/20/EC on the authorisation of electronic communications networks and services (Authorisation Directive), available at: http://eur-lex.europa.eu/legal-content/EN/ALL/?uri=CELEX:32002L0020 (accessed on 18 May 2015).

European Parliament and Council (2002c) Directive 2002/19/EC on access to, and interconnection of, electronic communications networks and associated facilities (Access Directive), available at: http://eur-lex.europa.eu/legal-content/EN/ALL/?uri=CELEX:32002L0019 (accessed on 18 May 2015).

European Parliament and Council (2002d) Directive 2002/22/EC on universal service and users' rights relating to electronic communications networks and services (Universal Service Directive), available at: http://eur-lex.europa.eu/legal-content/EN/ALL/?uri=CELEX:32002L0022 (accessed on 18 May 2015).

European Parliament and Council (2002e) Directive 2002/58/EC concerning the processing of personal data and the protection of privacy in the electronic communications sector (Directive on privacy and electronic communications), available at: http://eur-lex.europa.eu/legal-content/EN/ALL/?uri=CELEX:32002L0058 (accessed on 18 May 2015).

European Parliament and Council (2007) Regulation (EC) No 717/2007 on roaming on public mobile telephone networks within the Community and amending Directive 2002/21/EC, available at: http://eur-lex.europa.eu/legal-content/EN/TXT/?uri=celex:32007R0717 (accessed on 18 May 2015).

European Parliament and Council (2009a) Regulation (EC) No 1211/2009 establishing the Body of European Regulators for Electronic Communications (BEREC) and the Office, available at: http://eur-lex.europa.eu/legal-content/EN/ALL/?uri=CELEX:32009R1211 (accessed on 18 May 2015).

European Parliament and Council (2009b) Directive 2009/140/EC amending Directives 2002/21/EC on a common regulatory framework for electronic communications networks and services, 2002/19/EC on access to, and interconnection of, electronic communications networks and associated facilities, and 2002/20/EC on the authorisation of electronic communications networks and services, available at: http://eur-lex.europa.eu/legal-content/EN/ALL/?uri=CELEX:32009L0140 (accessed on 18 May 2015).

European Parliament and Council (2009c) Directive 2009/136/EC amending Directive 2002/22/EC on universal service and users' rights relating to electronic communications networks and services, Directive 2002/58/EC concerning the processing of personal data and the protection of privacy in the electronic communications sector and Regulation (EC) No 2006/2004 on cooperation between national authorities responsible for the enforcement of consumer protection laws, available at: http://eur-lex.europa.eu/legal-content/EN/TXT/?uri=celex:32009L0136 (accessed on 18 May 2015).

European Parliament and Council (2010) Directive 2010/13/EU on the coordination of certain provisions laid down by law, regulation or administrative action in Member States concerning the provision of audiovisual media services (Audiovisual Media Services Directive), available at: http://eur-lex.europa.eu/legal-content/EN/ALL/?uri=CELEX:32010L0013 (accessed on 18 May 2015).

OECD (2012) Fixed and Mobile Networks: Substitution, Complementarity and Convergence, OECD Digital Economy Papers, No. 206. Paris: OECD Publishing.

Parcu, P.L. and Silvestri, V. (2014) Electronic communications regulation in Europe: An overview of past and future problems, *Utilities Policy*, 31, 246–255.

RSPG (2013) Opinion on Licensed Shared Access, available at: https://circabc.europa.eu/d/d/workspace/SpacesStore/3958ecef-c25e-4e4f-8e3b-469d1db6bc07/RSPG13-538_RSPG-Opinion-on-LSA%20.pdf (accessed on 18 May 2015).

12

Policy and regulations in the postal sector

Fumitoshi Mizutani, Shuji Uranishi, Eri Nakamura and Christian Jaag

Introduction

This chapter discusses policy and regulatory aspects of the postal sector. The postal sector is undergoing significant changes, which are not only caused by technological progress. Whereas postal services have been traditionally provided by a monopolist, the sector has continued to be increasingly liberalized in recent years, and competition to the incumbent postal operator could still evolve. In the recent past, the discussion mainly focused on arguments concerning liberalization and sector-specific de- or re-regulation, especially regarding universal service obligations (USOs). In the present, the risks and opportunities for postal operators in the digital age have become the main issues for academics, policymakers, and regulators.

The market equilibrium in the postal sector is determined by regulatory policies in two major domains. On the one hand, market regulation aims to ensure fair and effective competition. On the other, USOs aim to ensure the provision of quality postal services to the entire population in all regions of a country.

The remainder of this chapter consists of four sections. The second section summarizes postal policy perspectives in the European Union (EU) and across the world. This section also concerns the movement toward liberalization of postal services, which has garnered much attention in recent years in many countries. We will give historical reasons for governments' decisions to pursue liberalization. The third section highlights various aspects of postal regulations in general. The fourth section discusses aspects of the scope and financing of postal USOs. The chapter concludes with an outlook on future postal-sector policy.

Postal-sector policy

In recent years, the postal sector has been liberalized in many countries around the world. Liberalization efforts began with the reduction of the reserved areas; namely, the weight or price threshold below which the incumbent postal operator maintains a monopoly. Such efforts have ranged from relatively minor upstream changes, as in the US, all the way to complete removal of reserved areas, as in the EU (Crew and Kleindorfer, 2011).

European perspectives on policy and liberalization

In the second half of the twentieth century, postal-sector policy in Europe was strongly influenced by the economic and political integration process. The main objective of postal policy in the EU is to establish a single market for postal services and ensure a high-quality universal postal service. The policy objectives for postal services have been pursued by opening up the sector to competition in a gradual way. The objectives were implemented in community law through a Framework Postal Directive in 1997, which established regulatory guidelines for European postal services (Directive 97/67/EC). The Postal Directive governs a series of aspects of postal markets and obligations for the universal service provider (USP). It defines the minimum characteristics of the USO to be guaranteed by each member state (within their territory); sets common limits for services that may be reserved for the USP in each member state, and a timetable for further liberalization; lays down the principles that govern the authorization/licensing of non-reserved services; defines the pricing principles applicable to the USO, as well as the transparency of the accounts of USPs; governs the quality of service standards for national and cross-border services; and requires the creation of national regulatory authorities independent of the postal operators. Within the framework of the Postal Directive, member states have considerable freedom in adopting country-specific postal policies (see Trinkner, 2009).

In 2002, the European Parliament and the Council adopted the Second Postal Directive (2002/39/EC), which amended the initial Postal Directive by defining further steps in the process of market opening, and by further limiting the services that can be reserved. Reserved areas are only allowed to safeguard the USOs. According to the new Directive, member states must open to competition items of correspondence weighing less than 100 grams and costing less than three times the basic tariff as of January 1, 2003 (approximately 9 percent of the market), and items weighing less than 50 grams and costing less than two-and-a-half times the basic tariff as of January 1, 2006 (approximately an additional 7 percent of the market). In addition, all outgoing cross-border mail has been open to competition since January 1, 2003 (approximately an additional 3 percent of the market opening to competition) (see Okholm *et al.*, 2010).

In 2008, the European Parliament and the Council adopted Directive 2008/06/EC, which amended the initial Postal Directive 97/67/EC as amended by Directive 2002/39/EC. According to this latest amendment, member states must have abolished any remaining reserved areas by the end of 2010, with the possibility for 11 member states to postpone full market opening by two more years at most.

Ambrosini *et al.* (2011) described the evolution of price regulation in the three Postal Directives as follows: Article 12 of the First Postal Directive (97/67/EC) stated that prices must be affordable, geared to costs, transparent, and non-discriminatory. It also proposed a uniform tariff throughout the national territory, although agreements with individual customers are possible. Article 1 of the Second Postal Directive (2002/39/EC) clarified the scope of price regulation, specifying that these prices: 'shall take into account avoided costs with the standard services covering the complete range of features offered for the clearance, transport, sorting and delivery of individual postal items'. Such pricing linked to avoided costs bounded two market segments (single-item and bulk), which had different demand characteristics (such as price elasticity), and therefore limited the ability for postal operators to compete on a level playing field (see Billette de Villemeur *et al.*, 2008). The Third Postal Directive loosened the avoided cost constraints on pricing; only the preamble now refers to this principle. Nevertheless, postal operators' price setting in all EU countries is restricted to at least USO products, and is likely to remain this way in the foreseeable future.

Non-European perspectives on policy and regulation

Variations have been observed in the liberalization of postal services among other countries. Two important factors are ownership and competition. Provision by the private sector through privatization is rather oriented towards productive efficiency, and it is necessary to introduce competition in situations where monopolistic organizations exist. The general trend in liberalization is toward privatization and competition, with the UK and Germany in the vanguard. Although Japan Post was ostensibly privatized in 2005, privatization is not yet complete because ownership of the organization remains in the public sector.

In the US, prior to 1971, the government provided postal services through its US Post Office Department, an agency that received heavy subsidies from Congress. The Postal Reorganization Act of 1970 transformed the Post Office Department into the United States Postal Service (USPS), which had increased authority over its own operations. USPS is now an independent agency of the executive branch, and is designed to be financially self-sufficient, relying on the sale of its products and services for revenue. USPS is required by law to cover its own costs, but can borrow from the US Treasury. Its basic function is still to provide postal services to bind the nation together through the personal, educational, literary, and business correspondence of the people. USPS is therefore mandated by Congress to provide the public with universal service, which includes uniform prices, access to services, and nationwide delivery six days per week.

In 2002, USPS published a transformation plan, which identified ways in which it could improve its service and control costs. Between 2003 and 2012, the volume of first-class mail fell by more than 20 percent, following decades of growth (see USPS, 2013). In December 2006, Congress passed the far-reaching Postal Accountability and Enhancement Act. This significantly changed how USPS operates and conducts business. In part, the Act provided new flexibility, particularly in competitive pricing for shipping services, enabling USPS to respond to dynamic market conditions and changing customer needs for packages.

Today, USPS still has a statutory monopoly on: (1) the delivery of ordinary letter mail, including addressed advertising mail (express services provided at premium rates are exempt from the monopoly); (2) delivery to residential mailboxes; (3) delivery to post-office boxes; and (4) household mailboxes. USPS does not have a monopoly on the delivery of periodicals, but the monopoly on mail gives it a de facto monopoly for the delivery of periodicals. As a federal organization, USPS benefits from numerous other privileges and is exempt from vehicle licensing requirements, sales tax, and local property tax.

Generally, regulations outside Europe are still heavier than in European countries. For example, there is no price regulation for competitive services in European countries, while there are still regulations for these in the US and Japan (prior approval in the US and subsequent reporting in Japan).

Finally, it is necessary to maintain the USOs, but procuring financial backing is problematic. While granting tax privileges is a financing method in Europe, this is not the case in non-European countries. In the US, borrowing and the right to issue bonds are permissible ways to finance the USOs, though these methods are used sparingly. Among various financing methods, a USO fund seems most reasonable.

Motivations for liberalization

In addition to the EU's general motivation for a single market, liberalization of the postal service was spurred by liberalization in other industries, notably air transportation, telecommunications, and energy (namely electricity and gas utility). Beginning in the early

1980s in the UK and the US was a move toward massive deregulation and privatization, which subsequently caught on worldwide, common trends being the privatization of state-owned corporations, the introduction of new regulation schemes such as incentive regulations (namely price-cap and yardstick regulation), the reduction or abolition of entry barriers, and the embracing of free competition to/in the market.

For several reasons, the postal service industry was a latecomer to liberalization, lagging about 10 years behind other public utilities industries, despite the increasingly urgent need for liberalization. The first reason was the clear necessity of integrating the postal service with other telecommunications tools, such as facsimile and the Internet. For example, according to Post and Parcel (2011), such integrated systems as E-Postbrief, run by Deutsche Post, and Digiposte, run by La Poste, have been in operation since 2010. Liberalization was also necessary because competition had severely increased against rivals, such as the private mail express services that proliferated in the 1980s. Furthermore, the traditional core business of the postal service industry – personal letters – was being supplanted in the 1990s by e-mail. Third, the decline in demand and the increase in the cost of postal services worsened managerial and financial situations. To solve these problems, national governments exhorted post offices to improve efficiency, ultimately leading to the liberalization of postal services through reforms in the post office, price setting, the introduction of competition, and other areas.

Sector-specific regulation

This section provides an overview of the main regulations and regulatory bodies related to postal services. As Table 12.1 shows, regulatory situations vary among countries.

First, as for entry regulations, while both the UK and the US have none, there are limitations on entry (through licensing or permission systems) in France, Germany, and Japan. There are differences in regulation only in services related to personal correspondence, such as letters. For parcel delivery services, there are no entry regulations at all.

Second, there is much variation in price regulation among countries, especially in non-competitive services. With no price regulation, the UK is the most liberalized country, while Germany and the US have stricter regulations: the price of non-competitive services must be approved by the regulator. Falling somewhere between are France and Japan, where price is not subject to strict limitations but must simply be reported in advance. For competitive service, there are no regulatory limitations except in the US, where price regulation is apparently still rather conservative.

Finally, Mizutani (2014) argued that the existence or non-existence of an independent regulator is an important factor affecting the fairness of judgment regarding incumbents and new entrants.

An important feature of postal service in Japan is that regulators and policymakers are one and the same – quite a different situation from that of many European countries and the US, where postal service regulators are separate from ministries (departments) involved in policymaking. In Japan, the government itself both creates and regulates policy, one reason being that competition in the postal service has not become fully open. The market itself is tightly limited to existing incumbent companies, and the idea of pursuing fair judgment from disinterested regulators has not taken hold in Japan.

The regulatory situation is more advanced in European countries such as the UK, France, and Germany, which have independent regulatory bodies, in compliance with Article 22 of Directive (97/67/EC), stipulating that the postal service in each country must maintain an independent regulatory body separate from the supervisory authority.

Table 12.1 Main regulations and regulatory bodies

Country		*UK*	*France*	*Germany*	*US*	*Japan*
Major Law		Postal Services Act (2011)	Postal Services and Electronic Communications Code	Postal Law (Postgesetz)	US Code (Title 39)	Postal Law
Entry reg.	Personal correspondence	None	License[a]	License[b]	None	Permission
	Parcel	None	None	None	None	None
Price reg.	Non-competitive services	None	Report in advance, Order of change and Suspension	Approval[c]	Approval[d]	Report in advance
	Competitive services	None	None	None	Approval[e]	Report after
Independent regulatory body		Yes	Yes	Yes	Yes	No
Regulator		Office of Communications (Ofcom)	Electronic Communications and Postal Regulation Authority (ARCEP)	Federal Network Agency for Electricity, Gas, Telecommunications, Post and Railway (BNetzA)	Postal Regulatory Commission (PRC)[f]	Ministry of Internal Affairs and Communication

Source: Ministry of Land, Infrastructure, Transport and Tourism (2003); Ministry of Internal Affairs and Communications (2012); Universal Postal Union, (2014); Ministry of Internal Affairs and Communications (2013a); OECD (2013); Bundesnetzagentur (2015); Royal Mail Group (2015).

Notes: (a) A license is not always necessary for domestic-only and non-delivery services; (b) a license is necessary for addressed letters (personal correspondence) of less than 1kg, and direct mail items; (c) prices should be approved for addressed letters (personal correspondence) of less than 1kg and direct mails. However, bulk mail with more than 50 items per unit is excluded; (d) the postal service may implement postage rate changes for market-dominant products, subject to a minimum of 45 days' advance review by the PRC, for consistency with the price cap and certain factors and objectives; (e) for competitive products, the Postal Service may implement competitive price changes on 15 days' notice for rates not of general applicability (negotiated service agreements) and on 30 days' advance notice for rates of general applicability, subject to filing with, and review by, the Commission; (f) the PRC is the regulator for USPS only, and private providers are excluded.

Universal service obligations

Universal service regulation intends to ensure the provision of quality postal services to the entire population in all regions of a country. Due to the strong influence of USOs on the postal sector, not only their scope but also their financing is a major aspect of postal-sector policy and regulation.

Definition and scope of universal service obligations

Although there is no concrete definition of 'universal service', there seems to be consensus about what it means. A report by the OECD (1991) defined universal service as having four components: universal geographical access, universal affordable access, universal service quality, and universal tariff.

For EU member states, the Postal Directive defines the minimum characteristics of the USOs as: (1) one collection from appropriate access points every working day; (2) one delivery to all addresses every working day; (3) including postal items and packages up to 20 kilograms; and (4) a service for registered items and insured items. The concrete specification and implementation is country-specific. Typical dimensions of postal USOs are displayed in Table 12.2.

Based on these ideas, the USOs can be characterized as the obligation of a provider to provide good-quality services to all users at uniform and affordable prices (Mizutani, 2012). In this section, we explain the characteristics of the USOs.

Table 12.3 shows an international comparison of the USO system for the postal service. It can be seen that selected countries have adopted similar approaches. Postal items to which the USOs apply are mainly letters, registered mail, guaranteed mail, and parcels. The postal tariff is applied at a flat rate nationwide.

Second, although the USOs are maintained in the postal service, a monopoly situation no longer remains. Competition is allowed in almost all fields of the service, except in the US, where the USO system appears to be conservative.

Third, although there are variations among countries in terms of the financial means for maintaining the USOs, there are four main sources: (1) tax privileges, (2) funds, (3) subsidies, and (4) loans. Obtained by exemption from value-added tax (VAT), tax privilege refers to a financing method used in European countries such as the UK, France, and Germany. Funds, used in France, Germany, and Japan, are another source for funding USOs, although there are slight differences among the countries as to who should contribute. For example, La Poste and new entrants contribute to the fund according to the amount of their sales. In Germany, organizations

Table 12.2 Dimensions of postal USOs

Product range	*Products and services covered by the USOs*
Coverage/accessibility	Requirements on where, when, and how these products are made available. Usually, services must be offered nationwide ("ubiquitous service") and be easily accessible.
Prices	Restrictions in pricing. For example, prices must be cost-oriented, affordable, uniform, or provide incentives for efficient service provision.
Quality	Minimum standards that must be met for USO products.
Infrastructure	Often, there are obligations to operate certain infrastructures, such as a certain number of post offices.

Table 12.3 The USO system in the postal service

Country	*UK*	*France*	*Germany*	*US*	*Japan*
Provider	Royal Mail	La Poste	Deutsche Post	USPS	Japan Post
Coverage business for USO	Postal service	Postal service	Postal service	Postal service	Postal service, banking, insurance[a]
Items for USO in postal service	Postal matters under 20 kg, registered mail, guaranteed mail[b]	Letters under 2 kg, newspapers, magazines under 2kg, parcels under 20 kg, registered mail, guaranteed mail	Letters under 2 kg (including registered mail, guaranteed mail, cash on delivery), parcels under 20 kg	Services provided by USPS	Postal items under 4 kg, registered mail, content-certified mail
Description of service standard[c]	Yes	Yes	Yes[d]	Yes	Yes
Competition field	All	All	All	All except monopoly field	All
Monopoly[e]	None (abolished in 2006)	None (abolished in 2011)	None (abolished in 2008)	Postal items with tariff lower than 6 times the standard tariff, and weighing less than 12.5 ounces (about 350 g), monopoly on postal receiving box	None (abolished in 2003)
Financial backing for the USO	Tax privilege: Exemption from VAT	Tax privilege: Exemption from VAT	Tax privilege: Exemption from VAT		
	Subsidies: Support from national government[f]	Subsidies: Support from national government[f]			
		Fund: Contribution to fund by each organization according to amount of sales[g]	Fund: Contribution to fund by each organization according to amount of sales[h]		Fund: A portion of Japan Post Holding company profits
				Others: Borrowing, issuing of bonds	

Source: Authors' own elaboration based on Mizutani (2012); the Ministry of Internal Affairs and Communications (2013a); the Ministry of Internal Affairs and Communications (2013b); ERGP (2012).

Notes: (a) According to the Ministry of Internal Affairs and Communications (2013b), the Postal Business Law was revised in 2012 to extend coverage of the USO to postal banking and postal insurance services; (b) Article 3.4 and Article 3.5 in the 1997 EU Postal Directives included different items to be covered by the USO. Here we follow Article 3.5, which stipulates that, at the discretion of individual countries, the minimum requirement be expanded to parcels under 20 kilograms; (c) For details of USO service standards, see Mizutani (2012); (d) According to information from the Universal Postal Union (2014), Deutsche Post currently provides all universal services nationwide without a formal legal obligation; (e) Before full liberalization, an exclusive reserve range had been approved in order to ensure financial sources for the USO in each country's postal service market. This exclusive reserve range remains in effect in, for example, the USPS. At the beginning of the EU Postal Directive in 1997, the exclusive reserve-range covered postal items with a tariff of less than five times the minimum tariff and less than 350 grams. Since then, the reserved area has shrunk, and it was decided in the EU Postal Directive in 2008 that it would be abolished by 2010 or (for some countries) by 2012; (f) According to the Ministry of Internal Affairs and Communications (2013a), subsidies in the UK and France are not used for the USO. However, as we consider them to be part of the USO, they are listed here; (g) La Poste and new entrants contribute to the fund according to the amount of their sales; (h) Organizations with annual sales of more than €500,000 contribute to the fund.

with annual sales of more than €500,000 contribute to the fund. In Japan, the fund is a portion of Japan Post Holding company profits. Subsidies from the national government can also support the obligations. In the US, borrowing and the right to issue bonds are also allowed as ways to finance the USOs, though these methods are used sparingly.

Finally, it is worth considering whether the USOs affect the corporate strategy of a postal service firm. The experience of Japan Post indicates that the USOs do indeed affect corporate strategy. For example, in Japan's postal privatization of 2007, the mail postal service and the postal office service were separated into different companies. However, in accordance with the definition of USOs, this was changed from 'provision of mail postal service only' to 'provision of mail postal service, postal banking and postal insurance'. As a result, these three services (mail postal service, postal banking, and postal insurance) came to be provided by the Japan Post Company as USO services. Furthermore, when the Japanese government reviewed the range of the special personal correspondence mail service (*Tokutei Shinshobin*) in 2014, the government set up the condition that the companies' expanding competition would not hurt the USO provision. Thus, the existence of the USOs clearly imposes restraints on corporate postal strategies, although the extent to which it does so is unclear.

The cost of universal service obligations

Regarding calculation methods of the cost of the USO, in general, four kinds of approaches have been used in industrial countries since 2000: (1) the deficit approach; (2) the net avoidable cost approach (NAC); (3) entry pricing (EP); and (4) the profitability cost (PC) approach. Each approach defines the cost of USOs differently.

Deficit approach

In the deficit approach, the deficits in postal service that a provider must supply are defined as the USO cost.

The advantage of this approach is that it is easily calculated, and counterfactual assumptions are not necessary because the approach can use actual financial data from providers of the postal service. The disadvantage is that we cannot judge whether the cost of USOs measured is the cost yield under the condition of the most efficient management by the provider. If the cost of USOs is approved without factual observation of the situation, the cost of USOs may include inefficiency.

Net avoidable cost approach

In the NAC approach, USO costs are defined as those that a provider need not incur if it does not provide services; that is, costs created in unprofitable areas (or services). This approach was originally developed for calculation of USO costs in the telecommunications industry. It was further developed by Elsenbast *et al.* (1995a, 1995b) with the aim of applying it to the postal service industry (see Maruyama, 2002).[1]

As an example, USO costs according to the NAC approach are shown in Figure 12.1, where the unit cost per postal item in a given area is arranged from lowest to highest on the horizontal axis. This shows that the unit cost per postal item delivered is increasing. The difference between the unit cost and the uniform tariff (the shaded areas in this figure) are the USO costs.

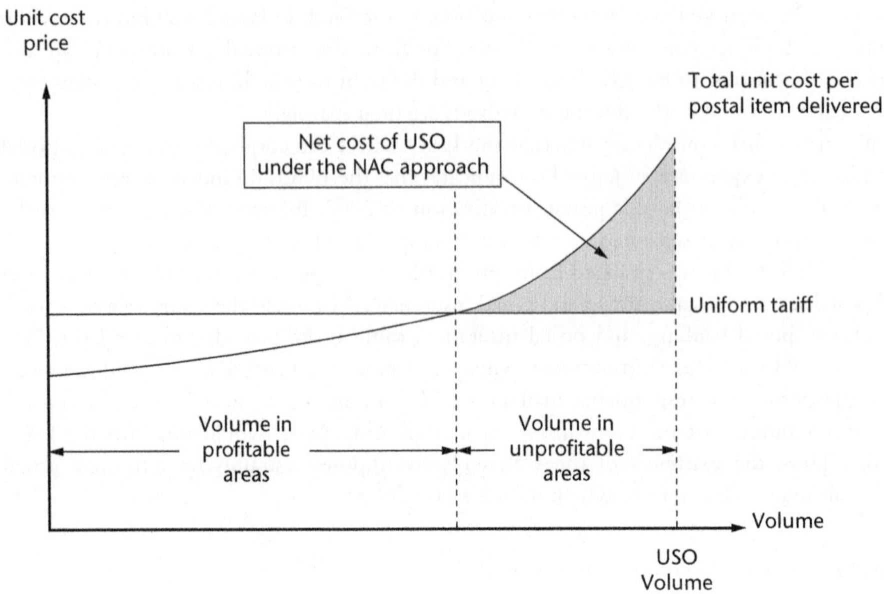

Figure 12.1 USO costs under the NAC approach

Source: Authors' own elaboration based on Frontier Economics (2013) (see also Jaag and Trinkner (2011a); Jaag (2013) for the same argument).

The calculated USO cost in this approach largely depends on the size of the delivery routes (or areas). If it is difficult to obtain information on delivery routes/areas, then their unit size will necessarily be manifested as large, resulting in underestimation of the USO cost.

Entry pricing approach

The USO cost obtained by the EP approach is defined as the reduction of profit of the incumbent postal service provider caused by competition from new entrants.

The EP approach makes certain assumptions. First, the USO is applied to an incumbent postal service provider. Second, the incumbent postal service provider maintains services financially by cross-subsidizing from profitable to unprofitable services under a uniform tariff. Third, a new entrant sets up variable pricing that is lower than the uniform tariff of the incumbent, and enters only postal service markets where the incumbent price is higher than its own ('cream-skimming entry').

The EP approach has the advantage of recognizing the necessary USO costs under competitive circumstances, as it makes assumptions regarding competition in liberalized postal service markets. However, the USO costs estimated here would vary with the range of assumptions made about competitive environments.

Profitability cost approach

The PC approach defines the USO cost as the difference between the profitability level at which the USO is in effect, and the profitability level at which it is not.

In a liberalized postal service market, a postal service provider without USOs can cross-subsidize between profitable and unprofitable postal services, thereby reducing costs by lowering service standards in the unprofitable postal service and thus attaining profit maximization.

On the other hand, a postal service provider with USOs must provide services with a consistent service standard, even if services are not consistently profitable. Therefore, it is difficult for the provider with USOs to improve profitability, which remains lower than that of the provider without USOs.

If the provider with USOs can be guaranteed compensation for the profit difference (the difference between the profit with and without USOs), then it can attain the same profitability level even while subject to USOs. The PC approach measures this profitability difference as the USO net cost.

According to Cremer *et al.* (2000), the PC approach is considered as the most sophisticated approach to calculating the USO cost in a liberalized competitive postal market.

Figure 12.2 illustrates the entry pricing approach and the PC approach: the net cost according to the PC approach results from a comparison of profit levels π^3 and π^4, both of which assume a competitive market. The net cost calculation must not be confounded with the effect of increased competition (due to reduced legal barriers to entry) on the incumbent's profit (comparing π^1 and π^3) according to the entry pricing approach. The latter expresses the effect of a change in market entry regulation, rather than a change in regulation of USOs. Hence, the calculation of the net cost according to the PC approach takes into account the effect of removing USOs and associated changes in the competitive environment, while other regulations/parameters are maintained.

If USOs represent a burden on the USP, it should be compensated appropriately in order to guarantee a level playing field for competition. Increasing direct and indirect competition also increases the net cost of inefficient services and infrastructures due to USOs: for example, the obligation of delivering mail items daily may not be economically binding if mail volumes are high. However, in the presence of considerable fixed costs in delivery, a decrease in volume results in daily delivery becoming increasingly unattractive, and hence in an increasing net cost of USOs. Instead of increasing compensation, postal policy has started to adapt USOs to better align them with consumers' needs, and thereby alleviate the USOs' burden.

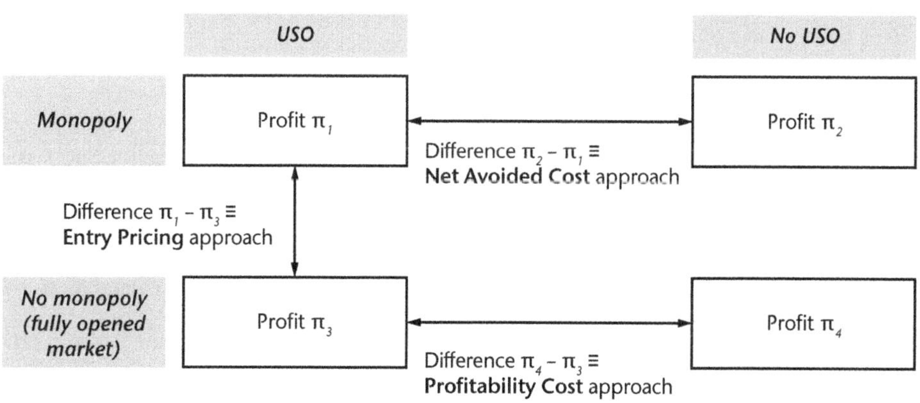

Figure 12.2 Calculating the net cost of the USO

Source: Jaag *et al.* (2009).

Conclusion and outlook

The postal sector has undergone significant change, mostly due to sector policy, but also as a result of electronic communication that has enabled e-substitution and e-commerce. The convergence between the postal and telecommunications sectors questions the EU member states' obligation to guarantee a specifically defined scope of universal service to all citizens. Regarding the developments and the spread of information and communication technologies (ICT), questions arise as to whether current regulation – especially USO – is still needed and desired by the customer in its current form. For example, Borsenberger (2014) argued that accessibility and proximity in connection with the USO should also contain a 'virtual' dimension regarding the progresses in ICT. She saw online services, which complement and extend physical postal services, as a solution to reduce economic and social costs of the USO. Jaag and Trinkner (2011b) took a similar path by presenting an outline for a future-oriented postal USO, which includes electronic complements and substitutes to traditional postal services. Their new USO concept combines old and new means to provide universal service and is based on the following five principles: output orientation, technological neutrality, product neutrality, necessity, and viability. In contrast to the current definition of the USO, this concept would allow USPs to adjust the universal service individually to the needs of their customers, to the portfolio of available products, and to the technological progress. Due to the convergence of postal and telecommunications markets, Jaag and Trinkner (2012) even proposed to establish an intermodal USO for postal and telecommunications services. Such an intermodal USO would consist of two basic services. The first is a physical delivery service for items of all kinds, meeting certain speed, reliability, affordability, and uniformity requirements. The second is a fast broadband service at an affordable, fixed rate. While the first service would require good accessibility and availability measured from the point of residence, the second would need to be available everywhere. In light of technological advances, especially in telecommunications, the convergence in communications' markets should also be reflected in converging, or sector-overlapping regulation.

Note

1 For estimation examples, see e.g. Castro and Maddock (1997) for Australia; National Economic Research Associates (1998) for 15 EU countries; Postcomm (2001) for Consignia data; Uranishi (2004, 2007) for Japan, and Mizutani and Uranishi (2006).

References

Ambrosini, X., Breville, S., Cornée, J. and Klargaard, O. (2011) Pricing strategies in regulated markets – Innovative pricing in the postal sector, *Competition and Regulation in Network Industries*, 12(1), 57–83.

Billette de Villemeur, E., Cremer, H., Boldron, F. and Roy, B. (2008) Worksharing: A calibrated model, *Review of Networks Economics*, 7(2), 272–293.

Borsenberger, C. (2014) Accessibility/proximity in the digital age: what does it mean for postal networks and postal services? in M.A. Crew and T.J. Brennan (eds) *The Role of the Postal and Delivery Sector in a Digital Age*. Cheltenham: Edward Elgar Publishing, pp. 267–279.

Bundesnetzagentur (2015) *Beschlusskammer 5*, available at http://www.bundesnetzagentur.de/cln_1421/DE/Service-Funktionen/Beschlusskammern/Beschlusskammer5/BK5_22_Entgeltregulierung/PreisregulierungNavNode.html (accessed on May 20, 2015).

Castro, M. and Maddock, R. (1997) The universal service obligation for post: Some Australian calculations, in M.A. Crew and P.R. Kleindorfer (eds) *Managing Change in the Postal and Delivery Industries*, Boston. MA: Kluwer Academic Publishers, pp. 258–269.

Cremer, H., Grimaud, A. and Laffont, J. (2000) The cost of universal service in the postal sector, in M.A. Crew and P.R. Kleindorfer (eds) *Current Directions in Postal Reform*. Boston, MA: Kluwer Academic Publishers, pp. 47–68.

Crew, M.A. and Kleindorfer, P.R. (2011) Liberalization in the postal and delivery sector, in M. Finger and R.W. Künneke (eds) *International Handbook of Network Industries: The liberalization of infrastructure*. Cheltenham: Edward Elgar Publishing, pp. 328–342.

Directive 97/67/EC of the European Parliament and of the Council of 15 December 1997 on common rules for the development of the internal market of community postal services and the improvement of quality of service, Brussels.

Directive 2002/39/EC of the European Parliament and of the Council of 10 June 2002 amending Directive 97/67/EC with regard to the further opening to competition of community postal services, Brussels.

Directive 2008/6/EC of the European Parliament and the Council of 20 February 2008 amending Directive 97/67/EC with regard to the full accomplishment of the internal market of community postal services, Brussels.

Elsenbast, W., Pieper, F. and Stumpf, U. (1995a) Estimating the universal service burden of public postal service, *Discussion Paper No. 150,* WIK, Bad Honnef.

Elsenbast, W., Pieper, F. and Stumpf, U. (1995b) *The Cost of Universal Obligation in a Competitive Environment*, Paper Presented at The Third Konigswinter Seminar on Postal and Delivery Economics, 6 - 8 November 1995, Konigswinter.

European Regulator Group for Postal Services (ERGP) (2012) ERGP report on net cost of USO – VAT exemption as a benefit or a burden, *ERGP,* 12(29), European Commission, Brussels, available at: http://ec.europa.eu/internal_market/ergp/documentation/documents/index_en.htm (accessed on September 25, 2014).

Frontier Economics (2013) *Study on the Principles used to Calculate the Net Costs of the Postal USO: A report for the European Commission*, Frontier Economics Ltd, London, available at: http://ec.europa.eu/internal_market/post/doc/studies/2012-net-costs-uso-postal_en.pdf (accessed on September 25, 2014).

Jaag, C. (2013) Price regulation and the financing of universal services in network industries, *Review of Law and Economics* 9(1), 125–150.

Jaag, C., Koller, M. and Trinkner, U. (2009) Calculating the cost of the USO – The need for a global approach, in M.A. Crew and P.R. Kleindorfer (eds) *Progress in the Competitive Agenda in the Postal and Delivery Sector.* Cheltenham: Edward Elgar Publishing, pp. 113–127.

Jaag, C. and Trinkner, U. (2011a) The interaction between universal service costing and financing in the postal sector: A calibrated approach, *Journal of Regulatory Economics*, 39(1), 89–110.

Jaag, C. and Trinkner, U. (2011b) The future of the USO – Economic rationale for universal services and implications for a future-oriented USO, *Working Paper 26, Swiss Economics*, Zurich.

Jaag, C. and Trinkner, U. (2012) Defining and financing an intermodal USO, *Working Paper 35, Swiss Economics*, Zurich.

Maruyama, S. (2002) Universal service obligation cost in postal service: Concept and measurement in foreign countries (Yubin no Yunibasaru Sabisu Kosuto: Kangaekata to Shogaikoku no Keisoku), *Institute for Posts and Telecommunications Policy Monthly Report (Yusei Kenkyusho Geppo)*, 161(2), 149–163 (in Japanese).

Ministry of Internal Affairs and Communications (2012) *Situations of Postal Fee (Yubin Ryokin no Genjyo nado ni Tsuite)*, available at: http://www.cao.go.jp/consumer/iinkai/2012/089/doc/089_120522_shiryou13-2.pdf (in Japanese, accessed on May 20, 2015).

Ministry of Internal Affairs and Communications (2013a) *Situations of Several Foreign Countries: Situations of the universal service obligations of postal services and introduction of entry competition of personal correspondence services in foreign countries (Shogaikoku no Jokyo: Shogaikoku no Yubin Jigyo no Yunibasaru Sabisu no Jokyo Oyobi Shinsyo Sotatsugyo heno Kyoso Dounyu no Jokyo)*, Ministry of Internal Affairs and Communications, Tokyo (in Japanese).

Ministry of Internal Affairs and Communications (2013b) *Current Situations and Background of the Universal Service Obligations of Postal Services (Yubin Jigyo no Yunibasaru Sabisu no Genjo to Keii)*, Ministry of Internal Affairs and Communications, Tokyo (in Japanese).

Ministry of Land, Infrastructure, Transport and Tourism (2003) *Situations of Truck Business (Truck Jigyou no Genjyo nado ni Tsuite)*, available at: http://www.mlit.go.jp/jidosha/whatsnew/low_track_gaiyo/track_syourei/track_syourei.htm (in Japanese, accessed on May 20, 2015).

Mizutani, F. (2012) *Regulatory Reform of Public Utilities: The Japanese Experience*. Cheltenham: Edward Elgar Publishing.

Mizutani, F. (2014) *Looking Beyond Europe with a Special Focus on Japan*, Discussion Paper, No. 2014–24, Graduate School of Business Administration, Kobe University.

Mizutani, F. and Uranishi, S. (2006) *Special Post Office, Privatization and Universal Service Obligation Costs*, Discussion Paper, No. 2006–05, Graduate School of Business Administration, Kobe University.

National Economic Research Associates (1998) Costing and financing of universal service obligations in the postal sector in the European Union, *Final Report for EC DH XIII*, available at: http://ec.europa.eu/internal_market/post/doc/studies/1998-nera_en.pdf (accessed on September 26, 2014).

Organisation for Economic Co-operation and Development (OECD) (2013) *OECD Indicators of Regulation in Non-Manufacturing Sectors (NMR)*, available at: http://www.oecd.org/eco/reform/Database_NMR_.xlsx (accessed May 20, 2015).

Okholm, H.B., Winiarczyk, M., Moller, A. and Nielsen, C. (2010) Main developments in the postal sector (2008–2010), *Report for European Commission*, DG Internal Market and Services, Copenhagen.

Organisation for Economic Co-operation and Development (OECD) (1991) *Universal Service and Rate Restructuring in Telecommunication Tariff*, OECD, Paris.

Post and Parcel (2011) La Poste Launches Digiposte Solution, *News, Views & Jobs for the Global Mail & Express Community*, March 3, 2011, available at: http://postandparcel.info/36736/news/la-poste-launches-digiposte-solution/ (accessed on September 20, 2014).

Postcomm (2001) An assessment of the costs and benefits of Consignia's current universal service provision, *A Discussion Document of Postcomm*, available at: http://stakeholders.ofcom.org.uk/binaries/post/508.pdf (accessed on September 26, 2014).

Royal Mail Group (2015) *Price Control*, available at: http://www.royalmailgroup.com/about-us/regulation/price-control (accessed on May 20, 2015).

Trinkner, U. (2009) Neue Postrichtlinie: Spielräume der Mitgliedstaaten bei der Umsetzung, Konsequenzen für den Binnenmarkt und Folgen für die Schweizer Postpolitik, in C. Baudenbacher (ed.) *Aktuelle Entwicklungen des Europäischen und Internationalen Wirtschaftsrechts*, Helbing und Lichtenhahn, Band XI, Basel, pp. 337–424 (in German).

Universal Postal Union (2014) *Status and Structures of Postal Entities*, Universal Postal Union, available at: http://www.upu.int/en/the-upu/status-of-postal-entities/about-status-of-postal-entities.html (accessed on September 9, 2014).

United States Postal Service (USPS) (2013) *Postal Facts 2013*, available at: http://about.usps.com/who-we-are/postal-facts/postalfacts2013.pdf (accessed on April 13, 2015).

Uranishi, S. (2004) Liberalization of postal service and maintaining universal service obligation: Estimation of providing costs (Yubin Jiyuka to Yunibasaru Sabisu Iji: Kyokyu Kosuto no Haaku), *Public Corporation (Koei Kigyo)*, 36(2), 2–9 (in Japanese).

Uranishi, S. (2007) Simulation of maintaining universal service obligation in postal service (Yubin Jigyo ni okeru Yunibasaru Sabisu Iji ni Kansuru Simyureshon), *Journal of Public Utility Economics (Koeki Jigyo Kenkyu)*, 59(2), 55–68 (in Japanese).

13

The future of electricity network regulation

The policy perspective

Michael G. Pollitt[1]

Introduction

Electricity networks consist of the transmission (high-voltage) and distribution (lower-voltage) transportation systems for taking power generated in large power stations to end-consumers. In a typical European country, network charges account for around 25 percent of the pre-tax price of residential electricity, with transmission and distribution charges accounting for roughly 5 percent and 20 percent, respectively.

In many countries, these networks consist of national or regional transmission monopolies that are connected to regional or local distribution monopolies. In some countries, transmission was historically integrated with distribution (such as within EDF in France), while in others transmission was integrated with generation (such as the CEGB in England and Wales). In most countries, distribution was integrated with retail supply (such as local distribution companies in the Netherlands or New Zealand). Electricity network asset ownership has traditionally been completely integrated into network operation (system operation).

However, there has recently been a considerable trend in transmission networks towards the creation of independent system operators (ISOs), such as PJM in the US, which exist separately from transmission asset owners (TOs). This is in contrast to transmission system operators (TSOs), such as the National Grid in Great Britain (GB), which continues to integrate transmission asset ownership and system operation (see Chawla and Pollitt, 2013). System operators can be thought of as platform providers that facilitate competition across their networks (in the same way as eBay or MasterCard facilitate competition between retailers across their platforms) for wholesale and retail energy services. As platform providers, they provide services in two-sided markets (in this case involving competing generators and competing retailers).[2]

The electricity transportation business involves the provision of network capacity to generators and to retailers. Transmission and distribution (T&D) systems predominantly consist of electrical wires (which can be on towers or poles, or underground) and associated transformers that step up or step down the voltages at which the electricity is transported. Electricity transported over long distances results in losses that are minimized at higher voltages; hence, electrical networks consist of relatively long-line segments at higher voltages and progressively shorter segments at lower voltages. Alternating current power networks give rise to the possibility of electricity flowing down multiple parallel pathways, subject to maximum flows of power on any given line. This gives rise to the possibility of running transmission networks with N-1 or N-2 security standards, meaning that if any 1 or 2 equivalent lines are congested or unavailable, power can still flow between the supply and demand points. At the lowest voltages of the distribution system, such redundancy does not exist. High voltage direct current power lines (such as those linking the UK and mainland Europe, or those crossing the US and China) are increasingly used for long-distance power links, as these involve lower electrical losses.

In common with most network industries, both transmission and distribution networks exhibit significant economies of scale, implying that actual competition in networks is not a cost-effective option. This has given rise to the network monopolies we see today in almost every country. Increasingly, these network monopolies have been separated from other parts of the electricity supply chain into separately regulated companies. Within the European Union (EU), the preferred model is for an ownership unbundled transmission monopoly, which both owns the assets and operates the transmission system, and for legally separate (from retail, transmission, and generation) distribution monopolies. However, in many countries, separate distribution network companies are being created (such as UKPN, which owns the electricity distribution network in London and much of the South and East of England), which are wholly separate from other parts of the electricity supply industry.

National (and sub-national) energy regulators (such as the Federal Energy Regulatory Commission and the state-level Public Utilities Commissions in the US) have responsibility for the economic regulation of transmission and distribution companies. Such economic regulation is usually most concerned with setting the overall revenue for the network companies and approving the charging methodology by which that revenue is recovered. In common with other aspects of the energy system, the policy goals for electricity networks are a combination of the achievement of decarbonization (that is, support for renewable generation and demand-side management (DSM) measures to reduce demand and match it to intermittent supply), the maintenance of energy security ('keeping the lights on'), and the delivery of affordability (an acceptable average level and distribution of the incidence of charges). These three policies represent the energy policy 'trilemma', where the achievement of two of the three objectives necessarily makes the third difficult to achieve.

This chapter discusses some of the challenges facing the future regulation of electricity network companies in light of the challenges of decarbonization and the attendant emphasis on renewable generation (which is often small scale), demand-side management, and the electrification of heat and transport. The chapter is divided into four sections. The first section examines some visions of the electrical future and their implications for network regulation. The second section considers the likely future interests of energy regulation. The third section looks at regulatory lessons from recent developments in Germany and New York State. Germany is interesting because it is a large country in which a very significant energy transition is taking place involving a substantial increase in distributed renewable generation. This transition has happened relatively quickly, straining the existing model of economic regulation of electricity networks. By contrast, the state of New York, which also has similar long-term ambitions for renewables, recently announced a major reform of its regulatory arrangements aimed at anticipating and promoting its energy transition. The final section offers some concluding thoughts.

Visions of the electrical future

Electrical networks have been largely designed to meet current demands on the electricity system, which involve matching supply and demand in real time with relatively small amounts of energy storage provided by pumped-storage hydro plants. Fleets of large fossil-fuel power plants (burning coal and gas) have been able to flexibly respond to fluctuating demands across the day, the week, and the season. Electrical networks have been largely passive mechanisms that have allowed this real-time balancing of supply and demand to take place. A key requirement on them has been the need to be sized to accommodate the annual peak demands on both transmission and distribution systems.

The future electricity network might evolve in very different ways, some of which would be radically different from today. In 2008 five network scenarios for a low-carbon future by 2050 in GB were produced for GB's energy regulator. They provide a useful starting point for our discussion of what future electricity network regulation might have to cope with. These five were:

> '**Big Transmission and Distribution**, in which transmission system operators (TSOs) are at the centre of network activity. Network infrastructure development and management continues as expected from today's patterns, while expanding to meet growing demand and the deployment of renewable generation.
>
> **Energy Service Companies**, in which energy service companies (ESCOs) are at the centre of developments in networks, doing all of the work at the customer side. Networks contract with such companies to supply network services.
>
> **Distribution System Operators**, in which distribution system operators (DSOs) take on a central role in managing the electricity system. Compared to today, distribution companies take much more responsibility for system management including generation and demand management, quality and security of supply, and system reliability, with much more distributed generation.
>
> **Microgrids**, in which customers are at the centre of activity in electricity networks. The self-sufficiency concept has developed very strongly in power and energy supplies. Electricity consumers take much more responsibility for managing their own energy supplies and demands. As a consequence, microgrid system operators (MSOs) emerge to provide the system management capability to enable customers to achieve this with the new technologies.
>
> **Multi Purpose Networks**, in which network companies at all levels respond to emerging policy and market requirements. TSOs still retain the central role in developing and managing networks but distribution companies also have a more significant role to play. The network is characterised by diversity in network development and management approaches.'
>
> Source: Ault *et al.*, 2008, Forward by Stuart Cook.

The two most sharply contrasting models are compared in Figure 13.1.

The 'Big Transmission and Distribution' scenario involves a much larger transmission (and distribution) network, which is capable of transporting larger amounts of power from the north and offshore to the load centers in the south (in and around London) from intermittent

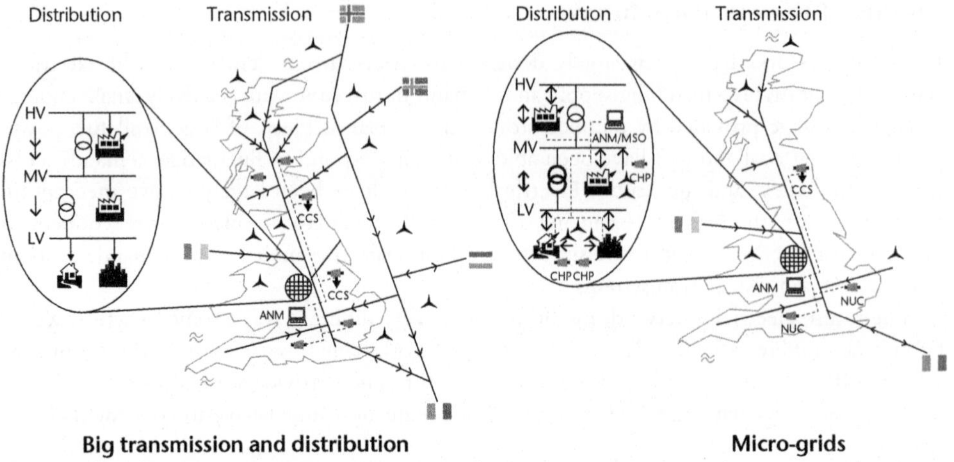

Figure 13.1 Two visions of the electrical future

Source: Ault *et al.*, 2008, p.v, viii.

renewable energy sources (mainly wind). The transmission network in particular needs to be perhaps three times larger than it is now to accommodate the peak power flows that would come from much larger and more remote wind generation, in contrast to the large fossil fuel power plants that supply demands today, which traditionally have been located closer to the centers of demand.

By comparison, the 'Micro-grids' scenario involves much more local generation of electricity, which can be accommodated within electricity networks that are of the same size as they are today. However, such micro-grids would require more active management of the local distribution system to match supply and demand more closely at the local level, rather than leaving supply and demand to be matched by the TSO via the turning on and off of large power plants. These different visions require very different emphases by energy regulators. In the first, the regulators would have to facilitate a massive investment by today's incumbent network companies; in the second, the regulators would have to emphasize efficient system operation of multiple individual small-scale companies, many of which do not currently exist.

Of the remaining three scenarios, the ESCO model sees the role of networks increasingly subsumed into the integrated energy service providers that seek to minimize consumption and consumers' utilization of public network assets. Arguably, this is the model that is gaining more serious attention in Germany, because it emphasizes consumer self-supply of energy and DSM. The DSO model sees the distribution utility taking on more of the activities of the transmission system operator, but at lower voltage levels. This is a model that is currently being debated in the State of New York (see *Promoting distributed system platform providers in New York State*), as it aims to make the distribution utility a promoter of local DSM and distributed generation (DG) within the distribution system. The final scenario – that of 'multi-purpose networks' – may be the most likely because it simultaneously combines features of the other models in proportions that may vary by jurisdiction according to their supply and demand characteristics.

Underpinning each of the scenarios outlined above are large variations in underlying conditions in which future networks may operate. These include the costs of different technologies (such as small-scale generation and storage), the commitment and ability to pay for decarbonization, and the willingness to undergo significant behavioral change on the demand side or in the security of supply. This is what gives rise to the diversity of the above visions. From the point of view of economic regulation, this diversity suggests a number of principles that should underpin regulation in the coming years.

First, there is value in keeping options open. It is not obvious that large network upgrades are required immediately, and indeed they might never be necessary. Overbuilding of network capacity (if that were possible given local planning constraints) is a strong possibility.

Second, given the diversity of possible futures and their exact local manifestation, there should be a presumption in favor of active engagement between industry participants and with the regulator. Regulators cannot easily predict the future and need to harness wide stakeholder expertise in order to make good regulatory decisions.

Third, it would seem sensible to use competitive mechanisms where possible in the provision of network services. The current geographical monopoly areas of ownership of existing network assets are unlikely to be optimal in the future. There needs to be further effort to identify genuine 'core' monopoly aspects from potentially competitive ones. For instance, system operation is clearly a natural monopoly function, while asset ownership is not. Thus, competition in the provision of new network assets and in the operation of existing assets is clearly possible, especially via auctions to be the monopoly provider (so-called 'competition for the field').

Fourth, the current level of vertical unbundling mandated by the EU and by many non-EU regulators was very appropriate in the environment of the 1990s when the initial restructuring of many formerly vertically integrated utilities was taking place. However, whether the vertical structure established at that time will continue to be appropriate is unclear. What may be the case is that many vertical models may be possible (an end-customer-owned micro-grid versus the current unbundled model) and the important thing for regulators is to understand when these are acting in the consumers' interests and when they are not.

Fifth, in line with the previous point, it might be desirable to allow a reconfiguration of existing distribution networks so that they can be better aligned with the interests of final consumers. This might necessitate the creation of more private wire networks within the distribution grid (owned by customers or ESCOs with long-term contracts). There is potential to carve out areas of existing networks into locally owned distribution utilities (which might be municipally owned). This is possible under existing US legislation that gives municipalities the right to buy public utility assets (at their current regulatory value) within their own jurisdictions if they think they can manage them better.

Finally, new kinds of regulatory licenses for heat networks or ESCOs might be needed to facilitate some of the possible futures envisaged that exhibit significant involvement from new companies.

It is worth observing that all of the core ideas within the five LENS scenarios are currently under serious consideration in multiple jurisdictions. It is also worth pointing out that the cost trends in some of the technologies that particularly impact on the distribution system and the possibility of the ESCO, DSO, and micro-grid scenarios all suggest that substantial disruption to the existing electricity network arrangements is possible. Thus, the declining costs of small-scale photovoltaics (PV), batteries, and associated communications technology all point to the potential for substantially moving away from the existing passive distribution grid in the medium term.

The likely interests of future network regulation

The political economy of regulation

In discussing the likely interests of future network regulation, it is worth considering some probable future infrastructure economics.

While individual networks, such as the low-voltage copper-wire network, are natural monopolies, this is not so obviously the case that the services provided by different network infrastructures will not compete more effectively than they have to date (as we already see between fixed-line, mobile, and cable infrastructures in telecoms). Thus, gas, electricity, and telecoms networks all compete for some parts of energy services provision. Final customers connected to multiple networks are thus contestable. One can see this most clearly with gas and electricity competing to provide heating services. This competition will intensify as heat electrifies. Similarly, petrol station networks will compete with electricity networks to provide energy services to private transport as electric vehicles become more prevalent. This suggests that parts of the electricity network could be duplicated or bypassed for the provision of some services, such as charging private cars at work to provide storage, which could be used to back up households that are disconnected from the local electricity grid. Energy regulators will need to be careful not to distort such network-on-network competition by the charging methodology that they allow distribution companies to employ.

There are some clear trends in the price of capital goods that may influence optimal regulation in the future. These are that smaller-scale, mass-produced pieces of capital equipment and their associated software will be subject to faster rates of learning and potential for commoditization compared to larger-scale, bespoke pieces of capital equipment and their associated software. This is especially true of large-scale capital provided by large multinational electrical equipment manufacturers. It will almost certainly mean that capital provided for the T&D grid (wires, transformers, and switchgear) will get more expensive relative to customer-level energy service equipment (such as local storage, and DSM software and equipment). Encouraging a pathway of development that allows such trends in costs to be exploited (rather than one that closes off their possibility) is likely to be optimal for society as a whole. Related to this, information processing, and perhaps labor itself, will get cheaper relative to grid-scale capital equipment, suggesting the importance of software and/or local labor-intensive solutions, rather than bespoke (let alone unique) capital investments.

Associated with these economic trends, there will be developments in the political economy of regulation. In liberal democracies, there will be increasing demand for clear justifications for, and democratic governance of, regulated charges. Monopoly revenues will be under increasing scrutiny, and it will be difficult to resist calls for potentially competitive aspects of current monopoly service to be market tested, or else face draconian regulation that is likely to result in a return to (or the continuation of) public ownership and/or underinvestment in monopoly networks. As the process of globalization continues, informed publics will increasingly expect good ideas emerging in one regulatory jurisdiction to be taken up in their own. This will mean that successful marketization of some monopoly network services in one jurisdiction will diffuse to others at increasingly rapid rates. A consequence of this will be that regulators (and the politicians who support them) will be become more subject to comparative regulation themselves, and hence compete with each other to implement new learning more rapidly.

The concerns of regulation

We are already seeing that the current uncertain nature of the low-carbon future for electricity means that economic regulators will face the choice between becoming more or less involved in corporate decision-making in the face of rising complexity. The multiplicity of investment options for simultaneously meeting decarbonization, energy security, and affordability goals will mean that a greater number of difficult-to-adjudicate decisions will be called for. These decisions will often involve higher bills in pursuit of government-imposed targets, and indeed higher levels of subsidy for early-stage technologies, such as is currently the case for renewables and distributed electrical storage. One response to this is for regulators to become larger and more involved in individual investment decisions. Another is to delegate decision making to the market via competitive processes or trusted third parties, such as the ISOs or the DSOs. This choice is largely about distinguishing between the actual decision and the process by which the decision is reached. Regulators, rightly, should be involved in the latter in terms of energy, but each jurisdiction will have to decide the extent to which they can reasonably be involved in the former. At the transmission level, we already see the global emergence of an ISO/'thin' regulator, as observed in the US, versus a TSO/'thick' regulator split, as is the case in the Netherlands (see Chawla and Pollitt, 2013; Strbac *et al.*, 2014).

In transmission, regulatory authorities already work closely with system operators. System operators are responsible for real-time balancing of the system, and as such act as 'regulators' by exercising regulatory functions over other market participants (for example, in wholesale energy, capacity, and ancillary services markets) on behalf of the sector regulator/ministry of energy. Often, such system operators are not-for-profit entities (as is the case with ISOs in the US). TSOs act as 'active' network managers. Traditionally, DSOs have been 'passive' network managers, simply taking wholesale power from the transmission system and transporting it to final customers. With increasing amounts of DG and DSM technologies in the distribution grid, distribution grids begin to need 'active' network management and to look more like TSOs. This strongly suggests that DSOs will undertake more short-term regulatory functions on behalf of the regulator.

National (and regional) regulatory authorities should encourage smart- and labor-based (local) solutions, rather than expensive unique capital investments. This is because the value added by a sector specific regulatory authority is precisely an ability to think about how regulation can adapt to local characteristics and make best use of national advantages in particular sectors. A locally sensitive regulation is likely to achieve the combined policy objectives for the electricity sector at less quality-adjusted cost, and with a greater degree of popular political support and a smaller degree of political opposition. This is essential for decreasing the energy policy trilemma mentioned above.

Economic regulation has traditionally focused on a number of key elements, which will be adapted in light of the above.

First, the regulatory scrutiny of the monopoly role of system operators in promoting competition will be extended beyond transmission into distribution, especially with respect to the management of DG and DSM. DSOs will be expected to facilitate the connection and operation of DG and DSM in a non-discriminatory way.

Second, there will be pressure to promote competition for the services currently provided by the DSO. TSOs have facilitated the creation of markets for reserve capacity and ancillary services, such as reactive power, rather than simply continuing to provide them within a vertically integrated company. Similarly, DSOs may come under pressure to provide some of their services via competitive markets. DSOs are currently monopoly providers of local reliability, start-up power, voltage support, power harmonics, and energy transactions with the rest of the system (EPRI, 2014). It is not clear that these need to be provided by – rather than simply procured by – a wide-area distribution monopolist, let alone that there is not scope for competition between distribution asset owners, customers, and specialist third parties.

Third, quality of service regulation is very important for network companies. Traditionally, in distribution, this has been about reducing the number of customer minutes lost or the number of interruptions, or increasing system availability in transmission. However, with the advent of more DG and DSM, a question will arise regarding how to better reflect the costs and benefits of their connection to the distribution grid. This may expose parts of the distribution grid to more fluctuations in power quality.

Fourth, an increase in the legal entities supplying services to the electricity system implies more financial regulation. The advent of micro-grids imposes potential financial risks on counterparties that trade with them, relative to the large, well-financed energy companies that characterize today's electricity system. The regulator will play a key role in monitoring the financial health of these new players and ensuring that 'reckless' business models[3] that expose customers to unnecessary financial risks are not followed.

Finally, energy regulators will continue to be under particular obligations to consider the implications of developments in network regulation on vulnerable (that is, the poor, the sick, and the elderly) customers. If increasing complexity only benefits richer consumers who can exploit the advantages of DSM or DG, then it is likely that there will be consequences for the progress of regulation. Specifically, it is unlikely that the charging methodology will be allowed to fully reflect the costs and benefits if the consequence is that poorer, less responsive customers pay disproportionately more for their electricity due to being forced to pick up more of the fixed costs of their associated electricity network. This is partly because there is considerable flexibility among similarly efficient choices for recovery of the fixed part of network costs, and society needs to work out how to target those costs on rich consumers. In the past, this was done reasonably well by charging the same price per unit of energy at any time of day, while richer consumers consumed more.

The practice of regulators

The above concerns of regulators will give rise to a number of likely responses. All of these responses have been observed as recent trends in energy network regulation in previous literature (e.g. Pollitt, 2008), including those that make use of surveys of national regulatory authorities (see Haney and Pollitt, 2009, 2013a).

These likely responses include: more use of negotiation between buyers and sellers of network services to deal with regulatory complexity; attempts to increase competition for the provision of network services via the creation of markets or use of procurement auctions; more focus on access terms and bottlenecks created by DSOs, meaning quality of access to DG and DSM; more use of innovation-funding mechanisms and incentives to use smarter solutions; and more use of horizontal and vertical unbundling within distribution networks, such as ISOs in transmission, and even in distribution.

The GB electricity and gas regulator, Ofgem, undertook a substantial review, beginning in 2008 and ending in 2010, of network regulation (see Ofgem, 2009). This 'RPI-X@20 review' followed almost 20 years of successful cost and price reductions for network services and improvements in quality of network service (such as reduced distribution-level interruptions and higher transmission system availability). This performance was delivered by incentive regulation based on a four–five year price control formulae (RPI-X) where network revenues were capped relative to inflation with an X factor that reflected the estimated scope for annual efficiency improvements over that period. These caps were successfully supported by specific incentive payments (penalties) for the delivery (or non-delivery) of quality of service improvements.

The RPI-X@20 review indeed led to progress on all of these likely regulatory developments as part of a new regulatory framework known as RIIO, or Revenue = Incentives + Innovation + Outputs (Ofgem, 2010). Under RIIO, regulated revenue for monopoly network companies has been more explicitly tied to incentive payments for doing the right thing, the delivery of innovative solutions, and a wider range of outputs that customers value. For instance, under the first price control review carried out under RIIO, National Grid Electricity Transmission (NGET) was subject to a wider range of output measures with incentives attached for the eight-year period 2013–2021 (see Ofgem, 2012: 22–23). The *outputs* included measures of: safety (including worker safety and asset health), network reliability (energy not supplied), network availability (preparation and maintenance of a network access policy), customer satisfaction (based on a customer/stakeholder satisfaction survey), connections (to the transmission grid), environmental (including reducing own emissions), and wider works (timely new investment). The associated *incentives* applied to each output measure were a combination of financial (such as +/-1 percent of allowed revenue for developing customer/stakeholder surveys) and reputational (such as worker safety). A new network *innovation* allowance was established of up to 0.7 percent of its revenue to finance large deployment and demonstration projects.

In GB, the result was greater emphasis on the use of negotiation between the parties in the industry over desirable investments and agreed levels of service quality (though less than has been observed in parts of the US and Argentina)[4]. There was room for increased competition in the provision of network services with a desire expressed to make more use of auctions for the procurement of new network assets, specifically if there was a doubt that the incumbent was procuring these effectively. Efficient network access was further encouraged; specifically, the speed of connection of DG was incentivized via DG customer satisfaction payments (under the first electricity distribution price control carried out under RIIO, ED1; see Ofgem, 2014). Innovation funding was substantially increased in light of RPI-X@20, with a 500 percent increase in the potential amount of research and development expenditure by electricity distribution companies, which was mostly provided through a competitive funding mechanism – the Low Carbon Network Fund (LCNF). While RPI-X@20 did not in itself lead to regulatory pressure to further unbundle system operation from network asset ownership, the subsequent Integrated Transmission Planning and Regulation project – initiated by Ofgem – looked explicitly at the future of transmission planning and recommended serious consideration of the creation of a GB ISO, breaking up the current TSO that exists in England and Wales (see Strbac *et al.*, 2014).

The interests of future regulation may be further promoted, with political support, by new business models and changes in the form of ownership. Keisling (2009) proposed a new ownership arrangement, which reduces the need for economic regulation of networks. This is a competitive joint venture (CJV), where competitive energy retailers are allocated shares in ownership of the network utilities in proportion to their changing share in the retail market. Owners of the CJV have an incentive to reduce quality-adjusted cost in order to maximize the value of their shareholding and effectively become regulators of the CJV. Haney and Pollitt (2013b) pointed out circumstances in which public ownership – broadly defined as state, municipal, community interest, or customer ownership – of monopoly networks makes sense. This is when public ownership reduces the cost of capital and/or reduces the need for complex third-party regulation. This approach continues for some transmission companies (for instance, via state ownership of the TSO, TenneT, in the Netherlands) and many distribution companies (such as consumer trust-owned distribution companies in New Zealand).

Recent developments in regulation from Germany and New York State

Promoting DG: The case of Germany

The US Electric Power Research Institute (EPRI) described the recent rapid addition of DG to the German network as 'unique' (EPRI, 2014: 12). By 2014, the German electricity network had 68 GW of distributed PV and wind connected to it, against a peak demand of 80 GW. As EPRI noted, from the perspective of other countries this high penetration of DG has not been an unqualified success. It has worsened security of supply, significantly increased prices, and is associated with higher carbon emissions from the electricity sector (as the carbon benefits of renewables have been offset by the closure of nuclear power plants and the addition of new coal-fired generation). The expansion of DG has created voltage control problems in low-voltage distribution circuits due to reverse power flows from end users who are now net exporters of power at times when embedded PV and wind output exceeds local demand. It has increased the risk of mass disconnection of end users in order to cope with frequency variation problems caused by the rapid ramping up and down of DG output. This problem is made worse by the lack of stabilizing inertia from large power plants – several of which have shut due to the rapid penetration of DG – which traditionally provide frequency response within integrated power systems. Priority dispatch of DG power means that larger power plants frequently have to be turned down or off in some areas, while more expensive power plants need to be turned on in other areas to maintain local supply and demand balance on the system (so-called generation re-dispatching), thereby raising total system costs. Germany has been fortunate in that its high degree of interconnection to surrounding European countries has allowed it to balance its system by exporting surplus renewable energy and to manage sharp reductions in renewable output with electricity imports.

Anaya and Pollitt (2014a) discussed the connection arrangements for DG in Germany, contrasting the successful support policies for adding DG with the lack of cost reflectivity in the grid integration costs, which were all socialized. This has led to the economically unregulated connection of DG to the network, with no regard for the wider system costs of connection.

Germany is now learning how to manage its electricity network in the face of this rapid and uncontrolled expansion of DG. One suggestion has been simply to massively increase grid investment. It has been suggested that the required investment by 2030 is €27.5–42.5 billion, in order to expand distribution circuit length by 43 percent (EPRI, 2014). This would be a version of the 'big T&D' scenario discussed for GB in the section **Visions of the electrical future**. Meanwhile, there are strong incentives (albeit created by inefficient connections) for system operators to pay third parties for DSM services, which are stimulating the growth of ESCOs to provide such services.

In the meantime, other changes are being introduced to manage the expansion of DG. Significant among these is a move away from 'net metering' whereby if electricity customers with DG export to the distribution grid, they only pay for their net consumption. This means that if, over the course of a year, an individual consumer were to produce as much power as they consume, they would pay no grid charges (related to usage) or make no contribution to the costs of environmental policies. This implies that these charges are borne by other users of the electricity grid (who include poor residential users unable to install their own PV). DG in these circumstances is promoted by a version of tax arbitrage where there is an inefficient incentive to invest in local generation in order to reduce one's 'tax' liability, while charging for distribution and transmission network use is not cost reflective. To partly address this Germany has introduced a new charge on own consumption of solar, a charge of 4.4 eurocent/kWh. Further regulatory changes to cope with the new reality of large amounts of DG on the system include: requiring frequency control on all generators; extending voltage control via the installation of inverters at a retrofit cost of $300 million; and upgrading network communications between DG and DSOs to allow active network management, which can turn down or off individual DG in order to better manage the social effects of renewable generation.

As Anaya and Pollitt (2014b) pointed out, large amounts of DG require better distribution charging methodologies, which allow distribution companies to impose cost-reflective connection charges. These might include offering non-firm connection to intermittent generation, which would allow them to pay less than they would under a firm connection to the grid in return for accepting curtailment of their generated output at times when the grid was at capacity. This could substantially reduce the capacity constraint and congestion problems of the type seen in Germany.

Promoting distributed system platform providers in New York State

New York State has significant electrical grid constraints, with supply located in the north (upstate New York) and demand concentrated in the south (in New York City). This, coupled with already relatively high electricity prices and a desire to decarbonize its electricity sector, has driven the pursuit of a new model to unlock valuable local DG and DSM. The New York State electricity regulator launched a Reforming the Energy Vision (REV) initiative in April 2014. The REV envisages an ambitious role for the DSOs within the state that will provide low-carbon DG and local DSM. Under REV, the six in-state distribution utilities are to become 'distributed system platform providers' (DSPs):

> 'The DSP operates an intelligent network platform that will provide safe, reliable and efficient electric services by integrating diverse resources to meet customers' and society's evolving needs. The DSP fosters broad market activity by enabling active customer and third party engagement that is aligned with the wholesale market and bulk power system.'
> (State of New York Department of Public Service, 2014: 6)

The REV vision is very much in line with the 'DSOs' scenario outlined in the section **Visions of the electrical future**, where the DSO takes on many of the functions currently undertaken by ISOs and TSOs at the transmission level. The aim of doing this at the distribution level is: to better identify distributed energy resources (DERs, essentially DG and DSM) which will reduce overall system costs; to extend the use of DSM within the distribution system; to promote the role of ESCOs in delivering DERs; and to create a level playing field for new entrants to DER markets (St John, 2014). The DSP might take a lead role in the promotion of 'transactive' energy business models,[5] where the grid is able to communicate with individual devices (such as washing machines and fridges) within customer properties in order to manage demand, frequency, and voltage (that is, the 'Internet of Things' in energy). The REV discussion did consider the creation of independent DSPs, separate from the incumbent distribution monopolies, but this was considered too radical at the current stage given the degree of overlap with existing DSO functions.

A comparison of the roles of the DSP and the traditional distribution utility is shown in Table 13.1. The table lists all of the current and potential roles and responsibilities of distribution utilities. It illustrates that the DSP will take on a number of new market functions (such as the creation of local markets for load reduction), all of which relate to extension of the market functions of the TSO to distribution. It will also take an interest in some of the existing functions of the distribution utility with a view to promoting the provision of these via DERs (the provision of ancillary services, such as the provision of reactive power).

The distribution utility will therefore be left to focus on metering, system maintenance, engineering, and capital investments, with a continuing role in interacting with the state transmission system operator (New York Independent System Operator – NYISO).

The REV vision is currently the subject of a significant consultative process with all interested stakeholders in New York State. It is clearly a very ambitious set of proposals for a radical overhaul of the DSO aimed at extending the 'thick' system operator/'thin' regulator model already observed in the US in the face of rising complexity and technological opportunity.

Table 13.1 A comparison of the traditional distribution utility in New York and the proposed DSP (X = role; NYISO=New York Independent System Operator)

Roles and responsibilities	*Utility*	*DSP*
Market functions		
Administer distribution-level markets including:		X
– Load reduction markets		X
– Ancillary services		X
Match load and generator bids to produce daily schedules		X
Scheduling of external transactions		X
Real-time commitment, dispatch and voltage control		X
Economic demand response		X
Demand and energy forecasting	X	X
Bid load into the NYISO	X	
Aggregate demand response for sale to NYISO	X	X
Purchase commodity from NYISO	X	
Metering	X	
Billing	X	X
Customer service	X	X
System operations and reliability		
Monitor real-time power flows	X	X
Emergency demand response program	X	X
Ancillary services	X	X
Supervisory control and data acquisition	X	X
System maintenance	X	
Engineering and planning		
Engineering	X	
Planning and forecasting	X	X
Capital investments	X	
Interconnection	X	X
Emergency response		
Outage restoration/resiliency	X	X

Source: State of NY Dept of Public Service (2014, p. 20).

Conclusion

The future of electricity network regulation will continue to be affected by the normal relationship between price-quality and income. This implies that as households get richer, they will be more willing to pay for value-added energy services, but less interested in a given quality-adjusted unit-price saving. Thus, network regulation will be forced to pay relatively more attention to the quality of services provided, as opposed to the recent emphasis we have seen on benchmarking costs in order to drive real price reductions in network services. Customers will likely value the same elements of distribution service as they do at present, and their interest in disruptive change, which visibly threatens quality of service at the DSO level, will be limited.

There is much optimism that charging methodologies within the distribution system will become more cost reflective, as we have seen in certain transmission systems (most notably via nodal pricing to reflect local transmission congestion in the US). However, the distributional implications of price discrimination by location and time of day and the associated unwinding of the current socialization of both energy and network costs between customers in energy bills will be politically difficult. There is a strong bias in many countries towards providing network services at the same price to all customers of a particular size, regardless of location (indeed, in some countries, such as Italy, these are explicitly equalized across the country for all distribution utilities). This sort of social preference will limit the ability to efficiently reward DERs.

The massively increased use of two-way communication within the distribution system envisaged by the exploitation of DERs (as part of the 'Internet of Things') raises significant privacy and cyber-security issues. Energy regulators will be drawn into data-management issues, and it is possible that in certain jurisdictions these will dictate the path of technological development; for instance, if restrictions are imposed on the transfer of data such that it has to be processed locally (at the level of the street), rather than by a DSP, an ISO, or central data manager. One can imagine that a single major electricity data security incident could have long-lasting effects on the course of technological development within the sector.

Electrical networks still only represent a relatively small part of the total cost of the energy services provided by electricity, especially if the cost of customer-owned equipment using electricity is included. Thus, it is important that electricity network regulation should facilitate, rather than prevent, socially useful technological developments with respect to electricity production and end-use. There are many significant developments induced by or interacting with network regulation, notably the large-scale customer-funded trials in GB under the LCNF; the impact of DG on German electricity transmission and distribution networks; and the New York State proposals for the creation of DSPs, which are worthy of close study by regulators and policymakers.

Notes

1 The author acknowledges the financial support of the EPSRC Autonomic Power System project and the helpful comments of Christian Jaag. The usual disclaimer applies.
2 See Weiller and Pollitt (2013) for a discussion of platform market concepts applied to electricity.
3 See House of Commons Treasury Committee (2008: 3).
4 See, for instance, the discussion in Pollitt (2008).
5 See http://www.gridwiseac.org/about/transactive_energy.aspx. Accessed March 10, 2015. 'Transactive' energy includes 'prices to devices', where each electricity-consuming device can be exposed to real-time prices.

References

Anaya, K. and Pollitt, M. (2014a) *Integrating distributed generation: regulation and trends in three leading countries*, Energy Policy Research Group Working Papers, No. EPRG1423. Cambridge: University of Cambridge.

Anaya, K.L. and Pollitt, M.G. (2014b) Experience with smarter commercial arrangements for distributed wind generation, *Energy Policy*, 71, 52–62.

Ault, G., Frame, D. and Hughes, N. (2008) *Electricity Network Scenarios in Great Britain for 2050: Final report for Ofgem's LENS project*. London: Ofgem.

Chawla, M. and Pollitt, M. (2013) Global trends in electricity transmission system operation: where does the future lie? *The Electricity Journal*, 26(5), 65–71.

Electric Power Research Institute (EPRI) (2014), *The Integrated Grid: Realizing the Full Value of Central and Distributed Energy Resources*. Palo Alto: Electric Power Research Institute.

Haney, A. and Pollitt, M.G. (2009) Efficiency analysis of energy networks: An international survey of regulators, *Energy Policy*, 37, 5814–5830.

Haney, A. and Pollitt, M. (2013a) International benchmarking of electricity transmission by regulators: A contrast between theory and practice? *Energy Policy*, 62 (November) 2013, 267–281.

Haney, A. and Pollitt, M. (2013b) New models of public ownership in energy, *International Journal of Applied Economics*, 27(2), 174–192.

House of Commons Treasury Committee (2008) *The Run on the Rock: Fifth Report of Session 2007–08, Volume I, Report, together with formal minutes*. London: HMSO.

Keisling, L.L. (2009) *Deregulation, Innovation and Market Liberalization*. Oxford: Routledge.

Ofgem (2009) Regulating Energy Networks for the Future: RPI-X@20 Principles, Process and Issues, Ref. 13/09. London: Ofgem.

Ofgem (2010) *RIIO:* A New Way to Regulate Energy Networks, Final decision, Ref. 128/10. London: Ofgem.

Ofgem (2012) *RIIO-TI Final Proposals for National Grid Electricity Transmission and National Grid Gas*, Ref. 169/12. London: Ofgem.

Ofgem (2014) *RIIO-ED1: Draft Determinations for the Slow-Track Electricity Distribution Companies – Overview*. London: Ofgem.

Pollitt, M. (2008) The future of electricity (and gas) regulation in low-carbon policy world, *The Energy Journal*, Special Issue in Honor of David Newbery, 63–94.

State of New York Department of Public Service (2014) *Developing the REV Market in New York: DPS Staff Straw Proposal on Track One Issues*, CASE 14-M-0101, August 22, 2014.

St John, Jeff (2014) 5 Key Proposals for New York's Grid Transformation, available at http://theenergycollective.com/jeffstjohn/494781/5-key-proposals-new-yorks-grid-transformation, Sept. 12 (accessed on March 10, 2015).

Strbac, G., Pollitt, M., Konstantinidis, C.V., Konstantelos, I., Moreno, R., Newbery, D. and Green, R. (2014) *Energy Policy*, 73: 298–311.

Weiller, C.M. and Pollitt, M.G. (2013) Platform Markets and Energy Services, Energy Policy Research Group Working Papers, No. EPRG1334. Cambridge: University of Cambridge.

14

The construction of a European gas market

Network investment under virtual trading

Michelle Hallack and Miguel Vazquez[1]

Introduction

About 15 years ago, when the first directive of the European Parliament on natural gas was issued, it was difficult to imagine such a commodity being priced by its own supply and demand curves. European natural gas industries were forced from the very beginning to rely on international flows from both within and outside of Europe. As a consequence, though networks became a virtual site at the national level, the importance of interconnection points increased. Market borders have changed over the years, but they do remain and they are likely the most significant challenge to the construction of a European gas market. On the one hand, market borders cannot be opened without investment in interconnection infrastructure. On the other hand, investment decisions are not trivial when networks are virtual sites (and hence invisible to market players) within borders, but relevant barriers at borders.

In order to analyze such infrastructure development, we look at the current European regulatory framework through the lens of coordination. The coordination of long-term decisions on network development requires coordination of players' information. We will show that the mechanisms adopted to facilitate coordination of national industries, which are based on building virtual trading sites, simultaneously create an informational gap. We will then analyze the complementary mechanisms that have been proposed to fill that gap. Put differently, we will point out the currently implemented mechanisms that have been designed to compensate for information lost in the creation of virtual trading sites.

Investments in networks, and the creation of a European market, rely on at least three different levels of information: the knowledge of market players (whose business is selling and buying gas at different places), the knowledge of network operators (who are able to see national networks), and the knowledge of policymakers (who are able to decide and analyze policy issues to secure supply). In this context, the set of tools to coordinate network investment decisions in Europe is a very particular combination of open seasons (to reveal shippers' information), the Ten Year Network Development Plan (TYNDP) (to reveal transmission system operators' [TSOs'] information) and the Energy Infrastructure Package (to sew up different common interests). The definition of tools adopted here is that they are the formal mechanisms defined at the European level to coordinate the players involved in pipeline investment. The outcome of these tools cannot be analyzed separately; they interact, and that interaction may create conflicting incentives. The ultimate outcome of such a set of mechanisms will depend on how incentives to behave strategically are dealt with. The regulatory framework forms the chessboard on which economic players use their private information. Therefore, a large part of the success of the investment framework depends on the design of how the three mechanisms interact.

The first step of our reasoning is a review of the European model for the gas market. We will show the importance of the logic for the implementation of virtual hubs in the current regulatory framework. The basic idea behind the design of virtual hubs is the creation of a zone of trade; players willing to sell gas must buy the right to enter into the market, and players willing to purchase gas must buy the right to potentially withdraw from it. In that context, the network system operator becomes responsible for the management of physical gas flows in order to deliver entry and exit services. Hence, flows resulting from trading activity in the virtual hub do not match the gas actually flowing through the system. The need to match contractual and physical gas flows motivates the existence of an additional set of services, managed by the network system operator, which are grouped under the umbrella of ancillary services; these services are paid for by all users through tariffs.

In this regulatory frame, TSOs become central players, as they are the link between flows and players' information. In this context, the information is fragmented and TSOs have information on the offer of network services. Shippers, on the other hand, have information on the potential demand for such network services. In the long run, the development of gas networks needs to include shippers' information (that is, information from buyers of simplified network services) and TSOs' information (data from those who transform network services demand into actual technical needs).

In addition, a third piece of information is necessary: policy and regulatory goals. In Europe, some of these goals are beyond the individual interest of shippers and networks, and also beyond the goals of national regulations, as they represent European Union (EU)-wide interests that individual negotiation or national regulation cannot achieve. These three groups of players need to coordinate the relevant information for long-term decisions. This explains the set of mechanisms that have been developed in Europe. This set of mechanisms is made up of tools for revealing shippers' information (open seasons and auctions), tools focused on TSOs' information that mix central planning and regulatory supervision (the TYNDP), and tools to transform energy policy pillars into information regarding network development (the process of cost–benefit analysis [CBA]).

The central message of this chapter is that the previous tools interact, and not necessarily in a constructive way. These tools have complementary dynamics, as they combine the information of different players that are relevant to the decision-making process. This complementarity is formalized, for instance, in the inclusion of open seasons and auctions in the definition of the TSOs' network planning, or in the inclusion of TSOs' planning in the decision-making process of policy incentives. However, this mix of tools may allow players to act strategically, so that one tool decreases the potential of other tools to reveal information. For instance, the ability of auctions to reveal shippers' willingness to pay is limited if shippers know that, as result of a TYNDP that forecasts available capacity for short-term trading, they will have free capacity in the short run.

The organization of this chapter is as follows. After this introduction, we define the basic logic of the European gas market model. In the second section, we show how the simplification of the EU regulatory model raises an informational gap, as different pieces of information are in the hands of different players. In the third section, we show that in order to decide on gas network investment, the different pieces of information need to be put together. We also show

how the European regulatory model has developed a toolkit to that end. The fourth section discusses the interaction of the European tools, as the outcome is not just the addition of the various tools. The last section concludes the chapter.

The European Model: aiming at market liquidity

The choices of European gas markets may be identified with the choice of building a regulatory framework to enhance national liquidity. The mechanism chosen was the simplification of gas network services that are coordinated through market arrangements, especially regarding time and spatial specificities. That simplified network is called commercial network (Vazquez *et al.*, 2012a).

The logic for virtual hubs

The previous design strategy can be motivated from the consideration that, in network industries, the use of the network defines the key features of the market, as it is the place where players meet and trade (Hallack and Vazquez, 2014). Consequently, access to the trading place limits the number of players, and, more importantly, the number of potential players. In the gas industry, the problem can be thought of as follows: one can only trade what the network can deliver. The network encompasses the spatial and time specificities of the product, and is central in the task of transforming it into a tradable commodity.

The spatial dimension of the network defines where to inject and withdraw gas, and thus sets the spatial dimension of trade. The time dimension of the network defines when to withdraw and when to inject gas; for example, it sets the temporal dimension of trade. These are not trivial characteristics. Historically, transmission specificities were seen as the key motivation for vertical integration in the gas industry, and for the impossibility to develop the gas market.[2] In Europe, the natural gas industry was developed based on long-term contracts of natural gas and transport. These two kinds of contracts were often bundled (if not formally, then informally), and they used to reinforce each other (Chevalier, 2004; Melling, 2010). No market value and no market equilibrium in any market are immune to when and where the commodity will be put in and taken from the market. Therefore, the precise definitions of the ways to trade gas as a commodity, as well as its related transmission and ancillary services, are at the core of any gas market design.

The EU approach to building gas markets is based on the socialization of some of the network costs associated with a reduction of the gas temporal and spatial specificities, which results in the commercial network. The current European market model implements the previous strategy through entry/exit zones (see Hallack and Vazquez, 2013 for details on the strategy and related costs).

The design of gas markets by means of trading zones is a peculiar model developed in Europe. As showed by Correljé *et al.* (2014), the institutional difference between the EU and the US has deep, historical roots and is a result of a sequence of conditions and choices. Makholm (2012) studied the historical development of gas industry institutions in the US and identified the existence of well-defined transmission property rights as the fundamental difference between US and EU markets. Vazquez *et al.* (2012b) showed that the absence of clear-cut transmission property rights is associated with the choice of gas markets based on virtual hubs. This aims to promote market liquidity by regulatory means, to some extent sacrificing the information and economic efficiency in gas infrastructure operation and investment. Using commercial networks creates virtual hubs: a virtual site for trade where some of the network specificities are simplified. It facilitates trade but, on the other side, an important part of information regarding the network can no longer be found in the market.

Moreover, this unawareness when trading in the marketplace has additional costs. Virtual trading of gas, regardless of its physical flows, can be done only in national or subnational zones. Each zone forces the network operator to lower time and spatial specificities of the gas being traded. However, among zones, the costs related to gas specificities reappear and become a negative incentive to cross-border trade. Therefore, in the EU, gas markets are designed and operated as if the physical network constraints within zones had to be placed at the border between entry/exit zones. The relationship between zones was not fully regarded until the Third Energy Package.

Cross-border barriers to trade

The market zones have favored liquidity within them. Following the last European legislation (Third Energy Package), new templates to rethink cross-border trade as foundations of a pan-European market have been discussed. They are condensed in several alternative 'European Gas Target Models' (CIEP, 2011; Frontier Economics 2011; Glachant *et al.*, 2013; Moselle and White 2011). Two typical measures have been proposed to facilitate cross-border trade: increasing the size of the zones by merging existing market zones; and allocating interconnection capacity according to a commodity merit order made across market zones (market coupling).

However, the challenges for integrating the existing zones in a pan-European setting go beyond these issues. The European entry/exit scheme also impacts on network tariff regimes and the incentives for new network investment. In an entry/exit scheme no direct link is made between the entry/exit points of a trade, so no tariffs based on the real use of the network exist: tariffs are not cost reflective. Within a certain zone, tariffs are calculated to recover the network costs on the whole zone, whereas each market player pays regardless of their real use of the network. When trading cross-border, the amplitude of economic distortions may even increase. In fact, network charges for transporting gas between zones are often higher than charges for transporting gas within each zone, independently of their real network costs (ACER, 2012). In practice, when a shipper crosses two zones, they need to pay charges that include cross-subsidies for the entire zones.

The informational gap associated with virtual hubs

Hence, the gas market design in the EU is based on commercial networks that abstract physical flows in order to facilitate trade. This abstraction means that market players receive less market signals about the costs and benefits of the actual gas flow within the network. As a consequence, the network operator role and the operation costs increase, which result in larger barriers to cross-border trade (Vazquez *et al.*, 2012b; Hallack and Vazquez, 2013). From this point of view, there is an additional effect that needs consideration. Removing market signals creates an informational gap, which complicates the coordination of network investment decisions.

The measurement problem

The logic of removing signals from trading arrangements is not an exclusive feature of the natural gas network. As shown by Barzel (1982), market arrangements tend to simplify commodity characteristics in order to create liquidity. Barzel's traditional example was trading of apples: not all apples in a market have the same attributes; however, traders often group apples under a few simplified types, which depend on how valuable the attributes are and how costly it is to measure the attribute. Differences can typically be found between rotten and fresh apples (so that not buying rotten apples is worth measurement), but there are not usually differences between Golden Delicious apples (they are similar enough not to be worth measurement).

In the gas industry, the cost of measurement is high. On the one hand, it is difficult to measure flow time (as it is continuous) and site attributes. Complete measurement would require continuous measurement and information management of the flow attributes at every point of injection and withdrawal (Hallack and Vazquez, 2014). On the other hand, measuring many attributes would decrease liquidity as it increases the number of differentiated products; as a consequence, the information contained in prices will be less relevant. Put differently, the larger the number of attributes taken into account, the higher the number of prices, and the lower the informational content of prices.

Long-term consequences of the choice of virtual trading

Choosing virtual trading brought significant short-term challenges, together with market liquidity (Hunt 2008; Vazquez *et al.*, 2012b; Hallack and Vazquez 2013). The informational gap in the gas flows prevent players from managing their own gas flows and force the development of a system operator, in order to bridge the gap between commercial and physical networks.

In addition, removing signals impacts investment mechanisms. On the one hand, the use of market mechanisms to determine cross-border investment may not be effective under this system. First, property rights of transmission capacity buyers are not clearly separated from entry/exit rights of any other player, and second, the value paid for the transmission services do not accurately reflect their costs. On the other hand, if one prefers to choose regulated mechanisms to determine cross-border investment, the calculations made by the TSOs, within their zones do not accurately represent the future characteristics of the physical gas flows between zones because of the entry/exit liberty given to market players by the zonal entry/exit rights. Consequently, there is a gap of incentive mechanisms, regulated or market based, to promote cross-border investment. This is where a third player appears: the policymaker. In Europe, one of the key policy objectives is the integration of the European market. The cross-zone becomes one of the key elements of policy in the gas market, as it is expected to enhance market integration, competition, and security of supply, and help to promote technologies with lower CO_2 emissions.

In this context, in the European choice for a natural gas virtual hub, we identify three basic dimensions of missing information: information on system characteristics, information on players' preferences, and information on policy objectives. This information is in the hands of different agents, such as TSOs, shippers, and regulators/policymakers, respectively.

The ability to reveal the different pieces of relevant information is a current challenge for the European system. In order to deal with this challenge, the European Commission (EC) has proposed a bundle of tools, each one of which concentrates on one kind of information. However, we cannot assume that the output of these tools is the mere sum of each one. They will interact, and this can reinforce or weaken the expected effect. The design of these tools must consider this interaction.

Mechanisms to coordinate infrastructure development: challenges for network investment

In this section, we describe the three different mechanisms that have been applied in Europe to decide on investments in natural gas networks: open seasons/auctions, the TYNDP, and the process for CBA. We will describe these mechanisms below, showing the kind of information that each one is intended to reveal.

Information from users: open seasons and auctions

Open seasons and auctions are sometimes used as equivalent mechanisms, as both are intended to reveal shippers' preferences on their interest in network capacity. Though both can be identified as mechanisms that reveal information for investment decisions, they are also used to allocate capacity. The key difference between these mechanisms – the way in which they have been applied in Europe – is the definition of capacity pricing.

Despite the fact that the definition of open season is quite broad, we will use the framework set up by the European Regulators Group for Electricity and Gas (ERGEG) good practice guidelines. The 'open season is a two-step process which allows a project sponsor to efficiently consult the market about how much infrastructure it needs, and under what terms it would like this infrastructure to be marketed. It also allows resulting capacity to be allocated on a transparent and non-discriminatory basis' (ERGEG, 2007: 5). In the first stage of the open season, the sponsor assesses the shippers' demand for infrastructure services, such as how much and what attributes are needed. The objective of this stage is to access information by asking and putting together shippers' information, and project information. The shipper and the sponsor are not responsible for this information (either the proposed project or the shippers' willingness to pay). Hence, this stage aims to facilitate the dialogue of the sponsor (frequently the network operator) and shippers in order to adapt potential projects (cost, volume, and designs) and shipper demands.

In the second stage, the sponsor offers capacity, and establishes the conditions and pricing mechanism for this service, to the open season participants. If they agree with the conditions of the service offered, they sign a binding agreement. Different methods can be chosen to offer this capacity, if they comply with the condition of being transparent and non-discriminatory.[3] ERGEG (2007) pointed out several elements that must be considered to guarantee the transparency and non-discriminatory features of the process; for instance, one of the critical points was the definition of the service characteristics, and the tariff methodology that should be applied if the agreement is signed.

Auctions are the preferred mechanism of the EC to allocate firm capacity, according to the Network Code Capacity Allocation mechanism (ENTSOG, 2012). The guidelines state that some standard capacity products should be defined by year, quarter, month and within-day. The main idea behind the choice of auction mechanisms is to allocate capacity to the shippers that most value it. On the other hand, as the European model seeks to retain short-term liquidity and does not believe that the secondary market can guarantee it, short-term capacity should be offered.[4] In both cases (auctions and open seasons), the European model highlights the need to retain some capacity for short-term allocation. The aim of this capacity reserve is to ensure available capacity for new entrants in order to promote market competition and liquidity. This reserve can be seen as promoting a policy objective, and shippers are not able to reveal this kind of information.

The open season was one of the first tools to be officially promoted by the EC, even before the Third Package. However, it has been regarded as an unsatisfactory mechanism to drive investments. Consequently, the EC has made an effort to regulate network plans at a national level, on a case-by-case basis.

Information from the system operators: Ten Years Network Development Plan

The TYNDP is a mechanism to aid in the short- and long-term planning of the investment in gas network infrastructures. It has both a national and a European dimension (ENTSOG, 2013). It started as an initiative of some national regulatory authorities, but became mandatory since the Third Package. Moreover, the TYNDP plan became European-wide after the last directive. At both levels, national and European, TSOs are responsible for proposing the plan. For the elaboration of the TYNDP, the TSO shall make public and reasonable assumptions of gas demand, supply, and exchanges with other countries. In addition, national or sub-national TSOs shall take into account investment plans for regional and community-wide networks, as well as investment plans for storage and Liquefied Natural Gas (LNG) regasification facilities. Regulators must supervise, propose modifications and enforce the actual application of the projects. In addition, at both levels we can find processes involving open consultations to all network users (ENTSOG, 2013).[5]

The process consists of modeling the gas network and developing the supply and demand scenarios of natural gas. The modeling tool used by the European Network of Transmission System Operators for Gas (ENTSOG) is structured along entry/exit capacity, as offered by TSOs, and is aggregated at balancing zones. In the scenario development, some key policy implications are taken into account as renewable policies[6]. After that, ENTSOG should explore network simulations, including new clustering projects, parameters for testing market integration and security of supply. The last TYNDP (2013–2022) included some elements for cooperation with the electricity network through the European Network of Transmission System Operators for Electricity (ENTSOE), as it aimed to cope with peak scenarios. We may conclude that it aims to avoid the situation of capacity scarcity in the short-term future (ENTSOG, 2013).

The Third Energy Package establishes that all independent systems operators must develop and comply with the national TYNDP (EC, 2009). On the other hand, national regulators must supervise and guarantee that national network development plans converge with the Europe-wide network development plan. The TYNDP shall indicate to market participants the main transmission infrastructures that need to be built or upgraded over the next 10 years, contain all the investments decided, and identify new investments that are to be executed in the next three years, and provide a timeframe for all investment projects. The TYNDP is a bi-annual non-binding plan of the EU-wide infrastructure development. While not binding, it represents a reference for the development of national network development plans.

Information from policymakers: cost–benefit analysis

Besides the two mechanisms detailed before, the EC included a third tool to improve the investment conditions in the region: the definition of projects of common interest (PCI) by using a CBA. In 2013, the EU defined new objectives through the Regulation 'on guidelines for trans-European energy infrastructure' (EC, 2013). According to this regulation, there is an urgent need to upgrade Europe's network in order to integrate networks at the continental level and allow the integration of renewable resources. The estimation of investment needs up to 2020 in electricity and gas transmission infrastructure is set at about €200 billion (EC, 2010). The amount and the urgency of this investment to face European policy priorities form the argument for new tools to boost investment in Europe. 'In line with the provisions of this

Regulation, the Commission presented on the 14 October 2013 the first Union list of energy infrastructure [PCIs]. The list contains 248 projects (107 on gas, 132 on electricity, 2 on smart grids and 7 on oil) spread over the 12 priority corridors and area' (EC, 2013: 2).

We can interpret the definition of PCIs as an institutional framework to introduce information on the European energy policy in the definition of new investments. We can divide the policy objectives into three groups: reduction of CO_2 emissions, improvement in EU market integration, and security of supply. These objectives are not new in European energy policy objectives, but many challenges have been observed in relation to meeting them. The three objectives are also broad, and may diverge in many situations (Glachant *et al.*, 2008).

The PCI regulatory framework aims to enhance investment by using regulatory and financial incentives. The market is expected to deliver half of the investments needed. For the remaining half, regulatory and political, and sometimes also financial, support will be needed. The Regulation foresees that permitting procedures shall take no longer than three-and-a-half years overall. It also requires member states to designate one national competent authority responsible for facilitating and coordinating the PCI permitting process (Meeus *et al.*, 2013). The role of national regulatory authorities is particularly important, as they need to find an optimal balance of the risks-reward ratio of infrastructure projects, which is attractive enough for investors to put sufficient capital into European infrastructures.

Following the entry into force of the trans-European energy networks (TEN-E) Regulation in May 2013, the first EU-wide PCI list was adopted in October 2013. At the same time, the ENTSOs were developing methodologies for the CBA to be performed on individual projects and on the TYNDP as a whole. In November 2013 these methodologies were presented to the Agency for the Cooperation of Energy Regulators (ACER), which provided its opinion to the EC in February 2014.

Interaction between tools: complementary and conflicting incentives

Each of the three tools described above is aimed at dealing with one aspect of the informational gap associated with virtual trading. Each of them involves different players. Open seasons and auctions are typically applied by TSOs at the national level to reveal shippers' information, even if they are prescribed within the EU regulatory framework (guidelines and network code). The TYNDP is developed by TSOs and submitted to national regulatory authorities. Moreover, the national/regional development plans are part of the ENTSOG's TYNDP, which in turn must be submitted to ACER at the European level. The EC ultimately decides the PCIs, but the project analysis is based on the CBA methodology developed by ENTSOG.

It is also necessary to combine the three tools in order to bridge the informational gap. Nonetheless, it is necessary to take into account that the three tools may interact, both complementing each other and creating conflicting incentives.

In fact, as each tool deals with one aspect of network investment, the existence of different tools may give room for strategic behavior. When players know that there are several steps of interactions with agents involved in network planning, they may use their private information strategically. Typically, their strategies consist in revealing less information to benefit from other tools.

In order to analyze the problem, we represent possible interactions in Figure 14.1. We labeled the first order for the possible interactions as the 'market-to-policymakers' direction. The intention behind this was to consider mechanisms to reveal shippers' information; for example, auctions or open seasons take place earlier than mechanisms to reveal regulated decisions, and those latter mechanisms take place earlier than mechanisms to reveal policy

'Market-to-policy-makers' direction →

Users' information	TSOs' information	Policy-makers information
Open season/auction	Ten Year Network Development Plan	Cost–benefit analysis

← 'Policy-makers-to-market' direction

Figure 14.1 Illustrative chart of interactions between EU investment tools

Source: Own elaboration.

options. The ordering is ultimately associated with representation of the relevant information available at each stage (when each mechanism takes place). Hence, TSOs' information regarding the gap is not available when auctions take place, and policymakers' information is not completely available when TSOs make decisions. However, the results of all previous mechanisms are available in the moment when policymakers decide which should be the priorities (as in the CBA and the PCI list).

On the other hand, in Figure 14.1 we labeled a second ordering for mechanism interaction as the 'policymakers-to-market' direction. This represents the opposite ordering of the former direction, as mechanisms aimed at revealing policy option would take place earlier than the others, and TSOs' mechanisms would take place before shippers' mechanisms. This direction might be viewed as introducing centralized decisions in gradually more decentralized mechanisms.

In practice, the market-to-policymakers interaction can happen through formal settings. For instance, in the Great Britain experience, auctions for contracting network capacity are a relevant source of shippers' information, which is then used by the national grid in the preparation of its network development plan. Nonetheless, interaction can happen in less formal ways. For instance, policymakers' tools (such as CBAs) would use both information from shippers and information revealed by TSOs, such as through the TYNDP.

In order to characterize the interaction, let us use the case of a participant of a certain open season. The binding part of the open season implies a cost for users, as they buy, partially or completely, the volume. In order to reveal the willingness to pay for the volume allocated through the open season, it is necessary that the player take the risk. That is, the player will bear the risk of buying capacity in advance if the cost of reserving capacity is lower than the valuation of the cost associated with waiting to buy the capacity in the future. However, if the player believes that there will be spare capacity in the future, and that capacity will be cheap (compared to buying capacity now), it will be better to wait and buy capacity in the future. Put differently, in the latter case the open season will not allocate capacity, but this will not mean that the player does not need the capacity, only that the required capacity will be cheaper in the future.

The above situation can be viewed as a consequence of the presence of other tools for network planning. The results of the open season cannot be viewed as isolated, as the availability of capacity in the short run, a key element of the previous analysis, is affected by other planning tools, particularly those associated with TSOs'/regulators' decisions. Moreover, if regulators set lower tariffs for short-term capacity, there will be a relatively strong strategic incentive for shippers to wait and contract short-term capacity.[7]

Figure 14.2 illustrates a decision tree in which we represent a certain shipper's decisions, starting from the point at which they have decided that they want more capacity in the future, including the risk assessment of a long-term agreement. The shipper's possible decisions are represented by dark grey boxes, while the light grey boxes show information coming from the environment. These light grey boxes are central in our analysis as they are the intersection with other tools. After the previous decision (where the shipper wants more capacity), the shipper analyzes their options to obtain capacity in the future. If the shipper expects that there will be no spare capacity in the future, so that it will not be possible to buy short-term capacity, then they will enter into the long-term contract, and hence reveal their information.

On the other hand, if the shipper expects to find spare capacity in the future, then the problem is deciding whether the price of short-term capacity will be lower than the price of the open-season capacity (where the future price valuation is affected by shipper's risk assessment). If the valuation of short-term capacity results in lower costs than the open-season capacity costs, then the shipper will not contract in the open season. Otherwise, the shipper will contract open-season capacity, and hence reveal their information.

From the depiction shown in Figure 14.2, we can observe several possibilities of a shipper not contracting in an open-season process, despite needing new capacity. The main lesson that can be drawn from the previous situation is that the result of an open season will be the result of the shipper's comparison between capacity today at today's price and (risk-affected) valuation of future capacity at future price. The latter valuation is affected not only by the rest of the planning tools (TYNDP or CBA), but also by regulatory measures affecting future capacity

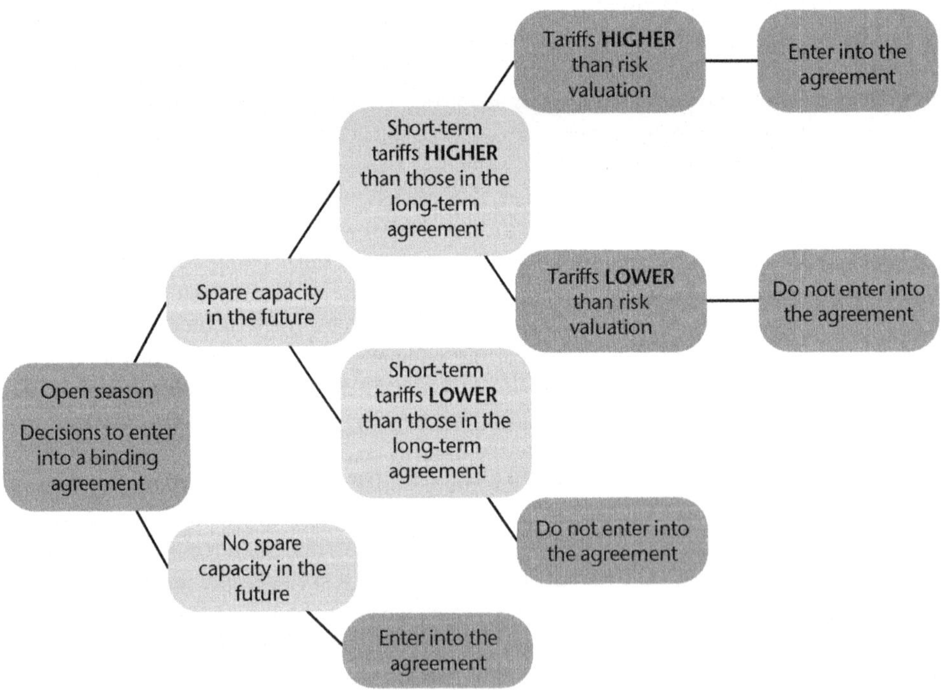

Figure 14.2 Illustrative decision tree for a shipper in an open season

Source: Own elaboration.

allocation and prices. For instance, the availability of short-term capacity is central to promote liquidity and trade in virtual hubs. According to EU guidelines, the network must retain some spare capacity for short-term trading, and both the TYNDP and CBA take this into account.

Analogously, if results of policymakers' mechanisms are introduced into TSOs' decision-making mechanisms, TSOs may have strategic incentives not to reveal their information and benefit from the knowledge of policy goals. For example, if the TSOs' planning takes place after, or at the same time as, the CBA mechanism, a certain TSO would have incentives to show that a certain project is of no interest for the national system, so that the TSO can benefit from the funds dedicated to projects of common interest. This is the motivation for adding a preliminary stage to the CBA methodology, which is called the TYNDP step, to avoid the previous kind of incentive for TSOs.

The interactions between the tools are summarized in Table 14.1. Columns in the table represent the effect that each mechanism has on each piece of information. For example, the first column represents that the open season takes place before any other mechanism, the second column represents that the TYNDP takes place before the other mechanisms, and the third column represents that the CBA takes place first. The first column represents that open seasons have the revelation of users' information as a primary goal, and that their results are useful input information for revealing the other pieces of information (held by TSOs and policymakers).

As we move to the right of the table, we find an increasing presence of conflicting incentives. The TYNDP has revealed TSOs' information as a primary goal, but if shippers know the output of the TYNDP, this will create incentives to behave strategically. The effects of the CBA are the extreme case, as knowing policymakers' decisions will create incentives to react strategically for both shippers and TSOs. Consequently, even if CBA is understood as a necessary tool for investment planning, using it must take into account its relationship with the other mechanisms.

Table 14.1 Summary of EU interaction – classifying the relationship between mechanism to reveal information and kind of information revealed (primary goal complementary and conflicting)

Piece of information	*Interaction*		
	Open season	*TYNDP*	*CBA*
User information	Primary Goal	Conflicting	Conflicting
TSO information	Complementary	Primary Goal	Conflicting
Policy-makers information	Complementary	Complementary	Primary Goal

Source: Own elaboration, Hallack and Vazquez (2015).

Conclusion

The EU has chosen to design gas markets based on virtual hubs. Consequently, together with the facilitation of gas trading, one needs to face an informational gap associated with the definition of a commercial network. From that point of view, we have shown that the set of mechanisms put into place to bridge the gap is made up of mechanisms to reveal players' preferences, TSOs' information, and energy policy goals. The current mix of open season processes, TYNDPs, and EU-wide CBAs represents a combination of the necessary tools.

Nonetheless, the interaction among them is relevant. Put differently, we have shown that the three kinds of mechanisms are necessary, so the question is not whether to use open seasons or TSOs' network planning, but how to combine those tools. This is motivated by the fact that one needs to combine mechanisms in a way that allows efficient coordination of the different players. Thus, the process to combine mechanisms matters.

We have shown that it is necessary to create a process for CBA where all agents' information is included (we ensure market-to-policymaker interaction), and not a CBA defined exclusively at the policy level, so we face policymaker-to-market interaction. Consequently, the results of the mechanisms should be considered in the broader sense. If the market does not contract capacity via auction, we need to understand that in the proper context, as shown in the last section. Many regulatory decisions affect that result, so it cannot be interpreted only as a market impact.

The institutional setting in the EU gas markets implies an informational gap. The mechanisms designed to bridge that gap requires the combination of three kinds of tools, which combine the information associated with three different kinds of players: shippers, TSOs and policymakers. Isolated tools that deal with one of the above mentioned kinds of agents cannot coordinate investment decisions for network development.

Notes

1 The authors thank the reviewer for their suggestions and comments, and also Professor Jean Michel Glachant for insightful discussion at the Florence School of Regulation about the issues tackled in this article.
2 The study of specificities and the transaction costs found in the natural gas network can be found in the authors arguing against the liberalization in North America. According to them, the specificities (and the associated transaction costs) of the gas transmission through pipelines would prevent industry coordination (see, e.g., Dahl and Matson, 1998).
3 In theory, this mechanism could include auction procedures, which explains why open season and auction are sometimes used indiscriminately.
4 'An amount at least equal to 10 percent of the Technical Capacity at each Interconnection Point shall be set aside for firm capacity services with a duration of less than or equal to one quarter, provided that the available capacity, at the time this Network Code comes into force, is equal to or greater than the proportion of Technical Capacity to be set aside' (ENTSOG, 2012: 11).
5 According to the Third Directive, the regulatory authority shall consult all actual or potential users in an open and transparent manner. Moreover, the regulatory authority must publish the results of the consultation process; in particular, the possible needs for investment.
6 For instance the achievement of the EU 20-20-20 targets are key elements to define gas flow scenarios. These targets are objectives to be introduced in 2020. CO_2 emissions should reduce by 20 percent compared to 1990 levels, 20 percent of energy should come from renewable sources and energy efficiency should increase 20 percent.
7 For instance, in the UK tariffs system the long-term capacity auctions have a reserve price, while the short-term auctions have a low or no reserve price.

References

Agency for the Cooperation of Energy Regulators (ACER) (2012) ACER/CEER Annual Report on the Results of Monitoring the Internal Electricity and Natural Gas Markets in 2011, Agency for the Cooperation of Energy Regulators.

Barzel, Y. (1982) Measurement cost and organization of markets, *Journal of Law and Economics*, v. 25 n.1, 27– 48.

Chevalier, J-M. (2004) *Les Grandes Batailles de L'énergie: Petit Traité D'une Économie Violente.* Paris: Gallimard.

CIEP (2011) CIEP: Vis*ion on the Gas Target Model*, Clingendael International Energy Programme.

Correljé, A., Groenleer, M. and Veldman, J. (2014) Understanding Institutional Change: The Development of Institutions for the Regulation of Natural Gas Supply Systems in the United States and the European Union, *Competition and Regulation in Network Industries*, v. 15 (2014), 2–31.

Dahl, C.A. and Matson, T.K. (1998) Evolution of the US Natural gas industry in response to changes in transaction costs, *Land Economics*, 74(3), 390–408.

European Commission (EC) (2009) Regulation N 715/2009 of the European Parliament. *Official Journal of the European Union*, v. 52, 36.

European Commission (EC) (2010) The EU Budget Review, Communication from the Commission to the European Parliament, the Council, the European Economic and Social Committee of Regions and the National Parliaments, COM(2010)700, Brussels, 19.10.2010

European Commission (EC) (2013) Regulation (EC) N 347/2013 of the European Parliament. *Official Journal of the European Union*, v. 56, 39.

Frontier Economics (2011) Target model for the European natural gas market. *Report Prepared for GDF Suez Branch Infrastructures*, London, Frontier Economics Ltd.

European Network of Transmission System Operators for Gas (ENTSOG) (2012) *Network Code on Capacity Allocation Mechanism*, Brussels, European Network of Transmission System Operators for Gas.

European Network of Transmission System Operators for Gas (ENTSOG) (2013) *Ten-Year Network Development Plan 2013–2022.* Available at www.entsog.eu/publications/tyndp#ENTSOG-TEN-YEAR-NETWORK-DEVELOPMENT-PLAN-2013-2022 (accessed 4 May 2015).

European Regulators' Group for Electricity and Gas (ERGEG) (2007) *ERGEG Guidelines for Good Practice on Open Season Procedures (GGPOS)*, Brussels, European Regulators' Group for Electricity and Gas.

Glachant, J-.M., Hallack, M. and Vazquez M. (2013) *Building Competitive Gas Markets in the EU.* Cheltenham: Edward Elgar Publishing.

Glachant, J-.M., Lévêque, F. and Ranci, P. (2008) *Some Guideposts on the Road to Formulating a Coherent Policy on EU Energy Security of Supply. The Electricity Journal*, 21(10), 13–18.

Hallack, M. and Vazquez, M. (2013) European Union regulation of gas transmission services: challenges in the allocation of network resources through entry/exit schemes, *Utilities Policy*, 25 (June), 23–32.

Hallack, M. and Vazquez, M. (2014) Who decides the rules for network use? A 'common pool' analysis of gas network regulation, *Journal of Institutional Economics* 10(3), 1–20.

Hunt, P. (2008) *Entry-Exit Transmission Pricing with Notional Hubs: Can It Deliver a Pan-European Wholesale Market in Gas?* Oxford Institute for Energy Studies.

Makholm, J.D. (2012) *The Political Economy of Pipelines: A Century of Comparative Institutional Development.* Chicago: University of Chicago Press.

Meeus, L., von der Fehr, N-H., Azevedo, I., He, X., Olmos, L. and Glachant, J-M. (2013) *Cost benefit analysis in the context of the energy infrastructure package.* THINK report. Available at: http://www.think.eui.eu (accessed 4 May 2015).

Melling, A. (2010) *Natural Gas Pricing and Its Futures: Europe as the Battleground*, Carnegie Endowment for International Peace.

Moselle, B. and White, M. (2011) Market design for natural gas: the target model for the internal market, *LECG Report for the Office of Gas and Electricity Markets.* London: LECG.

Vazquez, M., Hallack, M. and Glachant, J-.M. (2012a) Building gas markets: US versus EU, market versus market model, *European Energy Journal*, v3, 39–47.

Vazquez, M., Hallack, M. and Glachant, J-.M. (2012b) Designing the European Gas Market: More Liquid & Less Natural? *Economics of Energy & Environmental Policy*, v.1(3), 25–38.

15

Policy and regulatory perspectives on shipping

Laticia Argenti and Thomas Wakeman

Introduction

Maritime trade, or shipping, was one of the world's first network enterprises. A network industry is one in which the enterprise or its products consists of many interconnected nodes, where the node is a unit of the firm or its product, and connections among the nodes define the character of commerce in the industry (Gottinger, 2003). Maritime shipping is used to move people, goods, services, and information. Transportation is a demand-derived service that not only facilitates trade and communication, but historically has also facilitated cultural exchange of ideas. Maritime transportation enterprises began simply with individuals who owned cargo and hired ships to move it to a location that had a market demand. Over time, the enterprises came to be governed by small kingdoms or city-states, which grew into wealthy nations with strong merchant and trading classes (Paulsen, 1983). Often, cargo owners traveled with their goods on for-hire ships; however, in time, it became impractical for shippers to continue this practice, so they sought legal assurances, through contracts, that their cargo would be delivered undamaged and intact. This was the beginning of an energetic maritime jurisprudence forming around the private commercial transactions surrounding the carriage of goods by ships (Reynolds, 1990). However, vessel owners and their insurers were often treated more favorably than merchants by the various local maritime courts, so cargo owners began looking to governments to assist in developing international codes to govern trading transactions. What appeared to be mostly private law became a matter of public interest, and the body of maritime law grew to regulate cargo handling and shipmasters, cargo owners, and marine insurer interests.

The commercial marine industry has also matured as a profession. Maritime nations, such as Greece and Spain, have established marine academies focused on building maritime trade capabilities. Many governments began playing an active role in promoting their shipping industry, including the recruitment of mariner students. Through their marine academies and licensing procedures, these countries began exercising superintendence over their merchant marines, ensuring qualification standards were met.

Today, maritime shipping has grown under a regulatory scheme of standards that control the behavior and operations of the shipping industry and those who do business with it. What began as individual nation states regulating simple networks of merchants and shippers has evolved into a large and complex global maritime shipping enterprise that operates under a pervasive regulatory framework consisting of international conventions and domestic laws and regulations (Mukherjee and Brownrigg, 2013). Yet, despite heavy regulation of the shipping network, the maritime shipping industry drives a significant part of the world's economic growth by carrying ninety percent of the world's trade by volume on vessels (International Chamber of Shipping, 2015).

Due to stiff competition in the global marketplace among national and regional economic blocks, policy officials are challenged with balancing the regulatory reach of safety, security, and environmental protection with the efficient facilitation of trade. In the drive for a level ship safety, environmental protection, and competitive playing field, most nations strive for harmonization of legal obligations negotiated through international instruments (Hubner, 2003). These legal obligations often take the form of regulatory standards, expressed in vessels' design, operational or carriage requirements. For example, vessels are required to operate under a set of global navigational standards, and have certain lifesaving and firefighting equipment on board. However, sometimes a nation will go it alone, often with the result of influencing other nations to adapt to a higher regulatory structure than they might have otherwise negotiated by international agreement at that particular time, as was the case when the US required all tank vessels carrying oil in US waters to implement a number of oil-spill preventative and response regulatory measures in the aftermath of the *Exxon Valdez* oil spill of 1989. These regulations were in advance of ongoing work at the International Maritime Organization (IMO), a specialized UN agency for maritime shipping and the marine environment, which was addressing similar regulatory measures (USCG, 1994; Mukherjee and Brownrigg, 2013). Companies engaged in the maritime petroleum trade were forced to decide whether it was worth the investment to meet the more US stringent regulatory standard or no longer conduct trade with the US.

Singular state regulatory action is an inefficient manner by which to negotiate maritime shipping standards in a global economy. Naturally, the international shipping community heavily discourages unilateral nation-state action; but so does a nation's own shipping industry, fearing the precedence that unilateralism might set. Particularly during the last two decades, nations have primarily worked with the IMO in directing integrated efforts towards achieving global standards. For example, immediately after the September 11, 2001 terrorist attacks, the US worked diligently through the IMO to establish a comprehensive regulatory scheme that set regulatory standards and measures for vessels calling on any world port that may face an actual or probable terrorist threat (Mukherjee and Brownrigg, 2013). The ability of the IMO to move so rapidly illustrates the maturity of maritime shipping as a network system that can adjust, through the development and implementation of regulatory standards, when directed towards a common goal.

This chapter examines the complex nature of regulating maritime shipping as a network industry by exploring the challenges posed and successes achieved with respect to regulating ships that sail the world's waters and visit nations' ports carrying goods owned by private companies or citizens. Particular attention is given to the regulatory function and sovereignty interests of the nation that regulates the vessel, as well as the ability of the port state to exercise control over a foreign ship in its waters. The global commons, oceans and seas, the legal freedom to navigate, and the role of international governing bodies are also discussed.

Shipping as a network industry

Maritime shipping is a derived service-oriented enterprise for the waterborne commercial carriage of goods, freight, persons, or services (Rodrique *et. al.*, 2006). Shipping is a network industry in which transportation and storage are provided as services in the supply chain (Gottinger, 2003). The shipping service is a logistical characteristic of the network, in support of a commercial transaction between shipper and customer or consignee. Waterborne or maritime transportation is rarely a singular system, but is generally part of a larger, more intricate logistical system comprised of multiple surface-transportation modes with warehousing and distribution services encompassing part of the supply chain. The transportation transaction is controlled by both commercial terms, and governmental rules and regulations promulgated by international and national organizations. The ships, ports, waters, and personnel are also subject to myriad governmental rules and regulations covering topics including safety, security, environment, merchant marine qualifications, and labor. Financing and regulatory tax schemes also play an important role in ship and port operations.

The maritime shipping industry operates on a for-profit basis, and the multiple transactions that collectively form its transactional environment are a commercial network. Like all businesses, there is a need for fundamental controls to reduce risks (both commercial and public), including the rules of exchange between the master (ship owner) and the shipper (cargo owner) that must be settled before the ship sails. Governments may promulgate controls to reduce risks of monopolies or negative impacts (intended or unintended) during operation, including issues surrounding safety, security, labor, or environmental protection. The trend over the years, especially in the past few decades, has been for commercial and institutional risks to both private and public parties to decrease while world population and consumer demand have dramatically increased, creating a tremendous desire for worldwide shipping services. In fact, total waterborne trade estimates have quadrupled from just over 8 thousand billion ton-miles in 1968 to over 32 thousand billion ton-miles in 2008 (International Chamber of Shipping, 2015).

Global supply chain

Commercial transactions evolved from single suppliers of a single good to a single buyer delivered on a single ship to a wide variety of goods and products moving on a vessel or a fleet of vessels. With the great variety of goods and information, logistical services emerged to coordinate the movement, storage, and distribution of multiple goods going to multiple destinations, and since these goods were coming in on ships, many ports emerged as logistical centers. Logistics is the management of the flow of information and goods between their origin and their destination, or point of utilization. Today, the informational and material interchanges in the logistical process extend from the extraction of raw materials to the tracking of intermediary products to the delivery of a finished product. A supply chain is typically composed of multiple businesses, including vendors, logistics providers, and retailers that are linked to their customers through a network of production, logistics, marketing, and sales. Logistics had been a goods-movement practice for centuries; however, it was comprehensively developed by the military during World War II as a result of the volume of materials that needed to be moved in a timely manner. Goods transport, storage through warehousing, and distribution are the primary components of the logistics system, which is a key component of the global supply chain.

With the reduction in trade barriers and improvements in transportation, the global supply chain rapidly advanced in the maritime business world, particularly through the use of standard-sized containers to transport goods. Known as containerization, these containers are lifted onto trucks' chassis, rail cars, barges, or smaller container ships for further transportation to their destination point. Containerization has made the transfer of any good that could fit into a container a practical and efficient manner of moving chronologically through any transportation mode from origin to destination, and has facilitated efficient multi-modal transportation of goods while exponentially expanding the reaches of globalization (Levinson, 2008). For example, more than half of US imports are intermediary products used to produce finished products, which are then shipped in their final form to destinations, both domestic and foreign.

Supply chain management incorporates the management and planning of all sourcing, procuring, producing (conversion), and logistics-management activities from suppliers, intermediaries, third-party suppliers, and partners, wherever they are located in the world. Supply chain managers are integrators of business functions of all contributing links in the business supply chain. Maritime shipping plays an integral role in the logistical and supply chain system, despite the fact that it is a derived interest (dependent upon demand for the product transported). Because it is a service, any regulatory measures imposed may have a direct effect on the logistical and supply chain system. Supply chain managers must plan and prepare for possibilities and contingencies, while being practical and efficient in their business operations. Some regulatory standards require planning for such contingencies as a terrorist attack or pollution incident, and training requirements are imposed by nations on maritime companies to ensure that ships can adequately respond to or prevent events according to complex risk-based regulatory analysis (ISPS Code, 2002).

The cargo that ships carry is also targeted. Initially, business owners and shippers' attention was focused on preventing pilferage and cargo damage, but a growing concern among nations, and for academics, has been directed towards the security of containers from a terrorist attack or from being used to transport terrorists (Flynn, 2007; Acciaro and Serra, 2013). A disruption of the system due to a known threat (such as a terrorist attack on a port) has great consequences, but in many respects, disruption to the maritime transportation network due to unknown but suspected threats could have even greater consequences, because it is not possible to screen every container in the world. For example, in 2011 an estimated 154 million containers were traded (Mukherjee and Brownrigg, 2013). The ways in which businesses and policy officials manage risk through regulatory standards is described more fully under international conventions.

Regulation of commercial terms and transactions

Shippers and ship owners

If merchants wish to grow their businesses, they must seek new markets for their products and goods as local demand is met. In the past, new markets were often best reached by sea, and often the same holds true today. Maritime transportation services are arranged either through private or public shippers, also referred to as 'carriers' and the differences depend, in part, on how they are regulated, in addition to the types of services performed. Private carriers have relied upon unique contractual terms for hundreds of years covering each transaction that charters the use of a vessel's space and time. These contracts are known as 'charters', and there are generally four types of charter relationship: space, time, voyage, and bareboat. Courts act as interpreters and arbitrators of charters in disputes between the parties, and regulators play a small role in administrating the charter relationship. The burden of employing the vessel is dependent upon the nature of its use. For example, a space charter occurs when a shipper contracts an amount of space on a vessel; whereas a time charter, as the name suggests, is when a shipper contracts a vessel for a certain amount of time. The shipper is responsible for paying the freight for the entire amount of cargo that the vessel can carry for the space or amount of time contracted. The owner remains responsible for the vessel's operating expenses. If it is only needed for one voyage, the vessel owner will bear the entire cost of the vessel operations associated with the trip, and the fee charged will reflect the entire cost of the voyage in the charter contract. However, if a shipper needs to lease a vessel for a lengthy duration of time, then a bareboat charter is appropriate and the shipper will be required to cover the operating expenses of the vessel. This is common practice when a shipper wants to open a new business; for example, to transport produce on a regular basis from a Mexican port to a Florida port without the full investment expense of purchasing a vessel. With a bareboat charter, the owner transfers everything but title to the vessel. At this point, the charterer also becomes the operator of the vessel and is in control of all aspects of vessel operations. These four forms of contracting are still used in the tramp shipping industry today, primarily for bulk commodities such as coal or fertilizer. They have no fixed schedule or definite route, but carry general cargo to any destination and may be diverted to any port as required by potential business. Tramp shipping acquired its name from the appearance and unruly behaviors of the ships, similar to landside hobos. Tramp carriers transport nearly 30 percent of all US overseas commerce, with the remaining 70 percent of cargo moving on common carriers (Buckley, 2008).

The more regulated form of vessel service is known as 'common carrier'. Common carriers are vessel owners that transport cargo from all shippers in less than full shipload quantities. All common carriers must serve all shippers, although a carrier may limit its business to a certain type of goods. It operates on established trade routes, and has published sailing dates and published tariffs for its services. A common carrier that transports passengers is called an ocean liner. Cargo liners are a type of common carrier that ships goods. The contract takes the form of a bill of lading. The ocean carrier issues the bill of lading (generally filled on standard documents), which must be given to the consignee or receiver of the transported goods (Papavizas and Black, 2014). The bill of lading will contain the terms of the agreement between the carrier and the shipper, including the name of the ship to be used to transport the goods between named ports, and on specific sailing dates, in exchange for payment of the appropriate freight to the carrier. The bill of lading accompanies the goods and is an attestation as to the ownership and condition of the goods received for shipment and transferred to the consignee (United Nations Commission on International Trade Law (UNCITRAL), 2015).

Rules for transactions

Governments in countries such as the US responded with laws that stipulated the form of liabilities held by shipper and ship owner. However, there were problems with applying US law in foreign countries, or foreign laws in the US. Consequently, governments worked together to establish standardized rules governing the carriage of goods at sea, expressed in treaties and defined by international conventions and then implemented through national legal regimes. Known as the Hague Rules and later modified as the Hague-Visby Rules, the purpose was to balance the bargaining power between the carrier and the shipper by limiting the exclusions from liabilities claimed by a carrier and thereby increasing shipper protections. This could only be achieved by government intervention negotiated on a global scale (Reynolds, 1990). Two other conventions that have been adopted are the Hamburg Rules and the Rotterdam Rules. The Hamburg Rules formed a uniform legal base for the transportation of goods on oceangoing ships, and came into force on November 1, 1992 (Mukherjee and Brownrigg, 2013). The Rotterdam Rules, adopted by the IMO in 2008, provides a framework that takes into account the many technological and commercial developments that have occurred since the adoption of the other rules, including containerization, door-to-door carriage under a single contract, and the development of electronic transport documents (UNCITRAL, 2015). The convention provides shippers and carriers with a legal framework to support the operation of maritime contracts of carriage, which may involve other modes of transport in addition to a sea leg. Once ratified, these rules will broaden the scope and further define each party's obligations.

Today, ocean liners or cargo liners are container ships running designated trade routes, namely: Europe–Far East, trans-Atlantic, trans-Pacific, intra-Asian (major routes), and lighter routes consisting of Europe–South America, Europe–Australia/New Zealand and Europe–Southern Africa (Mukherjee and Brownrigg, 2013). Most ocean liners are organized in international associations or 'liner conferences', where they direct their efforts to stabilizing their trade (Mukherjee and Brownrigg, 2013). Ordinarily this behavior would be considered anti-competitive, and for the most part, governments permit agreements as necessary to ensure viability of the ocean-liner market (Shipping Act of 1984). Moreover, shipping companies have found it beneficial to work together to service trade routes, with government oversight (Mukherjee and Brownrigg, 2013). Control within regional or national borders is fairly straightforward because of political homogeneity. If a transport monopoly emerges, a government can use its domestic regulatory authority as a substitute for market controls to ensure reasonable prices (that is, competitive levels) and adequate service. If excessive competition develops between carriers (for example, rate wars), then this regulatory authority may be used to impose regulations to stabilize freight rates among competing rivals (Mukherjee and Brownrigg, 2013).

Maritime governance

The Vienna Convention on the Law of Treaties (1969) incorporates customary international law that each nation state has the right to negotiate treaties. Treaties are formal instruments governing relationships between nations and may take the form of bilateral (two party), multilateral (multiple parties), or international conventions, which include multiple nations that have signed the over-arching treaty and agree to incorporate its terms into their domestic laws (Bederman, 2011). In this chapter, maritime governance, when used narrowly, concerns the management, administration, and control of a nation's waters and vessels through legal regimes, including treaties, conventions, and international codes, as well as a nation's domestic legislative and juridical processes and administrative agency practices. An example of the latter is the administration of licensing and credentialing requirements for merchant mariners, or the documentation and inspection of vessels. Maritime governance may also be used broadly to denote the overarching regulatory rubric of global standards, including a nation's regulatory enforcement posture, combined with a nation's separate regulatory standard over the same activity. A nation's enforcement posture and interpretation, as well as a varied regulatory stance, can create confusion in the market and cause distortion, affect competition, and disrupt the smooth flow of shipping. A loose network of mottled legal regimes and practices challenge businesses that rely on international shipping. Progress has been made to establish global standards and protocols to alleviate some of the inherent tensions of conducting business in the global market, yet national and regional political regimes can still interfere with the efficient movement of goods (Wright, 2012).

The policy considerations that regulate the maritime shipping network system and manifest in regulatory standards reflect a variety of public-welfare concerns related to waterborne transportation; they are not limited to ship safety standards, but include other important considerations such as labor standards and climate-change mitigation. The recent prevalence of global outsourcing of manufacturing as a social and business phenomenon has forced shippers to rely especially on an efficient maritime shipping network to transport its intermediary products, as well as raw materials and finished goods. In turn, the maritime network has expanded and adapted – but also necessarily relies upon – an integrated governance posture driving international standards and consistent inspection and regulatory enforcement posture among nations (Mukherjee and Brownrigg, 2013).

Nationalism

With respect to vessel nationality and registration, the UN Law of the Sea Convention (UNCLOS or LOSC) provides that ships may sail under the flag of only one state and be subject to its jurisdiction on the high seas (LOSC, Article 92). Any nation may choose to register vessels, including those that are landlocked and have no merchant marine, and vessel nationality status has become rendered to a commercial enterprise for some, especially developing, nations. However, traditionally, a sovereign nation's extension of nationality could be considered a privilege and mutually beneficial. Nationality provides a form of protection, shielding the vessel from the amount of control other states may exert upon it, and extends national protection, especially during times of war or threat (e.g., Rules Applicable to All Ships, LOSC, 1982, subsection A). Nations benefit from having fleets of merchant vessels that they can draw upon in times of national emergency, by providing not only ready access to ships, but often to trained officers and crew who are its citizens. The nation, or, in the parlance of the international relations community, the state, exercises its political, social, and economic will on its vessels, especially over matters of trade, national defense, taxation, and labor.

The LOSC recognizes each state's sovereign right to formulate what it considers to be evidence of nationality for vessel ownership. Each state must establish a legislative and regulatory framework that 'effectively exercise[s] its jurisdiction and control in administrative, technical and social matters over ships flying its flag' (LOSC, Art. 94). The vessel must be registered in the nation's registry and meet certain documentation requirements specified by the maritime administration of the flag state. Once registered, vessels are required to fly the flag state ensign. It is open to interpretation what is meant by 'administration and social matters' (and perhaps even technical) jurisdiction over the vessel, but suffice it to say that it indicates that a flag state must have an adequate nexus with the vessel to which it confers nationality.

There are two types of registries: open and closed. Generally, maritime registrations using a closed registry require additional citizenship requirements imposed upon entities affiliated with the vessel (Mukherjee and Brownrigg, 2013). Closed registries are the traditional form of registry and grew through the experience of coastal trading nation states. However, a growing trend since the middle of the twentieth century is the preponderance of nations allowing foreign companies to document and register vessels under their flag, with very little or no connection to the nation. These types of registries are known as open registry and are considered less onerous in their regulatory requirements and enforcement. Because of regulatory leniency, these flag states are commonly referred to as 'flags of convenience', due to vessel owners choosing to register their vessels for the sole purpose of gaining relief from burdensome regulatory restrictions. Vessels that fly under open registries constitute more than half of the world's fleet by tonnage and are an increasingly popular business choice (UNCTAD, 2014).

Economic protectionism and cabotage laws

Governments usually use economic protectionism to promote a fledgling industry; however, often, economic protectionist policies are used to sustain an industry, to the detriment of competitive forces (International Chamber of Shipping, 2015). Maritime protectionist policies, it has been argued, have deeper policy reasons than pure economic protectionism, such as ensuring a merchant marine consisting of the nation's citizens is available in times of war or national emergency (e.g., Papavizas and Gardner, 2008). Often referred to as cabotage laws when directed towards protecting a state's maritime domestic trade, many nations have some form of protectionism, but the US is known to have the strictest by granting exclusive rights, in all its forms, to its domestic maritime industry (US Merchant Marine Act, 1920). For example, in the US, only ships built in the US and owned, operated, and crewed by US citizens may transport goods or people from one US port to another (US Merchant Marine Act, 1920; Papavizas and Gardner, 2008). The overall intended effect of maritime protectionism is to ensure a strong domestic merchant fleet; however, in the case of the US, it could be said that protectionist policies have had the unintended consequences of contributing to a strong trucking industry. In 2013, ships only carried less than 4 percent of US domestic trade, and even less than that along its coastline when subtracting the inland river trade (US Department of Transportation, Federal Highway Administration, 2013). The US has recently focused its attention on diverting some of its domestic trade from trucks to ships by promoting short-sea shipping through a program called 'America's Marine Highways' (Energy Independence and Security Act of 2007, 2007).

Role of selected international regulatory bodies

United Nations IMO

The burgeoning industrial revolution and advent of steamships, the frequency of steamship accidents, due in part to more complex mechanical ship systems and drew public attention to safety, especially after the 1912 sinking of the *Titanic* after she struck an iceberg on her maiden voyage between England and America, resulting in the loss of more than 1,500 passengers and crew (Wright, 2012). One of many safety concerns arising from this disaster was the lack of an adequate number of lifeboats for passengers and crew. A series of international conventions for the Safety of Life at Sea (SOLAS) were adopted over time, but the legal process could not keep pace with the realities of the maritime operating environment (Mukherjee and Brownrigg, 2013). Industry practices and technological advances benefitted pockets of society, and it became clear that an international coordinating body was necessary for more robust harmonizing of the various regulatory standards. This was the genesis of the IMO, a specialized UN agency, which first began as a consulting body, but now operates in a stronger leadership and regulatory role, driving global standards development through its technical committees of nation and industry representatives and interest groups (Mukherjee and Brownrigg, 2013).

The IMO consists of 170 member states and three associate members. It works closely with nearly 60 intergovernmental organizations through agreements of cooperation, and, as mentioned above, most of the IMO's work is conducted through technical committees including the Marine Safety Committee, Legal Committee, Marine Environmental Protection Committee, and subcommittees that identify areas for convention development (whether new or amended existing ones) to submit to the larger IMO body. The IMO also employs an agile legal mechanism, known as 'tacit acceptance'. This mechanism enables amendments to enter into force on a set date after being accepted by a specified number of parties to the original Convention. This provides a more timely and transparent regulatory effective date (IMO, 2015).

International Labor Organization

The International Labor Organization's (ILO's) genesis was the Paris Peace Conference of 1919. It is primarily focused on labor social justice matters, and, in the case of shipping, seafarer's rights. It has adopted over 25 recommendations and 30 international conventions relating to mariner labor conditions, but unfortunately its work, similar to the work of other international bodies, is only meaningful when implemented and enforced by individual nations (Mukherjee and Brownrigg, 2013). In 2012, the Maritime Labor Convention entered into force, addressing a broad number of seafarer welfare concerns, including ship working hours, living standards, and access to shore. Providing mariners' shoreside leave has proven problematic in many nations due to heightened concerns over terrorism in the past 15 years, and this issue continues to be a source of ongoing distress for the entire shipping industry (Mukherjee and Brownrigg, 2013).

Law of the sea and freedom of navigation

The intended global agreement governing the sea and navigation is the United Nations Convention on the Law of the Sea. Equally referred to as 'UNCLOS' or 'LOSC', it is actually the culmination of a treaty and four conventions between 1958 and 1982. Most notable is the US refusal to sign the 1982 convention regarding the deep seabed mining provisions. However, the US has acknowledged and incorporated portions of the treaty's terms in its domestic law through the codification of separate international instruments, including those discussed in this chapter (Norris, 2011). The US also stated that substantive provisions of the convention reflect 'customary international law' (Wilson, 2008). Aside from its provisions defining a nation's territorial boundaries, the LOSC establishes general obligations for safeguarding the marine environment and protecting freedom of scientific research on the high seas. It also provides for an innovative legal regime for controlling mineral resource exploitation in deep seabed areas beyond national jurisdiction, through an International Seabed Authority and the 'common heritage of mankind' principle (Frakes, 2003).

A merchant vessel's master is obliged to comply with a coastal state's laws when transiting its waters; the coastal state, in turn, is obliged, as a citizen of nations, to only exercise control over foreign-flag vessels that violate or threaten to violate its laws in certain instances governed by LOSC, other treaties, or areas covered by customary international law. The location of a foreign-flag vessel, the vessel's nationality, and its activity determines whether a nation state has the appropriate authority or jurisdiction over it. A foreign-flag vessel in the internal waters of a coastal state, such as a harbor or port, is most restricted in its conduct or activity and liberally subject to the coastal state's jurisdiction. On the other hand, for example, under LOSC, a foreign-flag vessel transiting 24 nautical miles seaward from a nation's territorial baseline – known as the contiguous zone – is subject to a nation's customs, fiscal, immigration, and pollution laws.

In those areas of the sea that are not defined by law (internal or archipelagic waters, territorial sea, the contiguous zone, or exclusive economic zone) the water is considered 'high seas' and under LOSC (and customary international law) 'freedom of navigation' applies, meaning that all vessels are free to navigate unimpeded unless they are boarded by their own flag state, which always has jurisdiction over its vessel, or by another vessel that relies upon a treaty with the vessel's flag state, where the boarding vessel has usually secured a contemporaneous agreement by that nation to board (e.g., SOLAS 1982; Wright, 2012; Norris, 2011). This is often the case with bilateral and multilateral treaties directed towards thwarting drug- or people-smuggling from certain nations (Wilson, 2008; Mukherjee and Brownrigg, 2013).

Legal obligation: Rescue at sea

The sea is a vast, and often harsh and unforgiving environment. Rules governing the obligations of a master to render assistance to persons in distress at sea are found in LOSC (1982 art. 98) and SOLAS (1974), various provisions including safety equipment, drills, training and competency, and other conventions (SOLAS, 1974). IMO member nations must require their registered vessels to render aid or undertake to rescue any person lost at sea or in distress whenever it is possible for the master to do so, provided doing so does not jeopardize the crew's safety. Coastal member nations of SOLAS must also have rescue centers for conducting adequate search and rescue operations at sea (SOLAS, 1974, Chapter Five). The 1979 International Convention on Maritime Search and Rescue imposes additional obligations on member states to ensure that parties provide assistance to persons in distress at sea. Importantly, no state or master can discriminate in their rescue and response activities. The obligation to render assistance extends to all persons (International Convention on Maritime Search and Rescue, 1979).

Technical regulations regarding shipping

Ship safety

The broad topic of marine safety includes ship safety, the conduct of which affects not only ship operations but also the navigational safety of the vessel in open waters and ports. The term 'ship safety' includes not only navigational safety, but also cargo safety, and personnel and occupational safety. Proposed regulatory standards frequently appear when a marine casualty occurs, especially when there has been a significant loss of life, as was the case with the sinking of the roll-on/roll-off car ferries, *Herald of Free Enterprise* in 1987, and *Estonia* in 1994, which together resulted in nearly 1,000 deaths (IMO Safety, 2015). From these incidents the International Ship Management (ISM) Code was adopted by the IMO in an effort to impress upon flag states, ship owners, and vessel crews the necessity of implementing a safety culture that focuses on identifying and preventing marine casualties, most of which are attributable to human error. The code requires owners to implement a management system on each vessel in their fleet. Flag states are required to inspect, certify, and audit ISM compliance (Mukherjee and Brownrigg, 2013; International Management Code for the Safe Operation of Ships and for Pollution Prevention, 1993). Other SOLAS conventions address ship design, construction, and technical standards, in addition to machinery and electrical installation. Fire protection, detection, and extinction for all ships, and specific safety provisions for certain ship types, such as tankers or passenger ships, have also been adopted. Life-saving equipment, including lifeboats and life jackets, are covered by another SOLAS chapter. Still another SOLAS chapter is dedicated to navigation safety. The Global Maritime Distress and Safety System genesis is found in another code. It is a carriage requirement for all passenger vessels and cargo ships of a certain size on international voyages to help improve their chances of rescue by use of satellite and communication equipment capabilities. With the exception of two codes (ISPS and the Polar Code), the remaining chapters are specific to ship types, such as those that carry dangerous goods (SOLAS, 1974).

Ship security

Although the focus of maritime safety and security seems to be two sides of the same coin, in reality and practice, the attentions are quite different. Maritime safety regulations are directed towards preventing or minimizing accidents at sea that may be caused by substandard ships or human error (Mukherjee and Brownrigg, 2013). Maritime security regulations, on the other hand, are directed towards outside criminal actors or terrorists. The regulatory standards are contained in the International Ship and Port Facility Security Code or ISPS (International Maritime Organization, 2002a), drafted in response to the September 11 terrorist attacks on the US. The purpose of the code is primarily to ensure that ship owners can restrict access to their vessel and its cargo to only authorized persons. Port facilities servicing vessels are required to employ similar access controls. Where the ISM Code goals focus on developing a culture of safety, the ISPS Code is centered on creating a culture of security; although it does not explicitly so state, it does require port facilities and ships to have security officers who can be crew members to perform security duties that include security risk assessments (International Management Code for the Safe Operation of Ships and for Pollution Prevention, 1993; IMO, 2002b). One objection directed towards ISPS is that it is unclear as to its linkage to the Convention for the Suppression of Unlawful Acts Against the Safety of Maritime Navigation, a criminal code pertaining to states' international legal obligations, and in particular, how the two can play out in instances of piracy and other criminal acts. This emerging issue will likely continue to be debated in the IMO for a number of years before there is resolution (Mukherjee and Brownrigg, 2013).

Environmental protection

There are 15 conventions that establish international rules, which are implemented by domestic legislation by states for the purpose of preventing, reducing, controlling, or responding to marine pollution. The overarching authority for each convention is found in LOSC articles 192, 193 and 194, which call for the protection and preservation of the marine environment. Some conventions are directed towards preventing ocean dumping (Protocol to the London Convention on the Prevention of Marine Pollution by Dumping of Waste and other Matter, 1972/96), or controlling trans-boundary pollution (Basel Convention on the Control of Transboundary Movements of Hazardous Wastes and their Disposal, 1989). The most recent conventions are focused on wreck removal and ship debris, including lost cargo, such as containers (International Conference on the Removal of Wrecks, 2007). This convention is a liability and compensation obligation on shippers, allowing for third-party claims. The MARPOL conventions regulate ship source pollutants: oil, noxious liquid substances, packaged harmful substances, sewage, garbage, and air pollution. Other conventions are specific to ship source pollution, such as those concerning ballast water to avoid the transfer of invasive species from one ocean source to another ocean environment (International Convention for the Prevention of Pollution from Ships (MARPOL), 1973/78).

Recently, environmental regulations have tightened for both ballast water and air emissions, despite the fact that ships have the lowest emission levels of all transportation modes per million freight ton-miles (US Government Accountability Office, 2011). Other transportation modes, especially trucks, are not subject to the same level of regulatory treatment, despite the focus on climate-change mitigation. This is likely to be due to the global nature of shipping, whereas competing transportation modes are more domestic. Nevertheless, ships are being required to use very low sulfur fuels, and are being prepared for the ability to switch to fuel alternatives. The trend over the past decade has been a larger supply of ships than the demand of cargoes seeking transport. This has resulted in industry consolidation and some are being driven out of the market. The emerging issue revolves around what shipping firms will do to meet these tighter environmental standards, while maintaining economic sustainability.

Port state control

The influence of IMO is ubiquitous in shipping, in terms of depth of technical regulations and breadth of its applicability to ship types. Its reach affects flag states' and coastal states' ability to regulate maritime shipping. Ordinarily, flag states ensure their vessels comply with IMO provisions, implemented through state legislation, audits, inspections, and other regulatory-enforcement activities. However, many nations believe that some flag states do not meet their IMO obligations, resulting in substandard vessels. UN article 218 of the LOSC permits coastal states to enforce IMO standards if a foreign-flag vessel is determined to be non-compliant within its waters. Known as 'Port State Control', this legal mechanism permits the port state to detain the vessel until it achieves IMO compliance. The concept began as a memorandum of understanding (MOU) between eight North Sea states in 1982, known as the Paris MOU. It was spawned from concerns about substandard vessels transiting their waters; most notably in the aftermath of the tanker vessel *Amoco Cadiz* oil spill (Wright, 2012; Takei, 2012).

The countries party to the Paris MOU target for additional inspection vessels that carry the flags of nations determined to be lax in their enforcement of IMO standards when those vessels are in the waters of the port state (Takei, 2012). Other regional agreements have emerged modeled on the Paris MOU, including the Tokyo MOU and US Coast Guard Port State Control Program (Takei, 2012). Port State Control inspections, detentions, and blacklists have influenced some vessel owners' decisions when choosing open or closed registry for their vessels' citizenship. However, half of the world's fleet remains registered by open-registry, reflecting the fact that significant economic factors still sway in its favor (UNCTAD, 2014).

Recognized organizations and classification societies

Classification societies play a unique and peculiar role in maritime shipping. These are the ship surveyors with the technical expertise to determine a vessel's seaworthiness (that is, the integrity of the ship's structure and operating capability). A ship's investors or equity interests, such as insurers and lenders, who lack maritime technical expertise, have traditionally relied upon class societies. Seaworthiness is a requirement in commercial maritime law, and the Hague Rules, Hague-Visby Rules, and Hamburg Rules require vessel seaworthiness (Mukherjee and Brownrigg, 2013). The IMO uses the term 'recognized organizations', when referring to the technical work conducted by surveyors, or the classification societies. Very often, flag states also rely upon classification societies to provide technical competence, allowable by IMO conventions and most countries' laws (Hormann, 2006).

Not all classification societies are equal, and because they are businesses, they can be subject to economic forces in the marketplace. Many vessel owners choose an open-registry flag because it is cheaper to comply. This similar rationale has proven true with the association of certain classification societies under identified flag states that are perceived to be more relaxed than others, making the relationship an even more economically advantageous choice for vessel owners (UNCTAD, 2014). Noting the causal relationship between classification societies and port state non-compliance, by 2001, the Paris MOU coordinating body began capturing data on classification societies as well.

Emerging trends

Climate change mitigation is an ongoing issue for any pollution-emitting sector, and will be for years to come. As discussed in the section under environmental protection, ships are already targeted to convert to lower sulfur fuels and other alternative fuel sources, despite the fact that they are the most environmentally effective transportation mode (US Government Accountability Office, 2011). As the world focuses on climate-change mitigation strategies, so it also must focus on adaptation, including in ports and the maritime industry. Scientists predict rising seas and an increase in sea storm activity, which would wreak havoc on shipping. As governments begin to grapple with the reality of climate change, the shipping industry must do so as well. According to the United Nations Conference on Trade and Development, the absence of significant climate change mitigation and evidence of rapid adaptation at ports and in the shipping industry renders it very vulnerable (UNCTAD, 2014). One area in which shipping has focused its attention is in the Arctic. Recently, the IMO developed the Polar Code, expected to become mandatory by tacit approval by 2017, for all vessels operating in arctic waters. With rapid icecap melting, newly opened Arctic shipping lanes could reduce shipping from certain regions by two days, and in the world of 'just-in-time delivery' this is significant (International Code for Ships Operating in Polar Waters, 2017). The remaining emerging issue is that of cybersecurity. As noted earlier, a key component of logistics is information; that is, information that tells logistics managers where ships and cargo are at all times. We have, indeed, entered the 'Internet of Things', where ship systems share information to other 'things' on a ship and share information back to the corporate office. This information relies on computerized networks, which are vulnerable to cyberattacks. Ship systems that control key functions are also vulnerable to cyberattacks. We can expect focused attention in this area, either relying upon existing regulatory authority (contained in ISPS Code, (IMO, 2002b) for example) or activity directed towards establishing new rules.

Conclusion

Maritime shipping drives a significant part of the world's economic growth by carrying approximately 90 percent of the world's trade by volume on its oceangoing vessels. The industry is subject to international governing policies, conventions and agreements, customary international law, and domestic laws and regulations, touching upon a variety of areas including maritime safety, security, and navigation, and labor, fiscal, tax, commercial, and environmental standards.

This network industry is a demand-derived commercial enterprise that moves people, freight, information, and services worldwide. An important aspect of this global business is its administrative and regulatory structure over both its commercial and operational sides. The ship must first be categorized by a classification society before it goes into service. Regulation begins when the ship is conferred registry status and is required to fly the ensign of the sponsoring nation state, also known as the flag state, of the vessel. With this status come responsibilities, privileges, and protections of the flag state over the ship and its owners. Because of the inherent risk to freight, cargo, passengers, and the environment associated with shipping, the shipping industry is heavily regulated by its flag state and the nation states visited by ships. Thereafter, a business transaction (such as a charter party) between a ship owner and a shipper may take place to commence the process of the transport activity (shipping) for the cargo to move from one port to another. As a ship conducts its trade, it continues to be subject to regulatory standards and requirements both by the flag state and coastal states. Maritime shipping is not a particularly profitable venture, but it is a necessary enterprise and its continued viability is expected long into the future.

References

Acciaro, M. and Serra, P. (2013) Maritime supply chain security: A critical review, *IFSPA 2013, Trade Supply Chain Activities and Transport: Contemporary Logistics and Maritime Issues*, 636.

Basel Convention on the Control of Transboundary Movements of Hazardous Wastes and their Disposal (1989). New York: United Nations.

Bederman, D.J. (2011) Law of the land, law of the sea: the lost link between customary international law and the general maritime law, *Virginia Journal of International Law*, 51, 299–351.

Buckley, J.J. (2008) *The Business of Shipping*, 8th Edition. Centreville, MD: Cornell Maritime Press.

Energy Independence and Security Act of 2007 (2007) Sections 1121, 1122, and 1123 of Public Law 110–140, approved December 19, 2007 (121 Stat. 1492); amended by 2010 National Defense and Authorization Act, Section 3515, Pub. L. 11–84, 46 U.S.C. 55601; US Coast Guard Authorization Act of 2012, Sec. 405 (H.R. 2838) (US).

Flynn, S. (2007) *The Edge of Disaster*, New York, NY: Random House.

Frakes, J. (2003) The common heritage of mankind principle and the deep seabed, outer space, and Antarctica: Will developed and developing nations reach a compromise? *Wisconsin International Law Journal*, 21, 409–434.

Gottinger, H.W. (2003) *Economies of Network Industries*. New York, NY: Routledge.

Hormann, H. (2006) Classification societies, what is their role, what is their future? *World Maritime University Journal of Maritime Affairs*, 5, 5–16.

Hubner, W. (2003) Regulatory issues in international maritime transport. *Prepared for the Organization for Economic Co-operation and Development (OECD), Directorate for Science, Technology and Industry, Division of Transport.*

International Chamber of Shipping (ICS) (2015) *Annual Review 2014*. London: International Chamber of Shipping Publications. Available at: http://www.ics-shipping.org/news/ics-annual-review

International Code for Ships Operating in Polar Waters (Polar Code), (expected to enter force by tacit approval January 1, 2017), International Maritime Organization, London.

International Convention for the Prevention of Pollution from Ships (MARPOL) 1973/78, available at: http://www.imo.org/KnowledgeCentre/ReferencesAndArchives/HistoryofMARPOL/Documents/MARPOL percent2073-78 percent20Brief percent20History percent20- percent20List percent20of percent20amendments percent20and percent20how percent20to percent20find percent20them.htm (accessed May 23, 2015).

International Convention on Maritime Search and Rescue, 1979 (with annex). (1979). London: International Maritime Organization.

International Management Code for the Safe Operation of Ships and for Pollution Prevention (1993). London: International Maritime Organization.

International Convention for the Safety of Life At Sea (SOLAS), International Maritime Organization, London.

International Maritime Organization (IMO) (2002a) *International Convention for the Safety of Life At Sea, IMO activities to enhance maritime security*, Conference of Contracting Governments to the International Convention for the Safety of Life at Sea. London: International Maritime Organization.

International Maritime Organization (IMO) (2002b) *International Ship and Port Facility Security Code (ISPS) and SOLAS Amendments 2002*. London: International Maritime Organization.

Levinson, M. (2008) *The Box: How the Shipping Container Made the World Smaller and the World Economy Bigger*. Princeton, NJ: Princeton University Press.

Mukherjee, P.K. and Brownrigg, M. (2013) *Farthing on International Shipping*. Heidelberg: Springer.

Norris, A.J. (2011) The 'Other' law of the sea, *Naval War College Rev*, 64, 78.

Protocol to the London Convention on the Prevention of Marine Pollution by Dumping of Waste and other Matter, 1972/96.

Papavizas, C. and Black, H.A. (2014) *Maritime Law Answer Book 2014*. New York, NY: Practicing Law Institute.

Papavizas, C.G. and Gardner, B.E. (2008) Is the Jones Act redundant? *21University San Francisco. Maritime Law Journal* 95–137.

Paulsen, G.W. (1983) An historical overview of the development of uniformity of international maritime law, *Tulane Law Rev*, 57, 1065.

Reynolds, F. (1990). Hague Rules, the Hague-Visby Rules, and the Hamburg Rules, *Austl. & NZ Mar. LJ*, 7, 16.

Rodrique, J., Comtois, C. and Slack, B. (2006) *The Geography of Transport Systems*. New York, NY: Routledge.

Takei, Y. (2012). Institutional reactions to the flag state that has failed to discharge flag state responsibilities. *Netherlands International Law Review*, *59*(01), 65–90.

Title 46 United States Code Chapter 556, *Short Sea Shipping*.

United Nations Commission on International Trade Law (UNCITRAL) (2015) United Nations Convention on Contracts for the International Carriage of Goods Wholly or Partly by Sea (New York, 2008) (the 'Rotterdam Rules'), United Nations, Commission on International Trade Law, United Nations, New York, available at: http://www.uncitral.org/uncitral/en/uncitral_texts/transport_goods/2008rotterdam_rules.html (accessed April 30, 2015).

United Nations Conference on Trade and Development (UNCTAD) (2014) Review of Maritime Transport, UNCTAD/RMT/2014.

United Nations Convention on the Law of the Sea Conventions (1982) 1833 U.N.T.S. 3 (hereinafter referred to as LOSC or UNCLOS).

US Coast Guard, (USCG) Navigation and Vessel Inspection Circular (NVIC) No. 10-94, Washington, DC, available at: http://www.uscg.mil/hq/cg5/nvic/1990s.asp#1994 (accessed May 25, 2015).

US Department of Transportation, Federal Highway Administration, Freight Facts and Figures, 2013. Washington, DC: Government Printing Office.

US Government Accountability Office, A Comparision of Road, Rail, and Waterways Freight Shipments That Are Not Passed on to Consumers, GAO-11-134, 2011. Washington, DC: Government Printing Office.

US Merchant Marine Act (1920) Public Law 66–221. United States.

Vienna Convention on the Law of Treaties (1969) 1555 U.N.T.S. 331. Available at: https://treaties.un.org/pages/ViewDetailsIII.aspx?src=TREATY&mtdsg_no=XXIII-1&chapter=23&Temp=mtdsg3&lang=en (accessed September 22, 2015).

Wilson, D.G. (2008) Interdiction on the high seas: the role and authority of a master in the boarding and searching of his ship by foreign warships, *Naval Law Review* 55, 157–211.

Wright, P.G. (2012) Shipping Regulatory Institutions and Regulations. *The Blackwell Companion to Maritime Economics*, 11, 281.

16
European rail policy and regulation

Matthias Finger

Introduction

This chapter focuses on railway reform in Europe, as the continent where the most significant and comprehensive policy and regulatory efforts have been undertaken over the past 25 years. Indeed, Europe is not only the 'continent of the railways' (as opposed to North America, for example) but also the only place in which deliberate policy efforts to revive railways have been undertaken. The driver for such profound railway reform covering the entire continent is clearly the European Commission (EC).

Importantly, this chapter starts from the observation that, despite 25 years of European railway reform, the outcomes are sobering, even in the EC's own assessment. Even though the modal share is slowly changing for the better, it is not doing so as fast as it should and remains at approximately 6 percent for passengers and 10–11 percent for freight (as of 2013) (Garofalo, 2014). Liberalization is progressing to some extent, but there is still a patchwork of different national systems, much of which is uncoordinated at the European level. Additionally, even though competition exists, it mostly occurs between former state-owned railway companies and their subsidiaries, most private operators having either disappeared or been acquired by incumbents. Of course, the EC is trying to promote a certain model of how railways should be governed nationally, but no clear framework has yet emerged and the existing models all appear to be somewhat unstable (Finger and Rosa, 2012). Finally, financing remains a taboo and very difficult topic, as most railways continue to be underfinanced and no clear way out is visible.

This chapter is not a policy evaluation; such an endeavor would be unfair, given that European railway reform is still underway. Such an evaluation would also be overly ambitious, since we are talking about a European policy implemented at the member-state level. Nevertheless, this chapter aims to conduct something of an intermediary assessment: after 25 years of railway reform in Europe, one may question whether the approach chosen for this reform is likely to yield the desired results. In this sense, this chapter raises, for the first time, the issue of whether European railway reform is actually on track.

Consequently, the chapter is structured as follows: first, we set the stage by highlighting the main relevant technological and institutional characteristics of the generic railway sector/industry, looking in particular at the financial dimensions of rail. These characteristics are important because any form of policy intervention into the sector needs to take them into account. After the stage is set, an outline of the EC's approach to (European) railway de- and re-regulation is provided. The EC's approach is unique and has no equivalent anywhere else in the world. It is important to understand the reasoning behind it, along with its unfolding. Next, we look at the specific approach to liberalization as conceived by the EC. This approach is basically characterized by regulatory policies and subsequently by regulations to be applied on a European-wide scale. We highlight the unique nature of this approach. We then ask whether other approaches to railway reform could have been possible. Finally, we try to answer the question of where European railway reform will ultimately end or lead.

Technological, economic, financial, and political characteristics of railways

In this section, we set the stage by highlighting the main relevant technological and institutional characteristics of the generic railway sector or industry, looking in particular at the financial dimensions of rail. These elements are important because any form of policy or regulatory intervention into the sector needs to take them into account (Nash, 2013).

Rail technology and economics

Historically, railways consisted – at the institutional level – of vertically integrated national public enterprises, most of which enjoyed a national monopoly. However, technologically, railways were – and still are – composed of several elements, altogether forming an integrated socio-technical system:

- First, there is the rail *infrastructure*, consisting of tracks and signals. Infrastructure features are long-lived assets, which, in economic terms, constitute sunk costs. Infrastructure must be planned and corresponding investment decisions must be taken into account. Once planned, infrastructure must be built and maintained. Rail infrastructure design and capacity basically determines transport capacity and potential discriminations. Time-lags are particularly important here.
- *Stations* are generally considered part of the rail infrastructure. They are the places where trains stop and passengers enter and exit the railway system. Railway stations are also long-lived assets, although their time horizon is somewhat shorter than that of tracks. Economically, stations also constitute monopolistic sunk costs.
- *Rolling stock* is the third element of the railways system, consisting of both locomotives and wagons. Rolling stock is also a long-lived asset, though the time horizon is shorter than for tracks or stations. To a certain degree, rolling stock is movable and does not necessarily constitute a sunk cost, provided it is interoperable with other tracks, which has not been the case in the past.
- In addition, there are a series of *systemic functions* that combine tracks, stations, and rolling stock. Typically, operation is such a systemic function, as it combines available tracks (train paths) with rail demand in an optimal way, building in particular on the interoperability between tracks and rolling stock. The two other main systemic functions are timetable construction and ticketing (or, more generally, sales). Indeed, even though the customer mounts a train, the product is ultimately an integrated one combining quality tracks with quality rail-transport services.

Rail financing and policy

Railways are subsidized socio-technical systems, at least up to today. Even the most market-oriented rail system, which today is the British rail system, covers only 50 percent of its operating costs, the other 50 percent being subsidies from various public actors. Most other railway systems are even more heavily subsidized – and this does not even include investments. It is important to remember that railways have come to exist – in Europe, in the late nineteenth and early twentieth centuries – because of national public policies and corresponding investments. In other words, rail finance is an essential element of the context of railways, liberalized or not. Over time, it has become widely accepted to break down such financing and to link it to specific objectives, resulting mainly from new public-management approaches to running public entities. Such breakdowns do not necessarily change anything in the overall amount public authorities will ultimately pay for a railway system, but it brings transparency and accountability, notably linking payments with public policy objectives. It makes sense to break down such financial support of a railway system along its technical characteristics, as outlined below:

- First, public authorities pay for *network* development and network maintenance, codified generally in terms of concession and/or service delivery (performance) contracts. This is the most costly block of a (national) railway system, and moreover one that cannot be billed to customers directly. Railway stations (of some size) are generally treated similarly.
- Second, public authorities pay for – that is, subsidize – *rail services* (train operations). Of course, over time, sophisticated mechanisms have been put into place to decide upon which type of train operations will be subsidized. The general agreement today is to distinguish between commercial services (not to be subsidized; such as most freight services, international passenger services, and long-distance national rail services) and services falling under public services obligations (PSOs). The latter are tendered (because of the use of public money) and generally enforced by way of concessions and/or contracts.
- Third, there are rail policy elements that fall under a systems perspective, namely *track access charges* and *priority rules*. Track access charges are basically an arbitration (and incentive) mechanism: even though they do not alter anything in terms of the ultimate amount of money that will be put by the public authorities into the overall railway system, track access charges basically decide upon how financing is divided between infrastructure and train operations. The second systemic element is priority rules; that is, the politically defined rules by which public authorities (by virtue of their subsidizing the entire railway system) decide which type of transport – freight, international, national, or agglomeration – has priority over the other in case of congestion and, more generally, in the case of slot attribution.

All of the above considerations pertain to a generic (technical) railway system; that is, they are valid regardless of ownership and (degree of) competition. The only factor that could eventually make these considerations evolve is technology; namely, technological developments that fundamentally alter the very nature of infrastructures, rolling stock, and the interaction among them. So far, no such fundamental rail technological changes are in sight.

EU railway reform

Having defined the key technical and institutional characteristics of a national railway system, we shall now outline the EC's approach to (European) railway de- and re-regulation. This is done in three steps: first we present the reasoning behind the EC's vision. We then outline the main policy – and especially regulatory policy – steps in implementing this vision. Finally, we briefly discuss the latest stage in the implementation process; namely the Fourth Railway Package that is currently under discussion, as this debate best illustrates the main issues that have arisen as part of this implementation process.

Europe's vision and approach

Europe's – or more precisely the EC's – vision has not changed over time, and has been reiterated on numerous occasions and in various policy papers. To recall:

> the backbone of the EC's idea [was] to insert more competitive pressure as an incentive to increase efficiency, achieve cost reductions and encourage innovation, not only in terms of technical progress, but also in terms of more customer orientation and better business models.
>
> (Garofalo, 2014)

The overall political objective is to make rail more competitive compared to road (for freight and passengers). This, in turn, is achieved by creating competition in the European rail sector, with the ultimate aim of creating a single European (internal) railway market or area. This is achieved by way of so-called unbundling; that is, separation between infrastructure and train services, as summarized in Figure 16.1.

The creation of the Single European Railway Area (SERA) consists, thanks to unbundling, of two separate elements: on the one hand the creation of an integrated, fully interconnected, and interoperable European railway infrastructure, whereby, ultimately, national infrastructures

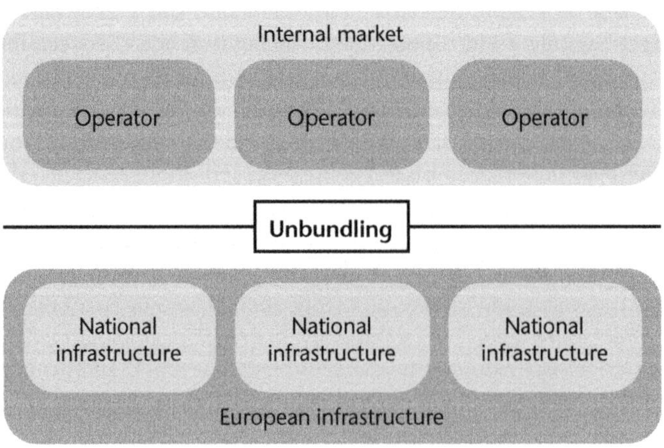

Figure 16.1 Unbundling and the creation of a single European railway area

Source: Author's own elaboration.

will be integrated into a higher, European railway infrastructure. On the other hand, and thanks to this fully integrated and interoperable infrastructure, a single European railway market will ultimately emerge, by which train-operating companies will compete on equal footing. Figure 16.1 also implicitly shows that this creation of a SERA is ultimately a political goal, namely the goal of European political integration. While this vision is perfectly logical and coherent, it is nevertheless a political vision, the market being simply a tool for realizing this vision. As such, this vision is up against the (political) reality of national, vertically integrated railway companies. These will ultimately have to be broken into (at least two) pieces if this vision is to be implemented. Moreover, this vision, and especially its implementation, works against the above technological (such as interoperability, interconnection, capacity), institutional, and financial realities, such as non-discriminatory third-party access to the infrastructure and state aid.

Steps towards implementation

Everything the EC has done in matters of railways since the early 1990s can be put into the broad context of implementing this very vision, notably by way of a stepwise approach. Figure 16.2 summarizes the main policy actions of the EC towards the realization of its vision.

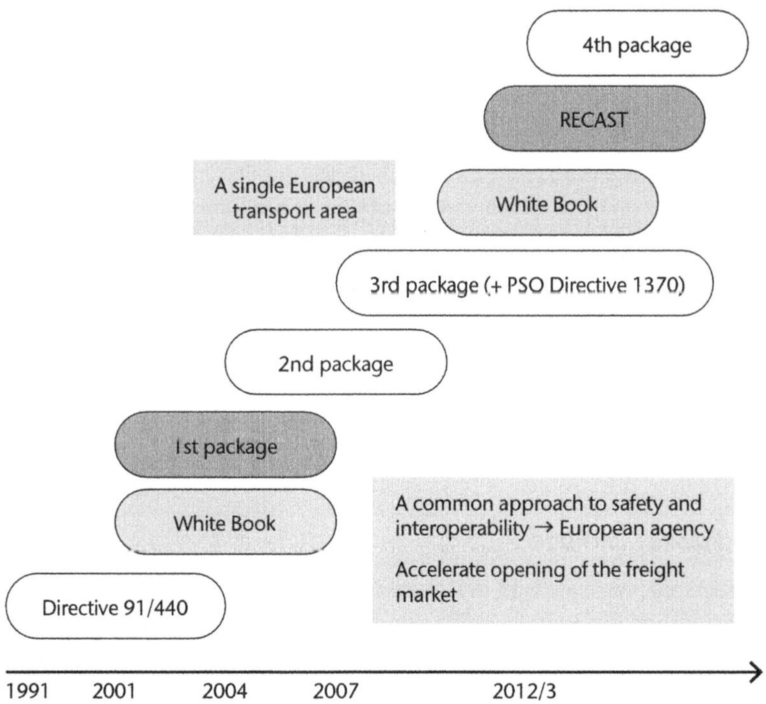

Figure 16.2 Main legislative steps of EU/EC railway reform

Source: Author's own elaboration.

The main elements of these different EC legislative actions can be described as follows:

- The trigger and first step, everybody agrees, is Directive 91/440. In it, the EC outlined principles of managerial independence of railway undertakings from their respective (government) owners, accounting separation or unbundling (between monopolistic infrastructures and competitive transport services), financial restructuring of railway undertakings, along with a first approach to non-discriminatory access to certain freight corridors.
- The next step – the so-called First Railway Package, which came in 2001, 10 years after the Directive – further promoted independence of the railway infrastructure (now called infrastructure manager) with clear financial accounting and access rules. The Package also aimed at extending freight liberalization beyond the corridors. Finally, it inaugurated the so-called independent rail regulatory authority, which became the prominent organization created to accompany Europe's railway de- and re-regulation process.
- The so-called Second Railway Package in 2004 saw the full European-wide (including national) liberalization of freight by 2007. However, its main focus was on the definition of common European interoperability and safety rules, along with the creation of a (single) European Railway Agency (ERA) charged with the implementation and supervision of precisely these technical (and safety) rules.
- The aim of the Third Railway Package (the most recent) was to open Europe's transboundary passenger market (including cabotage) by 2010, providing for some safeguards (against competition) in the case of some railways services of public interest. In addition, the Third Package provided for further technical harmonization (certification of rolling stock and drivers' licenses). Finally, the Third Package is also seen as the beginning of European-wide passenger rights. Though technically not part of the Third Package, the so-called PSO Directive (1370) distinguished, for the first time, between train operating services of public interest, which may be subsidized, and (domestic passenger) services that can be freely organized by train operating companies. Directive 1370 appeared to be somewhat problematic, as it was initiated from outside the railway sector (DG Internal Market); therefore it is slated to be revised in the Fourth Railway Package.
- Finally, the so called 'Recast' of the First Railway Package (2012/2013) focused mainly on accounting rules for clearly separating infrastructure from transport services, but went further in that it also defined non-discriminatory access to infrastructure-related facilities, or so-called 'essential facilities'. Additionally, the remit and powers of the independent regulatory authorities were further expanded and strengthened.

The Fourth Railway Package

In January 2013, only one year after the 'Recast', the EC proposed a Fourth Railway Package. This package was supposed to be a significant step towards the completion of European railway liberalization, notably by also opening up the domestic passenger markets. However, this Fourth Package has since run into problems. As such, the discussions around this Fourth Package perfectly illustrate the main issues to which European railway liberalization has led.

First, we should mention the non-controversial issues. These are all the issues that pertain to safety and interoperability, leading to a strengthening of the European Rail Agency. Indeed, everybody seems to agree that the creation of a SERA requires interoperability and a common approach to safety, monitored and enforced by a European authority.

What is contentious is the opening up of the domestic passenger markets by way of competitive tendering. Concrete issues here pertain to the 'economic equilibrium test' by which the regulator will have to judge whether tendering endangers public services provision. Moreover, it is not clear how lucrative (non-PSO) and subsidized (PSO) franchises could be combined. Even more contentious is the idea of reciprocity (the condition that only an unbundled operator may be able to bid for franchises). There are still other provisions aimed at further guaranteeing the independence of the infrastructure manager from the railway services operator. These provisions are criticized by the still (such as Deutsche Bahn, Ferrovie dello Stato) or newly (re-)integrated railway undertakings (such as SNCF in France). Of course, this all goes together with further strengthening the national railway regulatory authorities, along with the creation of a new European railway regulator, called the European Network Rail Regulatory Body (ENRRB). The latter, in turn, is criticized by the national regulatory authorities and their already existing (private) association, called the International Regulators Group – Rail (IRG-Rail).

Given the highly controversial nature of the Fourth Railway Package, it may be separated and only its non-contentious aspects implemented, at least in a first stage (see also last section of this chapter).

Policy by regulation and regulators

In this section, we look, in particular, at the specific approach to liberalization as defined by the EC. This approach is basically characterized by regulatory policies and subsequent regulations. Our aim is to highlight the unique nature of this approach. Railway regulation derives directly from the EC's approach to liberalizing, namely from the idea of unbundling, of a seamless European railway infrastructure, and of an international transportation market. We first present what is regulated, then discuss who regulates what, and finally offer some considerations about regulators, both national and European.

What is being regulated in railways?

The basic idea of the European approach is competition in the market; namely, competition among train-operating companies on a seamless European-wide infrastructure system. The main focus of railway regulation – with the exception of safety – follows directly from there and pertains to discrimination:

- First, there is the idea of *non-discriminatory access* to the infrastructure (system): regulations (and regulators) are there to ensure such non-discrimination (such as access to slots), whereby operators can complain if they are discriminated against by the infrastructure manager. Such non-discriminatory access is steadily expanded from simple access to the tracks to non-discriminatory access to service facilities and many other things. The end of discrimination, and therefore of regulating non-discriminatory access, is not (yet) in sight.
- Beyond access, *discrimination* must be prevented, requiring regulation in numerous areas that, directly or indirectly, affect train-operating companies, especially new entrants: such areas of discrimination are on the one hand *infrastructure* and on the other *transport*. On the infrastructure side, discrimination can be located in the way the network is planned, developed, built, and operated. In all these steps of the infrastructure cycle, discrimination – that is, favoring the incumbent by way of constructing, improving, and maintaining the infrastructure – is possible and regulation must prevent precisely that, for example, via

non-discriminatory planning or non-discriminatory maintenance practices. Since the infrastructure is a natural monopoly, economic regulation of course primarily pertains to efficiency (Cantos and Maudos, 2001; Friebel *et al.*, 2010; Finger and Messulam, forthcoming).

- On the *transportation* side there are other types of discrimination on top of the above-mentioned access to quality railway slots; namely, the question of priority rules. Often, these priority rules are set politically; in essence, this refers to the question of which of the transport modes – freight, international passenger transport, national passenger transport or agglomeration transport – has priority over the other. Related to this are questions pertaining to timetables, planning, and execution, as there is manifold potential for discrimination when slots are attributed both on a short-term and on a long-term basis. Another major discrimination potential in transport is the tendering process: do companies have equal chances to apply? Is tendering conducted correctly? Is the tender executed properly?
- The EC's general idea is that if unbundling is done properly, non-discrimination is much less of an issue, or is at least less systematically conducted in favor of the integrated (incumbent) firm. All the above discrimination factors must of course always be supervised, but the risk of discrimination is diminished if unbundling is done properly. Thus, a fourth area of regulation (pertaining to discrimination) is about supervising unbundling, especially in the case of not (yet) fully unbundled railway undertakings. This implies, in particular, the question of cross-subsidies, as well as information exchange between the train operating part of the railway undertaking and its infrastructure.

While discrimination and its prevention is the main focus of regulation in the railway industry, there are three other issues requiring regulation, two of which are technical and one political:

- First, there is the issue of *safety*, which is a major regulatory issue in all the network industries, especially transport. Safety pertains to tracks, but also to rolling stock and train drivers. As competition develops, the need for safety regulation generally increases in importance, as deregulated companies have the tendency to cut corners on safety.
- A second technical regulatory issue pertains to *technical harmonization*, namely interoperability rules and all kind of standards that need to be developed, and subsequently enforced by regulation so as to make the SERA possible. Of course, technical standards are also a source of discrimination, making technical harmonization an economic regulatory concern as well.
- A third, political aspect is regulating *passenger rights*: passenger rights were introduced more recently (Third Railway Package in 2007), as competition – just like safety – is likely to lead train-operating companies to cut corners on passenger rights. Therefore, such rights need to be defined and enforced.

The emergence of regulators

Historically, safety and technical regulation predate all other forms of regulation. Safety and technical regulation was traditionally located within a ministry. However, over time, such regulation has been made independent from the ministry and transferred, at least in some countries, to independent (safety) regulators. More importantly, however, safety has rapidly moved up to the European level, especially when the ERA was created in 2004. Since then, safety and technical regulation have become the clear prerogative of Europe – that is, the task of the ERA. The ERA's powers were defined in the Second Railway Package and are slated to be expanded in the Fourth Railway Package. As a matter of fact, safety and technical regulation is still considered to be a distinct area, as it is not politicized and there is significant consensus that technical harmonization, especially interoperability, is the only means by which the SERA is ultimately going to come about.

The novelty in matters of regulation is of course the non-discrimination regulation in the four areas described above. This new form of regulation – also called 'economic regulation' – is made necessary because of the introduction of competition into a formerly vertically integrated monopolistic system. The need for economic regulation was recognized early on and already set down in the First Railway Package (2001), in which the creation of independent National (economic) Regulatory Authorities (NRAs) was mandated for all member states. Remits and powers of these NRAs were expanded again in the Recast, and are set to be expanded further in the Fourth Railway Package (should it be adopted). In general, the need for, and the powers of, NRAs are not really disputed, at least not at the European level. The Recast also creates a new, European-wide regulatory body, the ENRRB, which is currently conceived as a coordinating mechanism – coordinated by the EC – so as to harmonize and streamline regulatory practices (Finger, 2011). The creation of this body follows the same logic as has already been observed in the other network industries. The ENRRB comes on top of IRG-Rail, a self-organizing mechanism set up by the NRAs themselves in 2011. It is clear that the EC wants to control these regulatory practices, which is why it created the ENRRB, much to the chagrin of IRG-Rail. However, in the long run, ENRRB will prevail (as in the other network industries), and will become ever more powerful and more controlling of the NRAs.

Third, then, is the question of *passenger rights*: regulating passenger rights is an eminently political task and the EC has not yet decided who is going to be in charge of it. At the present moment, member states, while obliged to comply, can attribute the task to any agency of their choice. So far, it is not clear to whom this task will ultimately be attributed, but it is conceivable, as in the case of electricity, for example, that passenger rights, as a form of consumer protection, will ultimately also end up with the NRAs.

There has also been a discussion, albeit an aborted one, to merge economic and technical regulations and make them all part of ERA. This is highly controversial and has, so far, no precedent in any other network industry. It may well not happen.

Towards the Europeanization of railway regulators

Figure 16.3 summarizes the process of creating NRAs, as well as the Europeanization of regulators.

While this process looks logical and straightforward, it hides a series of issues that remain mostly unaddressed. Indeed, setting up NRAs is far from a harmonious and straightforward process. While all member states (that have railways) have set up NRAs, there remain huge differences in terms of their remits, their powers, and especially their resources (European Transport Regulation Observer, 2013). There is also an issue of the focus of the regulator, most of which are very narrowly concentrated on specific discrimination matters. Only the German, and to a greater degree, the British regulators have a comprehensive view of, and approach to, rail regulatory matters.

However, the most important issue remains the question of the NRAs' independence. Especially in countries with integrated railway undertakings, the independence of the railway regulator is absolutely key. Yet, on numerous occasions, the EC has drawn the attention of member states to the lack of independence of their NRAs. And this is precisely the reason why

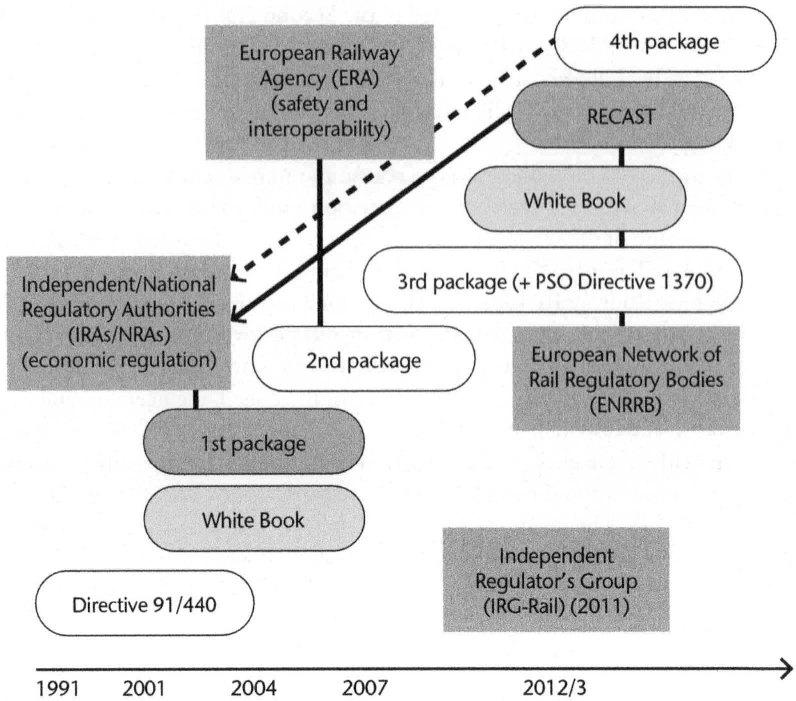

Figure 16.3 Creation of regulators

Source: Author's own elaboration.

the EC is now pushing for the Europeanization of NRAs in the form of the ENRRB. To recall, having an independent NRA is critical for making the European approach to railway liberalization work, given the many differences among European railway markets.

What alternatives would have been possible?

As shown above, there is a coherent European approach to railway de- and re-regulation. This approach proceeds from a political vision, as articulated most recently in the European White Paper on Transport (2011). Its aim is, among others, to create a Single European Transport Area by harmonizing and integrating the various infrastructures (rail, road, waterways), along with creating competition among the operators using this infrastructure. All policies, especially regulatory policies, contribute precisely to achieving this objective.

Despite all the regulatory policy efforts of the EC, there remain huge differences among the member states in terms of railway markets, the structure of the railway undertakings, their regulation, and regulators (Beria *et al.*, 2012; Finger and Rosa, 2012; Finger, 2014; van de Velde, forthcoming). For example, take the case of the fully fragmented British system, where there is no longer an incumbent train-operating company, but there is a strong regulator that basically holds the railway system together (Bowman, 2015; Cowie, 2015). A second example is the Swedish system, which is characterized by an infrastructure (including road infrastructure) that is integrated inside the ministry, which in turn encourages competing train (and bus) operating companies to use this infrastructure (Alexandersson and Rigas, 2013). Furthermore, there is the system as ideally conceived by the EC, with a fully unbundled infrastructure manager and (still very dominant) incumbents using this infrastructure. However, there is also the not yet fully unbundled holding company, which still owns the infrastructure along with the train operating company, and often also a freight company, as is the case in Germany (Link, 2012), Austria, Italy, and recently again France. It appears, in fact, that the EC no longer aims at harmonizing these different institutional systems. Consequently, we are far from a single European railway market, let alone a technically harmonized and interconnected infrastructure that allows for interoperable train operating companies to actually serve the European railway market and its users.

The question to ask at this point is whether alternatives would have been possible. However, before answering this question, I will briefly outline what possible alternatives are actually available by referring to concrete examples. To reiterate, the European approach banks on unbundling; that is, creating clear separation between infrastructure managers (to be harmonized and integrated at a European level) and train operating companies (to compete against one another at a European scale). In other words, alternatives are integrated railway systems, be they national or not, ideally with some elements of competition (following the liberal idea that markets are more efficient than monopolies):

- A first often-cited railway system is the Japanese one: Japan is indeed considered to be a very performing railway system, some of whose companies are privatized and profitable (Mizutani, forthcoming). However, this system reflects a very particular geographic situation, consisting mainly of one single line. Competition primarily takes the form of 'benchmark competition', whereby fully integrated railways are compared against each other because of some structural similarities, such as Japan Railway (JR) East, and JR Central. However, there is no access from one railway operator to the infrastructure of the other.
- A second often-cited railway system is the US one, as this system seems to be profitable (Mallikarjun *et al.*, 2014). Here, fully integrated (freight) companies are competing against each other, sometimes along parallel lines. Yet, once again, the US system is quite particular, inasmuch as we are only talking about freight, as well as about a system that is not very technologically advanced. This situation is hardly comparable with Europe, and even less so transposable to Europe.
- A third, generally cited railway system is the Swiss one (see also Chapter 25 of this book), as this clearly appears to be the highest performing one, at least among the European railways (see Desmaris, 2014; Duranton *et al.*, 2015). Despite the fact that the Swiss railway system is composed of several companies, there is no real competition and access by competitors is limited to freight transport. Competitors are basically agreeing with each other (corporatist model). However, again, the Swiss system is not really transposable to the European level, given its strong public-policy backing and corresponding financial support. As a matter of fact, the Swiss system more closely resembles an urban (or agglomeration) transport system, where competition, at best, can take the form of (some) franchises.

In other words, neither the Japanese, nor the US, nor the Swiss railway systems could qualify as alternatives to the European approach. First, they are all national systems and not transnational ones. Second, in all three systems, competition is very limited. The question therefore is whether the EC would have had other options than the one chosen. It is fair to say that there is no current alternative model available. Yet, one may argue, the EC could have chosen alternative paths to creating a SERA. Even this statement seems somewhat hazardous: indeed,

I consider that, given the EC's ambition to create a single European rail market, or at least a single European rail transport area, there is no intellectually sound alternative to the one chosen, with seamless infrastructure on the one hand and competitive access to this infrastructure on the other, all of which are accompanied by strong, sector-specific regulators and corresponding European harmonization efforts. Unfortunately, this intellectually sound vision may never actually see its full implementation.

Where will this all end?

So, where will this vision, accompanied by directives and other forms of EC regulations, all end? Before attempting to answer this question, it is worth returning to the beginning of this chapter, namely (1) to the current balance sheet and (2) to the key (technological and institutional) features of a railway system. It is clear that the balance sheet, as measured by the increase in modal shift, has not been a success thus far: railways have not really become much more competitive vis-à-vis the road in both passenger transport and freight. Railways are also not yet a success in terms of reducing public subsidies. The latter may have been an overambitious goal to begin with, as the very technological and institutional characteristics of railways inevitably lead to heavy public subsidies. However, public financing comes automatically with public policy objectives, and since the majority of public financing is still national, these public policy objectives will also be national, and thus will not necessarily contribute to the creation of the single European railway market. Needless to say, there are increasing constraints on (national) public finances, which will end up making national, and subsequently European, railways less competitive. Unfortunately, these are realistic constraints that will, as a minimum, slow down the creation of the single European railway market. So what is the likely outcome?

In our opinion, the foreseeable result of the combination of the above mentioned technological, institutional, and financial characteristics (constraints) of the (still very national) railway sector with the EC's vision and regulatory policies aimed at creating a SERA by way of seamless infrastructure and access competition will lead to the following six factors:

1. *Access competition* will not become the dominant form of competition in the European rail market, despite all efforts made by the EC to this effect. Access competition will prevail in freight, but probably not on the entire network, as there may simply not be enough of a market pull. It is likely that access may also prevail on some international passenger-transport lines.
2. The dominant form of 'competition' in the rail sector will be competitive tendering of franchises, called 'franchising'. The main question here, of course, will be the balancing (such as the economic equilibrium test the regulator will have to apply) between competitive franchises on the one hand and PSO franchises on the other, or, as it appears now, the possibility to combine both.
3. Subsequently, the main focus of the regulators will less be on discrimination issues, which should be solved by proper and transparent tendering procedures, and more on issues of market distortion due to state aid in the context of PSO Directive 1370. At this point, it is not clear whether this issue will actually be dealt with by the independent NRA or, more likely, by the competition authority – which would further fragment the regulatory landscape.
4. As a result, it may be that the EC will gradually redefine its original objective of creating a single Europe-wide railway market and rather – in light of the technological (such as interoperability), institutional (including unbundling) and financial (such as investments)

– focus on selected corridors, where it has the political clout and perhaps also the financial means to enforce its vision of free access. This vision will certainly be applied to freight, and probably also to some international passenger-transport lines.

5 Even to achieve the above, the EC will most likely further push the coordination, harmonization, integration, and ultimately Europeanization of the national independent regulatory authorities, as it has already started to do with the creation of the ENRRB. This may lead, in the end, to the creation of a European economic regulator, perhaps combined with the already existing European technical and safety regulator ERA.

6 Finally, I am convinced that the EC will also further push the question of passenger rights. Not only are passenger rights fully in line with the EC's philosophy and approach, but they are also relatively easy to implement, considering that it will be difficult for the railway undertakings to go against such politically accepted ideas.

In conclusion, I would like to highlight that, despite this likely evolution, the last word may not have yet been had. Indeed, it appears that all transport modes have entered into a more turbulent era recently, driven as they are by a combination of technological changes, notably in this case information and communication technologies, and changing customer/citizen demands. As a matter of fact, customers and citizens increasingly seem more interested in integrated mobility solutions that combine all modes of transport, rather than in isolated, though optimized, rail or car transport modes. It is conceivable that commercially operating intermediaries between customer needs and transport offerings will emerge (such as mobility solutions providers). These intermediaries, if they become widespread, will certainly create new dynamics in all the transport modes as well as across them. This will lead to the need for new regulatory approaches and policies at national, but even more so, European levels – an initiative that the EC has actually already started to tackle.

References

Alexandersson, G. and Rigas, K. (2013) Rail liberalisation in Sweden. Policy development in a European context, *Research in Transportation Business and Management*, 6, 88–98.

Beria, P., Quinet, E., de Rus, G. and Schulz, C. (2012) A comparison of rail liberalisation levels across four European countries, *Research in Transport Economics*, 36(1), 10–120.

Bowman, A. (2015) An illusion of success: The consequences of British rail privatisation, *Accounting Forum*, 39(1), 51–63.

Cantos, P. and Maudos, J. (2001) Regulation and efficiency: the case of European railways, *Transportation Research Part A: Policy and Practice*, 35(5), 459–472.

Cowie, J. (2015) Does rail freight market liberalisation lead to market entry? A case study of the British privatisation experience, *Research in Transportation Business and Management*, 14, 4–13.

Desmaris, C. (2014) The reform of passenger rail in Switzerland: More performance without competition, *Research in Transportation Economics*, 48, 290–297.

Duranton, S., Audier, A., Hazan, J. and Gauche, V. (2015) *The 2015 European Railway Performance Index. Exploring the Link Between Performance and Public Cost*, Boston Consulting Group. Available at: http://www.bcg.fr/expertise_impact/Capabilities/operations/PublicationDetails.aspx?id=tcm:105-182451andmid=tcm:105-182467 (accessed on 16 May 2015).

European Commission (2011) *White Paper on Transport. Roadmap to a Single European Transport Area – towards a competitive and resource-efficient transport system*. Available at: http://ec.europa.eu/transport/themes/strategies/2011_white_paper_en.htm (accessed on 16 May 2015).

European Transport Regulation Observer (2013) *Rail regulatory divergence – does it matter?* European University Institute: Florence School of Regulation, Florence. Available at: http://fsr.eui.eu/Documents/WorkshopPaper/Transport/2013/131129-ETRObserverRailwayRegulation.pdf (accessed on 16 May 2015).

Finger, M. (2011) Towards an European model of regulatory governance? In D. Levi-Faur (ed.) *Handbook on the Politics of Regulation*. Cheltenham: Edward Elgar, pp. 525–535.

Finger, M. (2014) Governance of competition and performance in European railways: An analysis of five cases, *Utilities Policy*, 31, 278–288.

Finger, M. and Rosa, A. (2012) *Governance of competition in the Swiss and European railway sector*, Final Research report, European University Institute/Florence School of Regulation, Florence.

Finger, M. and Messulam, P. (forthcoming) Rail Economics and Regulation, in M. Finger and P. Messulam (eds) *Rail Economics, Policy and Regulation in Europe*. Cheltenham: Edward Elgar.

Friebel, G., Ivaldi, M. and Vibes, C. (2010) Railway (de)regulation: A European efficiency comparison, *Economica*, 77, 77–91.

Garofalo, E. (2014) *The 4th Railway Package under Negotiation: Where do we stand?* Available at: http://fsr.eui.eu/Documents/WorkshopPaper/Transport/2014/141212MarketRailSummary.pdf. Accessed on 16 May 2015.

Link, H. (2012) Unbundling, public infrastructure financing and access charge regulation in the German rail sector, *Journal of Rail Transport Planning and Management*, 2(3), 63–71.

Mallikarjun, S., Lewis, H.F. and Sexton, T.R. (2014) Operational performance of US public rail transit and implications for public policy, *Socio-Economic Planning Sciences*, 48(1), 74–88.

Mizutani, F. (forthcoming) Looking beyond Europe, in M. Finger and P. Messulam (eds) *Rail Economics, Policy and Regulation in Europe*. Cheltenham: Edward Elgar.

Nash, C. (2013) Rail transport, in M. Finger and T. Holvad (eds) *Regulating Transport in Europe*. Cheltenham: Edward Elgar, pp. 61–81.

van de Velde, D. (forthcoming) European railway reform: Unbundling and the need for coordination, in M. Finger and P. Messulam (eds), *Rail Economics, Policy and Regulation in Europe*. Cheltenham: Edward Elgar.

17

Policy and regulation of air transport

The European experience

Benjamin Lehiany, Alain Jeunemaître and Hervé Dumez

Introduction

Policies and regulations governing the air transport industry find their roots in various motivations that go beyond purely economic reasons. These include safety, national sovereignty and defense, and environmental sustainability. Indeed, since the signing of the Paris Convention in 1919, which provided states with sovereign rights of the airspace over their territory, airspace has become a natural resource for governments, and the 'laissez-faire' approach that developed in the early years of aviation has been progressively replaced by state administration of publicly owned flagship monopolies (Doganis, 1973). Cross-border transportation was regulated through bilateral agreements between states, often supplemented by confidential arrangements on commercial issues between airlines. However, by recognizing the need to freely exchange 'air traffic rights', to regulate fares and tariffs, and to develop an optimized traffic flow management, states embarked on international negotiations that sought to develop multilateral agreements. Both the Chicago Convention in 1944 and the Geneva conference in 1947 failed to reach such agreements, leaving the International Civil Aviation Organization (ICAO) and the International Air Transport Association (IATA), created in 1944 and 1945, respectively, as the governing bodies in charge of common standards for international aeronautical activities.

In spite of these international initiatives, states remained ultimately responsible for safety, security, and economic oversight of airports and Air Navigation Service Providers (ANSPs). In particular, safety regulations included pilot certification, carrier licensing, and blacklists, as well as traffic management that would assist in avoiding collisions through ground handling and by systematically maintaining vertical and horizontal distances between flying aircrafts. However, there has been growing consensus that unnecessarily restrictive regulations may have led to significant shortcomings and economic inefficiencies regarding the ultimate objective of air transport policies and regulation, which is to ensure low-fare and safe air transportation to the largest possible proportion of the population.

> Recognising these shortcomings, several OECD governments have initiated reforms in the past two decades. Their aim was to improve efficiency and reduce airfares by increasing competition, encouraging the rationalisation of air networks, and enhancing airline governance.
>
> (Gönenç and Nicoletti, 2001: 184)

Along with institutional bargaining, introducing competition has been constrained by the particular technical and economic characteristics of the industry. Indeed, from an economic perspective, air transport can be seen as a network industry (Schmalensee, 1995; Dumez and Jeunemaître, 2001) that relies on an infrastructure network (airports, airspace routes, beacons, and radar) and associated air transport services (ATS). These components induce network externalities and natural monopoly characteristics such that specific regulatory designs come as a second-best option where markets cannot do the job (Dumez and Jeunemaître, 2001).

In this chapter, we first discuss the 'network industry' dimension of air transport by placing stress on the need to regulate the natural monopoly components of the industry. The second part introduces a narrative of the European policy and regulatory dynamics regarding the liberalization of the aviation market and the integration of the European sky.

The whys and hows of regulating air transport

The air transport industry exhibits particular techno-economic characteristics – including natural monopoly components (Schmalensee, 1995; Dumez and Jeunemaître, 2001) – such that efficiency and safety rely on relevant market and regulatory designs. Therefore, the main challenge faced by policymakers so far has been the attempt to introduce market-based mechanisms wherever they are workable, and to simulate competitive outcomes through economic regulation where a market-based solution appears inefficient. Competitive components would fall under common competition policy, including antitrust law related to abuse of a dominant position in airport capacity (Kosenina, 2013), whereas issues of natural monopoly would be subject to sector-based regulation defined as technical and economic. In other words, technical and economic rules would be applied to a particular sector to ensure transparency, non-discrimination, and proper functioning.

Air transport as a network industry

From a purely economic perspective, there is no robust rationale for restricting competition between airlines (Fu *et al.*, 2010) such that flag carrier monopolies were far more 'legal' than 'natural' (Pelkmans and Luchetta, 2013). Even if an aircraft could be somehow considered as infrastructure, it is not related to an infrastructure network that exhibits externalities and natural monopoly characteristics. On the other hand, airports (nodes), air corridors (ties), and associated ATS compose the infrastructure of the air transport network, and call for a specific regulatory design. Figure 17.1 depicts the architecture of the industry and specifies the natural monopoly and competitive components.

First, airports are infrastructure components that may be considered as natural monopolies, particularly the major hubs serving large capital cities, which are essentially compulsory points of entry. They face very limited competition from smaller airports in their city or region and enjoy market power, allowing them to arbitrarily set high prices that could result in excessive and unjustified profits. However, the monopoly power is mitigated by competition in less congested point-to-point airports (Kosenina, 2013).

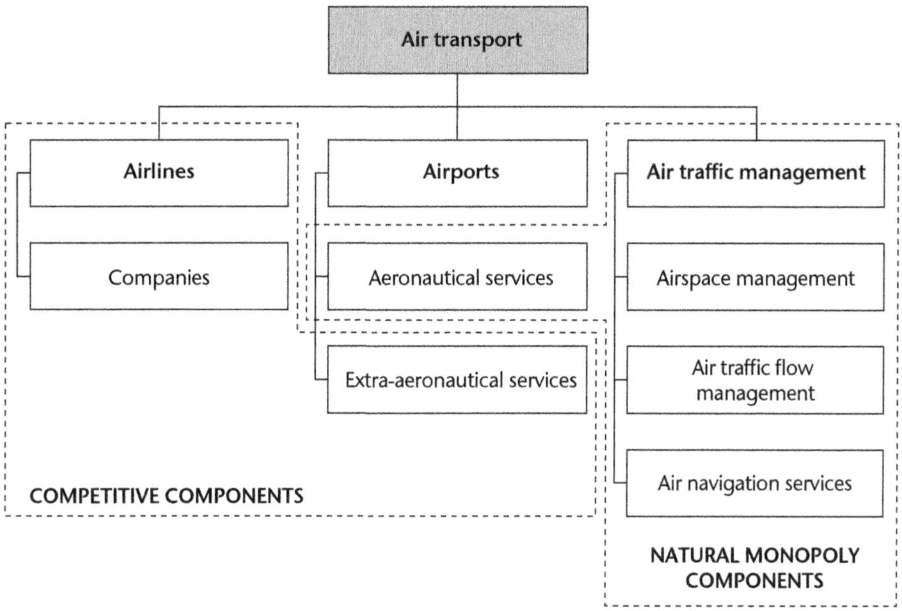

Figure 17.1 The architecture of the air transport industry

Second, from an economic perspective, air traffic management (ATM) can be viewed as a large technical system (Mayntz and Hughes, 1988), providing a range of services that ensure the safety of flights. It is composed of three main elements (see Figure 17.2 below):

- The network infrastructure, for example airspace design, route structures, and radar.
- Air traffic flow management, which aims to optimize the use of the infrastructure network.
- Air navigation services, which include air traffic control (ATC) (en-route and airport services), infrastructure services (communication, navigation, and surveillance), and advisory and ancillary services (alerting, meteorological forecasting, and other services).

ATC, in turn, is comprised of three components (Dumez and Jeunemaître, 2001):

- Airport ATC, which optimizes aircrafts' landing and take-off phases, as well as the use of runways;
- Approach ATC, which guides airplanes in the ascending and descending phases of flights in airport environs;
- En-route ATC, which controls airplanes during the cruising phase in upper airspace above 6,000 meters. Particularly, it ensures sufficient vertical and horizontal separation between planes in upper airspace to prevent collisions. The provision of service is based on ground radar infrastructure that provides ATC centers with information about airplane position, speed, and direction. Controllers track airplane movements, communicate with pilots through Very High Frequencies, and order them to make changes in altitude and speed when potential trajectory conflicts occur.

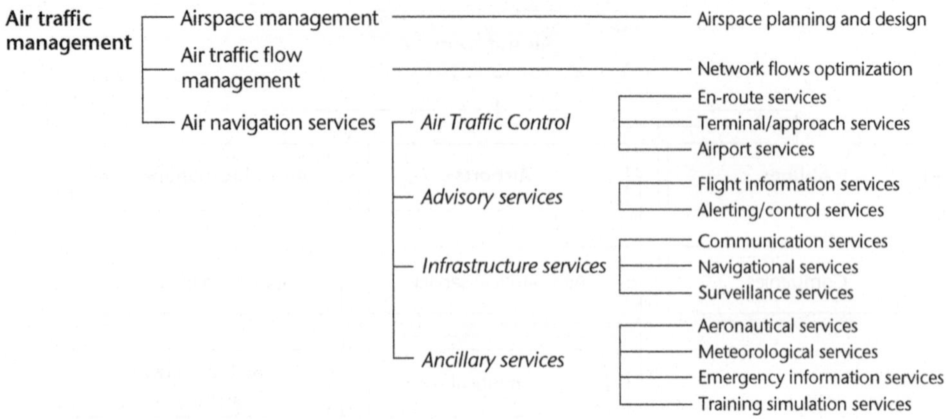

Figure 17.2 Components of air traffic management

Source: McCulloch *et al.*, 2001.

The upper and part of the lower airspace are sectorized into portions of, on average, 100 to 150 kilometers. Each ATC center manages a defined number of sectors with teams of two to three controllers simultaneously handling a maximum of 15 to 20 flights in each sector, depending on traffic complexity (that is, the number of crossing-routes at a particular time in a given sector). At low traffic hours, sectors are regrouped and the number of controllers is reduced, while the portion of airspace they manage is larger. Conversely, at peak hours, when airspace is more congested, sectors are divided up into smaller portions. This means the number of controllers increases in proportion to the number of opened sectors, as does capacity absorption. However, under such circumstances, coordination between sectors becomes more complex, such that dividing an airspace sector by two only increases capacity by 1.5 (Dumez and Jeunemaître, 2001). Moreover, increasing the number of sectors by division has a limit such that capacity absorption of an ATC center is constrained by three technical and economic variables: air traffic complexity, the number of sectors that an ATC center can open, and the decreasing returns in sectorization. Adjustment of capacity absorption to traffic fluctuations is made by regrouping and opening sectors (Dumez and Jeunemaître, 2001). From the above overview, one can deduce typical 'network industries' attributes:

- Air transport has network components made of 'nodes and links' (Schmalensee, 1995), namely airports and airspace routes, as well as the communications between controllers and pilots based on information about ground infrastructure, requiring data transmission and coordination between sectors in order to cope with network externalities.
- Air transport networks have capacity constraints (Dumez and Jeunemaître, 2001). For a pre-set route, ATC capacity equals the absorption capacity of the weakest node; that is, the ATC center that can cope with the smallest number of flights along the set route in a given period of time.
- ATC networks have natural monopoly components. As long as a given sector cannot simultaneously be controlled by two or more providers, airlines cannot choose a competing service provider for flying in that particular sector once the management of an airspace sector has been delegated to an ATC center.
- Economies of scale are likely to exist in the provision of service, such that large ATC centers could achieve cost-savings in management, coordination of control, and

rationalization of sectors. Nevertheless, the provision of service is labor intensive, with very few technological innovations, and still relies on strip bands and VHF frequencies (Grushka-Cockayne *et al.*, 2008).

To summarize, air transport exhibits the economic particularities of a network utility even if – by contrast to other utilities – the natural monopoly and infrastructure components are difficult to identify. If airports, beacons, and primary and secondary radars clearly appear as the tangible infrastructure of the network, it seems sensible to consider airspace as a structured and scarce resource composed of intangible infrastructure, such as routes and sectors, including communication navigation surveillance systems and ATC systems. Network externalities lie in the need for coordination and harmonization in defining routes, sectors, communication between ATC centers, air navigation, communication, and surveillance systems. As for the monopoly components, they prevail in airports, radar infrastructure, and the provision of service over an airspace portion (Dumez and Jeunemaître, 2001).

Regulating natural monopoly components of the network

All airports and ATS are subject to ICAO principles with regards to user charges, transparency, consultation, and cost-effectiveness. The three basic principles established by ICAO are expressed in Article 15 of the *Convention on International Civil Aviation*, usually referred to as the Chicago Convention, as follows (ICAO, 2013):

- Uniform conditions shall apply to the use of airports and air navigation services in a contracting state by aircraft of all other contracting states;
- The charges imposed by a contracting state for the use of such airports or air navigation services shall not be higher for aircraft of other contracting states than those paid by its national aircraft engaged in similar international operations;
- No charge shall be imposed by any contracting state solely for the right of transit over, entry into, or exit from its territory of any aircraft of a contracting state or persons or property thereon.

Ultimately states remain responsible for safety, security, and economic oversight of airports and ANSPs. Thus, along with these principles and traditional competition law, one can identify a number of potential needs for additional economic regulation (ICAO, 2013):

- Mitigating the risk that airports could engage in anti-competitive practices or abuse any dominant position;
- Ensuring non-discriminatory and transparent charging regimes;
- Incentivizing airports to invest in a cost-effective way to meet current and future demand;
- Protecting the interests of end users, namely passengers and shippers.

Several types of economic regulation could conceivably assist in reaching these goals and produce competitive outcomes – mainly in terms of investments, charges, and profits – when competition does not exist. As long as it is designed to provide the appropriate incentives while avoiding excessive regulatory burden, economic regulation of air transport is expected to promote competition over fares and cost of services to users (mostly airlines and passengers) and encourages efficiency through cost-effective new investment (Adler and Liebert, 2014).

The regulation of airports

Until the end of the 1980s, airports were state-owned and regulated by national administration. However, beginning in the 1990s they became corporatized or privatized under various shareholdership statuses (Gillen, 2011). This new form of governance did not exclude the potential for dominance by a privatized airport operator, which has raised concerns over industry competition, such as market dominance in case of owning several airports (Adler and Liebert, 2014), or discriminatory practices regarding airline competition, barriers to entry, or distortion of airport investment plans. Therefore, most privatized airports are subject to economic regulation (Gillen, 2011).

Furthermore, an aspect that is specific to airports is that they provide two types of services: aeronautical services for airlines (maintenance, investment in runways, and ground handling) and passengers (baggage handling, public facilities, and lounges), but also non-aeronautical services (parking services, restaurants, and shops) that are commercially related. Under the 'single-till' approach, both aeronautical and extra-aeronautical revenues are regulated simultaneously, whereas the 'dual-till' approach differentiates both types of services and associated revenues. In general terms, ICAO does not impose a particular form of economic oversight on airports depending on the profit or not-for-profit status (Adler and Liebert, 2014). Regardless of the ownership status or the use of single- or dual-till approaches, the range of possible forms of regulation goes from light-handed approaches (such as 'fallback regulation') to more invasive forms of economic regulation (such as 'price-cap' or 'cost-plus' regulatory approaches).

Fallback regulation

In the light-handed 'fallback regulation' approach, deterrence of monopoly power is found in the threat that price controls may be imposed in the case that an airport's behavior goes beyond 'acceptable' bounds. The main benefit of this *ex-post* approach is to avoid regulatory costs and distortions. The main issue is to state clearly what 'acceptable' means, so that airports have clear economic boundaries within which to operate. Nevertheless, defining those boundaries in detail may create precisely the regulatory distortions that this approach seeks to avoid.

Cost-plus regulation

Cost-plus regulation, also called 'cost of service' or 'rate of return' regulation, is designed to address the issue of unjustified monopoly profits. In this case, the airport may be required to obtain approval for the level of charges and investments in order to limit its rate of return on capital at the level prevailing in a competitive market. However, cost-plus regulation may provide the airport with a strong incentive for overinvestment in order to increase the volume of its profit (Littlechild, 1983).

Price-cap regulation

In the price-cap approach, also called RPI-X, the regulator sets a maximum price for airport services for a period of three to five years. The cap is periodically adjusted according to the fluctuation of general inflation – the Retail Price Index – minus a productivity factor for the considered period (the X factor). This approach has been used as an incentive for companies to improve their productivity in the short term by allowing them to reap the benefits when they outperform the cap, while in the long term increasing efficiency through the price review mechanism. Nevertheless, the choice of price-cap instead of cost-plus regulation has produced profits in excess for airports, and curbing them has introduced more bureaucratic controls than originally expected.

Under such forms of regulation it is possible to regulate airport revenues either under the single-till approach – including aeronautical activities and non-aeronautical activities in the scope of regulation – or the dual-till approach, in which economic regulation applies separately to aeronautical services, with no adjustment reflecting the costs of non-aeronautical services. The choice between both alternatives has been discussed at length (see Adler and Liebert, 2014); in particular, advocates of the dual-till approach stress that non-aeronautical services incentivize airports to make less use of their market power on aeronautical services. Generally, the price-cap associated with the dual-till regulation is more efficient than the fallback approach, the least appropriate form of economic regulation being cost-plus associated with whether single-till or dual-till 'reducing efficiency by 25 percent and 19 percent respectively' (Adler and Liebert, 2014: 102).

Regulating air traffic services

European ATM service provision has developed according to a national vertical integration governance with the bundling of services under administrative management procedures. Each country has organized its own ATM system. Each has designed a network of beacons allowing pilots and controllers to draw routes, a radar system that allows controllers to follow the aircraft in real-time, a telecommunication system between pilots and controllers, a weather information system, a rescue system in case of accidents, and ATC centers (Dumez and Jeunemaître, 2010).

- When an aircraft crosses a national boundary, it generally leaves one control system and enters another. The pilot takes leave of the controller of the country she is leaving and greets that of the country she is entering. Since VHF frequencies are saturated, and since it takes time to leave and to signal entry in a new airspace, national boundaries rarefy flows (Dumez and Jeunemaître, 2010, p. 159).

En-route charging is based on national unit rates, and is proportional to the flight distance. Therefore, regulating ATS must first involve increasing commitment to service quality through an appropriate charging regime for the provision of ATS, and second increasing network capacity through efficient congestion management mechanisms.

Charging regime for ATS

In a standard market, supply meets demand by means of a market price mechanism. As far as the provision of ATS is concerned, this market-based mechanism has not been introduced. Instead, pricing is based on collecting en-route charges through a cost-recovery mechanism. Indeed, since the Chicago Convention, states have agreed to charge users only enough to cover the costs of delivering safety, thereby preventing them from using their airspace as a financial asset.

In Europe, en-route charges are levied by the Central Route Charges Office, part of Eurocontrol, which collects payments on behalf of European member states. Charges are proportional to flight distance over national airspace and the square root of the maximum take-off weight of the airplane. For a given year, the national unit rate is the ratio of total cost of national ATC service provision (operational costs, capital expenses and investment, and contribution to Eurocontrol costs) divided by flights controlled in national airspace expressed in service units (Dumez and Jeunemaître, 2001). A service unit equals a 100-km-distance flight for a 50-ton airplane. This makes the charging regime uniform and independent of air traffic density and complexity to be handled in national airspace, without any differentiation between ATC centers and peak or low traffic hours. Thus, en-route charges do not reflect the real costs of providing the service at a particular time in a particular airspace portion. Furthermore, in practice, the costs of service provision are not related to airplane weight, which benefits companies that use small airplanes.

Network congestion management

At peak hours, supply cannot meet demand on a set route and queuing is organized at airports according to the available capacity of the weakest ATS network node (Dumez and Jeunemaître, 2001). This node corresponds to the most congested sector, which cannot cope with more than a certain number of flights along the route. In that case, regulation of congestion consists of take-off airport slots being allocated according to the available capacity declared by ATC centers a day in advance. Once capacity is known, slots are allocated to airlines on the basis of a 'first-planned-first-served' rule.

In short, airspace congestion is administered without taking into account users' preferences. Quality of service, including costs of delays incurred by users, has no impact on ATS national revenues. Thus, whatever a member state's investment policy in ATS capacity and quality of service is, costs are entirely recovered and passed on to users without any economic incentives for ANSPs to adjust to demand fluctuations. No credible monopoly regulation has been implemented for European member states or at the European level yet. Likewise, the en-route charges mechanism does not penalize or incentivize providers when service provision and quality of service do not meet demand requirements. Inefficiencies and lack of productivity that translate into insufficient traffic absorption are not penalized. As costs are fully recovered, under-capacity only causes lower traffic volumes and higher national unit rates. Furthermore, delays caused by mismanagement of national ATC systems are not internalized, and only users bear the costs of delays. From the ANSPs' viewpoint, there is no economic incentive for reducing delays (Dumez and Jeunemaître, 2001).

In terms of network flow management, the traffic is rarefied by national boundaries and depends on the organization of capability units decided at the national level (Dumez and Jeunemaître, 2010). From an economic perspective, national fragmentation results in losses in economies of scale regarding service provision; lack of coordination in the use of airspace infrastructure; duplication of costs through the multiplication of ATC centers;[1] lack of interoperability, and no harmonized status for controllers impeding intra-EU mobility. Thus, the fragmentation of ATM service provision has led the European Commission (EC) to pursue economic integration through the Single European Sky (SES) initiative. Regulatory packages have successively addressed the above shortcomings in order to improve ATM performance. The next section introduces a longitudinal study of the SES development through liberalization and market integration.

Air transport European policy: Liberalization and market integration

The Single Market European Act II issued by the EC identifies four drivers for growth, including 'developing fully integrated networks in the Single Market' and 'fostering mobility of citizens and business across borders' (EC, 2012: 5). It emphasizes that 'networks are the backbone of the economy and the aim is to achieve a Single Market where citizens and businesses benefit from one single transport and energy market' (EC, 2012: 5). In the air transport sector, as in other network industries, this ultimate objective is being achieved via a liberalization perspective (Dobson, 2010). The first step in this liberalization has been opening markets to competition from operators and service providers, which has had the effect of increased intra-European trade while putting pressure on infrastructure capacity (O'Reilly and Stone Sweet, 1998). A second step, still in progress, is to develop an SES through network integration, interoperability, and cross-border flow management.

Liberalization of air transport in Europe

Liberalization has meant dismantling flagship monopolies and allowing free movement across Europe with unrestricted competition among the European airlines (Baumgartner and Finger, 2014). At the same time, air transport liberalization has translated into airports' (partial) privatization and new forms of regulation (Reinhold *et al.*, 2010).

Creating a competitive aviation market

Liberalization of air transport has been achieved in three main institutional stages (Dobson, 2010; Baumgartner and Finger, 2014). In particular, Dobson (2010) showed how negotiations over the creation of a single European aviation market have been shaped by a small majority of member states and the EC, resulting in dramatic changes between 1987 and 1997. In 1987, the first liberalization package reduced fare restrictions and gave carriers additional flexibility for cooperation. In 1990, the so-called second liberalization package allowed all European airlines to carry passengers to and from their home countries to other EU member states (cabotage). In 1992, the third package introduced the common licensing of carriers and freedom of access to the market, with almost total freedom to set fares. According to Baumgartner and Finger (2014: 30), 'this freedom allows the airlines of a European Member State to operate to and from any EU member country, including on domestic flights'. Since 1997, the liberalization process has been considered complete and successfully achieved (Pelkmans and Luchetta, 2013).

Indeed, liberalization has led to effective economic and traffic growth thanks to increased competition and substantial efficiency gains (Fu *et al.*, 2010). Following the implementation of the final stage of liberalization, low-cost carriers such as Ryanair and EasyJet started to emerge. Today, they account for approximately 25 percent of total traffic in Europe (Eurocontrol, 2012) and their market share is expected to grow beyond 50 percent of intra-European traffic (Wulf and Maul, 2010). The direct response of surviving flag carriers has been to cluster in worldwide alliances – namely Star Alliance, OneWorld, and Sky Team created in 1997, 1999, and 2000, respectively – in order to maintain profitability through economies of scale and joint marketing strategies. Those alliances have also been naturally induced by the multiplication of bilateral agreements between states around the world.

Later, in order to boost this success, European institutions adopted Regulation 1008/2008, consolidating the three previous regulations. This guideline clearly sets the technical and financial conditions for an airliner to obtain the European operating license to be considered as a European air carrier entitled to provide air services throughout the EU. Regulation 1008/2008 also aims at protecting customers by banning price discrimination on the basis of nationality or place of residence. In other words, for the same product – that is, the same seat on the same flight bought at the same moment – no price difference should be observed. Transparency over pricing has been strengthened by asking air carriers to specify all the details comprising the final price, including charges, taxes, and fees.

As a result, the number of national and cross-border city pairs was estimated at 8,448 in 2009, compared to 692 in 1992 (Pelkmans and Luchetta, 2013). There is still a limited – but growing – number of competitive city-pair routes (less than 30 percent are operated by more than one carrier), keeping in mind that many submarkets do not structurally allow for more than a single operator. Where it is effective, competition has driven prices down, allowing more Europeans to travel by air, and has allowed airlines to optimize their networks within and across national markets (Fu *et al.*, 2010). Nevertheless, new market entry and increase in traffic remain constrained by congestion in airports and suboptimal ATM (Adler and Liebert, 2014) justifying new modes of regulation (Fu *et al.*, 2010).

Deregulating and re-regulating airports

As mentioned above, European airports were state-owned and regulated by national administrations until the end of the 1980s. At the time, they were regulated through a cost-plus mechanism according to the single-till approach (as outlined above). Liberalization started in 1987 when the British government privatized the three London airports, namely Heathrow, Gatwick, and Stansted, together with the Scottish airports. Whereas privatization and induced performance-based management proved successful in the UK, most EU member states were reluctant to lose total control over their airports, and thus engaged in partial privatization with a majority public stake (Gillen, 2011). Today, even though the vast majority of airports remain publicly owned, the new environment has facilitated the emergence of new business-models and more profit-oriented behaviors, calling for more systematic economic oversight. Indeed, from most airlines' viewpoints, major publicly owned airports are using their market power as much as partially privatized ones are (Reinhold *et al.*, 2010).

Experiencing the shortcomings of the cost-plus approach, notably in terms of incentives to reduce costs, price-cap regulation based on the RPI-X formula was introduced first in the UK (Littlechild, 1983), then progressively in major European airports. In 2000, the first airport to be regulated with a price-cap applied in accordance with the dual-till approach was Hamburg. This was soon followed by Malta (in 2001) and Budapest (in 2005; see Gillen, 2011), 'reflecting the view that regulation should be confined to the monopolistic bottleneck and incentives for developing the non-aviation business should not be lessened' (Reinhold *et al.*, 2010: 75).

Regarding regulation of slot allocation and non-discriminatory access to airports, Regulation 93/1995 was adopted to facilitate access of new entrants to newly available slots (Baumgartner and Finger, 2014). However, this measure has not been fruitful, and access to congested airports for new entrants has remained largely contested (Kosenina, 2013). To cope with this, Regulation 793/2004, which amended Regulation 93/1995, allowed member states to delegate seasonal slot-allocation to a national 'coordinator', providing air carriers with access to airports on a transparent, neutral, and non-discriminatory basis. The current slot-allocation mechanism in Europe relies on four rules (Combe, 2011; Kosenina, 2013):

- The 'grandfather' rule, which is a conservative rule according to which any airliner that has exploited slots in the past, in accordance with the coordinator, has priority over these slots for the next allocation season. This rule allows investment edging for incumbents, but acts as a barrier to entry.
- The 80/20 rule, or the 'use-it-or-lose-it' rule, aims at avoiding the retention of unused slots and stipulates that any slot that has not been used for more than 80 percent of a season should be relegated to a common pool to be reallocated to other companies. As a response,

and in order not to lose their slots, some companies have engaged in the so-called 'baby-sitting' strategy, which consists of operating small aircraft to increase the rate of utilization.

- The 50/50 rule, which states that 50 percent of the available slots in the common pool should be freely allocated first to new entrants (those owning less than 5 percent of available slots), the remaining 50 percent being offered to incumbents if they ask for them. Given the 5 percent threshold effect – which limits eligibility to the first round of slots allocation – this rule facilitates entry but limits small incumbents' growth.
- The 'swap' rule, according to which airliners are allowed to barter – but not sell – slots under the coordinator's supervision and following the 'one slot for one slot' rule.

In the UK, a secondary market for unused slots has been in effect since 1999, such that monetary compensations are allowed; but this is an exception to European regulations. In other words, to date no market-based mechanism for slot allocation is clearly recognized in Europe, which has resulted in a strengthening of incumbents' market power in congested airports.

To sum up, following the UK initiative to deregulate its aviation market in the late 1980s, the EU has entered into an institutional process of liberalization. Whereas market opening was successfully achieved in 1997, there remain some market power issues regarding non-discriminatory access to major publicly owned airports and slot allocation. In order to fully benefit from the competitive aviation market, the EU has engaged in the second phase of the process: the creation of an SES.

An attempt to market integration: the SES initiative

The EU's method for industry restructuring, which has brought about significant outcomes benefiting consumers through market opening, is now being applied to infrastructure and ATM integration. Integrating ATM across Europe goes back to the 1950s and 1960s. At the time, the core countries of Europe – France, Germany, Luxemburg, the Netherlands, and the UK – considered an agreement to delegate ATC in upper airspace (high-level flights crossing European airspace) to a central European agency, Eurocontrol (Mendes de Leon, 2007). The attempt failed due to opposition from the military, leaving Eurocontrol with the single task of creating a common ATC center (the Maastricht Upper Area Control Center), which only covered the airspace of Belgium, the Netherlands, Luxemburg, and adjacent German airspace. Consequently, from the 1960s to the 1980s no European integration progress occurred, meaning that ATC systems operations were run by national administrations with airlines paying charges to national states according to their flying distance over a country's respective airspace.

Towards the creation of a Single European Sky

ATM became an important issue for Europe when annual air traffic began to grow significantly, partly spurred by air transport liberalization (O'Reilly and Stone Sweet, 1998) which placed pressure on the system capacity and resulted in escalating flight delays (in 1986, 12 percent of intra-European flights were delayed by more than 15 minutes, which increased to 25 percent in 1989). After the first liberalization package on air transport, the then Commission of the European Communities issued its first Communication on 'Air Traffic System Capacity Problems' (COM/1988/577 Final). The 32-page blueprint Communication may be considered a landmark document, as it attempted to address all the shortcomings of European ATC management. ATC systems of member states across Europe were heavily interdependent, but non-interoperable. There was no coordination at the European level to manage air traffic flows.

The Communication also reiterated that the internal market had to be completed by 1992 in order to ensure free movement of goods and services and required an efficient air transport system upon which ATM would be central in reaching that objective.

In response, during the 1990s a number of initiatives were undertaken, such as the European Air Traffic Control Harmonisation and Integration Programme (EATCHIP) and the creation of a European Central Flow Management Unit (CFMU) within Eurocontrol. Furthermore, in 1998 the Performance Review Commission (PRC) was set up to monitor progress. Nevertheless, all initiatives proved disappointing, mainly due to the fact that they were not binding but depended on voluntary commitment by member states (Jacquard, 2000). To fix the situation, European countries embarked on changing the public-owned status of their ANSPs through privatization or corporatization (Dumez and Jeunemaître, 2001). In 1996, they regrouped as a private company association, the Civil Air Navigation Services Organization (CANSO), which would have its own agenda for air traffic performance and restructuring dynamics.

Because of persistent structural air traffic congestion and a lack of coordination at the European level regarding design of routes and flights, the Council asked the EC on June, 17 1999 to take new initiatives. Loyola de Palacio, the then Commissioner and Vice President of the EC in charge of transportation, decided to submit 'The creation of a Single European Sky' (COM/1999/614 Final). The new Communication did not diverge from the previous assessment, which stressed the need for an immediate and collective management of routes and airspace design regardless of national borders. It insisted on the need to establish an independent regulator for ATM within the member states and called for clear separation between safety and economic regulation. It also introduced the idea of creating incentives based on reward, penalties for delays, and a fund for particular restructuring projects. Finally, it proposed the establishment of a High Level Group chaired by the Commission that would bring together the parties responsible for ATM in the member states. The Commission was tasked with devising a report within six months. The main orientations of the High Level Group report did not differ significantly from the 1999 Communication, reflecting the willingness for an increased top-down approach (Commission, 2000). It also supported the creation of a strong independent regulator.

By December 2001, the EC submitted to the European Parliament and the Council an initial proposal on the organization and use of airspace (COM/2001/564 Final). It included the creation of a European Upper flight Information Region (EUIR) above flight level 285 (8700 meters), later to be extended to lower national airspaces. The upper airspace reconfiguration consisted of functional airspace blocks (FABs) of minimum size, free from national borders, and based on direct routes (Dumez and Jeunemaître, 2004). FABs would be decided by member states, which would define conditions of withdrawal, refusing to let the decision-making power to the comitology procedure. The final agreement remained a watered-down version of the initial proposal with the creation of an SES Committee to coordinate the implementation of FABs. By the same token, economic regulation was left at the discretion of member states, in spite of the opposition from users, the Airlines European Association, and the IATA. Both trade associations indicated their support for the top-down approach, with airspace charging blocks open to the possibility of tendering processes (IATA, 2003) in opposition to the views expressed by the Unions of Controllers, which did not want competition and liberalization, and by national services providers (CANSO) which were considering to have expertise in the management of ATM.

The end of the process was an initial regulatory package issued in March of 2004. It defined a general framework for creating separation between service provision and regulation (National Supervisory Authorities [NSAs]), set up a Single Sky Committee to assist the EC, established an

Industry Consultation Body, implemented a common charging regime, set up an airspace design structure (FABs), and addressed interoperability issues (Regulations [EC] No. 549/2004, No. 550/2004, No. 551/2004, and No. 552/2004).

From the first Single European Sky package (SES 1) to SES 2

Following the 2004 regulations, member states' bottom-up initiatives proved limited. The first moves on FABs consisted of one large country entering into association with a smaller adjacent one (UK–Ireland; France–Switzerland; Spain–Portugal; Germany–Benelux, etc.) with no ATC center restructuring except for the envisaged resectorization of airspace supported by mutual coordination to cope with congestion (Dumez and Jeunemaître, 2004). A first major appraisal of the situation was commissioned by the EC to the PRC. It conducted a general assessment of the impact of 2004 regulations on ATM performance (PRC, 2006). The conclusion was that it was too early for a clear-cut evaluation. The emphasis of the assessment was on strengthening the expertise of the newly established National Supervisory Authorities. The Single Sky Committee published its work program in 2006. It endorsed the view of an enlarged SES airspace, including lower airspace.

In March 2007, the Commission issued a formal evaluation (COM/2007/101 Final). The tone was unambiguous. Even the large states were seen as 'dwarfs' in terms of size of airspace. Fragmentation in service provision, divergent national airspace rules, operating procedures, and low productivity were stumbling blocks for air transport. The main principles guiding the conclusions of the report were 'performance' and 'governance', with general support given to accelerate the process. Moreover, the SES Air Traffic Management Research Joint Undertaking (SESAR-JU) was enacted in 2007 to promote new ATM technologies. The Commission announced it would strive in the course of the year for a new package to amend SES 1. This revision was intended to be performance driven, based on the path dependence of the initial framework with an insistence on the deployment of new ATC technologies through SESAR Single Sky Air Traffic Management Research.

Subsequently, the EC set up a second High Level Group that reported in June 2007 on aviation regulation, in particular making proposals on ATM and the future of the newly established European Aviation Safety Agency. A second major study was carried out on behalf of the EC by the PRC on the contribution of the member states' bottom-up approach to the redesign of European airspace. The PRC study (2008), which reported on the nine regional initiatives, was in line with the Communication, with an insistence on monitoring progress and ensuring convergence without asking for a change in the bottom-up approach. The study led to an amendment of the SES 1 framework in terms of reinforcing available regulatory tools. The new regulatory package placed particular emphasis on environmental issues. The latter aspect was not negligible as it gave additional credence to the Commission of the importance of the SES initiative (i.e., European inefficient routing meant longer distance, and therefore additional jet fuel consumption and pollution).

The mid-term evaluations, studies and High Level Group conclusions led the EC to issue a new proposal prefiguring SES 2 in June 2008 (COM/2008/389/2). This put the stress on quantified binding performance targets, on strengthening a European network management function and NSAs' power, on the need for introducing modern technologies, and on the environmental cost of fragmentation (estimated savings were on average 7 to 12 percent CO_2 emission per year). The move to reinforce the first regulatory package was much less contentious. Hence, in 2010, formal specific regulations were issued on common rules for charging (Regulation [EU] No. 1191/2010), the creation of a Performance Review Body in charge of defining a binding performance scheme inheriting the PRC approach (Regulation [EU] No. 691/2010), a Directorate Manager Network within Eurocontrol based on the CFMU with enlarged responsibilities (Regulation [EU] No. 677/2011), a European FAB coordinator SESAR, a public–private partnership with objectives by 2020 to save 8 to 14 minutes, 300 to 500 kg of fuel, and on average 948 to 1575 kg of CO_2 per flight.

At a later High Level Conference held in Limassol on October 2012, Siim Kallas, Vice-president of the EC and Commissioner for Transport, expressed his irritation about the progress of the situation: 'The Single European Sky: 10 years on and still not delivering'. The background data did not show significant improvement: in the enlarged EU there were still 37 national service providers and 60 control centers in a fragmented European airspace with concerns about delays and the capacity of the ATM system to cope with expected air transport growth. The next step was scheduled for Spring 2013, with consultation processes still underway to formulate new proposals in a new SES 3 regulatory package.

Conclusion

Air transport relies on an infrastructure network (airports, routes, beacons, radar, etc.) and an associated 'operating system', namely ATM, which must ensure safe and efficient traffic management. This infrastructure, whether tangible or not, produces network externalities and natural monopoly characteristics, such that specific regulatory schemes are needed. Historical industrial organization based on publicly owned flag carriers, airports, and ANSPs proved incapable of efficiently handling traffic growth, and did not generate sufficient technological innovation, which has necessitated industry restructuring processes in all developed countries.

The above narrative describes the European regulatory path regarding air transport industry restructuring. It shows that beyond technical and economic rationales presented in the first part of this paper, institutional bargaining over opposite governance perspectives – top-down versus bottom-up; centralized versus decentralized; and cooperation versus competition – translate into a sequential regulatory dynamic punctuated by packages of regulations reflecting consensual outcomes. As a result, this step-by-step approach has been successful for the first phase of the restructuring – namely liberalization of air transport – but seems to reach a limit when it comes to market integration. Indeed, despite many improvements in terms of harmonization, European airspace is still highly fragmented, with no proper 'single sky' or optimal flow-management mechanisms, and economic regulation remains at the national level.

Virtuous competition between airlines, including low costs, will depend on the ability of policymakers to design efficient regulatory frameworks for improving the network's capacity absorption at nodes (airports) and ties (en-route services) while ensuring transparent and non-discriminatory access. As for environmental sustainability, the aviation sector accounts for 2 to 3 percent of global carbon emissions, and expected air travel increases will necessitate economic incentives and technological innovation to reduce this environmental impact in the medium to long term. Notably, IATA calls for carbon-neutral growth by 2020, 50 percent absolute reduction in carbon emission by 2050, and zero-emission aircraft within 50 years. At the moment, technology innovation options for aircraft to cut CO_2 emissions remains very limited, but the EU has recently included airlines in the Emission Trading Schemes system that should provide economic incentives for internalizing such negative externalities.

Note

1 For instance, there are 42 ATC centers in Western Europe as opposed to 21 in the US, which handle six times as much traffic.

References

Adler, N. and Liebert, V. (2014) Joint impact of competition, ownership form and economic regulation on airport performance and pricing, *Transportation Research Part A: Policy and Practice*, 64, 92–109.

Baumgartner, M. and Finger, M. (2014) The Single European Sky gridlock: A difficult 10 year reform process, *Utilities Policy*, 31, 289–301.

Combe, E. (2011) *Le Low Cost*, La Découverte, coll, Repères, Paris.

EC (1988) *Air Traffic System Capacity Problems, COM/1988/577 Final*, Brussels.

EC (2000) *Single European Sky Report of the High Level Group, DG-TREN*, Brussels.

EC (2012) *Single Market Act II: Together for new growth, COM/2012/573 Final*, Brussels.

Dobson, A. (2010) Civil aviation and European integration: creating the seemingly impossible SEAM, *Journal of Common Market Studies*, 48(4), 1127–1147.

Doganis, R. (1973) Air Transport: A case study in international regulation, *Journal of Transport Economics and Policy*, 7(2), 109–133.

Dumez, H. and Jeunemaître, A. (2001) Improving air traffic services in Europe: The economic regulation perspective, in C. Henry, M. Matheu, and A. Jeunemaître, (eds) *Regulation of Network Utilities: The European Experience*. Oxford: Oxford University Press, pp. 290–311.

Dumez, H. and Jeunemaître, A. (2004) *Functional Airspace Block*, study for the Eurocontrol Experimental Centre, Brussels.

Dumez, H. and Jeunemaître, A. (2010) The management of organizational boundaries, *M@n@gement*, 13(3), 151–171.

Eurocontrol (2012) *Performance Review Report*. Brussels: Eurocontrol.

Fu, X., Oum, T.H. and Zhang, A. (2010) Air transport liberalization and its impact on airline competition and air passenger traffic, *Transportation Journal*, 49(4), 24–41.

Gillen, D. (2011) The evolution of airport ownership and governance, *Journal of Air Transport Management*, 17(1), 3–13.

Gönenç, R. and Nicoletti, G. (2001) Regulation, market structure and performance in air passenger transportation, *OECD Economic Studies*, 32, 183–227.

Grushka-Cockayne, Y., De Reyck, B. and Degraeve, Z. (2008) An integrated decision-making approach for improving European air traffic management, *Management Science*, 54(8), 1395–1409.

International Air Transport Association (IATA) (2003) *IATA Response to the Financial/Charges Aspects on the Draft Final Report of July 2003 of the RPI Study: Implementation Rules of Economic Regulation within the Framework of the Single European SkyI*. IATA, Montreal.

International Civil Aviation Organization (ICAO) (2013) *Airport Economics Manual*, International Civil Aviation Organization, Doc 9562, Montreal.

Jacquard, P. (2000) *Independent Study for the Improvement of ATFM*, September, Eurocontrol.

Kosenina, A.U. (2013) The role of competition law in promoting EU slot trading, *The Aviation & Space Journal*, 12(2), 2–16.

Littlechild, S.C. (1983) *Regulation of British Telecommunications: Report to the Secretary of State*. Department of Industry, London.

Mayntz R. and Hughes, T. (eds) (1988) *The Development of Large Technical Systems*, Campus/Boulder, Westview Press, Frankfurt.

McCulloch, R., Butler, M., Dumez, H., Jeunemaître, A. and Mendes de Leon, P. (2001) *Study on the Economic Regulation of Air Traffic Management Services*, report prepared with Logica for the European Commission, Brussels.

Mendes de Leon, P. (2007) The Relationship between Eurocontrol and the EC: Living Apart Together, *International Organizations Law Review*, 4(2), 305–320.

O'Reilly, D. and Stone Sweet, A. (1998) The liberalization and reregulation of air transport, *Journal of European Public Policy*, 5(3), 447–466.

Pelkmans, J. and Luchetta, G. (2013) Enjoying a single market for network industries? *Notre Europe, Studies & Reports* 95 (Feb), Jacques Delors Institute, Paris/Berlin.

Performance Review Commission (PRC) (2006) *An Assessment of Air Traffic Management in Europe in 2006*, 21 December, Eurocontrol, Brussels.
Performance Review Commission (PRC) (2008) *Evaluation of Functional Airspace Block Initiatives and their Contribution to Performance Improvement*, 31 October, Eurocontrol, Brussels.
Reinhold, A., Niemeier, H.M., Kamp, V. and Müller, J. (2010) An evaluation of yardstick regulation for European airports, *Journal of Air Transport Management*, 16(2), 74–80.
Schmalensee, R. (1995) *Testimony on Antitrust Issues Related to Networks*, 1 December, Federal Trade Commission, Washington D.C.
Wulf, T. and Maul, B. (2010) *Future Scenarios for the European Airline Industry*, Leipzig, Center for Scenario Planning, HHL–Graduate School of Management, Leipzig.

18

Local public transport

Didier M. van de Velde

Introduction

The organization of local public transport has undergone considerable change over the past 20 to 30 years. De facto area monopolies by municipal or state-owned companies dominated the sector in many European countries until the 1980s, with smaller local businesses only playing a marginal role under route authorization regimes. A very different and mixed picture has emerged since. Multinational private operators have appeared alongside municipally-owned operators and a decreasing number of local family businesses. Operators affiliated to state-owned railway companies that operate outside of their country of origin play a growing role in the sector. Time-limited exclusive rights submitted to contractual requirements, including various sets of financial incentives, have increasingly replaced old de facto area monopolies with ex post subsidization. Competition is playing a growing role as a means of organizing the production of public transport services, particularly through the competitive tendering of contracts, but also via deregulation.

The reforms behind these developments are embedded in the main streams of political thinking of the period, such as the growth of neoliberalism and new public management. They aim to address the problems observed at the time in the sector, such as productive inefficiency, the growth of public transport subsidies while public transport market share was declining, and a non-innovative or bureaucratic image in a rapidly changing world where new technologies started playing an increasing role.

These reforms are also interesting in the light of the wider local, national, or European policies that, over the course of the past few decades, have expected the sector to play a growing role in passenger mobility in view of the issues that characterized the period, such as a growing focus on environmental policy, sustainability, road traffic congestion issues, urban densification policies, and tighter public budgeting. Moreover, these reforms often took place within the context of a decentralization of local transport policies from central government to regional and local authorities. This decentralization presented an opportunity to adopt new regulatory approaches, which were fed by the growing practice and evidence provided by fellow authorities.

The next section summarizes the major influences that led to the appearance of competition within the institutional setup of the sector. The section after that summarizes the main policy options that have appeared in terms of institutional reform, along with the role of competition therein. Prior to drawing some general conclusions, there is a discussion about the size and scope of the transport authority as a major player in this sector, and the related issues of policy coordination.

Fundamental choice: What kind of competition, if any?

The most fundamental controversy related to regulatory reform in local public transport in the past three decades has been the choice for or against the use of 'competition' as a means to improve efficiency, customer orientation, and innovation in the sector in order to address the issues of sector inefficiency and low modal share of public transport. A complex related issue is that of the choice of the way to organize competition. This section starts with a summary of the main influences that have led to the introduction of competition in European public transport at the local level before presenting a classification, based on the concept of entrepreneurship, of the resulting organizational forms that can be encountered in European public transport.

Competition or not

The rising subsidy requirement of the public transport sector in the 1970s and 1980s, together with growing (suspicions of) inefficiencies in the public transport sector (Button, 1984), were triggers to start looking for new ways to organize the sector. The rise of neoliberalism in the 1970s, with such major proponents as the governments of Margaret Thatcher in Britain and Ronald Reagan in the United States, had already been a major trigger for market-based economic reforms in a growing number of sectors and countries. Influential ideas within that movement included the theory of contestable markets reinterpreting the ways in which competition can work in the free market (Baumol, 1982) and a renewed interest in competitive tendering (also called 'franchise bidding') as a mechanism to regulate utilities (Demsetz, 1968) and control monopoly operations in the absence of a free market. These market-oriented reforms – which were also inspired by the policies of 'New Public Management' (Hood, 1995), which aimed to improve the efficiency of the public sector – did not remain without impact in the public transport sector.

In the European public transport context, it was mainly the market-based reforms introduced in Great Britain since the 1980s under successive conservative governments that initiated significant waves of reforms and inspired other European countries to follow suit. This happened in various configurations and at various speeds, often in conjunction with decentralization policies and further local reforms generated by budgetary constraints. These changes in local conditions stimulated authorities (to which public transport regulatory powers had newly been delegated) to re-think the organization of the sector under the influence of this mixture of impulses from economic theory and concrete reform experiences that could be observed elsewhere.

Concrete reform experiences with deregulation had been present in the British long-distance coach sector since 1980. Deregulation spread to the bus sector outside London in 1986 with some clear influence from contestability theory, and later also to the long-distance coach sector in Scandinavia. In parallel, further reform experiences based on the usage of competitive tendering grew in the bus sector in London (1984) and later in Denmark (Copenhagen in 1991), Sweden (1989), France (reform of contracting in 1981 and stricter tendering rules in 1994) and the Netherlands (2001). The British government also introduced railway franchising in 1994, generating further policy developments across the world. These trends were further fostered by the growing involvement of the European Union in competition and transport policy towards the end of the 1990s. This resulted in a legal initiative by the European Commission in 2000, which resulted – albeit only in 2007 – in the adoption of EU Regulation 1370/2007 on public services obligations in passenger transport services by rail and by road. This legislation clearly favored the idea of imposing competition or by competitive tendering, while also allowing direct award to public operators in specific cases or the free market (van de Velde, 2008).

Most of the reforms that appeared during the last few decades have involved a combination of the following three elements: (1) deregulation (reducing the number of rules to which transport operators are subject to on the market in which they operate, resulting in an enhanced behavioral freedom for the transport operators in terms of the determination of their service characteristics and production processes); (2) liberalization (allowing other operators than the incumbent to get access to the market, whatever the degree of behavioral freedom allowed by regulation to operators present on that market); and (3) privatization (transferring the ownership of a company or agency from the public sector, such as the national or a local government, to the private sector). Many of these reforms share one of two common characteristics. The first is the instillation of at least some elements of competitive pressure into the institutional setting of public transport that was previously based on de jure public monopolies. The second is the reform of pre-existing competitive arrangements that had evolved into ossified structures with little or no market entry, often dominated by publicly owned operators (that is, de facto public monopolies), a phenomenon which can be the result of regulatory capture (Stigler, 1971).

The lack of adequate data has meant that few studies have attempted to quantify inefficiencies in local public transport. A report written for the European Commission's research program (ISOTOPE Research Consortium, 1997) attempted such a quantification and pointed at the efficiency advantages of competition-based regimes over monopoly-based regimes. Needless to say, there was disagreement about the idea of using competition as part of the institutional fabric of the public transport sector. The main sources of skepticism and opposition were certain political streams, labor unions, and established interests, such as municipal operators. Examples of good performances in terms of ridership and modal share of systems that are devoid of competition in their institutional setting (such as Switzerland or some German cities) have also been put forward, while noting the dramatic increase in public finance needed to support these system improvements (see, for example, Pucher and Kurth, 1995).

Competition under market initiative or under authority initiative

The second main controversy, for those who chose to adopt competition, is the shaping of the competition instrument. At first, two main interchangeable options seem to be present: free market competition and competitive tendering of monopoly rights by a transport authority. From this perspective, free competition on deregulated open markets is associated with the highest possible level of continuous – albeit potentially unruly – competitive pressure, while competitive tendering by an authority is associated with a more moderate, discontinuous but well-managed type of competition. From this same perspective, a simple regulatory reform is then associated with the lowest level of competitive pressure – namely its absence – even though such a regime could also include indirect competition via competitive regulation, such as yardstick competition.

However, such simplistic classification, in the form of a continuum from full via moderate to no competition, cannot fully grasp the essence of these reform options and their potential impact on market dynamics. In addition to this continuum, these reforms options also differ fundamentally in the role they give to the autonomous entrepreneur in the institutional setting and, consequently, in the potential dynamic of the sector. To understand this, it is important to realize that free market regimes, whether regulated or not, allow (in principle) any entrepreneur to initiate new passenger transport services where he or she sees a gap in the market and wants to take a competitive risk against other entrepreneurs on the market. On the other hand, regimes based on the award of monopoly rights by an authority, whether through contracted public sector operators or through contractual delegation via competitive tendering of temporary market rights to independent operators, concentrate the essence of the entrepreneurial rights in the hands of the authority as monopolistic *initiator* of contracted services, even though that authority is not necessarily the *producer* of the services (van de Velde, 1999). This is not fundamentally changed by the fact that tendered operators may be given some leeway within contractual boundaries to amend services (see below), as such contractual arrangements never approximate the position of the free entrepreneur on open markets and the continuous market dynamic to which the entrepreneur is potentially submitted.

Consequently, a classification of organizational forms in public transport based on the player(s) to whom the right to initiate and create services is attributed seems more useful than a classification based on the purported level of competitive pressure in terms of understanding potential market developments and related incentives. This introduces a fundamental distinction of organizational forms in public transport between 'market initiative' regimes and 'authority initiative' regimes (see Figure 18.1). Regimes based on market initiative can vary from full open entry to more regulated markets with more-or-less strictly regulated authorization regimes (which were historically based on private market initiative but were often dominated by publicly owned companies after the 1960s). Regimes based on authority initiative can vary from pure private concessions to public ownership regimes. The latter can be further subdivided into publicly managed operations and delegated management where the publicly owned assets (vehicles, garages, tunnels, etc.) are made available to an operator to whom the management of the services is delegated after a specific selection and awarding procedure. In principle, all of these modes of organization can make use of a further sub-contracting of (parts of) the operations to third operators selected, for example, by competitive tendering (van de Velde, 1999).

Observations on the fundamental choices

The reform that the European Union adopted in 2007 – after a great deal of compromise – has made it clear that competition is here to stay for the foreseeable future. Various forms of competition are allowed, although the EC's preferred option is clearly the awarding of exclusive rights by competitive tendering. Awarding monopoly rights without competition remains feasible, although it is essentially limited to public operators that, in exchange for this privilege, become confined to the area for which that right is granted.

The fundamental choices discussed above determine the functioning of the sector in the longer run. Changes to such fundamental institutional elements are likely to require legislation, which makes them unlikely to be frequent; only major policy shifts would generate a fundamental institutional re-engineering of the sector. On the other hand, the decisions pertaining to the functioning and fine-tuning of the regimes that are made possible by these fundamental choices (which will be discussed in the next section) are less likely to be anchored in legislation and are therefore more likely to be amendable in the medium to short term.

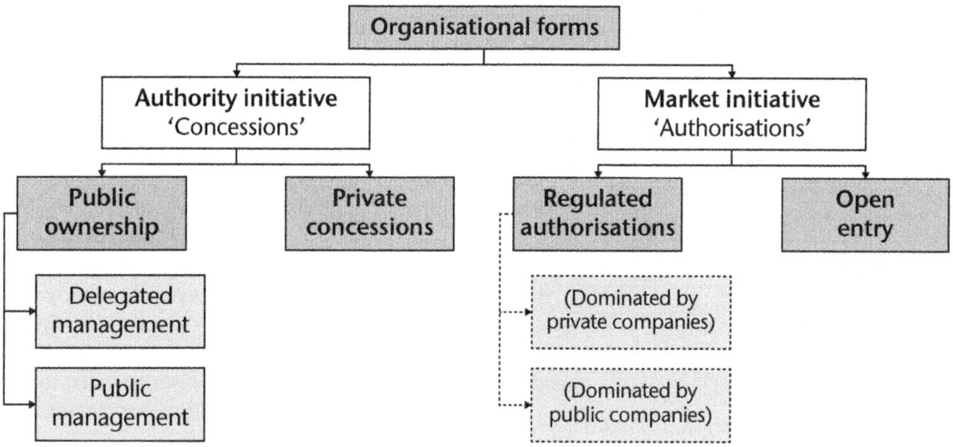

Figure 18.1 Organizational forms in local public transport

Source: van de Velde, 1999.

Main policy options for reforms

The 1986 British deregulation of the local bus sector outside London and the introduction of competitive tendering in London in 1984 marked the choice for competition-based regimes. It also marked the start of a fierce debate (Banister, 1985; Gwilliam *et al.*, 1985; Beesley and Glaister, 1985) on the relative merits of deregulation versus competitive tendering in addressing problems in the sector, such as productive and cost inefficiency, modal share decline, and lack of customer focus. Great Britain was the only European country at that time to choose a pure market initiative regime.[1] Other countries that engaged in competition-based reforms in the 1980s and 1990s precluded autonomous market initiatives in favor of regimes based on competitively tendered monopoly rights for the provision of integrated and centrally planned public transport systems. With this less extreme and more consensual way of introducing competitive incentives, transport authorities retained – or *obtained* – the monopoly to initiate the creation of public transport services. Others decided to maintain public monopolies, but to revise their regulations.

Several studies have reviewed the reforms that have taken place since the 1980s (Gwilliam and van de Velde, 1990; van de Velde, 2005; UITP, 2015). By summarizing these developments and attempting to categorize them on the basis of the two dichotomies presented above, we can distinguish four main reform options: market deregulation, introduction of competitive tendering, regulatory reform of monopolistic operators on the basis of indirect competition, and public operator governance reform (see Table 18.1).

The following sections discuss these four main avenues of reform and provide some implementation examples.

Deregulation

True deregulation usually includes all three of the elements defined above; that is, privatization of the pre-existing companies owned by the authorities, market liberalization by allowing the entry of new operators, and deregulation of market behavior giving operators more freedom in the determination of their transport services. This is exemplified by the 1986 deregulation of

Table 18.1 Categorization of reforms

	Direct competition between operators: Operators face direct competition from other operators	**Indirect or no competition between operators:** Operators are not directly threatened by other operators
Regimes based on market initiative: Operators are, in principle, free to take initiatives to provide services	**Market deregulation:** The possibility for direct and 'daily' competition between operators is introduced	**Competitive regulation of monopolistic operators:** Historic operators (public or private) are regulated on the basis of a mutual comparison of their performances (such as yardstick competition)
Regimes based upon authority initiative: A transport authority organizes transport services and/or assigns a temporary right to an operator	**Competitive tendering of operational rights:** Periodic competition between operators for temporary operational rights is introduced	**Public operator governance reform:** The governance of the publicly owned operator is reformed to instill new performance incentives

the local bus markets in Great Britain outside London. Operators should first hold an operating license issued by a regulator (the Traffic Commissioner) to ensure that operators are able to provide safe operations and proper maintenance. Operators then register the details of the services they intend to provide (routes and timetables) with the Traffic Commissioner, which will check whether restrictions should be applied due, for example, to traffic regulations imposed by local authorities (such as in cases of congestion). The Traffic Commissioner can also impose penalties for operating services in an unreliable manner. Barriers to entry are meant to be as low as possible and direct competition on the road between operators is allowed. In other words, there are no exclusive rights and operators are free to determine their own fares.

Deregulated regimes are never completely free of regulation. Apart from the safety and environmental regulations that are present in most cases, deregulated markets can also be submitted to different types of regulations that could perhaps be better termed as the 'rules of the game'. These are behavioral rules for the operators on the market that are meant to enhance the functioning and outcome of the free market. Examples include requirements for integrated ticketing and fares arrangements and compulsory participation in information integration systems. Such rules of the game limit the freedom of the entrepreneur, but do not preclude autonomous market entry; they can even stimulate market entry by reducing the market power of incumbents or by addressing market failures such as network benefits that could not be realized otherwise. The fine tuning of the British bus deregulation, carried out in small re-regulatory steps by legislation introduced in 2000 and 2008, is an example of such measures (see White, 2010), but more options could be designed. Financial incentives are another example of entry stimulation, guiding entrepreneurship to provide socially desirable services that would not otherwise be provided due to a lack of profitability. One example is fare rebates for specific groups of customers, reimbursed by the ordering authority – a mechanism present in Great Britain. Another example is a generic subsidization of an increased supply of service at specific times (peak hours, late evening, etc.) or in specific areas (remote or deprived) by such means as a bus-kilometer-based subsidy (or tax reimbursement, such as a fuel duty rebate), which may be linked to the provision of specific features (such as reasonable fares, accessible information, etc.)

Further rules may also be introduced to reduce entry by imposing entry selection on the basis of a 'desirability' test carried out by a regulator. This was the case in many regulatory regimes in Europe between the 1930s and the 1980s (and was abolished by the deregulation implemented in 1986 in Great Britain). Various types of tests can be devised. While old practices were based on regulatory expertise, new tests have also appeared, based on objective measures of duplication versus complementarity with existing services (as used, for example, in the regulation of the Japanese bus markets) or by measures of balance between revenue generation and revenue subtraction from existing services (as is the case for open access services in the British railway sector).

Competitive tendering

In the competitive tendering option, reforms are often constrained to liberalization, entitling new operators to compete in a formal tendering procedure for public transport contracts. Their competitors may be incumbent operators that are not necessarily privatized. Such contracts can be referred to as 'service contracts', 'concessions' or 'franchises', all of which depend on their characteristics in terms of risk allocation and the legal regime in place. They entitle the operator to a temporary and often exclusive right to operate the services covered by the contract.

The services procured within a competitive tendering regime are typically based upon a transport policy document established by the local or regional transport authority, which embodies the main transport policy aims and a more or less detailed sketch of the expected public transport services. The development of this document is often handled by a specialized authority body or company owned by the political authority that ultimately ratifies the proposed plan. In cases such as London, Copenhagen, and Stockholm, this body emanates from the former public operator that was, with the introduction of the reform, put in charge of gradually sub-contracting its own service operations to independent operators or to its own operational divisions that were eventually privatized within the reform process.

Routes, bundles, or network areas are put out to tender under a list of service obligations. Potential operators submit bids and an evaluation procedure is used to award the contract to the 'best' bidder. Some authorities choose to give operators some leeway in terms of service design, while others very tightly specify the services (fares, routes, and timetables) to be provided, which severely limits the possibility for service design innovation by the operator and restricts its action to efficiency improvements and innovation in service production. For this reason, this type of contracting can usually hardly be classified as 'deregulation'.

Two main tendencies exist. The first came to be known in Europe as the 'Scandinavian model', even though this regime was actually based upon the London bus tendering as introduced in 1984. Cases are most commonly found in London, Denmark, Sweden, Finland, and to a lesser extent in Germany. Contracts tend to be small in size (one or a few bus routes) and are typically short (approximately five years). The operator usually assumes the production cost risk, but not the revenue risk, which is borne by the transport authority (so-called 'gross-cost contracts'). The tendering body determines the services tightly prior to tendering, as routes, frequencies, fares, and vehicle appearance are fixed. Operational quality incentives are often added (such as punctuality incentives). This case clearly illustrates the monopolistic entrepreneurial role of such authorities on the market for passenger transport.

The second tendency, which can be observed on a large scale in France and the Netherlands, for example, is based on larger contracts (whole networks) where the operator is usually given both the cost and revenue risks in so-called net-cost contracts that are typically longer (10 years). The operator is usually asked to suggest innovations and options during both the tendering procedure and contract realization. To this effect, invitations to tender should describe the services to produce in a more functional way, avoiding stifling details. Incentive regimes are often added in the contracts to increase the incentive for operators to develop and implement innovations that will increase ridership and/or reduce costs. This practice grew in France on the basis of older awarding practices of urban networks to private operators, which had been gradually codified with contracting obligations (1981) and competitive tendering obligations (1994). The Netherlands adopted a similar network tendering approach in 2001, but with the intention of giving operators substantially wider market development freedom using a functional specification; an intention that has not proven to be self-evident to realize in practice (van de Velde *et al.*, 2008). The awarding of large franchises in the British railway sector is similar to this type of contract, while rail tenders in Germany are more comparable to the gross-cost contracts presented above. While this type of network contracting gives the operator more freedom than smaller gross-cost contracts, it remains remote from deregulation as the authority, through competitive tendering of a monopoly right, decides on the geographical area and core characteristics of the services provided. This fixes core items of what an entrepreneur would otherwise be free to decide upon in a deregulated market.

The dichotomy between these two contractual tendencies masks a wider variety of options that differ in allocation of planning prerogatives, incentive regimes, and financial risk allocation between an authority (or its planner) and operators. Further elements that need to be considered here are contractual completeness and the building of trust and partnerships, which also relates to the mechanisms used to award contracts. Competitive tendering is the favored option under EU Regulation 1370/2007,[2] which gives some (tightly regulated) space for choice in awarding procedure between more negotiated tendering procedures and more 'mathematical' awarding procedures.

Importantly, criticism has also been heard about competitive tendering compared to performance-based contracts negotiated with incumbents. According to Hensher and Stanley (2010), for example, competitive tendering has frequently failed to live up to expectations and negotiation is often likely to deliver better value for money.

Competitive regulation

A less common alternative is competitive regulation of monopolistic operators, such as historic operators (public or private), on the basis of a mutual comparison of their performances. This option uses competition only indirectly. The best example in the economic literature is yardstick competition (Shleifer, 1985), whereby comparative performance levels between regulatees are calculated by econometric means and used as a regulatory tool. The implementation of this tool requires the existence of comparable observation units. The fact that this is not always available can be one of the reasons why this regime is less widespread.

Yardstick competition, when introduced, is likely to entail a light deregulation or re-regulation of the sector. It can be combined with privatization, but it does not necessarily involve liberalization, other than indirectly, through a piecewise privatization of former public companies.

Yardstick competition is currently uncommon in European public transport, although elements of cost comparisons between operators did play a role in former, negotiated bus contracting regimes such as those managed at the national or regional level until the end of the 1980s in the

Netherlands, Belgium, and elsewhere. The clearest example of yardstick competition in public transport is that used in Japan in the regulation of rail passenger transport (Mizutani *et al.*, 2009).

Another example of competitive regulation is the institutionalized use of competitive tendering when the incumbent's performances stray from set benchmark levels and when negotiation does not manage to bring the incumbent's performance back in line with the benchmark levels determined by peer performance levels or competitive tendering outcome in similar conditions or areas. This option is used in the Zürich region of Switzerland.

Reform of the governance of the public sector

The fourth main direction is that of reforming elements of the governance of publicly owned transport operators without directly questioning the operators' position. Liberalization is not part of this reform as the choice is to keep the public monopoly in place. Neither is privatization, obviously, although the corporatization of a branch of a public administration is a common element of this type of reform. This type of reform could be qualified as 'light deregulation' when the revision of the existing regulation leads towards a more contractual, functional, less detailed operational guidance of the operator.

This widespread reform option, which has been adopted by many cities, fits with one of the main options given by EU Regulation 1370/2007, which allows authorities to entrust the realization of their public transport services to an internal operator. One of the conditions is to establish a public service contract that determines in advance the public service obligations of the operator and the compensation payment parameters in a way that prevents overcompensation.

Such reform can be accompanied by the appointment of a new management, which is often selected on the basis of experience in the competitive sector to bring greater efficiency and customer focus to the public sector. It can also be accompanied by a benchmarking exercise ahead of reform to determine efficiency improvement targets. Although indirect competition is usually not part of such an approach, it could still be introduced in the context of the contract negotiations via a threat to introduce competitive tendering. Such options were implemented in the Amsterdam case, for example.

General observations on the main options for reform

The cost efficiency improvements brought about by competitive tendering vary greatly, from a few percent up to 50 percent, all according to a complex set of circumstances (see, for example, Hensher and Wallis, 2005; Alexandersson, 2010; Beck, 2011). Additionally, data availability for international comparisons between regimes remains problematic (van de Velde, 2015), the information available in academic literature on the effects of the other reforms remains limited, and proper benchmarking of the available evidence remains scarce, or leads to nuanced or inconclusive results in terms of global performances (see also Karlaftis and Tsamboulas, 2012). In his review study, Karlaftis concluded that privatization and competition had led to efficiency improvements and lower operating costs, but also that the question of whether the composite effects of privatization on efficiency, ridership, fare increases, and levels of service had had a positive effect on welfare remained largely unanswered (Karlaftis, 2008: 94). These conclusions point to the complex changes in circumstances and transport policy priorities (fares policy, network coverage policy, social policy, etc.) that have developed during the period under study. The upshot is the absence of a clear consensus regarding the best regime in terms of global performance. What is best might depend more on circumstances and the realization of the necessary conditions of the chosen regime than on the regime choice itself.

Real-world cases do not always fit perfectly in the four options presented above. One key component of hybridity is the possibility to reduce the level of exclusivity granted by a contract. This introduces a share of free-market in regimes based hitherto on monopoly regulation, including competitive tendering regimes. One example is the 2012 reform of Swedish local public transport, since which tendered public transport contracts no longer grant exclusivity rights to the operator, as commercial competitive entry is now allowed. Another example is the British rail sector, where open-access entrants can infringe upon the exclusive rights of franchised operators, but can only do so after agreement by the railway regulator who developed a test to refuse entry when this would be primarily more abstractive of existing passenger streams rather than creating new passenger movements. Another component of hybridity is the opportunity to combine monopolistic regimes with the threat of tendering, as presented in one of the options above.

The transport authority and wider policy coordination

This chapter has focused on the regulatory regime of local passenger transport, paying particular attention to the role played by competition. It has not yet discussed the institutional setup of transport authorities or their remit in terms of geographical area and policy domains. Nevertheless, these are important, albeit controversial, issues in the context of reform design and implementation as they often entail major impacts on the balance of political and budgetary power between existing authorities. The opportunities for coordination and synergies between policy domains will be largely determined by the choices made in relation to these issues. This, in turn, could be an important determinant for public transport performance within the regional mobility system and, through this, for regional performance in economic and livability terms.

Several elements should be mentioned briefly here. The first is the institutional setup of the transport authority, as one of the elements determining its clout or leverage. This includes how political control and funding is organized, staff expertise and professionalism, the administrative setup of the authority, etc. These choices codetermine decisional swiftness and quality. One example is whether to locate the professional staff of the authority in a separate company-like structure. Such an arrangement can often be found in larger conurbations, where a choice is made to locate all marketing functions on the authority's side. While this can enhance professionalism, it can also become a contentious issue when – depending on the chosen governance – the political level feels that it is losing control on public money spending (see, for example, the 2012 Swedish transport authority reform).

A second element is the authority's geographic area, as urban sprawl and mobility growth necessitate authority cooperation and policy coordination at higher administrative levels. For example, local cooperation in Germany and Austria started with operators associations (Pucher and Kurth, 1995), many of which later became associations of local authorities. The French case shows how the adoption of a specific local transport tax linked to thresholds in the authority's population created an incentive to generate local authority cooperation (Menerault, 1993).

A third element is the scope of policy coordination. While many authorities are responsible only for public transport, there is also a tendency to develop authorities with a wider remit to facilitate policy coordination across all urban mobility issues. Transport for London is a good example, as it is also responsible for taxi regulation, shared bicycles, river services, and even roads management, including a congestion charging system. Similar schemes exist in Singapore and Budapest (without congestion charging but including parking). A further integration level involves coordination of transport with land-use planning issues, which is likely to be facilitated when the same political authority is responsible for both fields – a condition that is often not realized.

Conclusions

Substantial developments in the organization of local public transport can be seen over the past few decades in the context of reforms that aimed to address issues of inefficiency, declining market share, and lack of innovation.

The role of contracting and competition has grown. Competitive tendering, in particular, has become dominant in places such as Sweden, Denmark, the Netherlands, London, and France, and has, as a relative newcomer, grown the most over the past decades in term of its 'market share' amongst institutional setups. However, not all reforms have moved in the direction of competition and privatization. A large share of public transport services is still organized without competition via the public sector; examples include Germany, Austria, Belgium, Italy, and Ireland. Furthermore, recent examples from France show that some local authorities have decided to re-create publicly owned companies due to earlier disappointments with competitive tendering; this could point at the existence of a regulatory cycle (Gwilliam, 2008a). Reforms based on an increased role for competition have also gained ground outside of Europe, although not necessarily along the same path. Competitive tendering under authority initiative is increasingly used in Australia, New Zealand, the United States, South America, and China, albeit in various configurations. Some countries, such as New Zealand and Japan, have reformed and enhanced the role of market initiative, again in different guises. In many cases, however, traditional de facto or de jure public monopolies continue to play a major role across the world, as do market-based, more or less unregulated services provided by the so-called 'informal' sector in many (mostly developing) countries. Note also that an internationalization of the sector occurred – paradoxically perhaps – with a growing role for the European state railways.

As a result, the international institutional setup remains varied. The multiplicity of objectives and actors generates issues of sector management and regulation (Gwilliam, 2008b), which adds complexity. The options available are themselves complex – not in principle, but in terms of how to implement them. How much regulation should there be for deregulated markets? What contractual details should tendered regimes involve? Which incentives should there be within public sector governance? Past choices in legal regime influence and limit options available for the foreseeable future. Regime choices, which vary by country, seem to be (unsurprisingly) linked more to ideological or political preferences than to rational economic performance analysis.

Challenges lay ahead. New types of mobility systems made possible by mobile phone and the Internet have appeared, such as new ways to hail taxis or rent cars and bicycles for short periods of time. More innovations will develop, such as the self-driving car, but also mobility-on-demand services made possible by aggregating in real time individual requests over mobile phone and the Internet to provide users with combined individual, shared, or collective services delivered by various providers. A characteristic that many of these new systems share is that they are autonomous market initiatives and constitute intermediates between purely individual transport modes (car, bicycle, taxi) on the free market, and collective services such as traditional public transport that are often organized via monopolies (tendered or not). By challenging this traditional regulatory approach, these trends – together with recent initiatives to deregulate long-distance coach services in several European countries, and the European policy's policy initiatives to allow competition on the track in the rail sector – could increase the relevance of market-initiated regimes and deregulation for the future setup of collective transport (van de Velde, 2014).

Ultimately, the main challenge for those managing existing regimes, and those in a position to co-determine the design of new regimes, is to avoid ossification such as to accommodate the needs generated by future socio-economic changes and collective priorities, at the same time as avoiding inefficiency and facilitating innovation.

Notes

1 Albeit complemented by local authorities organizing the provision of additional non-commercial services on the basis of competitive tendering. On average, 80 percent of services are provided on a commercial basis, with the remainder provided on the basis of competitive tendering or negotiations in specific smaller cases.

2 This text, applicable to public transport within the European Union, regulates the award of financial compensations and exclusive operational rights in return for the discharge of public service obligations. Its requirements have been applicable since 2009 and must be fully implemented by 2019.

References

Alexandersson, G. (2010) *The accidental deregulation – Essays on reforms in the Swedish bus and railway industries 1979–2009,* EFI, Economic Research Institute, Stockholm School of Economics, Stockholm.

Banister, D. (1985) Deregulating the bus industry in Britain – (A) The proposals, *Transport Reviews,* 5, 99–103.

Baumol, W.J. (1982) Contestable Markets – an Uprising in the Theory of Industry Structure, *American Economic Review*, 72, 1–15.

Beck, A. (2011) Experiences with Competitive Tendering of Bus Services in Germany, *Transport Reviews,* 31, 313–339.

Beesley, M.E. and S. Glaister (1985) Deregulating the bus industry in Britain – (C) A response, *Transport Reviews,* 5, 133–142.

Button, K.J. (1984) Subsidies and the Provision of Urban Public Transport, *International Journal of Transport Economics,* 11, 177–188.

Demsetz, H. (1968) Why regulate utilities? *Journal of Law and Economics*, 11, 55–65.

Gwilliam, K.M. (2008a) Bus transport: Is there a regulatory cycle? *Transportation Research Part A: Policy and Practice,* 42, 1183–1194.

Gwilliam, K.M. (2008b) A review of issues in transit economics, *Research in Transportation Economics,* 23, 4–22.

Gwilliam, K.M., C.A. Nash and P.J. Mackie (1985) Deregulating the bus industry in Britain – (B) The case against, *Transport Reviews*, 5, 105–132.

Gwilliam, K.M. and D.M. van de Velde (1990) The Potential for Regulatory Change in European Bus Markets, *Journal of Transport Economics and Policy*, 24, 333–350.

Hensher, D.A. and J. Stanley (2010) Contracting regimes for bus services: What have we learnt after 20 years?, *Research in Transportation Economics*, 29, 140–144.

Hensher, D.A. and I.P. Wallis (2005) Competitive Tendering as a Contracting Mechanism for Subsidising Transport: The Bus Experience, *Journal of Transport Economics and Policy*, 39, 295–321.

Hood, C. (1995) The 'new public management' in the 1980s: Variations on a theme, *Accounting, Organizations and Society*, 20, 93–109.

ISOTOPE Research Consortium (1997) Improved Structure and Organization for Urban Transport Operations of Passengers in Europe, 51, Office for Official Publications of the European Communities, Luxembourg, p. 177.

Karlaftis, M.G. (2008) Privatisation, Regulation and Competition: A Thirty-year Retrospective on Transit Efficiency, In: *Privatisation and Regulation of Urban Transit Systems* (Ed. OECD International Transport Forum), 67–108, OECD Publishing, Paris.

Karlaftis, M.G. and D. Tsamboulas (2012) Efficiency measurement in public transport: Are findings specification sensitive? *Transportation Research Part A: Policy and Practice*, 46, 392–402.

Menerault, P. (1993) Les effets territoriaux d'un outil de financement des transports publics: le versement-transport, *Transports Urbains,* 78 21–24.

Mizutani, F., H. Kozumi and N. Matsushima (2009) Does yardstick regulation really work? Empirical evidence from Japan's rail industry, *Journal of Regulatory Economics*, 36, 308–323.

Pucher, J. and S. Kurth (1995) Verkehrsverbund: the success of regional public transport in Germany, Austria and Switzerland, *Transport Policy*, 2, 279–291.

Shleifer, A. (1985), A Theory of Yardstick Competition, *Rand Journal of Economics*, 16, 319–327.

Stigler, G.J. (1971) Theory of Economic Regulation, *Bell Journal of Economics and Management Science,* 2, 3–21.

UITP (2015) Organisation and major players of short distance public transport, UITP, Brussels, p. 160.

van de Velde, D.M. (2014) Market initiative regimes in public transport in Europe: Recent developments, *Research in Transportation Economics,* 48, 33–40.

van de Velde, D.M. (2015) Chapter 16: Local and regional public transport, in C. Nash (ed.), *Handbook Of Research Methods And Applications In Transport Economics And Policy*, Handbooks of Research Methods and Applications series. Cheltenham: Edward Elgar.

van de Velde, D.M. (1999) Organisational forms and entrepreneurship in public transport (Part 1: classifying organisational forms), *Transport Policy*, 6, 147–157.

van de Velde, D.M. (2005) The evolution of organisational forms in European public transport during the last 15 years, in Hensher, D.A. (ed.), *Competition and Ownership in Land Passenger Transport, Selected Papers from the 8th International Conference (Thredbo 8), Rio De Janeiro, September 2003.* Amsterdam: Elsevier, pp. 481–513.

van de Velde, D.M. (2008) A new regulation for the European public transport, *Research in Transportation Economics*, 22, 78–84.

van de Velde, D.M., W.W. Veeneman and L.R. Lutje Schipholt (2008) Competitive tendering in The Netherlands: Central planning vs. functional specifications, *Transportation Research Part A: Policy and Practice*, 42, 1152–1162.

White, P.R. (2010) The conflict between competition policy and the wider role of the local bus industry in Britain, *Research in Transportation Economics*, 29, 152–158.

19

Economic regulation of water utilities

The US framework

Janice A. Beecher

Introduction

Even among fixed utilities and network industries, providers of water services are distinctive. Water and sanitation necessities can be self-supplied; yet provision through the piped infrastructure of public utility systems offers substantial individual and social advantages. Water services are understood as particularly essential to everyday life and marked by positive externalities associated with public health and welfare, as well as environmental protection and economic development. Water and wastewater services are intrinsically related, but water service also enables urban fire protection. Affordable access to a subsistence level of safe drinking water and sanitation is increasingly regarded as a human right (United Nations, 2010).

The provision of water and wastewater services is in many respects quintessentially monopolistic. Water systems are especially capital-intensive, with relevant economies manifested in vertical integration of the production and distribution functions (see Stone and Webster, Consultants 2004). The problem of monopoly is a primary form of market failure that argues for authoritative governance by direct control or economic regulation. Given the critical roles of water and water-delivery networks, related issues and policies also are inevitably political. Successful reform requires an appreciation of water's social and political dimensions, along with its technical and economic dimensions.

Generally, the water sector has not experienced the same technological and structural dynamics as the telecommunications and energy sectors. Nor does water supply lend itself to many of the institutional models and regulatory reforms implemented in other sectors. In many respects, water continues to offer special insight about the essential nature of utility services and the networks through which they are provided. This chapter provides a basic introduction to, and overview of, economic regulation as applied to the water sector, drawing primarily on the US model and experience and focusing on emerging policy issues.

Properties of water

Water in its various forms can uniquely be characterized as a public good (ocean water), a private good (bottled water), a common-pool resource (groundwater), or a toll good (publicly supplied water). The focus here is on the latter, or the provision of water as a toll good or utility service through public or community water systems. The water utility sector can be further distinguished in terms of fundamental supply, demand, and infrastructure characteristics. These technical and economic features in turn relate directly to structural options for water-service provision, as well as institutional governance.

Properties of supply

The physical resource properties of water play an important role in distinguishing water services from other utility services. Although resources may be temporally and spatially transient and vulnerable, and natural forces continually govern availability, water is a relatively abundant and renewable resource. All of the water ever on earth remains on earth, so despite the prevalent concept of 'consumptive use' in resource management, water is basically borrowed and returned. This is not to say that water resources cannot be stressed – sometimes severely. Practical availability is a function of the interrelated dimensions of water quantity and quality. A global perspective recognizes that water scarcity has both physical and economic dimensions (Molden, 2007), but local scarcity can be understood as a social construct reflecting the imposition of human demand on natural supplies (see Rijsberman, 2006). Water-resource management is thus as much a governance as a technological challenge.

Water supply and treatment, along with system operations, tend to enjoy scale economies, although these are not absolute or unlimited (see Shih *et al.*, 2004; Pollitt and Steer, 2012). Because water is heavy, incompressible, and corroding, diseconomies emerge for its conveyance across long distances (especially withouth the advantage of natural gravity). With exceptions, water systems tend to be more localized, less interconnected, abundant in number, and diverse in structure. Water is also storable in its raw and treated forms, which facilitates both supply and demand management. Raw water can be stored in surface or underground reservoirs; treated water can be stored in water tanks or towers located throughout distribution territories.

In the US, the volume of water withdrawn for domestic purposes is less than water withdrawn for agricultural irrigation or thermoelectric power-plant cooling (Maupin *et al.*, 2014), and water is generally not priced systematically for these much larger uses. Competition for available resources will intensify with population growth and climate events. Proposals for diverting large volumes of water from one watershed to another tend to be controversial, and may be subject to regulatory or legal scrutiny. A related concern is for water 'footprints' and 'virtual' transfer in the form of exported foods and goods (see Hoekstra and Chapagain, 2007). Water for energy development, particularly hydraulic fracturing, can be a source of pressure on supplies. Fortunately, increased efficiency is apparent across the major withdrawal categories. Wastewater is also now recognized as a resource for reuse (including 'greywater' distributed through segregated irrigation systems), or for recharging of supplies. Desalination is another option, but one that tends to raise concerns about energy requirements, brine disposal and related externalities.

Properties of demand

Like other utilities, water systems serve a mixture of residential, commercial, and industrial customers (or customer classes). Other possible classes include wholesale, irrigation, public-use, and fire-protection customers. Many smaller water systems serve residential properties only; the customer base is more diversified for larger systems. Water demand is best understood in terms of usage per connection for a given customer classification. Patterns of water demand or system load relate directly to system design and operation (see Howe and Linaweaver, 1967).

Water usage varies according to a variety of known factors: population, demographics, and economic conditions; seasonal precipitation and temperature; customer composition and activity within classes; efficiency standards and technology deployment; water conditions and mandated restrictions; and price and income elasticities. Water demand is understood to be relatively income elastic and price inelastic (see Dalhuisen *et al.*, 2003). However, indoor usage is expected to be less price responsive, while outdoor residential usage (which tends to vary seasonally) and nonresidential usage are expected to be more price responsive.

For residential users, water systems essentially deliver multiple products through a single set of pipes, which is relevant to understanding demand and informing water pricing (Table 19.1). Water usage can be divided into less discretionary and more discretionary usage, the latter of which involves the use of water for lawn watering and other outdoor purposes. Irrigation, which tends to rise during dry conditions that also affect sources of supply, plays a significant role in system design and costs. Standards, pricing, and other programs are aimed at improving efficiency across all end uses.

Properties of infrastructure

Community water systems operate as localized infrastructure networks that today might be characterized as 'micro-grids.' Most systems are vertically integrated, providing all supply, treatment, and distribution functions (Figure 19.1), although some purchase raw or treated water on a wholesale basis from another system. Water systems and water utilities are structurally distinct. A water system can generally be defined in terms of the closed network that distributes treated water in compliance with regulatory standards. In the US, a water utility (public or private) or holding company might operate multiple water systems that may or may not be geographically proximate or physically connected.

Water services can be self-supplied in the form of individual wells and septic systems, but these are not perfect substitutes for networked services. Thus, piped water can also be understood as a 'value-added' commodity. For most systems, the majority of costs are associated with treatment and distribution, rather than the water itself (see USEPA, 2009). Water supply and wastewater collection are infrastructure-intensive, and piping is typically buried below all other infrastructure. Water distribution systems in the US generally are specified in terms of sizing and pressure to meet fire-protection requirements guided by industry standards and imposed by local authorities. In other words, systems must have sufficient capacity to serve peak-hour demand, plus flow needed for fire suppression. As pressurized water distribution is energy-intensive, elevated water storage is a form of energy storage.

Table 19.1 Products delivered to residential customers by public water systems

Type of usage	*Specific function*
Consumption	Drinking and cooking
Personal hygiene	Washing and sanitation
Home hygiene	Laundry and cleaning
Discretionary	Irrigation and other outdoor usage
Fire protection	Fire suppression

Source: Author's own elaboration.

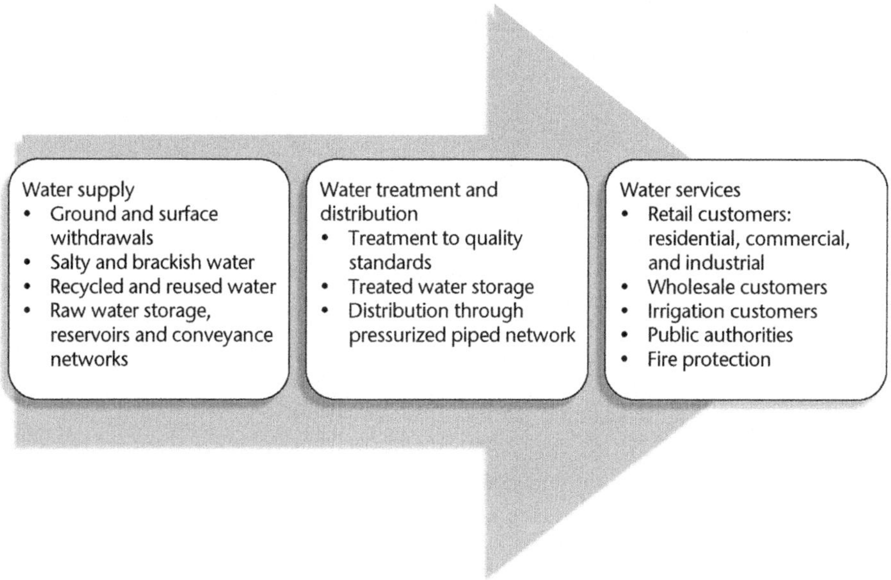

Figure 19.1 Water systems: a functional overview

Source: Author's own elaboration.

Industry structure

For utilities, including water utilities, industry structure is a function of alternative models that delineate ownership and operation (Table 19.2). Ownership of water systems is generally defined in terms of legal possession and control of the system's physical assets. The three basic ownership options (with additional variations) are public, private, and nonprofit.

Globally, governmental authorities are largely responsible for water services. A notable exception is the UK, where the country's many systems were first regionalized around watershed areas in 1973 (see Okun, 1977). In a separate historical event, they were privatized in 1989 and placed under the scrutiny of a national economic regulator, Ofwat. In the US, early water systems were privately owned, but municipal ownership took hold and remains dominant (see Masten, 2011). All of the largest US systems are municipal utilities with sizable regional service areas. They are generally fiscally autonomous and governed by boards of directors. Another form of public ownership includes districts and authorities. Nonprofit systems are in the minority, but include not-for-profit corporations, associations, and cooperatives or customer-owned systems.

Private ownership of water utilities invariably invites more formal economic regulation due to the monopolistic nature of water services. About half of US water systems are privately owned but they account for less than one-tenth of water deliveries USEPA, 2009). Only a handful of large companies are publicly traded on stock exchanges. A few of these (such as American Water and Aqua America) are organized as holding companies operating multiple systems across several states, but most privately owned water systems are much smaller in scale. The US water sector is essentially bifurcated, where large and mostly municipal systems serve the majority of the population and many small systems serve a relatively small number of people (USEPA, 2009).

Table 19.2 Models of ownership, operation, and governance for water systems

		Operation of system	
		Public	*Private*
Ownership of assets	Public	Publicly owned utility Public capital Local governance	Contracts and concessions Public capital Local governance
	Private	Transfers and leases Limited private capital Local governance	Privately owned utility Private capital Economic regulation

Source: Author's own elaboration.

Water privatization

Although public ownership dominates the water sector globally, some publicly owned utilities engage in public-private partnerships (also known as 'PPPs'). Despite considerable speculation, global data reveal little momentum in terms of private participation in water-related projects (World Bank, PPI database, 2015). Some cities have sought to take over private operations (municipalization or reverse privatization).

Publicly owned systems may delegate the operational role under broad agreements known in France as concessions. Partnerships are also used for the construction of major capital projects, such as treatment plants, under 'build-own-and-operate' or 'build-own-and-transfer' agreements (see National Research Council, 2002). Various other contracting and leasing arrangements can be found. The market for major privatization engagements is specialized and oligopolistic. Because contracts involve a limited field of contenders at the onset and provide long terms of engagement, they are suggestive of private oligopoly and monopoly. Separation of ownership and operations may lead to suboptimal outcomes or even failure if conflicts arise. Nonetheless, these agreements are typically subject only to local oversight, and not to economic regulation.

The rates charged for services provided by privately owned utilities are generally higher due to the effects of taxes, returns on private investment, and financing and ratemaking practices. Smaller private systems also lack scale economies. Regulated private systems have no choice but to impose 'full-cost pricing' to be sustainable. Full-cost pricing covers all capital and operating costs with revenues from user rates, which in turn sends strong price signals. Full-cost pricing is not always followed by publicly owned systems; some municipalities may undercharge while others may charge at or above the cost of service, but divert revenues to other purposes.

Limits to competition

As noted above, the water sector is characterized by monopoly and vertical integration. Many (often smaller) systems purchase treated water under wholesale agreements and wholesale-only systems may provide water to multiple distribution systems (USEPA, 2009). This is also the case for wastewater, where local collection systems may feed into regional sewage treatment facilities. However, vertical separation of functions or unbundling of services is generally not regarded as a means of promoting workable competition. Any perceived market opportunities, if they could be cultivated, would be offset by redundancy costs and lost economies of scope and scale (see Stone and Webster Consultants, 2004).

More apparent for the sector is institutional contestability in the form of rivalry between publicly and privately owned water systems. Poorly performing systems, public and private, are sometimes threatened with takeover. Environmental and economic regulators can encourage acquisitions to resolve drinking water compliance issues. In the US, privately owned systems can be acquired under local powers of eminent domain if 'just compensation' can be provided; such cases are always controversial. Short of ownership change, regulators can promote comparative competition by publishing water-system performance data.

Evidence of how ownership affects water utility performance is generally inconclusive (Beecher, 2013), although different performance incentives apply. The chief advantage of 'investor' ownership is the infusion of private capital into a capital-intensive industry, along with the potential to harness profit motives toward efficiency and innovation. In fact, the potential for investment returns is a powerful motive for infrastructure expansion under the prevailing regulatory regime. Profit motive becomes a disadvantage if it leads to potential abuse of market power power (hence the need for regulatory review). Conversely, publicly owned systems may face fiscal and political pressures that cause them to avoid both making infrastructure investments and raising financial capital and tariffs. In some cases, under-investment materializes in the form of infrastructure decay and high rates of water loss. Both public and private managers are sensitive to the politics associated with providing and pricing an essential service.

Regulatory framework

In many countries, the US included, regulation of the water sector is multi-layered, multi-faceted, and complementary (Table 19.3). Because their product is physically ingested, water systems are subject to substantial environmental and public-health regulation related to quality; because water resources can be locally constrained, water systems may be subject to quantity regulation in the form of permits for withdrawals; because water services are essential, providers may be eligible for government funding; and because water utilities are monopolistic, they are subject to some form of direct control or economic regulation with respect to pricing.

Table 19.3 Water federalism and governance in the US

	Water quality	*Water quantity*	*Water funding*	*Water prices*
Federal	Congress and Environmental Protection Agency	Court review as applicable	Congress and Environmental Protection Agency	Judicial review as applicable
Interstate	River basin commissions (varies)	River basin commissions (varies)	Generally not applicable	Generally not applicable
States	Primacy agencies for federal health and environmental standards; public utility commissions for aesthetics	Resource agencies	Federal and state funded revolving-loan agencies	Public utility commissions for private utilities and others (varies); judicial review as applicable
Substate	Management districts (varies)	Management districts (varies)	Generally not applicable	Generally not applicable
Local	Local health departments	Local zoning and fire officials (pressure)	Local financing (bonds)	Municipal and other local boards

Source: Author's own elaboration.

The water delivered by community systems is subject to stringent quality regulation (see Pontius, 2003) regardless of ownership, although specific requirements vary by system characteristics to the extent that these may affect level of exposure to particular contaminants. In the US, federal standards for drinking water are authorized by Congress (Safe Drinking Water Act), developed by the US Environmental Protection Agency, and implemented and enforced by state primacy agencies. Unlike the UK, the US does not have a federal economic regulatory presence in water, although water-quality regulators have focused considerable attention on ensuring that new and existing water systems have adequate technical, managerial, and financial capacities. State economic regulation applies to all privately owned and some publicly owned systems. However, because the vast majority of water utilities remain in public hands, governance in the economic area often falls exclusively to local government.

Economic regulation

Economic regulation of utilities is considered a balancing act that takes into account the interests of utility investors and ratepayers as well as the broader public interest. US regulators practice what is known as the 'rate-base with rate-of-return' form of regulation, whereby a utility's annual revenue requirements are a composite of capital costs (including an authorized return on investment) plus expenses for operations, maintenance, depreciation, and taxes. By comparison, UK regulators implement a multi-year price-cap model.

Economic regulation in the US is generally a quasi-judicial and reactive process that is initiated by a specific filing by the jurisdictional utility. The regulatory process imposes a degree of uniformity in accounting, financing, and ratemaking. Ratemaking begins with detailing all relevant costs for a specified test year (essentially, the utility's total budget for a 12-month historical, forecast, or hybrid period). For each of the key components of the revenue requirements formula, the utility must justify and the regulator must judge whether each cost element is ultimately translated into rates charged to customers.

Ratemaking follows the principle of 'full-cost pricing', wherein ratepayers cover the cost of operations as well as compensate debt and equity holders for capital-related costs. The costs incurred by regulated utilities are held to long-established standards of review that are embedded in the law and reinforced by regulatory practice across the utility sectors. Utility costs must be deemed 'prudent' and 'used and useful' to ratepayers for recovery to be allowed. Proper expenditures associated with maintaining appropriate levels of service, including compliance with environmental and other mandates, will generally be accepted. An imprudent cost is borne by shareholders in the form of a disallowance that reduces amounts available for paying dividends (return on investment). Equity shareholders are entitled only to a reasonable opportunity to earn a 'fair return' on their investment; that is, profits are not 'guaranteed'. Regulators often allow a return that exceeds the utility cost of capital to encourage socially beneficial investment (Beecher and Kihm, 2016).

Cost allocation generally involves the functionalization of costs by major activities (such as water supply, treatment, and distribution), cost classification (customer, capacity, and commodity), allocation by usage based on analysis of usage patterns (including on-peak and off-peak), assignment of costs to customer classes (residential, commercial, industrial, and others), and finally tariff or rate design (the determination of fixed and variable charges, as well as rate tiers and tier breakpoints) (see AWWA, 2015). For larger water systems, the process is often informed by usage or billing analysis and cost-of-service studies. Efficiency and equity argue for allocating costs and designing rates based on cost causality. Rate design can be controversial because of the implications for differential burdens on customers. It is not unusual for advocates of special interests (such as low-income customers or large-volume customers) to intervene in rate cases and present evidence with regard to utility rate-design proposals.

Once approved, rates remain in place until the utility files another rate case. For privately owned systems, efficiency between rate cases will affect profitability. In a rising cost environment, annual rate cases are common. For some smaller utilities, cost indexing may provide for rate adjustments between cases. For some larger utilities, special adjustment or surcharge mechanisms allow utilities to pass through certain operating costs (such as purchased water or energy costs), and even some capital costs (such as those for distribution improvements) on a limited basis and subject to regulatory review and reconciliation.

The US regulatory model has advantages and disadvantages, but it has endured and generally enjoys a high degree of institutional acceptance. Investment incentives under the model are powerful, which can work to the benefit of society if tempered by checks on the prudence of capital expenditures and their usefulness to ratepayers.

Water pricing

No cohesive system exists for pricing the water commodity across all usage sectors. For the most part, the water 'ratepayers' are those served by utilities. Regulated or not, water pricing is generally guided by traditional cost-of-service and rate-design principles that prevail for most larger utility monopolies. This is not to say that all systems recover or allocate costs based on a common approach. Ideally, from an economic perspective, water utilities will spend to an optimal level of service and price according to associated expenditures (Table 19.4). In other words, cost-based ratemaking discourages both underpricing and overpricing and implied subsidies to and transfers from the water system. Despite wide acceptance of the principle of full-cost pricing and the model of fiscally autonomous utilities, and evidence of price inflation (as reported annually by the US Bureau of Labor Statistics), concerns about underpricing of water services relative to accounting and economic costs are persistent.

Water tariffs and customer bills consist of fixed and variable charges. Some water utilities provide a water usage allowance as part of the fixed (or 'meter') charge. Most water utilities will recover some of the fixed capacity costs of the water system through variable charges. Putting

Table 19.4 Expenditures and pricing for sustainable water systems

	Expenditures relative to optimal service level		
Price revenues relative to expenditures	< 1 expenditures are below optimum ("cost avoidance")	= 1 expenditures are optimal	> 1 expenditures are above optimum ("gold plating")
< 1 price revenues are below expenditures ("price avoidance")	Deficient system	Subsidized system	Budget-deficit system
= 1 price revenues are equal to expenditures	Underinvesting system	SUSTAINABLE SYSTEM	Overinvesting system
> 1 price revenues are above expenditures ("profit seeking")	Revenue-diverting system	Surplus system	Excessive system

Source: Author's construct.

some fixed costs in variable charges promotes economic efficiency by recognizing the long-run variability of costs and allowing for possible avoidance of both capital and operating costs through price signals that promote end-use efficiency.

Three basic forms of variable (unit) pricing are uniform, decreasing-block, and increasing-block rates (see AWWA, 2015). Decreasing-block rates were once more prevalent, and supported to some extent by cost studies, but increasing-block rates are widely recognized as more efficiency oriented. Seasonal rates can also be used to target discretionary use (namely, for irrigation and other outdoor uses). Wastewater prices are often tied to off-season (for example, winter) water usage. Rate structures can be modified for policy purposes (such as affordability, drought management, and economic development), although substantial departures from cost-based rates may invite controversy.

Regulatory jurisdiction

Independent regulation of water services is essential in the context of privatization because privatization introduces investment and profit motives, but not necessarily competition. For privately owned monopolies, regulation substitutes for competition by providing standards, incentives, and accountability for efficient performance, while also considering equity. In fact, uniform economic regulation has the potential to improve public confidence in the water system performance and pricing, regardless of ownership structure.

Publicly owned water utilities are 'regulated' at the local level by applicable governing boards and elected officials. Economic regulation by the state may be undesirable or unnecessary if cities are capable of self-regulating. Many municipal water boards are independent and very effective in their oversight function for what is essentially a local service. For the public sector, profit motive and market power are not factors. Regulation also imposes a bureaucratic process and an additional expense on regulated entities. Local officials and the public may be concerned that regulators may be unresponsive to local concerns. Finally, perceived weaknesses in regulators or regulatory institutions make the prospect of state regulation less appealing.

Nonetheless, a compelling case can be made for extending regulatory jurisdiction to publicly owned water utilities. In the US, the state of Wisconsin applies economic regulation to municipal utilities providing water or energy services. Comprehensive regulation recognizes the value of transparency and accountability for all utility monopolies. A centralized regulatory agency may have advantages over disparate local agencies in terms of oversight capacity and expertise. A regulator can impose uniform accounting, auditing, reporting, consumer protection and appeals processes. Regulation also tends to level the playing field among structural options, which may allow for contestability (namely, public vs. private ownership).

Rates under regulation that reflect full accounting costs are considered economically efficient as well as reasonably equitable (or, at least, not arbitrary). Regulated, cost-based ratemaking also reduces subsidies and transfers, thereby promoting fiscal autonomy and institutionalizing a 'willingness to charge' for water services. In addition, regulation tends to advance common standards and expectations for resource management and service quality. Economic regulation can also reinforce other forms of regulation and provide coordinated incentives. Regulation can ideally provide for less politicized infrastructure investment and ratemaking decisions. In the context of private operations of publicly owned systems, regulation provides additional oversight and protection. In these cases, regulation provides institutional checks that can help build both public and investor confidence in ratemaking, planning, and other decision-making processes.

Contemporary policy issues

On the surface, the water sector lacks some of the structural complications of the communications and energy sectors. In recent years, however, a convergence of forces has elevated popular awareness of, and academic interest in, water services. In fact, 'crisis' rhetoric often permeates discourse about water, suggesting an intractability that thwarts technological progress and governance capability. Some key contemporary trends and policy issues affecting the water sector and its regulation are summarized below.

Rising costs

Many water and wastewater utilities, having last upgraded in the post-war period, find themselves at an advancing age (see AWWA, 2012). Leakage and loss rates can be unacceptably high, the value of the water lost is related not just to the water but to the value of energy and chemicals required for water treatment and distribution. Infrastructure replacement and improvement is disruptive and costly. It requires financial capital, as well as a means of spreading capital costs over time (through the use of debt and depreciation) to align costs with usage. As infrastructure is renovated, utilities should practice sound principles for asset management and planning and explore opportunities to re-optimize water systems relative to contemporary supply and demand conditions.

Falling usage

Although developing economies will experience rising demand for water, associated with population and economic growth, many developed economies are actually seeing declining per-capita usage for the public-supply sector (see Beecher and Chesnutt, 2012). In the US, efficiency standards for toilets, faucets (taps), showerheads, clothes washers, and dishwashers are credited for this trend, but rising prices and a growing conservation ethic are likely relevant as well. Unlike energy, there are few new uses for water at the household level. Declining sales revenues present a fiscal dilemma to utilities. Due diligence on the part of water utilities calls for better demand forecasting, as well as for incorporating both usage trends and price effects into planning and ratemaking.

Price pressure

The combination of rising costs and falling usage is placing considerable pressure on prices for water services (Beecher and Chesnutt, 2012). In the US and Europe, the movement toward fiscal autonomy and cost-based ratemaking is also contributing to more frequent rate adjustments and higher prices. As noted above, prices for water services in the US are rising at a pace far greater than the overall rate of inflation. Higher prices tend to invite controversy over cost allocation, calling for transparency in ratemaking. Higher prices also suggest the need to consider price response, particularly with regard to more discretionary and price-elastic forms of water usage (namely, outdoor and nonresidential usage). Finally, higher prices raise a number of issues with regard to affordability. Water bills might gradually command a larger share of household budgets for utility services.

Access and affordability

As mentioned above, access to water and sanitation is increasingly regarded as a basic human right, as well as a global public-health imperative (United Nations, 2010). However, universal service through public supply is not necessarily a well-established principle for the water sector. A persistent tension is found in the challenge of providing affordable service while pricing water in a manner that encourages efficient resource allocation and usage. Affordability issues tend to arise prominently in the consideration of rate-design options, including the specification of fixed and variable charges and rate tiers. In the interest of universal services, many systems may need to explore alternatives to disconnecting customers, such as low-income assistance programs, prepaid metering, and flow restriction.

Resource issues

For public supply, access to a clean and reliable water source is critical to sustainability. In terms of water resource availability, the US enjoys relative abundance, although examples of local stress are easily found (particularly in the southwest region). Public supply competes for water used by the agriculture and energy sectors, and awareness of the water–energy–food nexus is growing (see United Nations World Water Assessment Programme, 2014). Even when water resources are plentiful, efficiency can be rationalized on the basis of water's energy intensity. For all water systems, excessive withdrawals relative to natural availability, as well as climate change and extreme weather events, can jeopardize the temporal and spatial balance of supply and demand. Local and regional water scarcity will intensify interest in demand-side management, as well as supply alternatives (including storage, reuse, recharging, and desalination) that will be judged in terms of cost effectiveness, environmental impact, and public acceptance.

Other change drivers

In some respects, water may lack technological complexity, but it is not exempt from long-term forces of change. As already noted, end-use efficiency standards have been a significant change driver. Joint opportunities for water and energy management are also relevant. Water storage allows for electricity load shifting, which could benefit both water utilities and their energy suppliers. Opportunities may also exist to pair location, production, and usage of renewable energy with water and wastewater services perhaps on a distributed basis. Energy issues are especially important with regard to desalination technologies. desalination technologies. Other innovations that could change water requirements include modifications to turf grass and alternative methods of fire suppression. Regardless, rising water prices are likely to continue to have a significant impact on usage, and thus on system capacity requirements.

Regulatory policy reform

Along the spectrum of network services, water utilities are sometimes characterized as the 'last monopolies'. For the most part, vertical integration and limited competition are accepted as pragmatic. Monopolistic structures thus strongly urge either public ownership or private ownership with effective economic regulation to guard against abuse of market power. At least until recently, however, the water sector has also been a rather forgotten stepchild in the economic regulatory realm.

One size does not fit all when it comes to water policy. Nonetheless, although not necessarily codified by jurisdiction or authority, a number of 'generally accepted regulatory principles' are available to guide policies and reforms, as well as build institutional legitimacy for regulating the water sector. Their practical purpose is to support sustainability so that water utilities in turn can continue to serve social goals. These principles, which are well understood by many water-sector professionals and increasingly reflected in public policy, tend to fall within interrelated conceptual areas, some of which are briefly considered here.

Cost knowledge and reporting

All water utilities benefit from comprehensive and detailed knowledge of actual capital and operating costs, a practice enhanced by professional accounting standards and practices for the public and private sectors. Cost knowledge is supported by uniform methods of cost accounting that establish the content of balance sheets and income statements, along with supporting documentation. The National Association of Regulatory Utility Commissioners publishes a system of accounts for water utilities that many state and municipal jurisdictions adopt or adapt (NARUC, 1996). Cost knowledge and uniform accounting facilitate performance benchmarking, prudence and rate reviews, and transparent financial reporting, which in turn enhance water-utility accountability.

Full-cost pricing

As noted above, full-cost water pricing based on total accounting costs is increasingly recognized as an important means of resource management. Many water utilities today have no choice but to support the cost of service through rates. Prices that are based on costs can help reduce inefficient usage and thus avoid associated operating costs in the short run and capital costs in the long run (Beecher and Chesnutt, 2012). The use of a forward-looking test year can help ensure cost recovery. Although community goals and values can and should come into play, the ratemaking process should be professionalized rather than politicized to the furthest extent possible. Frequent and thorough reviews and audits can ensure that costs are reasonable and rates sufficient.

Tariff design

A variety of rate forms can be used to cover utility revenue requirements. Cost allocation and rate design should be revenue neutral; in other words, tariffs should collect no less but no more than the system's established revenue requirements. Rate design should account for price elasticities and possible effects of rate adjustments on subsequent usage. Incorporating marginal-cost pricing principles in the rate-design process can promote efficiency in consumption and production. Rate design ultimately involves consideration of values, and these should be addressed explicitly, along with the need to make tradeoffs among competing goals. The rate design-process should be approached experimentally, including empirical evaluation. No rate structure will be perfect from either a theoretical or practical perspective, but some methods will serve purposes and mediate impacts better than others.

Ensuring service

Although much attention is paid to the role of prices in promoting efficiency, the equity dimension of rates is as relevant from a societal perspective. All utility rates have distributional consequences, and low-income households pay a disproportionately higher share of their income for utility services (that is, rates are regressive). Rate regulators must be cognizant of the consequences of rate levels and structures. Even though water utilities have relatively high fixed costs, translating these into high fixed charges will be burdensome for some ratepayers. Public health and safety priorities may argue for ensuring that a basic level of service is accessible and affordable (including water allowances and lifeline rates), and that service disconnection is limited. The scope of the poverty issue, however, is generally beyond utilities and regulators (that is, broader household subsidies may be needed).

Performance standards

Regulation works best when performance standards make expectations clear. Some performance standards may be professionally established as a form of self-regulation. Standards for service quality are essential, and some of these will come from agencies other than the economic regulator. Standards should recognize differences in resource endowments and system capacities, while aiming for optimal performance relative to goals and constraints. Well-established standards allow for benchmarking by regulators and possibly a degree of comparative competition. In the context of a rate review, standards can also be used to evaluate the prudence of investment and expenditure decisions. Standards can also extend to forecasting and modeling, integrated resource planning, and asset management.

Communication and engagement

All utility service providers must find effective means of communicating and engaging with customers. Because water might be viewed as an entitlement or a public good that should be free, and because so much water-related infrastructure is not visible, utilities and regulators should actively engage ratepayers in ways that build interest in and understanding of what water services entail. Water emergencies, such as droughts and contamination events, provide teachable moments, but ongoing effort is needed as well. A well-educated public may be more willing to pay for investments necessary to meet social goals. The communication and engagement process is especially crucial when transitioning from subsidized to full-cost pricing, and when raising prices in the context of falling usage.

Alternative models

Policymakers should be open to considering structural and institutional alternatives for the provision of sustainable water services, and viable models may exist beyond the public–private dichotomy. One variation involves placing water assets under a public trust (as in Indianapolis, Indiana) so that the public owns them in perpetuity. Regional and cooperative models of ownership and governance can be explored, and convergence models that capture economies across services may be relevant. Fiscal autonomy with transparency and accountability should be given priority, and comprehensive economic regulation may help achieve these ends. In any case, regulatory models and capacities should be adaptive and responsive to the sector's evolution.

Observations

Among the fixed network utilities the water sector offers a valuable perspective. Any sectoral reforms must take into account an understanding of water's unique character and social relevance. In many respects, the water industry is positioned to lead the way on sustainability because it already manages a finite but renewable and storable resource. Although the sector has achieved notable gains in water quality and end-use efficiency, considerable challenges remain. Water issues are complicated, and can be fully addressed only if all water-intensive sectors of the economy are engaged and governance is effective.

Economic regulation of water utilities remains essential for addressing market failure in the form of monopoly and facilitating efficient and equitable pricing, among other social goals. Of course, regulation is only as good as jurisdictional authority and those entrusted with its implementation. Building regulatory capacity and efficacy for the water sector is therefore central to institutional legitimacy and acceptance.

References

American Water Works Association (AWWA) (2012) *Buried No Longer: Confronting America's Water Infrastructure Challenge*, AWWA, Denver.

American Water Works Association (AWWA) (2015) *Principles of Water Rates, Fees and Charges (M1)*, AWWA, Denver.

Beecher, J.A. (2013) What matters to performance? *International Review of Applied Economics* 27, 150–173.

Beecher, J.A. and Chesnutt, T.W. (2012) *Declining Water Sales and Utility Revenues: A Framework for Understanding and Adapting*, Alliance for Water Efficiency and Johnson Foundation, Chicago, IL.

Beecher, J.A. and Kihm, S.G. (2016) *Risk Principles for Public Utility Regulators*. East Lansing, MI: MSU Press.

Dalhuisen, J.M., Florax, R.J.G.M., Groot, de H.L.F. and Niijkamp, P. (2003) Price and income elasticities of residential water demand: A meta-analysis, *Land Economics* 79(2), 292–308.

Hoekstra, A.Y. and Chapagain, A.K. (2007) Water footprints of nations: Water use by people as a function of their consumption pattern, *Water Resources Management*, 21(1), 35–48.

Howe, C.W. and Linaweaver, Jr., F.P. (1967) The impact of price on residential water demand and its relation to system design and price structure, *Water Resources Research*, 3(1), 13–32.

Masten, S. (2011) Public utility ownership in 19th-century America: The 'aberrant' case of water, *Journal of Law, Economics and Organization*, 27(3), 604–654.

Maupin, M.A., Kenny, J.F., Hutson, S.S., Lovelace, J.K., Barber, N.L. and Linsey, K.S. (2014) *Estimated Use of Water in the United States*, US Geological Survey Circular 1405. Reston, VA: USGS Publications Warehouse.

Molden, D. (ed.) (2007) *Water for Food, Water for Life: A Comprehensive Assessment of Water Management in Agriculture*. England and International Water Management Institute, Colombo, Sri Lanka. London: Earthscan.

National Association of Regulatory Utility Commissioners (1996) Uniform System of Accounts for Class A Water Utilities. Washington, DC: NARUC.

National Research Council (2002) *Privatization of Water Services in the United States*. Washington, DC: National Academy of Sciences.

Okun, D. (1977) *Regionalization of Water Management: A Revolution in England and Wales*, Essex, UK: Applied Science Publishers.

Pollitt, M.G. and Steer, S.J. (2012) Economies of scale and scope in network industries: Lessons for the UK water and sewerage sectors, *Utilities Policy*, 21, 17–31.

Pontius, F. (2003) *Drinking Water Regulation and Health*. New York, NY: Wiley-Interscience.

Rijsberman, F.R. (2006) Water scarcity: Fact or fiction? *Agricultural Water Management*, 80(1–3), 5–22.

Shih, J.S., Harrington, W., Pizer, W.A. and Gillingham, K. (2004). *Economies of Scale and Technical Efficiency in Community Water Systems*, Resources for the Future, Discussion Paper 04–15. Washington, DC.

Stone & Webster Consultants (2004) *Investigation into Economies of Scale in the Water and Sewerage Industry in England and Wales*, Report to Ofwat, London, UK.

United Nations (2010) *The Human Right to Water and Sanitation*, General Assembly Resolution 64/292. New York, NY: United Nations General Assembly.

United Nations World Water Assessment Programme (2014) *World Water Development Report 2014*, United Nations Educational, Scientific, and Cultural Organization, Paris, France.

United States Environmental Protection Agency (USEPA) (2009) *2006 Community Water System Survey*. Office of Water, Washington, DC.

World Bank (2015) *Private Participation in Infrastructure (PPI) Project Database*. Available at: http://ppi.worldbank.org/ (accessed on 18 May 2015).

Part III

The strategy and management perspective

20

Innovative and disruptive effects of the Internet on strategy in the communications and media markets

Pier Luigi Parcu and Maria Luisa Stasi

Introduction

The Internet ecosystem is rapidly and constantly expanding. By the end of 2014, almost three billion people around the globe had used the Internet – roughly 40 percent of the world's population. In addition, current statistics show that about half of Internet users have bought products or services online; these simple numbers provide an idea of the continuously growing importance of the Internet for industries and businesses.

The Internet has dematerialized physical assets and services, lowered production and distribution costs, strongly contributed to the diffusion of 'free' goods and services, and multiplied multi-sided markets. In numerous economic sectors, the Internet is acting as a 'black hole', attracting the majority of transactions and reducing space for offline businesses and traditional means of performing economic activities.

In order to cope with the disruptive effect of the Internet on preexisting businesses, traditional firms have had to react in order to survive. In practice, they have had three choices: to transfer their businesses online in their existing forms, to adapt their business models to the digital world, or to create completely new businesses online.

In each case, the changes have been driven by the particular features of the markets and of the market dynamics established by the Internet. Often, the outcome of such transformations creates profound tensions within the regulatory environment where preexisting businesses used to operate, thus confronting decision-makers and rule-enforcers with unprecedented challenges.

In this chapter, we begin by providing a brief picture of the economic impact of the Internet revolution on traditional businesses. We then narrow the focus and specifically concentrate on the disruptive and revolutionary effects of the Internet on the communications and media markets, analyzing how such effects have altered the specific dynamics and characteristics of these markets. We examine a number of firms' reactions to these changes, looking at common trends. This allows us to identify those business models that seem better placed to take advantage of the possibilities brought about by the Internet and show better prospects for long-term survival within this new environment.

The Internet revolution

Never in history has a new technology experienced such rapid growth as the Internet,[1] Europe's Internet penetration, in terms of European citizens using the Internet reached 75 percent at the end of 2014 – today the highest percentage penetration worldwide – bringing the European Union (EU) closer to its Digital Agenda Goals related to broadband access.[2] In the Americas, about 65 percent of the population is currently using the Internet, making it the second highest regional penetration rate in the world. In the Asia-Pacific Region, the rate is more than 35 percent (which, in absolute numbers, signifies around 45 percent of the world's Internet users). In Africa, almost 20 percent of the population was online by the end of 2014, doubling the region's 2010 percentage (ITU, 2014).[3]

Internet connections can be provided at different speeds, through fixed, mobile, or other networks. Fixed broadband subscriptions are now growing more slowly, while mobile broadband subscriptions continue to grow everywhere at double-digit rates.[4] An important trend to take into account is the move, especially in developed countries, towards fixed-mobile integration. In general, the relative irrelevance of the specific medium of transport of Internet content is commoditizing traditional networks and unavoidably reducing their economic value.

The vast and rapidly growing base of Internet users has encouraged businesses to innovate in order to offer an ever-evolving array of online products and services. Different business players are active within the Internet ecosystem. From a vertical-industrial perspective, presently we can best represent the Internet as silos with four main levels: network builders at the bottom; network operators in the low-middle layer; equipment, device, and application manufacturers in the high-middle layer; and content and service providers at the top (see Figure 20.1). In order to correctly understand the core technical and economic dynamics of the Internet, it is key to pay simultaneous attention to all four levels and, in particular, to explore the evolving relationships of competition and complementarity among players that are apparently located at different levels of the silos.

The Internet is not the first technology to have a strong impact on the global economy and on previous methods of doing business. Since the Industrial Revolution, the world has experienced several steep peaks in productivity and corresponding economic growth fuelled by major advances in technology; steam engines, electricity, telephones, automobiles, airplanes, and computers have all brought about epochal changes in the methods for performing human tasks, and have given rise to completely new types of businesses, disrupting many old approaches. However, Internet technology is particularly powerful because it is extremely pervasive. It introduces new ways of communicating, sharing, and using information, exploiting knowledge, and creating content, which in turn enables major innovations and new dynamics in very different and apparently quite remote industries and markets. In many sectors, the Internet is

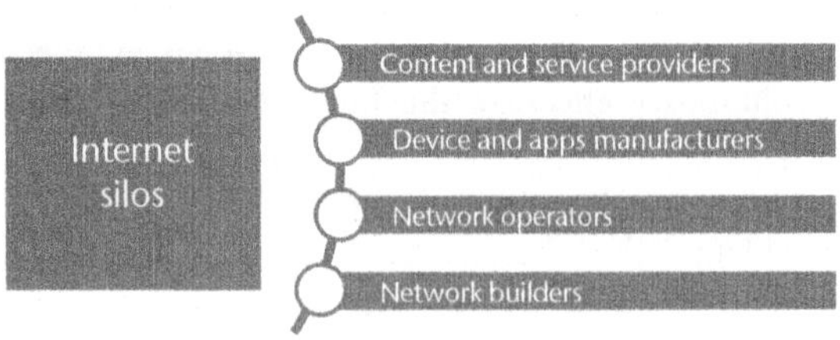

Figure 20.1 The Internet silos

Source: Authors' elaboration.

changing value chains, disrupting traditional commercial relationships, and enabling new forms of competition to an unpredicted extent. It is also creating new customer expectations, obliging firms to continuously develop and adapt business models, services, and even physical products.

This explains why, on the one hand, the Internet is generating immense value,[5] while on the other hand it is doing so through a highly disruptive process. Unfortunately, a relevant part, or in some cases most, of the revenue acquired via the Internet is subtracted from traditional means of producing and distributing offline, thus creating the progressive and large-scale disappearance of entire areas of economic activity. In this sense, the Internet exercises an impressive gravitational pull, obliging firms to make substantial changes in their businesses to avoid being relegated to oblivion.

The Internet has lowered marginal costs of both production and distribution processes, and has allowed for massive dematerialization of physical assets and services. In some cases, dematerialization has touched both the product or service provided and the distribution channels, while in others it has simply created more efficient and economic online channels of distribution.

The steep drop in marginal costs often allows suppliers on the Internet to sell at a lower or negligible price. In doing so, they compete strongly with firms operating in the traditional way, challenging the latter's economic viability and changing the industry as a whole. The Internet has also created conditions for the wide diffusion of *free* goods and services in many markets. This is because the Internet has expanded the possibility of intermediation among different groups of agents, and has generated a number of businesses in which the costs incurred to provide a product or service to one group can be more than compensated through the reliance of the provider on the satisfaction and financing of the other group. In other words, the Internet has multiplied so-called 'two- or multi-sided' markets.[6]

On a different note, the Internet is also significantly changing the balance between suppliers and customers, as well as the latter's expectations. It has created fairly open trading regimes, giving customers more choices and providing responses to various needs. Supply alternatives are nowadays easily accessible and more transparent; therefore, traditional firms are currently exposed to increasing competition. Moreover, the Internet has amplified opportunities for interactions among suppliers and consumers, giving the latter the possibility to combine by themselves the product or service they are interested in.

Finally, the Internet has questioned the common parameters used to measure the value of transactions. Within the Internet ecosystem, very often the absence of monetary value does not necessarily correspond to the absence of economic value. In a number of cases, the price of the good or service can be seen in less direct, non monetary forms, such as customers' attention and information concerning their interests and preferences; this, in turn, provides firms with the ability to design specially targeted and more efficient advertising and sales activities. From this specific perspective, it can be said that the Internet has completely revolutionized the field of marketing, and that in the Internet ecosystem the importance of personal data is continuously growing. The ability to gather data and find efficient ways to monetize its use is one of the major current challenges for firms operating online.

While dealing with the disruptive impact that the Internet has had on traditional markets and businesses, it is worth mentioning the 'sharing economy' phenomenon. By facilitating the circulation of information and the interconnections among users, and therefore making it cheaper and easier than ever to match supply and demand, the Internet has dramatically enhanced opportunities for sharing choices and requests among consumers. By sharing these aspects, users are able to significantly cut down costs, which are divided among a wide group. Moreover, with the sharing model users often no longer need to 'own' the goods, as long as they can buy the service when they need it. Furthermore, users have become more involved in the demand–supply dynamics of the market; they can act as suppliers, customers, or both, and they have the ability to influence how and at what cost the goods or services are offered, and to personalize them according to their needs.

From the above, it is clear that the Internet has had a strong impact on offline markets and businesses. By pervading all stages of the value chain, and by reshaping the means of interaction among the different market players, the Internet has condemned to death a number of traditional businesses, substituting them with new ones. This has forced traditional firms to cope with various challenges that have, in many cases, rendered totally unviable their previous business models.

In the following paragraphs, we narrow our focus to analyze the specific disruptive effects and the innovations that the Internet has introduced to traditional communications and media markets. We will concentrate on the new dynamics that have been established within these markets, and look at how firms have reacted to these changes, while identifying common trends and best business practices.

Effects on communications and media markets, and firms' reactions to the new ecosystem

The widespread diffusion of the Internet and advances in technology are determining both a quantitative and qualitative increase of the services and contents available through all kinds of electronic communication networks.

From a quantitative perspective. Global IP traffic has increased fivefold over the past five years, and forecasts indicate that will increase threefold over the next five years. More specifically, annual global IP traffic will pass the zettabyte (1000 exabytes) threshold by the end of 2016, and will reach 2 zettabytes per year by 2019 (Cisco, 2015).[7]

From a qualitative angle, the availability of broadband networks gives stakeholders the possibility to offer an ever-increasing variety of digital services and contents. In addition, the morphology of traffic is changing; the transmission of data has been overtaken by audiovisual content, which constitutes a future challenge for all players active in the sector.[8] In this regard, it must be noted that the wide accessibility of devices and applications, as well as the proliferation of social networks, has given rise to a new kind of content – mainly user-generated – that is gaining a dimension unexpected only a few years ago. Even more typically, the Internet allows top-down content and services to be partially modified and affected by the interaction with user-generated 'additional' content.

Moreover, the massive dematerialization provoked by the Internet now allows players to directly reach end users; service and content providers are enabled to essentially bypass network providers and traditional aggregators. In this sense, the Internet has created conditions for substituting services and contents that were previously only available through traditional, dedicated channels (such as telecommunication networks and broadcasting networks) with similar services and content delivered over the Internet.

By way of example, traditional voice services are currently subject to the competitive pressure of voice-over-Internet-protocol (VOIP) services such as Skype, Viber, and Google Voice; and SMS is being substituted with instant messaging apps, such as WhatsApp, WeChat, iMessenger, and Facebook Messenger.[9] Furthermore, the technical possibilities created by the Internet continue to transform the way people interact and communicate. One consequence of these changes is that social networks, such as Facebook, Twitter, LinkedIn, and Instagram are at least in part competing directly with the traditional telcos' services.

A similar pattern is identifiable within the media sector. Online newspapers are progressively substituting paper ones,[10] and online video and television services are acquiring consumers at the expense of traditional linear and non-linear content services.[11] Moreover, user-generated additional or integrative content is putting direct pressure on professional content production in both the information and the entertainment industries. YouTube, Vimeo, YouReporter, and similar websites directly compete with broadcasters and 'professional' content creators. Here, again, advances in technology have allowed people to act as directors or reporters by simply using a smartphone, and to share their produced content online with potentially no limits.

Another sector-specific effect of the Internet revolution has been to overcome the conventional division within the communications and media universes. In fact, the boundaries between communication, information, and entertainment services are now blurred. The technological developments have created conditions for the different actors to change their roles in the market and to modify their relationships with other players.

Once a user has access to the Internet, voice calls, texts messages, and videos are essentially available for free; music and movies can be downloaded or streamed for a very low or even no price; and vast amounts of editorial content can be accessed without extra payment. Moreover, technology developments allow consumers to decide when and where to benefit from the services, making it possible to easily time-shift and/or space-shift the consumption. This is also a reason why ubiquitous connectivity has become essential.

Because of the proliferation of services and content that can be offered over the Internet, firms active in the communications and media industries tend to establish themselves as platforms, internally breaking and mixing the levels of the silos with the aim of linking all components of the ecosystem and intermediating among different actors in search of value creation and viable businesses' activity preservation. In doing so, successful firms distinguish themselves as gatekeepers of the system, hoping to influence the general level of prices and the relationships among non-integrated players. The capacity of intermediation and the internalization of externalities among different groups of consumers and other actors in the market have become a fundamental asset for the most successful companies.

Furthermore, the Internet has tremendously increased the amount of data about customers that players can gather. The ability to process this data is extremely relevant; it allows firms to take advantage of the widespread interaction possibilities within the ecosystem, to profile consumers and personalize offers, and to become more attractive to advertising companies. The capability of effectively gathering and processing data provides the possibility to monetize data in a number of ways, and has become a relevant economic factor in Internet economics.

The technical and market convergence between communications and media markets, the multiplication of services and players, the strengthening of the interdependence among them, the diffusion of integrated offers, and the process of *platformization* of companies are all direct effects of the Internet revolution that now influences the competition dynamics within the electronic communications and media industries. Firms are currently called to compete symmetrically – that is, with players whose core business is at the same level of the value chain – and asymmetrically – with firms that are mainly active at different levels. Moreover, competition can take place both among different platforms and/or within the same platform.

In the following paragraphs we will analyze – without the pretention of being all-embracing – how preexisting communication and media firms have reacted to these changes, and will try to identify which business models and strategies appear to be best placed to take advantage of the new market scenario. In this exercise, we identify three main categories of reactions: (1) firms that have tried to resist by simply transferring their business online; (2) firms that have adapted to the new ecosystem not only by going digital, but also by modifying their business models in a variety of ways; and (3) firms that have been able to use the innovative features of the Internet to create unknown businesses and become new business stars (see Table 20.1).

Table 20.1 Firms reactions to the new ecosystem

	Communications and media markets	
Transfer online	Dematerialization Consolidation	BBC Telefonica/E-Plus H3G/O2 Ire Time Warner/Comcast Virgin Media/Liberty Global
Adaptation/modification	Personalization Vertical integration Scale	Financial Times Huffington Post Netflix Microsoft/Skype TeliaSonera/Spotify
Creation of new business	Platformization Vertical integration Intermediation Lock-in Scale	Google Facebook Twitter

The first category, that is simply migrating online, appears to be rare in the communication and media industries. For example, a number of newspapers are now available online only, as they have stopped distribution of a paper edition. However, it should be noted that, as we will see below, in most of the cases, firms, in migrating to the online world, have modified their product in order to possibly create more value or better monetize it.

The same is true for traditional linear and non-linear broadcasting services, which, while migrating online, tend to modify their business models to offer more comprehensive and customized services. Examples can be found in almost every national market, but here we limit ourselves to mentioning the BBC and CNN as the most resounding cases.

We should also add to the first category of reactions the process of national and/or cross-border consolidation. The reasoning behind this reaction appears to be the same as the one that drives firms to transfer their business online: to resist the impact of the Internet by preserving previous ways of doing business through cost reductions realized through consolidation and scale economies.

This is the case for a number of telcos, which, by acquiring direct competitors, are trying to widen their consumer bases to gain scale, and therefore to better resist the competitive pressure of other industry actors. However, especially in cases where such mergers have effects on one national market only, the competent authorities closely scrutinize these trends in order to guarantee that the increase of market power of the merging entities does not create competition concerns, nor harm consumers, or that at least such risks are counterbalanced by merger-specific efficiencies that are passed on to consumers.[12]

Another direction that the consolidation process appears to take, especially within the EU, is the cross-border one. In this case, firms move towards a more international dimension, which can allow them to invest more in the networks and to better compete with 'over-the-top' (OTT) players, which usually have global offerings.[13]

Consolidation, and thus the need to safeguard the position on the market in order to resist stronger competitive pressure, is not an exclusive move of network providers. Broadcasters are also pursuing this strategy, especially within the US market, where the convergence between the communications and media sectors already appears to be at a more advanced stage compared to in the EU.[14]

Adaptation, the second category of media firms' reactions to the impact of the Internet, appears to be quite prevalent. Returning now to the example of communications and online newspapers, we can highlight the *Financial Times* as a publication that, while going online, has substantially enriched its content, adding specialized sections, blogs, video, and tools for user involvement; therefore, the product it offers to subscribers cannot be thought of as the same as the paper version on offer at newsstands.[15]

Another meaningful example of a very successful adaptation and evolution of a daily newspaper business is the *Huffington Post*, the American online news aggregator and blog founded in 2005 by Arianna Huffington. Its site offers news, blogs, and original content, covering politics, business, entertainment, the environment, technology, popular media, and many other sectors, as well as local news. It is currently available in English, French, Spanish, Italian, Japanese, German, Portuguese, and Korean. All these editions apply the same business model: they publish news (paid) and blogs (unpaid), and generate revenues mainly from display advertisements. We may classify the *Huffington Post* as a very successful adaptation of an old business, verging on a new creation, because the organization has distanced itself from the journalist–reader dichotomy typical of the traditional press. Instead, it is mainly based on interaction between those actors (via comments on articles) and on user-generated content (via a vast number of blogs). Both these elements have become possible only because of the Internet.

Turning to video content services, we have Netflix, a US-based firm that initially enabled customers to order DVDs online and have them delivered at home by permit reply mail. Thus, back in the 1990s, Netflix simply transferred the DVD renting business online. However, Netflix's capacity to adapt to and take advantage of the transformations caused by the Internet went much further. In February 2007, the firm delivered its billionth DVD and began to add other services to its portfolio by introducing the provision of video-on-demand via the Internet. Currently, the old DVD rental arm of Netflix amounts to a truly minor part of the firm's revenues. By contrast, its streaming library is constantly expanding and includes a growing element of Netflix-produced original content. It is true that, in this case, the border between adapting a traditional business and creating a new one is blurred. Nevertheless, we believe that the criterion used to decide on the prevalent feature is whether we can identify an – at least partial – competing service in the offline world, in this case, 'traditional' satellite and cable pay-TV businesses.

Another type of successful business model commonly used by firms to adapt to the new communications and media ecosystem is vertical integration, both intra-sector and inter-sector. The industry convergence might stimulate a reconfiguration of the value chain through the addition, by acquiring other firms, of new activities to their core business. This can also be achieved by developing new in-house capacity, but it is more quickly facilitated by cooperating closely with other players. Thus, in this scenario it becomes essential for companies to carefully orchestrate their relationships with players coming from different market segments in order to expand and complete their offer.

For example, mobile telcos began buying cable operators with the aim of bundling their names and enlarging their customer bases for a more inclusive triple-play offer of mobile and fixed telephone, television, and Internet services.[16] Furthermore, the pull towards integration has been felt by software providers and device manufacturers as well.[17]

The vertical integration process does not always happen via mergers. Sometimes, different players enter into strategic partnership agreements that are generally transnational in scope. These kinds of alliances have been shown to provide competitors with the additional opportunity of imposing technological standards and becoming market pioneers by creating lock-in effects. A clear example of this is the series of agreements among telcos and online music players.[18] Another layer of partnership concerns the provision of video services, and thus the integration of broadband-broadcasting.[19]

However, it must be noted that in some cases the telcos have tried to compete in broadcasting markets not by way of alliances with broadcasters, but rather through the direct acquisition of premium content, which in recent years has acquired a strategic value and currently constitutes an essential asset for competing in this market segment.[20]

All the examples above depict a tendency towards vertical integration along the value chain among players, be it realized though merging activities or strategic agreements. By bundling their services with those of companies competing at different levels of the value chain, firms aim to enlarge their customer base and resist the competitive pressure of new and traditional market actors. Furthermore, mergers, partnerships, and commercial agreements provide the right incentive to invest in the launch of products and services, for which new technologies are needed. One major example is 4G in mobile communications, which allows users to access video and music content through streaming to their smartphones. Another meaningful example is smart TV, which, among others, has made possible the offer of so-called social TV services.

Moreover, the provision of bundled services permits firms to diversify their revenue sources and to put in place different pricing strategies. Players can offer flat-rate, usage-based, and freemium mechanisms, thus better targeting each consumer's specific willingness to pay. Furthermore, some operators leave to users the choice of composing their package of services in the way they prefer, and to pay accordingly.[21]

Irrespective of the pricing strategy used, the provision of multiple-play offers has become a way for firms to move their business models toward an industry platform approach. In this process, different participating players can attempt to leverage their specific strategic assets. Telecoms operators hope to take advantage of direct management of the networks, of network presence in a given territory, and of direct contact with the client base. Broadcasters, meanwhile, are seeking to exploit the quality of content and their consolidated system of advertising management. Device manufacturers can influence the ways in which the services are made available. Finally, service providers can count on their ability to process data and personalize offers.

Nevertheless, even this platformization process will not subtract these old players to the actual very difficult challenges that the Internet environment brings about. They remain exposed to the direct competitive pressure of operators that have superior capacity with regard to one or another aspect of their traditional or new platform businesses. By way of example, telecoms operators are bypassed by OTTs, which can directly reach their (potential) customers; broadcasters' traditional advertising strategies appear outdated in comparison to those used by other service and content providers (such as Google and Facebook); and traditional service providers are often unable to process data and personalize offers in the same way that new players can. Therefore, adaption appears to be a possible solution for survival, but the challenge remains daunting and economic decline a sizable risk.

We conclude this closer look at potential options by focusing on the third category of firms' reaction: those that have resulted in taking advantage of potentialities that the Internet has brought with it, in order to create original businesses and become business stars.

The first and most resounding name in this category is Google. Founded in 1998, the firm began as a simple search engine company and went on to develop its proprietary search technology to navigate the Internet. Thus, Google's core business (an online search engine) was created to solve a fundamental question that did not exist, nor could it have been imagined, before the Web revolution: that is, how to find things in the labyrinth of the Internet, with its millions of websites, documents, and online content. How Google answered this question is well known: it used a link-based approach to develop a proprietary algorithm that proved to be extremely valuable to users. However, the most powerful answer that Google gave was another: it found an effective way to make money with the Internet by revolutionizing the advertising business and redesigning the relationships between advertisers and Internet users. Moreover, Google adopted a business model that transformed its Internet search technology into an industry platform. As platform leader, and in order to beat its competitors, Google has constantly invested in creating economic incentives for its ecosystem members to develop complementary innovations, and to keep doing so over time.

Since its foundation in 1998, Google has expanded its scope of activity by providing an ever-growing variety of Internet-related services and products, both by developing in-house capacities and by acquiring other companies. Within the communications and media ecosystem, it is currently present in most sectors of the industry, although with varying degrees of incisiveness and presence.[22]

A second type of business star created by the Internet is comprised of the major social networking firms, such as Facebook and Twitter. Facebook is the largest one, with more than one billion individual users. It started off by offering an online platform where users could create their own content (profiles) and share these with other users. It then acted as a platform leader, creating incentives for developing and offering, over its social network, an increasing variety of products and services (applications).[23]

The strategy aimed at leading the platform and creating lock-in effects is justified by Facebook's monetization channel: the company generates profit primarily through selling advertisements; therefore, direct and cross-side network effects play a fundamental role in Facebook's business model.[24] On the one hand, the more users Facebook has, the more attractive it will be for new users to join the network. On the other hand, the more users who create profiles on Facebook, the more companies will be interested in advertising their products and services on it.

Overall, Facebook's business model has many similarities with that of Google. They both operate on multi-sided markets and adopted the platform model, and they are both platform leaders. They also offer their main service for free and make money from advertising. For both, continually increasing the number of users is their greatest challenge, and data constitutes the essential resource: the more data they are able to gather about their users, the stronger their appeal to advertisers becomes.

The future scenario

We have seen that in recent years the communications and media industries have drastically changed due to the impact of the Internet. Having to cope with a significantly different marketplace, firms have migrated their businesses online and attempted to consolidate their position in the market, modified or adapted their business models, or been able to sense the potentialities that the Internet has brought and take advantage of the new scenario to create original businesses and become business stars.

The driver of the above-mentioned transformations appears to be the offer of personalized communication and infotainment products and services. In fact, literally billions of customers own devices and want to choose freely how to communicate: what to read, listen to, and watch, and when to do these things. Therefore, industry players should have this target in mind when defining their future business models. Yet, as we mentioned at the beginning of this chapter, we cannot exclude that in the future the scenario will not change again; thus, not only connecting people but also connecting 'things' or connecting 'cities' will become a major challenge driving businesses.

The last step before concluding is to look ahead and try to imagine future developments within the industry, and thus likely future scenarios for market players. At present, we can identify in the marketplace a number of different platforms. Competition takes place both within and among platforms. The platforms can be telco-centric, content-centric, service-centric, or device-centric, depending on the typology of actors that play the leading role. In any case, what characterizes the Internet marketplace is the growing interdependencies among different sectors.

In this situation we can try to identify, for each of the presently prevailing platforms, which business models can be more efficient in terms of attractiveness of the offers and capability of monetizing them. For networks, as we have already mentioned, the trend appears to be towards a fusion between fixed and mobile networks. Therefore, we might abandon the current binary system and adopt the idea of offering integrated, ubiquitous, and non-differentiated connections. The service's discriminating factors are then likely to become the quality, in particular the quality of data rates, or of the connection provided, which acquires different values depending on the specific needs of each customer. Furthermore, it seems likely that information transport will become simply a commodity; this, in turn, will have significant consequences on the ways in which network providers shape their business strategies, and on their monetizing capability.

Due to the multiplication of content and of the channels on which users can watch it, even content providers can no longer rely on traditional monetization schemes to produce revenues. Until recently, their value chain consisted of a number of steps that took place in a chronological order and implied peaks in revenue generation (for example, for a movie being shown in cinemas, the DVD sales, the film on premium TV services, and the film on free-to-air TV channels). Nowadays, apart from a limited number of premier live events (mainly sports) and other limited premium content, it appears to be extremely difficult for providers to monetize even live or first-pay window (that is, the first time a movie is shown on a consumer platform) shows. As a consequence, it seems more attractive and functional to combine the offer of premium content with the offer of a vast library of movies and other types of TV programs that customers can watch on demand.

Looking at device manufacturers, we can see that technology developments have the greatest impact. On the one side, device manufacturers have a somehow privileged position: in a connected world with an ever-increasing array of contents and services available online, they are the players that are well positioned to influence the way in which users can access the Internet and benefit from the content and services available. However, on the other side, due to the short-lived nature of the product's lifecycle and of the corresponding technologies, device manufacturers have to constantly innovate, or they risk lagging behind. Therefore, their future business strategy should be soundly innovation-oriented; in addition, it might be expected that the better they are able to offer a complete array of interoperable devices, enabled through an applications platform, the less consumers will feel the need to switch to a competitor. Apple, by far the most capitalized company in the world, has been successfully moving along this trajectory for years.

Similar dynamics seem to characterize the current and future scenario for service providers. In order to establish themselves as industry platforms, they are under pressure to continuously innovate. In this case, the objective might be achieved through external growth, which plays the role of an innovation integrator. As mentioned in previous parts of this chapter, a number of players are already putting this strategy to use; the major challenge here is to continue the innovative attitude to avoid being overtaken by the next 'winner-takes-all' innovation by an industry outsider.

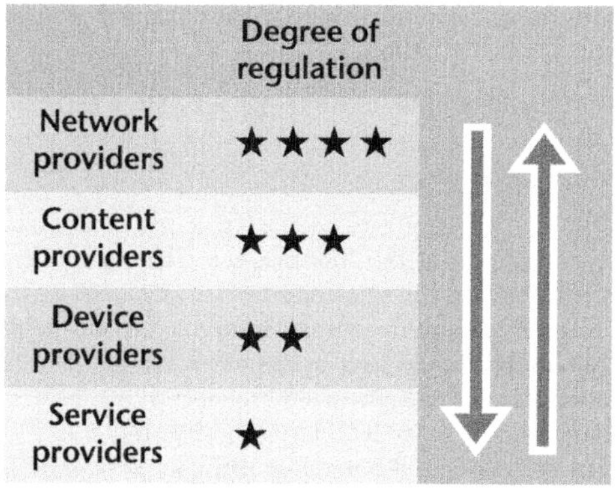

Figure 20.2 Different degrees of regulation

Source: Authors' elaboration.

To conclude, as businesses do not take place in abstract contexts, while shaping their strategies firms will have to take into account and comply with a number of laws and regulations that discipline the specific sector in which they operate. In this regard, it is worth noting that, at present, the regulatory environment influences the firms' activities to a different degree depending on the firms' core business. If we had to make a classification, we could affirm that the more regulated actors appear to be the network providers, followed by the content providers, and device and applications providers, while the least regulated seem to be the service providers. In a scenario where different market segments converge into a single marketplace, and thus a number of different market players start to directly compete with each other, it will be necessary to harmonize the regulatory regimes applicable to each players' category in order to ensure a level playing field for all actors. The question remains as to whether the preferable direction to follow would be towards widespread deregulation, or the opposite (see Figure 20.2).

Conclusions

The Internet revolution has had a strong impact on both society and the economy, and has yielded a sort of gravitational pull on a number of traditional businesses. In the communications and media industries, the Internet has blurred the boundaries among different market segments, leading to a more expansive environment in which traditional and new players compete, but are at the same time becoming continually more interdependent.

By observing these industries, we have identified the major types of reactions from firms in order to cope with the new scenario. Some are trying to consolidate their presence in the market, both at national and transnational levels. Others are moving towards a vertical integration strategy, either by acquiring new businesses or by entering into partnerships and alliances with competitors active at a different level of the value chain. Finally, a variety of firms are investing in multi-product and multi-service packages, personalizing their offers and diversifying their pricing strategies.

While there seems to be no doubt about the fact that platforms will dominate the marketplace in the future, the question remains as to whether the number of platforms will grow or shrink, and which kinds of players are better placed to be able to lead them. In addition, the future will reveal which business models are most efficient, depending on the firms' core activities. Finally, in order to guarantee a level playing field in this converged scenario, it appears to be important to harmonize the regulatory regimes applicable to different market players. The major challenge here seems to be the direction to be followed: towards a common form of deregulation, or towards a balanced legislative intervention with regard to all actors.

Notes

1 For a description of the emergence of the Internet, see Chapter 2 'Telecommunication networks: Technology and market development' in this volume.
2 The Digital Agenda for Europe has set three targets related to broadband access, two of which refer to broadband coverage: (i) all homes should have access to broadband of at least a basic quality by 2013, and (ii) all homes should have access to high-speed broadband of at least 30 Mbps by 2020.
3 Source: ITU (2014): The World in 2014: ICT Facts and Figures.
4 Fixed-broadband penetration grew at 4.4 percent globally in 2014. The slowdown is mostly evident in developing countries, especially Africa where the penetration has been lower than 0.5 percent by the end of the year. Europe's fixed-broadband penetration is much higher compared with other regions, and almost three times as high as the global average (28 percent compared with 10 percent). On the other side, mobile-broadband uptake continues to grow everywhere at double-digit rates. By the end of 2014, 32 percent of the global population had access to mobile broadband – five times the penetration rate of 2009. The number of mobile cellular subscriptions worldwide has reached 7 billion, corresponding to a penetration rate of 96 percent; more than half of these (3.6 billion subscriptions) have been in the Asia-Pacific region. Contrary to the case for fixed connections, Africa leads in mobile-broadband growth with a rate of over 40 percent – twice as high as the global average. By the end of 2014, mobile-broadband penetration in Africa had reached almost 20 percent, up from less than 2 percent in 2010. Source: ITU (2014): The World in 2014: ICT Facts and Figures. In Europe, the average penetration rate has approached 60 percent; however, penetration rates overall in Europe lag behind markets such as the US and Japan, although there are several European countries with penetration rates over 100 percent (GSM Association [2013], Mobile Economy Europe 2013).
5 By way of example, Internet advertising revenues in the US reached US$11.6 billion for the first quarter of 2014, marking a 19 percent increase over the same period in 2013. Source: IAB and PwC US, 2014). Global digital music revenues amounted to US$5.9 billion in 2013, 4.3 percent more than the previous year (IFPI, 2014). Global online travel and tourism sales are steadily growing and are expected to reach US$830 billion in 2017 (Euromonitor International, 2014).
6 'A market is two-sided if the platform can affect the volume of transactions by charging more to one side of the market and reducing the price paid by the other side by an equal amount; in other words, the price structure matters, and the platform must design it so as to bring both sides on board' (Rochet and Tirole, 2003).
7 Source: Cisco (2015), The Zettabyte Era—Trends and Analysis.
8 The transmission of audiovisual content is also rapidly expanding over mobile devices. It is foreseen that in 2016 the mobile networks themselves will process 4749 petabytes of video every month, which is +90 percent if compared with the available data for 2011. See: AGCOM, *Relazione Annuale 2014.*
9 The data shows that the consumption of voice services over traditional telecommunications channels is decreasing over both fixed and mobile services; the same is true for SMS. By way of example, in Spain, in the period 2011–2012 the minutes of voice services consumed over fixed networks went from 64 to 61 billion, those over mobile networks fell from 71 to 70 billion, and the number of SMSs sent went from 8 to 6 billion. Over the same period, in Brazil, the numbers were 181 to 172 billion minutes for the fixed network, and 310 to 277 billion for mobile. However, it is difficult to calculate what this data means in terms of loss of revenues; in fact, the revenues of the telecoms sector have been largely stable over recent years, although the number of players has increased due to the reduction of entry barriers, especially for Internet-based firms. See: Ofcom, International communications market report 2013.
10 See: Ofcom, International communications market report 2013.
11 See: Ofcom, International communications market report 2013.
12 Good examples of the telcos' consolidation process on a national basis are the recent mergers between Hutchison 3G UK and O2 Ireland in Ireland, and between Telefonica Deutschland and E-Plus in Germany. Both concentrations have been recently approved by the EC, which gave clearance conditional upon commitments packages presented by the parties that were considered to guarantee a

competitive scenario, notwithstanding the fact that the number of mobile operators active in the respective countries would have decreased from four to three. In the Hutchison 3G (H3G) and Telefonica Ireland (O2 Ireland) merger (case M.6992), the merging parties offered a package enabling Mobile Virtual Network Operators (MVNOs) entry in the Irish market. This includes the sale on 'attractive terms' of up to 30 percent of the combined entity's network capacity in the form of dedicated bandwidth to each MVNO, on a fixed-payments (as opposed to usage) model. Each MVNO will be required to take 'significant' minimum capacity for at least five years. The combined entity will provide technical assistance and ancillary services. In order to enable such MVNOs to eventually become network operators in their own right, H3G also committed to divest spectrum. The commitment is 'up front' in character, in that the transaction cannot complete until at least one MVNO agreement has been entered into. The combined entity also committed to maintaining the existing network-sharing agreement between Eircom and O2 Ireland, on improved terms. This secures Eircom's options in terms of coverage and the roll-out of new services such as 4G, and thus ensures the continued competitiveness of Eircom. In the Telefonica Deutschland and E-Plus merger in Germany (case M.7018), the commitments package submitted by Telefónica is composed of three parts: (i) Telefónica commits to sell, before the acquisition is completed, up to 30 percent of the merged company's network capacity to one or several (up to three) MVNO(s) in Germany at fixed payments; (ii) Telefónica commits to offer to divest radio wave spectrum and certain assets, either to a new Mobile Network Operator (MNO) entrant or subsequently to the MVNO(s) who will have taken up the network capacity thanks to the first part of the commitments; and finally, (iii) Telefónica commits to extending existing wholesale agreements with Telefónica's and E-Plus' partners (that is, MVNOs and service providers) and to offer wholesale 4G services to all interested players in the future.

13 This direction seems to be more in line with the goals of a European Single Market for telecommunications. Among the meaningful examples we can mention Deutsche Telekom, the German incumbent, which in June 2014 purchased GTS Central Europe (case M.7109), the company that provides communications services in the Czech Republic, Romania, the Slovak Republic and Hungary. Another example is Telenor, a Norwegian operator already present in Sweden and Denmark, which in 2013 expanded its scope of activities to the Bulgarian market by acquiring Cosmo Bulgaria Mobile (case M.6948).

14 For instance, Time Warner Cable and Comcast are awaiting the authorization for their merger from the US federal antitrust authority, while Virgin Media has been recently acquired by the US company Liberty Global.

15 The cases of the *Wall Street Journal* and of the *New York Times* are similar: more content, better differentiated, and more interactive, and partially available under freemium models.

16 One significant European example is Vodafone, which, in September 2013, acquired Kable Deutschland, the largest cable television operator in Germany (case M.6990). Shortly afterwards, Vodafone bought the Spanish company ONO, which offers broadband communications and entertainment services to residential customers (case M.7231). On the other side of the Atlantic, the telecommunications giant AT&T has seemed to move in the same direction, with the acquisition, in July 2014, of Direct TV, the second largest cable/satellite provider in the US, after Comcast (MB Docket 14-90).

17 By way of example, in May 2011 Microsoft acquired the VoIP service provider Skype (case M.6281), and, in September 2013, it brought Nokia's mobile phone business (case M.7047).

18 Just to mention a few, Spotify, the largest music-streaming service provider in Europe, has entered into partnership agreements with Telia Sonera, the Swedish telecommunications incumbent, in Sweden, and with Vodafone in a number of other European countries. In the UK, O2, the telecommunications operator part of the Telefónica's group, has a partnership with the start-up MusicQubed to provide O2Tracks, the premium music service for mobiles. The same Telefónica has also more recently entered into an agreement with Napster, the cross-platform online music store, to offer bundle of offers to its customers. In Europe, there are currently more than 50 partnerships active among telcos and online music service providers (Mulligan and Jopling, 2013).

19 By way of example, in Spain, Telefónica, the incumbent operator, and Canal+, the Spanish satellite broadcasting company, have signed a commercial agreement that will enable the former to sell all of Canal+'s TV services to its customers alongside its home line, mobile, and broadband products.

20 One of the first examples has been BT UK, which, in 2012 and in response to the fast expansion of Virgin Media and SKY in the broadband market, invested in purchasing the premiership rugby rights in order to offer attractive packages of bundled services and acquire new customers. The move paid

off, and since then BT has been constantly pursuing this strategy. Orange, the French telecommunications company, acts similarly and since 2008 has provided a live TV service offering movies, TV series and documentary, buying the rights from Warner Bros and HBO. Over the years, to this basic offer Orange has added a number of sports channels, a movie channel, and video on demand and remote storage services from the catalogue of available contents on the main French free-to-air channels.

21 An interesting example is Vodafone's initiative in Italy called *Scegli tu*, which allows customers to combine the different parts of the package of services offered by Vodafone in the way they prefer, and to pay accordingly.

22 The acquisition of YouTube in 2006 enabled the firm to compete directly with video and music content providers. The 2011 purchase of Motorola Mobility (case M.6381) was essential in order to continue to freely offer the operating system Android, and thus to be a relevant player at the device- and application-manufacturing level. The creation of the social network Google+ allowed the firm to compete with its more direct competitors, the service providers. Finally, Google is making its first moves at the network-provider level: its Google Fiber initiative aims to provide super-fast connectivity in a number of US cities; in addition, the firm is working to build and help run wireless networks in emerging markets such as sub-Saharan Africa and Southeast Asia, with the aim of connecting a billion or more new people to the Internet. In the case of Google, the vertical integration, platformization, and winner-takes-all mechanisms, so common in the industry at stake, can be observed in one single firm.

23 To this end, in March 2014 Facebook acquired WhatsApp, one of the most globally diffused cross-platform mobile messaging apps, for roughly US$19 billion (case M.7217); this transaction was most probably driven by Facebook's intention to incorporate the application into the Facebook platform and thus offer it to all its users, thereby lowering their incentives to switch to a competing service.

24 An extremely significant example comes from Facebook's declarations a few days before the start of the last football World Cup that they had identified 500 million users with an interest in football, based on links these users had clicked on or pages they had liked (this is almost double Twitter's total monthly active user base of 255 million). This transformed Facebook into the 'biggest stadium in the world', with a global audience for advertisers to target during the World Cup.

References

AGCOM (Autorità per le Garanzie nelle Comunicazioni) (2014), *Relazione Annuale 2014*, available at: http://www.agcom.it/relazioni-annuali, last access: 15 May 2015.

BBC (2015), Premier League TV rights: Sky and BT pay £5.1bn for live games, available at: http://www.bbc.com/sport/0/football/31357409, last access: 16 May 2015.

Cisco (2015), The Zettabyte Era—Trends and Analysis, available at: http://www.cisco.com/c/en/us/solutions/collateral/service-provider/visual-networking-index-vni/VNI_Hyperconnectivity_WP.html, last access: 30 August 2015.

Euromonitor International (2014), Global Online Travel and Tourism Sales to Reach US$830 Billion in 2017, available at: http://www.marketwired.com/press-release/global-online-travel-and-tourism-sales-to-reach-us830-billion-in-2017-1885494.htm, last access: 15 May 2015.

European Commission (2011), Case No. 6281 – Microsoft/Skype, available at: http://ec.europa.eu/competition/mergers/cases/decisions/m6281_20111007_20310_2079398_EN.pdf, last access: 16 May 2015.

European Commission (2011), Case No. M.6381 – Google/Motorola Mobility, available at: http://ec.europa.eu/competition/mergers/cases/decisions/m6381_20120213_20310_2277480_EN.pdf, last access: 16 May 2015.

European Commission (2013), Case No. M.6948 – Telenor/Globul/Germanos, available at: http://ec.europa.eu/competition/mergers/cases/decisions/m6948_20130703_20310_3167385_EN.pdf, last access: 16 May 2015.

European Commission (2013), Case No. M.6990 – Vodafone/Kabel Deutschland, available at: http://ec.europa.eu/competition/mergers/cases/decisions/m6990_20130920_20310_3307840_EN.pdf, last access: 16 May 2015.

European Commission (2013), Case No. M.7047 – Miscrosoft/Nokia, available at: http://ec.europa.eu/competition/mergers/cases/decisions/m7047_20131204_20310_3495212_EN.pdf, last access: 16 May 2016.

European Commission (2014), Case No. M.6992 – Hutchinson 3G UK/Telefonica Ireland, available at: http://ec.europa.eu/competition/mergers/cases/decisions/m6992_20140528_20600_4004267_EN.pdf, last access: 15 May 2015.
European Commission (2014), Case No. M.7018 – Telefónica Deutschland/E-Plus, available at: http://ec.europa.eu/competition/mergers/cases/decisions/m7018_20140702_20600_4149735_EN.pdf, last access: 16 May 2015.
European Commission (2014), Case No. M.7109 – Deutsche Telekom/GTS, available at: http://ec.europa.eu/competition/mergers/cases/decisions/m7109_20140414_20310_4178052_EN.pdf, last access: 16 May 2015.
European Commission (2014), Case No. M.7217 - Facebook/ Whatsapp, available at: http://ec.europa.eu/competition/mergers/cases/decisions/m7217_20141003_20310_3962132_EN.pdf, last access: 16 May 2015.
European Commission (2014), Case No. M.7231 – Vodafone/ONO, available at: http://ec.europa.eu/competition/mergers/cases/decisions/m7231_20140702_20310_4002660_EN.pdf, last access: 16 May 2015.
European Commission (2015), *Fast and ultra-fast Internet access – analysis and data*, available at: http://ec.europa.eu/digital-agenda/fast-and-ultra-fast-internet-access-analysis-and-data, last access: 15 May 2015.
Federal Communications Commission (2015), AT&T ad Direct TV, MB Docket 14-90, available at: https://www.fcc.gov/transaction/att-directv, last access: 16 May 2015.
Financial Times (2014), Facebook takes on Twitter and TV in World Cup marketing battle, available at: http://www.ft.com/intl/cms/s/0/119fa1b8-edd6-11e3-8a00-00144feabdc0.html#axzz3aDzWqWTd, last access: 15 May 2015.
GSM Association (2013), Mobile Economy Europe, available at: http://gsmamobileeconomyeurope.com/, last access: 15 May 2015.
IAB (Interactive Advertising Bureau) and PwC US (2014), At $11.6 Billion in Q1 2014, Internet Advertising Revenues Hit All-Time First Quarter High, available at: http://www.iab.net/about_the_iab/recent_press_releases/press_release_archive/press_release/pr-061214#sthash.HVsRA7Ru.dpuf, last access: 15 May 2015.
IFPI (International Federation of the Phonographic Industry) (2014), Digital Music Report, available at: http://www.ifpi.org/resources-and-reports.php#/digital-music-report.php, last access: 15 May 2015.
ITU (International Telecommunication Union) (2014), *The World in 2014: ICT Facts and Figures*, available at: http://www.itu.int/en/ITU-D/Statistics/Documents/facts/ICTFactsFigures2014-e.pdf, last access: 15 May 2015.
Mulligan, M. and Jopling, K. (eds) (2013), Building the New Business Case for Bundled Music Services: A media consulting report commissioned by Universal Music, July, available at: http://musicindustryblog.files.wordpress.com/2013/10/building-the-new-business-case-for-bundled-music-services.pdf, last access: 15 May 2015.
Ofcom (2013), International Communications Market Report 2013, available at: http://stakeholders.ofcom.org.uk/market-data-research/market-data/communications-market-reports/cmr13/international, last access: 15 May 2015.
Rochet, J-C. and Tirole, J. (2003), Platform Competition in Two-Sided Markets, *Journal of the European Economic Association*, MIT Press, vol. 1(4), pp. 990–1029, 06.
Virgin Media Transaction (2013), available at: http://www.libertyglobal.com/ir-virgin-media-transaction-2013.html, last access: 16 May 2015.

21

Governance and strategies in the postal sector

Fumitoshi Mizutani, Shuji Uranishi and Eri Nakamura

Introduction

The modern postal service began in the UK in 1840 (Royal Mail Group, 2014) with a system characterized by universal pricing regardless of origin or destination, and involving prepaid postal stamps. This basic arrangement for postal services has since been adopted in countries around the world, and has become the international norm.

An important network industry, postal services have traditionally been provided by national governments in the form of a monopoly (Le Groupe La Poste 2013; Deutsche Post DHL Group 2015a; Japan Post Holdings 2015; Royal Mail Group 2014; USPS 2015a). While postal services at first comprised only the exchange of letters for personal correspondence, the service soon expanded to include the delivery of parcels, newspapers, periodicals, direct mail, and many other items. In some countries, postal organizations have evolved to encompass even banking and insurance businesses (Le Groupe La Poste 2013; Japan Post Holdings 2014).

However, postal services now face an important turning point in their mission to deliver information and goods. Hard-copy letters are becoming obsolete as they are rapidly replaced by electronic messages and quick, easy cell phone calls. Another challenge in the postal industry is the introduction of competition among postal service providers, which is part of the recent trend toward deregulation designed to mitigate the lack of efficiency of traditionally monopolistic government-run postal services.[1] In other public utility industries – for example, industries providing electricity, gas, water, and rail services – competition policies have been implemented and privatization carried out either wholly or in part. This chapter aims to examine where postal services stand today based on the perspectives of governance and strategies, and to provide advice relevant to their future policy and management.

This chapter consists of four sections following the introduction. The second section provides a description and discussion mainly focused on postal services in five countries: the UK, France, Germany, the US, and Japan. The second section also provides an overview of postal services' size and organizational form.

The third section concerns the governance structure of postal operators. We explain general perspectives on corporate governance and apply them to postal operators in order to discuss the current governance system in the postal industry.

The fourth section discusses strategies such as diversification and internationalization. It is important to note that liberalization which includes privatization spurs more radical reforms in management compared to liberalization without it, and that this topic might have particular relevance to deciding future policy.

The last section summarizes the main points of this chapter from the perspective of governance and strategies in postal services.

Summary of postal services in selected countries

In this section, we provide an overview of postal services in the UK, France, Germany, the US, and Japan. We focus on the size of postal services, and ownership and managerial types.

Size of postal services

Table 21.1 shows a comparison of the size of postal service organizations in the 2012 financial year (FY). As there are variations among these countries in terms of population and total land area, we use the unit number per population and land area.

The number of post offices is on average about 30 to 50 per 1,000 km^2 of land area. The US, with its huge land area, has a much smaller number than the average, and Japan, 70 percent of whose land area is comprised of mountains, has a much larger number. It is also worth noting that the UK's number is slightly larger because its non-permanent post offices are included in the total.

Second, the number of employees is similar among these countries, except for Germany, which has between two and four employees per 1,000 people. The number of employees for Germany includes part-time staff.

Table 21.1 Comparison of postal service sizes in FY2012

Country	*UK*	*France*	*Germany*	*US*	*Japan*
Main provider	Royal Mail	La Poste	Deutsche Post DHL	United States Postal Service (USPS)	Japan Post
Population (thousand)	62,798	63,458	81,991	315,791	126,435
Area (1000 km^2)	242.9	551.5	357.0	9,629.0	377.9
Number of post offices[(a)] (per 1000 km^2 area)	48.7[(b)]	30.9	36.4	3.1	64.9
Number of employees (per 1000 population)	2.39[(b)]	3.57	5.17[(c)]	1.99	3.09
Number of delivery items[(d)] (per 1000 population)	0.29	0.24[(e)]	0.25	0.47	0.17
Postal service revenues[(f)] (per 1000 population)	127.2	293.0	581.2	134.4	105.4

Source: Universal Postal Union (2014).

Notes: (a) includes both permanent post offices and post offices under contract; (b) number is for FY2011; (c) total number of employees, including both permanent employees and part-time staff; (d) total number of letter-post items (domestic service) and ordinary parcels (domestic service); (e) number is for FY2011 and includes international service (dispatch), but excludes unaddressed advertising items; (f) unit is special drawing rights (SDR), where 1SDR = 140.8846 yen as of January 2014.

The number of delivery items is also similar among these countries, except for the US where the number is inflated by the high letter-post volume, which is most likely the result of massive direct mailing advertising activities.

Finally, postal service revenues per population appear similar among these countries, except for Germany, which has revenues of roughly four to five times higher than those of other countries, presumably because Deutsche Post has likely included in its total revenues those of DHL, a leading global postal service provider with which it has merged. We will discuss this type of international business strategy in a later section.

Organizational form

Postal services can be organized in several ways. In this section, by considering ownership, managerial type as organizational structure, and the range of related services in the five selected countries, we examine the organizational forms that postal services may take. Table 21.2 shows the organizational form of postal services.

Royal Mail is a member of the Royal Mail Group Ltd. Royal Mail Group Ltd, which is owned by Royal Mail plc (a holding company), has two brands, 'Royal Mail' and 'Parcelforce Worldwide', and three affiliated companies: Royal Mail Investments Ltd, Royal Mail Estates Ltd, and Romec Ltd. In 2013, Royal Mail was privatized and about 70 percent of its shares were sold to the private sector.

According to Le Groupe La Poste (2013), France's La Poste Group has six main subsidiaries to the parent company La Poste SA, and many others associated with these six companies. La Banque Postale, the former postal savings division of La Poste SA, now works as a main financial services provider in the group, and became a subsidiary in 2006. Although La Poste SA became a public limited company in 2010, 73.7 percent of its shares were still held by the French government as of 2013.

Germany's Deutsche Post DHL is an independent company with two internal brands, Deutsche Post and DHL. Deutsche Post DHL has four divisions in addition to a corporate center: Post-eCommerce-Parcel, Express, Global Forwarding and Freight, and Supply Chain. According to Deutsche Post DHL (2013), the Post-eCommerce-Parcel division handles mail, e-post, press services, export and import, and global eCommerce. The corporate center provides office functions for the entire company, including board services, corporate controlling, corporate finance, and human resource management. Deutsche Post DHL has many affiliated companies, associated companies, and joint ventures around the world. The origin of Deutsche Post DHL was Deutsche Post AG, created during the privatization of Deutsche Bundespost in 1995. Deutsche Post acquired DHL in 2002 and integrated related business operations under the DHL brand. It is worth noting that Deutsche Postbank AG and Deutsche Telekom AG were separated from Deutsche Bundespost when it was privatized, and now have no capital ties with Deutsche Post DHL.

USPS falls into the category of a public corporation, since it is a quasi-independent organization operated by the government, with one segment incorporating mailing, shipping, packages, and international services. USPS began operations in 1971, after the Postal Reorganization Act of 1970 stipulated that the post office would be transformed into a self-funding entity (USPS, 2013).

Japan Post Group, which is a holding-company-type organization, has three main service providers – Japan Post, Japan Post Bank, and Japan Post Insurance – in addition to 16 affiliated companies and consolidated subsidiaries. These three service providers were created under Japan Post Holdings when Japan Post was privatized in 2007. One hundred percent of the

Table 21.2 Organizational form of postal service

Country		*UK*	*France*	*Germany*	*US*	*Japan*
Provider		Royal Mail	La Poste	Deutsche Post DHL	USPS	Japan Post
Establishment year						
State-owned:		1660	1804	1876	1775	1871
Public corporation:		1969	1991	–	1971	2003
Corporatization:		2001	2010	1995	–	2007
Privatization:		2013	–	2000	–	–
Company type		Holding company	Single corporation	Single corporation	Public corporation	Holding company
Public ownership (%)		30[a]	100	21[b]	100	100
Postal service		100% subsidiary of holding company	Corporation	Corporation	Public corporation	100% subsidiary of holding company
Other business	Banking	None	100% subsidiary of post company	None	None	100% subsidiary of holding company
	Insurance	None	Associated company of post company	None	None	100% subsidiary of holding company
	Front customer service	100% subsidiary of holding company	None	None	None	100% subsidiary of holding company[c]

Source: Adapted from Ministry of International Affairs and Communications (2013), Hough and Booth (2014), Royal Mail Group (2014), Deutsche Post DHL Group (2015a), Deutsche Post DHL Group (2015b), Le Groupe La Poste (2015), Japan Post Holdings (2015), and USPS (2015b).

Notes: (a) the number is the ratio of public ownership (government and government-related financial organizations); (b) number is the ratio of public ownership (government-related organizations) (Deutsche Post, 2014); (c) this company was integrated into the Post Company on October 1, 2012.

shares of Japan Post Holdings are still held by the government. Japan Post Insurance and Japan Post Bank also subcontract operations to Japan Post.

From these descriptions, we can summarize the following. First, postal services are largely publicly owned. Among the selected countries, in France, the US and Japan postal service organizations have 100 percent public ownership. In the UK and Germany, ownership is more private sector or business-oriented.

Second, with respect to company type, these postal organizations can be divided into three groups: (1) the single corporation type, which includes Deutsche Post DHL and La Poste; (2) the holding company type, which includes Royal Mail and Japan Post; and (3) the public corporation type, which includes USPS. Deutsche Post DHL, La Poste, Royal Mail, and Japan Post are all stock companies with several divisions and affiliated companies.

Finally, the postal service industries in France and Japan also provide banking and insurance services. This strategic behavior is discussed in the section on corporate strategy.

Governance structure

This section describes the governance structure of postal services, with Deutsche Post DHL (Germany), La Poste (France), Royal Mail (UK), USPS (US) and Japan Post (Japan) selected as the main providers.

General theory of corporate governance

In general, corporate governance of an organization can be described from certain conventional perspectives: (1) board type, (2) board size and composition, (3) appointment of board, (4) relationship with government, (5) important shareholders, and (6) type of corporate governance. Through these perspectives, we can categorize each organization's board structure as follows.

First, according to Douma and Schreuder (2013), boards can be categorized into one-tier or two-tier types. In a one-tier system, all board members are appointed by a shareholders' general assembly and belong to the same board. In contrast, a two-tier system consists of the executive board (top-management members) and the supervisory board (external directors). The main difference between these systems is in the type of monitoring. In a one-tier system, executive members are monitored by non-executive members of the same board, while in a two-tier system, top-management members are monitored by external directors. The one-tier system is frequently used in the US and the UK, while the two-tier system is common in continental Europe and Japan.

The second important point on governance structure involves the monitoring system (either market-oriented or network-oriented). In the market-oriented system, the markets play an important role in monitoring through, for example, shareholders' active interference by addressing the claim directly to the company, called 'voice', and selling the shares of the company to withdraw, called 'exit'; and threats of takeovers in the stock market, which can strongly influence corporate management. In a network-oriented system, various organizational or individual networks with stakeholders play a major role, with important factors being relationships and connections between business groups, large shareholders, banks, and individuals in top management. In a network-oriented system, a company can be heavily influenced by a few large shareholders, such as banks and the government.

Governance structure of postal services

The governance structure of each postal organization is summarized in Table 21.3, with attention to the above six points.

First, Royal Mail and USPS have adopted the one-tier system, while Deutsche Post DHL and Japan Post use the two-tier system. However, La Poste and Japan Post Holdings, the parent company of Japan Post, have one-tier boards.

Second, the governance system of these five organizations has been network-oriented. Since postal service providers are regulated by the government to varying extents, they have been owned totally or primarily by the government through certain organizations even after privatization, or have remained in some way connected to the government. However, as the example of Deutsche Post DHL shows, governance systems for some operators have progressed toward the market-oriented type. Shareholder composition has become diversified in Deutsche Post DHL, though large shareholders have retained their influential power. In contrast to other organizations examined here, USPS remains in the public sector, although it is organized as a public corporation.

Table 21.3 Governance structure of postal organizations

Organization	*Royal Mail*	*La Poste*	*Deutsche Post DHL*	*USPS*	*Japan Post*
Board size and composition	1 chairman, 3 executive directors, 7 non-executive directors.	21 members (as required by law).	6 on board of management, 20 on supervisory board. (Number of board members is determined to be at least 2 by law. When the company requires more members, a supervisory board decides the number).	9 governors, postmaster general, deputy postmaster general.	Japan Post Holdings: 13 members (8 are external directors). Japan Post: 9 members on board of management (6 are external directors), 3 on supervisory board (2 are external auditors).
Appointment of the board	Appointed by an ordinary resolution of the company or by the board.	12 recommended by the government and appointed at the annual general meeting of shareholders, 2 appointed by decree, 7 elected by employees, CEO selected by board of directors.	On supervisory board, 10 representatives of shareholders, 10 elected by employees. Supervisory board appoints board of management.	The president appoints 9 governors, and 9 governors appoint postmaster general and deputy postmaster general .	Shareholders' general assembly appoints the management and supervisory board. Board of management appoints and monitors CEO.
Relationship with the government	Through Postal Services Holding Company, the government has the right to nominate one non-executive director to maintain at least 10 percent control in voting rights.	Representatives of the government can attend board of directors' meetings, though they do not have voting rights.	The government holds 21 percent of the shares via KfW Bankengruppe.	Quasi-independent organization in the government.	Japan Post is totally held by Japan Post Holdings, and Japan Post Holdings is totally held by the government.

(continued overleaf)

Table 21.3 (continued)

Organization	*Royal Mail*	*La Poste*	*Deutsche Post DHL*	*USPS*	*Japan Post*
Important shareholders	Postal Services Holding Company (totally owned by UK government), which has 29.98 percent voting rights.	French government (73.7 percent) and French public financial institution, Caisse des Depots et Consignations (26.3 percent).	KfW Bankengruppe (21 percent, largest shareholder). Other shareholders: institutional investors (67.8 percent), private investors (11.2 percent)	–	Japan Post Holdings (100 percent) in Japan Post, government (100 percent) in Japan Post Holdings.
Type of corporate governance	Market-oriented and partially network-oriented (shareholder composition is diversified, while the influential power of the government is consolidated in managerial decision-making).	Network-oriented (the government has large, direct, influential power on the management).	Market-oriented and partially network-oriented (the floating stock ratio is relatively high: 79 percent at the end of 2013. Shareholder composition is diversified but maintains the influential power of government).	Network-oriented (directly involved in governmental policy).	Network-oriented (under high influential power of the government via Japan Post Holdings).

Source: Authors' own elaboration based on Deutsche Post DHL (2013), Le Groupe La Poste (2013), Royal Mail plc (2014), USPS (2013), and Japan Post Holdings (2014)

It is worth noting that governance structure is frequently subject to regulation in the postal industry. For example, board size and composition, appointment of the board, or the share owned by the government in Royal Mail, La Poste, USPS, and Japan Post are restricted by the specific laws regarding each country's postal industry. This means that postal operators are highly controlled by the government due to the public nature of the postal industry, compared with other industries whose boards are subject to regular corporate law.

Corporate strategy

This section considers the corporate strategies of postal operators in selected countries. Since the postal industry is highly regulated by the government in many countries, the business strategies of postal operators have so far been relatively unfocused. However, due to recent developments in the Internet and electronic exchanges, the core mailing business has been steadily declining. Moreover, as deregulation and privatization of the postal industry have recently been widely discussed and implemented in many countries, postal operators now face the same need for strategic decision-making as their private sector counterparts do.

General theory of corporate strategy

In general, there are two types of corporate strategy: growth strategy and competitive strategy. The former aims for the future growth of a whole company, while the latter aims for divisional success in each market. Since corporate growth is achieved mainly by diversification, growth strategy can be relabeled 'diversification strategy'.

Diversification strategy can be categorized into two types: related and non-related diversification. The former is diversification into areas related to existing business resources, such as markets and technology, and is frequently implemented by dividing internal business into portions and creating affiliated companies from these. The latter type is diversification into new areas or markets, frequently implemented through mergers and acquisitions.

Competitive strategy can be categorized into various types according to the researcher's definition. Common types are cost-leadership and differentiation strategies. The former aims for low cost and thus low price, so that a division dominates with a large share of the market, while the latter aims for a niche market with a product of high price but with special value.

A relatively important strategy in postal services has been diversification, as it can compensate for the decline in core mailing business through a shift to more profitable activities, even though providers face severe competition from rivals. Thus, here we mainly discuss the diversification strategy of postal operators. However, as diversification advances, operators enter competitive areas where competitive strategy becomes equally crucial. In fact, some operators have already diversified into such areas and face severe competition from rivals.

Moreover, corporate internationalization strategy is frequently combined with diversification strategy. In the postal industry, while Deutsche Post DHL, La Poste, and Royal Mail have taken active steps to expand their international operations, the less internationally active USPS and Japan Post have been left behind.

Diversification strategy of postal services

Postal providers have most commonly diversified into the logistics, parcel, express, and finance industries, all of which utilize the existing synergies of networks, markets, and/or technology. Providers can realize combined innovations and shared costs through collaborations among business lines. In contrast, diversifying into non-related business requires additional management resources that are not commonly or readily available to providers of postal services.

This related diversification strategy is common, and can be classified into two types: the post-banking-insurance service type and the postal-service-only type.

La Poste and Japan Post are included in the post-banking-insurance diversification type. La Poste has diversified through affiliated companies and joint ventures, with La Poste SA, for example, engaged in the banking business (La Banque Postale) and the mobile telephone business (La Poste Mobile). Other business diversification includes real estate activities (such as industrial platforms, small- and medium-sized retail spaces, and commercial premises) by Poste Immo. Revenue for the whole group comprised 47.4 percent for mail, 26.9 percent for parcels and express, and 25.0 percent for banking in 2013. According to Le Groupe La Poste (2013), the group plans to proceed with related diversification based on existing assets as part of its new strategic plan 'La Poste 2020: Conquering the Future'.

There are legal restrictions related to how Japan Post may diversify. Affiliated companies are subject to legislative limitations, and their operating plans require permission from the government. As a result, Japan Post Group is limited to banking (Japan Post Bank) and insurance (Japan Post Insurance), logistics, and real estate, in addition to its core mail business. Its revenue comprised 60 percent for mail, 20.5 percent for banking, and 12.4 percent for life insurance in 2013.

On the other hand, the postal-service-only type is mainly limited to activities such as letter and parcel delivery. Deutsche Post DHL, Royal Mail, and USPS are included in this type. Deutsche Post DHL has focused on the specific areas of mailing and global logistics, in fact withdrawing from the banking business completely when all shares of Deutsche Postbank AG were sold to Deutsche Bank AG in 2012. As a result, the divisional revenue of Deutsche Post DHL comprised Post–eCommerce–Parcel (27.8 percent), express (21.5 percent), global forwarding, freight (27 percent), and supply chain (25.9 percent) in 2013.

Royal Mail has affiliated companies that operate non-mailing services, such as Royal Mail Investments Ltd, Royal Mail Estates Ltd, and Romec Ltd. However, the main activity is restricted to post-related services. The divisional revenue of Royal Mail comprised 82.4 percent for UK Parcels, International & Letters (UKPIL) and 17.5 percent for General Logistics Systems (GLS) in 2013.

Diversification of USPS is legislatively restricted. Congress also requires USPS to adhere to the core business of the mailing and package service. Thus, USPS has only one segment based on the same network. According to USPS (2013), the major service categories are first-class mail, which is offered mainly for letters and postcards, standard mail, which is offered for any item, including advertisements and marketing packages, shipping and packages, international, periodicals, and other. Services involving first-class mail, standard mail, and periodicals are dominant in the US market.

Internationalization strategy of postal services

Diversification strategy frequently includes corporate internationalization. First, Deutsche Post's DHL operates in Europe, the Americas, Asia Pacific, the Middle East, and Africa. DHL has expanded its business through vigorous acquisition of local companies: Danzas in Switzerland and Van Gend & Loos in the Netherlands in 1999, Airborne Express in the US in 2003, Blue Dart in India in 2005, and Professional Parcel Logistics in the Czech Republic in 2006, to name just a few.

La Poste Group works actively on internationalization through affiliated companies. For example, SofiPost has Asendia, a joint venture with Swiss Post. GeoPost also has affiliated companies in various countries, such as GeoPost Intercontinental Entities, DPD Germany

Entities, DPD UK Entities, and SEUR Spain Entities. Moreover, the group actively acquires foreign companies. For example, Asendia purchased Pitney Bowes in the UK and invested in 40 percent of eShopWorld in Ireland in 2013.

Royal Mail also aims for internationalization. According to Royal Mail plc (2014), its UKPIL division operates in the UK and on an international basis under the 'Royal Mail' and 'Parcelforce Worldwide' brands. In addition, as an international logistics company, GLS operates in 37 European countries. Moreover, Royal Mail is investing in joint ventures with the Bank of Ireland: Midasgrange Ltd for financial services and First Rate Exchange Services Holdings Ltd for foreign exchange services.

USPS, which is operated by the government and subject to heavy regulation and government policy, had no branches in foreign countries as of 2014.

Japan Post has a Chinese consolidated subsidiary, Japan Post International Logistics Co. Ltd., for logistics in Japan and China. However, Japan Post had no other branches in other countries as of 2014.

In summary, Deutsche Post DHL, La Poste, and Royal Mail have taken active steps to expand their operations internationally, while USPS and Japan Post are lagging behind in this respect.

Conclusion

This chapter aimed to provide useful information for policymakers involved in planning for the management of postal services. Five countries were selected – the UK, France, Germany, the US, and Japan – and the characteristics of their postal services were described in terms of regulation, governance, and strategies. Variations were noted in their regulatory structures. Governance structure and corporate strategies were deemed to be of increasing importance as postal service providers adopt a more corporate style. The important points made in this paper can be summarized as follows.

First, the governance structure of postal service providers varies from country to country, according to corporate law. Regarding company type, postal organizations are divided into three groups: single corporation (Deutsche Post DHL and La Poste), holding company (Royal Mail and Japan Post), and public corporation (USPS). It is not yet clear whether there is one best solution for general postal operators and, if there is, which type is the best. These issues should be examined in future research.

Second, with regard to diversification strategy, postal operators mostly choose related diversification, such as expansion in the logistics, parcel, express, and finance industries, using the existing network. Non-related diversification is not yet common in the postal industry. The future direction of diversification strategy can vary among operators, depending on the company's vision and management style.

Finally, regarding internationalization strategy, Deutsche Post DHL, La Poste, and Royal Mail have taken steps to expand their operations internationally, while USPS and Japan Post have been slower to make inroads abroad. Although the strategy depends heavily on regulations and public involvement in each country, internationalization is expected to progress in the general postal industry due to liberalization, changes in technology, and the subsequent increase in the necessity of obtaining a broader customer base.

Note

1 With regard to the effects of competition and ownership in the postal industry, see, for example, Mizutani and Uranishi (2003).

References

Deutsche Post DHL (2013) *2013 Annual Report*, Deutsche Post DHL, Bonn.

Deutsche Post (2014) 'Shareholder structure', available at: http://www.dpdhl.com/en/investors/shares/shareholder_structure.html (accessed September 4, 2014).

Deutsche Post DHL Group (2015a) *History of Deutsche Post DHL Group*, Bonn, available at: http://www.dpdhl.com/en/about_us/history.html (accessed May 18, 2015).

Deutsche Post DHL Group (2015b) *Shareholder Structure*, Bonn, available at: http://www.dpdhl.com/en/investors/shares/shareholder_structure.html (accessed May 18, 2015).

Douma, S. and Schreuder, H. (2013) *Economic Approaches to Organizations*, fifth edition. Harlow: Pearson.

Hough, D. and Booth, L. (2014) 'Privatization of Royal Mail plc', *Briefing Paper of House of Commons Library*, SN/EP/06668, available at http://researchbriefings.parliament.uk/ResearchBriefing/Summary/SN06668#fullreport (accessed May 18, 2015).

Japan Post (2014) *Documents Pursuant to Section 13 of Act on Japan Post Holdings Co., Ltd. (Nihon Yubin Kabushikikaisha-ho Dai 13 jo ni Motoduku Shorui)*, Japan Post, Tokyo (in Japanese).

Japan Post Holdings (2014) *Summary of Statement of Accounts in March 2013 (2014 Nen 3 Gatsuki Kessan no Gaiyo)*, Japan Post Holdings, Tokyo (in Japanese).

Japan Post Holdings (2015) *History of Japan Post*, available at: http://www.japanpost.jp/en/ (accessed May 18, 2015).

Le Groupe La Poste (2013) *Registration Document 2013*, Le Groupe La Poste, Paris.

Le Groupe La Poste (2015) *Postal Activity Statistics*, Paris, available at: http://www.laposte.fr/chp/pages/statistiques_uk.php (accessed May 18, 2015).

Ministry of International Affairs and Communications (2013) *International Trend of Postal Business (Yubin Jigyo wo Torimaku Kokusaitekina Doko)*, Ministry of International Affairs and Communications, Tokyo (in Japanese).

Mizutani, F. and Uranishi, S. (2003) The post office vs. parcel delivery companies: competition effects on costs and productivity, *Journal of Regulatory Economics*, 23(3), 299–319.

Royal Mail Group (2014) *Fact Sheets of Royal Mail Group: History of Royal Mail Group*, available at: http://www.royalmailgroup.com/media/fact-sheets (accessed September 17, 2014).

Royal Mail plc (2014) *Annual Report and Financial Statements 2013–14*, Royal Mail plc, London.

United States Postal Service (USPS) (2013) *Annual Report Pursuant to Section 13 or 15(d) of the Securities Exchange Act of 1934*, USPS, Washington, DC.

United States Postal Service (USPS) (2015a) *Postal History*, Washington, DC, available at: http://about.usps.com/who-we-are/postal-history/welcome.htm (accessed May 18, 2015).

United States Postal Service (USPS) (2015b) *Significant Dates*, Washington, DC, available at: https://about.usps.com/who-we-are/postal-history/significant-dates.htm (accessed May 18, 2015).

Universal Postal Union (UPU) (2014) *Status and Structures of Postal Entities*, Berne, available at: http://www.upu.int/en/the-upu/status-of-postal-entities/about-status-of-postal-entities.html (accessed September 4, 2014).

22

Electricity distribution utilities and the future

More than just wires

Rahmatallah Poudineh, Wenche Tobiasson and Tooraj Jamasb

Introduction[1]

This chapter reviews the main challenges facing electricity distribution network utilities along technological, economic, and social dimensions. It also discusses the implications of challenges ahead for network utilities and provides some insights into the likely features of their future business models.

Electricity networks are a crucial part of the power system as they transport electricity from generators to end users. The power grid consists of transmission and distribution networks that differ in voltage level, size, operation, and objectives. The transmission grid comprises high-voltage circuits designed to transfer bulk power from power plants to load centers, using step-up transformers to raise the voltage to the required level. Distribution networks deliver electric energy to end users after receiving bulk power from the transmission grid. Circuits with different voltage levels in transmission and distribution networks are connected by substations.[2] Electricity is delivered through underground cables or overhead lines. Underground cables are often used in urban areas, whereas overhead lines are used for less densely populated and rural areas.

In a liberalized and unbundled model of the electricity sector, distribution networks are owned and operated by distribution network operators (DNOs). Each DNO serves a specific service area but has no direct financial relationship with final consumers (that is, DNOs do not sell electricity). End users buy electricity from or sell to, retail suppliers. In many countries, prior to the liberalization of the sector in the 1990s, distribution networks were part of vertically integrated monopoly structures that owned and operated the four basic functions of the electricity system: generation, transmission, distribution, and retail supply. Power sector reforms led to the introduction of wholesale and retail markets for electricity. However, competition is not feasible in the electricity networks, and consequently, network companies are subject to economic regulation.

In the coming years, distribution networks will likely experience extensive changes in their operating environments. Networks that were originally designed as passive transporters of electric energy will face a shift in their operational paradigm in terms of bi-directional power flows and their use of information and communication technologies. Moreover, penetration of distributed generation sources, electric vehicles (EV), and storage facilities create techno-economic challenges that require grid upgrade, reinforcement, technological improvement, and, ultimately, the development of new business models (see Figure 22.1). Furthermore, the DNOs are the main point of interaction between the power grid and the end users; therefore, implementing new concepts such as demand response, smart metering, and consumer empowerment involves changes in planning and operation at the distribution level.

These developments will lead to fundamental changes to the relationship between utility companies and their customers, which will result in the emergence of new business models. Future distribution network utilities will adapt their conventional business models based on the provision of unidirectional wire connection to innovative and interactive service-based business models.

The outline of this chapter is as follows. The following section discusses penetration of new technologies and their implication for network companies. The third section explains the role of consumers and society and the change in the nature of demand. Regulatory challenges and possible solutions are discussed in the fourth section. The fifth section investigates the problem of the current stylized business model of the DNOs and explores some possibilities in this respect. Finally, conclusions are drawn in the final section.

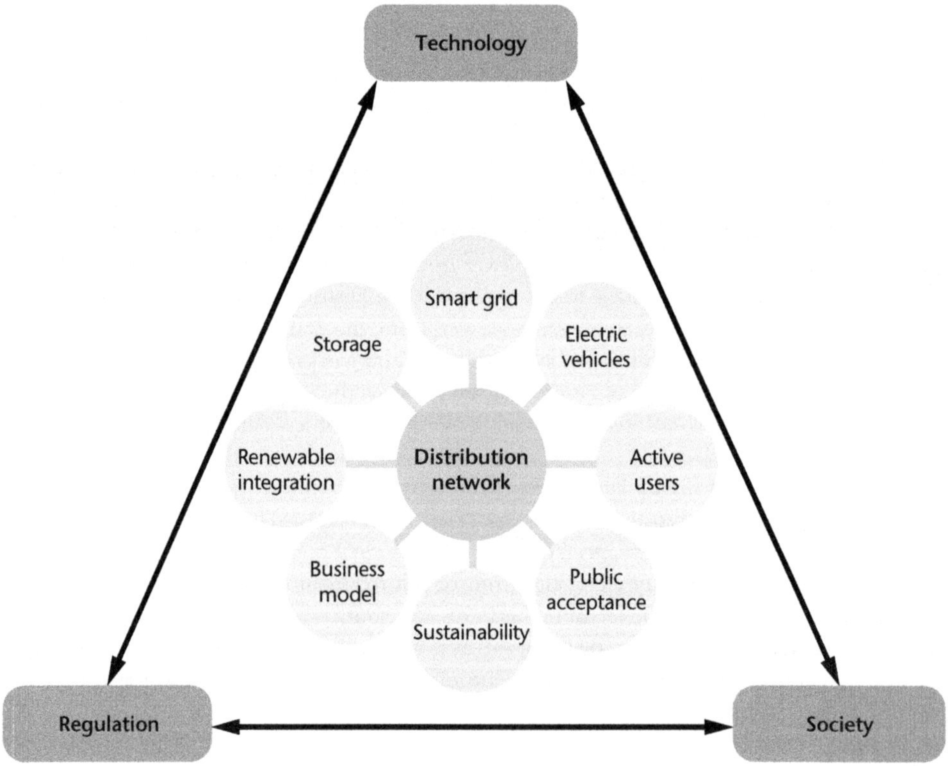

Figure 22.1 Electricity distribution networks in a dynamic environment

New technologies: Game changers

Distributed energy resources

Distributed energy resources are facilities that can generate electricity (and heat) using several small- and medium-scale technologies. These include different types of distributed generations (DGs) such as small turbines, fuel cells, combined heat and power (CHP), and photovoltaic systems (IEA, 2002). These facilities either connect to the distribution network or serve customers directly on-site. This differs from the traditional system, which produces electricity in a few large facilities that is then transported over long distances through transmission and distribution networks to reach consumers.

Distributed sources have several possible benefits. A greater number of local generation facilities can potentially reduce congestion in the network and defer upgrades to transmission and distribution systems. Additionally, quality of supply can increase as energy is generated closer to demand, and system losses may also decrease (IEA, 2002). Distributed generation currently accounts for a small proportion of total capacity, but this share is set to increase as these technologies improve. Furthermore, growing concerns over climate change, constraints in upgrading the transmission grid, and supply security are increasing the number of generators connected to distribution networks (IEA, 2002).

However, large volumes of distributed generation can also negatively affect the quality of supply, voltage levels, and phase imbalance (Putrus *et al.*, 2009), whilst large increases in renewable sources can create new bottlenecks in distribution networks. In passive networks, the distributed generation capacity that can be connected is limited as network stability is essential for a safe and secure supply, and large volumes of distributed generation may cause system volatility (Lopes *et al.*, 2007). Therefore, the networks require substantial investment for upgrades and expansion to accommodate the diverse distributed energy sources.

Alongside the increased focus on distributed generation is the prospect of development of storage technologies. Depending on the duration of storage, benefits include voltage and frequency control (short storage), peak load topping, renewable power smoothing (medium storage), smoothing of weather effects, and annual smoothing of loads (long storage). Thus, energy storage can increase the penetration of distributed generation by ensuring a smoother supply and offering greater demand predictability (Barton and Infield, 2004). This holds out the potential for electricity customers to become less dependent on the networks, so that DNOs will need to find alternative methods of securing their revenue base.

The smart information and communication technology era: Smart grids and meters

Conventional distribution networks are passive and operate based on predefined values, and are thus unable to respond to short-term customer behavior. They are also unable to accommodate the wide range of renewable and distributed energy sources. Therefore, large increases in distributed generation and EVs necessitate the development of active networks with the ability to respond to changes in demand and supply. A smart grid uses information and communication technology (ICT) to collect and respond to information about customer and supplier behavior. With two-way communication technologies and smart meters, the networks can better respond to changes in demand, aggregate consumption, and grid condition, enabling informed participation by their customers (Byun *et al.*, 2011).

However, the implementation of smart technology does not automatically lead to smart network operation. The transition must be comprehensive, and requires retraining of staff as well as development and implementation of new protocols that are compatible with the new operating environment (Arends and Hendriks, 2014). Moreover, the costs associated with active smart networks are substantial, and their benefits need to justify and outweigh their costs. In the conventional business model, DNOs do not normally have an incentive to implement a responsive grid as they would only be able to offer limited benefits (Lopes *et al.*, 2007).

Electric vehicles

Whilst CO_2 emissions from some sectors of the economy are decreasing, emissions from transportation are increasing (DECC, 2014). The UK government has implemented a number of measures to incentivize the public to switch from traditional vehicles, which run on petrol or diesel, to EV. These measures include grants, road tax waivers, and exemption from London congestion charges (TRL, 2013). With costs being a major motive behind purchases (TRL, 2013), financial incentives and technological progress can increase the uptake of EVs in the UK (Putrus *et al.*, 2009). However, to date, interest in the UK has been slow, and only 5 percent of consumers were considering buying an electric car or van in the near future as of 2014 (Department for Transport, 2014). On the other hand, strong incentives in countries such as Norway have resulted in a greater demand for electric cars.

Electric vehicles have yet to make a substantial impact on the distribution network; however, since the vehicles use batteries with large storage capacity, allowing them to travel longer distances, an upsurge in uptake may place strain on the network. One potential problem relates to a mismatch of supply and demand due to uncertainties regarding when and how owners charge their vehicles. The distribution grids can only safely carry up to a certain load, and if owners charge their vehicles at peak demand hours, a congested network may overload. Therefore, substantial local infrastructural reinforcements are required to accommodate the integration of EV (Lopes *et al.*, 2011).

As the number of vehicles increases, the DNOs will need to upgrade the network to supply the charging points and other required infrastructure (Pieltain Fernández *et al.*, 2011). However, provided that the necessary infrastructure is in place, the vehicles may be able to deliver electricity back to the grid. This opens the possibility for electric cars to provide peak-demand relief, which would reduce the need for grid capacity enhancement. Additionally, the potential mismatch between demand and supply can be eliminated through improved communication and provision of price incentives to consumers to encourage off-peak charging (Putrus *et al.*, 2009).

The aforementioned changes in the operating environment of distribution networks will necessitate a shift in the operating paradigm of these companies from being network operators (DNOs) to distribution system operators (DSOs). Figure 22.2 illustrates this likely transition, and depicts and relates the above-discussed aspects of technological change in the operating environment of the DNOs, including distributed generation, storage facilities, ICTs, and EV.

The consumer and society: The changing nature of demand

Governments across Europe have set ambitious green energy targets to curb carbon emissions. The policies, including increased generation of renewable energy and adoption of EVs, largely depend on public and local support for their success. The role of the individual and the community in energy policy issues is thus on the rise (Akcura *et al.*, 2011). This trend is also noticeable in the transportation of electricity. The technical challenges of DNOs to ensure a sustainable energy future include extensive expansion and modernization of the networks to allow for smaller but more numerous generation facilities, uptake of EV, and active grid

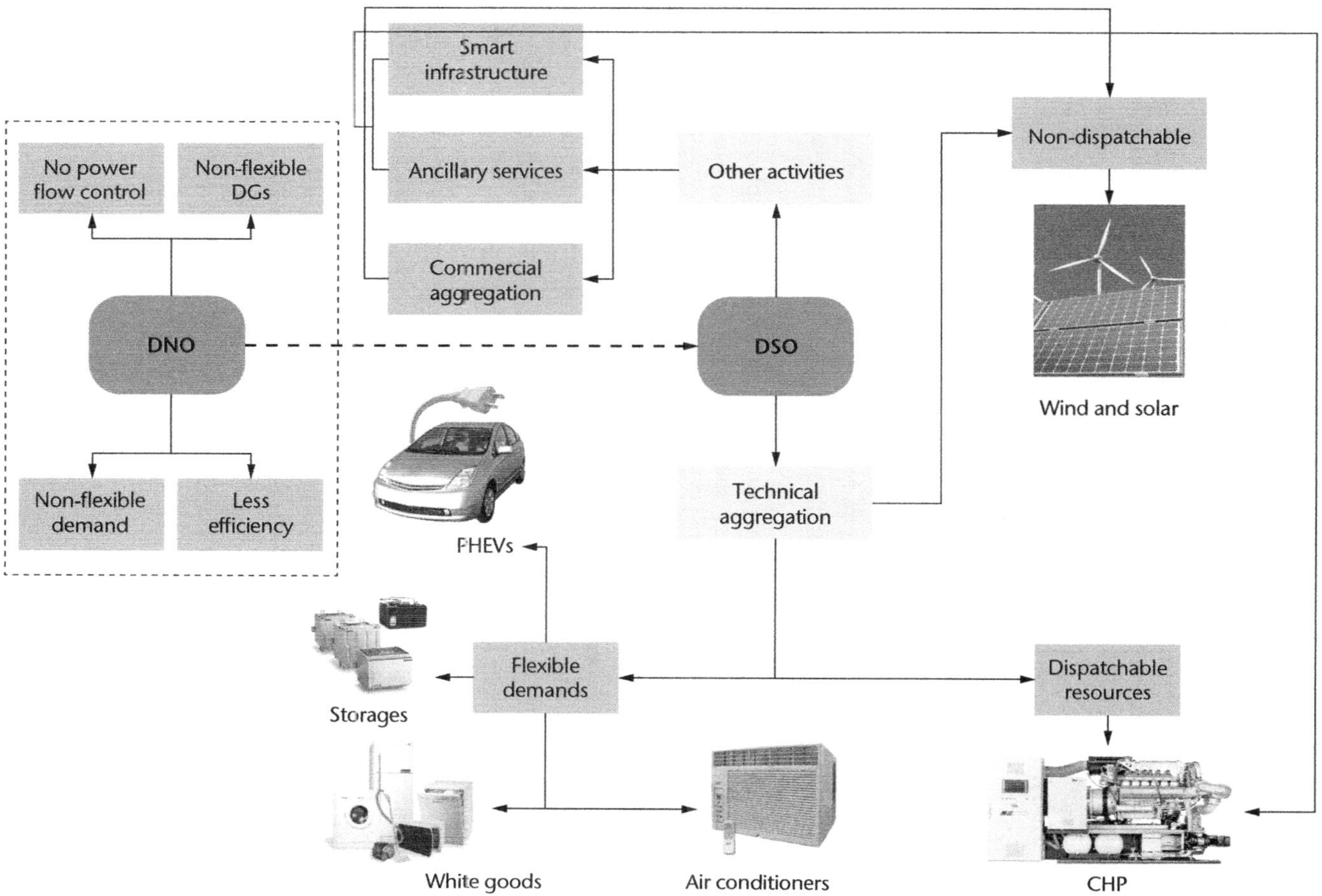

Figure 22.2 A shift from DNO to DSO

management. However, whilst the technical and economic aspects receive more attention from the sector and academics alike, they are only part of the challenge. As the nature of electricity demand and supply is changing, so is the role of the society and consumer engagement in the sector.

Societal and consumer acceptance of green energy innovations plays an important part in addressing and curbing climate change. Whilst it is generally thought that public attitudes towards renewable energy are positive, local opposition to large facilities remains significant. The importance of public acceptance has been discussed with regards to large infrastructural projects, such as transmission lines (Ciupuliga and Cuppen, 2013), renewable-energy-generation technologies (Devine-Wright, 2011), and hazardous facilities (Johnson and Scicchitano, 2012). However, where large infrastructure, put simply, only needs 'passive' consent (see Ciupuliga and Cuppen, 2013; Tobiasson and Jamasb, 2014), distributed generation, EV, and smart networks depend on 'active' acceptance from consumers. This includes the willingness to invest, install, and change behavior to adapt to these technologies (Sauter and Watson, 2007). The slow progress from simple acceptance to participation and changing behavior shows how priorities expressed by citizens sometimes fail to translate into actions by customers (Cotton and Devine-Wright, 2012).

The shift to a decentralized generation mix creates a flow of electricity that is less predictable and less flexible to operate. Shifts in both demand and supply will have an effect on the operation of DNOs. Through increased uptake of demand–response, smart grids, and distributed generation, customers are more involved and can actively contribute to increased energy efficiency, energy saving, and peak load shifts. Not only are customers able to affect the demand side through altering electricity consumption patterns, but also the supply side, where consumers can take on the role of producer through distributed generation (Mah *et al.*, 2012).

Moreover, customer action is the main driver behind reaching the policy goals to curb climate change, and customer engagement should therefore be a priority (Honebein *et al.*, 2011). Smart grids and distributed generation require communication between utility companies and their customers. The relationship is likely to change from a one-way information flow to a two-way interactive discussion. However, not only will the DNOs be required to engage actively with customers once new technologies are implemented, through dialogue at an early stage, but DNOs can also learn about their customers' priorities and concerns, and adapt these technologies accordingly. Early communication and customer participation is important for building trust and confidence among consumers, which in turn is important for achieving customer acceptance of new technologies (Gangale *et al.*, 2013).

Ultimately, increasing communication and participation with customers will bring to light the heterogeneity of customer behavior, as the same technology may be perceived differently among different groups in the same or different communities (Batel and Devine-Wright, 2015). The role of the consumer in the sector is shifting. As distribution networks change from passive to active utilities, the public is also changing from being a passive to active stakeholder. On the other hand, DNOs face the challenge of adapting to a new nature of demand. However, rather than adopting a 'wait and see' approach, the DNOs can also choose to act early and smooth the transition from passive transporters of electricity to active participants in between both demand and supply. Therefore, policymakers and regulators have the challenging task of providing incentives that increase public acceptance and participation in implementing green-energy innovations.

Regulation: Incentives work

Maintaining a well-functioning liberalized sector requires supervision and regulation of the wholesale and retail markets as well as the networks services. At grid level, this becomes more important as there is no competition and the networks are subject to incentive-based regulation. The incentive regulation regimes aim to induce the market outcomes in this segment of the sector. The expectation is that incentive regulation better realizes the objectives of regulators. However, the post-liberalization experience has shown that incentive regimes give rise to new challenges, including those related to investments and innovation. Additionally, promotion of low-carbon technologies and objectives has resulted in new challenges that require regulatory innovation and solutions. In what follows, we review some of the most important regulatory challenges that will likely affect future development of electricity distribution networks.

Investment and innovation

The post-liberalization policies of achieving a low-carbon economy have changed the dynamics of the electricity sector. This is reflected in the need for smart technologies, distributed-energy resources, EV, network security, and integration of electricity markets. Achieving these objectives calls for substantial innovation and investments, and ensuring sufficient and efficient investments in the networks is among the most challenging tasks facing regulators.

The current regulatory models of investment treatment are either ex ante, ex post, or a combination of the two. Under the ex-ante model, network companies submit business plans that contain details of their investment needs over the subsequent regulatory period. The regulator uses auditing, cost–benefit analysis, and consultants to verify the prudence of investments plans. At the end of the regulatory period, if there is a deviation from the agreed level of capital expenditures in the business plan, the regulator might partially or totally disallow the excess investment.

The ex-ante approach has been criticized on the grounds that it provides incentive for strategic behavior. For example, network companies will have incentive to inflate their capital costs by reporting high volumes of work or by capitalizing their operational expenditures. Averch and Johnson (1962) demonstrated that under this model firms will, for a given level of output, employ more capital compared to non-regulated companies. The incentive for overcapitalization will be higher if there is no incentive attached to downward deviation from the agreed level of investment in the business plan. The planned RIIO (Revenue= Incentives+Innovation+Output) which is a framework for regulating the network companies in the UK aims to promote innovation and efficiency by allowing the DNOs to retain some of their capital cost saving if they deliver the same output with less investment.

In ex-post regulation, the regulator adds the controllable costs incurred to the company, including the operating and capital expenditures, in order to construct a single variable reflecting the total cost. The total cost is then benchmarked against the similar companies in the sector to obtain the cost efficiency. The firms' revenue is set based on their deviation from the optimum frontier. The threat of financial loss from the benchmarking process can lead to an efficient level of operating and capital expenditure. Poudineh and Jamasb (2016) show that this model is vulnerable to harmonized behavior, such as over- and under-investment by utilities. Harmonized behavior changes the costs for companies uniformly, and within-group comparisons cannot detect the incidence of overcapitalization. Additionally, the minimum productivity level to pass a benchmarking exercise (that is, no-impact efficiency) is also vulnerable to harmonized behavior.

Regulatory treatment of investment presents a trade-off between intervention in firms' operation and distribution of risk between the firms and their consumers. The ex-ante model is more interventionist, but the firm bears little risk compared to the consumers. This is because consumers are more likely to be exposed to the actual costs of the firm rather than the efficient costs. The ex-post model, on the other hand, is less interventionist, but firms bear more risk compared to consumers. The choice between the two approaches depends on the regulator's view of intervention and risk. Nevertheless, both models suffer from a lack of incentive for dynamic efficiency.

As noted by Müller *et al.* (2010), under incentive regimes (both ex ante and ex post), efficiency gain has mainly been achieved in operating costs, but regulatory models do not incentivize dynamic, efficient behavior among firms. In the case of ex-post regulatory treatment of investment, Poudineh *et al.* (2014) showed that persistent inefficiency due to the presence of quasi-fixed inputs, such as capital costs, can affect companies' short-run productivity and regulated revenue. This can create disincentives for long-term investment and innovation. In the case of ex-ante regulation, although capital costs are excluded from benchmarking, the model does not provide explicit incentives for dynamically efficient behavior.

Incentives and alignment of benefits

In order to unlock the system-wide benefits of dynamic networks, the incentives that guide the behavior of players need to be realigned. Additionally, policies need to serve the diverse interests of distributed resource developers and consumers. The public, as well as community engagement with the sector as consumers and as citizens, can affect the development of the network and energy infrastructures. Some projects have stood still because local communities perceive them as failing to meet their objectives. The need for involvement of customers in the planning of new projects or through demand-side participation requires a new consumer–distribution utility relationship.

Consumers with micro-generation, EV, and storage capability are no longer passive users, but can benefit or harm the system. The load from EV varies with respect to time and location. In the absence of incentives, the EV owner indifferently charges and discharges at any time and place. However, the power system would benefit from charging during off-peak periods and in uncongested areas, and discharging at peak times and in congested zones. Thus, there is a need for incentive signals that coordinate the actions of players to the advantage of power system reliability and efficiency. However, current regulatory models do not provide such incentives and thus are contrary to the paradigm of a sustainable power sector.

The current incentives for the integration of distributed resources are not directly relevant in terms of impact on network infrastructure and generation supply. For example, siting a distributed generation (DG) close to demand centers or areas served by frequently congested lines will be beneficial for a DNO as it can reduce network energy losses and have an impact on demand-driven investments. DG can have various effects on the grid, depending on factors such as location, technological specification, and timing of investments (Vogel, 2009). The lack of a mechanism that aligns these benefits between the DG developer and the DNO might reverse the expected advantages of DG integration.

An example of this is network energy losses. Networks are incentivized to reduce such losses and are rewarded or penalized for outperforming or underperforming on the loss targets. Although DG can reduce these losses, it is generally bound by time and location and, under the condition that capacity exceeds the demand, it can increase overall energy losses because the relationship between capacity and loss is U-shaped (Harrison *et al.*, 2007). Therefore, DNOs might be exposed to DG-induced losses, with consequences for their revenue. On the other hand, generators are not incentivized for their positive or negative effect on network energy losses. Hence, there is a conflict between the interest of developers wishing to increase DG penetration and the DNO that wants to avoid DG-induced losses.

One solution is to use efficient and effective connection and 'use of system' (UoS) charges – a mechanism that not only includes the real cost of connection but also rewards the developer when DG installation is in line with the optimal operation of the network (Jamasb *et al.*, 2005). The distribution UoS charges can play a role, as DGs' connection charges could be based on their capacity and the sole-use network asset used. On the other hand, rewards can be offered based on generator-exported power at system peak, proximity to frequently congested zones, and network assets utilized (Poudineh and Jamasb, 2014). This ensures that rewards will reflect the benefits from integration of the resource. Taking into account the cost drivers when devising the charges and rewards will help to guarantee that they are aligned with the costs imposed by DGs on the network.

Managing uncertainties

There are several sources of uncertainty in the operating environment of distribution network companies, which call for uncertainty to be incorporated into regulatory models. These include future tightening of environmental policies, change in price of fossil fuels and its effect on the rate of growth of renewable resources, cost and performance of networks, carbon prices, uncertain demand and economic growth, availability of capital, and finally, change in the behavior and expectations of consumers.

DNOs face significant uncertainty from unexpected changes in the aforementioned factors. These factors can impact the existing infrastructures in terms of planning and operation, as well as development of new assets. The network infrastructures are long-lived assets and irreversible investments. Hence, insufficient consideration of uncertainty in the regulatory and decision-making process can lead to negative consequences for the firm and consumers. The regulatory framework should also recognize the increasing importance of local communities as part of the low-carbon solution, and provide incentives for these communities to become part of the solution for future networks.

Thus, given the importance of uncertainty, there is a need for regulatory models that reduce the exposure of firms and society to the adverse effects of changes in the operating environments of network companies. Furthermore, uncertainty is not welcomed by investors, who are interested in a stable return on their investments. Uncertainty means risk, which is likely to erode creditworthiness of the utilities and manifest in the form of higher capital costs and thus higher bills for consumers. This will lead to reduction of capital availability, which affects DNOs' future investment plans. These cycles have previously been experienced in other network industries, including telecommunications and airlines.

The utility business model: What future?

There is limited consensus on the definition of a business model (Desyllas and Sako, 2013). However, there is more agreement that business models are at the core of strategies for surviving in a dynamic environment. In recent years, electricity distribution networks have experienced rapid changes in their environment as a result of energy and sustainability policies. These changes not only influence technical operation of the grid, but also its economics and revenue generation. Evidence suggests that network companies cannot continue with traditional business models in the new environment (Poudineh and Jamasb, 2014). The next section reviews the effects of large-scale integration of distributed energy resources on the business model of distribution companies, and explores possibilities for alternative models.

Disruptive technologies and DNO revenues

A variety of new technologies and factors can have disruptive effects on the revenue of distribution network companies. These include photovoltaic cells, micro turbines, micro CHP, fuel cells, storage facilities, demand response, and energy efficiency. As distributed technologies are on a descending cost trajectory, the traditional generation–transmission–distribution paradigm comes under increasing pressure to be changed. The threat to the traditional centralized supply will be exacerbated by behavioral change, which may lead to reduced load. The proximity of distributed resources to demand sites reduces the volume of energy transported in the grid and consequently erodes the revenue base of network companies over time.

The current incentives to promote renewable distributed generation are characterized by a tendency to work at cross-purposes with the original objective. It is conceivable that some consumers will choose to leave the grid entirely if there are other cost-effective possibilities available. For example, this can occur when storage facilities such as those of plug-in vehicles are combined with suitable distributed generation. In a more optimistic scenario, consumers will use the grid only as a backup and aim to be self-sufficient otherwise. In this case, the networks will not be able to recover their costs from consumers who install self-generation facilities, especially those installed behind the meter because they do not pay for grid connection.

Furthermore, while the total network cost will barely change with the exit of an existing customer, the remaining consumers will incur the cost burden of the network. These are often the same consumers who cannot afford self-generation in the first place. The increase of electricity rates will create positive feedback, which results in more independence from networks. Moreover, due to the structure of retail tariffs in some countries, penetration of distributed resources has not led to a reduction in peak demand, but rather a reduction in average demand (Nelson *et al.*, 2014). This implies a rise in the network costs imposed by other consumers who do not pay for network charges.

Furthermore, the paradoxical nature of consumer-side renewables with the business model of utilities deters integration of small-scale, low-carbon technologies from gaining sufficient momentum. Although in recent years, some incumbent utility companies have been providing various services for their consumers, such as consulting services on energy efficiency and financial support to install rooftop PV (photovoltaic), managers of these utilities often acknowledge that such activities are inherently counterproductive given their current business model (Richter, 2013). Thus, as residential renewable generation currently does not benefit utility companies, in practice the promotion of these resources is not supported by these companies, and where there is evidence to the contrary, it is mainly to show political goodwill or to manage the consumer–utility relationship.

The challenge of disruptive technologies gives rise to the idea that the power industry needs to shift from the traditional business model of selling energy in terms of kWh (or MWh) to something that is not in conflict with other policy objectives, such as sustainability. As demand for energy is a derived one – that is, consumers do not gain utility from energy itself but rather from the services they obtain, such as heat, light, computer hours, and entertainment – a solution for utility companies to adapt to their dynamic environment is to consider selling the unit of 'energy service'. In this view, the consumer bill can resemble a list of energy-based services, such as heating, cooling, interior and exterior lighting. These ideas are not completely new. Indeed, during the last four decades some pioneering energy-policy thinkers have suggested that utility companies should sell energy services. Such a model will push utility companies towards the business of end-use hardware appliances. Similar models have been developed in the telecommunications industry, where consumers actually receive kilobits per second (Kbps) while the service providers charge their consumers for minutes of talk, number of text messages, amount of data downloaded, etc.

The emergence of smart technologies brings such ideas closer to reality. Two-way communication and advanced sensors that are becoming increasingly commonplace within the current power infrastructure reduce measurement problems that were considered an impediment to implementation of this kind of model in the past.

Innovation in business models

There have been important discussions around the future business models for distribution network companies and potential regulatory models that can support these companies through a rapidly changing landscape. Common among many of the discussions is that the network companies need to go beyond only connection and UoS charges. The utility companies will need to work closely with consumers, resource developers, and other stakeholders to create an integrated-value partnership. Decoupling the revenue of network companies from aggregate energy usage is not only important for the companies, but also for achieving energy-efficiency initiatives that can be opposed by distribution networks (Brennan, 2014).

An issue is that even if utility companies have the resources to introduce new ideas and products, they often fail to successfully commercialize them. Experiences from the past in other industries show that this has sometimes been the case. For example, at the end of the 1990s, IBM was among the first companies to develop new technologies such as commercial routers and speech recognition, but these entered the market later, produced by other companies and not IBM (Richter, 2013). Another issue is that network companies are regulated businesses and innovation in such an environment is only derived from incentives and institutional frameworks.

Despite these challenges, there are potential areas that can be utilized in an extended business model of distribution network companies. Although some research suggests that the critical skill for traditional players is not to create new business models but instead to identify and implement the already existing ideas into a mass-market scale (Nillesen *et al.*, 2014). These arguments are based on experiences from other industries, where the majority of new business models have been created by newcomers but implemented on a large scale by incumbents.

An important dimension of any future business model is digital-communication capabilities. The ICT revolution in the last century has embraced all sectors, including electricity distribution. The change from capital-intensive to information-intensive business has already been initiated in this segment of the power sector. This provides valuable system data for distribution utilities, which can be shared with developers of distributed energy resources and retail suppliers for efficient planning and operation in return for a payoff.

Figure 22.3 presents an extended business model for distribution network companies. Transmission system operators (TSOs) often procure balancing services. Penetration of distributed energy resources provides an opportunity for DSOs to contribute to national balancing services and be compensated for it by the TSO. As seen in Figure 22.3, the costs of a DSO consist of grid reinforcement, use of (transmission) system charges, ancillary services procured from the transmission operator, operation and maintenance, and finally, energy losses.

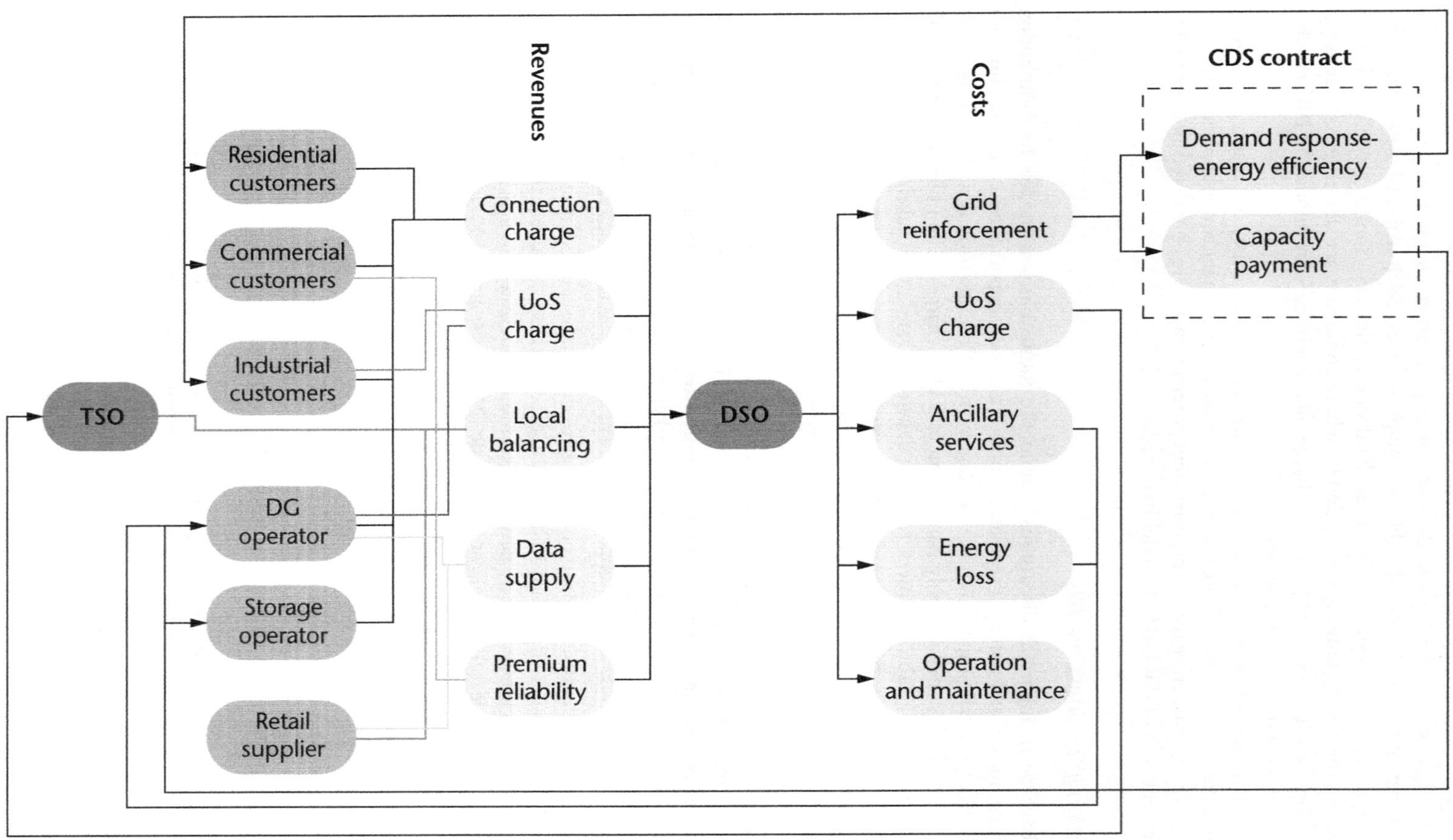

Figure 22.3 An extended business model for distribution networks

On the cost side, a DSO can optimize its capital expenditures through adopting innovative approaches to the problem of grid reinforcement. The traditional asset-based network service is capital intensive and costly. DSOs can optimize on network infrastructures by combining asset-based service and an alternative approach based on procurement of distributed energy resources that can provide network capacity. These resources can deliver energy at the time of network congestion, and thereby reduce the need for costly redundant transformers.

Another important feature of this approach is that it provides more flexibility to DSOs compared with traditional network reinforcement. Integrating distributed resources to offer services, such as voltage control and congestion management, could provide various benefits for utilities, grid users, and wider society. However, for this to happen, a suitable business model is required. Poudineh and Jamasb (2014) introduced a contract for deferral scheme (CDS) that integrates distributed generation, storage, demand response, and energy efficiency as alternatives to grid capacity enhancement. This method can lower capital costs for network companies and also boost deployment of low-carbon technologies.

On the other hand, as shown in Figure 22.3 the revenue of a DSO comprises connection and UoS charges, data supply to resource developers and retailers (this is likely to be a possibility as the future smart grid becomes a reality), contribution to the national balancing service, and offering premium reliability. A DSO with smart grid technology can communicate with generation facilities and consumption equipment on the consumers' site through a secure connection. This means that the DSO can increase generation or reduce demand at times of stress to the national grid, hence stabilizing electricity supplies. Furthermore, in many industries the production process is sensitive to electricity inputs, and DSOs can be reimbursed by these industries for providing a highly reliable connection (Poudineh and Jamasb, 2014).

Conclusions

Electricity distribution networks are an important part of the power system that deliver energy to end users and play a key role in the integration of distributed energy resources, security of supply, and demand-side participations. The post-liberalization era has necessitated technological, regulatory, and business-model evolution in electricity-distribution companies.

Adoption of distributed energy resources and EV require innovation and large-scale investment as the grid requires reinforcement and reconfiguration to accommodate them. The ICT revolution has extended digital communication capabilities to the grid level, with ample opportunities for new services. The DNOs can integrate virtual power plants by aggregating many small-scale renewables, thereby providing greater efficiency and flexibility. This is important, given that the installed capacity of variable generation from wind and solar power is increasing every year.

At the same time, the regulatory framework of network companies needs to evolve in order to better align with the objective of an efficient, low-carbon power sector. The current regulatory models for investment treatment do not take into account the dynamic nature of investment and innovation. Strong emphasis on short-run cost efficiency can result in reduction of research and development and capital expenditure as network companies cannot afford persistent inefficiency caused by long-term investment plans. Therefore, there is a need for innovative regulatory models that incentivize innovation and the right investments without compromising other objectives, such as cost efficiency.

Moreover, a shift from an asset-based, capital-intensive business model of distribution utility is crucial in order to adapt to an environment with high levels of penetration of distributed energy resources. Along with the traditional connection and use of system charges, future business models of network companies can tap into smart ICT technology to create new and value-added services.

Notes

1 This chapter draws substantially from different parts of Poudineh (2014).
2 There are two main types of substations associated with the distribution system: the primary substations, which act as load centers located near populated areas, and the customer substations, which are situated close to consumer sites and convert the voltage to a suitable level for consumption.

References

Akcura, E., Haney, A.B., Jamasb, T. and Reiner, D. (2011) From Citizen to Consumer: Energy Policy and Public Attitudes in the UK, in T. Jamasb and M.G. Pollitt (eds) *The Future of Electricity Demand: Customers, Citizens, and Loads*. Cambridge: Cambridge University Press, pp. 231–248.

Arends, M. and Hendriks, P.H. (2014) Smart grids, smart network companies, *Utilities Policy*, 28, 1–11.

Averch, H. and Johnson, L.L. (1962) Behaviour of the Firm under Regulatory Constraint, American Economic Review, 52, 1059–1069.

Barton, J.P. and Infield, D.G. (2004) Energy storage and its use with intermittent renewable energy, *Energy Conversion, IEEE Transactions on Energy Conversion*, 19(2), 441–448.

Batel, S. and Devine-Wright, P. (2015) A critical and empirical analysis of the national-local 'gap' in public responses to large-scale energy infrastructures, *Journal of Environmental Planning and Management*, 58(6), 1076–1095.

Brennan, T. (2014) An expanded distribution utility business model: win-win or win-maybe? in F. Sioshansi (ed.) *Distributed Generation and its Implication for the Utility Industry*. Oxford: Academic Press.

Byun, J., Hong, I., Kang, B. and Park, S. (2011) A smart energy distribution and management system for renewable energy distribution and context-aware services based on user patterns and load forecasting, *Consumer Electronics, IEEE Transactions on Consumer Electronics*, 57(2), 436–444.

Ciupuliga, A.R. and Cuppen, E. (2013) The role of dialogue in fostering acceptance of transmission lines: the case of a France–Spain interconnection project, *Energy Policy*, 60, 224–233.

Cotton, M., and Devine-Wright, P. (2012) Making electricity networks 'visible': industry actor representations of 'publics' and public engagement in infrastructure planning, *Public Understanding of Science*, 21(1), 17–35.

Department of Energy and Climate Change (DECC) (2014) UK Greenhouse Gas Emissions – 1st Quarter 2014 Provisional Figures, Department of Energy and Climate Change, London, available at: https://www.gov.uk/government/uploads/system/uploads/attachment_data/file/328695/GHGQuarterly_statistical_release.pdf (accessed August 21 2014).

Department for Transport (2014) Attitudes to electric vehicles, *Statistics on Public Attitudes to Transport*, London, available at: https://www.gov.uk/government/uploads/system/uploads/attachment_data/file/321157/electric-vehicles-2014.pdf (accessed August 21 2014).

Devine-Wright, P. (2011) Place attachment and public acceptance of renewable energy: a tidal energy case study, *Journal of Environmental Psychology*, 31(4), 336–343.

Desyllas, P. and Sako, M. (2013) Profiting from business model innovation: evidence from pay-as-you-drive auto insurance, *Research Policy*, 42(1), 101–116.

Gangale, F., Mengolini, A. and Onyeji, I. (2013) Consumer engagement: an insight from smart grid projects in Europe, *Energy Policy*, 60, 621–628.

Harrison, G.P., Piccolo, A., Siano, P. and Wallace, A.R. (2007) Exploring the trade-offs between incentives for distributed generation developers and DNOs, *IEEE, Transaction on Power Systems*, 22(2), 821–828.

Honebein, P.C., Cammarano, R.F. and Boice, C. (2011) Building a social roadmap for the smart grid, *The Electricity Journal*, 24(4), 78–85.

International Energy Agency (IEA) (2002) *Distributed Generation in Liberalised Electricity Markets*, OECD/IEA, International Energy Agency, Paris, available at: http://library.umac.mo/ebooks/b13623175.pdf (accessed August 8 2014).

Jamasb, T., Neuhoff, K., Newbery, D. and Pollitt, M. (2005) *Long-Term Framework for Electricity Distribution Charges: Report for the Office of Gas and Electricity Markets* (Ofgem). London: March.

Johnson, R.J. and Scicchitano, M.J. (2012) Don't call me NIMBY: public attitudes toward solid waste facilities, *Environment and Behavior*, 44(3), 410–426.

Lopes, J.A.P., Soares, F.J. and Almeida, P.M.R. (2011) Integration of electric vehicles in the electric power system, *Proceedings of the IEEE*, 99(1), 168–183.

Lopes, J.A., Hatziargyriou, N., Mutale, J., Djapic, P. and Jenkins, N. (2007) Integrating distributed generation into electric power systems: a review of drivers, challenges and opportunities, *Electric Power Systems Research*, 77(9), 1189–1203.

Mah, D.N.Y., van der Vleuten, J.M., Hills, P. and Tao, J. (2012) Consumer perceptions of smart grid development: results of a Hong Kong survey and policy implications, *Energy Policy*, 49, 204–216.

Müller, C., Growitsch, C., and Wissner, M. (2010) Regulation and Investment Incentives in Economic Theory, IRIN working paper for working package: Advancing Incentive Regulation with Respect to Smart Grids, No. 349, WIK Wissenschaftliches Institut für Infrastruktur und Kommunikationsdienste GmbH, Germany: Luneberg.

Nelson, T., McNeill, J. and Simshauser, P. (2014) From throughput to access fees: the future of network and retail tariffs, in F. Sioshansi (ed.), *Distributed Generation and its Implication for the Utility Industry*. Oxford: Academic Press.

Nillesen, P., Pollitt, M. and Witteler, E. (2014) New utility business model: a global view, in F. Sioshansi (ed.), *Distributed Generation and Its Implication for the Utility Industry*. Oxford: Academic Press.

Pieltain Fernández, L., Roman, T.G.S., Cossent, R., Domingo, C.M. and Frías, P. (2011) Assessment of the impact of plug-in electric vehicles on distribution networks, *Power Systems, IEEE Transactions On*, 26(1), 206–213.

Poudineh, R. (2014) Electricity Distribution Networks Post-liberalization: Essays on Economic Regulation, Investment, Efficiency and Business Model. PhD thesis, Durham University Business School. UK.

Poudineh, R. and Jamasb, T. (2014) Distributed generation, storage, demand response and energy efficiency as alternatives to grid capacity enhancement, *Energy Policy*, 67, 222–231.

Poudineh, R. and Jamasb, T. (2016) A new perspective: investment and efficiency under incentive regulation, *The Energy Journal* (forthcoming).

Poudineh, R., Emvalomatis, G. and Jamasb, T. (2014) Dynamic Efficiency and Incentive Regulation: An Application to Electricity Distribution Networks, Cambridge Working Papers in Economics 1422/ Energy Policy Research Group Working Paper 1402. Faculty of Economics, University of Cambridge, Cambridge.

Putrus, G.A., Suwanapingkarl, P., Johnston, D., Bentley, E.C. and Narayana, M. (2009) Impact of electric vehicles on power distribution networks, *Vehicle Power and Propulsion Conference, 2009. VPPC'09*, IEEE, pp. 827–831.

Richter, M. (2013) Business model innovation for sustainable energy: German utilities and renewable energy, *Energy Policy*, 62, 1226–1237.

Sauter, R. and Watson, J. (2007) Strategies for the deployment of micro-generation: implications for social acceptance, *Energy Policy*, 35(5), 2770–2779.

Tobiasson, W. and Jamasb, T. (2014) Sustainable Electricity Grid Development and the Public: An Economic Approach, Cambridge Working Papers in Economics 1432/Energy Policy Research Group Working Paper 1411. Faculty of Economics, University of Cambridge, Cambridge.

Transport Research Laboratory (TRL) (2013) Assessing the role of the plug-in car grant and plugged-in places scheme in electric vehicle take-up. Published Project Report PPR668, available at: https://www.gov.uk/government/uploads/system/uploads/attachment_data/file/236748/research-report.pdf (accessed August 8 2014).

Vogel, P. (2009) Efficient investment signals for distributed generation, *Energy Policy*, 37, 3665–3672.

23

Strategy challenges in the natural gas market

Sergio Ascari

Introduction

This chapter addresses the natural gas industry, with special attention to the company perspective. In an industry that is heavily and increasingly affected by regulation, all companies must devote at least as much attention to regulation as to other elements of the market. For several companies, the regulator is the market, and the relationships between companies' results and regulations are so deep that they could be analyzed under literature that addresses the issue of 'Regulatory Capture'. However, even companies that are subject to only partial regulation often know that a remarkable share of their outcome is related to regulatory developments.

Other chapters in this book consider, in more detail, how natural gas regulation has evolved, and what have been its objectives and tools, and its achievements. However, this chapter does not address regulatory capture, but rather how companies have been thriving between regulation and the market. In the energy field, oil and coal industries are most affected by the market, even though regulation matters. The opposite can be seen in electricity, including nuclear, hydro, and other renewables; gas lies somewhere in between.

Natural gas is not only a network-based industry. In fact, its exploration and production (i.e., upstream activities) are closely associated with oil, and share its main characteristics. High-risk investments limit access to this industry to a few large international or state-supported companies, although some areas, such as North America, have also seen smaller enterprises playing a remarkable role. Long-distance transportation, in the order of thousands of kilometers, can hardly be regarded as a network industry. Transportation through the liquefied natural gas (LNG) chain is increasingly flexible and its characteristics are increasingly closer to oil transportation, although most of it still occurs via dedicated facilities that are built and operated for the service of one or more trading contracts. Yet even long-distance transportation via pipelines is technically akin to domestic transmission; however, the pipelines' size usually requires different models from those of networks shared by several users, and is more likely undertaken by companies that take their own risk in return for the exclusive benefits of using the necessary infrastructure. Other important sectors of the gas industry, such as underground storage, are also often developed on a relatively small scale and through competitive market models. Chapter 5 described the gas market evolution in its own right, with more attention to the development of supply and demand drivers.

On the other hand, transmission over shorter distances, as is typically performed within national borders of small to medium-size countries[1] and even more so distribution, are often close to natural monopolies, and are heavily affected by regulation. Once gas reaches its destination market, it is injected into a network that shares several features of electricity transmission. This process occurs, to an even larger extent, in the final stage of local distribution.

Therefore, this chapter will mostly take the perspective of companies, rather than that of the regulation, or of general market developments. It will outline how companies have reacted to regulatory, as well as market, developments with a particular focus on Europe, in view of the peculiar position of natural gas, which is stuck between market and regulation.

Since the focus of this book is on network industries, and a summary illustration of the upstream activities is provided in Chapter 5, the current focus will be mostly on downstream and midstream activities; that is, the business of purchasing and trading natural gas and selling it in the wholesale market through its complex network logistics. The discussion will be focused mostly on Europe; some insights will also be provided on the huge and dynamic markets of the rest of the world, including highlighting similarities and differences in their regulatory frameworks and organization models.

The historical development of the American and European gas market models

Unlike many other network-based services, natural gas started as a competitive business in Europe, fighting against other energy sources. Unlike electricity, for most uses, other fuels (mainly oil derivatives) could substitute natural gas. For approximately 30 years after World War II, natural gas actually struggled to gain its market share against them. In the upstream activities (exploration, development, production, and treatment), natural gas is often associated with oil and shares its regulatory status. However, this has been far from uniform; in North America, tight regulation of wellhead prices until the 1970s was followed by deregulation. In other cases, including in Europe, state-owned concerns were often given the mission of developing natural gas in competition with other fuels, with a view to developing national (as opposed to imported) resources. These concerns acted on a pure market basis, although they were sometimes subject to formal price controls.

Particularly in cities, the natural gas industry met the old-town gas networks, and increasingly replaced the costly and often noxious manufactured gas, opening new perspectives for a cleaner way of heating heavily polluted urban environments, as its reduced cost often allowed it to beat the competition of coal and oil derivatives. Given the higher political sensitivity and reduced competitiveness of the residential and small commercial market, national or local governments often took control of local distribution or introduced formal price regulation.

On the other hand, the status of transmission and wholesale supply companies was rather heterogeneous, and often in line with the prevailing attitude of countries. Those in favor of state ownership of the key industries typically included natural gas among these industries, and formed national companies for gas (for instance, Belgium, France, Great Britain, the Netherlands, and Spain), or worked in association with those in charge of the oil sector (such as in Austria, Italy, Finland, and Norway). Other countries had a mix of private and local government control, such as Canada, the US, and West Germany. Countries of the Soviet Bloc saw the industry under tight state control, or even directly run by ministries, much like in the Soviet Union.

In the US,[2] the gas industry has been traditionally tightly regulated, with interstate trade in private hands but under the control of the Federal Power Commission (and later the Federal Energy Regulatory Commission [FERC]). After the removal of the cumbersome wellhead price controls in the 1980s, and due to macroeconomic and industrial evolution, a gas glut emerged, which sent the integrated transportation and wholesale companies into a crisis. In return for their bailout in the 1990s, the FERC required progressive separation of the transportation and trading business (unbundling), which is still the main feature of the American model. Unlike in Europe, transporters (pipeline companies) are free to negotiate their services, although they are subject to maximum tariffs (rates) and a remarkable transparency of accounts and contracts. However, since transportation is their main business and they cannot trade in their own gas, they have no choice but to open their services to all suppliers (shippers), and even to compete for them.

The large and geographically integrated size of the North American market (including Canada), the availability of large domestic and scattered resources, and a common regulatory framework, have fostered the development of a competitive industry. Private transportation rights were traded and the development of the transportation capacity market coincided with that of the gas itself, after private initiatives, although subject to FERC oversight.

On the other side of the Atlantic, the precursor case was the UK. The country's market was concentrated on a relatively small territory, which was largely isolated from other markets but for limited LNG supplies and imports from Norway by pipeline. In this situation, the dual process of privatization and liberalization, launched in the mid 1980s, opted for a rather different model compared to that of the US. The transportation and distribution network was unbundled from supply, though left as a monopoly. Its services were to be open to suppliers and customers alike (in the role of *shippers*). A new regulatory body, (the Office of Gas Supply, OFGAS, later merged with the electricity regulatory body to become Office of Gas and Electricity Markets, OFGEM), was empowered to set access tariffs and approve other market rules, which were assembled into a Network Code. The dominant position of the former state-controlled integrated concern was addressed by forcing a gas release towards other suppliers, almost halving its market share.

For several years, this remained the single example in Europe. The European Union (EU) undertook liberalization of the gas industry only in the late 1990s, just after that of electricity, with the intention of curbing the market power of dominant companies, as well as that of the external suppliers, as the continent's production was increasingly being replaced by imports through the integration of national markets. At that point, the availability of the British model and lack of political support for a stronger European integration and regulation led to a moderate imitation of the British model, rather than of the American one.

The EU liberalization has been based on partial unbundling of transmission and distribution from supply and other services, third-party access (TPA) to transportation, distribution, storage and LNG regasification, and the gradual freedom of customers to choose their suppliers. However, the combined effect of resistance from incumbent, dominant suppliers, which were sometimes partly or completely privatized, and the lengthiness of EU procedures, have prolonged this process. In particular, legal unbundling and regulated TPA have been mandated with the Second Energy Legislation Package and became effective around 2005, and a substantial separation of transmission system operators (TSOs) from suppliers' control has been achieved only with the Third Energy Legislation Package, introduced in 2009 (see FSR, 2013).

However, the process has suffered more than electricity from the lack of an EU-level regulator, whereas the industry is inherently continental in scope: with increasing interconnection and the decline of European production, nearly 60 percent of all natural gas crossed at least one border in Europe by 2010, compared with only three percent for electricity. Weaker regulatory control of access to cross-border interconnection points has limited the availability of long-distance capacity transportation, and caused a slower-than-expected development of effective competition. Only action by the EU and national competition authorities in the middle of the decade has imposed the opening and reinforcement of interconnection capacity.

Markets and companies in European gas supply

Gas market liberalization in Europe has required a major restructuring of the energy industry. The ingredients of this adaptation have been privatization, internationalization, convergence with the electricity industry, and a wave of mergers and acquisitions (M&A). However, as unbundling was starting its slow progress through the three EU Packages, the midstream gas industry originally consisted mainly of integrated, mostly state-owned companies that controlled monopolies or very large market shares in their own countries, but were rather small with respect to the EU market as a whole. On the other hand, just after 2000 it was already clear that the unbundling and liberalization process was going to deepen, albeit at an uncertain pace, and many new actors were ready to take action, often at a faster pace than that of institutional change.

As the liberalization process started, some of its supporters expected the development of an integrated and competitive gas market, much like in the way of the North American one, with many producers and suppliers emerging, vibrant competition and diminishing prices.[3] This expectation was matched by the attempt of many smaller operators to enter markets, which challenged the position of former incumbents. Optimism about the liberalization process attracted the support of politicians, consumers, regulators, and financial partners. Success attained in other network industries, such as telecommunications, provided a model. Natural candidates to enter the market and challenge the incumbents included:

- Electricity companies
- Gas (and electricity) incumbents of other markets and countries
- Distributors
- Large consumers
- Producers
- Utilities from external markets
- Holders of capital in search of opportunities.

In fact, the first two groups were the most successful. Overall, sales of companies that can be classified as incumbents, or former monopolists, have grown more than the market overall (see Figure 23.1).[4] Their strategy was based on several objectives that had to be pursued at the same time:

1 The defense of domestic market shares was the most apparent and common feature of the decade. Its pursuit was aided by several regulatory and other barriers, as well as by their (only partly limited) control over TSOs, domestic production, storage, and imports. Yet this led to the most notable and widely discussed development of the industry in the past decade. However tough this defense may have appeared in several cases, most incumbents were probably aware that it was a way of buying time and slowing down processes, rather than the ultimate goal.
2 Just as important was the internationalization effort, where companies' approaches have varied. Some have been very active in their offensive side, leading to the start of a new integrated, transparent, and competitive market, where the main objective was entering new markets. Yet entry by simply establishing branches in other countries was rarely successful, for several reasons:
   a Limited access to infrastructure, given the inadequate regulatory framework until the end of the decade, notably for cross-border interconnections and storage.

b A very large share of the end-user value consisted either of natural gas, often imported by all players at similar prices, or of regulated network components; therefore, the part of the value chain that was actually open to competitive efforts was rather small – sometimes less than 10 percent. As a consequence, benefits for consumers of switching to other suppliers were also scant.

c The traditional consumers' perception that gas was a monopoly of the well-known incumbent also contributed to their loyalty; this was even more prominent if the choice was to leave a national supplier for a foreign one.

3 Another requirement was convergence with the electricity industry. Power utilities were often larger, but feared the opening of the gas market, mostly due to gas companies' tight control of domestic reserves and relationships with foreign suppliers. Therefore, the radical decision often came to invest in M&As, with the intention to integrate towards gas supply and hedge the risk of lower electricity-generation margins compared to those of gas. For several years, after the takeoff of the combined technology cycle in the 1990s, gas had become the fuel of choice for the power generation within and outside of Europe. The *spark spread* (a measure of the margin of gas-fired electricity generation, calculated at conventional transformation rates and at market prices), became a popular index of how the energy industry margins were parted between the two 'brothers' of energy liberalization. The convergence was also fostered by regulatory models and the related opportunity of pooling increasingly important regulatory departments.

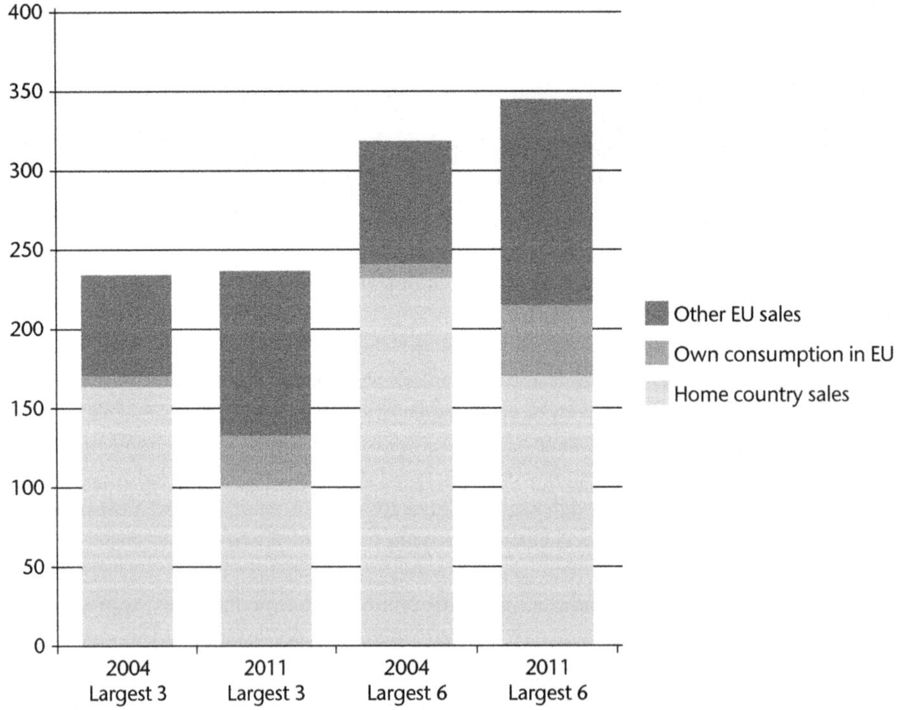

Figure 23.1 Sales of the largest EU gas companies by destination market (billion cubic meters, bcm)

Source: REF-E elaborations based on companies' Annual Reports (owner of the data: Gestore dei Mercati Energetici S.p.A.).

Considering the above conditions, it is not surprising that a wave of mergers and acquisitions has swept the industry, pursuing:

1 Consolidation of domestic positions, between both electricity and gas companies and those operating in different market sectors (wholesale and retail), and in different geographical areas (where applicable). This led to some vertical reintegration, which partly offset the unbundling of transmission and distribution businesses.
2 Establishment of bridgeheads in new markets, through the acquisition of smaller old players, such as distributors or their retail branches and storage operators.
3 Control of gas suppliers by electricity generators, or, less frequently, the opposite case of control of the power-generation destination market by gas suppliers, or the expansion of gas companies into power generation.

While the goals were clear, the terrain to pursue them was uneven. The EU sets harmonized market liberalization and regulation objectives and criteria, but, due to its own fundamental statutes, it refrains from addressing ownership. The choice of privatizing a largely government-controlled industry was in the hands of national, and sometimes state- or local-level government. The starting points were also rather different, as shown in the previous section; state, local, and private ownership was unevenly spread among countries. Politics, and even more traditional policy orientation towards markets, as well as the need to raise money for public finances, played a role. Hence countries that were more open to privatization have largely played the role of 'prey' in the M&A game, sometimes with benefits for their consumers: in Western Europe, this was notably the case in the UK, but also of Belgium, the Netherlands, and Spain. Thus, most Dutch and British distributors and some Spanish ones, as well as their sister supply companies and customers, were taken over by (mostly) French, German, Italian and Swedish large gas and power suppliers. For other reasons, mostly related to the need to raise hard currency revenue for public coffers, state-owned monopolists with dominant supply positions have been partly sold to foreign interests in the Czech Republic, Hungary, Lithuania, Portugal and, more recently, Greece.

On the opposite side, governments that feared loss of control over former monopolists that turned into national champions supported their consolidation through mergers of national operators, hence the birth of E.ON Ruhrgas in Germany, GDF Suez in France, and EconGas in Austria. This strengthening was the basis for an aggressive role in countries less prone to defending national ownership. Others have simply stuck to public ownership, such as Bulgaria, Poland, Slovenia, and Sweden, or have chosen an intermediate path by retaining control and allowing the privatization of minority shares of national champions, with a view to raising further finance to support their external growth (Denmark, Italy, Slovakia, and partly also France). The M&A wave occurred mostly in the first decade of the century, and has shaped the current structure of the gas industry, with limited events in later years.

Given the different attitudes of national governments towards privatization and liberalization, the strategies of incumbents have varied. In the early stages, the retail sector was partly closed by law, as the EU rules allowed member states to postpone eligibility of residential customers until 2007. In fact, even the wholesale market was initially largely closed due to the limited role of national governments and regulators in the promotion of competition at cross border level.[5] Thus, control of integrated, albeit possibly legally unbundled, concerns allowed de facto control over the whole market. In the retail market, this situation lasted even longer and is often still true today, with limited switching rates by smaller end-customers; in these cases, control of the distribution system operators (DSOs) involves control of the largest market share.

To summarize, incumbents have remained the primary protagonists of the gas industry in Europe. A significant wave of restructuring has not really modified this fact, and few new players have managed to achieve a leading role in the same way as has occurred in telecoms.

In the UK, where the market was already far more advanced and competitive, the network business had been privatized as integrated, regulated transmission and distribution companies, such as BG Transco, and later National Grid Gas. In this situation, foreign and domestic hunters also preferred to acquire the less concentrated electricity companies and use them as bridgeheads to win the gas retail market. Four of the six largest electricity and gas retailers have fallen, and remain, under the control of large international concerns.

Spain has seen parts of all of these strategies. Similar to the UK, the network business has been privatized as a public company, and the largest power utility (Endesa) has been acquired by Italy's Enel and entered the gas market. The supply branch of the former integrated gas company (Gas Natural), which is controlled by the main Spanish oil company (Repsol), has merged with the country's third utility (Unión Fenosa), while the second power company (Iberdrola) has acquired Scottish Power and gained a limited market share in gas as well.

Some gas positions have also been sold to comply with competition authorities' requirements. The most significant case is probably Belgium's Distrigas, which had to be spun off the new GDF Suez group and was ceded to Italy's ENI. Larger foreign majors in Germany, Italy, and other countries have purchased DSOs, and large (though not dominant) energy companies. Overall, takeovers have been friendly and hostile bids have failed, after staunch government defense of incumbents, as in the attempts by Italy's ENEL with Suez, and by Austrian national champion OMV with Hungary's MOL.

Overall, the evolution of the EU midstream gas industry, which mostly addressed the wholesale market, shows that within a few years, the largest EU companies have increased their overall market shares, even if they have 'lost at home', by ceding significant parts of their original market (see Figure 23.1). In fact, the same companies have often been put under pressure at home by regulators, competitors and consumers alike, whereas they have been simultaneously hailed in other countries as newcomers and competition standard-bearers. The most active hunters have been companies from France and Germany, and the most passive prey those from the Netherlands, the UK and Central-Eastern Europe, with Italy and Spain in the middle.

The achievements of the above-mentioned candidate market players have been mixed at best. Distributors have in most cases become prey rather than expanding their market shares, and their hope of strengthening their independence and absorbing the margins of the former monopolists have rarely been achieved, except where they have been backed by strong public ownership. The reason for this destiny is clear: awareness of end-users' loyalty in a market where competitors can offer only limited improvements in prices, and even less in service quality, has made it quickly clear that control of distributors has usually included that of their sister supply companies.[6] Given consumers' stickiness, limited unbundling and the lifting (albeit slowly and with many exceptions) of end-user price caps, control of distributors was clearly an asset. This was another major driver of the M&A wave: British, Dutch, Hungarian, Italian, Spanish and other distribution companies became the main targets. Control of already owned distributors was reinforced, as was the case of ENI, which withdrew its main distribution subsidiary from the stock market.

A major exception was RWE, which emerged from a merger between German local utilities with limited gas activities. As early as 2002, RWE purchased both the state-owned Czech wholesale operator and TSO (Transgas), as well as all DSOs but one, becoming the dominant gas company in the Czech Republic. In the Netherlands, the state retained the midstream business but promoted consolidation and privatization of older distributors, and the two largest among them were taken over by RWE and Sweden's Vattenfall. In both cases, this represented the first landing of electric utilities into the gas business. Similar deals also occurred in Hungary, with the government selling supply and storage interests of the former monopolist to E.ON,[7] and in Slovakia, with the sale of a 49 percent share and management control over the state enterprise (SPP) to E.ON and GDF Suez.

In other countries, such as Austria, Germany, Slovenia, and parts of Italy, local government control over distributors has hampered the incumbents' expansion. On the contrary, the UK has split its single national distributor, with a view to achieving benchmarking and spread the distributor's control.

Turning to other companies that might have achieved a greater role in the market, entirely new suppliers mushroomed at first, though these sometimes failed and never managed to achieve a large role due to the control of large imports through long-term legacy contracts and of remaining (though declining) domestic production by incumbents, and the difficulties of procuring new gas from imports due to unsatisfactory cross-border regulatory control.

Advances of national companies from producing countries were much expected, and were feared by some, including incumbents. In fact, producer country companies have hoped to 'disintermediate' mid-streamers and sell directly to final (wholesale) markets – for instance, to retailers and large industrial customers or power generators. In fact, this development has rarely succeeded. Russia's Gazprom has been the most active, with the creation of Wingas, first as a 50/50 joint venture with a large German chemical and energy group (BASF–Wintershall), and later, in 2013, with full control. Similarly, smaller incursions in the Czech Republic, Hungary, Italy and Slovakia have achieved less remarkable results, and have not added much to the actual penetration of the Russian giant into Europe's markets, despite its declared willingness to do so. Wingas is also a significant success case of reintegration upstream by a large consumer, becoming its own supplier (and technically shipper).

Likewise, oil and gas majors have not significantly increased their role. Even Western majors that would not face political hostility akin to that of Europe's external suppliers have not increased their market shares. State-controlled integrated companies such as ENI, Gasunie, and OMV, or private concerns such as BP, British Gas, and Total have often struggled to retain market shares, and their retailing business has not been particularly profitable.

This failure may have been due to several reasons. First, mastering of market rules and consumers' knowledge and trust have turned out to be more important success factors compared to control of the raw material, such as gas production. Second, vertical integration has been an obstacle more than an asset, which has strengthened the suspicious attitude of regulators and shareholders alike – the latter fearing a blurring (and ensuing cross-subsidization) between lower risk downstream or network-based regulated businesses and higher-risk exploration and production. Overall, oil and gas majors have preferred to stick to their upstream and oil activities. Total and ENI have eventually disposed of their transmission networks and have not been very successful in the gas market once their original monopolistic position eroded.

It is worth noting that newly integrated gas and power companies have somehow tried to integrate upstream, again with limited success. Upstream branches of EDF, E.ON, and RWE have had limited developments.

Both Western and other gas producers (including Gazprom and Algeria's Sonatrach) have preferred to focus on the new major development of the industry: organized hubs. These have gained importance as markets have become more competitive, and balancing requirements on suppliers and other networks users have become tighter, requiring the quick purchase or sale of small amounts of gas, which could be more effectively traded in open and transparent markets.

The growing availability of LNG from several producers, the appearance of more players (also through the above-described processes), and the interest of market operators and the financial sector have triggered the hubs' development. 'Hub' has often become a magic word, able to solicit support from politics, and a new dimension of competition between countries has emerged, with several countries trying to become the basis of the most successful wholesale markets. In turn, this has required several objective and subjective conditions:

- The availability of gas from several resources, possibly including LNG.
- The possibility to generate flexible short-term flows from storage or local production at, or near, the hub.
- A clear regulatory framework, reassuring traders about the legal status of their transactions.
- Transparent and timely information about the market players' trading positions.

Depending on the market design and transportation tariff system, hubs have been physical locations, situated at major pipeline junctions, such as Baumgarten, Austria, and LNG terminals like Zeebrugge, Belgium and some Spanish terminals; or, more frequently, virtual, as in the case of all others, pioneered by the British National Balancing Point. In these cases, the marketplace is the whole (or part) of the transmission network that is subject to the same entry/exit tariff system.[8] The development of hubs has thus far favored the British and Dutch, where most of the liquidity is available and longer-term products have been offered. Others have been mostly used for local balancing purposes and feature far less liquidity, with some already declining. Access to organized markets based on hubs is easier for large, upstream companies, as it does not require specific involvement in local market regulations.

After the implementation of the Third Package, all hubs became virtual. Some convergence of hub prices has also been noted, thanks to greater viability of interconnecting pipelines and the possibility to re-route LNG vessels. However, some difficulties remain and liquidity remains rather concentrated in the leading hubs (Petrovich, 2014).

Regulated network businesses

The status of the transmission business has changed most with European market liberalization. From being a logistics branch or subsidiary of integrated gas companies, pipeline (and sometimes also LNG and storage) operators have mostly turned into power-like TSOs. Yet the inherent business may be more risky in gas, as demand swings may be much larger in this commodity. In fact, energy regulators have often preferred to take the majority of risk out of TSOs by guaranteeing their income (or allowed revenue) through various mechanisms that change tariffs, as necessary. In this way, reduced market risk has allowed the reduction of regulated return rates and of transmission tariffs, which was a major regulators' goal.

Low returns and the complex and pervasive regulatory framework entailed by the Third Package have led to even lower interest for suppliers to retain control of TSOs. Abundant capacity allocated by competitive procedures and subject to congestion management has lost its strategic value; hence, most gas companies have decided to opt out of any remaining integration. As a low-risk, low-return business, gas transmission raises the interest of institutional investors, like pension funds, who have been eager to take significant shares, and even control; most TSOs have been sold by incumbents (see Table 23.1).

Whereas the majority of large TSOs have been happy to achieve this independent, regulated status, others have continued to face inherently higher risks. This is particularly notable in the case of those most involved in cross-border transits, which suffer competition from other infrastructure, and the evolution of producer areas' market shares. Moreover, these TSOs may

Table 23.1 Main gas companies in Europe: sales and TSO control

Parent company	*TSO of origin country*	*2011 sales (Bcm)*	*Type of TSO unbundling, 2013*	*TSO control in origin country*
E.ON–Ruhrgas	Germany	88.4	Ownership	None
ENI	Italy	77.6	Ownership	State
GdF-Suez	France	70.9	Legal (ITO)	Yes
Gasunie	Netherlands	38.1	Ownership	State
RWE	Czech Republic	37.5	Ownership	None
Gas Natural	Spain	32.1	Ownership	None
Wingas	Germany	30.0	Ownership	None
OMV	Austria	24.3	Legal (ITO)/Ownership	Partly
Centrica	Great Britain	16.8	Ownership	None
EDF	France	16.4	Ownership	None
PGNiG	Poland	14.4	Legal (ITO)	State
Enel	Italy	13.9	Ownership	None
TOTAL	France	12.9	Ownership	None
DONG	Denmark	11.6	Ownership	State
Iberdrola	Spain	7.4	Ownership	None
Vattenfall	Sweden	6.1	Ownership	None
EDP	Portugal	6.1	Ownership	State

suffer from the decline of natural gas demand, which actually began to materialize after 2005. Little state or regulatory protection is available for those businesses, which have often retained a peculiar status, remaining under direct or indirect control of suppliers. The most significant cases are in Austria, Belgium, the Czech Republic, Poland, and Slovakia, where cross-border flows exceed those aimed at domestic markets. In the long term, continuing demand decline would require higher average tariffs.

Some TSOs have also undertaken consolidation efforts by acquiring other, similar companies with a view to take control and promote the development of critical gas routes. Benefits are not only in coordination and economies of scale, but also in liquidity improvements for related hubs, which are often partly run by the same or by affiliated companies. The most interesting cases are the expansion of Dutch Gasunie in Northwestern Germany, and Belgium's Fluxys acquisitions in Germany and Switzerland and its strategic alliance with Italy's Snam Rete Gas. Further acquisition by the latter of two smaller TSOs, French TIGF and Austrian TAG seem to envisage an attempt to create a continental vision of transmission. However, this remains a minority perspective in the industry.

Overall, transmission and distribution businesses, unbundled from supply roles, have become companies of high public interest, protected by a factual (and sometimes even legal) monopoly, with guaranteed income (except for transit activities), through the provision of tariff compensation in case of transmission or capacity-booking decline. For these companies, the market – in the sense of who decides how much the company sells and at which price – is the regulator. It is not surprising that these companies – whatever their ownership status – are now endowed with large regulatory offices, which represent (in a sense) their marketing division. In turn, the high competence and role of regulatory offices require a similar capability on the regulatory side. This triggers a significant evolution of the network companies' business model, which in the gas case (unlike in electricity) leads to an opposite direction than the liberalization process has intended, with an actual increase of regulation burdens with respect to the previous regime. This is usually regarded as a necessary price for the liberalization of gas supply, yet North America has followed a different approach, where pipeline companies have maintained a certain competitive attitude towards each other. This has been almost impossible in Europe, due to the national (rather than continental) dimension of markets, until recently, and the related national dimension of most TSOs. It remains to be seen whether this approach can survive the new challenges of the gas market.

Outlook and conclusion

Whereas demand growth and a bright outlook have supported the long process of market liberalization, this trend reverted after 2005. In fact, the US shale revolution has had a double effect: LNG bound for America has become available for Europe, but American coal that has been displaced has depressed the coal price. The Fukushima events in 2011 and the uncertainty of carbon policies, together with a boom of incentive-driven renewables, have led to a remarkable loss of the gas market share in power generation in any country where there has been room for such a switch. The decline is also probably related to several phenomena, such as the emergence of thermal renewable energy, industry migration towards Asia and other regions, and efficiency improvements of appliances starting to affect the traditional market sectors. Parts of the decline are, indeed, seen as permanent (demand destruction).

This development has jeopardized the gas-power convergence strategy of several large European companies, which have often invested in gas-fired plants that are now running at low rates. For several years, spark spreads have allowed little amortization of such investments, and significant losses have emerged. After turning continental from national, and having survived liberalization, the old gas incumbents may have to further globalize in order to survive the decline in fossil fuel use in Europe.

On the other hand, the electricity industry seems to have merged with gas just to sink with it, as the stranded gas-fired generation is currently (as of early 2015) its major headache. The future of the gas industry in Europe (unlike in the rest of the world) remains closely connected with that of environmental policies and with other less predictable factors, such as the reliability of the traditional (and objectively less costly) external resources of Russia and North Africa.

The European gas industry seems unable to replicate the US shale gas revolution. Though such replication would probably be the only way of substantially reducing European gas prices, it is widely seen as unlikely, given the difficulty of developing more domestic, unconventional (and possibly even conventional) resources against a mostly hostile public opinion and to ever achieve the economies of scale that have allowed US success.

Nevertheless, most gas demand forecasts are cautiously optimistic: the International Energy Agency (IEA) still sees a slight increase into the next decade (about 1 percent per year). In fact, coal is likely to be at least partly removed by the new Large Combustion Plant Directive, and other carbon policy enhancements after the Paris 2015 Climate Conference may restore some competition margins for natural gas. The recent cut of subsidies to renewables, due to their accumulating costs, could also open some more room for natural gas in the mid term. On the other hand, even the most ambitious decarbonisation scenarios assume that natural gas is necessary as a backup for uncontrollable renewable resources. Hence, gas infrastructure is probably necessary in almost all its full scale, even though it may be used at full capacity for only a few hundred hours each year.

In such conditions, it is clear that the financing of infrastructure can hardly follow the traditional, market-based model. No market forces can pay for huge infrastructure with a very low load factor, whether it is pipelines, storage sites, or LNG terminals. Similar needs emerge from the security of supply requirements, with redundant capacity necessary to face (or possibly avert) the economic or political exploitation of pivotal positions by external suppliers. Europe has done much in this direction, notably after the 2009 Ukrainian crisis and the introduction of the new Security of Supply Regulation (No. 994/2010/EC). However, the cost of maintaining and possibly expanding such infrastructure is far from granted. Union-level financing is only slowly expanding; incentives for infrastructure aimed at further integrating the market and enhancing its supply security are being introduced, as well as procedures to better rank infrastructure (in terms of benefit/cost ratios) and to share its costs in line with benefits.

Overall, as the IEA itself noticed, the Golden Age of Gas is probably here, but it may be already over in Europe. The gas industry is diversifying its targets and getting increasingly global, with a view to making good use of the remarkable European expertise, possibly in other continents.

Notes

1 That is, in countries that are not as large as the Russian Federation, the United States, China, India, Australia or Brazil.
2 For further details see Makholm (2012).
3 Others feared that liberalization and competition would have actually led to a loss of role of the traditional gas companies, which could be successfully outcompeted by smaller, flexible, and more efficient new competitors in the downstream, and by the downward integration of gas producers (national companies of exporting countries and international oil and gas majors) selling directly into the wholesale (or even retail) internal markets, see Hall (2002).
4 The analysis is not as easy as one may think. Data for each company must be collected individually and is not stored, except in some costly private databases. Data found in annual reports and other corporate publications may be overestimated in order to impress shareholders and other stakeholders. Furthermore, the market churn rate has significantly increased, with the same quantities resold several times, unlike what happened in monopolistic markets in the past. Although the utmost care was taken to include only final sales, duplication cannot be ruled out. Nonetheless, the data shows a clear increase of total sales by large companies, as listed in Table 23.1: even if this is partly a statistical, rather than a real effect, it means that the 17 companies listed in the Table – all but one of which are former incumbents – clearly have a role in trading that encompasses almost the whole market.
5 Only after 2002, and mostly around 2005–6, the European Commission actively enforced cross-border competition through DG Competition, its antitrust branch. This took the form of probes against several of the main incumbents of large member states, for foreclosure of markets through hoarding or reduced expansion of cross-border transmission capacity.
6 In fact, only a few governments have been willing to alienate the support of strongly unionized workers by forcing a real unbundling between distributors and retailers.
7 In a rare opposite move, this was nationalized back in 2012 through purchase by the state Hungarian electricity company, MVM.
8 An entry/exit tariff, typical of Europe, is a system in which access to a transmission network is paid (mostly) by the sum of an entry tariff for each injection point or zone, independent of the withdrawal

area; and of an exit tariff for withdrawal, which is in turn independent of the gas provenance. In this way, the tariff is not directly path-related and a large amount of gas is available 'between' the entries and exits of the transmission systems, where it can be traded a number of times. The cost of this approach, requiring more flexibility by the transmission system, is a loss of the total transmission capacity.

References

FSR, Florence School of Regulation (2013) EU Energy Legislation Packages, available at: http://fsr-encyclopedia.eui.eu/eu-energy-legislation-packages/ (accessed on 22 September 2015).
Hall, D. (2002) Energy liberalisation and concentration in Europe, PSIRU, University of Greenwich.
Makholm, J. (2012) *The Political Economy of Pipelines.* Chicago: University of Chicago Press.
Petrovich, B. (2014) 'European gas hubs price correlation – barriers to convergence', OIES Paper NG-91.

24

Maritime transport company strategies

How to be sustainable in the future

Raimonds Aronietis, Christa Sys and Thierry Vanelslander

Introduction

Together with growth in international trade, transport and maritime volumes have strongly grown over recent decades. Vessel sizes have increased, requiring ever-increasing volumes of capital. This has led to a greater concentration of shipping activities, in particular in the container segment and in segments such as dry bulk, where historically the number of major operators has been lower (Meersman *et al.*, 2013). At the same time, larger ships contribute to lower costs. van Hassel *et al.* (2014), Sys (2010) and Stopford (2009) showed that the general total chain cost will decrease if larger ships are deployed. However, the shipping company's position will worsen due to the deployment of larger ships. It can therefore be expected that shipping companies want to increase their power in the total chain by acquiring hinterland transportation companies and establishing vertical integration.

The recent economic crisis and the prior major capacity expansions of the shipping fleet have created a particular shipping market that is characterized by overcapacity and low freight rates. Shipping companies have resorted to alliance forming to optimize their operations, thus creating an even greater price pressure in the market. This has led to issues of reduced competition (Sys *et al.*, 2011)[1], in response to which many nations and an increasing number of supra-national authorities (e.g. the European Commission) have started to take action.

Also in the social field, maritime transport features issues and challenges. The most recent BIMCO[2]/ISF[3] (2010) report highlighted that crewing is likely to be a future challenge, as continuing tight labor markets will lead to recurrent shortages for some officers. Seafarer skills and training are also linked to safety. Schröder-Hinrichs *et al.* (2013) reviewed documents submitted to the International Maritime Organization's (IMO) Maritime Safety Committee, and confirmed that IMO work related to the human factor was reactive in the 1990s. The typical reaction to an accident has been a combination of (mainly technical) regulations, and changing procedures and training. There are a limited number of examples of more recent regulations that can be considered proactive.

Furthermore, greener waterway transport is an overarching aim. It is important to monitor the impact of cap-and-trade systems on CO_2 emissions and on the organization of containerized shipping lines and ports of call. The current market situation with shipping companies unable to invest in new technologies presents a major challenge for current and future transport policies. Taking into account the current age of the shipping fleet and the average lifetime of ships, providing ships with green technologies, or, in a weaker version, applying green shipping practices, is one of the realistic options considered for achieving the goals set by the policies.

This chapter further explores the challenges identified in the previous sections, their impact, and how their achievement is impacted on by ship strategies. The chapter ends with a number of recommendations and fields for attention.

The second section summarizes the regulation and key research results on the main shipping challenges identified in the introduction. The third section presents the evaluation model that can be applied to analyze the impacts of any strategy taken by shipping companies. The fourth section applies the model to a selected sustainability innovation strategy. The fifth section is an overall assessment of a wider set of innovation strategies. The final section concludes with an overview of findings.

Review of shipping regulation practice and strategies

This section deals with the regulation practice as it applies to the above-mentioned challenges and issues, and with the reaction pattern encountered in the shipping business.

A main objective of European policy regarding shipping is to create a competitive European shipping sector. According to the European Commission (2008), 'the priority is to achieve and maintain an attractive framework for quality shipping and quality operators in Europe including financial measures. This will help maritime transport achieve sustainable development goals'.

Sys (2010) stated that competition in the shipping sector, both at industry and at trade level, increased over the last few years. Wang (2014) developed a statistical model to the level of competitiveness on shipping routes as a consequence of the US 1999 Ocean Shipping Reform Act. In line with Sys (2010), Wang (2014) found that the market structures of both the Transatlantic and Transpacific trade lanes are competitive. All this imposes no need for immediate measures, but at the same time makes a permanent shipping competition observatory more than desirable, as the vast majority of all traded commodities use maritime shipping.

Furthermore, econometric results reveal a significant positive impact on profit persistence for the leading liner operators, while subsequently competition has intensified (Sys, 2010). Intensified competition forces competitors to set low prices. In theory, inefficient liner operators are forced to exit the market. As a reaction, shipping companies are now regrouping in an effort to gain economies of scale. Next to regrouping, innovation can also lead the ship and/or its operations to reduce operating costs. Imposing green shipping measures will impact the power of existing big players, and is likely to re-enforce it, as these big players are the ones with most potential to spread investments over their capital stock. In such a case, greener practices can go along with cheaper operations.

Regarding chain cost structure and power division, the decreasing generalized chain cost observed by van Hassel *et al.* (2014), if larger ships are deployed, is especially observed for the liner route from the Far East to Europe. On this trade, the maritime part of the chain is the dominant element. However, now that the ships are increasing in scale, this dominant position is decreasing. As a result, the influence of the port and the hinterland is increasing. When a shipping company deploys ships of +18,000 TEU[4], the chain cost share of the port and the hinterland phase are as large as the share of the maritime section. Thus, ensuing vertical integration can be very important when deploying larger container ships, if the shipping company wants to maintain its dominant position in the total chain. Yip *et al.* (2012) also referred to the liner shipping market entering a phase in which liner shipping companies (LSCs) reap economies of scale. However, the results of enlarged capacity may be uncertain. By examining empirical data between 1997 and 2008, the same authors investigated the relationship between capacity and firm performance in the liner shipping industry, and attempted to apply an S-curve to describe the association between capacity and firm performance in liner shipping operations. The findings suggest that the S-curve is robust. Introducing green shipping measures may be expected to make the share of maritime shipping in total transport chain costs increase again, thereby re-enforcing the power of shipping companies over those chains. This all depends on the extent to which external costs will be internalized on the landside: if that happens, the power balance may shift in favor of the hinterland again.

For the human factor, as the European Commission (2008) stated:

> There is a genuine European interest in making maritime professions more attractive to young people and thus improving employment of seafarers. Positive measures may include facilitating life-long career prospects in the maritime clusters; enhancing the image of shipping; supporting the work of international organization (IMO and ILO) on fair treatment of seafarers; and implementing simplification measures which aim at reducing the administrative burden on masters and senior ship officers.

Statements made by IMO in recent years claim a shift towards a proactive approach in maritime safety. Thai *et al.* (2013) recommended that the tripartism between maritime governing bodies, training institutions and shipping and ship-management companies will be essential to the effective attraction and retention of quality seafarers for the maritime industry. Innovation is key here, but that same innovation should also apply to the way ship crews are trained.

Safe and secure shipping is another target in European shipping policy. The European Commission (2008) gave priority to the enforcement of existing Community and international rules and the speedy implementation of measures introduced with the 3rd maritime safety package. The work already started should be completed by establishing a comprehensive framework for security measures in terms of prevention, reaction capacity and resilience.

An aspect related to safety is the risk of explosions or fire in cases where fuel is being switched. The latter happens when Emission Control Areas (ECAs) are reached. The North Sea, one of the busiest shipping areas in the world, could therefore be particularly vulnerable. However, Stevens *et al.* (2014) showed that safety is not jeopardized. On the security side, Pristrom *et al.* (2013) analyzed the contributing factors to piracy based on cases reported to IMO. Their study confirms that maritime security and piracy issues have received increased policy attention over the years. Hallwood and Miceli (2013) argued that failure to adequately enforce international law is symptomatic of inherent weaknesses in that law: namely, that as 'cooperation' between States Parties (Article 100 of the Law of the Sea) is undefined, investment in enforcement by multiple-enforcement agents is left open to free-riding problems.

With respect to environmental sustainability, European Commission (2008) stated that, 'The Commission, the Member States and the European maritime industry should be working together towards the long-term objective of 'zero-waste, zero-emissions'. The measures announced in the Greening Transport Package should be fully implemented'. More specifically, the policy aims at the introduction of cleaner engines, design and shift to sustainable fuels (see STTP[5]); work with international partners and in international organizations such as IMO [...] to promote European competitiveness and climate goals at a global level. For maritime, in particular, the target of reducing emissions by at least 40 percent from bunker fuels can be met by operational measures, technical measures, including new vessel design, and low-carbon fuels.

Given the global nature of shipping, these measures need to be worked on in the international context of the IMO to be effective (European Commission, 2008).

Those are exactly the sustainable innovation strategies that are dealt with as case examples in section four of this chapter.

Stevens *et al.* (2014) also examined the potential effects on the deep-sea shipping competition between seaports of the emerging international maritime emission regulations on the one hand, and the potential underlying economic motivations fostering discussion of introducing ECAs on the other. Through a policy-related analysis, it was found that the political theory of public choice suggested that not the green lobby, but rather the petrochemical lobby, is the major driving factor provoking the very strict emission caps. An alternative explanation can be traced to international energy policy and the greening of this policy. The potential port shift from Northern Europe towards Mediterranean ports often indicated by Northern European ports as a consequence of ECA measures in the North seems fairly unlikely due to logistics disadvantages and service problems in South European ports, and port consolidation, economies of scale, and the specific nature of long-distance container shipping and a growing environmental awareness in Northern European ports. Finally, no convincing proof has been delivered that the main liner companies would be unprepared for this legislation and should be persuaded to rearrange their routes, in favor of Mediterranean ports, solely due to the various emission regulations. However, the legal analysis points out that the current enforcement regime of MARPOL[6] Annex VI should be improved in order to rule out the possibility of a low degree of compliance in order to protect the competiveness of compliant ships. Shipping companies also take measures by themselves to move towards greener shipping practices. Section three 'Strategy analysis framework' will illustrate the extent to which such measures have positive private benefit/cost ratios for the ship operator-investors.

There is no shortage of environmental technology innovation options. Some studies have compiled lists of up to 50 or more technological options, although only some of these are in the stage of commercial development (www.retrofit-project.eu; Stevens *et al.*, 2014). Technologies suitable for innovating include propeller optimization techniques, machinery enhancements, alternative energy adoption (for example, LNG) and a long list of others (Yella *et al.*, 2012; Stevens *et al.*, 2014). The vast range of available technologies is one of the reasons why innovating ships and shipping practice presents a challenge.

Lirn *et al.* (2014) identified three critical green shipping-management capability dimensions; namely, greener policy, greener ships, and greener suppliers. Greener policy turns out to impact greener ships and greener suppliers positively. The latter have positive impacts on financial shipping company performance through improved environmental performance.

Related to green shipping is the sustained implementation of slow steaming. Yin *et al.* (2014) and Maloni *et al.* (2013) looked into the motivations for, and impacts of, slow steaming. Oversupply of shipping capacity is clearly a main reason; furthermore, bunker prices and environmental pressure expressed by the price of CO_2 emissions are negatively correlated to speed increases. The latter implies that higher bunker and CO_2 prices both lead to slower steaming. Design speed of the vessels is positively correlated to actual speed increase. Woo *et al.* (2014) considered whether slow steaming could also achieve lower CO_2 emission levels and operating costs by testing a threefold relationship between speed and emissions, speed and operating costs, and finally between emissions and operating costs.

A number of the above-mentioned challenges in shipping can be covered, or at least supported, through innovation and technological development. The European Commission (2008) stated that, the competitiveness of the European maritime industries and their capacity to meet the environmental, energy, safety and human challenges is positively influenced by increased efforts in research and innovation. There is wide scope for improving energy efficiency in ships, reducing environmental impact, minimising the risks of accidents or providing better quality of life at sea. In the years to come, innovation and technological research and development in shipping should be further promoted.

The next section develops a framework for assessing the cost and benefit impacts of selected innovation strategies.

Strategy analysis framework

This section proposes an approach for evaluating the impacts that the introduction of shipping innovation solutions would have. To assess the impacts of the shipping strategies, this chapter uses simulation. In the modeling, the cost and benefit implications of the solutions are important.

Cost components

A review of literature on cost components shows three major private cost categories and one benefit center in the cost algorithm (Yella *et al.*, 2012).

The capital cost, sometimes referred to as the initial cost or investment cost, is an upfront cost that constitutes the fixed cost component of an investment. Typically, it will include design, equipment, installation, commissioning, and transaction costs. Most of the expenditures will become sunk costs and cannot be recovered in case the technology is removed from the ship.

The lost service cost, sometimes referred to as opportunity cost, is primarily the lead-time cost and cost of space lost due to installing the innovation. This results in lost deadweight, which is tonnage carrying ability or deck space for handling volume. An estimate of the forgone revenue due to giving up this space must be made for the lifetime of the measure or the ship – whichever is shorter. Lead time refers to the amount of time the ship spends when docked for installation and maintenance of the innovation technology.

The service or running cost typically includes repair and maintenance costs, and in some cases the cost of alternative fuel, extra personnel, and training. This cost category is not always stable, because it depends on variables that include, for instance, fuel prices.

There are also benefits that arise from introducing innovation solutions. According to Yella *et al.* (2012), internal or economic benefit during the operational lifetime of the measure is basically savings for the shipping line that come from innovating.

Externalities from innovating are those costs and benefits that are incurred to society because of a certain technology adopted in the market. Examples of externalities include reduction of pollution (benefit), or extra CO_2 emissions (cost).

The model

The aggregate simulation model developed and used in this chapter focuses on ro-ro and ro-pax ships[7]. The model makes it possible to calculate various parameters that describe the impacts, including direct and external, which the introduction of a tested innovation solution would have, as shown in Figure 24.1. In general, for the model, the impacts of an innovation solution can be defined with several variables. For a shipping company applying an innovation strategy, the following can be defined as a result of innovation:

- ΔR_p – change in private revenues;
- ΔC_p – change in private costs.

For society, as a result of applying an innovation strategy, the following can be defined:

- ΔB_S – change in social benefit;
- ΔC_S – change in social cost.

The impacts of introducing a ship innovation solution for the shipping company would therefore be: $\Delta R_p - \Delta C_p$, and the impacts for society: $\Delta B_S - \Delta C_S$.

Figure 24.1 summarizes the structure of the aggregate simulation model. The formula that describes the impacts of an innovation solution in general is given above. The impacts of the reference scenario, which describes business-as-usual situations, are shown as: $\Delta R_p = 0$, $\Delta C_p = 0$, $\Delta B_S = 0$ and $\Delta C_S = 0$. The modeled innovation scenarios are shown below, demonstrating the impacts they have and the model outputs that are generated. This allows for the economic, energy, and emission performance of the modeled innovation strategy to be assessed.

Scenarios

There are two types of scenarios in the model: the reference scenario and the innovation scenario (see Figure 24.1). The reference scenario simulates the business-as-usual situation with the aim of providing a comparison reference for the modeled innovation scenario. In the reference scenario, it is assumed that no ship innovation strategy is applied in the market. Furthermore, the economy follows normal historic development patterns.

The innovation scenario assumes that an innovation strategy is applied in the market. Each of the selected solutions has certain economic parameters, which serve as inputs for the model at the second data level. The model allows for a number of such innovation strategies to be tested. The strategies are detailed in the Assessment Approach section below.

Input data

Two data levels are used in the model. Top-level data is used in all calculations and does not change, but the scenario-specific data is changed to reflect the characteristics of the modeled scenarios.

Top-level data

The top data level includes data that is permanently used in the model and that does not change with the scenarios. It includes a range of macroeconomic data, but also specific energy, emissions, and transport activity data.

In literature, the following sources can be consulted for macroeconomic data and short-term forecasts. The European Commission (2012), through its DG ECFIN, provides short-term economic forecasts for the EU member states and some non-EU countries. The OECD (2012) Economic Outlook Database is a comprehensive and consistent set of macroeconomic data. It contains the bi-annual macroeconomic forecasts for each OECD country and the OECD area as a whole. The World Economic Outlook 2012 database by the International Monetary Fund (2012) also provides short-term forecasts of main economic indicators. Longer-term forecasts

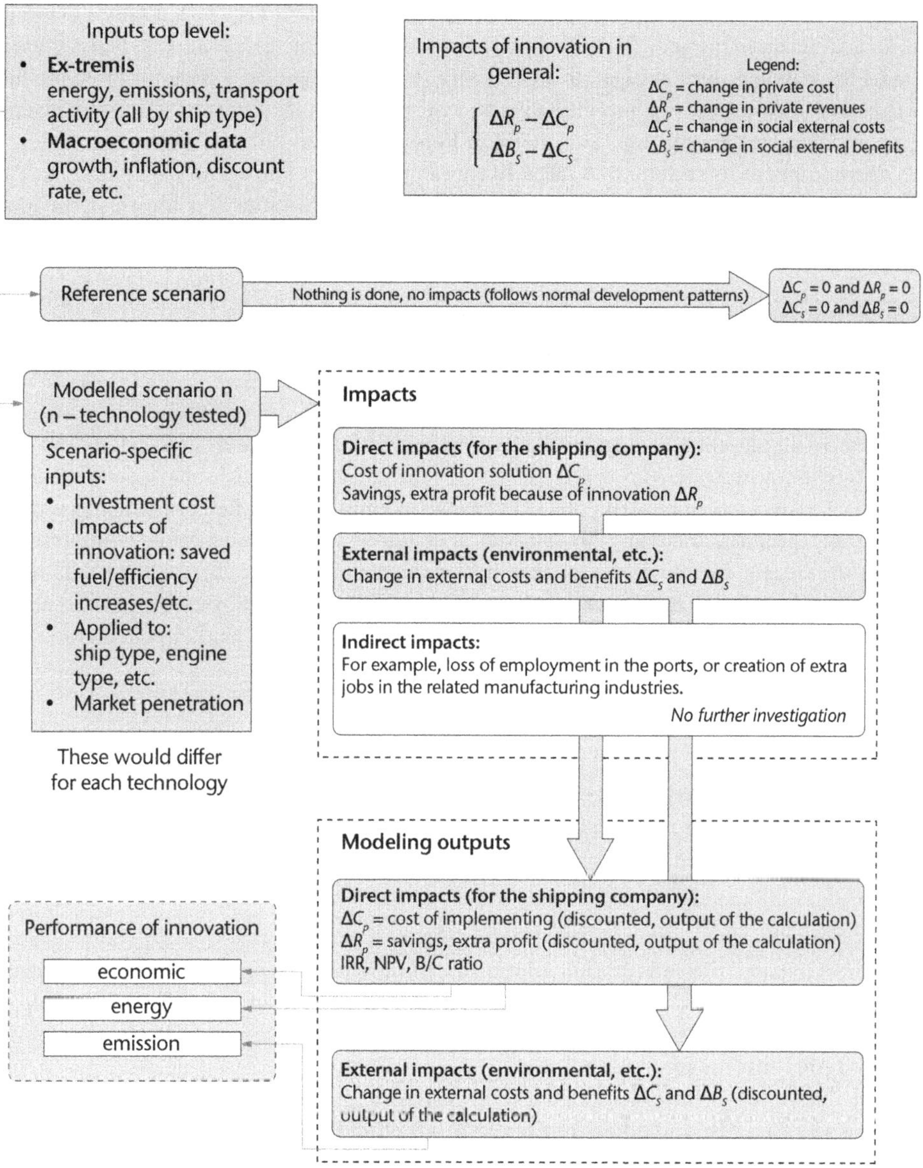

Figure 24.1 Aggregate economic model

can be consulted in the 'European Energy and Transport Trends to 2030 – update 2009' (European Commission, 2009).

With respect to the social discount rate, some controversy exists over the appropriate rate to be used for calculation of the net present value for a project (Anthony *et al.*, 2006). Cruz Rambaud and Torrecillas (2006) described different possible options. For the purpose of the modeling, the exponential discount rate of 5 percent is chosen.

The data on energy used in shipping is available from the EX-TREMIS database developed in an EU-financed project (VITO, 2007). Extremis Maritime is an activity-based emission model for seagoing ships engaged in EU seaborne trade. The model is built on three modules: a fleet module, an activity module, and an emission module. Emission estimates given in Extremis Maritime are for ship movements in European waters of the EU-27 countries.

The number of ro-ro ships that call at European ports is not known. Based on data from ISL (2010) and Lloyds List Intelligence (2013), the passenger/ro-ro cargo fleet for use in the model is estimated.

Scenario-specific data

At the second level comes scenario-specific data. This includes items such as investment cost, impacts of innovating and market data.

Investment costs are needed to put the innovation solution into operation. They are usually covered by the shipping companies that would benefit from the innovation. Here, the direct impacts of innovation are considered. For each of the scenarios, it means that quantified data on saved fuel, reduced or increased costs, and change in emissions of different pollutants is used.

For any product, including an innovation solution, market penetration is important. It shows the degree to which the market has adopted the product. In this research, market penetration is defined as a percentage of the ships fit for the innovations that are actually applying it. Estimation based on expert evaluation of the probable market penetration is used here.

Model outputs

The outputs of the model include calculations of various parameters. These parameters describe the impacts that the introduction of the tested innovation solution would have. Three types of impacts are distinguished and described as they appear in the model.

Direct impacts

The direct impacts of the innovation solution are those that the shipping companies introducing the innovation solution would generate. The introduction of an innovation for a shipping company is associated with a certain cost, ΔC_p, which in turn is compensated for by the financial benefits, ΔR_p, that the innovation brings.

The outputs of the model at the direct-impacts level provide the discounted values of costs ΔC_p and revenues ΔR_p caused by innovating. Also, other substantial financial parameters, such as internal rate of return (IRR), net present value (NPV), and benefit/cost (B/C) ratios are calculated.

External impacts

When innovating, external impacts are present. These are costs or benefits imposed on others that are not taken into account by the person taking the action. For example, in innovating, an increase of social benefit could be related to the reduction of harmful emissions.

The outputs of the model at the external impacts level provide the discounted values of the change in social benefit ΔB_S and cost ΔC_S caused by innovation.

Indirect impacts

The authors of the present research acknowledge the multitude of various indirect impacts that an introduction of an innovation brings. For example, the indirect impacts of an innovation strategy could be price changes in related markets, or increased sales, profits, or unemployment in related industries (Starrett, 2011). Quantification of the indirect impacts at aggregate level is beyond the scope of this research.

Strategy simulation and results

In this section, the aggregate simulation model from the previous chapter is applied to environmental sustainability strategies with ro-ro and ro-pax ships. As shown in the first two sections, environmental sustainability and regulation are key challenges for the shipping sector. Furthermore, the ro-ro ship type is interesting because its sailing pattern has specific characteristics that are particularly favorable to the implementation of green innovation solutions: a relatively high number of port calls, and sailing close to shores where higher external costs are incurred. In this section, the tested scenarios are described in detail and examples of modeling results are shown.

Scenarios tested

Several scenarios are constructed to model the impacts of each of the above innovation strategies. Every scenario is a combination of input data that characterizes the strategy investigated. This includes associated investment costs and generated savings, achieved energy savings or waste, and assumptions on the environmental performance that the retrofit solutions bring. This is done for the following nine innovation strategies, which were selected from a long list of strategies based on their commercial availability:

- Dual-fuel engine (LNG/diesel);
- Wind propulsion;
- LNG-powered generator (for harbor approach);
- Variable speed operation of propeller;
- Enable power take-off (PTO)/power take-in (PTI) to improve loading of the engine;
- Speed reduction;
- Voyage optimization (weather, waves, current, speed);
- Selective catalytic reduction (SCR) system;
- Scrubbing (SOx).

Tables 24.1 and 24.2 provide a summary of the economic and environmental characteristics of the nine modeled innovation strategies. The number of scenarios calculated differs for each technology according to the assumptions shown. If a cell contains several values related to the characteristics of the strategy, a separate scenario is calculated for each possibility. Using this approach, 117 scenarios are generated and calculated. For some scenarios, the specific values of emissions are not available for each emission type. In those cases, the total change in emissions is used (Table 24.2).

Table 24.1 Economic, lifetime and market characteristics of the modeled technologies

	Strategy	*Average investment cost (m€)*	*Savings (%)*	*Lifetime (years)*	*Market penetration (%)*
1	Dual-fuel engine (LNG/Diesel)	10; 15; 20	2; 3; 4	27	5; 10; 15
2	Wind propulsion	0.34	4; 8; 12	10	0.5; 1; 2; 3
3	LNG-powered generator (for port use)	1; 2; 3	0	20	1; 2; 3
4	Variable speed operations of propeller	0.5; 0.7; 1	1; 3; 5	27	5; 10; 15
5	Enable PTO/PTI to improve loading of the engine	0.1	1; 2; 3	27	10; 20; 30
6	Speed reduction	0.1	15	30	20; 30; 40
7	Voyage optimization (weather, waves, current, speed)	0.1	4	10	20; 30; 40
8	SCR system (catalyst)	2; 3; 4	0	7	5; 10; 15
9	Scrubbing (SOx)	2; 3; 4	4	10	5; 10; 15

Table 24.2 Environmental characteristics of the modeled technologies

	Strategy	*Total Δ of emissions (%)*	*ΔCO_2 (%)*	*ΔNOx (%)*	*ΔP (%)*	*ΔSO_2 (%)*	*Δ energy consumption (%)*
1	Dual-fuel engine (LNG/diesel)		−25	−85	−45	−100	−2; −3; −4
2	Wind propulsion	−4; −8; −12					−4; −8; −12
3	LNG-powered generator (for harbor approach)		−0.125	−0.425		−0.5	0
4	Variable speed operations of propeller	−5					−5
5	Enable PTO/PTI to improve loading of the engine	−3					−3
6	Speed reduction	−15					−15
7	Voyage optimization (weather, waves, current, speed)	−4					−4
8	SCR system (catalyst)			−80			0
9	Scrubbing (SOx)				−45	−97; −80	2

The exact number of passenger ships and the number of ro-ro cargo ships calling at European ports is not known. For use in the model, it is assumed to be 1,560, based on data from ISL (2010) and Lloyds List Intelligence (2013).

In this chapter, the decision is made to present calculation results for voyage optimization, as an illustration of the framework in action.

The modeling results shown further for these strategies apply to the entire ro-ro and ro-pax market in Europe, under the assumption that a certain part of the fleet adopts the innovation strategy ('market penetration' column in Table 24.1). The results are indicative and demonstrate the likely outcomes under the assumptions that are used in the model.

Voyage optimization

Voyage optimization is the best performing strategy, if the speed reduction – which seems to be an outlier, and which has a lot of adverse chain and service aspects – is not taken into account.

The purpose of voyage optimization is to find the optimum route for long-distance voyages, where the shortest route is not always the fastest. The basic idea is to use updated forecast data on weather, current, and waves, and choose the optimal route. Water depth can also be taken into account.

To further optimize the voyage, it is important to encompass the traffic on the planned route, as well as the time slot and waiting time in which a ship can be handled at a certain port. Having access to the timeslot in real time gives the possibility of 'just-in-time' arrival.

As shown, the investment costs for implementing a voyage optimization system on a ship are approximately €100,000, and the predicted average lifetime of the system is 10 years. The savings come from a reduction of energy consumption. Due to its high potential, the market penetration of voyage optimization is estimated to be between 20 and 40 percent. The reduction of emissions amounts to 4 percent for all emission types, as shown in Table 24.2.

Figure 24.2 shows the impacts of the voyage optimization on the private costs ΔCp and private benefits ΔRp for scenarios 7.1 to 7.3, depending on the market penetration. Scenario 7.1 assumes a market penetration of 20 percent, scenario 7.2 of 30 percent, and scenario 7.3 of 40 percent. For voyage optimization, other changes in characteristics of the strategy are not tested (see Table 24.1 and Table 24.2). It can be observed that in the investigated scenarios, the discounted benefits or savings for the ship owners, ΔRp, outweigh the relatively small costs, ΔCp, that are associated with the introduction of voyage optimization.

Figure 24.2 shows the impacts of voyage optimization for the ship owners (the difference between private benefits, ΔR_p, and private costs, ΔC_p), the impacts for society, ΔB_S, and the sum of the NPV (private + external).

From Figure 24.3 it can be observed that for all three scenarios, the NPV (private + external) is positive. As a result of voyage optimization, reduction of emissions (see Figure 24.4) and reductions of fuel consumption (as shown in Figure 24.5) are expected.

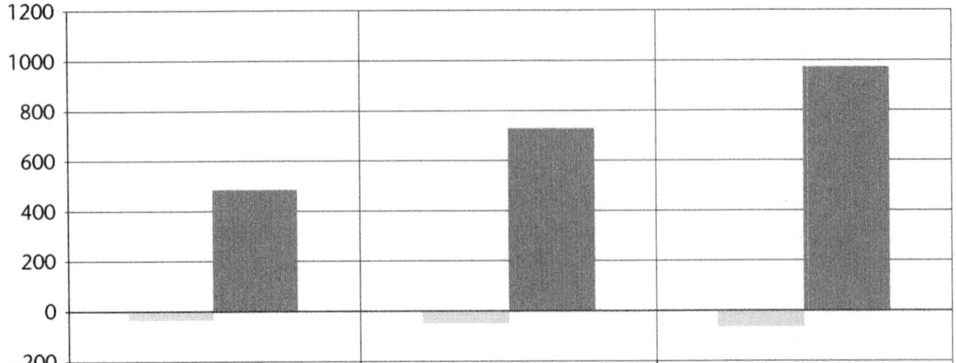

	7.1	7.2	7.3
ΔC_p	–31	–47	–62
ΔR_p	484	726	969

Figure 24.2 Impacts of the voyage optimization solution on private costs, ΔC_p, and private benefits, ΔR_p, per scenario (m €)

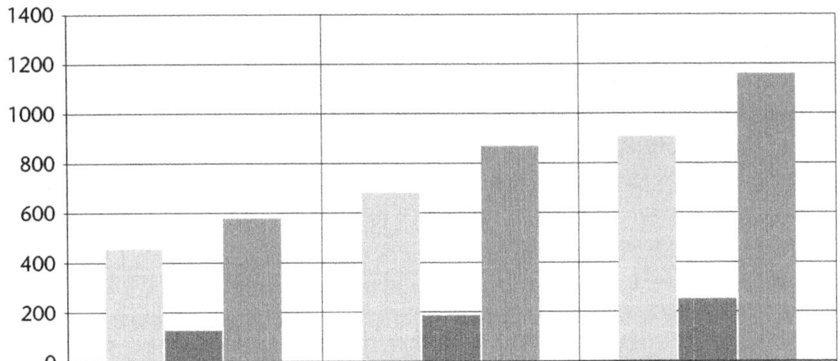

	7.1	7.2	7.3
$\Delta R_p - \Delta C_p$ (NPV, private)	453.1	679.7	906.2
ΔB_s (NPV, external)	125.4	188.1	250.9
NPV, private + external	578.5	867.8	1157.1

Figure 24.3 Impacts of the retrofit solution on social benefit, ΔB_S, private NPV and NPV (private + external) per scenario (m €)

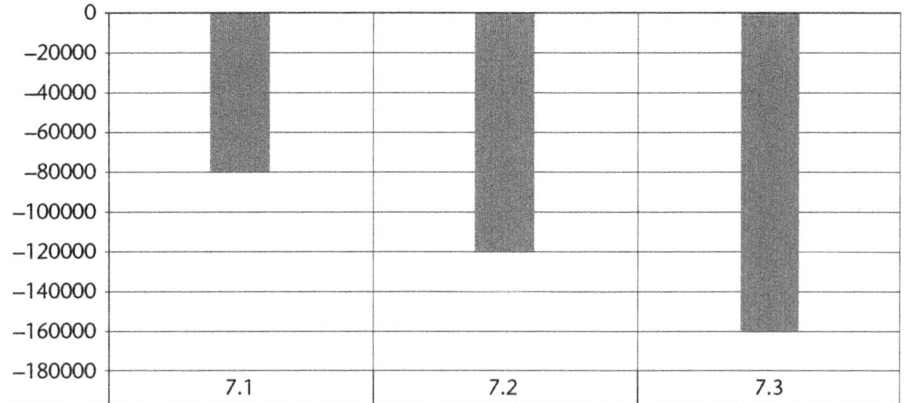

	7.1	7.2	7.3
Δ emissions	-79979.97508	-119969.9626	-159959.9502

Figure 24.4 Changes in average yearly emissions per scenario, t

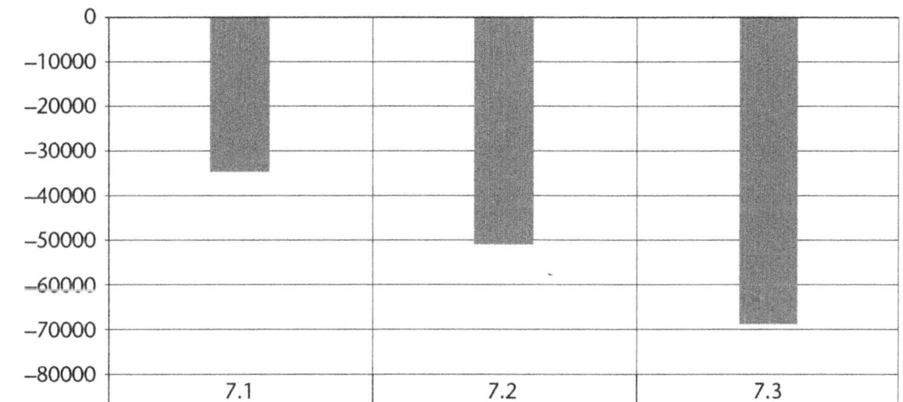

	7.1	7.2	7.3
Δ fuel cons.	-34361.44183	-51542.16274	-68722.88365

Figure 24.5 Changes in average yearly fuel consumption per scenario, t

Assessment of possible strategies

An assessment is necessary to compare the different innovation strategies based on modeling results and assist in choosing the best-performing innovation option.

Assessment approach

An assessment of the impacts is conducted to compare the different innovation strategies based on economic, emission and energy performance. The assessment criteria are shown in Figure 24.6.

In order to perform the assessment in practice and make the assessment criteria comparable, a strategy assessment index is used. This index is calculated for each of the assessment criteria in comparison with the other scenarios calculated in the model. A value of 1 is assigned to the best or most desired value of the criterion amongst those achieved in all the model runs. The value 0 is assigned to the least desired value. The other index values (in bold) are calculated depending on the values obtained for the criteria in the model runs. This allows three indexes to be assigned to each of the calculated scenarios. An example of strategy assessment index calculation for economic performance of voyage optimization is shown in Table 24.3.

Table 24.3 Calculation of strategy assessment index value for economic performance of voyage optimization

	Scenario	*Economic performance, (m €)*	*Index value*
Worst-performing scenario	1.21	–4274.4	0
...	...	...	...
Average performance of voyage optimization	7	679.7	**0.3828**
...	...	...	...
Best-performing scenario	6.3	8667.5	1

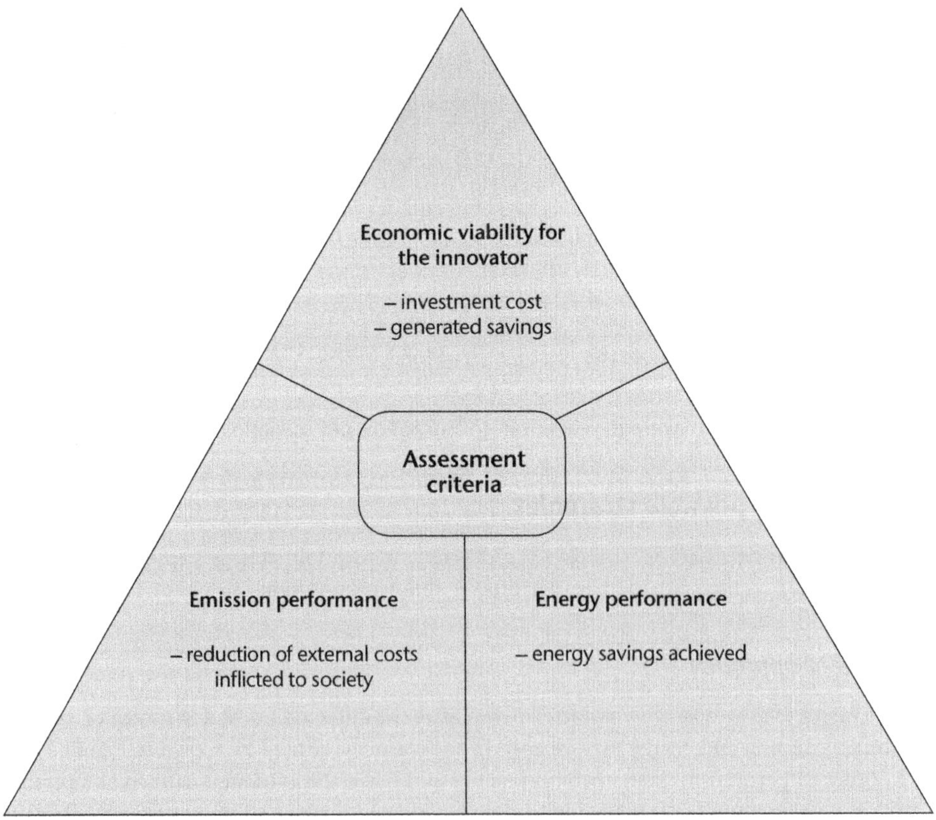

Figure 24.6 Assessment criteria

Assessment of the innovation strategies

For each of the scenarios in the model, the index values for economic, energy and emission performance are calculated. Figure 24.7 shows graphically the obtained strategy assessment index, with average values for each strategy. The value for each of the performance characteristics is marked on the corresponding axis, creating triangles that indicate the performance of each strategy.

Figure 24.7 shows which of the tested strategies are best for achieving specific policy targets, and which have the best overall performance. The strategies that have the best performance are those with the largest triangle areas, which is speed reduction in the case of Figure 24.7. The shape of the triangle describes in which of the performance areas the strategy gives best results. For example, scrubbers perform well economically, but the emission and energy performance is worse than that of the other strategies.

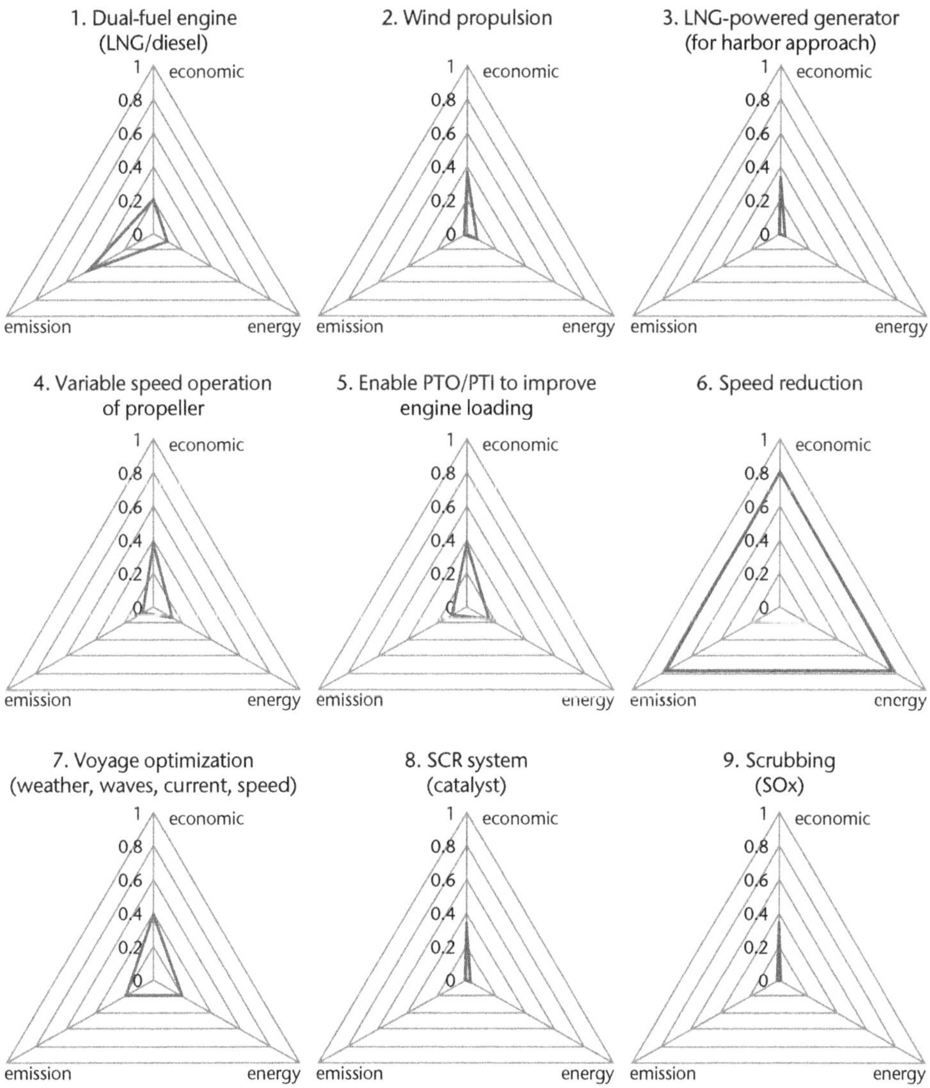

Figure 24.7 Retrofit strategy assessment index

In order to compare the technologies, the values of the strategy assessment index can also be summarized in a radar graph (see Figure 24.8). It can be seen that speed reduction (strategy 6) brings most benefits. The economic benefits that can be observed for this technology are probably one of the main reasons why speed reduction is a commonly used practice. The emission performance of the dual-fuel engines (strategy 1), which in normal operations are assumed to run on LNG, is also very good. For dual-fuel engines, the high investment cost is the reason for the poor economic performance, although the emission performance is very good. The economic performance of voyage optimization (strategy 7) and enabling PTO/PTI to improve loading of the engine (strategy 5) are good due to low investment costs.

It is not surprising that for maritime transport, which is by definition a slow transport mode, applying speed reduction shows high performance. The shipping lines are aware of this, and this approach, known as slow steaming, is commonly used. However, it must be taken into account that there are practical limitations to the application of speed reduction. For example, for ro-ro traffic, speed reduction often cannot be used, because ships have weekly schedules that need to be met.

To put the results into perspective without the bias of the speed reduction as an outlier, Figure 24.9 shows a performance comparison that excludes speed reduction. The performance of the other strategies can be clearly discerned.

It must be noted that combinations of technologies are not investigated here because of data unavailability. If sufficient data were available on the impacts of combinations of strategies, the model would permit the calculation of such results as well.

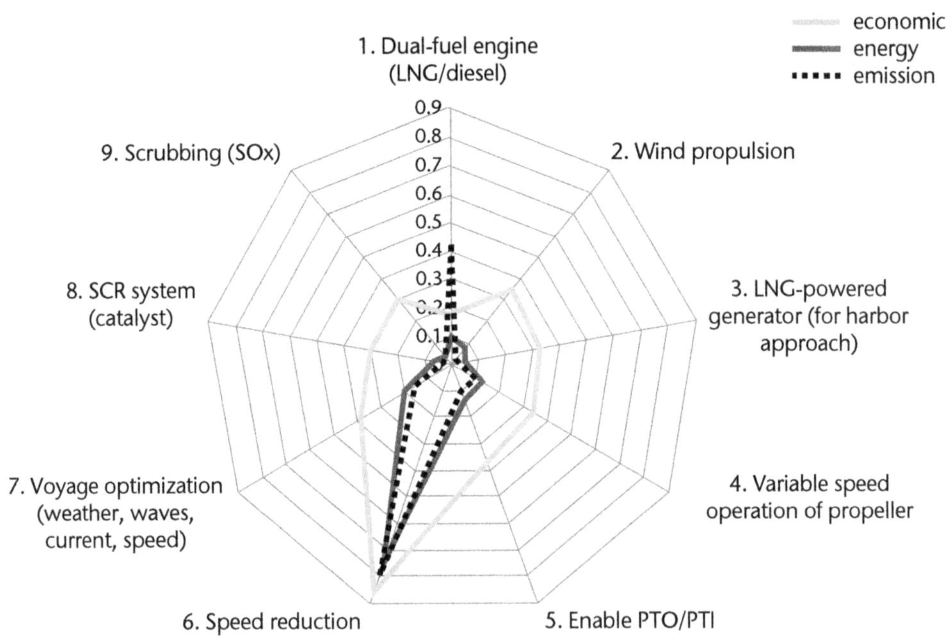

Figure 24.8 Performance comparison of the tested strategies

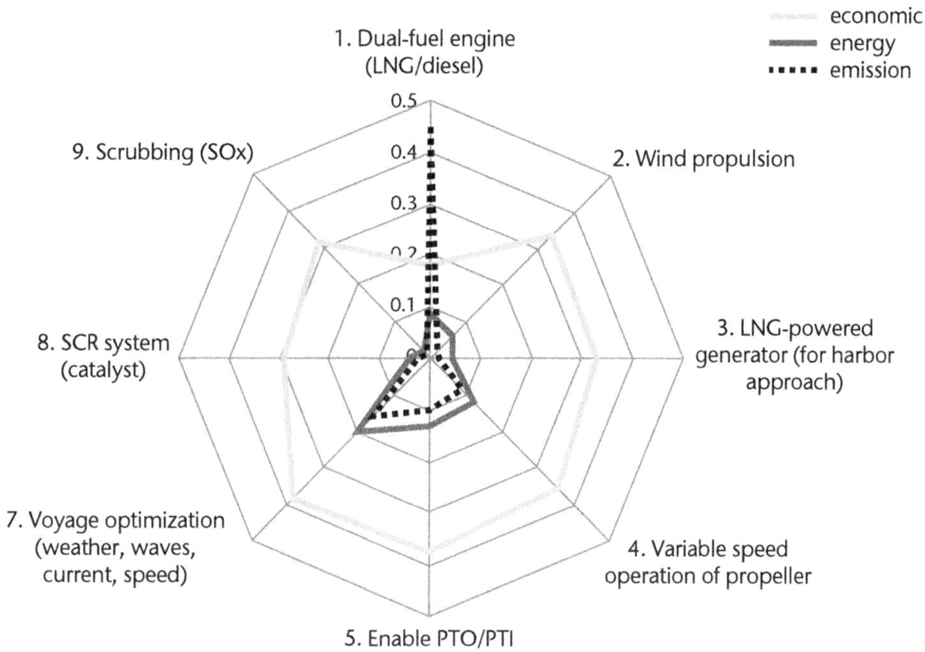

Figure 24.9 Performance comparison of the tested strategies with speed reduction excluded

Conclusions

This research set out to investigate the selection of innovation strategies for maritime shipping. This was achieved by creating an aggregate simulation model of the impacts innovation strategies would have if they were implemented in the market. The model was run for a set of nine commercially available environmental sustainability strategies, which have clear impacts on economic performance, safety, and the human factor.

The developed assessment approach allows the impacts of each strategy to be evaluated in order to compare the alternatives based on their economic, emission and energy performance. The evaluation of relative performance of the strategies allows for a selection of the best-performing option, depending on the goals that a specific actor has. If the actor were a shipping company, the economic performance, and also existing and future regulation, would be taken into account. For governments, the most important aspect would be emissions and overall performance of the solution.

The results of the environmental sustainability assessment confirm what can be observed in the market. Those strategies that are performing better at the economic and/or energy level are most likely to be followed by shipping companies. Others, which may have higher social cost/benefit ratios, may require incentives – financial or regulatory – from governments.

Speed reduction seems to be substantially outperforming all of the other technologies tested. While the calculation results seem valid, certain aspects should be taken into account when interpreting them. The relatively good performance is mainly due to the small investment that is required for application of this approach. At the same time, this measure is often not applicable, not only for ro-ro ships but also in general. This is due to the technological limitations, sailing schedules, and other issues that shipping lines face.

For policymakers, next to private cost/benefit analysis, this research also shows the welfare benefits and costs of the tested green innovation strategies. It also shows that good economic performance of a strategy is not always in line with good welfare characteristics. This should be taken into account for the development of efficient and viable policies.

It seems that out of the three performance criteria (economic, energy, and emission), the economic performance of the strategy chosen could be left for the market, as an investor will always choose the strategy with the best economic performance. At the same time, developed policies could look into setting benchmarks for the energy and emission performance of the innovation strategies.

The developed model is flexible and can be extended for use on other shipping segments (bulk, tanker, etc.), and also for other strategies (economic, social, etc.). The input data regarding energy use, emissions, transport activity and other characteristics of those segments should then be added to the model to allow for these calculations.

The results of this research are most relevant for ship owners and policymakers, but other stakeholders might be interested as well. For ship owners, this research shows which strategies are economically viable and worth considering. For policymakers, it shows the welfare benefits and costs for ship owners in relation to the tested solutions, which is applicable for development of efficient and viable policies.

Notes

1 Recent developments regarding cooperative agreements (e.g. 2M, Ocean three) and mergers (Hapag Lloyd and CSAV, Hamburg Süd and CCNI) increase the degree of competition?
2 Baltic and International Maritime Council.
3 International Seafarers Federation.
4 Twenty foot equivalent unit or a measurement of cargo-carrying capacity on a containership.
5 Strategic Transport Technology Plan.
6 International Convention for the Prevention of Pollution from Ships (MARPOL).
7 The developed model is flexible and can be extended for use on other shipping segments (bulk, tanker, etc.). The input data regarding energy use, emissions, transport activity, and other characteristics of those segments should then be added to the model to allow for these calculations.

References

Anthony, E., David, H. and Aidan, R. (2006) *Cost-benefit Analysis: Concepts and Practice*. Vol. 3. Upper Saddle River, NJ: Pearson Education. Available at: http://anet.ua.ac.be/record/opacua/c:lvd:6875424/N, accessed 22 September 2015.

Cruz Rambaud, S. and Munoz Torrecillas, M.J. (2006) Social discount rate: a revision, *Anales de estudios economicos y empresariales*, XVI (6), 75–98.

European Commission (2008) The European Union's maritime transport policy for 2018. Available at: http://europa.eu/rapid/press-release_MEMO-09-16_en.htm?locale=en, accessed 26 October 2012.

European Commission (2009) European energy and transport trends to 2030 – update 2009. Available at: http://www.energy.eu/publications/Energy-trends_to_2030.php, accessed 29 October 2012.

European Commission (2011) Roadmap to a single European transport area – towards a competitive and resource efficient transport system. White paper.

European Commission (2012) Economic forecasts. Available at: http://ec.europa.eu/economy_finance/eu/forecasts/index_en.htm, accessed 26 October 2012.

European Commission (2013) Integrating maritime transport emissions in the EU's greenhouse gas reduction policies, COM (2013) 479. Brussels. Available at: http://ec.europa.eu/clima/policies/transport/shipping/index_en.htm, accessed 20 September 2014.

Hallwood, P. and Miceli, T. (2013) An examination of some problems with international law governing maritime piracy, *Maritime Policy & Management*, 40(1) 65–79.

International Monetary Fund (2012) World Economic Outlook Database October 2012. Available at: http://www.imf.org/external/pubs/ft/weo/2012/02/weodata/index.aspx, accessed 29 October 2012.

ISL (2010) *Shipping Statistics and Market Review*. Bremen: Statistical Publications.

Lirn, T., Lin, H. and Shang, K. (2014) Green shipping management capability and firm performance in the container shipping industry, *Maritime Policy & Management*, 41(2), 159–175.

Lloyds List Intelligence (2013) Ship Sailings Ro-Ro 01-Mar-13. Available at: http://www.lloydslist.com/ll/marketdata/containers/shipRoroPage.htm, accessed 13 June 2013.

Maloni, M., Paul, J. and Gligor, D. (2013) Slow steaming impacts on ocean carriers and shippers, *Maritime Economics & Logistics*, 15(2), 151–171.

Meersman, H., Van de Voorde, E. and Vanelslander, T. (2013) Nothing remains the same! Port competition revisited, in T. Vanoutrive and A. Verhetsel (eds) *Smart Transport Networks: Market Structure, Sustainability and Decision Making*. Cheltenham: Edward Elgar Publishing, pp. 9–28.

OECD (2012) Economic outlook, analysis and forecasts. Available at: http://www.oecd.org/economy/economicoutlookanalysisandforecasts/economicoutlook.htm, accessed 26 October 2012.

Pristrom, S., Li, K., Yang, Z. and Wang, J. (2013) A study of maritime security and piracy, *Maritime Policy & Management*, 40(7), 675–693.

Schröder-Hinrichs, J.U., Hollnagel, E., Baldauf, M., Hofmann, S. and Kataria, A. (2013) Maritime human factors and IMO policy, *Maritime Policy & Management*, 40(3), 243–260.

Starrett, D.A. (2011) Economic externalities, *Fundamental Economics*. Vol. 1. *Encyclopedia of Life Support Systems* (EOLSS). Available at: www.eolss.net/Sample-Chapters/C04/E6-28B-02-00.pdf, accessed 21 January 2014.

Stevens, L., Sys, C., Vanelslander, T. and van Hassel, E. (2014) Is new emission legislation stimulating the implementation of sustainable (retrofitting) maritime technologies? International forum on shipping, ports and airports, *2014 Conference Proceedings*, Hong Kong: Hong Kong Polytechnic University.

Stopford, M. (2009) *Maritime Economics*. London: Routledge.

Sys, C. (2010) Is the container liner shipping industry an oligopoly? *Transport Policy*, 16(4), 259–270.

Sys, C., Meersman, H. and Van de Voorde, E. (2011) A non-structural test for competition in the container liner shipping industry, *Maritime Policy & Management*, 38(3), 219–234.

Sys, C., Vanelslander, T. and Adriaenssens, M. (2012) Worrying clouds? International emission regulations and the consequences for deep sea shipping and European ports, in M. Martinez de Osés and X. Fransesco (eds) *Proceedings of Maritime Transport 5 Technological, Innovation and Research*. Barcelona: Technical University of Catalonia.

Thai, V., Balasubramanyam, L., Yeoh, K. and Norsofiana, S. (2013) Revisiting the seafarer shortage problem: the case of Singapore, *Maritime Policy & Management*, 40(1), 80–94.

Yella, G., Sys, C., Vanelslander, T. and Frouws, J. (2012) An economic analysis of the costs effectiveness function for measuring ships' technology abatement potential, *Proceedings of NAV 2012 17th International Conference on Ships and Shipping Research*. Naples: Centro Congressi Università di Napoli Federico II.

Yin, J., Fan, L., Yang, Z. and Li, K. (2014) Slow steaming of liner trade: its economic and environmental impacts, *Maritime Policy & Management*, 41(2), 149–158.

Yip, T., Lun, V., and Lau, Y. (2012) Scale diseconomies and efficiencies of liner shipping, *Maritime Policy & Management*, 39(7), 673–683.

van Hassel, E., Meersman H., Van de Voorde, E. and Vanelslander, T. (2014) Impact of scale increase of container ships on the generalized chain cost, Proceedings of the IAME Annual Conference, International Association of Maritime Economists, Norfolk, 16–18 July 2014.

VITO (2007) Trasporti e Territorio Srl, Flemish Institute of Technological Research and Institute for Prospective Technological Studies (IPTS) *EX-TREMIS. Exploring non-road transport emissions in Europe*. Available at: http://www.ex-tremis.eu, accessed 26 October 2012.

Wang, D. (2014) Ocean shipping deregulation restructures the liner shipping industry, *Maritime Policy & Management*, 41(1), 97–111.

Woo, D. and Moon, D. (2014) The effects of slow steaming on the environmental performance in liner shipping, *Maritime Policy & Management*, 41(2), 176–191.

25

Developments in the European railway sector

Challenges for railway service providers[1]

Reto Bleisch, Bernhard Meier and Gregory Smith

Introduction

Railways in Europe began to struggle during the late 1960s, with both rail freight and passenger transport finding it difficult to compete with the increasing popularity of road and air transport and to adapt to new customer requirements. This triggered a reaction from the European Commission (EC), which has sought ways to overcome this declining competitiveness of rail vis-à-vis road. According to the EC, greater competition will help to create a more efficient and customer-responsive industry. EU rail legislation has consistently encouraged competitiveness and market opening, with the first major law in this direction dating back to 1991. Since then the EC has continuously proposed 'railway packages' with the aim to introduce competitive and structural regulatory tools to open and foster international and national rail freight and passenger transport markets to solve the problems identified.

Parallel to the ongoing implementation of the First, Second, and Third Railway Packages – as well as the Recast of the First Railway Package – the EC has taken a further step towards more competitive railway services in Europe by publishing its proposal of the Fourth Railway Package at the beginning of 2013. This proposal contains remedies similar to what has been applied in other network industries, notably regarding structural (vertical) separation and the opening of the national railway markets by mandatory competitive tendering of public service traffic (PSO) contracts, and opening access on commercially viable routes. Overall, the objective stated by the EC through introducing competitive elements is to increase the attractiveness of railway services, and, as such, service quality for customers, as well as more efficient provision of transport services, which ultimately should lead to lower fares for customers and a decrease in government spending.

This chapter addresses the question of possible implications of this approach to railway liberalization (and regulation) on railway companies and their respective strategies. More generally, it aims to discuss managerial implications of the current process in Europe.

In the second section, the regulatory developments in Europe are described from a high-level perspective. The third section focuses on outcomes in various railway markets in Europe. The fourth section briefly presents the Swiss railway operator as a case in point to illustrate the strategic options of a historical railway operator in light of European railway liberalization. The last section generalizes from the Swiss case and highlights the main strategic challenges European railway undertakings face (and will face) in a de-, yet at the same time, re-regulated environment.

Railway liberalization in Europe

Since the late 1980s, the European railway industry has undergone significant changes in regards to its governance structure, ownership, and the regulatory framework that applies across member states. Some of these changes have been driven at the national level, others at the supranational (European) level. Two themes have emerged as central drivers behind restructuring the industry: first, the desire on the part of some countries to open their markets to a liberalization of services, and second, in order to facilitate liberalization, the structural unbundling of services from infrastructure. The ultimate goal has been to increase efficiency and performance of the whole system. Some countries, such as Sweden in 1988 and the UK between 1993 and 1996, implemented unbundling and liberalization in the sector based on a national political desire to open their railway markets. At the European level, various directives have been enacted with the goal of implementing both liberalization and unbundling. Due to differences in interpretation of the European framework for railways across European member states, divergent railway market structures have developed.

European railway regulation

Rail infrastructure is considered to be a natural monopoly, and in order to enable a competitive intramodal framework, remedies have been applied in various forms in order to grant non-discriminatory access to the bottleneck input. In order to facilitate the opening of markets, the inherent theoretical assumption is that any infrastructure manager that is integrally owned and operated by an incumbent train-operating company has a significant incentive to abuse its monopoly position to keep new entrants out and, therefore, hinder competition on the network. This assumption is not unique to the railway sector and has been the basis for infrastructure access regulation in other network industries, such as telecommunications, water, gas, and electricity. A standard approach to enabling market opening and the entry of third parties to markets is to separate vertically integrated incumbent providers from service providers (Pfund, 2003: 4–6). Therefore, the EC's assumption is that a full vertical separation between the infrastructure manager and the incumbent railway undertakings is key to achieving market opening for the benefit of end users of the rail sector.

Starting in 1991, European institutions have adopted a series of directives aimed at harmonizing the safety and interoperability, governance, and structure of European railway markets, with the explicit goal of liberalization. Directive 91/440 'on the development of the Community's railways' developed the framework for market opening in freight markets, followed by two other 'packages' as well as a Recast of the First Railway Package. The following overview shows the scope and extent of each of the individual Railway Packages, and demonstrates the rapid pace of implementation of this approach.

The First Railway Package, adopted in 2001 (Directive 2001/12/EU), was constructed to develop clear guidelines for the European railway industry and governments. Specifically, it was devised to clarify the formal relationship between the state and industry, in particular the accounting separation of the infrastructure manager. The goal was to increase transparency regarding cross-financing between incumbent infrastructure managers and incumbent operators. A component of this was the standardization of track access regimes. It also sought to liberalize the international rail freight market, including the licensing regimes under which freight operators must work (Office of Rail Regulation, 2015).

The Second Railway Package was adopted in 2004 (Directive 2004/51/EU), with the aim of harmonizing legal and technical regulations in the industry. The package was constructed to further liberalize both national and international freight services as of 1 January 2007. It also increased the interoperability of rail networks by establishing the European Railway Agency (ERA), and harmonized safety regulations in the rail industry (Office of Rail Regulation, 2015).

The Third Railway Package, in 2007 (Directive 2007/58/EU), was adopted with the specific aim of liberalizing international passenger services by harmonizing the certification processes for rolling stock, locomotives, and train drivers. Passenger rights were also addressed in the legislation as a foundation for international market opening (Office of Rail Regulation, 2015).

The Recast of the First Railway Package (Directive 2012/14/EU) was adopted in 2013. The explicit goal of the package was to further clarify areas in which the EC felt that there was long-run non-compliance among member states regarding the First Railway Package. In many ways, it went further than simple clarification measures. The package was constructed to set out specific guidelines regarding the accounting separation of the infrastructure manager and focused on the accounting separation of so-called 'essential facilities', including central service facilities needed to operate a passenger rail service. It also sought to strengthen the role and structure, including the independence, of regulatory bodies, to ensure non-discriminatory access to those facilities (Office of Rail Regulation, 2015).

Based on the Third Railway Package, international passenger traffic (including cabotage) has been liberalized since 1 January 2010 with safeguards for PSO. In other words, EU member states may decide not to open domestic passenger traffic to competition if public-service contracts are adversely affected.

From a legislative point of view, two types of passenger service markets are defined at a domestic level: public service traffic and other passenger traffic. According to the Community of European Railways and Infrastructure Managers (CER) the definition of these two types of services is as follows:

- Public service (PSO) traffic relates:
  to passenger services that an operator, if it were considering its own commercial interests, would not assume or would not assume to the same extent or under the same conditions without payment. Those services, including their precise specifications as required by these authorities, must be contracted with competent authorities in the context of a so-called public service contract. The legal basis for this type of traffic is Regulation 1370/2007[2] which defines that public service traffic must be compensated by public authorities by direct financial influx and/or the granting of exclusive rights. The compensation methodology is decided by public authorities.

  (CER, 2011a: 14–15)

- Other (non-PSO) passenger traffic:
  relates to the rest of domestic passenger traffic which is freely organised by railway undertakings. This concerns purely commercial traffic freely organised by the operator without public subsidy or exclusive rights. It is currently only governed by national law, except for the cabotage element of cross-border services, which will be opened up to competition by the Third Railway Package's amendments to Directive 91/440.

  (CER, 2011b: 15–16)

Both types of traffic must be carried out as commercial activities if railway undertakings are to finance their activities without cross-subsidies. Public service traffic is to be subsidized, including a reasonable profit, and non-PSO traffic is per se provided on a commercial basis (EC, 2014).

In January 2013, the EC published its latest legislative proposals regarding a Fourth Railway Package (EC, 2014), largely based on further propagating the regulatory model of market liberalization. The Fourth Railway Package aims to:

- Open domestic markets through competitive tendering for PSO services and ensure open access in domestic services;
- Provide separation guidelines for the infrastructure manager and the incumbent operator, introducing de facto full vertical separation, through amending article 7 in 2012/34/EU (EC, 2014);
- Further harmonize technical standards and interoperability between countries through strengthening the role of the ERA.

In terms of the dynamics and pace of new legislation in the railway sector, a number of questions can be raised, notably regarding stability and certainty for urgently needed long-term investment – an essential dimension of railway strategy. Indeed, stability in the regulatory framework for long-term planning and infrastructure investment appears to be one of the ingredients for high-quality service provision.

Developments in European member states

The implementation of the legislative framework – the Railway Packages – as well as the developments of national regulatory frameworks, has varied substantially across member states, regarding both market opening and separation of the infrastructure manager and operations. Some countries, such as Sweden and Great Britain separated their infrastructure managers in the 1980s and 1990s, largely or, in the British case, fully liberalizing their markets. In some countries such as Germany and Austria, railway markets have been partly liberalized, retaining the incumbent operator as the de facto infrastructure manager. Other countries, such as France, separated out their infrastructure manager, retaining market protections, particularly in the case of PSO services.

In 2009, the EC brought 14 legal infringement cases against member states, mostly regarding separation of the infrastructure manager from the incumbent. These cases met with little success, most notably in Germany, where it was ruled in 2013 that the current structure of the incumbent Deutsche Bahn AG, which owns its infrastructure subsidiary as a holding, is permitted under the current European legislative framework.

Also notable is that although markets for international passenger services, and in some member states for domestic passenger services, have been open, there have been a strikingly low number of new entrants, and those who have entered have experienced varied amounts of success. In the British case, where competition for the market and in the market has existed since 1996, there have been few instances of new open-access providers entering the market. Tendered, franchised services have been partially awarded to European incumbent railways or their subsidiaries.

Analytical considerations regarding the proposal for the Fourth Railway Package

For the following analysis, we draw a distinction between vertical and horizontal separation. In vertically separated models, the infrastructure manager is separated from the transport service provision. There are various degrees of this form of vertical separation, ranging from operationally separated business units to full ownership unbundling (an overview can be found in Bleisch and Marcus, 2010). In a horizontally separated market, structure in rail transport contracts is tendered out and the service is subsequently offered by different railway providers.

With regards to the EC's proposal to introduce competition in railway markets (horizontal separation) and to enable it to separate railway infrastructure from the service provision (vertical separation), a number of analytical elements can be derived, for example:

- The advantages and disadvantages of a vertically integrated service provision;
- The costs and benefits of a vertical separation model;
- The correlation between vertical separation and a workable competitive outcome;
- The objectives to be achieved and the instruments to be used;
- The adequacy of competition instruments to achieve these objectives;
- The competitiveness of individual railway markets, taking into account the cost structure and the system wide optimization of service quality; and
- The effect on intramodal, as well as on intermodal, competition between different modes of transport.

In the literature on industrial economics and network industries, much empirical evidence can be found about each of these topics across different sectors. Since the publication of the EC's proposal on the Fourth Railway Package, there has been some debate on the specific features of the railway market and the extent to which the new elements support the goal of higher quality and efficiency.

When analyzing the proposal for the de facto full vertical separation of railway infrastructure managers and operators, opponents of the EC's proposal argue that there is no robust relationship between the structure of a market (fully integrated vs. separated service provision) and the outcome in terms of quality or efficiency generated. Especially in high-density networks, the costs of full vertical separation are likely to increase (van de Velde *et al.*, 2012).

There is broad consensus between market participants and member states that there is no 'one-size-fits-all' approach to both structural models and market-opening instruments that can serve as a benchmark for increasing efficiency and quality. On the contrary, interfaces that have to be established between the vertically separated units needed for high-quality rail service provision are likely to lead to substantially higher transaction costs than in an integrated model (van de Velde *et al.*, 2012).

When employing a cost–benefit analysis, the costs of artificial interfaces between fragmented units – as well as the ongoing dispute potential – have to be compared to the potential benefits arising from a theoretically reduced incentive to discriminate. Systems with an independent regulatory authority overseeing non-discriminatory access to the network may offer a more

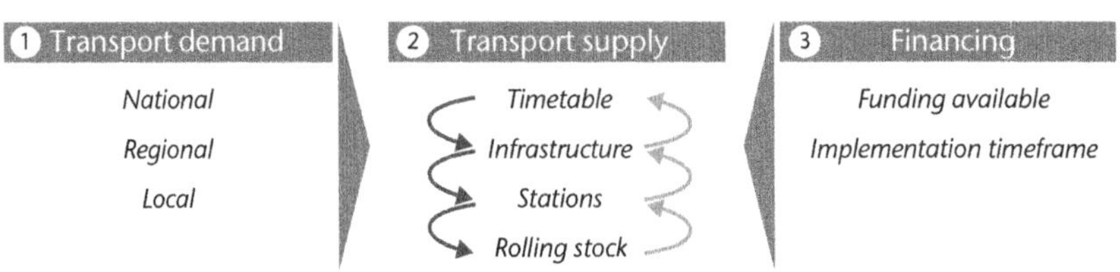

Figure 25.1 The integrated system of demand, transport supply, and financing

Source: Own illustration.

cost-effective method than full vertical separation, especially in light of the fact that systems with higher usage incur higher costs when separated. This position has recently been supported by the French government, which decided on integration of the infrastructure manager, RFF, back into the structure of the incumbent operator, SNCF, combined with more competences for the regulatory authority ARAF (Autorité de Régulation des Activités Ferroviaires).

The EC's proposal on domestic market opening has been broadly debated and, to some extent, criticized. Some member states are in favor of keeping direct awards for transport contracts as an option. This is reflected by the notion that there are examples where direct awarding mechanisms have led to high performance. In particular, small- to medium-sized countries and member states with complex, high-density (metropolitan) railway systems have felt that the overall cost of mandatory competitive tendering would outweigh the potential one-off dynamic welfare benefits.

The EC's proposal foresees a low threshold for direct awards, and a de facto phasing-out of this form of transport contract. Specifically, the EC proposes a provision that introduces specific upper limits on the value of direct awards for small-volume contracts for rail transport (<€5 million per year or an annual provision of less than 300,000 kilometers of public passenger transport services). The EC estimates the efficiency gains from competitive tenders to be 20–30 percent (derived from selected tendering procedures in the past).

Looking at SBB Passenger Service's cost structure as an example of a railway operator, it is likely that the EC's efficiency estimation is at the high end. For SBB, approximately 30–40 percent of the total costs of passenger services are charges for track access, which are set in Switzerland on a non-discriminatory basis and standardized. In other words, there is hardly any possibility to differentiate on prices. Cost on and of capital invested is estimated to be somewhere between 20 and 30 percent of the total cost, based on SBB's figures. Again, it can be hypothesized that in a fully competitive world a differentiation with regards to rolling stock costs is rather challenging, if possible at all.

The remaining 40–50 percent of the total cost for the service provision are labor costs (SBB Annual Financial and Sustainability Report, 2014). In the context of a competitive tendering process, it is assumed that labor costs are variable despite the fact that the work force is part of the labor unions. Thus, mandatory tendering favors new entrants without social obligations. It eventually becomes a policy choice as to the extent to which wages should or could be cut.

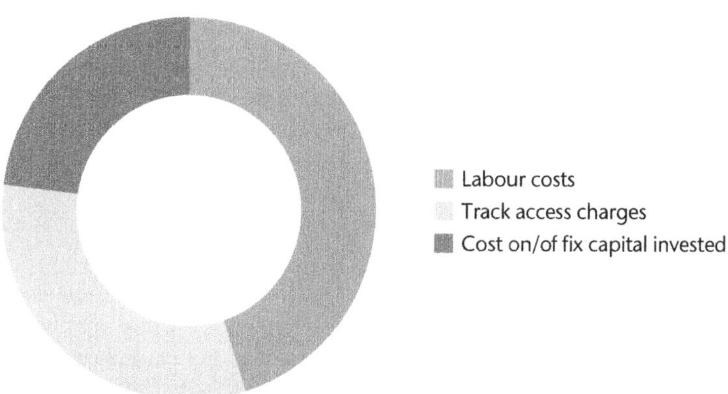

Figure 25.2 Total costs for providing passenger rail transport services

Source: SBB internal estimation.

The potential efficiency gains from competitively tendered transport contracts for rail estimated by the EC are intuitively likely to be one-off effects that may occur in the first round of bids, but are unlikely to be sustainable in the long run. This argument is based on the notion that labor cost can be reduced in the first round of bids, but not on a sustainable long-term level (static efficiency gains as opposed to dynamic). The key question with regards to the cost–benefit analysis arises as to whether the tendering process itself might be more expensive than any efficiency gained from the process. The ability of the competent bodies to carry out such tenders, the specific know-how required by operators to participate in tenders, as well as the oversight mechanism and the legal proceedings are highly costly to railway systems overall, and in particular for small- to medium-sized jurisdictions, and thus must not be underestimated.

Preliminary conclusions

Based on the observations from the theoretical framework, as well as from the market developments across EU member states, there are a few preliminary conclusions that can be derived.

First, market opening does not necessarily lead to an increased number of open-access players entering the market. Competition, in its ultimate form, might lead to fewer market players rather than more. In other words, it is likely that today's national rail monopolies are simply replaced by an oligopoly on a pan-European level with regional monopoly provision of transport services.

Second, where competitive elements are introduced, it is likely that, based on the cost structures of standard railways, the efficiency gains are largely attributable to labor cost savings. Hence, companies without social labor contracts are likely to benefit most from the first round of tendering procedures. It is also likely that efficiency gains are high where service quality is at a low level. In countries with a high level of service quality, or where it has improved substantially over recent years, the costs of tendering procedures may exceed potential benefits.

Railway markets in Europe

Thus far, it is clear that an integrated European railway market has not (yet) emerged as a result of de- and re-regulation. Markets, if they have come to exist at all, are mainly national, owing to the large differences among countries in matters of railway sector liberalization and governance. Markets are de jure open in freight and international passenger transport (including cabotage), and, in some countries, in domestic passenger transport via tendering. However, this does not necessarily mean that competition has emerged. For a railway services provider, a series of factors are important from a competitive perspective – that is from the perspective of seeking to enter new railway markets or defending one's own market shares, namely volumes, quality, funding, and modal split. None of these central factors for firm strategy seem to be directly correlated neither with the degree, nor with the type, of liberalization.

Transport volume

European countries have experienced divergent amounts of absolute growth in passenger kilometers, passenger train kilometers, and freight traffic, as well as the speed at which volumes have changed. Certain countries, such as the UK, the Netherlands, Germany, Austria, and especially Switzerland, have experienced relatively high levels of growth in passenger numbers, while others have experienced stagnation. The performance of individual railway systems in producing growth may be due to the structure of their markets, but also to a number of exogenous factors, including the physical constraints of the network and national policies regarding the construction of public transport systems.

Figure 25.3 shows the absolute number of train kilometers per inhabitant, as well as the number of trains per line in selected European countries and Japan (Swiss Federal Railways, 2015).

Countries with high volumes or, even better, high-volume growth, are more attractive for any rail services operator. However, these are not necessarily the most liberalized and easy-to-enter markets.

Punctuality

Figure 25.4 indicates levels of punctuality across selected European passenger rail service operators. It can be argued that punctuality is another relevant indicator of a functioning rail market. Higher punctuality would presumably lead to higher patronage, and subsequently to market growth. Again, punctuality is not directly related to liberalization, even though it might be related to regulation.

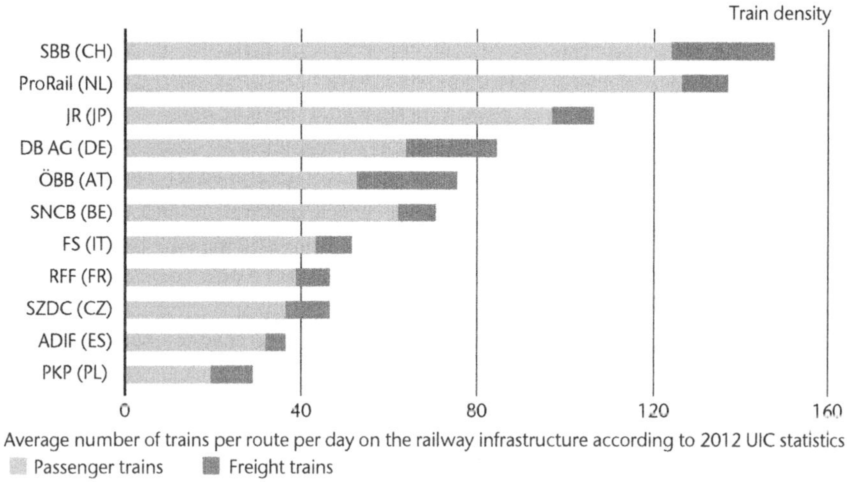

Figure 25.3 Comparison of network loads

Source: SBB, 2014.

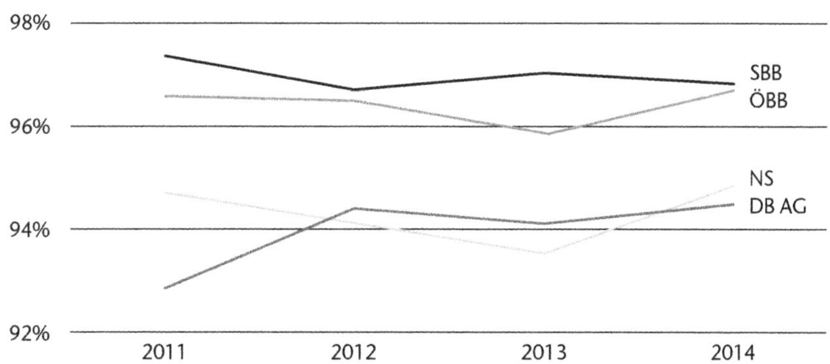

Figure 25.4 Punctuality comparison

Source: SBB, 2014.

Public funding

Public funding is another key factor impacting the attractiveness of a railway market. To recall, each railway system has various sources of income, such as passenger fare revenue, income from track access charges, third-party business (for example, income from contracts with shops in stations), and direct state funding for PSO/non-PSO services, along with infrastructure grants. Various approaches can be used to compare the relative cost of a system, ranging from a per-unit cost analysis to sophisticated econometric analyses.[3] No one approach is correct, and the more disaggregate method (such as comparing only PSO funding across countries) does not capture other effects, such as policy decisions and differing financing mechanisms for the industry.

One approach used to compare public funding across various jurisdictions is to consider a measure of both freight and passenger usage on the network. It stands to reason that the higher the usage of a particular network, the higher the corresponding operating, maintenance, and renewal costs will be (and therefore the funding required). The underlying reasoning is that there is an efficient level of usage of the network reflected through a relatively high number of passenger kilometers, as well as freight ton kilometers transported on the network. A number of studies have used this approach to make comparisons, including the CER EVES rail study (van de Velde *et al.*, 2012).

A comparison of a measure of usage of both passenger kilometers and freight ton kilometers, which form a 'transport unit', has been conducted compared with overall state funding for the whole industry. This approach offers the advantage that both passenger usage and freight usage on the whole network are taken into account. When considering the year 2010, the picture shown in Figure 25.5 emerges.

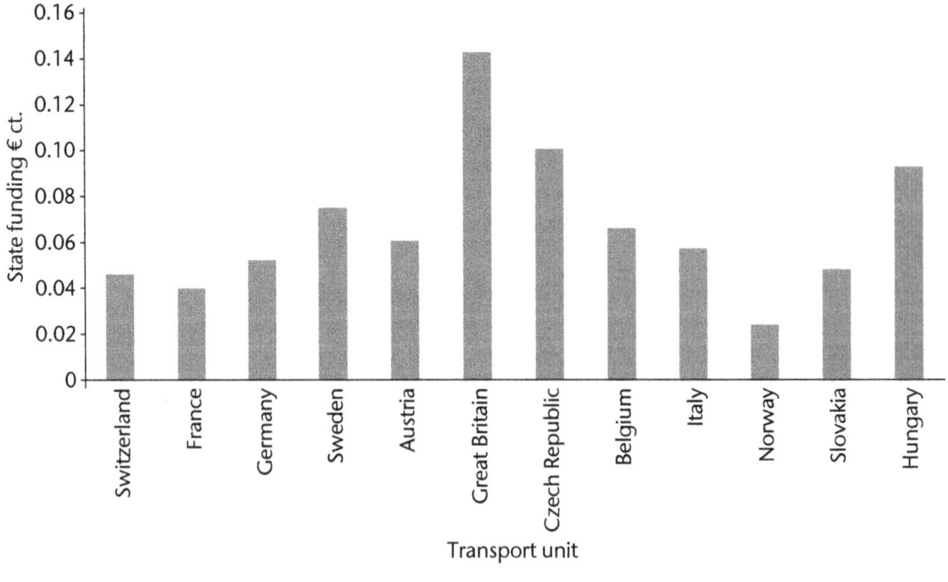

Figure 25.5 State funding for railways

Source: Boston Consulting Group, 2012; Eurostat, 2015; SBB in facts and figures; authors.

It should be noted of course that this approach has various downsides. For example, it is a yearly snapshot only, and funding levels vary. Still, in countries that have liberalized their railway markets, such as the UK, one would expect to see levels that are lower than in those that have not. However, based on this analysis, this appears not to be the case. Further research would have to be conducted into this matter, as a one-year comparison is not sufficient to derive a conclusion. This holds in particular for an industry in which investment cycles last several decades and cash flows should be reasonably stable from a funding perspective.

Modal split

One of the key performance indicators of railway reform is the relative level of the modal share generated against other modes of transport. One of the stated goals of the EC in its 2011 Transport White Paper is indeed the shift of traffic from road to rail. Market opening was considered the means to achieve precisely that. But modal share is of course also a highly relevant indicator for any competitor seeking to enter a market.

Figures 25.6 and 25.7 show the modal share for both rail passenger and rail freight services, compared across countries. In both cases, Switzerland shows the highest modal split for rail. Considering the structural setup and the degree of market opening of the countries chosen for the benchmark, there is no one distinct trend that can be derived from observing the different railway markets.

Overall, it appears clearly that the attractiveness of Europe's railway markets – as measured by volumes and volume growth (a proxy for patronage), quality, public funding, and modal split – is hardly related to their degree of market opening. While it is true that the country with the highest per-unit funding is also the most liberalized one, other well-funded railway systems are highly liberalized.

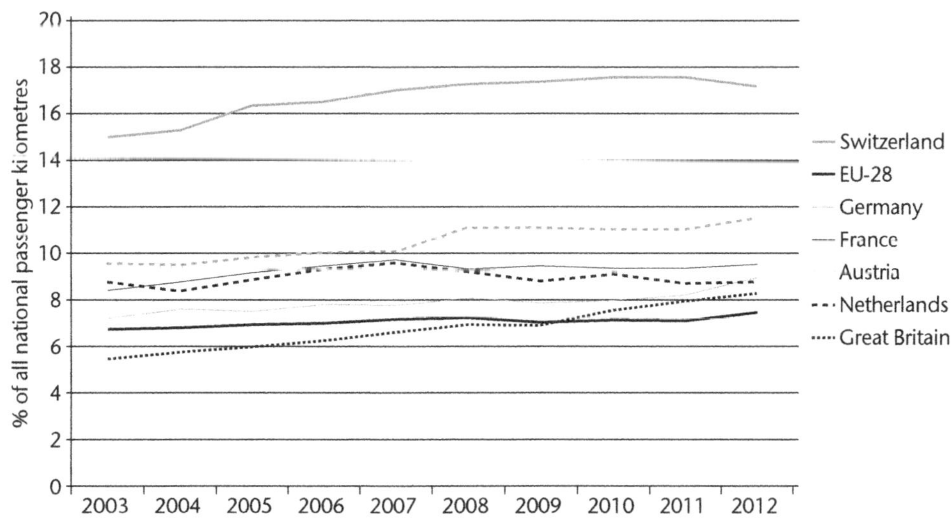

Figure 25.6 Comparison of modal split for passenger rail

Source: Eurostat, 2014b.

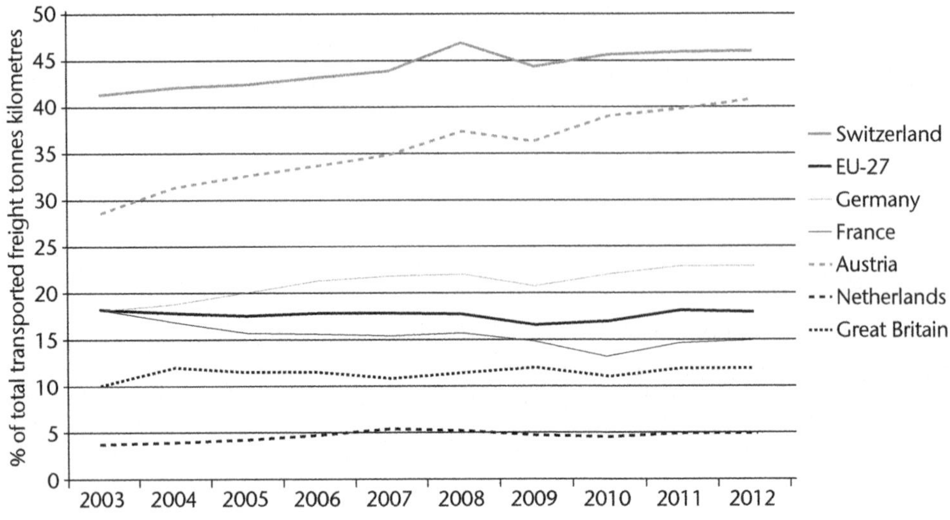

Figure 25.7 Comparison of modal split of freight rail

Source: Eurostat, 2014a.

Perspective of a national railway operator: The case of Switzerland

In this section, we take the example of one historical national railway operator to illustrate what European liberalization and national railway policies mean. Switzerland is, in many ways, atypical: it has the highest network load (Figure 25.3), the highest modal split (Figures 25.6 and 25.7), and the highest punctuality (Figure 25.4) when compared within Europe. Furthermore, it enjoys solid public financing along with strong public support. European railway legislation is adopted in Switzerland on the basis of the 'equivalence principle', and hence has a substantial impact on the market outcome. Therefore, it is justifiable to take the Swiss case as an illustration for firm strategic implications. In order to do so, we first briefly recall the market structure in Switzerland, and then move on to the financing of the Swiss railway system.

Market structure

The Swiss railway system is characterized by several fully integrated railway undertakings that provide their (infrastructure, passenger, and freight) services in a high-density, multi-modal network. SBB is the largest, but not sole, railway undertaking in Switzerland. Overall, there are more than 35 railway companies providing freight and passenger services across the country. In this section, we examine the market structure in Switzerland for international, national long-distance, and regional services.

Concessions for passenger rail services fall into two categories, namely a long-distance concession, currently running from 2007–2017, and numerous regional passenger-service concessions. At present, concessions for national long-distance and regional passenger services are awarded directly, although there is legal ground for open tendering procedures.

The current long-distance concession is held exclusively by SBB.[4] As part of this monopoly, SBB must offer a high level of tightly defined services, in most cases on a half-hourly basis, between major Swiss urban conglomerations, regardless of ridership. In some cases, most notably in peak hours, these services are increased to quarter-hourly. The concession for national long-distance services contains approximately 37 lines. One of the key features of the long-distance rail service concession is the embedded cross-subsidy mechanism between profitable and unprofitable routes. The long-distance concession must be self-financing and is not subject to PSO compensation.

There are over 30 regional passenger service concessions for the Swiss normal-gauge network. The majority of concessions for regional traffic run from 2009–2019 in the current period, with the following exception: the largest of the regional passenger service concessions is the Zürich S-Bahn network, which is currently held by SBB from 2014–2024. Under the legislation, competent local authorities (cantons and municipalities) may choose to award public service contracts following a competitive tendering procedure.

Although there is legal ground for competitive tendering in regional passenger services, regions award local transport contracts directly, either to SBB or to other regional railway operators. SBB's current market share in regional services is approximately 60 percent measured in terms of train kilometers, and 80 percent in terms of passenger kilometers. Contracts are characterized by a cost-recovery mechanism, not taking into account an appropriate rate on return (cost of capital). In other words, there is no profit to be earned. The overall volume for regional passenger rail transport increased between 2008 and 2012 in terms of passenger kilometers by 13.1 percent (SBB: 10.5 percent), and in terms of train kilometers by 11.2 percent (SBB: 4 percent).

The main objective of the Swiss government, and embedded in the Swiss constitution, is to shift goods from road to rail, where possible. In order to achieve this political objective and increase the rail modal share, there are specific rules in place to increase the attractiveness of rail transport, such as limits to the weight of road vehicles (40 tons), a ban on road transport from 10pm to 5am and on Sundays, or a heavy-vehicle charge.

In 1999, the freight market in Switzerland was fully opened to open-access competition, well ahead of the European member states. Currently, there are more than 11 freight operators active in the market for block trains, predominantly on the North–South axis along the Rotterdam–Genoa corridor, whereas single-wagonload remains a business run by SBB only.

Railway financing

Overall, the volumes for both passenger and freight services (measured in train kilometers) increased between 2004 and 2014. The overall growth is largely attributable to passenger services, with approximately 50 percent growth in train kilometers over 10 years. Simulations of the period between 2012 and 2030 show that the demand for railway services will further increase, overall and on a per-line basis. Growth estimations range between 20 percent and up to 80 percent (in terms of passenger kilometers), depending on the line considered.

In order to facilitate this growth, the Swiss infrastructure-financing mechanism was reconsidered in 2014. In recognition of the fact that infrastructure maintenance costs have to be balanced against the costs of any future enhancements, a new legislation proposal was introduced under the name of FABI (*Finanzierung und Ausbau der Bahninfrastruktur* or in English, Financing and Upgrading Switzerland's Railway Infrastructure).[5] It aims at balancing limited public funding between new infrastructure enhancements and the necessity of ongoing maintenance for the existing infrastructure. The goal is to combine both funding streams into one central fund, whereby the Federal government, cantons, and railway undertakings would finance future projects with a whole-system cost approach. This means that the costs of upgrades today are balanced against future maintenance costs, thus taking a long-term approach to infrastructure financing. Swiss citizens approved the FABI framework in February 2014, with 62 percent of voters favoring the plan, thus ensuring the support of the Swiss citizenry for the railway system as a whole.

Public expenditure for the Swiss railway system includes subsidies for railway infrastructure and for the provision of regional rail passenger services. Figure 25.9 shows the development of subsidies for both infrastructure and PSO contracts with an increase from 2002–2014, predominantly due to higher maintenance costs for infrastructure caused by an increase in transported goods and passengers.

Despite the increase in subsidies, the average state funding per passenger kilometer decreased from 2002–2014 by about 7 percent, as passenger kilometers increased more than the public contribution. In other words, productivity for the transportation of rail passengers increased.

In short, infrastructure funding and developments of EU legislation constitute the main strategic risks, but also opportunities, for a railway operator. In that respect, the case of Switzerland is typical, even though market and policy conditions may well be a little more favorable there, which in turn is likely to lead the incumbent to more fiercely defend its position.

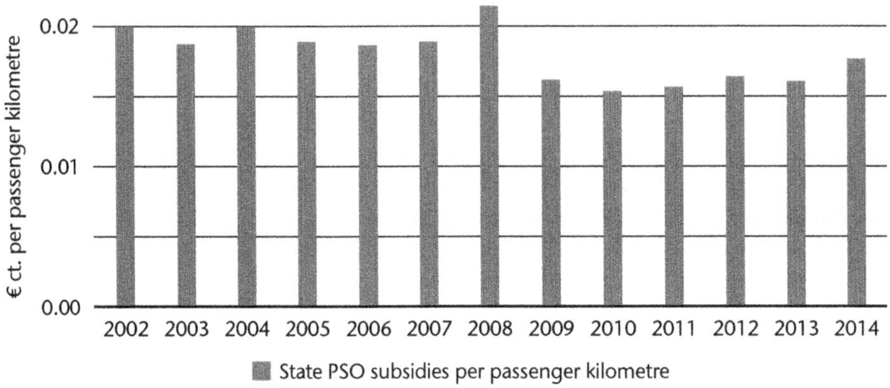

Figure 25.8 Swiss government subsidies for SBB PSO obligations

Source: SBB internal calculation.

Conclusions: Challenges for railway services providers

In the context of the intrusive regulatory remedies that have been adopted in the railway sector over the last two decades, railway incumbents have limited strategic options, at least with regards to their traditional business model. In this conclusion, we will derive four types of implications for traditional railway markets and service providers on the basis of what has been presented above.

Railway liberalization has led to market opportunities for railway service providers, at least in theory. Most obviously, such opportunities have arisen in the freight sector which has been completely liberalized in the EU since the start of 2007 (in Switzerland since 2002), for both national and international services, on the basis of an 'open-access' regime. This means that any licensed EU railway company with the necessary safety certification can apply for capacity and offer national and international freight services by rail throughout the EU. Market entry has occurred in certain segments, in particular for block trains. Yet, at the same time, margins have decreased continuously over time following strategies to compete on price. Most freight service operators in Europe are close to or even below the break-even threshold. Factors such as the competitive cost advantage of road vis-à-vis rail freight transport, a lack of the quality or availability of the underlying rail infrastructure, burdensome tax regimes and treatments, cross-border controls, or innovation cycles are imposing risks for rail freight transport providers. Thus, the attractiveness for long-term private investments in rail freight market appears to decline over time and a consolidation process has been seen and is still expected to happen across Europe. Overall, these challenges are to a large extent caused by a strong intermodal competition in combination with regulatory uncertainty, hence a big question mark has to be put on the ongoing claim for additional intramodal competition remedies. Rather a stabilization of the regulatory framework in combination with a cross-sectorial legal framework for road, air and rail – or in other words competition on an level playing field – is key to achieve a striving rail freight transport market.

The market for international rail passenger services has been liberalized in the EU from 1 January 2010. Any licensed, certified rail company established in the EU is, in principle, able to offer such services, and in doing so has the right to pick up and set down passengers at any station along the international route. Yet, again, there are only limited cases of effective and sustainable market entry partly due to the limited amount of revenues that can be generated for cross-border passenger transport compared to the cost for such a service provision. Where market entry effectively has happened, it appears to be the subsidiaries of the large railway operators in Europe competing with each other. Business models based on cooperation agreements between two providers seem to be an alternative way in which to provide a high-quality transport service for customers. Cooperation models allow for an effective allocation of costs and revenues between contracting partners, as well as a mitigation of risks according to market considerations. Furthermore, cooperation between railway undertakings appears to be a more promising strategy in an intermodal competition set up between rail, road or air transport.

In the national rail passenger transport markets, market access models reach from open access through to PSO tendering and franchising. Whereas market entry in long-distance rail passenger transport has been very limited, competitive tendering for regional PSO rail transport contracts has occurred (notably in Germany and the UK), and also – under certain conditions – has been successful in terms of lower public subsidies, higher volumes, or higher performance indicators. Again, as described in previous sections, the risks and opportunities with regards to open access and PSO tendering need to be assessed carefully on a national level, in particular the potential long-run benefits from tendering compared to the significant system costs that occur through a fragmentation of an existing market. The financial viability of business models is highly dependent on the ability to earn an appropriate rate of return on and of capital invested. Besides specific national quality requirements such as through-ticketing or cross-modal timetabling, stranded long-term investments in infrastructure or rolling stock that is not yet at the end of its lifetime appear to be key elements for the sustainability of traditional business models.

Finally, examples show that one of the success factors for a competitive and high-quality rail transport service provision is the state and the condition of the railway infrastructure. As railway infrastructure is an essential input for the production of rail transport, the investment required funded by governments, and the investment/planning cycles long term, a stable regulatory and funding framework is key. Such a funding framework not only has to take into account the growth pattern of traditional rail transport, but also factors such as the cost to maintain the investments in place and innovative new transport concepts (combined and automatized mobility such as self-driving cars or car sharing models) that may cause investments to be stranded.

Building on the above, possible means for a traditional rail transport company are to increase revenues using intelligent demand management or introducing supplementary products and services. Indeed, on the demand side, innovative and more incentive-based pricing schemes could potentially lead to new revenue streams or to incentivizing customers to change their travel behavior. Such mobility pricing schemes may be suitable to balance out traffic flows over time, hence avoiding stranded investments for both infrastructure as well as in rolling stock procurement. The pace of the adoption of new technologies, as well as the use of economic concepts to optimize traffic flows – in particular in the areas of customer information, pricing schemes and product offers – will be key to bringing forward some of the benefits to end users and companies alike. Investments into digital products, innovative services and the use of 'big data' will be essential here to boost innovative solutions in both rail freight and passenger transport. However, overall, the scope of these approaches may be limited when it comes to growing the railway business internationally, expanding it beyond the traditional rail operator's national borders.

Thus, somewhat more disruptive approaches will be needed in light of the current EU legislation regarding the international and national service provision. Railway operators will have to think beyond the boundaries of railways and analyze customer needs much more carefully, along with their willingness to pay. This probably means that traditional rail transport providers will have to think in terms of mobility – of goods and people – beyond today's traditional rail service provision. This might well lead them to become mobility providers, a process that has already been started. Some railway service providers have expanded into road transport services (e.g. national or international bus connections as a complement to existing railway links) or even have become important in terms of urban development (e.g. 'mobility hubs'). However, this trend may well take them further into offering integrated mobility solutions including car-sharing, bike-sharing, taxi services, and so on. The active usage of information and communication technologies will certainly (have to) play a central role in this strategic (re-) orientation of railway service providers.

Strategic evolution into all of the above directions will of course have to be actively supported by corresponding strategies in the field of regulation, in particular when it comes to (1) strengthening rail vis-à-vis other transport modes; (2) ensuring a sustainable rail infrastructure funding scheme; (3) fencing off overly intrusive (EU) legislation about firm organization and, more generally, (4) creating conditions for railway service operators to move into broader mobility.

Notes

1 The views expressed in this paper are solely those of the authors, and do not necessarily reflect the views of Swiss Federal Railways (SBB/CFF/FFS).
2 Regulation 1370/2007 entered into force on 3 December 2009. It replaced Regulation 1191/69 on public service transport for inland transport.
3 Recent publications, most notably an Inno-V study completed for SNCF, compared relative levels of state subsidies with the relative level of track access charges.
4 The current long-distance concession runs for 10 years. By law, a concession may run for up to 20 years.
5 For more information, see http://www.sbb.ch/en/group/the-company/projects/upgrading-the-rail-network/national-projects/fabi.html.

References

Bleisch, R. and Marcus, S. (2010) International Experience with Vertical Separation in Telecommunications: The Case of New Zealand, available at: http://papers.ssrn.com/sol3/Delivery.cfm/SSRN_ID1587438_code333755.pdf?abstractid=1587438&mirid=3 (accessed 1 May 2015).

Boston Consulting Group (2012) *European Railway Performance Index*, SNCF Report.
Community of European Railway and Infrastructure Companies (2005) *Reforming Europe's Railways – An Assessment of Progress*, Brussels, Eurailpress, CER.
Community of European Railway and Infrastructure Companies (2008) *European Railway Legislation Handbook*. Second Edition, Brussels, Eurailpress, CER.
Community of European Railway and Infrastructure Companies (2011a) Public Service Rail Transport in the European Union: an overview, Brussels, CER.
Community of European Railway and Infrastructure Companies CER (2011b) Reforming Europe's Railways – Learning from Experience, Brussels, Eurailpress.
EC European Commission (2014) Proposal for a REGULATION OF THE EUROPEAN PARLIAMENT AND OF THE COUNCIL amending Regulation (EC) No 1370/2007 concerning the opening of the market for domestic passenger transport services by rail, Brussels, available at: http://eur-lex.europa.eu/LexUriServ/LexUriServ.do?uri=COM:2013:0028:FIN:EN:PDF (accessed 1 May 2015).
EC European Commission (2014) Railway packages 1–4 and Recast of the First Railway Package. Communication from the Commission on interpretative guidelines concerning Regulation (EC) No 1370/2007 on public passenger transport services by rail and by road, available at: http://eur-lex.europa.eu/legal-content/EN/TXT/?uri=CELEX:52014XC0329(01) (accessed 1 May 2015).
Eurostat (2014a) Table tran_hv_frmod.xls. Güterverkehr nach Verkehrszweig, available at: http://ec.europa.eu/eurostat/de (accessed 1 May 2015).
Eurostat (2014b) Table tran_hv_psmod.xls. Personenverkehr nach Verkehrszweig, available at: http://ec.europa.eu/eurostat/de (accessed 1 May 2015).
Eurostat (2015) Table purchasing power parities (PPPs), price level indices and real expenditures for ESA2010 aggregates [prc_ppp_ind], available at: http://ec.europa.eu/eurostat/de (accessed 1 May 2015).
Office of Rail Regulation (2015) *EU Law*, available at: http://orr.gov.uk/about-orr/what-we-do/the-law/eu-law (accessed 1 May 2015).
Pfund, C. (2003) *Separation Philosophy of the European Union – Blessing or Curse?* LITRA.
SBB Annual Financial and Sustainability Report (2014) Swiss Federal Railways, Berne, Switzerland.
Swiss Federal Office for Statistics (2014) Tables 1–9. Zeitreihen der Eisenbahnstatistik, BfS, Biel, available at: http://www.bfs.admin.ch/bfs/portal/de/index/themen/11/07/blank/01/01.html (accessed 1 May 2015).
Swiss Federal Railways SBB/CFF/FFS (2013) Berne, available online at: http://www.sbb.ch/en/group/the-company/projects/upgrading-the-rail-network/national-projects/fabi.html (accessed 1 May 2015).
Swiss Federal Railways SBB/CFF/FFS (2015) SBB in Facts and Figures 2014, Berne, available at: https://www.sbb.ch/en/group/the-company/facts-and-figures.html (accessed 1 May 2015).
van de Velde, D., Nash, C., Smith, A., Mizutani, F., Uranishi, S., Lijesen, M. and Zschoche, F. (2012) EVES-Rail – Economic effects of vertical separation in the railway sector, Full technical report for CER – Community of European Railways and Infrastructure Companies; by inno-V Amsterdam, University of Leeds, ITS, Kobe University, VU Amsterdam University, and Civity Management Consultants (accessed 1 May 2015).

26

Airport structure, strategy and performance

A review

Peter Forsyth, Jürgen Müller and Hans-Martin Niemeier

Introduction

The institutional nature of airports has changed substantially over the last 40 years, from a public utility to a business with private involvement, with increasing variations of competition and regulation, management strategies, and policies. The trend towards privatization began in 1987 with BAA in the UK. It has led to an almost fully privatized industry in the UK. Only a few countries, such as Australia, followed the UK. In the rest of Europe, only a minority of airports have been privatized; those minority are only partially privatized, and very often with a minority share for a private investor (Gillen and Niemeier, 2008). There are no signs that US airports will be privatized in the near future.

Separately from privatization, although certainly enhanced by it, runs the trend of commercialization. Airports are businesses with large shares of commercial revenues, and commercialization has also led airports to be more profit orientated. Large airports have become more profitable than airlines (IATA, 2011).

Deregulation of airlines has led to more footloose airlines, even for those with large hubs, which created some countervailing power. Now, airports in similar catchment areas often have different owners, and competition is feasible and likely. It has intensified, thereby lessening the case for regulation; for example, in the UK, Manchester has been de-designated from regulation. London's major airports (Heathrow, Gatwick, and Stansted) now have different owners, and compete against one another. Some claim that with this new environment airports are an ordinary industry with imperfect competition (Copenhagen Economics, 2012).

This change in institutions – with a move to privatization and commercialization – means that airport strategies have become much more of an issue. Pricing strategies have always been pertinent, but now they are often implemented in a competitive environment. The idea of airport marketing is now a real one (see Halpern and Graham, 2013), and airports seek to raise revenues and profits from traditional sources, such as aeronautical services, but also retail, parking, and other services, which are becoming increasingly important. Airports choose to make use of their operational expertise through contracting out at other airports, so the vertical organization of the industry changes. Mergers and the emergence of private airport groups indicate also a change in the horizontal organization. Not all airports are deregulated, often – especially with larger airports – their strategies need to be employed in a regulated environment.

We start this chapter by considering structural aspects, including economies of scale and scope, vertical relationships, and competition. Next, we look at strategies towards commercial revenues and pricing, which are often implemented in a competitive environment, and sometimes with a strong overlay of regulation. Airports face difficult issues regarding provision of capacity, which constrain their strategies. We also look briefly at the outcomes of strategies in this new environment, in terms of performance, and conclude by highlighting some of the policy implications.

Structure of the airport industry and the nature of competition

In this section, we first analyze how production technology affects competition among airports. Thereafter, we look at the constraints of market power due to the airline market. We summarize the results in a section on the nature of competition.

Economies of scale and scope

Traditional airports were seen as natural monopolies; surprisingly, however, this view lacked empirical support (Lechmann and Niemeier, 2013). Early studies showed that the benefits of scale economies were running out at 3 to 5 million passengers. This would imply that the threshold for a natural monopoly would be in the range of 6 to 10 million passengers, so that those airport markets that are subject to entry need not be regulated. However, research by Martín and Voltes-Dorta (2008, 2011), in particular, has suggested that economies of scale do not run at that level. Even large airports of 60–80 million may have decreasing average costs. This view is also compatible with patterns of market entry, which reflect a combination of scale economies, constrained by regional planning and environmental restrictions.

Market entry and exit in the industry have been infrequent. In Europe, only 21 airports entered the market and 18 exited it in the period from 1955 to 2012 (Müller-Rostin *et al.*, 2010; GAP Database, 2014). Entry has not occurred in regions with excess demand. These patterns of market entry and exit, as well as the large number of regional airports, indicate that airports are seen as instruments for regional development, in terms of providing access to air transport and developing tourism and connectivity. Military aspects also play a role.

Unlike with airlines, no network effects drive the structure of the airport industry (Forsyth *et al.*, 2011), though network connectivity effects exist. While there are economies of scope within an airport, there is no evidence of substantial gains from multi-airport operations. Nevertheless, a number of countries use one state company to run all or most of their airports, across many cities, in an airport system.[1] In contrast, airport alliances and mergers have been rare and rather unsuccessful. International airport companies have also emerged, but on a limited scale (Forsyth *et al.*, 2011). These forms of geographic integration do not follow a pattern of building networks. Only a few activities, such as marketing and information technology (IT), can be integrated centrally, while the bulk of activities remain local. Knowledge transfer seems to have played a role, as many airports bid for international projects such as building and operating a terminal or an airport. Gaining market power is also a motive. An example of this can be seen in the alliance between Schiphol and Aeroport De Paris, as well as the attempt of Vienna airport to take over neighboring Bratislava airport.[2] Overall, the airport industry is not highly concentrated on a national (unless a national airport system is operated), or an international level. For origin destination traffic, the market is certainly much more local, while for transfer flights the relevant market is geographically much larger (Bilotkach and Müller, 2012).

Vertical relationships in aviation

Airports do not sell to the traveler directly, except when they provide non-aeronautical services. They provide services to airlines, which, using the services of the air traffic control system, carry passengers and freight. Airlines are essentially competitive or oligopolistic. In most city pair markets only a small number of airlines operate. In addition, there is potential competition: sometimes, airlines serving related routes (for example, from the same or nearby airports) have some impact on the pricing on a route (this is termed the 'Southwest' effect). The presence of only a small number of airlines suggests oligopoly, and economists very often model airline markets as oligopolistic. On the other hand, the returns on investments in airlines are anything but oligopolistic. For many decades returns have been poor, with less than normal profit levels. This suggests that prices are closer to competitive, rather than oligopolistic. To date, there have been no convincing explanations for this (IATA, 2011).

Regulation has long been a component of airline markets, though its significance has been declining. Starting with the US in 1978, most countries have deregulated their domestic air transport. International aviation is a different story; there is still considerable regulation, though it has lessened over time. The bilateral system of regulation is still in place, and countries regulate air transport jointly with bilateral partners. Some countries are liberal, while others remain restrictive. This bilateral system of regulation between countries A and B means that it is still not easy for an airline from country A to serve markets between B and C.

As with domestic air transport, the US has been a leader in international aviation liberalization through its Open Skies agreements, which allows relatively competitive conditions between the US and its partner country's airlines (though not with airlines from other countries). There have been some significant deregulations at a regional level. In particular, there is an open market between European countries. Other regional markets, particularly those of the ASEAN countries have also been liberalizing.

Another part of the air transport industry is the air traffic control system. This governs the airways, and the approaches and departures to and from airports. The system is characterized by natural monopoly, and government departments or government enterprises[3] typically provide these services as legal monopolies. Normally, prices are set at a certain level to cover costs, though there are questions surrounding how productive and efficient these systems are.

Thus far, we have not highlighted air transport as a network industry. Indeed, except for some aspects of the industry, most discussion has not emphasized it as a network industry. The most obvious aspect is that the industry is structured in terms of hubs and spokes to reduce transport costs by taking advantage of economies of scale and scope on transport between the hubs. While most countries have used a hub-and-spoke system, where regulators arbitrarily chose airports to act as hubs, the US system developed without much use of hubs. This changed with deregulation, which saw airlines developing their own hubs. In Europe and Asia, although there were hubs, deregulation meant that airlines were free to choose, and optimize, their own networks.

This network structure has several implications. One is the possibility of competition for transfer traffic between hubs; thus, Frankfurt airport may be competing for hub traffic with Paris and Amsterdam. Some airlines will be dominant at the hubs they fly from, and this gives rise to 'hub' premium, which is a higher air fare when flying from a hub as compared to flying through a hub (Borenstein, 1989; Morrison and Winston, 1995). Not all airlines have chosen a hub-and-spoke network. In particular, many low-cost carriers (LCCs) have chosen to emphasize point-to-point services. This is particularly true when they fly to less central (but cheaper) airports. This said, the lure of hubs has been affecting them as well; several LCCs are now using major hubs to enhance the connectivity of their flights.

Connectivity is now increasingly regarded as an important aspect of airline networks. In essence, airline networks gain from having good connections. An airport that has many flights to different destinations is likely to be well connected, and there has been considerable effort to devise measures of connectivity between airports and cities. Good connections give rise to time and convenience savings, along with operating-cost savings. Research on connectivity is in its infancy, but what is available suggests that connectivity is valuable. For example, there is evidence that connectivity for a city or country is associated with higher GDP (InterVISTAS, 2006; Pearce and Smyth, 2007). Improved connectivity is of value to business travelers, and there will be gains in GDP as a result of increased productivity. However, leisure travelers, who constitute the majority of travelers on most routes, also gain from increased connectivity, even though their gains do not increase GDP. While there is increasing evidence that connectivity is valuable, it has yet to be proven that it constitutes a wider economic benefit (WEB) of air travel, and creates an external gain not taken into account by travelers when buying their ticket. This is similar to the WEBs of ground transport, which have recently been analyzed intensively (for a discussion of WEBs of ground transport, see Venables, 2007).

The nature of airport competition

Connectivity, together with scale economies, are relevant in determining the nature of competition amongst airports, both for transfer and origin-destination (OD) traffic, but it is important to keep their different geographic markets in mind.

For OD traffic, a major cost of using an airport is not just the production cost, but also the cost of accessing it. For most people, the cost of a taxi to the most convenient airport is much higher than the average production cost per passenger, which is an approximation to price. Other cheaper ways of accessing the airport are used, but these are also relatively time consuming. This suggests that, looking at this aspect alone, we should expect there to be many airports in all but small cities, unless economies of scale are more significant than often assumed. However, this is not the case: most cities have only one airport, except for the very large ones such as London, Paris, and New York.

There are several reasons for this. One is geographical; it is notoriously difficult to aggregate large areas suitable for airports. This is obvious when new airport developments are being contemplated. Possible lower property values, noise, and local emissions make airports unpopular. However, economies of density are present as well. Single large airports are convenient. They can provide frequent services to a range of destinations, serving not only OD traffic, but also hub flights. Smaller, more dispersed airports may be convenient, but they would not be able to provide frequent services to many destinations. Such airports would also not be able to operate as hubs.

The consequence of this is that it is population density, rather than returns to scale, that determines the intensity of airport competition for OD traffic. The UK is perhaps the prime example of airport competition. The UK is a densely populated country that uses aviation extensively. There are many cities with airports, and travelling times between airports are modest. Thus, travelers have a choice of which airports to use. Airports other than the major London airports are not regulated, even though they are mainly privately owned. In countries such as France and Australia, airports are further apart and competition is less effective or not feasible. Some cities have multiple airports and the potential for competition is thus present. In several cities, such as Paris, the same firms own all of the airports, but in some cases, notably London, airports have been demerged and competition is possible.

With small, high-cost airports, competition is unlikely to be strong. These airports are able to maintain high prices because of the barriers to competition – they may be on an island or remote. Because of their convenience to local populations, they are able to survive. There are also some small, high-cost airports that operate in niche markets.

The extent to which an airport operates in a competitive OD market depends primarily on how close it is to other airports. Thus, studies of airport competition for OD traffic focus on measuring how many airports are in the catchment area of another airport (for example, one or two hours' driving distance of each other). However, these types of studies are essentially arbitrary, since they rely on assumptions of how far travelers are prepared to drive to access an airport. Interestingly, they do not use extensive evidence regarding values of time. A recent study by Copenhagen Economics (2012) for the industry association for airports, ACI Europe, argued that there is a great deal of competition between airports in Europe, though another study by InterVISTAS for IATA (the International Air Transport Association) (Pearce and Wiltshire, 2013) argued that there is much less competition amongst airports than that suggested by the Copenhagen Economics report. Maertens (2012) and Malina (2010) assessed market power quantitatively.[4] Their results were more in line with the InterVISTAS study and showed that, in general, small airports are facing competition, but in each European country there is at least one, which is often the major airport, that has persistent market power, which needs to be further assessed by the regulatory authorities.

Strategy: Managing the value chain, market conduct and regulatory implications

In this section, we provide an overview of the strategy of airports by first analyzing the production spectrum of an airport. This is followed by an analysis of the commercial revenues and the debate on complementarity, which leads to issues of pricing and regulation, as well as managing airport capacity.

Management of the production spectrum of an airport

There are various ways in which the activities in an airport's value chain can be organized. In general, an airport is a complex system in which several processes are interlinked, such as passengers, baggage, freight and mail, and aircraft handling. Figure 26.1 provides a simplified overview of the value chain in terms of aircraft handling, passengers, and baggage processes, and identifies some links between these processes.

The airport itself can operate these activities in the value chain, or they can be delegated. However, many depend on access to critical bottleneck infrastructure under the control of the airport. Generally speaking, three possibilities exist:

- A single supplier provides infrastructure or services; for example, the airport becomes the sole infrastructure or service provider.
- Multiple suppliers provide infrastructure or services (including the airport and the airlines), but non-airport suppliers need access to the bottleneck infrastructure of the airport.
- The airport operator does not offer these services, and instead concentrates on the provision of bottleneck infrastructure.

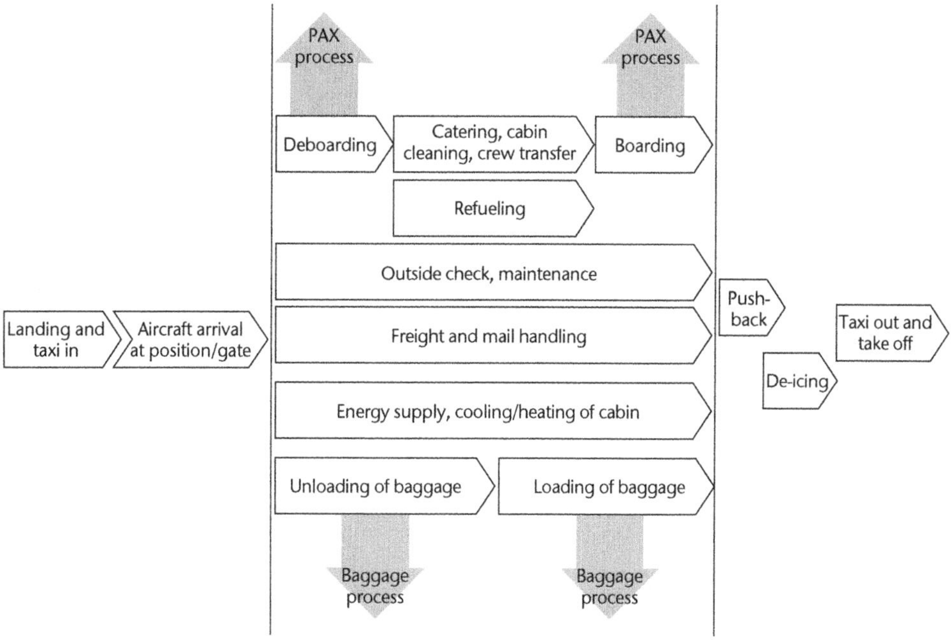

Figure 26.1 Aircraft handling process (key elements) with linkages to passenger and baggage process

Source: GAP, 2014.

Many of these activities can be handled by third parties, such as catering, cleaning, crew transfer, refueling, maintenance of aircraft, energy supply, and luggage handling; and the range of the product spectrum covered by an airport varies greatly around the world. The key determinants for this choice are economies of scale and multi-plant advantages for each of these processes, and economies of scope across activities. The institutional and regulatory environment also matters greatly, as does the governance structure of the airports for some of these undertakings.

Small airports are more likely to outsource activities for which economies of scale matter, as do airlines with only a few daily flights. On the other hand, large airports would have an economic base to offer some of these activities at a competitive level, but many choose not to do so. Atlanta airport, being the extreme of a vertically disintegrated airport, offers only runway infrastructure and air traffic control (ATC) for the approach, while third parties and airlines operate the terminals and all of the associated services. On the other hand, German airports tend to be highly vertically integrated, offering a full range of ground handling services in addition to non-aviation activities such as retail and parking.

Multi-plant economies also matter for some of these activities, so that even large airports will outsource services such as ground handling, and the operation of restaurants, retail shops, and parking operations. Figure 26.2 illustrates the importance of multi-plant activities for large ground handling operators in Europe. Single airports would find it difficult to compete with such multi-plant operators.[5]

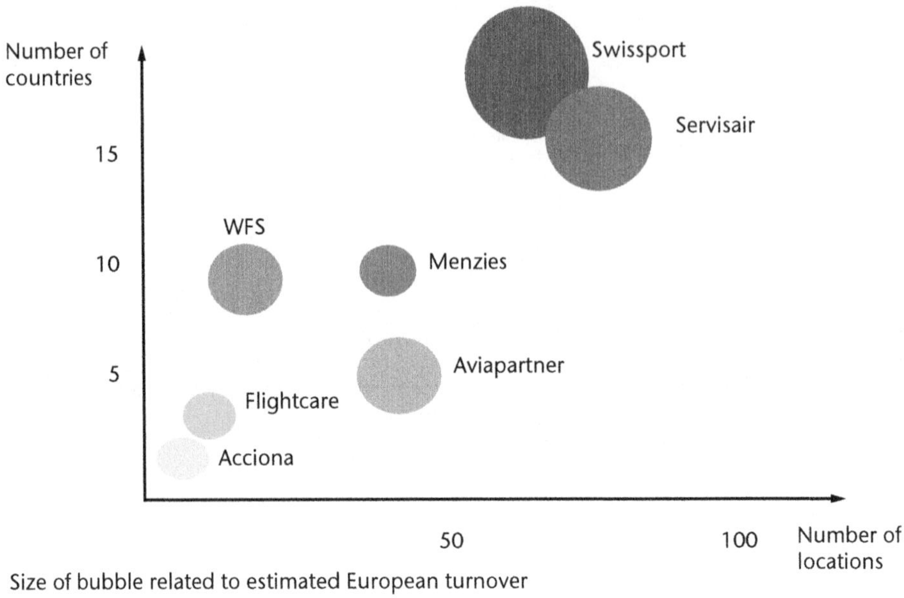

Figure 26.2 Importance of multi-plant activities for ground handling services in Europe

Source: Bluth, 2008.

Regulatory implications

The airport plays a crucial role in providing access to the bottleneck infrastructure. It provides access to the infrastructure required (such as to the airport ramp and the terminal; the central baggage system; energy and utilities; and rental space) to offer such services at the airport. The question to be answered is whether this provides possible leverage that airports can use to exercise market power to the disadvantage of third-party suppliers.

Commercial revenues and debate on complementarity

When airports decide on the level of vertical integration, how important, in financial terms, are these different activities? We can illustrate these financial dimensions with a few examples. Airport revenues normally consist of:

- Aviation charges that are paid by airlines for the use of the airport infrastructure.
- Concession fees that are paid by third parties for the right to offer services at the airport; for example, refueling companies, ground transport, or service providers such as taxis, restaurants, or shops.
- Rents that are paid by tenants for the use of rental property, entire buildings, storage facilities, etc.
- Other revenues received, such as for consultancy, equity holdings, etc.

Some of these revenues are directly related to the level of aviation activities, such as refueling and ground handling, while others are revenues based on passengers, who might spend money in restaurants or shops, or on car parking.

In the US, aviation funds tend to be the most important revenue stream, while at many large airports in Europe and Asia non-aviation revenues tend be larger than aviation incomes. Figures from the US also give us some idea about the monetary importance of the major airports' activities, and the large importance of parking in the US. Again, in Europe and parts of Asia, parking is less important and retail dominates, as can be seen in Table 26.1. However, the most important aspect is that these non-aviation revenues are often more important than the core aeronautical services are. What strategic impact does this have on policies of airports? And what are the regulatory implications of the growing importance of non-aviation revenues?

In order to understand the strategic implications of these developments, it is useful to employ the concept of the two-sided market approach developed by Armstrong (2006).[6] This suggests that an airport is a platform that enables retailers, restaurant owners, and other shops and passengers to meet (Malavolti, 2010). The parking and retailing activity depends on how many passengers are circulating and connecting at the airport, as well as the time they spend in the airport. Starkie (2002) has argued that this complementarity leads the airport to favor lower aeronautical charges, and that this lessens the need for regulation to control the use of market power. However, others have argued that this complementarity is not strong (Zhang and Zhang, 2010). Empirically speaking, the issue of a two-sided market depends largely on the cross-price elasticity between the two markets; for example, what the reaction is in one market to a changed strategy in another. The two-sided market literature, which is applied to airports by Gillen (2011), provides a means of analyzing this issue.

Pricing and regulation

Optimal pricing of airport capacity differs between non-busy, busy, and very busy airports. Setting marginal prices at a non-busy airport would lead to a deficit; therefore, some form of price differentiation, such as Ramsey pricing, is needed to cover the fixed costs. Airports have traditionally used weight-based charges. Operators oflarge aircrafts will have a higher willingness to pay than those using smaller aircraft, this might be an approximation of a Ramsey scheme, although it is not clear how much welfare can be gained from better-structured charges (Morrison, 1982; Hakimo and Müller, 2015). Weight is also a proxy to measure the wear and tear of an additional flight; however, Starkie and Hogan (2003) have argued that weight is not a good indicator for the damage to a runway.

Table 26.1 Airport commercial revenues by world region (2007)

Region	*Commercial revenues (US$ billion)*	*Commercial as % total revenues*	*Commercial revenues per passenger (US$)*
Africa/Middle East	1.80	52.9	8.00
Asia/Pacific	6.92	45.7	7.06
Europe	16.61	48.1	12.15
Latin America/Caribbean	0.85	29.0	3.13
North America	9.05	52.6	5.92
Total	35.23	48.1	8.06

Source: ACI, 2008.

At busy airports, demand exceeds capacity and delays build up at peak times. If demand grows even further, the peaks are extended and excess demands are spread over the whole day. An example of a very busy airport is London Heathrow. If such airports were still to charge weight-based fees, capacity would not be managed well. Large aircraft pay more than small aircraft do, although the two groups use the runway for more or less the same time. Some form of time-related pricing thus seems to be necessary. Airports use such pricing for managing their car parks, but generally do not adopt peak and congestion pricing to manage their airside capacity (a few examples of peak pricing exist in Australia). Therefore, excess demand has to be rationed by some other instrument; in the case of airports, slots perform this role. The extent of excess demand is reflected in the slot prices (except in the US where queuing is the norm), and this should indicate whether to invest.

As airports are run as businesses and very often have persistent market power, regulators face a challenging task, including the information asymmetry that airports know the relevant supply/ cost and demand characteristics, while they do not. It is therefore necessary to design contracts that provide incentives to produce efficiently, and set prices at an optimal level. Cost-based regulation cannot achieve this, as airports are encouraged to use cost padding and gold plating, and to invest too early. The structure of charges is usually cost related, and therefore airports have no interests in adopting peak and congestion pricing. Price caps and other forms of incentive regulations could, in principle, reduce X-inefficiency, and promote costs being near efficient levels. A well-designed price cap also sets incentives to adopt peak pricing and manage capacity effectively (Forsyth and Niemeier, 2008); however, in practice these aspects are often not achieved (see below).

Airport capacity in the short and long term

Airports embody assets that are fixed and indivisible. This is true of airport runways and, to a lesser extent, terminals. The availability of these key assets determines the effective capacity of the airport. Terminals can be more easily expanded than runways, but even these usually take several years to expand. The capacity of an airport's runways is relatively fixed, given the ATC arrangements.

Most airports have sufficient runway capacity to serve all users, though a minority do not. These airports have a capacity rationing problem, at least for some hours in the day, and occasionally all of the time they are open. In effect, there are two main ways in which capacity is rationed: one is via queues and delays, and the other is via slots. In the US, for most airports excess demand is rationed by the delay mechanism, whereby aircraft movements are served on a first-come, first-served basis. Economists have noted the high cost of this approach for several decades (for a recent estimate of the cost, see Morrison and Winston, 2008). To some extent, airlines may internalize the delay costs, lessening the problem (Brueckner, 2002).

Slots ration airport capacity for most airports outside the US (and a few within the US) (for a detailed analysis see Czerny *et al.*, 2008). The airport capacity is predetermined, and only those flights that have a slot are permitted to use the airport at the specific time. The result is that demand does not exceed capacity, and delays are minimized. In reality, for busy airports there is pressure to maximize the throughput of movements, and delays can be significant (though not at US levels). While capacity may be nearly fixed, demand is subject to uncertainty (for example, flights can be late); as a result, slots do not eliminate all delays. The slot system has grown up over time. Most airports do not control their own slot system; rather, there are slot coordinators, which are often dominated by the major airline customers at the airport. In this respect, an important aspect of strategy is beyond the airport's control. There are also some very rare examples of prices being used to allocate airport capacity.

In the long run, capacity can be increased by investment. If demand is increasing, capacity will become more and more inadequate and additional investment will be needed. Additional capacity can be warranted in runways, terminals, and non-aeronautical areas such as retail and car parking. Currently, the UK Airports Commission is using cost–benefit analysis and computable general equilibrium models to investigate options for new capacity for London (Airports Commission, 2013).

Given that many airports are now privatized but regulated, regulators will become much more involved in the investment decision. Airports will be loath to invest in costly new capacity unless they are assured that they will be able to cover their costs. As a result, regulators will need to adjust price caps upwards to enable the airport to cover its costs. As an example, the regulator of London Heathrow, the UK CAA (Civil Aviation Authority), increased the price cap when Terminal 5 was being built. Again, parties other than the airport take key strategic decisions.

Performance: The effects of privatization and regulation

The performance of airports has been increasingly analyzed. The Air Transport Research Society and Transport Research Laboratory (2002) benchmark airports yearly on a worldwide scale. Liebert and Niemeier (2013) critically reviewed the research in depth.[7] The following discussion confines itself to the effects of the three major changes discussed above; namely privatization, regulation and competition, and management strategies.

Effects of privatization

Empirical studies of the effects of ownership on the efficiency of airports are inconclusive. Two different approaches have been used. The first assesses the airport's efficiency before and after privatization, while the second compares public and private airports. Parker (1999) estimated the technical efficiency prior to and after privatization of the British Airport Authority (BAA) for 1979–1996, and found no evidence that privatization had increased technical efficiency. In contrast, Yokomi (2005) argued that BAA airports have become more efficient for the period 1975–2001. Studies of the second approach initially also found a significant relationship between privatization and efficiency (see Oum *et al.*, 2003; Vasigh and Gorjidooz, 2006). However, in contrast to previous studies, Oum *et al.* (2006, 2008) found evidence that fully privatized airports and public airports perform better than airports with mixed ownership; in particular, the European partially privatized airports did not score highly.

Effects of regulation and competition

The problem with studies of privatization is that they do not separate the changes that come from regulation and competition, which is very often accompanied with privatization. Adler and Liebert (2014) combined all factors in an Australian–European comparison and separated the effects. They argued that if airport competition is not possible, any ownership form should be subject to incentive regulation. However, effective competition is preferred as it ensures cost efficiency. Assaf and Gillen. (2012) showed that price-cap-regulated airports tend to be more efficient than non-price-regulated airports in the UK. Given the diversity of incentive regulation (see below), Adler *et al.* (2015) analyzed these different forms, and showed that a move towards incentive regulation improves productive efficiency. They found no evidence that an independent regulator improves performance, but this might be due to the limited practice of independent regulation in Europe.

Effects of management strategies

Benchmarking studies consistently show that commercialization and outsourcing have a positive effect on airport performance (Adler *et al.*, 2013; Oum *et al.*, 2006; Tovar and Martín-Cejas, 2009). Commercialization usually leads to higher commercial revenues and better performance. Outsourcing is particularly important for ground handling. Here, most German airports have preferred to produce in-house, which largely explains why they do not perform well in benchmarking (Kamp *et al.*, 2007).

Commercialization and outsourcing are also key in the management of small regional airports, which have often been subsidized by larger airports or directly from taxpayers' money. Starkie (2008b) questioned the rationale for these subsidies, as even small private UK airports in a competitive environment are profitable. Adler *et al.* (2013) found for European airports that they cover their operational costs at 460,000 passengers. This break-even point can be lowered to 160,000 passengers if airports are efficiently managed.

Conclusions: Policy implications and further research

As outlined above, the changing institutional nature of airports has constantly influenced the development of the industry. These changes have often been triggered by policy. Therefore, below we discuss the implications for policies towards slot allocation and regulation, and highlight some questions for further research.

Slot allocation

As noted above, slots are potentially an efficient means of rationing scarce airport capacity. However, this does depend on how efficiently the slots are allocated. There are serious questions about this. In most airports, slots are allocated on administrative criteria; existing airline users have priority, though there may be some scope for new entrants. In some international airports, slot allocations are linked to air traffic rights; if an airline has a traffic right, it also gets a slot. There have been some cases of auctions being used to allocate slots in the US, though these have not lasted.

In practical terms, the most promising option for reform of the slot system lies with secondary trading (see Starkie, 2003). While the original allocation of slots may be inefficient, if slots could be traded the ultimate outcome could be efficient. If an airline is allocated valuable slots but cannot use them effectively, it may sell them to airlines that can use them effectively. The questions then arise as to the extent to which slot markets exist, and whether they are efficient. There are some slot markets that are relatively open and appear to function well, in particular those for the London airports. There have been occasional reports of slot trades at high prices, and there are also some grey markets in other airports. Airlines may swap slots, perhaps for undisclosed cash considerations, and perhaps with their alliance partners. The European Union has, several times, attempted to facilitate trading, though not to permit full secondary trading. The overall impression is that there is some slot trading, but it is far from an efficient market.

Airport regulation: Europe

Traditionally, airport charges were cost regulated. This changed with the price-cap regulation of the UK airports. The 1985 Privatization Act set up an independent regulator. The government, based on the advice of the Competition Commission, defined the scope of regulation. Initially, Manchester and the three BAA London airports were regulated, while all other airports had to report their charges, and were observed. This threat of regulation seems to have faded out with the de-designation of Manchester Airport in 2008, along with further evidence that UK airports were facing effective competition. This institutional setting was not mimicked by other European states Niemeier (2009). In countries such as France and Germany, the regulatory function has not been separated from ownership. Although airports frequently claim to be a competitive industry, this has not been studied or assessed by governments, with the exception of Schiphol Airport, where two studies confirmed that Schiphol has a persistent market (Müller *et al.*, 2010; Frontier Economics, 2000).

The UK adopted a hybrid form of price cap. Every five years, the price cap was determined through the regulated asset base. The price cap was based on a single till. The relatively high commercial revenues raised the X (in particular at Heathrow), thereby lowering charges although the airport was in greater demand. Although the single-till principle was heavily criticized (Starkie, 2008a), it was not abandoned. In the 1990s, the level of prices was substantially lowered; however, it later increased to allow for substantial investment, such as Terminal 5 at Heathrow. Quality was monitored, but later on regulated as well. This form of price cap was only implemented at a few other European airports, and often complexity was added, particularly to reduce risks. A so-called sliding-scale mechanism, which relates traffic growth to the inverse of level of charges, and which stabilizes revenues, was introduced in Vienna, Hamburg, and Paris. Malta and Hamburg airports switched from a single till to a dual till, and others, such as Paris have gradually followed suit. Quality and investment is regulated in Paris. Overall, cost-based regulation is still the dominant form, but slowly some incentives have been introduced (Niemeier, 2009).

Airport regulation: Australia and New Zealand

In contrast to other countries, Australia and New Zealand have opted for forms of light-handed regulation (LHR) (Forsyth, 2008; Arblaster, 2014). This is interesting, granted that the market power of Australian airports is relatively strong, since many airports are located relatively far away from their competitors.

After privatization, Australia implemented a price-cap system modeled on the UK. In 2001–2002 an LHR system replaced this. There were several reasons for the change; for instance, there was a fear that the price caps would deteriorate to a form of cost plus regulation; the price caps were seen as inflexible when airports needed to invest, and the price caps were making it difficult for airports to cover costs at times of crisis.

Currently, the four largest city airports are subject to LHR. This works through a system of periodic reviews conducted by an independent body. If an airport is shown to be abusing its market power it can be subjected to a sanction, such as re-regulation. Overall, the system has worked well and no airport has been subjected to any sanctions. There is some evidence of good productive efficiency performance, and the airports have been able to make investments, though airlines would argue that some charges are higher than they need to be. At present, the most controversial issue is that of the level of car parking charges, which have risen markedly (though in the price-cap period, there was a dual till in place, and car parking charges were not subject to any regulation). The Australian approach to LHR is now influencing thought elsewhere, particularly in the new arrangements for London's Gatwick and Stansted airports.

Further research

The wide range of issues discussed in this review shows that airports are a deceptively complex industry. This is reflected in the research on airports, which is largely comparable to that on airlines – a much larger industry. While many issues have been settled, there is still debate on a number of areas. Some of these are:

- To what extent are there economies of scale in airports, and what is the scale elasticity?
- How strong is competition in various country markets, and to what extent is regulation needed or desirable?
- Are the complementarities between aeronautical and non-aeronautical services strong? If so, do they weaken or eliminate the case for regulation?
- Why is peak pricing almost entirely absent from airports, and are slots an efficient alternative for rationing scarce capacity?
- Is new capacity being built where it is needed? If not, to what extent is regulation helping or hindering the matching of demand to capacity?
- Why are so many countries privatizing their airports only partially, although such a form yields poor results in terms of efficiency?
- Why is it so difficult for policy to reform slot allocation, and reform regulation to set strong incentives for efficiency?

Addressing these and other issues should not only result in airport economists being gainfully employed for some time, but more importantly, should also produce research that is directly relevant for transport policy.

Notes

1 As in Spain, Norway, Sweden, Denmark, Ireland, etc., Italy gave up its national company by moving to privatization and Portugal also sold off most of the airports from the national company ANA.
2 The latter was approved by the Austrian, but not by the Slovakian, Competition Authorities.
3 The most prominent exception is the ATC of the UK, which is a partly privatized firm.
4 They use a market power indicator based market share of airport in the NATS 3 region within 100 km, and switching options for airlines and passengers.
5 Some airports have separated ground handling activities into a new company, which can then be active at a number of airports, as Hamburg does with AHS. We observed similar multi-plant activities in retailing; for example, Frankfurt airport operates retail concessions at Boston, Baltimore, Washington International, Cleveland, and Pittsburg, as does the BAA Airport Group.
6 A market is said to be two-sided when the volume of transactions on both sides is affected by a change in the price of one side of the market, keeping the total price constant.
7 This line of research is limited to short-term cost efficiency, as investment and capital cannot be analyzed due to data restrictions.

References

ACI Airport Economics Survey (2008) Airport Council International, Montreal, Canada.

Adler, N., Forsyth, P., Müller, J. and Niemeier, H-M. (2015) An economic assessment of airport incentive regulation, Transport Policy, 41, 5–15.

Adler, N. and Liebert, V. (2014) Joint impact of competition, ownership form and economic regulation on airport performance and pricing, *Transportation Research Part A*, 64, 92–109.

Adler, N., Ülkü, T. and Yazhemsky, E. (2013) Small regional airport sustainability: Lessons from benchmarking, *Journal of Air Transport Management*, 33, 22–31.

Airports Commission (2013), *Airports Commission: Interim Report*, Airports Commission, London, December.

Arblaster, M. (2014) The design of light-handed regulation of airports: Lessons from experience in Australia and New Zealand, *Journal of Air Transport Management*, 38, 27–35.

Armstrong, M. (2006) Competition in two-sided markets. *RAND Journal of Economics*, 37, 668–691.

Assaf, A.G. and Gillen, D. (2012) Measuring the joint impact of governance form and economic regulation on airport efficiency, *European Journal of Operational Research*, 220, 187–198.

Bilotkach, V. and Müller, J. (2012) Supply side substitutability and potential market power of airports: Case of Amsterdam Schiphol, *Utilities Policy*, 23(C), 5–12.

Bluth, P. (2008) The commercial future of ground handling at airports, ACI Europe Airport Exchange Conference, 28 October 2008, Berlin.

Borenstein, S. (1989) Hubs and high fares: dominance and market power in the US airline industry, *RAND Journal of Economics*, 20, 344–365.

Brueckner, J. (2002) Airport congestion when carriers have market power, *American Economic Review*, 92, 1357–1375.

Copenhagen Economics (2012) *Airport Competition in Europe*. Copenhagen: Copenhagen Economics.

Czerny, A., Forsyth, P., Gillen, D. and Niemeier, H-M. (eds) (2008) *Airport Slots, International Experiences and Options for Reform*. Burlington: Ashgate.

Forsyth, P. (2003) Replacing Regulation: Airport Price Monitoring in Australia, in P. Forsyth, D. Gillen, A. Knorr, W. Mayer, H-M. Niemeier and D. Starkie (eds), *The Economic Regulation of Airports: Recent Developments in Australasia, North America and Europe*. Aldershot: Ashgate, pp. 3–22.

Forsyth, P. (2008) Airport Policy in Australia and New Zealand: Privatization, light-handed regulation and performance, in C. Winston and G. de Rus (eds), *Aviation Infrastructure Performance: A Study in Comparative Political Economy*. Washington, DC: Brookings Institution Press, pp. 65–99.

Forsyth, P. and Niemeier, H-M. (2008) Price regulation and the choice of price structures at busy airports, in A. Czerny, P. Forsyth, D. Gillen and H-M. Niemeier (eds), *Airport Slots. International Experiences and Options for Reform*. Aldershot: Ashgate, pp. 127–148.

Forsyth, P., Niemeier, H-M. and Wolf, H. (2011) Airport alliances and mergers – Structural change in the airport industry? *Journal of Air Transport Management*, 17, 49–56.

Frontier Economics (2000) *Schiphol Airport: Market Definition Study*, prepared for the NMa, London.

GAP Database (2014) available at: www.GAP-projekt.de (accessed 18 August 2015).

Gillen, D. (2011) The evolution of airport ownership and governance, *Journal of Air Transport Management*, 17, 3–13.

Gillen, D. and H. M. Niemeier (2008) *The European Union: Evolution of Privatization, Regulation, and Slot Reform*, in C. Winston and G. de Rus (eds), Aviation Infrastructure Performance *A Study in Comparative Political Economy*, Washington, Brookings Institution Press, pp. 36–64.

Hakimo, R. and Müller, J. (2015) Charges of uncongested German airports: do they follow Ramsey pricing scheme? *Research in Transportation Economics*, Elsevier, forthcoming.

Halpern, N. and Graham, A. (2013) *Airport Marketing*. London: Routledge.

IATA International Air Transport Association (2011) Vision 2050 – Shaping Aviation's Future, Singapore. Available at: http://www.iata.org/pressroom/facts_figures/Documents/vision-2050.pdf (accessed 18 August 2015).

InterVISTAS (2006) *Measuring the Economic Rate of Return on Investment in Aviation*. Vancouver: InterVISTAS.

Kamp, V., Niemeier, H-M. and Müller, J. (2007) What can be learned from benchmarking studies? Examining the apparent poor performance of German airports, *Journal of Airport Management*, 1(3), 294–308.

Lechmann, M. and Niemeier, H-M. (2013) Economies of scale and scope of airports – a critical survey, *Journal of Air Transport Studies*, 4(2), 1–25.

Liebert, V. and Niemeier, H-M. (2013) A survey of empirical research on the productivity and efficiency measurement of airports, *Journal of Transport Economics and Policy*, 47, 157–189.

Maertens, S. (2012) Estimating the market power of airports in their catchment areas – a Europe-wide approach, *Journal of Transport Geography*, 22, 10–18.

Malina, R. (2010) Competition in the German airport market – an empirical investigation, in P. Forsyth, D. Gillen, J. Müller and H-M. Niemeier (eds) *Airport Competition. The European Experience*. Farnham: Ashgate, pp. 239–260.

Malavolti, E. (2010) Single till or dual till at airports: a two-sided market analysis, 12th World Conference on Transport Research, 11–15 July 2010, Lisbon, Portugal.

Martín, J.C. and Voltes-Dorta, A. (2008) International airports: economies of scale and marginal costs, *Journal of the Transportation Research Forum*, 47(1), 1–22.

Martín, J.C. and Voltes-Dorta, A. (2011) The dilemma between capacity expansions and multi-airport systems: Empirical evidence from the industry's cost function, *Transportation Research Part E*, 47, 382–389.

Morrison, S.A. (1982) The structure of landing fees at uncongested airports, *Journal of Transport Economics and Policy*, 16, 151–159.

Morrison, S.A. and Winston, C. (1995) *The Evolution of the Airline Industry*. Washington, DC: Brookings Institution Press.

Morrison, S. and Winston, C. (2008) Delayed! US Aviation Policy at a Crossroads, in C. Winston and G. de Rus (eds) *Aviation Infrastructure Performance A Study in Comparative Political Economy*. Washington, DC: Brookings Institution Press, pp 7–35.

Müller, J. Bilotkach, V., Fichert, F., Niemeier, H-M., Pels, E. and Polk, A. (2010) The economic market power of Amsterdam Airport Schiphol. Study commissioned by the Netherlands Competition Authority (NMa), April. Available at: http://www.nmanet.nl/nederlands/home/Actueel/Publicaties/Consultatiedoc/Consultatie_NMa-rapportage_economische_machtspositie_Schiphol.asp (access date: 18 August 2015).

Müller-Rostin, C., Ehmer, H., Hannak, I., Ivanova, P., Müller, J. and Niemeier, H-M. (2010) Market entry and market exit in the European airport market, in P. Forsyth, D. Gillen, J. Müller and H-M. Niemeier (eds) *Airport Competition: The European Experience*. Aldershot: Ashgate, pp. 27–46.

Niemeier, H-M. (2001) On the use and abuse of impact analysis for airports: a critical view from the perspective of regional policy, in W. Pfähler (ed.) *Regional Input Output Analysis: Conceptual Issues, Airport Case Studies and Extensions*. Baden-Baden: HWWA Studies, Nomos Verlagsgesellschaft, pp. 201–222.

Niemeier, H-M (2009) Regulation of large airports: Status quo and options for reform, OECD/ITF Joint Transport Research Centre Discussion Paper, No. 2009–10.

Niemeier, H. (2010) Effective Regulatory Institutions for Air Transport: A European Perspective, OECD/ITF Joint Transport Research Centre Discussion Papers, No. 2010/20, OECD Publishing, Paris.

Oum, T.H., Adler, N. and Yu, C. (2006) Privatization, corporatization, ownership forms and their effects on the performance of the world's major airports, *Journal of Air Transport Management*, 12(3), 109–121.

Oum, T.H., Yan, J. and Yu, C. (2008) Ownership forms matter for airport efficiency: A stochastic frontier investigation of worldwide airports, *Journal of Urban Economics*, 64(2), 422–435.

Oum, T.H. and Yu, C. (2004) Measuring airports' operating efficiency: a summary of the 2003 ATRS global airport benchmarking report, *Transportation Research Part E*, 40(6), 515–532.

Oum, T.H., Yu, C. and Fu, X. (2003) A comparative analysis of productivity performance of the world's major airports, summary report of the ATRS global airport benchmarking research report – 2002, *Journal of Air Transport Management*, 9(5), 285–297.

Parker, D. (1999) The performance of BAA before and after privatisation: A DEA study, *Journal of Transport Economics and Policy*, 33(2), 133–145.

Pearce, B. and Smyth, M. (2007) *Aviation Economic Benefits*, IATA Economics Briefing 8, IATA (International Air Transport Association), Geneva.

Pearce, B. and Wiltshire, J. (2013) *Airport Competition*, IATA Economics Briefing 11, IATA. (International Air Transport Association), Geneva.

Starkie, D. (2002) Airport regulation and competition, *Journal of Air Transport Management*, 8, 53–72.

Starkie, D. (2003) The economics of secondary markets for airport slots, in K. Boyfield (ed.) *A Market in Airport Slots*, IEA, Readings 56, London, pp. 51–79.

Starkie, D. (2008a) A critique of the single-till, in D. Starkie (ed.) *Aviation Markets*. Aldershot: Ashgate, pp. 123–130.

Starkie, D. (2008b) The airport industry in a competitive environment: A United Kingdom perspective. Discussion Paper No. 2008–15, OECD/ITF.

Starkie, D. and Hogan, O. (2003) Calculating the Short-Run Marginal Infrastructure Costs of Runway Use: An Application to Dublin Airport, in P. Forsyth, D. Gillen, A. Knorr, O. Mayer, H-M Niemeier, and D. Starkie (eds) *The Economic Regulation of Airports: Recent Developments in Australasia, North America and Europe*. Aldershot: Ashgate, pp. 75–82.

Tovar, B. and Martín-Cejas, R.R. (2009) Are outsourcing and non-aeronautical revenues important drivers in the efficiency of Spanish airports? *Journal of Air Transport Management*, 15(5), 217–220.

Transport Research Laboratory (2002) *Airport Performance Indicators*. Wokingham: TRL.

Vasigh, B. and J. Gorjidooz (2006) Productivity analysis of public and private airports, A causal investigation, *Journal of Air Transportation*, 11(3), 144–163.

Venables, A. (2007) Evaluating urban transport investments: cost-benefit analysis in the presence of agglomeration and income taxation, *Journal of Transport Economics and Policy*, 41(2), 173–188.

Yokomi, M. (2005) Measurement of Malmquist index of privatized BAA plc. Paper submitted to the 9th Air Transport Research Society Conference 2005, 3–7 July 2005, Rio de Janeiro.

Zhang, A. and Zhang, Y. (2010) Airport capacity and congestion pricing with both aeronautical and commercial operations, *Transport Research*, 44, 404–413.

27

Strategic challenges in urban transport

Beat Mueller

Introduction

In this chapter we will discuss the view of operators towards the challenges of urban public transport. After setting the context and explaining the regulatory environment, we will highlight current and future challenges facing urban public transport operators, and provide possible responses to these challenges.

The chapter is written from the operator's perspective while trying to take into account the effects on passengers, authorities and other stakeholders. Although it includes experiences and examples from all continents, the focus will be on the situation in developed countries, mainly Europe, North America and Asia.

The context

Of the world's population, 54 percent (UN Department of Economic and Social Affairs, 2014) reside in urban areas, and seven out of every 10 people will live in cities by 2050, with about 90 percent of the growth in developing countries (UN-Habitat, 2013). Public transport has a very important role in the life of most citizens. In the European Union (EU), approximately 57 billion trips were made using local public transport (UITP, 2014b). In comparison, long-distance rail had only about one billion journeys and commercial air services only about 800 million (UITP, 2014b). The 57 billion trips in local public transport represent, on average, over 182 million journeys per day or about 50 trips per year for each inhabitant. The sector employs over two million people and contributes around €140 billion to the economy, representing about 1.1 percent of the EU's gross domestic product (UITP, 2014b).

Over the last 12 years, public transport growth has continued despite the negative effect of the 2009 crisis. In the European Union alone, in 2012 an average of 8 percent more public transport trips were taken than in 2000; this was about level with the pre-crisis peak of 2008 (UITP, 2014b). This average growth is underpinned by a complex picture when considering national contexts, with some countries showing 20 percent or more growth (Austria, Belgium, France, Sweden, and the UK), others around 10 percent growth (Germany, Italy), and some close to stagnation (Denmark, Finland, and Ireland) or even having a negative demand evolution (Baltic States, Eastern Europe, Portugal, and Spain).

Regulatory context and industry setup

Public transport started as a private initiative for a new commercial service with the state only acting as an observer and eventually intervening with safety regulations. As shown by Veeneman (2002: 10–11) the state involvement followed a gradual approach, moving from observation to regulation of safety and of operations, then supporting the service financially, before finally taking over the services provided – often in the case of the private promoter's bankruptcy. Since the 1980s, the growing complexity of public transport services and concerns over the lack of cost efficiency in the public provision of services has driven the delegation of service provision to private operators. Based on theoretical research from the Chicago School of Economics, this trend started in the US and the UK in the 1980s. It lead to the deregulation of public transport and other industries under the presidencies of Ronald Reagan in the US and Margaret Thatcher in the UK (Demsetz, 1968).

The UK bus market outside of London was fully deregulated in the Transport Act of 1985, meaning that any operator could start or stop any new line and freely define its timetable and tariff (Stanley, 2011). This extreme withdrawal of the state from the organization of public transport initially led to increased competition, but also rapidly to complaints about service, quality, and safety issues regarding UK public bus transport. Other European countries adopted a more nuanced attitude towards privatization and deregulation, either not opening their public transport to competition at all, or choosing an intermediate form of outsourcing to the private sector, mainly through competitive tendering. Thereby, the state no longer provides the public with transport services, but concludes a public-service obligation contract with a private operator that is chosen via an open tender (Stanley, 2011).

Spain adopted this tendering system in the 1980s (Garcia-Pastor *et al.*, 2013). Similarly, France rendered compulsory competitive tendering in places where there was no public operator, mainly outside the Paris region and some big cities (Loi Sapin, 1993). In parallel, the European Commission pushed hard towards competitive tendering, but had to accept a compromise in 2007 that continued to allow both internal service provision by the state and competitive tendering, while proscribing for both organizational approaches the conclusion of a public-service obligation contract (European Union, 2007).

Therefore, currently in European public transport organization there is a parallel system of either direct awarding to an internal operator or competitive tendering of services to private operators. In general, the bigger cities have kept their internal, city-owned public operator while the smaller cities have opted for competitive tendering. Exceptions are the cities of London and Copenhagen, which have set up a strong transport authority in charge of planning, ticketing, and marketing, and tender out only the operational part of bus and rail public transport on a line-by-line basis (UITP, 2015).

Outside Europe, the same basic organizational setup exists, where the bigger cities retain their internal operator and smaller cities and countries prefer competitive tendering.

To summarize, Table 27.1 shows the main features and applications of the three primary organizational setups.

Interestingly, there has been very little change in the design and application of the above-described organizational regimes. More than 20 years ago, Berechman (1993) argued for a distinction between direct awarding and competitive tendering based on the size of the urban transport area. In his view, competitive tendering was inefficient for large urban areas above

Table 27.1 Organizational forms of urban public transport

Type of organizational regime	*Description*	*Application*
Direct-awarding to an internal, state-owned operator	The state itself provides the service, usually through a state-owned public company that has an exclusive right to provide public transport in a given area.	Still a primary organizational regime in urban public transport used in almost all big cities worldwide and in some smaller cities, mainly in China and Eastern Europe.
State concessions awarded through competitive tendering	Intermediate form where exclusive right to operate a given service is awarded competitively to an independent operator.	Urban transport in smaller cities and regional services worldwide, especially Northern Europe, France, Spain, Australia and New Zealand.
Full deregulation and market initiative	Any operator can start their own service without state intervention in the planning or financing of the service.	Commercial services, mainly long-distance coach, and some urban and suburban services in the UK, Sweden, Africa and Latin American countries.

Source: Author's own elaboration based on Macario (2014) and van de Velde (1999).

100,000–150,000 inhabitants. Although the limit Berechman proposed seems low, this distinction has largely remained in practice.

The only exceptions have been the line-tendering models developed in London and Copenhagen, where a strong public planning authority tenders the pure operation of lines. However, some might argue that in these cases the role of the urban transport authorities encompasses such operational responsibilities as planning, timetabling, ticketing, marketing and quality control, and therefore is indeed just a sub-form of the direct in-house provision of urban transport (UITP, 2015).

Current challenges to operators

This section will list and explain the main challenges that public transport operators face today. It will first describe the challenges individually, before presenting some response strategies to these challenges for operators.

The chosen list of challenges and its grouping into three main aspects – increasing requirements, fare revenue, and public sector constraints – follows an approach where we will first look at the cost or expense side, then consider the revenues available to finance these costs, which come from fares from passengers and contributions from the public sector.

Increasing requirements regarding quality and service

In addition to the increase in the urban population, another phenomena influences public transport demand: the ageing of the world is a demographic phenomenon characterized by a decrease in fertility, a decrease in mortality rate, and a higher life expectancy among populations. The consequence is a structural change of public transport users with a much higher proportion of elderly and disabled. In turn, this has led to new legislation for the accessibility requirements for elderly and disabled passengers on public transport. The necessary adaptations to vehicles and infrastructures, as well as the creation of specific on-demand transport services for elderly and disabled people, has put heavy pressure on transport authorities and operators to divert investment funds in order to comply with this new regulation (European Union, 2014).

Environmental concerns have also influenced the public transport sector (European Environment Agency, 2015). For many years, concerns – mainly about air quality and noise – were pushing for the further development of public transport. The more recent concern about global warming, and in consequence the goal of reducing greenhouse gases, has changed this slightly. The transport sector has high greenhouse gas emissions and more than two-thirds of transport-related greenhouse gas emissions are from road transport. As the car industry has improved its energy efficiency and decreased its greenhouse gas contribution, the environmental requirements for cleaner vehicles and CO_2 reduction have been extended to public transport vehicles that have been lagging behind in reducing their pollution. This has led to new pollution standards for buses and a strong push for hybrid and electricity-powered public transport, as per the example of Euro6 in Europe. These cleaner vehicles are still not economically self-financing, meaning that their fuel savings do not recoup the additional cost of purchase. This, therefore, creates another financial strain on operators and authorities, which can lead in cases of fixed budgets towards the acquisition of fewer, but cleaner, vehicles and, therefore, less public transport on offer. Extreme calls in several cities to abandon diesel-powered buses altogether, in favor of electric or hybrid buses (China, Paris, and Oslo), have placed additional uncertainty on operators' long-term investment plans. Electric buses, except for trolley buses that run on fixed electric power lines, are still in a development stage and uneconomic. It is to be expected that improvements in battery technology might improve this in 10 to 20 years from now. Other alternative fuels have either been abandoned (biogas, biofuel, and liquid gas) or are still in an early development stage (hydrogen). In Europe, the European commission has been trying for several years to stimulate the development of fuel-cell buses that run on hydrogen through their 'Clean Hydrogen Initiative in Cities' project (CHIC, 2014). The scope of this project is to demonstrate the feasibility of hydrogen-powered fuel-cell buses in everyday operations in nine European cities over a five-year period. Currently, negotiations are under way for the establishment of a follow-up project that is intended to extend the trial from 56 to over 200 buses via a massive reduction in the price of these buses from manufacturers (CHIC, 2014).

In the meantime, public transport passengers are becoming used to having real-time information in vehicles, at stations, and increasingly on mobile devices. Generic mobility information platforms are created by transport authorities and private information technology (IT) providers in order to avoid users needing to open one specific mobile application or Internet site per operator. This means that public transport operators will have to be able to produce and provide real-time data on their operations; this data will not be valued by the operator, but considered public data to be put on open platforms (open data movement), thereby depriving operators of a potential revenue source to pay for this additional service. Of course, the fear in the industry is that these new private mobility platforms will, in time, monopolize ticket sales, as has happened in the travel industry with hotel bookings. Nevertheless, potential distribution commissions to be paid to new intermediaries, such as mobility information platforms, have to be offset against additional sales. For example, tourists and other foreign visitors are usually reluctant to use public transport for fear of failing to find their way or not being able to buy the correct tickets easily. Also to be considered are lower distribution costs on traditional channels, such as the hugely expensive-to-maintain ticketing machines and sales offices.

Fare policy and the effect on cost coverage ratios

The recognized positive contribution of urban public transport to social integration and to the environment (reduction of pollution, noise, and congestion) has tempted politicians all over the world to advocate for low public transport tariffs in order to attract more passengers to the service. Often, these promotional tariffs start as temporary measures, but end up as permanent price reductions. In particular, the price reductions offered to certain groups of users and voters, such as the elderly or families, have proven very difficult to resist or to revert. It has therefore become a well-used practice to partially or completely exempt large groups of users from paying for the use of public transport.

In consequence, despite the fact that usage of public transport has increased, the revenues from passengers have stagnated or even decreased over the last decade (UITP, 2014a). In some cities, the share of passenger revenues has become so low (typically below 10–20 percent of costs), that calls for the general gratuity of the service in order to save the proportionally high costs of distribution and fraud prevention have emerged (Reynolds, 2008).

The few real examples of free urban transport, such as in Tallinn/Estonia, Aubagne or Boulogne-Billancourt/France, Hasselt or Mons/Belgium have had rather mixed results (Cats *et al.*, 2014; UTP, 2010). Some initial increases in passenger numbers have quickly ebbed and been offset by problems with the squatting of vehicles by the homeless and other problematic populations. Gratuity has lost most of its proponents and some of the early adopters, such as the city of Hasselt in Belgium, have since reverted to a paying service.

The continued deterioration of the cost-coverage ratios of public transport has been worsened by the requirements of the modified international accounting standards, on the one hand from the European System of National and Regional Accounts 2010 (ESA) (Eurostat, 2013) and on the other hand from IPSAS/IFRS (IPSASB, 2015) that force operators to include infrastructure costs (such as depreciation and financing) and to exclude non-transport-related revenues, such as real estate developments and commercial activities.

In consequence, the target ratio of at least 50 percent of the total costs being covered by passenger revenues on urban transport becomes increasingly difficult to reach, which creates a negative image of public transport in the majority financed by taxpayers rather than passengers.

Public finance constraints

Despite the general political will in favor of a further development, and even extension, of public transport, the state contributions for public transport have also come under pressure in the aftermath of the financial and economic crisis following the collapse of the Lehman Brothers in September 2008. As an example, Spain and Italy had to cut their respective contributions by 30–40 percent, leading the operators to cut their service offerings and, at the same time, increase fares for passengers. The result has been a substantial reduction in ridership by 10–20 percent, also partly motivated by lower tourism and leisure activity in those countries in the aftermath of the financial crisis (UITP, 2014b).

The financial crisis has also slowed the pace of investments in public transport infrastructure. Financial markets have become much more risk-averse and have also suddenly factored in the possibility of default or renegotiation of government support in their appraisal of public infrastructure projects financed as public–private partnerships. Private (co-) financing of investment projects has therefore become more difficult to obtain. On the other hand, the public sector could not compensate either, having seen its debt ratios explode after the costly banking bailouts. Therefore, they have had to cut their investment envelopes and put on hold plans for new public transport infrastructure such as train, tramway, or metro lines. As a consequence, old-fashioned bus transport and conventional rail has seen its attractiveness increase, as these modes necessitate much lower investments and offer greater flexibility for eventual service adaptations.

Responses of operators to the current challenges

The increasing requirements regarding the quality and service of urban public transport described earlier have put enormous demands on operators over recent years. It has become almost impossible for a medium-sized company to fulfill the technical and commercial requirements of a current urban transport service, at least in places where the state has not set up a strong transport authority to provide at least part of these services for the operators, as in London or Copenhagen.

Parallel to this, public transport operators had to increase their productivity and learn to adapt to a new world of savings and service reductions after years of expansion and growth. Increased scrutiny of their profit margins by contributing authorities and increased competition through tendering under public finance constraints have also reduced the profitability and, therefore, attractiveness of the sector to investors.

Operators' first response strategies have been to increase requirements, and pressure for productivity has led to consolidation of the industry into larger, more efficient companies that are able to respond to the increasing requirements of passengers and authorities with sufficient specialist expertise, while at the same time being big enough to reap economies of scale in operations and purchasing (Di Giacomo and Ottoz, 2010).

In reaction, a lot of small and medium-sized family enterprises and small public companies have been bought by, or merged with, bigger operators, private or public. The remaining family-owned operators are either specialized in niche services, such as taxis or tourism, or act as subcontractors for the bigger operators that then assume the planning, marketing, and IT aspects.

Uncertainty exists about further tightening of the legal framework in the European Union (EU 1370 Directive) and about the measures of liberalization of the railway sector contained in the Fourth Railway Package that are currently stalled in the EU parliament. The combination of lower (or inexistent) growth, lower (or inexistent) profits, and uncertainty about the future regulatory environment have led to a loss of interest from private capital, notably in the stock markets. Several stock-listed companies have divested their public transport sectors – Macquarie Bank and Veolia France being the biggest examples. Others have been taken over by public companies due to a lack of interest from other private investors: for example, Abellio was taken over by Dutch railway company NS in 2009; Arriva by Deutsche Bahn in 2010; Arriva Germany by Italian Railway Company FS in 2011; and Veolia/Transdev by the French State Bank Caisse de Dépôts in 2013 (UITP, 2015).

A second strategy by transport operators (and their owners) has been the increased trend towards public (state) ownership. This has happened either through the cancellation or reversal of planned privatizations of state-owned operators, or the absorption via mergers of formerly privately owned operators by public ones.

As a result, we have seen an emergence of a handful of international/global players that are mainly state owned. These are shown by order of size in Table 27.2.

Besides the seven global players shown in Table 27.2, there exist a great number of local or national operators, which are mainly state-owned and concentrated in their home city and surrounding urban areas. A few of these state-owned city operators have tried to expand

Table 27.2 Biggest international (urban) public transport players in 2014

Company	*Main areas of activity*	*Owner*	*Number of employees*
First Group	North America and UK	Listed on the London stock exchange	117,000
Transdev	Worldwide	Caisse de Dépôts (French State-owned bank)	86,000
RATP Paris	Paris area and through RATP Dev worldwide	French State and Paris city authority	70,000 (of which 13,400 in RATP Dev)
Arriva	All over Europe	German state rail company Deutsche Bahn	55,000 (excluding Deutsche Bahn)
Keolis	Worldwide	French state rail company SNCF	55,000 (excluding SNCF)
National Express	Germany, North America, Spain, and the UK	Listed on the London stock exchange	42,000
MTR Hong Kong	Australia, China, Sweden, and the UK	Listed on the HK Stock Exchange, but majority owned by the Hong Kong government	22,000

Source: Author's own elaboration based on UITP (2015).

nationally, and some even internationally, such as RATP Paris, ATM Milan in Copenhagen, or TMB Barcelona in France, usually under the form of technical assistance or joint ventures. On the other hand, plans to privatize, which were highly popular in the 1990s, have been postponed or abandoned altogether; for example, in Amsterdam and Rotterdam/the Netherlands, or in Eastern Europe. On one side, there seems to be little interest from private investors in such operators with only one major customer – their own city authority – and there is not much to gain from privatization as potential productivity gains might be quickly offset by the necessary profit margins in the private sector. There is also a growing conviction that above a certain size within the public transport system, traditional network tendering is no longer efficient or even possible, and therefore the expected productivity gains from competition are illusory.

After a wave of consolidation in the aftermath of the financial crisis, the current organizational setup with a handful of global players and big local or national champions seems stable; no major changes have happened in recent years, either between global or local players.

On the revenue side, about half the revenues of urban public transport operators come from passengers; thus, these are also called fares or 'farebox' revenues. In Europe, a study from the association of transport authorities has come up with an average of 46 percent of the costs covered by fares (EMTA, 2015) in 25 of the larger European metropolitan areas. In order to keep this ratio close or above the symbolic barrier of 50 percent of costs covered by passengers (and therefore less than 50 percent from public contributions), the operators and their industry association have identified the following measures:

- A clear separation of social and environmental policies from transport policies. This means that the politically motivated lowering of tariffs for certain groups has to be financed and accounted for as a social expense, and not charged to public transport.

- The necessity for regular price increases in order to compensate for general inflation and continued service and network improvements.
- Freedom given to operators to exploit other commercial revenue sources such as advertisements, shops and food stalls at stations, car parks, and real estate developments at stations.

Finally, concerning public contributions, the strategy of public transport operators is to avoid the squeeze on public transport investments and operational contributions by putting public transport financing on a new, more solid basis. Italy created a public transport fund in 2012 to be financed mainly by an increase in petrol taxes, which will eventually cover about 80 percent of the public transport contributions, replacing the uncertain part coming from the national general budget (Buglione, 2014). Early results suggest that the complete dependence on volatile petrol tax revenues that are due to higher fuel efficiency tend to decrease over time and will pose a challenge to that setup. A more balanced financing approach has been adopted by the new infrastructure investment fund in Switzerland, approved by a national referendum in February 2014, that combines various sources on top of petrol taxes, such as a part of value added tax (VAT) or a levy on lorries (OFT, 2013). Germany also has plans to create a permanent infrastructure fund, including public transport infrastructure (Hickel, 2015), and the US are debating how to reform and extend the notoriously underfunded federal highway fund (Kelly, 2015).

Other governments are looking into consolidating and decentralizing all transport-related competencies to local or regional authorities, which can then apply a differentiated approach and also experiment with local solutions. Some ideas tested and implemented in several countries include better parking management and taxation, road tolls and congestion charges, and better integration of urban, regional and school transport. Therefore, the financial crisis of 2009 and its aftermath may at least have advanced the cause of stable, well-defined and well-sourced financing for public transport, particularly through new funds earmarked for infrastructure.

Future challenges and possible evolutions

This section will list some future challenges that public transport operators will face over the coming years. It will first describe these challenges individually, and then assess the readiness and possible strategies for operators to prepare for these challenges.

For many years, experts have been predicting a reduction of mobility needs through a combination of the effects of workplace decentralization, urban densification, and new teleworking practices. So far, none of the three underlying causes have produced an actual reduction of mobility:

- Workplace decentralization of public sector jobs in some countries has been more than compensated for by the opposite trend in the private sector, with multinational companies setting up regional or national head offices and shared service centers in urban centers.
- Urban densification has been promoted for over 50 years, but the actual trend is clearly against the building of new dense housing estates and back to smaller apartment blocks with a maximum of green space around them. Skyscrapers, although popular with architects and multinational companies, are almost exclusively built for office purposes, forcing more people to commute to the city, rather than fewer. On the other hand, the decline in population within cities has been halted in the Western world and most cities now see positive growth rates in jobs and residents. In Asia, Africa, and Latin America the rampant

urbanization, fueled by an overall population growth and rapid economic development, has continued and even accelerated.

- Teleworking has definitely become a reality in the sense that modern communication technology allows access to information from almost anywhere. This has led to a real trend in favor of 24-hour and seven-days-a-week accessibility for modern workers, but without provoking a reduction in the need to move around or to commute to the office. Even readily available and cheap videoconferencing technologies have not replaced the need for face-to-face communication and for coming together in the office. These tools seem to have increased individual productivity, but without bringing a reduction to commutes and overall mobility.

In consequence, there is no observable trend for an expected halt in mobility growth, or even a reduction in mobility needs (Mbeche, 2013). On the contrary, the underlying positive drivers of urban mobility and public transport will continue over the next decades, notably in the form of:

- Overall population growth and continued urbanization;
- Economic growth, allowing for higher incomes and more spending on leisure activities, thereby increasing mobility demands;
- Environmental concerns favoring public transport over private cars in order to reduce air pollution and global warming.

Challenges to operators include the effects of the 'sharing economy' on the demand for public transport. Although the sharing economy, in which people will share their belongings rather than own them, is a rather idealistic, almost utopian, concept that is unlikely to go beyond the circles of modern revolutionaries, the appearance of IT-based solutions has made some concepts, such as bike sharing, car sharing, or car pooling rather popular. Almost all cities in the Western world offer a bike-sharing system that allows consumers to rent a bike for short periods at one of the many unmanned stations in the city and to leave the bike at another station at the end of the rental period. As these systems are strongly supported by city governments and have been initially cross-financed by advertising on nearby public ground, the user fee is almost zero and is usually limited to a low annual membership fee and a symbolic per usage fee. Bike sharing (or renting) systems do not pose a threat to public transport and have to be seen as a complement providing the 'last mile' transport inside the hyper center.

A different situation arises if the concept of bike sharing is extended to short-term, automated car rentals, often confusingly referred to as car sharing. Most large European cities now have one or several such systems, allowing members to use a car for one-way, very short-term rentals, by simply searching for the nearest available car using their mobile phone. The newest of these systems do not require designated stations or parking spots, which lowers their costs even further. The car industry is actively supporting these new offers and most cities are happy to offer residents an additional form of mobility, without having to invest themselves. It is yet to be seen whether these offers will cannibalize public transport, or, on the other hand, complement and help it by allowing people to forego ownership of a car by offering cheap rentals on the few occasions they want or need such transport.

A less controversial form of new mobility is car-pooling, which allows car owners to advertise and share (actually rent seats) on their trips. These pose a challenge to long-distance buses and trains, but not to urban transport. Another more threatening application of the car-pooling concept is its commercial application, in which car owners actually act like taxis without being affiliated with traditional, often strongly regulated taxi organizations. After years of self-employed 'black' taxis and small limousine companies, the recent emergence of the mobile service provided by American IT company Uber is the best example of this new application. The advantage of the Uber offer is that it renders commercial car-pooling safe and easy for users (through Uber's reputation and payment features) while optimizing productivity through the company's routing optimization software. The result is a very easy to use and cheap service, which threatens traditional taxis as well as public transport. Despite protests by taxi owners worldwide that have led to regulatory restrictions in many countries, Uber was valued at $41 billion in December 2014 (Bradshaw, 2014), compared to $1.5 billion of First Group, the biggest stock-listed public transport operator with 117,000 employees (FirstGroup, 2015).

The hottest current topic, and probably the most serious potential threat to public transport in the long run, is the development of autonomous vehicles that might one day replace the need for public transport for people unable to drive, as well as reduce the attraction of public transport for other passengers. As the recent RAND report states:

> By providing a new level of mobility to some users, it may siphon riders (and support) from public transit systems. Currently, one of the key attractions of public transit is riders' ability to undertake other tasks in transit. Autonomous vehicle technology may erode this comparative advantage.
>
> (RAND, 2014, page xvii of summary)

Public transport operators currently hesitate between ignoring and downplaying the subject and are actively trying to engage in it by participating in trials that integrate these self-driving vehicles into their service offering. There are two potential applications put forward for autonomous vehicles in public transport: short-distance shuttle services, as in inner cities or between airport car parks, such as the small service that has been running along the seafront since 2011 in La Rochelle/France (Négroni, 2011), and, potentially, on-demand off-peak services.

Operators' responses to the new challenges

The big worry about the development of ever more complex IT-based transport solutions, such as Uber and autonomous vehicles, relates to the capacity of existing operators to follow and integrate this technology, rather than become dependent on or replaced by new competitors such as Uber or Google. These IT companies have the luxury of concentrating exclusively on the newest technology, without having to run existing operations. They also benefit from enormous capital to invest, either from their profitable other business, as in the case of Google, or from capital markets. State-owned public transport operators have to justify each investment with an almost immediate payoff, and cannot invest in uncertain, early-stage technologies.

Therefore, the only viable strategy for public transport operators is to cooperate with these pure technology companies in more or less loose partnerships in which both parties' interests are catered for. Typically, with respect to timetable data, after initial hesitation operators have come around to an 'open data' policy where they openly share their timetable and real-time operations data, allowing any technology company to use the data in their proprietary applications. Of course, the interest for operators is to provide better and more integrated information to passengers while avoiding the need to build expensive travel information platforms.

The same approach is gaining ground concerning the attitude to adopt versus suppliers of sharing mobility solutions: public transport operators are increasingly willing to partner with the sharing providers as they see their offer as a complement to traditional public transport, rather then as competition. Indeed, despite rapid growth and expansion of the various sharing solutions, these remain minor in terms of number of trips made, but can actually provide an attractive complementary offer to public transport, notably in areas and times of day where little public transport is offered. Therefore, they can actually provide a cost-effective complementary offer in place of an expensive extension of traditional public transport.

With respect to autonomous cars and buses, it is debatable how quickly these will reach normal traffic and how easily the public will accept them. Nevertheless, public transport operators have every intention to follow the development in order to adopt the technology for their own service. In more developed countries, the driver is the most expensive component of a public transport service. Therefore, autonomous buses, trams, or metros might provide significant cost savings to public transport (RAND, 2014).

Conclusion

With an end in sight to the economic downturn following the financial crisis and the consequential reduction of passenger increases, and therefore service extensions, the public transport sector has every reason to be optimistic about the future. Environmental concerns about air pollution and global warming are strongly supporting renewed public support in the extension of public transport networks. The financial crisis has also shown potential limits to the once-championed introduction of private capital and competition into public transport. Therefore, the current setup, with a handful of global players and some local champions, most of them state-owned, seems to be durable.

Public transport operators and transport authorities have understood that a solid financing setup for public transport is a necessary basis for stable and predictable long-term development. Therefore, many initiatives are underway all around the world to improve the resilience of public transport financing, higher passenger contributions, regular tariff increases or even indexation formulas, and increased local competence and resources through parking levies and value-capture systems (Suzuki *et al.*, 2014). Even on the infrastructure side, the crisis-induced underinvestment phase of the last decade has brought awareness of a need for a better long-term planning and funding solution for infrastructure, notably through dedicated taxes, such as fuel or road taxes.

The future looks rather bright for public transport operators worldwide. Due to population growth, urbanization, and environmental policies, there will be light growth in public transport offers in Europe and North America and fast development in Asia, Africa, and Latin America. Even in Europe, the modal share of public transport in urban areas is only around 20 percent, with over 50 percent still using their own private car, leaving plenty of room for growth in public transport. Even the new technologies and sharing services (car, bike, and taxi), do not seem to pose a threat to traditional public transport, and might even be actively integrated by public transport operators to enhance their offer and reduce costs.

References

Berechman, J. (1993) *Public Transit Economics and Deregulation Policy*. Amsterdam: North-Holland.

Bradshaw, T. (2014) Uber valued at $40bn in latest funding round. Financial Times edition of December 4. Available at: http://www.ft.com/cms/s/0/66a76576-7bdc-11e4-a7b8-00144feabdc0.html, accessed 18 March 2015.

Buglione, E. (2014) Italian regionalism: between unitary traditions and federal processes, *Essays on Federalism and Regionalism*, Vol. 1, 307–334.

Cats, O., Reimal, T. and Susilo, Y. (2014) Public transport pricing policy: Empirical evidence from a fare-free scheme in Tallinn, Estonia. *Transportation Research Record TRR*. Washington: Transportation Research Board, pp. 89–96.
Clean Hydrogen in European Cities (CHIC) (2014) CHIC (Clean Hydrogen in European Cities) Project Overview. Available at: http://chic-project.eu/about-us/what-is-chic/chic-in-brief, accessed 20 March 2015.
Demsetz, H. (1968) Why regulate utilities? *Journal of Law and Economics* 11(1), 55–65.
Di Giacomo, M. and Ottoz, E. (2010) The relevance of sale and scope economies in the provision of urban and intercity bus transport, *Journal of Transport Economics and Policy*, 44(2), 161–187.
European Environment Agency (2015) *The European environment, State And Outlook 2015*. Copenhagen: European Environment Agency.
European Metropolitan Transport Authority Association (EMTA) (2015) Cost coverage by fare revenues in 24 European urban transport areas. *EMTA Barometer 2013*, EMTA Paris, January.
European Union (2007) Regulation no. 1370/2007 on public transport services by rail and by road, European Parliament and the Council of Ministers of the European Union, Brussels, 23 October.
European Union (2014) Guidelines for (the introduction of) accessibility and safety concepts in future design of bus systems, 3iBS (Intelligent, Innovative, Integrated Bus System) project, European Commission, Brussels, March 25.
Eurostat (2013) European System of National and Regional Accounts 2010 (ESA 2010), European Commission, Brussels, 26 June.
Federal Office of Transport (OFT) (2013) *FAIF: Comment Fonctionne le Financement*, Federal Department of the Environment, Transport, Energy and Communications, Berne, 2 December.
FirstGroup (2015) Share price details: First Group Investors information. Available at: http://www.firstgroupplc.com/investors/share-price/share-price-details.aspx, accessed 20 March 2015.
Garcia-Pastor, A, Gonzalez, J-D., Cristóbal-Pinto, C. and López-Lambas, M. (2013) The Spanish situation of road public transport competition. European Transport Conference, Strasburg, 8–10 October.
Hickel, R. (2015) *Öffentlicher Infrastrukturfonds für Deutschland*. Bremen: Institut Arbeit und Wirtschaft (IAW), Universität und Arbeitnehmerkammer Bremen. Available at http://rhickel.iaw.uni-bremen.de/ccm/homepages/hickel/aktuelles/oeffentlicher-infrastrukturfonds-fuer-deutschland, accessed 20 April 2015.
International Association of Public Transport (UITP) (2014a) Better Public Transport Fare Policy for more resilient funding, Position paper, UITP Transport Economics Commission, Brussels, January.
International Association of Public Transport (UITP) (2014b) Local public transport trends in the European Union, Statistics brief, UITP, Brussels, June.
International Association of Public Transport (UITP) (2014c) The Benefits of Open Data. Position paper, UITP Information Technology and Innovation Commission, Brussels, May.
International Association of Public Transport (UITP) (2015) *Organisation and Major Players of Short-Distance Public Transport. New Developments in the European Union*. Updated and revised edition, UITP EU committee, Brussels, January.
International Public Sector Accounting Standards Board (IPSASB) (2015) *International Public Sector Accounting Standards*. New York: International Federation of Accounts.
Kelly, E. (2015) Congress struggles to find highway funding, *USA Today*. Available at http://www.usatoday.com/story/news/politics/2015/04/09/highway-trust-fund-gas-tax/25361567/, accessed 20 April 2015.
Loi Sapin (1993) *Loi de transparence des procédures publiques, dite 'Loi Sapin'*. (Law for the transparency in public procurement processes, also called 'Loi Sapin'), French legal collection No. 93–122, 29 January.
Macario, R. (2014) Urban public transport in M. Finger and T. Holvad (eds), *Regulating Transport in Europe*, Cheltenham: Edward Elgar, pp. 140–168.
Mbeche, U. (2013) Sustainable urban mobility: Visions beyond Europe, *UN Habitat Contribution to Civitas Forum Sustainable Urban Mobility: Visions Beyond Europe in Brest on October 3*, Civitas, Bruxelles.
Négroni, A. (2011) Un bus électrique sans chauffeur à La Rochelle, *Le Figaro*, edition of 26 May. Available at http://www.lefigaro.fr/actualite-france/2011/05/26/01016-20110526ARTFIG00749-un-bus-electrique-sans-chauffeur-alarochelle.php, accessed 20 April 2015.
RAND Corporation (2014) *Autonomous Vehicle Technology: A Guide for Policymakers*. Santa Monica, CA: RAND Corporation.
Reynolds, J. (2008) Zero fare public transport, *CIV5314: Transport Planning and Policy*. Clayton, Australia: Monash University.

Stanley, J. (2011) Public transport liberalization: achievements and future directions, in M. Finger and R. Kuenneke (eds) *International Handbook of Network Industries: The Liberalization of Infrastructure*. Cheltenham: Edward Elgar, pp. 269–289.

Suzuki, H., Murakami, J., Hong, Y-H. and Tamayose, B. (2014) *Financing Transit-Oriented Development with Land Values*. Washington, DC: World Bank.

United Nations Department of Economic and Social Affairs (2014) *World Urbanization Prospects: the 2014 Revision Highlights*. New York: United Nations.

United Nations Human Settlements Program (UN-Habitat) (2013) *The State of the World's Cities 2012/2013: Prosperity of Cities*. New York: Routledge.

Union des Transports Publics et Ferroviaires (UTP) (2010) *La gratuité dans les transports publics urbains: une fausse bonne idée*. Paris: UTP.

van de Velde, D.M. (1999) *Organisational Forms and Entrepreneurship in Public Transport (Part 1: Classifying Organisational Forms) Transport Policy*, 6th ed., pp. 147–157. Amsterdam: Elsevier.

Veeneman, W. (2002) *Mind the Gap: Bridging Theories and Practice for the Organisation of Metropolitan Public Transport*. Delft: DUP Science.

28

Innovation and public management

Comparing dynamic capabilities in two Swiss wastewater utilities

Eva Lieberherr, Bernhard Truffer and Damian Dominguez

Introduction

Potable water and flushing toilets in households are taken for granted in today's Organization for Economic Co-operation and Development (OECD) countries. Close to 100 percent of the population in most OECD countries has access to safe drinking water, and ca. 70 percent is connected to wastewater treatment plants (Aubin and Varone, 2007; OECD, 2011; OECD Environment Directorate, 2008).[1] This taken-for-granted situation is largely possible due to extensive governmental planning, management, and investments in water and wastewater infrastructure (OECD, 2009). The expansion of domestic water service provision occurred via public subsidies, with service provision provided by primarily local and regional governments and, hence, predominantly public organizations (Citroni, 2010). Indeed, the water and wastewater sectors in OECD countries have been developed as centralized systems of treatment plants and waterworks with vast, integrated networks of water supply mains and wastewater pipes. Accordingly, these sectors can be considered 'typical' public network utility sectors (Luis Manso, 2007: 2).

Despite the high level of water and wastewater service provision in OECD countries, challenges remain in this network industry (OECD, 2011; OECD Environment Directorate, 2008). These include both quality and quantity concerns, such as (micro)pollution, conditions of floods and droughts in the context of climate change, as well as financing (OECD, 2011). For example, dry periods can lead to low run-off in surface waterways, and pollution concerns. Despite high connection rates and extensive infrastructure, OECD countries face major challenges in terms of the costs involved to renovate their water and wastewater systems (OECD, 2011). One OECD report notes a 'significant gap between the funding that is currently available and the investment that is needed [which] will require significant efforts by governments and the private sector around the world' (OECD, 2009: 3).

In light of these challenges, the governance and management of water and wastewater by the government has become questioned (Citroni, 2010). This questioning emerged during the general deregulation and privatization debates in the early 1990s, which swept across different utility sectors. Following these arguments, competitive market set-ups, private-sector participation and new public management (NPM) reforms in the water and wastewater sectors have been proposed to offset the deficits of the public model of service provision (Aubin and Varone, 2007; Massarutto *et al.*, 2007). A primary argument for these reforms has been that private companies are bound to be innovative as they have to survive in a market environment (Eisenhardt and Martin, 2000; Teece *et al.*, 1997). Accordingly, private firms have been regarded as more likely to develop the necessary (dynamic) capabilities; that is, the organizational and strategic routines that enable organizations to create, evolve, and recombine resources (ranging from physical assets to competences such as specific skills) to generate new 'value-creating' strategies and even change the market (cf. Dominguez *et al.*, 2009; Eisenhardt and Martin, 2000: 1107; Gebauer, 2011; Teece, 2007).

There has been an incremental shift toward private actor involvement, via private law, private capital or semi-private organizations, in the water and wastewater sectors since the 1970s (Citroni, 2010). However, most water utilities worldwide remain as some form of public organization (Dominguez *et al.*, 2009; Palaniappan *et al.*, 2004). Moreover, privatization processes and the inclusion of market principles in the water and wastewater sectors have had mixed success in terms of achieving policy goals (Lieberherr, 2012; Lieberherr *et al.*, 2012). However, given the wide range of long-term challenges that the sector faces, public utilities need to take a strategic approach to managing their infrastructure. This in turn requires the development of capabilities to identify and implement innovative solutions. In other words, the utilities need a sufficient amount and quality of dynamic capabilities. How can they achieve this goal under the condition of being publicly owned and having to operate under public law? This question will be addressed in the present chapter.

In a recent comparison between public, private, and mixed utilities (Lieberherr and Truffer, 2015), we found that a public utility can compensate for the lack of internal dynamic capabilities with external collaboration (for instance, with research institutes, professional associations, or consultancies) to a degree. Drawing on this work, in this chapter we compare two public utilities in the Swiss wastewater sector (Zurich and Berne) that are operating under different public governance frameworks (direct versus delegated public management).[2] While our focus is on the organizational form of utilities, we also consider the broader context (external) on which these utilities draw for building up their dynamic capabilities (for example, regulatory context and the major collaboration partners, such as research institutes and associations). Together, the organizational level (internal means) and the regulatory-industry level (external means) comprise what we call a governance mode.

The next section provides an overview of the organizational forms and governance types that exist in the water and wastewater sectors in Western Europe. We then outline and define the concept of dynamic capabilities, drawing on the management literature to assess firms' internal means to develop dynamic capabilities. Specifically, we employ Teece's (2007) framework of sensing, seizing and reconfiguring, which provides a spectrum through which to assess the range of developing capabilities from strategy to structure. Drawing on the governance types in the next section, we introduce the two public utilities (Zurich and Berne) embedded in different governance frameworks. We then show how they have taken varying approaches for developing dynamic capabilities. We thus provide insights regarding hindering and supporting conditions at both the organizational and the regulatory level for public utilities to develop such capabilities. We end with lessons learned from these two cases for both infrastructure managers and policymakers.

Organization of the water and wastewater sectors in Europe

The organizational forms providing water and wastewater services in Western Europe are heterogeneous, with great variation between, as well as within, countries. Yet the majority is vertically integrated with no true competition. Competition measures have been proposed in the water and wastewater sectors in the context of liberalization (Allouche *et al.,* 2007). However, unbundling of integrated activities by separating infrastructure from service provision (for example, water treatment, local water distribution, sewage collection, and treatment could all be autonomous activities) is regarded as having limited potential due to the need for strong coordination between the different segments, as well as high prices to access the network (Allouche *et al.*, 2007; Garcia, *et al.*, 2007). Thus, competition is typically considered as limited to being 'for the market', where the European Commission (EC) advocates for the competitive tendering of service concessions to third parties in the water supply sector (Moss and Hüesker, 2010).

Within the context of 'competition for the market', there is a range of possibilities for transformation in terms of the responsible entity for water and wastewater service provision, as well as infrastructure ownership. Involving private actors in order to gain from private capital is a rising trend in Western Europe (Correlje *et al.*, 2007). Moreover, internal restructuring within the public mode, toward adopting NPM practices, has also been taking hold (Massarutto *et al.*, 2007).[3] However, despite being 'typical' public utility sectors, the water and wastewater sectors have purportedly taken a different reform trajectory from that of many other such sectors, due, in part, to the limited potential for competition (Allouche *et al.*, 2007; Prosser, 2005).

As summarized in Table 28.1, the literature indicates that there are five main governance types or models in today's Western European water and wastewater sectors at the operational level, which range from strong public involvement to full privatization (Aubin and Varone, 2007; Luis-Manso *et al.*, 2007; Moreau-Le Golvan and Breant, 2007; Schouten and Pieter van Dijk, 2007):[4]

1 Direct public management: the water and wastewater infrastructure is publicly owned and operated (Schouten and Pieter van Dijk, 2007).[5] Direct public management often does not involve explicit regulation. Instead, there is typically hierarchical monitoring by government departments (Massarutto *et al.*, 2007). Exemplary countries of direct public management include Luxembourg, Switzerland, and Denmark (Schouten and Pieter van Dijk, 2007).

2 Delegated public management: ownership is public and the government (typically local or regional) retains indirect control over the operations, through delegates. Some call this 'formal privatization' as it typically involves a shift to private law (Rothenberger, 2002). Within this model, the public actors increasingly hire third parties to accomplish certain tasks in the water and wastewater value chain. An exemplary country with respect to this model is the Netherlands (Schouten and Pieter van Dijk, 2007).

3 Delegated private management: public actors award a private actor the right to sell water services within a public ownership frame. This relates to public–private governance. Only two countries have this as their main means of service provision – France and Spain (Schouten and Pieter van Dijk, 2007). This model is commonly known as the 'French model of privatization' (that is, in terms of delegation or affermage), where operational responsibility is transferred to private operators. While ownership is public, the operator accepts the responsibility to maintain the infrastructure for the duration of the contract. Through franchise bidding there is 'competition for the market' as operators compete for the right to temporarily provide services (Schouten and Pieter van Dijk, 2007). Regulation typically involves exogenous quality and environmental standards, which are set in contracts between water and wastewater providers and the government, and regulated via governmental oversight involving tenders (Massarutto *et al.*, 2007).

Table 28.1 Summary of governance models in the Western European water and wastewater sectors

Form	*Known as*	*Predominance*	*Ownership*	*Service provision*
Direct public	Public works	Widespread	Public	Public
Delegated public	Formal privatization	Increasing	Public	Public
Delegated private	French model	Rare	Rare	Rare
Direct private	English model	Rare	Private	Private
Joint ventures, PPPs	German model	Increasing	Shared	Private

Source: Lieberherr, 2012.

4 Direct private management: involves a transfer of infrastructure ownership and operations to private actors – that is, divestiture or material privatization, which relates to private governance. This model is commonly known as the 'British (Anglo-Saxon)', or, more accurately, 'the English (and Welsh) model of full privatization'. Competition in the market is stimulated by semi-independent regulators (Garcia *et al.*, 2007). Direct private management entails explicit regulation with quality, environmental, and economic regulators using price-caps and performance standards (Massarutto *et al.*, 2007).

5 Joint ventures, such as public–private partnership (PPP): the government divests a percentage of the assets to private actors. The ownership is shared between public and private actors, but the actual management typically occurs through private actors (OECD, 2009; Thom and Ritz, 2006). This model has been called the 'German privatization model', where regulation occurs via supervisory boards and competition happens in the product and service markets for providing water services (Moreau-Le Golvan and Breant, 2007; Wackerbauer, 2008).

Overall, we find a range of governance models with a blurring between public and private involvement. The trend is that public providers are becoming increasingly autonomous from political decision-making, via delegated management (Allouche *et al.*, 2007). However, the reality remains that public organizations predominate. Given the fundamental challenges that the water and wastewater sectors have to confront, it is therefore legitimate to ask how public water utilities should be governed and managed, so that they improve their capabilities for strategic planning and management, ultimately becoming more innovative. We address this query by drawing on the innovation literature on dynamic capabilities.

Dynamic capabilities

Often, the assumption is that public organizations can improve their ability to innovate if they adopt strategies from the private sector. Indeed, the innovation literature stems primarily from the private sector or management literature, where the focus is on profit-maximizing firms (Hartely, 2013). Drawing on this literature, our focus is on the organizational forms of utilities. However, as we are assessing a public sector, where public organizations remain predominant, we also consider the broader context (external) on which these utilities draw to build their dynamic capabilities (such as regulatory context and the major collaboration partners, including research institutes and associations).

An organization's means to innovate relates to management theory's concept of 'structure follows strategy' (Chandler, 1962). To accomplish such innovation, a firm must have certain capabilities. Stemming from this well-established concept and embedded in the resource-based view of the firm (Barney, 2001), management scholars have employed the concept of dynamic capabilities; that is, the organizational and strategic routines of a firm, which enable it to innovate (Eisenhardt and Martin, 2000; Helfat and Peteraf, 2009; Zollo and Winter, 2002). Teece (2007) is one of the most prominent scholars in this field. In his seminal article (2007) he categorized dynamic capabilities as consisting of sensing, seizing, and reconfiguring. Teece's framework provides a spectrum of dynamic capabilities, which ranges from strategy to structure: *sensing* relates to having foresight, searching for new products and processes, and moving beyond daily business. *Seizing* entails responding to sensed options and translating these into products and services, by experimenting with new technologies or alternative approaches. Finally, *reconfiguring* refers to restructuring the core business of the firm, implementing new routines (Teece, 2007). This framework thus presents a continuum from planning to implementation of organizational and strategic routines that enable organizations to create, evolve and recombine resources. Table 28.2 summarizes Teece's three categories.

These capabilities can be developed internally, within the firm, as well as by collaborating with other actors in a specific sectoral context (Gebauer, 2011). Indeed, innovation research by public-management scholars (Osborne and Brown, 2005) has emphasized 'the importance and influence of the external societal environment on the public service sector' (Hartely, 2013: 49). In summary, dynamic capabilities enable an organization to innovate (Gebauer, 2011; Gebauer *et al.*, 2012).

Table 28.2 Dynamic capabilities

Capability	*Definition*
Sensing	– Searching for and/or creating new opportunities. – Investment in research and development (*R&D*) in order to scan and search for, as well as learn about, new customer needs and technological possibilities. – Occurs in relation to competitors, regulators, standard-setting bodies, the judiciary, and educational and research institutions.
Seizing	– Ability to respond to and exploit sensed opportunities or threats by implementing new/altered *products, processes or services*, or adopting *alternative approaches or strategies*. – Selecting or creating a specific *business model* that defines its strategy, investment priorities and related incentives. – From incremental innovation in terms of optimizing processes and technologies, to radical innovations such as implementing novel products.
Reconfiguring	– Implementing actions to maintain the potential for *change* through continuously aligning and realigning tangible and intangible assets through mergers, acquisitions and divestments. – (In relation to transitions), long-term strategic planning and a willingness to take risks to adopt new technologies or processes.

Source: Adapted from Teece, 2007 and Lieberherr and Truffer, 2015.

Comparison of two public organizations

We focus on the public domain and provide in-depth insight into two public utilities in the Swiss wastewater sector (Zurich and Berne) that have taken different approaches to developing dynamic capabilities. First, the governance modes are presented, and then we assess the respective dynamic capabilities.

Governance mode

No independent, sector-specific regulator (economic or environmental) exists in Switzerland. The responsibility to monitor the wastewater treatment operators in both Zurich and Berne has been delegated to the cantonal (constituent state) departments. In Zurich, it is the cantonal specialist department for Waste, Water, Energy and Air (Zurich Cantonal Department) and in Berne it is the Water and Waste Department (Bernese Cantonal Department) that are responsible for monitoring environmental performance and compliance in terms of water protection mandates (see Figures 28.1 and 28.2). Hence, in terms of regulation, the Berne case does not differ greatly from Zurich: it also remains under the jurisdiction of the cantonal department (shown by the grey arrows in Figure 28.2). However, the enforcement policy of both cantonal departments is diametrically opposed. The Berne Cantonal Department defines water protection goals, but leaves implementation of these goals to the infrastructure owners. As long as they fulfill water protection goals, the infrastructure owners are free to pursue other objectives. In contrast, the Zurich Cantonal Department is often involved in the very definition of projects, and is skeptical about wastewater organizations engaging in fields other than the treatment of wastewater.

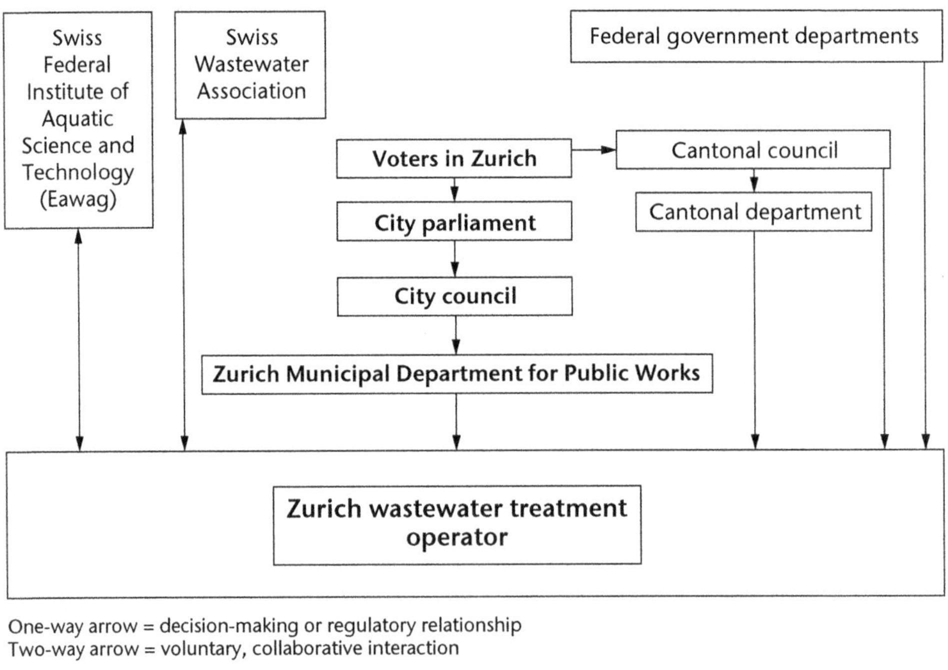

Figure 28.1 Direct public management in Zurich

Source: Adapted from Lieberherr and Truffer, 2015.

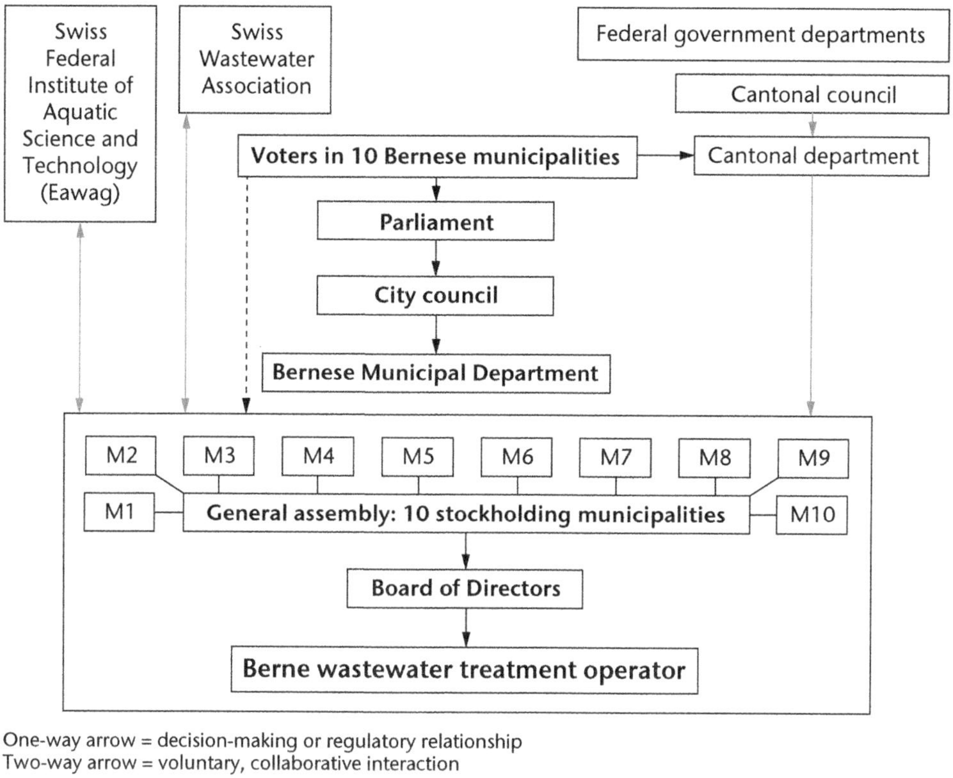

Figure 28.2 Delegated public management in Berne

Source: Adapted from Lieberherr, 2015.

While both are public organizations, Zurich's approach takes the form of direct public management and Berne uses delegated public management. As such, the Zurich operator has no legal personality and is embedded within the Zurich municipal department, under public law (see Figure 28.1). As shown by the black arrows in Figure 28.1, the operator is tied to the political decision-making chain (from voters to the city council). The grey arrows indicate the formal oversight structures and the operator's link to the cantonal public administration. With regard to collaborations with research institutes and professional associations, both operators engage with the Swiss Federal Institute of Aquatic Science and Technology (Eawag) and also interact with the national wastewater association to varying degrees (Figures 28.1 and 28.2).

In contrast to Zurich, the operator in Berne is no longer embedded within the public administration. Ten municipalities have joined together to form a joint-stock corporation. Therefore, Berne has its own legal personality and is under private law. In other words, it is a joint-stock corporation and has a private legal form. Each municipality (indicated by M1–M10 in Figure 28.2) is a stockholder and thus integrated within the General Assembly. Figure 28.2 shows that the operator no longer has direct links to the municipal department and the political decision-making system. However, voters in the participating municipalities can still have an indirect link (dotted arrow) in relation to the municipal delegates in the operator's board.

In terms of financial decisions, Zurich is under far more direct control by the city and the canton than Berne, as the city and cantonal politicians have the capacity to pass such decisions and appoint the operator's director in Zurich, which is not the case in Berne. In addition, the city government in Zurich has direct control over the operator's financial decision, whereas the city government in Berne lacks such control, as this organization is under private law whereby such decisions are transferred to the operator (Lieberherr, 2015).

Dynamic capabilities

We now analyze the extent to which the two utilities have developed differing dynamic capabilities. We assess how the diverging links to the political decision-making system – Zurich having a direct link, as it is embedded in the public administration, while Berne has an indirect link – affect the utilities' degrees of freedom for developing routines for sensing, seizing, and reconfiguring. In addition, we take the political and regulatory context, as well as major collaboration partners (such as research institutes and associations) into account.

Sensing

Sensing capabilities refer to the tactical identification of future opportunities and threats by searching for new products and processes, which can involve foresight and strategic planning or R&D. Besides formal in-house capacities for detecting and creating opportunities, utilities may draw on competencies in their broader environment by engaging in regular collaboration and exchange with experts in research institutes, consultancies, universities, or professional associations.

In Zurich, the operator lacks internal sensing capabilities, as it does not have its own R&D department that focuses on new technologies or designs. This can largely be attributed to Zurich's direct public management, which has led to little leeway to develop such internal structures. However, the operator has thought about alternative strategies, such as (1) becoming an integrated waste service provider; that is, expanding its scope beyond wastewater to include other waste-related tasks; (2) having its own incinerator; and (3) merging or taking over wastewater tasks of more municipalities, and becoming a larger organization with fiscal sovereignty; that is, becoming more autonomous from the political system (Lieberherr and Truffer, 2015). The objective behind these considerations has been to move towards delegated public management. However, these have remained ideas, proposed by an individual, rather than being part of foresight-based strategic planning processes. Strategic planning processes have focused on process optimization rather than on more radical change. For example, the focus has been on defining goals and strategies and delegating responsibility (Pauli, 2009).

Zurich has focused on process optimization, conducting studies on new filtration methods to combat micropollution. For instance, Zurich has emphasized the importance of knowing the state-of-the-art in its field, which it accesses through contracting consultancies for specific tasks, as well as through active participation in the Swiss National Association for Wastewater and Water Protection (see Lieberherr and Truffer, 2015). The wastewater association is a platform for the interaction of actors dealing with drainage, water purification/quality and water protection, which focuses on incremental innovation in terms of optimizing technologies, outlining technical regulations, making recommendations for best practices, and holding informational events. This industry association is wary of moving into new areas of technology or radical changes in the means of service provision. Hence, this association does not support the Zurich operator to develop strong sensing capabilities (Lieberherr and Truffer, 2015). The only driver for identifying new opportunities was found to stem from Eawag (Lieberherr and Truffer, 2015; see Figure 28.1), which is an internationally leading aquatic research institute encompassing research, education, consulting and knowledge transfer about water science and technology.[6] This institute is an important partner for the Zurich operators as it addresses not only optimizing current technologies (for instance, to become more energy efficient) but also focuses on alternative pathways, such as onsite treatment plants (Lieberherr and Truffer, 2015).

In contrast to Zurich, Berne has not focused on the process optimization of its existing (wastewater) infrastructure. It regards itself as part of the whole infrastructure sector. Consequently, the sensing capabilities required for the identification of adequate future opportunities, threats, and the corresponding activities differ from those required to optimize the existing infrastructure. Like Zurich, Berne lacks its own R&D department, while its contact with research institutes is scarce. However, this shortcoming is uncritical, as the organizations' scope lies on growth opportunities within the infrastructure sector and not solely in the wastewater sector. Corresponding sensing capabilities have thus been developed through regularly engaging in foresight-based strategic planning processes and by influencing the policymaking process. To achieve the latter, the management of the organization actively participates in different national working groups with a strategic character. For example, the Swiss Federal Government is planning to introduce new regulations regarding the elimination of micropollutants in wastewater treatment plants and the recovery of phosphorus from digested sludge. Both amendments will have important technical, financial and organizational implications for the wastewater and waste sector. Berne is a member of the steering committees that oversee the definition of the new requirements, and can thereby sense the future implications and, to a certain degree, influence the direction. At the same time, Berne has a leading role within the Communal Infrastructure Association, a lobby group whose scope is not limited to the wastewater sector, but also includes waste treatment, road transport infrastructure, communal development, and energy production. In contrast to Zurich, the involvement of Berne in the purely technical Swiss National Association for Wastewater and Water Protection is minimal.

Seizing

The seizing capability involves translating sensed options into new product and process innovations within the utilities by experimenting with different strategies and projects.

The Zurich operator has sought to expand its organizational size, as well as existing business model, by defining new strategies and prioritizing investments accordingly. At the time of analysis in 2010, the operator expected that it would be able to seize the strategy to implement its own sludge incinerator through which it can produce biogas, instead of shipping the dewatered sludge to external waste incinerators. Moreover, the wastewater operator has pursued a strategy to extract phosphate from dried sludge, where the planned investments for this were ratified by the City Council in 2010 (as data collection ended in 2010, we are unable to say what has happened since then) (Lieberherr and Truffer, 2015).

While the Zurich operator has been able to invest in projects in order to implement some new products (such as biogas and phosphate), its ability to engage in large-scale projects remains restricted due to the fact that these would have to be passed through the political system; for example, the city council, parliament, and, for large new projects (over 20 million), voters. Due to this link, the operators face difficulties in implementing major changes, as such, projects are often not ratified and large projects take a long time to be approved (Lieberherr and Truffer, 2015). Such restrictiveness is mainly the case in terms of organizational expansion, but also affects new technologies and processes.

As of 2014, the Berne management has succeeded in implementing the detected opportunities into actual projects. The aim of these projects is expansion into new or related markets, rather than technical optimization. For example, Berne has taken over customers from wastewater plants outside its original region of operation, and is leading negotiations with neighboring treatment plants to continue this path. Over the past 15 years, it has managed to drastically increase its biogas production by acquiring and processing energy-rich wastes with its infrastructures. Currently, Berne has planned to boost the biogas production by separately cleaning industrial wastewater with an alternative process that produces biogas as a by-product.

The successful implementation of the sensed opportunities in Berne can be attributed to the organizational structure (delegated public management) and the low investment volume. Due to its legal form, the management of the organization can make decisions that are detached from the political process, which results in high flexibility and quick implementation. At the same time, the investment volume of the targeted activities is relatively low (<10 million Swiss francs), which further reduces the need to involve politicians and the public administration.

Reconfiguring

Reconfiguring relates to the ability to change the core business of the organization. This can be assessed in terms of whether experimentation with new technologies or strategies has led to an actual change in the organizations' routines and practices, or whether the new activities remain at the periphery, without affecting the core business of the organization.

The Zurich operator has undertaken restructuring reforms to become more autonomous than a traditional public bureau. The operator underwent a procedure to increase its autonomy in 2000 with the objective of becoming process-, customer- and employee-oriented (Wiederkehr, 2004). As such, its management was restructured in terms of devolving vertical decision-making, decoupling decision-making from the city hierarchy, and simplifying and clarifying processes (Lieberherr and Truffer, 2015). In addition, at the time of the empirical analysis more focus was being placed on strategic planning in terms of clearly defining goals and strategies and delegating responsibility (Pauli, 2009). Although the Zurich operator's financial decision-making competency is linked to political decision-making paths, operational, subject-specific competencies are delegated to a low level within the organization.

Despite the above changes, Zurich has not been able to change its core business. Indeed, the operator has neither been able to expand its size nor become an integrated waste-service provider. This inability to develop reconfiguring capabilities can be attributed to the political system, as cantonal decision-makers have blocked initiatives by the organization to expand and to become more autonomous (Lieberherr and Truffer, 2015). However, less radical changes, such as the project to extract phosphate from sludge, have been ratified by the city council.

In Berne, the pursued growth strategy has led to a change in the routines, role, and, to a certain degree, the self-conceptualization of the organization. In the past, the treatment of energy-rich waste was seen as surplus to efficient use of temporary overcapacities in the sludge treatment infrastructure. If possible, overcapacities were to be filled with sludge from other wastewater treatment plants, and not with waste. Meanwhile, the acquisition of energy-rich wastes is now part of the core business and is favored, when possible, over the treatment of external sludge. Along the same vein, there are plans to increase the flexibility of biogas production by creating two different statutory corporations, one focusing on biogas production and one on wastewater treatment.

The geographical expansion has also left its mark on the organization. Ten years ago, the ten municipalities owned the sewerage pipelines, while the Berne organization owned only the wastewater treatment plant. The organization realized that the connection of customers that are currently linked to another treatment plant could be drastically simplified if it owned the main sewerage pipelines. Otherwise, Berne would have to undergo negotiations with each municipality. As a consequence, Berne has started to acquire parts of the main sewerage pipelines (that is, the large mains connecting the municipality to the wastewater treatment plant, but not the pipelines within the municipality). As the organization lacks the skills to operate its newly owned sewer system, it has outsourced the operation to the municipalities. However, the decision-making procedure has been simplified, as Berne now has the ability to make decisions about the infrastructure directly, without negotiating with the municipalities.

Discussion and conclusion

Table 28.3 provides a comparison of Zurich and Berne, showing that they have developed their dynamic capabilities differently. It is apparent that Berne has developed dynamic capabilities to a further degree than Zurich, as it has moved beyond process optimization and towards expansion into new markets, ultimately changing its core business. Instead of focusing solely on the wastewater treatment side, Berne has been able to develop seizing and reconfiguring capabilities to focus on the whole infrastructure sector. In Zurich, the operator has only been able to sense the opportunity to expand its business beyond the wastewater sector, without changing its core operations.

Given the wide range of long-term challenges that the water and wastewater sectors face, public utilities need to take a strategic approach to managing their infrastructures. We have thus assessed how two public utilities in the Swiss wastewater sector (Zurich and Berne) that operate under different governance frameworks (direct versus delegated public management) have developed capabilities in order to identify and implement innovative solutions. By comparing these two utilities, we have found that a utility under direct public management is more

Table 28.3 Comparison of dynamic capabilities for innovation activities in Zurich and Berne

Capability	*Zurich*	*Berne*
Sensing	– No R&D department. – Ideas about new approaches, expanding beyond wastewater sector. – Focus on process optimization of status quo. – External: best practices via wastewater associations and new opportunities via Eawag.	– No R&D department. – Holistic approach: whole infrastructure, not just wastewater. – Foresight/strategic planning, focusing on growth opportunities in infrastructure sector. – External: little contact with research institutes and wastewater association, but influencing policymaking.
Seizing	– Limited ability to exploit sensed opportunities: optimizing processes and technologies, but large-scale projects/changes restricted by political system.	– Ability to implement detected opportunities into actual projects, focusing on market expansion rather than technical optimization.
Reconfiguring	– Restructuring to become more autonomous, but core business unchanged; focus remains on wastewater.	– Change in core business, operating in the infrastructure field, focusing not just on wastewater but energy-rich waste in general.

Source: Own representation, 2015.

restricted in developing dynamic capabilities (Zurich) than a utility under delegated public management (Berne). Returning to our question posed in the first section, we find that public ownership is not the decisive factor affecting how a utility can develop dynamic capabilities: both organizations in this analysis were publicly owned, but developed different dynamic capabilities. Instead, the legal component – that is, whether the utility is under public or private law – was found to have far more of an influence: as a private legal form, Berne had more entrepreneurial freedom than Zurich. This ultimately enabled Berne to develop dynamic capabilities to a further degree, achieving more innovative solutions than Zurich.

From both cases, lessons can be derived for infrastructure managers and policymakers in the water and wastewater sectors and beyond. For infrastructure managers, autonomy from the political and regulatory system is key: both cases emphasize the relevance of a certain degree of entrepreneurial freedom. Without this, we argue that the development of dynamic capabilities would have been hindered in the Berne case. Indeed, in the Zurich case, it was particularly the lack of autonomy from the political and regulatory system, and hence its low degree of entrepreneurial freedom, that restricted the organization's development of dynamic capabilities. The restrictiveness of the political and regulatory system in the context of direct public management came to the forefront when assessing seizing and restructuring. Here, Zurich struggled to implement major changes, due to either veto from politicians or the lengthy process for such projects to become approved. Following from this, a second key lesson is that the development of dynamic capabilities can differ widely between organizations, depending on the scope of the organization and its political and regulatory context.

Lessons can also be drawn for policymakers. The approach taken by Berne would have been unthinkable in Zurich, as the latter cantonal decision-makers are quite restrictive regarding strategies outside the traditional wastewater treatment sector. The results on restructuring capabilities serve as valuable insights to policymakers: we have shown how delegated public management can enable changes in the core business of the organization. The case of direct public management was unable to achieve such restructuring. Policymakers may thus need to weigh the trade-off between losing a degree of control, and having a more innovative organization.

It would also be interesting to compare how these cases in the Swiss context relate to utilities in different national contexts. Such a comparison can be found in Lieberherr and Truffer (2015), where we assessed the Zurich case in relation to Leeds, England, and Berlin, Germany. This latter study supports the analysis in this chapter: entrepreneurial freedom plays a key role for fostering the development of dynamic capabilities. Our comparative analysis has shown that public utilities can tap into dynamic capabilities to a degree, but that delegated public management leads to a greater ability to develop these, and thus take a more strategic approach to managing the infrastructure.

Notes

1 Spain and Portugal are two exceptions.
2 The data stems from an interview campaign conducted by the authors in 2010 (cf. Dominguez 2008; Lieberherr and Truffer, 2015; Lieberherr, 2015). For the Berne case we have additional insight provided by one of the authors, who worked for the Berne Cantonal Department. Hence, while the analysis on Zurich is largely limited to 2010, the Berne case involves insight up until 2014.
3 For instance, even in a country such as Switzerland, where the government is a strong actor and direct public management is predominant, there is some delegated management and private-sector involvement (Luis-Manso, 2005). Only in Luxembourg and the Netherlands (for water supply, not for wastewater) is there no private participation (Luis-Manso *et al.*, 2007).

4 This classification serves only as an indication of overall trends, with variations within each country: 'huge differences are noticed inside each country from one sub-sector to another' (Aubin and Varone, 2007: 45).
5 This governance model provides over 90 percent of water and wastewater services (Luis-Manso *et al.*, 2007).
6 http://www.eawag.ch/index_EN (accessed May 2015).

References

Allouche, J., Luis-Manso, P. and Finger, M. (2007) Introduction: liberalisation, privatisation and network industries: a similar path for water?, in M. Finger, J. Allouche and P. Luis-Manso (eds) *Water and Liberalisation: European Water Scenarios*. London: IWA, pp. 1–10.

Aubin, D. and Varone, F. (2007) Policies regulating the water supply and sanitation sector in nine European countries, in M. Finger, J. Allouche and P. Luis-Manso (eds), *Water and Liberalisation: European Scenarios*. London: IWA, pp. 34–53.

Barney, J.B. (2001) Is the resource-based theory a useful perspective for strategic management research? Yes, *Academy of Management Review*, 26(1), 41–56.

Chandler, A. (1962) *Strategy and Structure*. Cambridge, MA: Harvard University Press.

Citroni, G. (2010) Neither state nor market: Municipalities, corporations and municipal corporatization in water services: Germany, France and Italy compared, in H. Wollmann and G. Marcou (eds) *The Provision of Public Services in Europe: Between State, Local Government and Market*. Cheltenham: Edward Elgar, pp. 191–216.

Correlje, A., Francois, D. and Massarutto, A. (2007) Economic implications of water scenarios, in M. Finger, J. Allouche and P. Luis-Manso (eds), *Water and Liberalisation: European Scenarios*. London: IWA.

Dominguez, D. (2008) *Handling Future Uncertainty: Strategic Planning for the Infrastructure Sector*. Doctoral thesis, Swiss Federal Institute of Technology, Zurich (ETH), available at: http://dx.doi.org/10.3929/ethz-a-005779391 (accessed March 2014).

Dominguez, D., Worch, H., Markard, J., Truffer, B. and Gujer, W. (2009) Closing the capability gap: Strategic planning for the infrastructure sector, *California Management Review*, 51(2), 30–50.

Eisenhardt, K.M. and Martin, J.A. (2000) Dynamic capabilities: What are they?, *Strategic Management Journal*, 21, 1105–1121.

Garcia, S., Guerin-Schneider, L. and Breuil, L. (2007) Analysis of the European Union explicit and implicit policies and approaches in the water supply and sanitation sectors, in M. Finger, J. Allouche and P. Luis-Manso (eds) *Water and Liberalisation: European Scenarios*. London: IWA, pp. 54–81.

Gebauer, H. (2011) Exploring the contribution of management innovation to the evolution of dynamic capabilities, *Industrial Marketing Management*, 40, 1238–1250.

Gebauer, H., Worch, H. and Truffer, B. (2012) Absorptive capacity, learning processes and combinative capabilities as determinants of strategic innovation, *European Management Journal*, 30, 57–73.

Hartely, J. (2013) Public and private features of innovation, in S. Osborne and L. Brown (eds) *Handbook of Innovation in Public Services*. Cheltenham: Edward Elgar, pp. 44–59.

Helfat, C.E. and Peteraf, M.A. (2009) Understanding dynamic capabilities: Progress along a development path, *Strategic Organization*, 7(1), 91–102.

Lieberherr, E. (2012) *Transformation of Water Governance and Legitimacy: Comparing Swiss, German and English Water Supply and Sanitation Service Providers*. Doctoral thesis, Swiss Federal Institute of Technology, Lausanne (EPFL).

Lieberherr, E. (2015) Trade-offs and synergies: Horizontalization and legitimacy in the Swiss wastewater sector, *Public Management Review*, doi: 10.1080/14719037.2015.1014397.

Lieberherr, E., Klinke, A. and Finger, M. (2012) Towards legitimate water governance? The partial privatization of the Berlin waterworks, *Public Management Review*, 14(7), 923–946.

Lieberherr, E. and Truffer, B. (2015) The impact of privatization on sustainability transitions: A comparative analysis of dynamic capabilities in three water utilities, *Environmental Innovation and Societal Transitions*, 15, 101–122.

Luis-Manso, P. (2005) Water institutions and management in Switzerland, *Chair in Management of Network Industries Report*. Lausanne: Swiss Federal Institute of Technology.

Luis-Manso, P. (2007) *Reform and Risk Management in the Urban Water Sector: The Role of Regulation*. Lausanne: Ecole Polytechnique Federale de Lausanne.

Luis-Manso, P., Finger, M. and Allouche, J. (2007) Analysis of the strategies of the water supply and sanitation operators in Europe, in M. Finger, J. Allouche and P. Luis-Manso (eds) *Water and Liberalisation: European Scenarios*. London: IWA, pp. 82–103.

Massarutto, A., Linares, E. and Paccagnan, V. (2007) Liberalisation and private sector involvement in WSS: The European experience, in M. Finger, J. Allouche and P. Luis-Manso (eds) *Liberalisation and Water: European Water Scenarios*. London: IWA, pp. 196–216.

Moreau-Le Golvan, Y. and Breant, P. (2007) *Organisation and Financing Models of the Drinking Water Sector – Review of available information on trends and changes*, Jan, Techneau, European Commission, Brussels, pp. 1–31.

Moss, T. and Hüesker, F. (2010) Wasserinfrastrukturen als Gemeinwohlträger zwischen globalem Wandel und regionaler Entwicklung – Institutionelle Erwiderungen in Berlin-Brandenburg, *Interdisziplinären Arbeitsgruppen IAG Globaler Wandel – Regionale Entwicklung*, Diskussionspapier 4) Berlin-Brandenburgerische Akademie der Wissenschaften, Berlin, pp. 32–41.

Organisation for Economic Co-operation and Development (OECD) (2008) *Environment Directorate: Key OECD environmental indicators*. Paris: OECD Publishing, pp. 1–38.

Organisation for Economic Co-operation and Development (OECD) (2009) *Managing Water for All: An OECD perspective on pricing and financing*. Paris: OECD Publishing, pp. 1–150.

Organisation for Economic Co-operation and Development (OECD) (2011) *Meeting the Challenge of Financing Water and Sanitation: Tools and approaches*. Paris: OECD Publishing.

Osborne, S. and Brown, L. (2005) *Managing Change and Innovation in Public Service Organizations*. London: Routledge.

Palaniappan, M., Gleick, P.H., Hunt, C. and Srinivasan, V. (2004) Water privatization principles and practices, in P.H. Gleick (ed.), *The World's Water 2004–2005: The Biennial Report on Freshwater Resources*. Washington, DC: Island Press.

Pauli, U. (2009) *Geschäftsbericht 2008*, Stadt Zürich, Entsorgung und Recycling, Zürich.

Prosser, T. (2005) *The Limits of Competition Law: Markets and Public Services*. Oxford: Oxford University Press.

Rothenberger, D. (2002) Optionen für die Deregulierung der Siedlungswasserwirtschaft, *Kommunal-magazin*, 6, 45–47.

Schouten, M. and Pieter van Dijk, M. (2007) *The European Water Supply and Sanitation Markets*. London: IWA.

Swiss Federal Institute of Aquatic Science and Technology (2015) Eawag: Welcome. http://www.eawag.ch/about/index_EN (accessed May 2015).

Teece, D.J. (2007) Explicating dynamic capabilities: the nature and microfoundations of (sustainable) enterprise performance, *Strategic Management Journal*, 28(13), 1319–1350.

Teece, D.J., Pisano, G. and Shuen, A. (1997) Dynamic capabilities and strategic management, *Strategic Management Journal*, 18(7), 509–533.

Thom, N. and Ritz, A. (2006) Die organisatorischen Gestaltungselemente des Public Managements, *Public Management Innovative Konzepte zur Führung im öffentlichen Sektor*, Vol. 3. Wiesbaden: Verlag Dr. Th. Gabler, pp. 211–298.

Wackerbauer, J. (2008) Public or private water management: Experience from different European countries, *IOP Conference Series: Earth and Environmental Science*, 4(1), 1–10.

Wiederkehr, P. (2004) ERZ/Geschäftsbereich Kompositier- und Klärwerke, *Abwasserpreis Schweiz*, VSA, FES, Zurich, pp. 1–3.

Zollo, M. and Winter, S. (2002) Deliberate learning and the evolution of dynamic capabilities, *Organization Science*, 13(3), 339–351.

29
Conclusion

Matthias Finger and Christian Jaag

Introduction

In this handbook we wanted to offer a comprehensive and systematic overview of the evolution of the main network industries from three perspectives: the perspective of the industry into which infrastructure sectors are rapidly evolving; the perspective of policy and regulation; and the perspective of the firms operating in these industries. This is, to our knowledge, the first such systematic overview. In this conclusion, we will proceed in two steps: first, we will look at each of the network industries separately and try to crystallize the most striking issues as they emerge when one compares, or at least looks at, these three perspectives together. Subsequently, we will consider the three perspectives separately and identify the most striking features in terms of industry evolution, policy and regulation, and firm strategies when taking into account all of the network industries covered in this book.

Telecommunications

Of all the network industries, telecommunications is, without doubt, the one that has undergone the most radical changes over the past 20 to 25 years, owing mainly to technological dynamics. While the liberalization of the telecommunications sector – along with the privatization of some important players such as AT&T in the US and British Telecom in the UK – probably played a role in triggering this technological evolution in the early 1990s, it is clear that technological change has developed a life of its own since. As highlighted by the three contributions on telecommunications in this handbook, this technological evolution was first characterized by mobile technology and subsequently by the dynamics in fixed, and later mobile, broadband. However, more importantly, this technological evolution rapidly led to industry uptake and subsequently a convergence – or vertical integration – between telecommunications infrastructures and content, facilitated, of course, by the rapidly expanding and developing global Internet. Thus, today, the converging telecommunications infrastructure and content industry appears to be challenged, once more, by a new type of firm, whose business model is based on the exploitation of information received from its customers (such firms include Google, Facebook, and Amazon). Needless to say, in the context of this rapid and often disruptive technological environment, telecommunications policy and regulation lag behind, where regulation is now mainly focusing on the abuse of dominant position (for example, competition regulation). Thus, the efforts of the European Commission (EC) have been to place telecommunications policy and regulation within the much broader context of the promotion of the information society and the knowledge economy. Nevertheless, telecoms operators were privatized early on (in the 1990s) and this privatization has helped them to grow.

Postal services

Among all the historical operators of the network industries, postal operators are probably the most challenged, as their 'industry' has undergone the most radical changes of all. However, this may actually be due to the fact that postal services were never an 'industry' to begin with. Historical postal operators were active in the communications, logistics (parcels), and financial services industries. In many countries, policy changes led to privatization of the postal financial services early on, thus leaving postal operators basically with the letters and parcels. Two decades of postal market liberalization (1990–2010) significantly shook up the industry and led to competition and significant loss of market share in express and courier services, as well as parcels, whereas letters remained almost exclusively under the control of the incumbents despite total market opening, at least in Europe. The main reason for this became obvious from the 2010s, when a new wave of much more radical technological changes transformed the postal industry even further and much more radically; that is, information and communication technologies (ICTs). As a result, historical operators are now also losing significant market shares in letter mail through a phenomenon called 'substitution', and are struggling to remain relevant in the parcels business, where e-commerce firms have emerged as the new competitors to historical postal operators. Needless to say, postal regulation and regulatory policies are equally challenged, trying first to remain relevant and second to catch up with the new electronic reality into which postal operators are increasingly integrated, and by which they are perhaps even absorbed. Indeed, postal regulation was mainly concerned with guaranteeing a universal postal service, which appears to be becoming increasingly obsolete in light of the new communications behaviors of customers. In adapting to these new challenges, traditional postal operators have 'hyper-diversified' into previously unknown territories (for them), while governments seem to have started considering (so far partial) privatization of their historical operators.

Electricity

The electricity industry has been facing profound transformations as of late, driven mainly by the emergence of renewable-energy production. This, at least, is the picture that is emerging from the three chapters in this book. Energy production by renewables, but especially the ability to manage such production in the electricity system, is itself the result of technological change, notably due to ICTs. However, even more so, it is the result of a change in policy, at least in certain countries – notably Germany – whereby such renewables are being heavily subsidized. Consequences pertain to generation on the one hand and grid management on the other. Not only have prices fallen as a result of such massive subsidizing of renewables; thus making certain types of production unattractive and even creating negative prices at times. For some producers specializing in peak-load production, this leads them to even change their business models. With respect to grid management, renewables generate much bigger volatility and thus an increased need for balancing activities, load, as well as demand management (for example, smart grids). In turn, these factors challenge regulators, who have to find creative solutions to financing grid reinforcements, along with incentive mechanisms that will prevent this smart energy revolution from falling onto the shoulders of the grid operators – high-voltage transport and distribution – and thus ultimately onto consumers. Even though this transformation of the electricity sector is not addressed to a great extent in the three chapters mentioned above, it must be borne in mind that the transformation is itself the result of electricity-market liberalization, leading to sector unbundling and consumers' free choice regarding producers. This latter is particularly challenging for distribution companies, who are currently developing new business models, notably moving into the direction of energy-services companies, with a special focus on 'smart energy'.

Gas

Gas is yet another, quite different, network industry. As the chapters in this book show, it is simultaneously a global, a regional and a national industry. Globally, gas – or at least the price of gas – is tied to oil and coal. Technological innovation in the area of gas liquefaction (for example, liquefied natural gas) has made global gas-transport possible, whereas historical gas was mostly transported by pipelines. Another global feature of gas is its production locations, which are limited to certain countries (for example, Russia, the Middle East). However, a profound technological change in the form of fracking has enabled gas production in other parts of the world, notably in the US, with consequences on prices and more regional consumption. However, gas is also a regional industry: there is an East Asian regional market, a North American market, and a European market. The European approach to creating a gas market is particularly highlighted in this book, characterized as it is by the creation of gas trading (for example, virtual hubs) on the one hand and infrastructure development and investments on the other. The creation of such (artificial) market mechanisms cannot hide the fact that gas is ultimately a natural monopoly infrastructure, leading to a highly regulated industry. Business models and business development only exist inasmuch as the EC and the member state regulators, or the US federal regulator (FERC), for that matter, create the conditions for gas markets, notably by regulating access to the transportation system, and also by regulating trading and investment. Given the importance of the state – and its strategic interests – gas is therefore ultimately also a very national network industry.

Maritime transport

Maritime transport constitutes yet another type of network industry. Of all the network industries discussed in this book, maritime transport is probably the most global and (consequently) the least regulated. Unlike the gas industry, it is not really regional and basically combines national (public and private) ports (and terminal operators) with global (private) carriers and global (private) cargo owners. Technological changes in maritime transport have taken place in the past and pertain mainly to containerization and subsequent interoperability, and to growing vessel size and increased transport capacity. In turn, this has led to overcapacity and price wars among carriers. In terms of global regulation, which is generally sponsored by the International Maritime Organization (a UN organization), security and safety are the most widespread and also the most accepted regulations in the industry. However, there are also global regulations pertaining to liability. The European Union especially, is pushing for the greening of the maritime transport industry with corresponding rules on maritime pollution and CO_2 emissions, the latter being promoted by way of incentives for green technological innovation. However, none of these global regulations are easy to enforce, and many loopholes remain. At national levels, regulations are tougher and easier to enforce, and pertain, in the large maritime transport countries (for example, the US), to routes of national relevance and cabotage rules, and of course to port and terminal access – another area in which the EC is aiming at European-wide harmonization. Finally, and in the context of a global industry that is mainly characterized by price competition, carriers have little leeway except perhaps the shopping of registry (also called 'flags of convenience').

Railways

The railways industry is clearly not a global one; rather, railways are national, the most important railway nations being India, China and Japan, or continental in Europe (including most European countries, such as Germany, France, Italy, Spain, and Switzerland). Of all the network industries, railways is certainly the most subsidized, and at the same time not particularly known for technological innovation, with the exception perhaps of high-speed trains. However, this is not to say that railways do not constitute a growth industry. Such growth takes place especially in emerging countries (China, India, and Korea) in both freight and passenger transport. It is also worth mentioning growing rail patronage in agglomeration transport, notably in Europe. Chapter 7 looks at the different models and distinguishes between the integrated state-owned monopoly (the main rail companies in the world still following this model), private integrated monopolies (for example, American freight companies), and the emerging European model of rail competition. Chapters 16 and 25 of this book focus exclusively on the unique European approach to railway liberalization by way of unbundling of the historical operators and creation of competition on the tracks, but increasingly also via tendering of monopolistic (public-service) franchises. This approach creates unique regulatory challenges in terms of both (technical) interoperability and (economic) market distortions. Yet, in the long run and on a global scale, the main future challenges for railways are the need for (and the difficulty to obtain) investments in rail infrastructures on the one hand and intermodal competition from the road (trucks, buses, and cars) on the other.

Air transport

For some (chapter 8), air transport is 'the archetypal network industry', while for others (chapter 26) it is not a network industry at all. This controversy can probably be explained by the fact that air transport has, historically, never been vertically integrated. Airlines (air transport) were originally state-owned flag carriers, whereas air traffic control (ATC) was, and still is, mostly a national public monopoly – airports being locally or regionally owned public monopolies. This situation is also reflected in this book, where the three chapters (8, 17 and 26) focus on the three different elements of the air transport industry. Clearly, liberalization of air transport started with US deregulation in 1978, followed by deregulation in Europe throughout the 1990s, leading to the creation of low-cost airlines. Yet, beyond these two continents, air transport remains characterized by bilateral and increasingly multilateral agreements among nation states. However, despite this liberalization of air transport, the sector remains highly regulated, beginning with safety, which is the overarching regulatory intervention into the sector. Chapter 26 focuses on airports and the deregulation of many of their services (for example, ground handling). Yet airports remain regulated, especially in Europe, and their performance is monitored. In addition, airport capacity and (competitive) slot allocation remains a concern in many airports and today is probably the major concern when it comes to further liberalizing the air transport industry. Chapter 17 focuses primarily on ATC, which, especially in Europe (and the US) is undergoing a major transformation, driven by the EC's initiatives to create a Single European Sky. However. this initiative has more or less ended in gridlock and, at least in Europe, prevents significant further efficiency gains and thus diminishes the competitiveness of the European air transport sector.

Urban public transport

Urban public transport is yet again a quite particular network industry, as it is basically made up of local public monopolies, owned historically by municipalities and rarely by regional or national governments. Overall, urban public transport is also heavily subsidized (approximately 50 percent on average). Probably for these reasons, it has been a relatively stable industry to date. Changes have come since the 1990s, at least in Europe, from national and European liberalization initiatives. However, the main underlying trends affecting urban public transport are primarily urbanization; that is, the rapid growth of cities and related transportation problems, namely congestion and lack of parking spaces, but also environmental concerns, namely vehicle pollution. These trends alone make urban public transport a very promising industry. In particular, chapter 9 and to a certain extent, also chapter 27 highlight changes in the way urban public transport has been provided in Europe – that is, as a result of local authorities' efforts to engage in new forms of public–private partnerships, whereby urban public transport services are tendered, and subsequently increasingly provided by franchised private (or public) operators. Regulation of these relationships is mainly conducted via contracts between the local transport authorities and the franchised operators. This evolution in the mode of provision has led to the rise of large global urban transport players, such as FirstGroup and Transdev.

However, new challenges are on the horizon, resulting mainly from technological changes. On the one hand there are autonomous vehicles, which will further individualize transport, and on the other is the growing role of ICTs, leading to new concepts such as digital urban transport or 'transport as a service' – an approach now also taken on by the EC. Transport as a service will go far beyond integrated timetables and integrated ticketing, and has the potential to reduce urban transport operators to simple carriers without direct access to their customers.

Water

Drinking and wastewater (sewerage) are typical local monopolies, water being locally sourced and locally discharged. They are also essential public services, probably more 'essential' than any other network industry. Consequently, water, and especially water distribution, has a strong political dimension, making it particularly susceptible to politization and (local) political intervention. In addition to public-service considerations, the water sector is transcended by environmental (for example, water scarcity and pollution) and public-health issues. Thus far, technological evolution in the water sector has been quite limited, if not absent. Only very recently have the ICTs started to penetrate the drinking-water sector, mainly for water savings (and not for commercial) purposes. However, what have drawn most academic attention in the context of water as a network industry are the various efforts by the World Bank and national and local governments to 'privatize' water (for example, chapter 10 in this book), or, more precisely, to introduce private participation into the sector. As a result, as shown by chapter 28, various new forms of governing water distribution and sewerage have emerged, first in developing and emerging countries, and later on in Europe. Besides public management (often by way of corporatized local public enterprises), joint ventures between public and private

Table 29.1 Summary

Industry		*Industry characteristics*	*Drivers of change*	*Public policy*	*Regulation*	*Firm behavior and strategy*
Telecommunications	Most dynamic	Strong dynamics; creative destruction	Technology (mobile telephony, Internet, ICTs)	Promotion of information society	Competition regulation (market power)	Business-model innovation
Postal services	Most challenged	Still mainly dominated by incumbents, becoming increasingly privatized	Deregulation (1990–2010) and technology (substitution since 2000)	No longer any clear public-policy objective	Regulation of increasingly outdated public or universal services obligations	Hyperdiversification into electronic and increasingly unrelated businesses
Electricity	Most recently dynamized	Unbundling, privatization and subsidies for renewables	Deregulation and, most recently, ICTs	Climate-change policies and promotion of renewables	Heavy regulation, especially in transmission, distribution, and, most recently, trading	Energy services companies as new business models; energy trading as funds generator
Gas	Most strategic	Simultaneously global, regional and national; industry concentration	New technologies such as liquefied natural gas and fracking	Energy security policies; climate-change policies	Considerable regulation in matters of network access, investments and trading	Backward and forward integration
Maritime transport	Least regulated	Global players	Containerization	Safety and environmental policies	Regulation of port access	Supply chain management strategies

(continued overleaf)

Table 29.1 (continued)

Industry		*Industry characteristics*	*Drivers of change*	*Public policy*	*Regulation*	*Firm behavior and strategy*
Railways	Most subsidized	Strong presence of national governments, mainly because of financial subsidies	Little technological innovation, except for high-speed trains	Public-service objectives; transfer from road to rail policies	Strong economic regulation, especially in Europe for on-track competition and access; safety regulation	Still little strategic behavior and innovation
Air transport	Most global	Industry concentration (alliances); strong national presence (in ATC). dynamics at airport level	Little technological innovation	Environmental policies; Single European Sky in Europe	Safety regulation predominant; regulation of airports and ATC	New business models resulting from deregulation (low-cost airlines); new strategies from new global carriers (Turkish, Gulf carriers)
Urban public transport	Most local	Redefinition as a mobility industry	Pressure from new technologies, especially ICTs	Environmental and mobility-related policies; subsidies	Regulation by contract	Emergence of global players; public–private partnerships (PPPs) as a business model
Water distribution and sewerage	Most politicized	Still a large variety of governance models; some industry concentration	Main driver comes from new forms of private participation; little pressure so far from technological change	Strong policy intervention in terms of public service, public-health and environmental objectives	Regulation by contract in most parts of the world; typical monopoly regulation in the US	PPPs as a business model; emergence of global players
Balance sheet – sector overview		Concentration; global players in almost all network industries; emerging threats from information integrators such as Google	Growing importance of technological change, notably ICTs	Climate change and environmental policies; security of supply concerns; politization remains high	Growing (economic) regulatory pressure in all industries; safety and technical regulations omnipresent	New business models emerging, especially in terms of new forms of PPPs; pressure to vertically integrate remains

enterprises, delegated private management (the so-called French or concession model) or even private management (the UK) have seen the light of day over the past 20 years. This of course raises the question of regulation; or more precisely the question of regulating public, and increasingly also private, local monopolies. This task is made particularly challenging by the public-service nature of water distribution and sewerage, as highlighted by chapter 28 of this book. Quite logically, as a result of such private-sector participation, global water and sewerage companies, most of which are French (such as Veolia and Suez) have emerged in the sector, adding new dynamics to this increasingly global water industry.

The evolution of network industries

If one looks across all of the network industries addressed in this book, it becomes clear that the main initial drivers have been deregulation and private-sector participation and, to a certain extent, even privatization (air transport, telecommunications) as of the late 1980s, but mostly during the 1990s. More recently – that is, mostly after the 2000s – technology has started to play a role as the most powerful driver of industry change; this is most prominently illustrated in the postal sector, but is increasingly also present in electricity and mobility (especially urban public transport). The only exception to this rule may be telecommunications, where technology may have been the most prominent industry driver from the very beginning. In any case, network industry dynamics are best captured, at a conceptual level, by the co-evolution between institutions (institutional changes such as liberalization, deregulation, and privatization) and technology (technological changes, especially by pervasive technologies such as ICTs). Another striking feature of network industries dynamics is certainly their globalization, which now affects local network industries such as urban public transport, water distribution and sewerage, and airports. The most obvious illustration of such globalization is without doubt the emergence of global players in all network industries, most of whom, interestingly, are of European origin.

Policy and regulation

Despite their growing dynamization, privatization and globalization, politics (and corresponding policies) and subsequent regulation have not disappeared from the network industries. On the contrary, there is no doubt that regulation in and regulatory pressure on the different network industries has increased overall, and this not only in Europe, where the very model of network industry liberalization consists, quite paradoxically one may say, of their growing regulation. Safety and technical regulation has always been there (especially in aviation, transport, and energy), but the area of regulation that has been developing exponentially since liberalization is clearly economic regulation pertaining to access to infrastructures, non-discrimination (especially of new entrants), and unbundling of historical operators. In the case of Europe, such economic regulation (and of course technical and safety regulation) is increasingly moving to the European level. This is mostly because network industries remain ultimately integrated socio-technical systems, with regulation increasingly taking the role of coordinating the overall system wherein as a result of liberalization, unbundling and market dynamics have become increasingly fragmented. In addition, network industries remain in the policy focus, and perhaps increasingly so. The most prominent policy areas are of course safety and security (for example, air transport, telecommunications, and energy), climate change and the environment (energy and transport), security of supply and national independence (energy), public services (water and urban public transport, railways), as well as overall national competitiveness (telecommunications) and employment (postal services, railways).

Firm strategies and behavior

Industry dynamics, globalization and the continued, and even growing, persistence of policy and regulation altogether determine firms' strategies and behaviors in network industries. To recall, historically, firms in the different network industries were generally locally or state-owned monopolies. However, this has already changed in many network industries, where firms have first become corporatized and even privatized (for example, airlines, telecommunications operators, and postal services). Some of these firms have become global players, such as the major airlines (Lufthansa, Air France, and British Airways), telecommunications operators (T-Telekom, Vodafone, and Orange), postal operators (DHL, TNT), electricity companies (EDF) or railway companies (Deutsche Bahn Schenker). In the local monopolies, the emerging global players are actually new private entrants, such as Veolia and Suez in the water and wastewater industry, and FirstGroup and Transdev in urban transport. Given the political nature of the different network industries, along with omnipresent regulation, it is not surprising that an important, if not the dominant, business model pertains to 'partnering' with national and local governments in providing the services, including creating political and regulatory framework conditions that are favorable for network-based services. As of late, and thanks to the rapid penetration of network industries by ICTs, a new type of actor has emerged, which is probably best characterized as information intermediaries, whose business model is the exploitation of the electronic interfaces with users (for example, Google, Amazon, smart-metering companies and so on). This may well announce a fundamental change in the way business will be done in network industries in the future.

Index